TROUT FISHING
in the
CATSKILLS

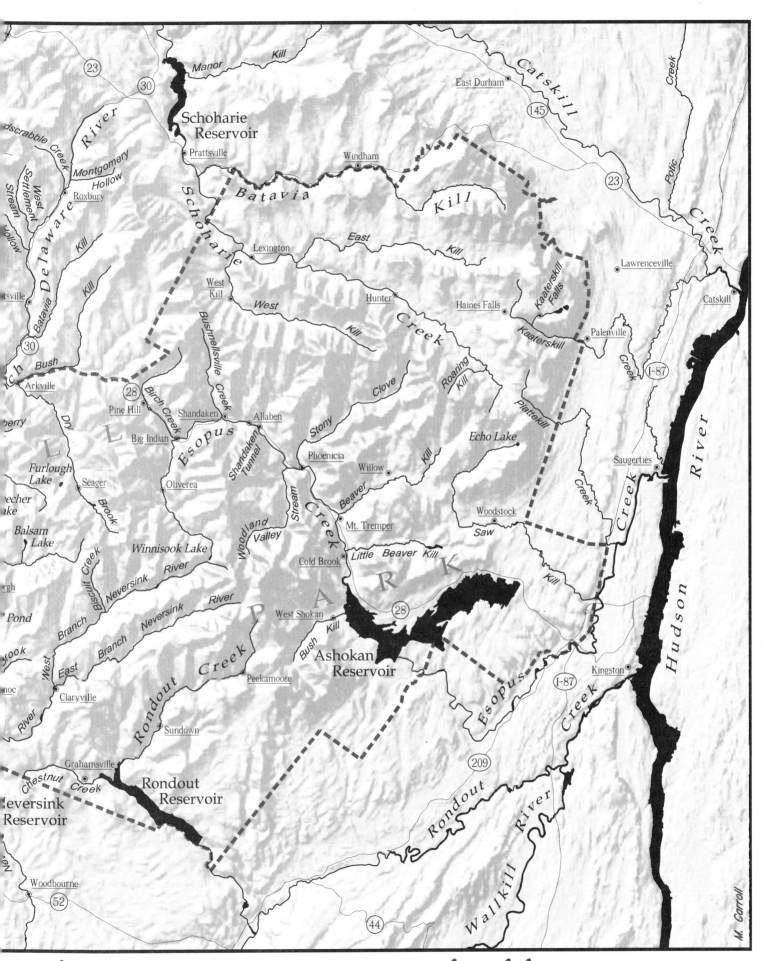

The Great Catskill Rivers

TROUT FISHING
in the
CATSKILLS

Ed Van Put

Introduction by John Merwin

Skyhorse Publishing

To my wife Judy O'Brien

www.skyhorsepublishing.com

10 9 8 7 6 5 4 3 2 1

Library of Congress Cataloging-in-Publication Data
    Van Put, Ed.
    Trout fishing in the Catskills / introduction by John Merwin ; written by Ed Van Put.
        p.   cm.
    Includes bibliographical references and index.
    ISBN-13: 978-1-60239-049-2 (hardcover : alk. paper)
    ISBN-10: 1-60239-049-5 (hardcover : alk. paper)
    1. Trout fishing—New York (State)—Catskill Mountains.   2. Trout fishing—New York (State)—
Catskill Mountains—History.   I. Title.

    SH688.U6.V363   2007
    799.17'5709747—dc22
                                                                    2007006390

Printed in the United States of America

CONTENTS

⊶

Acknowledgments

The idea for this book came about as the result of an event that occurred more than twenty years ago, while I was looking through the Delaware River files at the fisheries office of the New York State Department of Environmental Conservation in New Paltz. I was curious to learn if there were records that would reveal the date when the Delaware was originally stocked with rainbow trout. That information was not found, but I discovered a note that stated "*Hancock Herald*, May 21, 1942. Write-up on history of salmon culture as related to Delaware River." The note went on to say that the article that was referred to contained the history of salmon stocking in the Delaware.

This stirred my curiosity. Several weeks later, while traveling through Hancock, I decided to find out if the paper was still being published, and if so, whether I could obtain a copy of the article. I found the newspaper office located on a side street and spoke to a woman about locating the article; she directed me to the local library, where I was assured bound editions of the paper were kept. At the library I was given a bound volume of the *Hancock Herald* from the year 1942 and easily found the item I was looking for.

This incident led me to another weekly newspaper. I had read that the *Liberty Register* had published a series of letters written by Edward R. Hewitt, noted fly fisherman, regarding the posting of his water along the Neversink in 1920. This paper was also bound in yearly volumes, and while searching for the Hewitt letters, I found a number of interesting fishing-related articles.

As with many of the weekly newspapers published in the Catskills, the editor was a trout fisherman, and the paper often reported on fishing. I learned that almost every local library had bound editions of newspapers or had them on microfilm. I was hooked! Some papers originated in the 1820s, but most covered the period from the 1840s to the present—or when they became defunct.

I began visiting libraries all over the Catskills seeking weekly newspapers and reading microfilm on days off, on weekends, at night, even during lunch breaks. It did not take long for me to realize that the articles I found relative to trout fishing were an untapped source of historical information that had been, for the most part, buried in the fading pages of the newspapers and most likely would remain there. I began Xeroxing articles when it was possible and copying them in longhand when it was not.

It took about two hours to go through one year of a weekly newspaper—that is, only after I'd become familiar with the format and knew where to concentrate my efforts. The work was tedious and time-consuming, and at times disappointing. There were some papers that were researched for several years, with no information found worth recording. The only satisfaction I got was that I had in fact covered those years and knew there was nothing that may have been missed. This happened in many instances.

My wife was recruited, and together we visited additional libraries all over the state. In addition, we traveled to college and university libraries at Orange, Ulster, and Sullivan County Community Colleges; State Universities of New York at Delhi and New Paltz; and the Cornell, Vassar, and Yale University libraries. We spent many days at the New York Public Library in New York City, as well as countless hours at the New York State Library in Albany, where we brought sandwiches, took a break, ate our lunches on benches in the busy Grand Concourse, and then resumed our work.

For more than twenty years we researched newspapers and periodicals, and studied every book published on local history. In addition, I read every old fishing book I could find, as well as sporting periodicals, magazines, and articles relative to fishing. My research was exhaustive, and I took great pains not to take shortcuts. The work required dedication and was very time-consuming, which led me to believe that no one would repeat my journey.

I was greatly assisted through local libraries by the interlibrary loan system that enables researchers and library patrons to receive books, periodicals, and microfilm from such places as the New York State Library, the Library of Congress, and the Smithsonian Institution.

I am especially indebted to the New York State Library, and to the libraries of Delhi, Livingston Manor, and Walton; to the Jerry Bartlett Memorial Library Collection at the Phoenicia Library; as well as to the Historical Societies of Greene and Sullivan counties, the New-York Historical Society in New York City, and the New York Historical Association in Cooperstown, all of whom were helpful with my research.

My gratitude is also extended to the following individuals and organizations who gave advice and direction or allowed access to their photographs, libraries, files, records, and collections: the Anglers' Club of New York, the Balsam Lake Club, Tony Bonavist, Emerson Bouton, Jean Boyd, Phil Chase, Francis Davis, the Catskill Fly Fishing Center, Mary Dette Clark, Karl Connell, Dr. Paul D'Amico, Richard Frisbie (Hope Farm Press & Bookshop), Clem Fullerton, Barbara Jaffe, Walter (Bill) Kocher, Dan Myers, Ed Ostapczuk, Judie Darbee Smith, Charlotte Steenrod, Delbert Van Etten, the Woman Flyfishers Club, and Bob Wood. A special thanks to my son, Lee Van Put, for all of his assistance with the art work.

It is my hope that I have put together a book that is educational and entertaining. I know that I have done my absolute best to describe and present an accurate accounting of what trout fishing was like from the time of settlement until the era of fisheries management.

Introduction

There are few things as timeless as rivers, but Ed Van Put's latest incarnation of Catskill angling history comes awfully close.

You'll find, first, that there is life beyond the fabled Beaverkill; that rivers like the Neversink, Esopus, Mongaup, and Schoharie are also vital parts of a rich tradition grown up across the mountains of midstate New York, along with dozens of smaller streams and feeder creeks. Whether you fly fish for trout in Michigan, Wyoming, or beyond, chances are at least some of the tactics, flies, and tackle you use have their roots here. In that respect, Van Put's work is a trout-fishing genealogy for all of us, a look back at where we as anglers came from and why we fish the way we do.

His writing about the Esopus in the eastern Catskills, for example, reminds me of an afternoon I spent there a half-century ago, struggling to wade the murky currents as a twelve-year-old and marveling with stiff-jawed determination at the numbers of rising trout I was unable to catch. Lightning was snapping about the nearby hills, and sharp claps of thunder came rolling through as if reborn from Rip Van Winkle's classic dream. I finally acceded to my mother's bankside pleading and left both the river and the thunderstorm on her promise of a trip to Folkerts in nearby Phoenicia, where I could find more and better and local dry flies.

At that old village drugstore and general emporium, there were cases of exquisite Catskill-style dries, as much a part of local lore as the monster brown trout hanging in stuffed splendor on the wall overhead. I bought a few flies and later actually managed to catch a trout on one. It was only years afterward, though, that I began to learn the history behind the flies, the store, the river, and yes, even that monster trout. All of those stories are in these pages, along with a great deal more.

History in general—and fishing history in particular—is a rather odd thing. It starts with current events that are often of no great note, things that happen and then fade in memory like evaporating water. Reconstructing long-past fishing events, people, and even towns can thus be extraordinarily difficult, like trying to assemble a jigsaw puzzle with missing pieces.

It is a task for which Van Put is ideally suited, if for no other reason than because his job involves searching out possible riverbank fishing access areas for the state. This has long taken him not just to rivers but also into the dustiest corners of town clerks' offices and records rooms across the Catskills. In such places he has discovered details and images that are then saved and savored much like a well-organized box of trout flies that are drawn out when there's a special fish to catch— or a story to tell.

I don't know of anyone else who could have done such a thorough and thoroughly enjoyable fishing history of the Catskills. You will probably not catch more fish because of this book. But your fishing will be more rewarding as you learn where your own flies are landing in the timelessness of rivers.

—John Merwin, Fishing Editor
Field & Stream
2007

PART 1

Fontinalis: Pre-1800s to 1870s

1

The Catskill Mountains

The Catskill region is a densely forested mountainous area renowned for its rivers, streams, waterfalls, and scenic landscape, as well as for influencing many of America's earliest and most famous writers, poets, artists, and naturalists.

The Catskills have also been pivotal to the history of American fly fishing, and streams like the Beaverkill, Willowemoc, Esopus, Neversink, and Rondout have been revered by generations of trout fishermen. These are historic trout waters steeped in tradition, held dear by men and women who fly fish, not only in this country, but all over the world. There are more than 1,500 miles of trout streams in the region; thirty of these streams are greater than 10 miles in length.

The eastern Catskills provide the Hudson River with picturesque views of wilderness peaks and fresh water from major streams like the Esopus, Rondout, and Catskill Creeks. In the northern region, the Schoharie Creek flows into the Mohawk River, which then flows into the Hudson near Albany. The western and southern slopes are part of the Delaware River watershed and are drained by the Neversink, Beaverkill, Willowemoc, and Callicoon Creeks, and the East and West Branches of the Delaware River.

Geologists tell us that the Catskill Mountains were formed from the eroding soils of much larger mountains located in what is now New England and southeastern New York. Hundreds of millions of years ago, rivers and streams flowing from these mountains carried soil, sand, and gravel into a vast inland sea that covered western New York, Pennsylvania, and parts of the Mississippi Valley.

This eroding material deposited into a great sinking delta, or alluvial fan. Eventually, as the mountains were worn low, deposits into the delta halted, and rock strata were formed. The strata, piled layer upon layer, accumulated to a thickness of several thousand feet; and approximately 225 million years ago, the delta was uplifted far above sea level to form a plateau. In time, the plateau took on a mountainous form, as it was dissected into deep valleys by weathering, stream erosion, and the breakdown of the flat-lying rocks.

A further event in creating the physiography of the Catskills occurred approximately twenty-one thousand years ago when the mountains were completely covered with glaciers. The glaciers reworked the soil, scattering rocks of all sizes and shapes through it. When the ice moved over the landscape, it scraped off the loose soil, sandstone, and rocks, and carried everything in, on, and under the ice. As the ice melted, glacial drift piled up at the ice borders was either carried away by streams coming off the melting ice or spread out as a sheet of till. This glacial till covers much of the region and is composed of an unsorted mixture of clay, sand, silt, and rock fragments of various sizes.

Following deglaciation, an arctic-alpine flora first covered the region. In time, milder climate allowed the arctic-alpine flora to be replaced by a boreal forest of red spruce, balsam fir, paper birch, and mountain ash. From the south, a northern hardwood forest of beech, birch, maple, and hemlock ascended the mountain slopes and slowly took over, in varying degrees, the boreal forest. (Although hemlock is not a hardwood, it is often associated with this type of forest.)

The present form of the Catskill Mountains is the result of the continuing actions of the many streams and rivers that cut narrow valleys into the landscape. All Catskill streams are basically unstable; the glacial till that is found in the area forms fragile banks and forever-changing streambeds. Understandably, banks composed of clay, sand, and unsorted gravel form a loose, erodible soil and collapse quite readily. Streams are steep gradient, soil is thin, and runoff from rains and melting snow is rapid. Streams rise quickly and overflow their banks often. Flooding is a common occurrence, and erosion is evident on all streams.

Where the Catskills begin and end has been the subject of many interpretations; there is only one obvious boundary, and that is in the east and northeast, where a rock precipice rises more than 2,000 feet from the valley floor below, just a few miles from the Hudson River. At first, the name Catskill Mountains applied only to the region west of the hamlet of Palenville and this great escarpment. Included were the headwaters of the Schoharie Creek and only those mountains visible from the mouth of Catskill Creek where it enters the Hudson River.

Visitors to the summit ledges of the escarpment are treated to unequaled views of a vast panorama

Haines Falls (at the head of Kaaterskill Clove). *Harper's New Monthly Magazine*, September 1883.

of the Hudson Valley and beyond. Spread before the eye is a patchwork of cultivated fields, meadows, farmland, woodland, wetlands, villages, cities, and the distant states of Massachusetts and Connecticut. The most spectacular scenery in the Catskills is found in this area and includes the famous Kaaterskill Falls and the Kaaterskill and Plattekill Cloves: deep gorges carved through the towering rock wall.

The view from the escarpment is the most dramatic in the Catskills and inspired the prolific and popular American author James Fenimore Cooper to put into words this remarkable scenic vista in his classic book *The Pioneers* (1823). It is Cooper's work that is most often quoted when writers attempt to describe the inexpressible view. In *The Pioneers,* Cooper's character Natty Bumppo and his companions are fishing. When one of them praises the nearby scenery, Natty then tells of the beauty of the Catskills:

> "I have travelled the woods for fifty-three year, and have made them my home for more than forty, and I can say that I have met but one place that was more to my liking; and that was only to eyesight, and not for hunting or fishing."
>
> "And where was that?" asked Edwards.
>
> "Where! Why up in the Cattskills. . . . Next to the river, where one of the ridges juts out a little from the rest, and where the rocks fall for the best part of a thousand feet, so much up and down, that a man standing on their edges is fool enough to think he can jump from top to bottom."
>
> "What see you when you get there?" asked Edwards.
>
> "Creation!" said Natty. . . ."[1]

The Catskills were also an inspiration to another of America's most distinguished authors. Washington Irving described the wonders of the mountains and created a public awareness of the region at a very early date when he wrote his classic story "Rip Van Winkle" in 1819. According to author Kenneth Myers, "Irving's fiction both introduced the Catskills to large numbers of European and American readers and gave the mountains a history with which they have been identified ever since."[2]

Years later, in an essay titled "The Catskill Mountains," Irving recalled when he first saw the mystical mountains as a young boy, before the advent of steamboats. "The interior of these mountains is in the highest

Kaaterskill Falls. *Forest Rock and Stream,* 1886.

degree wild and romantic; here are rocky precipices mantled with primeval forests; deep gorges walled in by beetling cliffs, with torrents tumbling as it were from the sky; and savage glens rarely trodden excepting by the hunter."[3]

Washington Irving was not a fisherman, but he contributed to the lore of trout fishing when he produced an essay titled "The Angler." The work was published in 1820 in the *Sketch Book of Geoffrey Crayon, Gent.,* and it has been hailed as "the first description of fly fishing in America."[4] "The Angler," however, is a story of an aging British fly fisher whom Irving befriends and observes fishing along the Alun, a tributary of the Dee, which flows down from the Welsh hills.

In the essay, Irving does recall his own attempt at angling in America years before. He had read, and greatly enjoyed, Izaak Walton's *The Compleat Angler,* and with several of his friends traveled to the "highlands of the Hudson;" a stretch of river 15 miles in length between Peekskill and Newburgh.

They fished a "mountain brook," apparently with little success, as Irving states he was always a "bungler" at sports that necessitated "either patience or adroitness." He had only fished a half hour before he convinced himself of this fact: "I hooked myself instead of the fish, tangled my line in every tree, lost my bait, broke my rod, until I gave up the attempt in despair, and passed the day under the trees reading old Izaak, satisfied that it was his fascinating vein of honest simplicity and rural feeling that had bewitched me, and not the passion for angling."[5]

Although the name Catskill Mountains was first associated with the area around Catskill Creek and took in the headwaters of the Schoharie Creek, in time the name *Catskill* spread to the southwest and south, absorbing the then-called Shandaken Mountains of the Esopus Valley. Later, a good portion of the upper Neversink and Rondout Creek were included in the description, and eventually the name *Catskill* began to be applied to the westerly side of the mountains that took in all of the Beaverkill, Willowemoc Creek, East Branch of the Delaware River, the headwaters of the West Branch of the Delaware River, and part of the Callicoon Creek.

Perhaps the best description of the physiographic boundaries of the Catskills can be found in a report by Karl L. Brooks titled "The Catskills and Their Flora—An Overview." The report delineates that nearly all of Delaware County, parts of the towns of Gilboa and Conesville in Schoharie County, the southwestern half of Greene County, the western half of Ulster County, and the northern third of Sullivan County make up the Catskill Mountains.

The exact origin of the name *Catskill* is unclear. It was derived in the time of Dutch domination, appearing at least as early as 1656, when the name was depicted on a map of New Belgium or New Netherland by Adriaen Van der donck as *Landt van Kats Kill.* The most common explanation is that the mountains were so named because they contained large numbers of wildcats (bobcats) and mountain lions.

Catskill streams and rivers often have the word *Kill* attached to them, as in Beaverkill, West Kill, Batavia Kill, or Bush Kill. The word *Kill* is Dutch for creek. Early maps reveal that streams like the Neversink, Rondout, and Schoharie were once known as the Neversink Kill, Rondout Kill, and Schoharie Kill. Many streams, such as Stewart Brook, Benton Hollow Brook, or Darbee Brook, are named for early settlers. Others were named for the wildlife of the region, such as Pigeon Brook, Elk Creek, and Mink and Wolf Hollows; and some retain names dating back to the time of Indian culture, such as Willowemoc, Neversink, Esopus, and Mongaup.

Throughout our history, angling has been a favorite pastime of Americans, and in particular to New Yorkers, who have developed a tradition for the sport dating back to colonial times. The first law in the New World aimed at protecting and preserving freshwater fisheries was enacted in New York City in 1734. Overfishing forced the Common Council to restrict fishing methods on a pond known as Fresh Water Pond or The Collect. The law banned netting of all kinds and limited the taking of fish to "Angling, with Angle-Rod, Hook and Line only: Every Person so offending against the Tenours of this Law, shall for every such Offence forfeit and pay the Sum of *Twenty Shillings* of current Money this Colony . . ."[6]

Andrew Burnaby, an English clergyman and traveler who visited the colonies in 1759 and 1760, wrote of the popularity of angling among women in New York and of the desire to leave the city and pursue the solitude of the less-inhabited areas: "The women are handsome and agreeable; though rather more reserved than the Philadelphian ladies. Their amusements are much the same as in Pennsylvania; viz. balls, and sleighing expeditions in the winter; and, in the summer, going in parties upon the water, and fishing; or making excursions into the country."[7]

The earliest reference to trout fishing in the Catskills is found in Jay Gould's *History of Delaware County* (1856), and women once again are referenced. Gould writes of the years 1785 to 1790 and of the early settlement of Walton. The village of Walton lies along the banks of the West Branch of the Delaware River in Delaware County:

> Fish and game were plenty. Shad were, if reports were true, near Pine-hill, in quite large numbers; and trout, those delicious fish, the river is said to have been full of them—we being a regular disciple of Isaac Walton, it fairly makes our mouth water to think of them; the women would go out with a pole and line, and in a few minutes catch enough for tea or breakfast; and to use their own expression, some of them would make a pan-full. Those were indeed the days of *women's rights*, when they were allowed to catch fish and manufacture their own clothes; and we should like to be transported back to those good old times, were it only for a day or two, just to breakfast on those delicious trout, dine on samp-porridge and sup on choice bits of dried elk-meat.[8]

Many of the first residents of the region were not tillers of the soil. The high elevation predicated late spring and early autumn frosts, and the steep slopes of a mountainous terrain, combined with stony soils and rock outcroppings, prevented deep plowing. Settlers lived in cabins or log huts with no floors or furniture, and although they may have had a small garden for beans, potatoes, and pumpkins, they mostly lived off the land, and their principal foods were wild meats taken by hunting and fishing.

Log home. *The American Angler's Book*, 1864.

The Catskills' abundant natural resources and scenic beauty have attracted visitors from the earliest days of settlement. Hunting and fishing parties traveled to the region even when accommodations were poor and transportation difficult, slow, and uncomfortable. At times, trout fishermen found a night's lodging at the humble homes of settlers, and if the settlers' locations were in the more accessible valleys, they would turn their residences into country inns or public houses.

When settlement in the region began, men either walked or rode on horseback; most trails were too narrow to allow travel with a team, be it oxen or horses. As more people migrated to the area, Indian trails and bridle paths became wagon roads, yet travel remained difficult. These roads were crudely cut through the forest; stumps, boulders, and other obstructions were left in the roadway, and because wagons had no springs, people traveled only by necessity.

By the early 1800s, roads were slowly improved, and a small number of tourists began finding their way into the Catskills. In 1810, there were three major roads running west from the Hudson into the mountains. The northernmost was the Susquehanna Turnpike, which opened in 1803. It began at the village of Catskill and traveled into Schoharie County and through Delaware County. The central road was the Ulster and Delaware Turnpike, which ran from Kingston through Ulster and Delaware counties to Bainbridge in Chenango County. The southerly route was via the Newburgh and Cochecton Turnpike. This road began along the Hudson River at Newburgh and traveled through all of Orange and Sullivan counties to Cochecton on the Delaware River.

As road conditions improved, stage travel was extended into more villages and became a popular means of transportation for trout-fishing tourists. Stagecoach travel in the Catskills lasted for more than a half century, and the four-horse stagecoach with its lofty driver's seat was a sight to behold. Upon reaching a destination at an inn, boardinghouse, or tavern, the driver announced the arrival with a blast from his bugle, signaling villagers that the stage was arriving. Stage drivers were the envy of country boys who rarely got the opportunity to leave their village and found the occupation of stagecoach driver glamorous and exciting.

By 1820, New York City was fast becoming America's principal center of trade, intellect, and culture. The city's population was growing rapidly, and over the next ten years, all semblance of rural life was being swept away by development and expansion. As streets and avenues were constructed, streams and wetlands were drained, filled, placed in culverts, covered over, and built upon.

Steamboat travel had begun on the Hudson as early as 1808, but it was not until

Stagecoach through the Catskills. *Lippincott's Magazine*, September, 1879.

the Supreme Court removed all barriers to free navigation that service was expanded. In 1825, there were steamboat lines running regularly to most of the important points along the river between New York and Albany. Soon boats were traveling both day and night, and the increased transportation made the Catskills easily accessible to major population centers.

By 1835, the Hudson became the busiest waterway in the nation, and boat traffic was such a common sight that author Nathaniel P. Willis remarked, "There is a suburban look and character about all the villages on the Hudson which seems out of place among such scenery. They are suburbs; in fact, steam has destroyed the distance between them and the city."[9] And steam also made it possible for city anglers to commute to the pristine trout streams of the Catskills on a more regular basis.

Trout fishing in particular held a fascination for many early Gothamites who may have inherited a love of the sport from their English, Scottish, and Irish ancestors. For recreation and tranquillity, city dwellers in ever-increasing numbers made excursions into the countryside. Throughout the next decade, angling was widely practiced, and New Yorkers were well on their way to establishing fishing as a primary form of recreation. Evidence of its popularity can be found in the comparatively large number of tackle shops in the city in the 1830s dealing in fishing paraphernalia.

The oldest shop was T. J. Bate, the parent firm of William Mills & Son, which was established in 1822. Fishing enthusiasts also frequented Abraham Brower's on Water Street, Charles Taylor's on Maiden Lane and Broadway, and Lewis's at New and Wall Streets. On Fulton Street alone were the shops of T. W. Harsfield, J. B. Crook's, Thomas Conroy's, John Brown's Anglers Depot, and the famous Pritchard Brothers.

Before 1825, there was little written history regarding trout fishing in America; sporting magazines that were available were published in England, and newspapers at the time rarely reported on field sports. Even years after Americans had achieved their political independence, they remained a principle market for English books, periodicals, and sporting literature.

One of the earliest references to trout fishing in the Catskills appeared in a scientific journal in 1823. The article was written by James Pierce and was published in the *American Journal of Science and Arts*. Its title was "A Memoir on the Catskill Mountains with notices of their Topography, Scenery, Mineralogy, Zoology, economical resources, &c." Pierce's essay is informative and covers many aspects of the Catskills, including descriptions of forest vegetation, mountain scenery, wildlife, and fishery.

He writes that trout are abundant, particularly in the Plattekill, Kaaterskill, and Schoharie Creeks, and he claims that other

Trout fishing on a mountain stream. *Frank Forester's Fish and Fishing of the United States and British Provinces*, 1849.

mountain streams are "uncommonly well stored with trout," citing that one angler caught five hundred trout in a single day. Pierce also mentions a mountaintop lake located deep in the forest at the head of the Saw Kill known as Shue's Lake (Echo Lake):

> About three miles south of the Platterkill and at a great elevation above the Hudson, a deep body of water one mile in circumference, called Shues lake is situated, and is environed by an amphitheatre of wild, rocky, and steep mountains. It contains trout of large size.[10]

Pierce was the first to draw attention to Shue's Lake, a body of water that has figured prominently in Catskill trout-fishing lore. The lake was a favorite rendezvous of some of the earliest hunters and fishermen who found their way into the region seeking deer, bear, mountain lions, and the large brook trout for which the lake was famous.

One of the earliest haunts of hunters and fishermen in the mountains was the roadside tavern of Merchant Lawrence, located near the great escarpment in Kiskatom Valley in the town of Catskill, Greene County. Lawrence purchased land near the foot of the mountains in 1798 and a few years later constructed an inn, which was for many years a well-known resort to sportsmen from New York, Albany, and other populated areas.

Fishermen would spend the night at Lawrence's tavern and fish Kiskatom Brook, the Shingle Kill, Kaaterskill Creek, and other nearby waters. The tavern was especially popular with bear hunters, both novices and veterans, who were known to tell of their adventures while enjoying the comforts of the bar. A special feature at the tavern were the live bears tamed by Lawrence; for a fee of three cents, guests would get to see the bears, which were kept on chains in pens, and be entertained by them.

The native black bear was common to the region and became a symbol of the mountain wilderness; in the Catskills, February 2 was known as "Bear's Day." It was long believed that on that date, bears would wake up from their long period of hibernation, come out of their dens, and "take a knowing observation of the weather for a few minutes, and then retire to their nests and finish their repose of some weeks or months."[11]

It was claimed that if the sky was clear and the bear saw its shadow when it came forth, it would return to its lair and sleep until the first of April, knowing that cold weather would continue until that date. If upon emergence the bear finds the weather mild and cloudy, it looks toward an early spring and often leaves its den. This practice by the bears is said to have been witnessed by veteran bear hunters and also proven by the discovery of tracks made by bears on that particular date each year.

Bear meat was a regular staple on the menu at Lawrence's, but on New Year's Day, he would serve a special feast of bear meat to which friends and his most favored customers of the rod or gun would be invited. Tales of bears were told and retold in the famous barroom as guests enjoyed the camaraderie of this unique event.

Trout fishermen are disposed to accepting hardship and travel in pursuit of their sport, and with the completion of the turnpikes, parties of anglers journeyed deeper into the Catskills. Another early destination of trout fishermen was the inn of Milo Barber, which was located near the Esopus Creek, where it is joined by Stony Clove Creek at Phoenicia in Ulster County. Barber purchased 90

A bear wallow. *Harper's New Monthly Magazine*, May, 1877.

acres in 1812, and while he farmed the land, he operated a small store on the road along the Stony Clove and boarded trout fishermen as early as 1826. Upon the death of Milo Barber, his son, Milo Barber Jr., continued to take in boarders and guide trout fishermen for many years.

Those anglers who first cast their lines into the mountain streams of the Catskills encountered only one species of trout: the brook trout, *Salvelinus fontinalis*. Although they prefer cold, clean, well-oxygenated waters and thrive in streams, their natural habitat includes lakes and ponds. *Salvelinus* means "char"; *fontinalis*, "living in cold springs"; and, as their name implies, brook trout prefer to live where water temperatures are coolest.

Samuel L. Mitchell first named the species, and it was in 1814 that the first important work on fish or fishing in America appeared. Mitchell authored a small book titled *Report, in part, of Samuel L. Mitchell . . . on the Fishes of New-York*. Mitchell, a professor of natural history at the University of New York, examined and dissected fish and wrote physical descriptions of his findings. In 1815, an expanded version of his report was published in *The Transactions of the Literary and Philosophical Society of New-York*.

Mitchell named the "common trout" or brook trout, *Salmo fontinalis*. In *The Inland Fishes of New York State*, C. Lavett Smith explains, "Fontinalis is the genitive of the Latin *fons*, fountain or spring, and refers to the habitat of the brook trout."[12] However, in classifying the brook trout in the genus *Salmo*, Mitchell was mistaken. The fish was later found to be a char and not a true trout, and in 1878, fisheries scientists reclassified it and changed the Latin name to *Salvelinus*. Today the brook trout is known as *Salvelinus fontinalis* (Mitchell), retaining Mitchell's name as the authority, a lasting tribute to America's pioneer ichthyologist.

Early fishermen found brook trout to be plentiful, every stream had an abundance of the fish, and all of the larger waters contained excellent populations along their upper and middle reaches. Though their number was great, the brook trout of our forefathers' day was a predominantly small fish. In the early days of trout fishing, anglers measured their success by the pound—not of individual fish, but of the total catch! Trout fishermen who first waded the waters of the Catskills carried baskets that, when filled, contained an approximate weight of the accumulated fish. The most popular sizes held 15, 18, and 24 pounds of trout!

Native brook trout. *The American Angler's Book*, 1864.

The lack of size was of small concern to those who delighted in stream fishing; they found attributes in the brook trout that were unequaled by other fish:

> The lines of grace and beauty, so gratifying to the poet and the artist, culminate in absolute perfection in the trout. The perfect symmetry, the harmonious blending of colors, the graceful motions of this exquisite of the brook, give it a value of great price, to all who look at it with appreciative eyes. Look at its large round eyes, orbs of light nev-set; its snow white body; look at its sides clad in mail of rainbow hue dotted with pink stars in sky blue tints.[13]

Brook trout were the favorite fish of many of the old-time fly-fishing masters, such as artist/angler Charles Lanman, who wrote, "He always glories in the coldest and purest of water, and the regions of the country to which he is partial are commonly distinguished for the wildness of their scenery; and therefore it is that to the lover of nature this imperial fish has been exceedingly dear."[14]

Throughout much of the nineteenth century, the western portion of the Catskills, primarily Delaware and Sullivan counties, were accessible only by horseback, wagon, or in some areas by stagecoach. In Delaware County at the headwaters of the East Branch, the oldest inn in Roxbury, which dated back to 1798, evolved into the Hendrick Hudson House. By the 1840s, this hotel became a favorite resort of trout fishermen who fished not only the upper East Branch but also nearby tributaries, such as the Batavia Kill, Hardscrabble Creek, Meeker Hollow, and Montgomery Hollow, streams that abounded in native brook trout. Some guests even ventured overland to the upper Beaverkill and Balsam Lake.

Long before they were considered to be part of the Catskills, the trout streams of Sullivan County were the destination of most urban trout fishermen. By the 1830s, fishing tourists with regularity were casting lines, with flies attached, into the waters of the Neversink, Beaverkill, Callicoon, and Willowemoc Creeks. These were well-known names to all serious anglers, and whereas today's fly fishers place these famous streams in the Catskills, pioneer fly fishermen always referred to the region as Sullivan County and praised its trout and streams in prose, poetry, and paintings.

Many of the first anglers to fish the waters of Sullivan County headed for the Darbee House, located at the junction of the Beaverkill and Willowemoc Creek; Samuel and Hannah Darbee constructed their early fishing resort in Westfield Flats (Roscoe) in 1806. With the accidental death of Samuel, this "publick house" became known to sportsmen for many years simply as "Mrs. Darbee's." "Eminent doctors, artists and men of letters came for the excellent nearby trout fishing, relaxation, and charms of the wild countryside."[15]

The 1830s were an important era in the development of sportfishing in America. It was the decade Americans began developing their own angling identity and started drifting away from the strong influence English angling traditions had previously held.

The first sporting magazine to appear in the United States made its debut in 1829. It was published in Baltimore and titled *American Turf Register and Sporting Magazine.* Founded and edited by John S. Skinner, the magazine was devoted to horse racing, shooting, hunting, fishing, and other outdoor activities. Although the magazine featured articles written about American sportfishing, many were still of English origin.

A more significant publication of the period, however, appeared two years later. It was in 1831 that William T. Porter began publishing the *Spirit of the Times* in New York, and fishing enthusiasts enjoyed an all-around weekly sporting journal that reported regularly on American sportfishing. The *Spirit* specialized in field sports, horse racing, hunting, and fishing, but it also included literature and the stage. In New York City at that time were a large number of men who extracted themselves from their business professions each year and devoted time to field sports with rod or gun.

While some Americans were still hunting and fishing out of necessity, others, who were seeking recreation, began exploring the unsettled and remote regions of New York State. By the end of the decade, the number of anglers had increased greatly, causing Porter, in the summer of 1838, to write in the *Spirit*:

> There are hundreds upon hundreds of our citizens scattered about the country within two hundred miles of us and probably there is not a brook, river, or pond, within that circle in which they have not wet a line.[16]

The *Spirit of the Times* played an important role in promoting sport or recreational fishing. Editor William T. Porter was an avid trout fisher, fly fisherman, and prominent journalist. Fishing was Porter's passion, and so he penned most of those articles himself. He pioneered sporting literature and, importantly, reported on fishing for pleasure. He was determined to free his paper from the influence of English sporting literature and to "fashion truly *American* ones in their place."[17] Americans, on a regular basis, could now read angling articles about their own waters that were written by Americans. And more often than not, early fishing enthusiasts read about the trout streams of Sullivan County; particularly those flowing into the Delaware River watershed.

2

Sullivan County

"THE TALL SON OF YORK" and "THE LARGEST TROUT IN THE WORLD"

No one wants to be lugged out of bed, precisely as no one wanted to travel beyond Sullivan County; the best shooting and fishing in the world was to be found there.

—ROBERT BARNWELL ROOSEVELT, *Game Fish of the Northern States of America and British Provinces,* 1862

In the earliest days of sportfishing, the most well-known trout streams in America were the Beaverkill, Willowemoc, Neversink, and Callicoon Creek. These waters were held in high esteem by all serious trout fishermen, not only for the number of trout they yielded, but for the size of the trout as well.

Many anglers traveled arduous routes to reach these streams, and the region they occupied was then known to pioneer fly fishers as Sullivan County. The Sullivan County portion of the Catskills had not yet been included in the general description of what we now call the Catskill Mountains.

The Beaverkill was the favorite, and although its source was located in Ulster County, the uppermost section of the stream was almost uninhabited, mountainous, and difficult to reach in the 1820s and 1830s. The Sullivan County portion of the Beaverkill had early settlements and accommodations for trout-fishing tourists at Westfield Flats (Roscoe) and Shin Creek (Lew Beach).

Located in the western Catskills, the source of the Beaverkill is a narrow, rocky ravine between the mountains Graham and Doubletop. The elevation is approximately 2,900 feet, and the stream flows in a general direction westerly through a dense forest with a steep and stony mountainous landscape. At its headwaters, the Beaverkill recruits many springs and a few larger tributaries such as Black Brook, Balsam Lake Brook, and Beecher Brook.

After a course of approximately 10 miles, the stream forms Beaverkill Falls, one of the most picturesque sites on the Beaverkill. The falls is notable in that it combines an impressive vivid scene of great natural beauty with some of the best trout fishing on the upper Beaverkill.

Source of the Beaverkill. Ed Van Put.

It is from the area upstream of the falls that the Beaverkill received its name. When the first settlers scouted the region, they found an abundance of abandoned beaver dams, lodges, and ancient beaver meadows. The beaver were gone; they had been hunted by the Indians to trade with European fur buyers many years before.

Approximately 3 miles downstream of the falls, the Beaverkill flows near the base of Touchmenot Mountain, where the stream's elevation is approximately 1,770 feet; a drop of about 1,130 feet in 13 miles. Along the way, tributaries named Scudder Brook and Alder Creek add their cold waters, and after Touchmenot the Beaverkill turns in a southwesterly direction, recruits Upper Beech Hill Brook, and flows another 4 miles before reaching Shin Creek, which was, at one time, the name of a small settlement.

Shin Creek itself is a prolific trout stream that adds volume as well as trout to the Beaverkill as it continues flowing southwesterly. The Beaverkill continues to receive waters from tributaries both named and unnamed, but three streams of note that enter the flow are Mary Smith Brook, Berry Brook, and Spring Brook. After traveling approximately 28 miles, the Beaverkill joins the Willowemoc Creek, a stream of equal size and flow.

At the time of settlement, the Willowemoc was known as the Whelenaughwemack, and the Beaverkill upstream of this union was known as the Great Beaverkill. A tributary 7 miles upstream on the Whelenaughwemack was called the Little Beaverkill, an appellation deferring to the larger of the two Beaverkills. The river downstream of the junction was known as the Whelenaughwemack until it was joined by the "Papagonk," "Pawpacton," or "Pepacton" river, now known as the East Branch of the Delaware River.

Whelenaughwemack is derived from the name used by the Lenni-Lenape, who lived at the mouth of the river, which was a noted rendezvous of the Indians before, during, and after the Revolutionary War. Over time, "Whelenaughwemack" evolved into "Welawemacks" and, eventually, Willowemoc; the portion of the river downstream of the junction would become known as the "lower" or "big" Beaverkill.

When the first settlers came into the region, they learned the meaning of the name directly from the Indians: "It is 'the kettle that washes itself clean,' and the stream was so called because of the spring freshets, which carry off all the driftwood, etc., from its banks."[1]

The Beaverkill headwaters wind through an ancient beaver meadow. Ed Van Put.

The entire Beaverkill Valley is narrow and steep-sided, and mountainsides are densely forested with beech, birch, maple, and, as is often the case in northern hardwood forests, hemlock.

By 1785, a trail had been measured and cut from Lackawack, in the Rondout Valley, through the forest and across the headwaters of the Beaverkill to Pawpacton on the East Branch of the Delaware River. This trail had marked and numbered "mile trees," 1 through 35, and was known as "the common road." The road crossed the waters of the Neversink, Willowemoc, and Shin Creeks and the Beaverkill, and was used by the earliest hunters, trappers, and trout fishermen.

Settlement along the Beaverkill began where the stream joined the waters of the Whelenaughwemack. Most of the earliest settlers came from Connecticut, and many were veterans of the Revolutionary War. According to local lore, these men were told of good flatland located along the "Great Beaverkill" by scouts who had been in the region during the revolution keeping an eye on the remaining Indians, who, it was feared, would aid the English.

The source of the Willowemoc Creek is also in Ulster County, in the town of Denning. The stream begins at an elevation of approximately 2,940 feet and flows through a mountainous land-scape of unbroken forest in a southwesterly direction, falling approximately 286 feet per mile for the first 3 miles. The gradient continues dropping but changes sharply, becoming less steep after 3 miles, averaging approximately 55 feet per mile over the next 7 miles. The stream recruits many

The spectacular beauty of a Willowemoc tributary.
Ed Van Put.

springs and small tributaries, but only two streams of note—Butternut Brook and Fir Brook—enter the Willowemoc before reaching a hamlet of the same name.

Downstream of the hamlet of Willowemoc, the stream runs in a more westerly direction, picking up a few unnamed tributaries before reaching DeBruce, where it is joined by the Mongaup Creek, a moderate-sized trout stream with a fine reputation. The Willowemoc continues growing in size as it flows westerly, adding water from Frog Hollow and Sprague Brook before reaching Livingston Manor. There it is joined by its largest tributary, the Little Beaverkill, and Cattail Brook.

The Willowemoc becomes a large trout stream between Livingston Manor and Roscoe, and within these 7 miles the gradient drops only 20 feet per mile. In this stretch of river, notable tributaries are Elm Hollow Brook, Bascom Brook, Hazel Brook, Bennett Brook, Stewart Brook, and Abe Wood Brook. The total length of the Willowemoc from source to its confluence with the Beaverkill is approximately 26.3 miles.

Not only was there great fishing along the Willowemoc and Beaverkill, there was more of it. The two streams combined offered approximately 54 miles of native brook trout fishing. By comparison, the Rondout Creek had 10 miles, as did the Esopus. Only the Neversink was comparable: Including its two branches, it totaled about 26 miles of brook trout water.

In the earliest days of trout fishing, tourists found their way to Sullivan County via the Newburgh and Cochecton Turnpike, which opened in 1808. This route had stagecoach lines through Orange and Sullivan counties from Newburgh all the way to the Delaware River. When travelers departed from the stage route, they were usually transported by horse and wagon to their destination.

Many of the first trout fishermen to fish the Beaverkill headed to the Darbee House, which was located on a small knoll overlooking the junction of the Beaverkill and Willowemoc Creek. Samuel and Hannah Darbee's hotel was known for its fine meals, and the cost was "a shilling, or one and eight pence, if toddy was ordered."[2] There were seven huge stone fireplaces and a ballroom, and many fine paintings hung on the walls painted by artists who boarded there while trout fishing. The kitchen contained a bake oven and two fireplaces with iron cranes for supporting cauldrons.

Before 1825, there is very little written history regarding the Catskill region, especially as it relates to trout fishing. This is primarily due to the fact that the Catskills had barely been settled, and those newspapers available rarely reported on activities other than politics. In addition, historical data relative to trout fishing in America before 1830 is also rare.

When the *American Turf Register and Sporting Magazine* made its debut in 1829, the Beaverkill was already well-known to trout fishermen. Though the magazine featured fishing articles of predominantly English origin, the reputation of the Beaverkill and Mrs. Darbee's found their way onto its pages:

> Make your headquarters at Mrs. Darbys [sic] and you will be sure to find excellent accommodations, and capital fishing. The Williewemauk, Calikoon, and Beaver Kill, are three of the finest trout streams in this country; the trout are large, very numerous, and of the most delicious flavor.[3]

In the 1820s, some New York City fishermen headed to the nearby waters of Long Island, where placid streams and ponds contained native brook trout. But even more sought their piscatorial adventures along the mountain streams of Sullivan County, which, in addition to abundant trout, offered unparalleled scenic beauty and the pleasant musical sounds of flowing water that are found only along streams of rapid descent.

Through diary entries and articles in sporting journals, we learn that Henry Inman, William T. Porter, and Henry William Herbert (Frank Forester) were among the earliest trout fishermen, and that Sullivan County played a key role in the history of American fly fishing.

HENRY INMAN

Henry Inman (1801–1846) was a pioneer sport fisherman who spent many days' trout fishing the Beaverkill and Willowemoc, as well as other nearby waters, while staying at the Darbee House at Westfield Flats (Roscoe). Inman achieved great fame as an artist of portraits, and coupled with his talents with a fly rod, he was looked upon as one of this country's most celebrated trout fishermen.

Although he was born upstate in Utica, Henry Inman spent most of his life in New York City, where his family relocated in 1812. At the age of thirteen, he began studying art under John Wesley Jarvis, a well-known portrait painter. Inman's apprenticeship with Jarvis lasted seven years, and at the age of twenty-two, he opened his own studio on Vesey Street in lower Manhattan.

The versatile Inman belonged to the first generation of American-trained artists. He worked in landscapes, miniature, and genre, but he was primarily a painter of life-sized portraits. During the 1830s, he was considered New York's finest portrait painter, and his studio was visited by an imposing list of patrons, including many famous men and women such as President Martin Van Buren, DeWitt Clinton, John J. Audubon, Nathaniel Hawthorne, and Clara Barton.

As his popularity and reputation increased, his income soared. His portraits were "realistic," and he possessed great skill in reproducing the eyes. A critic once stated, "Perhaps we have never had a painter who could paint a better eye than Inman—few so well." It was also said that the eyes looked "at you more than you at them."[4]

It was believed that Inman's personality and his skill as a conversationalist gave him an edge with those he painted; he put them at ease and thus captured a sitter's natural expression. In this he excelled, and while his paintings may have improved the appearance of those who posed, there was always a "likeness" that he captured better than others who painted portraits. When he painted Wordsworth, the famous poet told him that he had sat twenty-seven times for many different artists, and he stated that Inman's picture was a better likeness than any of the others.

Because of his artistic skills, Henry Inman commanded a good price for his work. Costs were generally fixed in conjunction with the size of the painting; he received, at times, $500 for half length and $1,000 for full length. Artists are known for their temperament and sensitivity toward their work, and a story is told about Henry Inman of an instance when he received a sum far less than he expected for a group painting. Inman asked that the painting be returned to him so that he could make some improvements; instead, he proceeded to reduce the size of the painting by cutting off all of the subjects' legs, and then returned it, along with $200!

Henry Inman made regular pilgrimages to the distant wilds of Sullivan County and was one of the first to explore the exceptional trout fishing found along the Beaverkill, Willowemoc, and Callicoon Creeks. His devotion to trout fishing was well known to the New Yorkers of his day.

He was a man who found solace away from the brick walls and turmoil of the city, and like many anglers, he recognized that trout fishing is more than just catching fish. Inman found great joy in the natural beauty of a stream environment. In an article published in the *Atlantic Souvenir,* he wrote:

Who that has enjoyed the pleasures of wandering free and far among scenes of rural beauty; has not learned to loathe more deeply the irksome bondage of a city life. Give me the blue and lofty mountain shutting out another world behind it—the sequestered valley where I may quietly muse among overhanging rocks, soothed by the murmurs of the bubbling stream.[5]

In the days when Henry Inman fished the Beaverkill and stayed at the Darbee House, there were, on the side of the building drawn and cut in outline, large brook trout that were taken from the nearby Beaverkill and Willowemoc. One such fish was placed there by Inman, who drew the outline on the plain surface of a window shutter. Even after many years, it was still remembered how excited he was when he held up the large trout to an admiring crowd, before "taking its likeness." This unique fish, a brook trout of extraordinary size, was caught in late June in the year 1841.

Your most sincerely
H. Inman.

Henry Inman 1826. Print Collection, Miriam and Ira D. Wallach Division of Art, Prints and Photographs, The New York Public Library, Astor, Lenox and Tilden Foundations.

It is difficult today to imagine what trout fishing was like for those anglers who first cast their lines into the lakes, ponds, and streams of the Catskills, before trout populations were depleted by overfishing or altered by the introduction of domestic fish or a competitive species. Documented accounts are rare, and when they are found, they usually reveal a fishery dramatically different from today.

Fortunately, a diary kept by one of Henry Inman's close friends gives us some insight into the trout fishing of his era and the particulars of the large trout he drew on the side of the Darbee House. Richard T. Fosdick recorded information on several trips that he and Inman made together to Sullivan County:

> 1841. June 21.—Inman, Warner, Dawley and I left for Chester Darbie's,* [sic] in Sullivan Co. Took 7 o'clock train at Jersey City and arrived at Hankin's Station at 1:30. Hired two wagons to take us across mountains over the most infernal road ever invented. Arrived at Darbie's [sic] about ten at night; took rest next morning and spent the day fixing tackle. Tried sundown fishing, but with no success. In morning was fishing by 5 o'clock and kept busy until 8. Upon show of hands we counted ninety-eight of as pretty fish as man could wish to see; seven about 1 lb. each and the balance averaging a half. Next day same success, and so on for six days. In figuring up we found the number of fish caught to be 548; the largest was a beauty, weighing 3 lbs. 3 oz. Inman was so delighted that he sketched the trout on the woodwork of Darbie's [sic] porch.[6]

A few weeks later, Inman, Warner, and Fosdick returned to Darbee's, and in addition to their stream fishing, they spent a couple of days and nights camping and fishing at Russell Pond. The pond is located in Delaware County, approximately 10 miles northwest of the junction of the Beaverkill and Willowemoc Creek and is at the headwaters of a Beaverkill tributary called Russell Brook:

> 1841. July—Inman, Warner and I at Chester Darbie's, [sic] Sullivan Co. Three day's fishing brought 271 trout. Camped out by Mother Russell's Pond two nights. Splendid time. Inman caught 69; Warner, 65; and I, 66. Pretty even fishing, as there was not 3 lbs. difference in the catches; some weighing 1¼ lb. down to ¼ lb. The united weight was 107½ lbs.[7]

Two years later Fosdick recorded another trip made with Henry Inman to the Beaverkill and Misner's Pond (Tennanah Lake), known for many years for its large brook trout:

> 1843. August—Sam Warner, Dr. Jim Quackenboss, Henry Inman, John Farren, Dr. Bill King, Henry Muir and myself start for Sullivan County to fish the Beaverkill and Willowhemack Rivers. A lively party, ready for any thing. First day caught 103 trout and kept increasing to the end of the week. Camped out one night on the mountains to fish Misenor's [sic] Pond. Great catch of fish; more than was wanted; 792 trout in all, 38 weighing 2 lbs. and over each, the average of balance being over a pound.[8]

Henry Inman was a popular New Yorker; his notoriety as the city's leading portraitist led to contacts with many of its prominent citizens. He was cultivated, possessed great wit and humor, and was an eloquent conversationalist. This personality endeared him to many, and he had a wide circle

---

*Chester Darbee was the son of Hannah Darbee.

of friends and acquaintances in the intellectual life of New York. He knew and socialized with many of the famous men then living in the city, such as Washington Irving, Charles Fenno Hoffman, Fitz-Greene Hallock, George P. Morris, Asher B. Durand, and William Cullen Bryant. Most everyone connected with art and literature knew of his love of trout fishing.

Inman suffered from poor health for many years, and annually he had debilitating bouts with asthma. By the time he reached forty years of age, his illness had worsened, and he would be sick for days with constant fevers. As his health declined, it caused him to cease work and go into depression. His income was greatly reduced from previous years, and on January 3, 1843, he wrote:

> Fine prospect of starving to death this year. Not a soul comes near me for pictures. Ambition in Art is gone. Give me a fortune, and I would fish and shoot for the rest of my life, without touching a brush again.[9]

With his health improving somewhat in 1844, he decided to go abroad to seek commissions painting portraits and landscapes. His traveling to Europe was considered a special event, and his good friend William T. Porter, of the *Spirit of the Times,* wrote a humorous article to celebrate the occasion:

> This poet, wit, and painter—as ardent a disciple of old Izaak Walton as ever threw a fly, and who never wet a line out of season, is about to sail for Europe, having recovered, we are delighted to add, his usual health. . . .
>
> Personally, and purely from selfish impulses, we hate to hear of his going abroad at all! Who shall now put us up to the trick of hornswoggling a salmon trout of forty pounds? Who will teach us the art and mystery of fabricating a fly that will induce a sockdolager* to "rise" at its first pirouette, though lying over a spring hole in ten feet of water?[10]

Inman returned to New York on April 16, 1845, and his health soon worsened. He had bad attacks of asthma throughout the year, and his income was reduced to the point to which he was barely meeting expenses. In December, his condition became critical, and in January, he died of heart disease at his home on Murray Street: "His death, which occurred January 17, 1846, called forth an unusually deep expression of public feeling; the press, throughout the country, teemed with the warmest eulogies of his social character, and his artistic abilities."[11]

Seven or eight hundred people attended Inman's funeral. Relatives, friends, and dignitaries from New York and other cities formed a long procession of mourners who followed the artist's casket, on foot, 2 miles through the winter evening. Pallbearers included Richard Fosdick and the artist Asher B. Durand and several members of the National Academy of Design.

Inman was interred at Greenwood Cemetery. Immediately after his funeral, a meeting of his friends was held, and it was decided to hold an exhibition of his work to benefit his family. The exhibition was held at the American Art-Union and was open to the public; 126 paintings were exhibited, and all proceeds were given to Inman's widow and five children.

"HENRY INMAN is no more!" wrote William T. Porter in the *Spirit of the Times.* Porter was one of Inman's fishing companions and closest friends. The terse statement exudes the sorrow Porter must have felt over the death of his dear friend. Porter continued:

---

*An old-time term for a very large trout.

Next to his devotion to his friends and his art, was Inman's fondness for Field Sports. In trout fishing, especial excelled . . . And a more ardent, accomplished, or, delightful disciple, good old Izaak Walton never had.[12]

One of the paintings exhibited at the Inman Memorial Exhibition to aid his family was a landscape titled *Trout Fishing in Sullivan County, New York.* The painting had been exhibited in New York at the sixteenth annual exhibition of the National Academy of Design on May 3, 1841, at the third Boston Artists' Association exhibition in 1844, and again at the annual exhibition of the Pennsylvania Academy of the Fine Arts in Philadelphia in 1847.

At these exhibitions, *Trout Fishing in Sullivan County, New York* was well received and thought to be the artist's most celebrated landscape. In time, the painting disappeared and was only known from an engraving that appeared in *New York Illustrated Magazine of Literature and Art* in 1847.

Fortunately, in 1983, the painting resurfaced and was purchased by the Munson-Williams-Proctor Institute, Museum of Art. The museum, located in Utica, New York, Inman's birthplace, has acquired an extraordinary collection of American art, including paintings by many of our most famous artists. When the Museum of Art purchased the painting, the price was greater than had been spent on any other American work—perhaps deservedly, as the acquisition gives the public an opportunity to view not only a work of art, but an important historical work as well. Angling scenes, especially of Inman's era, are quite rare.

It is most likely that the scene painted by Inman is the junction of the Beaverkill and Willowemoc Creek, one of the most celebrated pools in angling history. The site is but a short walk from the old Darbee House, where Inman spent so many days fishing in Sullivan County. In a catalogue titled *The Art of Henry Inman,* William H. Gerdts, professor of art history at the City University of New York, has written of the painting, "It was in its time the most renowned landscape effort, and is probably also the most autobiographical, for it documents the artist's piscatorial enthusiasms, for which he was almost as well known as for his artistry."

Henry Inman left behind many fine paintings. Some are found in New York's City Hall, in Washington, D.C., and in museums from Boston to San Francisco. They are reminders of both his wonderful talent as an artist and of the fact that Sullivan County was a special place to Henry Inman; he enjoyed the scenic beauty of the countryside and the challenge of its trout fishing. It is his *Trout Fishing in Sullivan County, New York* that goes beyond artistic achievement and serves as a lasting monument, reminding contemporary fly fishers that Henry Inman was here, that he loved their sport, and that he, too, walked the stream banks, waded the riffling waters, and cast his fly in those difficult places a wary trout would likely rise. And while the famous artist applied his skills with the fly more than 160 years ago, we remember that he was one of the first, and his memory is yet retained in a beautiful landscape he painted of a special pool formed by two streams he had a deep affection toward.

"THE TALL SON OF YORK"

William Trotter Porter (1806–1858) is known as the founder of American sporting literature. Born in Newbury, Vermont, Porter began his editorial career in 1829 with the *Farmers Herald,* a small newspaper in St. Johnsbury. A year or so later, he moved to New York City with the intent of starting a sporting journal; by 1825, the city had become the literary capital of America and was attracting young writers from other parts of the country.

Porter founded the *Spirit of the Times,* the first sporting journal, in the closing days of 1831. From the beginning, the newspaper maintained a classical literary reputation. It had contributors who were among the brightest names in American literature, many of whom were of the first generation of sporting writers. Porter's publication of the *Spirit* coincided with the development of steam presses that were capable of printing thousands of copies at greatly reduced costs and an improved postal system with faster distribution.

At first, however, Porter's venture was not successful, and after a few months, the *Spirit* merged with the *Traveller,* with Porter in charge of the sporting department. A year later, he resigned and took charge of the *New Yorker* and then the *Constellation.* As these papers had limited space for sporting topics, Porter acquired the *Traveller, and Spirit of the Times* from C. J. B. Fisher, who had united the two, and the paper was again published under its original name, the *Spirit of the Times.* In 1839, Porter also purchased the *American Turf Register and Sporting Magazine,* which, along with the *Spirit,* gave him an even larger readership. By the early 1840s, circulation of the *Spirit* was estimated at 40,000 and was even larger by the end of the decade. It was said that for every subscriber, ten additional people read the paper.

William T. Porter was a knowledgeable fisherman who gave good technical information. The trout fisherman was informed of the pleasures of fly fishing, the type of rod and what flies to use, where to go, and what to expect when he got there. Porter's knowledge of where to fish for trout was vast:

> As for places where to find sport, every reader of the *Spirit,* in this vicinity, well knows. There is not a babbling brook, or tide stream, nor a pond, public or private, of any repute, within a hundred miles of our sanctum, in which we have not, at some time, wet a line.[13]

During the 1830s, 1840s, and 1850s, Porter wrote frequently about trout fishing in the streams and ponds of Long Island; the lake trout of Piseco, Long, and Pleasant lakes in Hamilton County in the Adirondacks; and of the wonderful trout fishing he found in Sullivan County along the Beaverkill, Willowemoc, and Callicoon Creeks.

He was an advocate of fly fishing, and his reputation was large enough that in the fall of 1841, the firm of Thomas Conroy, one of the best tackle shops in the city, produced a fly rod with the given name of Porter's General Rod. The rod was of lancewood with varying sections and several different tips; its length could be adjusted between 10 and 16 feet. The rod could be used as a light trout rod or be made into a powerful rod for salmon and bass; its weight was about 3 pounds!

William T. Porter was known for his wit, humor, and genial magnetism. In appearance he was striking. He dressed flawlessly, had a long flowing beard, and vivid blue eyes with an "almost effeminately sweet smile" that contrasted with his athletic build and unusual height. Porter was 6 feet, 4 inches in his stocking feet and known throughout the city as "the Tall Son of York." This sobriquet was used for years, affectionately, by writers referring to Porter and by his friends in conversation.

He was very social, and his personality endeared him to a large circle of friends and innumerable acquaintances. He was known for his generosity, and everyone who made his acquaintance desired to cultivate it. Henry William Herbert, a close friend of Porter's who wrote under the name of Frank Forester, once wrote a touching description of his personal appearance:

> . . . serious or merry, solemn or sentimental, still so calm and serene and softly smiling, in thy ruby-colored waistcoat, with thy soft silky hair, unchanged by a streak of gray, cooly disparted from thy high, white unwrinkled forehead, with the luxuriant flow of that grand beard, which a Mussulman might envy, with that mild, clear blue eye, that almost effeminately sweet smile, singularly contrasting the athletic frame, the six-foot-four in his stockinged feet, the chivalrous and gallant spirit, the free, open speech, the high soul made up all of honor, the simple-minded straight-forwardness of thought and action, which go together in thee to make up that noblest of God's works, a real man,
>> Loyal and firm, and kind and true,
>> That fear or falsehood never knew.
>> Long may'st thou flourish, dear Bill, the spirit of *The Spirit of the Times*, the glory of not yet utterly degenerated Gotham, the best as the tallest son of York.[14]

Sensitively written, Herbert clearly had a special relationship with Porter, who was his dearest friend. And while he was beloved by all, other close friends included Richard T. Fosdick, the noted sportsman from Greenwich Village, and Henry Inman, the artist. In these early years of American sportfishing, there existed in the city a "piscatorial club" that met at Ward's hostelry, of which Fosdick, Inman, Herbert, and Porter were leading members: "In those good times the sportsmen of New York and its vicinity constituted a veritable fraternity, united by the strongest bond of friendship; consequently, intimacy with one implied a familiarity with the entire brotherhood."[15]

Invariably, whenever Porter went on an extended fishing trip to the trout waters and wilds of Sullivan County, he was accompanied by Henry Inman. Richard Fosdick was a friend of both men, and being somewhat older and known for his anecdotal stories, he was affectionately called "Uncle Richard." Fosdick was one of the city's veteran sportsmen and was

William T. Porter. *Ballou's Pictorial*, August, 1856.

acquainted with all the famous actors, musicians, artists, and sportsmen of his era. William F. Brough rounded out the group; nicknamed the "Merchant Vocalist," Brough was retired from the stage and was an avid disciple of the rod and gun.

Porter also moved in the same literary circles as Knickerbocker writers Nathaniel P. Willis, Charles Fenno Hoffman, George P. Morris, and Fitz-Greene Halleck. Sportsmen and literary men of celebrity could not pass by the *Spirit's* office, which was on Barclay Street and Broadway, without paying homage to the "Tall Son of York." Porter's office was dubbed "The Sanctum"; it contained a high desk where he wrote while standing, and along the wall were a series of wooden shelves containing a thousand or so sporting volumes neatly bound and systematically arranged. Other furnishings included a massive armchair, a small table, and a used bureau. It was here that Porter was visited by many of the first sportsmen of our country, and for many years, Henry Inman made almost daily visits to the *Spirit* office and conversed for an hour or so with him.

Among the popular public resorts, alehouses, and taverns of the day frequented by "sporting gentlemen" were the Widows, the Pheasant, the Old Reynolds Beer Shop, and Frank's, a saloon conveniently located on Barclay Street. Frank's was dubbed by sportsmen "the lower office," as visitors to the *Spirit* frequently were entertained there by William T. Porter.[16]

Another habitual resort of Porter's was Windust's, which was located in the theater district and was a rendezvous for actors, critics, journalists, and sportsmen. It was here that Porter, Herbert, Fosdick, Brough, and Inman, with other members of their piscatorial club, held their famous "all-game dinners." Richard Fosdick was the originator of these affairs, which were usually limited to six in number, with each guest contributing fish or game that he "killed by his own hand." For years, Edward Windust personally prepared the feast: ". . . the like of which have never been set before kings, were discussed by the elect alone, the vulgar herd of his frequenters being uncompromisingly denied access to a 'parlor,' whose very walls were redolent with ancient and fish like smells."[17]

Sportsmen, at the time, "occupied an almost despicable position" in our society. This tenet may have been influenced by Puritan work ethics and the "Yankee" dislike for field sports. Men who hunted or fished for amusement were regarded as fools, and there was contempt for any man who could be lured away, even for a single hour, from his "righteous duty of amassing dollars."[18]

William T. Porter died a relatively young man; he was only fifty-two when he passed away in the summer of 1858. He was mourned by the entire city. A writer for the *New York Times* reported, "Few men have had truer and warmer friends, and fewer men deserved them more."[19] Porter was the founder and, for many years, the voice of American sporting literature; he wrote frequently of trout fishing, and more than anyone else of his era, influenced the sport of angling and helped make it a common pastime of several generations of Americans. His reputation in sporting matters was greater than anyone's, and he is considered the father of a school of American sporting literature.

FRANK FORESTER

Henry William Herbert (1807–1858)—author, poet, horseman, and scholar—achieved fame as a sporting writer named Frank Forester. Born in London, England, Herbert belonged to a distinguished and titled family; his father was the Reverend William Herbert, son of Henry Herbert, first Earl of Carnarvon.

Herbert received the classical education of British gentry. He was tutored at home until the age of twelve, then went to a school at Brighton for a year, followed by Eton, which he attended until the summer of 1825. In 1830, he graduated with honors from Caius College, Cambridge. He was taught early in life how to shoot and to ride a horse, and his knowledge of horsemanship was extensive.

Herbert came to America as a condition of an involuntary exile. He was twenty-four years old at the time and had recently finished his education. Rumor said he was forced to leave England because of debt, having lost his property because of the dishonesty of a trustee or perhaps because of an unfortunate love affair. Whatever the reason, he reached New York in the spring of 1831 and began employment as a teacher of Greek and Latin at a prestigious private school.

Within a couple of years, he had made the acquaintance of many of the leading writers in the city and had begun a literary career. He and A. D. Paterson founded the *American Monthly Magazine* in 1833, and Herbert was the editor until the end of 1835. A year later, he began writing romance and historical novels, articles, poetry, and editorials for such prestigious magazines as the *Knickerbocker,* the *Literary World, Godey's Ladys Book,* and *Ladies Companion.* His writings were very popular, and there was hardly a magazine of note to which he did not contribute.

Herbert had a keen interest in field sports, and when not in the classroom or actively writing, he went on hunting and fishing expeditions, primarily in New York State, but also up the East Coast and into Canada. In 1839, after William T. Porter purchased the *American Turf Register and Sporting Magazine,* he asked Herbert to write a series of outdoor articles. This was the beginning of Herbert's career as a sporting writer, and he titled the articles for Porter "The Warwick Woodlands." Although they were well written and well received, Herbert chose to write them under the name Frank Forester, believing that writing about field sports would bring harm to his reputation as a serious writer.

It was also in 1839, while on a hunting trip to Maine, that he met and married Sarah Barker. The couple had a son two years later; sadly, following the birth of their second child, Sarah died at the age of twenty-three. The child, a daughter, lived only but a short time after her first birthday. Herbert then decided to send his son to England, where his family assured him that the child would receive educational advantages Herbert could not provide.

Shortly after he sent his only child to England, his father advised him that he would be willing to purchase a parcel of land for Herbert and pay for the construction of a home that the exiled Herbert could use as long as he lived. New Jersey was chosen, as the state of New York had a law that prohibited "aliens" from taking title to land in that state. In 1845, he chose a small parcel of land along the Passaic River in New Jersey, lying between Newark and Belleville. The area was sparsely settled and bordered a newly opened cemetery. Herbert constructed a small cottage with a large bay window facing the river and dubbed his new home "The Cedars." It was here that he composed his best sporting writing.

Herbert was very knowledgeable about horses, dogs, and hunting; an excellent rider, his favorite area for hunting was the area around Warwick, New York, though he also hunted sections of New Jersey, Long Island, and the Catskills. He wrote articles about fishing, but he was more comfortable with a gun than a rod: "With the rod Forester was incontestably a moderate proficient, and although he frequently accompanied Porter, avowedly a rodman of the very first order, and Inman, who worshipped Isaac Walton almost as a demigod, on their piscatorial excursions, it was mainly to glean practical information as to methods in fishing and the customs of fishermen."[20]

Henry William Herbert was among the first to write about field sports and, like Porter, he was writing to an ever-increasing number of outdoorsmen. He was an excellent writer who provided vivid descriptions of hunting; he possessed great ability to describe in detail the natural landscape and the habitat of wild game. As an outdoor writer, he was one of the first to plead for game protection, especially for laws restricting the taking of quail and woodcock.

From his series of articles, Herbert published *The Warwick Woodlands, or Things as They Were There Ten Years Ago* (1845), an extremely popular book that has been reprinted many times. Other favorite works included *My Shooting Box* (1846), *The Deerstalkers* (1849), *Frank Forester's Field Sports of the United States and British Provinces of North America* (1849), and *Frank Forester's Fish and Fishing of the United States and British Provinces of North America* (1849). Herbert's writing influenced much of the American angling literature that came after him.

His *Fish and Fishing* went through many editions and was a popular book with American anglers. The book contains information on species, methods of capture and equipment (including fly fishing), and even preparing the various fish for table. Special attention is placed on trout and salmon and, writing about brook trout, Herbert mentions the "unrivaled excellence" of the brook trout fishing found in the Beaverkill and "Callikoon Creek."

Herbert made fishing trips to Sullivan County with Henry Inman and William T. Porter, and he wrote about trout fishing at a very early date and "sang the praises" of the Willowemoc. In the 1850s, *Graham's Magazine* published a couple of his trout-fishing articles, such as "Among the Mountains; or Taking Times Along a Trout-Stream" and "Trout and Trout-Fishing." In these articles, in addition to informing readers on methods, tackle, and flies, Herbert wrote of the joys of trout fishing and directed anglers to the Catskills: "On Long Island, in May, trout-fishing is nearly at an end; on the Callicoon, the Beaverkill, and the various tributaries of the upper Delaware and Susquehanna, it is then beginning, and is shortly after in its perfection."[21]

Surprisingly, Herbert advocated, even at this early date, the use of flies to catch shad, a fish he wrote favorably of as a game fish at a time when many believed shad could not be caught with a hook and line. He also tells his readers to try flies for striped bass, another recommendation that appears well ahead of its time.

He became a celebrity in New York and was the type of individual that liked to draw attention to himself, even by the manner of his dress. When he strolled down Broadway, he usually wore a striking sporting costume, a plaid shawl tossed over one shoulder, with cavalier boots and large imposing King Charles spurs. He wore his hair rather long below his coat collar and donned a huge black mustache:

> Setting aside outward adornment, he was a "man of mark," graceful in bearing, athletic in form, and of attractive features, with eyes through which glowed the true fire of genius. In any assemblage he would have attracted more than passing notice. Among the *literati* of old Gotham he became known and admired as an able writer, a conversationalist of rare powers, and a gentleman well versed in *belles lettres*.[22]

Despite living in America for many years, Herbert never rid himself of his English prejudices, and he made no attempt to conceal his dislike for everything American. He was quick-tempered and unable to drink alcohol without having serious confrontations that brought him great embarrassment and shame. He had few friends, was impulsive, eccentric, egotistical, impetuous, pretentious, headstrong, and easily angered. In addition, he possessed a terrible temper, and his relationships with his friends were often strained, for he was vain and touchy, and inordinately proud of the social position he had held in England.

Herbert once stated that he was "an American author of English birth." While he was a tireless writer and appeared to earn a living from his writing, he had a reputation of being extravagant and living beyond his means; this led to borrowing money, and he was often in debt. By the time he was forty, he had lost most of his friends, though Porter always remained loyal.

After the death of his first wife, Herbert remained a bachelor for fifteen years, and it was not until February 1858 that he remarried. Unfortunately, his second wife left him rather abruptly, and it was rumored that he had married her for her money, something he vehemently denied. The breakup disturbed him greatly, and it was said he began to suffer moods of melancholy and became very despondent. He certainly had reasons to be depressed: He was exiled from his homeland; he lost the love of his life when she was very young; after sending his son to England, he never saw the boy again; a second marriage failed; he was poor of purse; and even the home he resided in was not his own.

On May 16, 1858, Herbert, said to be heartbroken, invited friends to dinner at the Steven's House on Broadway. Only one person came. In the early morning hours, after dinner, Herbert shot himself in the head. On May 18, three months after his marriage, the lead story of the *New York Times* read "SUICIDE OF 'FRANK FORRESTER'" [*sic*]. William Henry Herbert committed suicide at about 2 o'clock in the morning in a room at the Steven's House. The news of his death shocked the country. Before shooting himself, he left two letters on a table: one addressed to the "Press of the United States," and the other to the "Coroner." His letter to the coroner began:

Henry William Herbert (Frank Forester). Print Collection, Miriam and Ira D. Wallach Division of Art, Prints and Photographs, The New York Public Library, Astor, Lenox and Tilden Foundations.

> Tuesday, May 18, 1858
>   Three months since, the happiest day of my life. To avoid all trouble, and simplify your duty, I have to state that I have taken my own life by a pistol shot, no one being privy to my doing it, or to my design.[23]

The letter contained additional comments by Herbert and gave his reason for taking his life:

The reason for this act, then, is simple. My life, long, sad, solitary and weary, and without an object has become utterly hopeless, hateful and unendurable. A hope had been kindled in my heart again; my home had got a light in it brighter than sunshine; my life had a purpose; I loved her unutterably. I was immeasurably happy—all this has been dashed down—all is lost forever.[24]

In his letter to the "Press of the United States," Herbert wrote about his weaknesses and asked for forgiveness. His letter seemed almost like a religious confession; he requested no praise, and stated that he probably deserved none. He basically asked for "silence" and that the press not dishonor his name. He wrote, "I die forgiving every man who has wronged me, asking forgiveness of every man whom I have wronged." He also stated that he had a most unhappy life; "No counselor, no friend, no country, have been mine, for six and twenty years."[25]

One friend, who also wrote for the *Spirit*, Gen. H. H. Sibley, always believed that there was an event connected with Herbert's self-exile from England that caused deep depression, which he experienced at intervals and, combined with his unfortunate domestic relations, caused his suicide.

Before his death, Henry William Herbert also wrote a letter to his friend Miles I'Anson, asking him to allow his body to be buried in I'Anson's cemetery plot. Herbert did not even have enough money for a grave site, and he feared he would be buried in a potter's field. He also asked that I'Anson make the arrangements for his burial and funeral. Before taking his life, Herbert wrote to the clergyman who had married him, asking that he perform a grave-side service; unfortunately, this request was denied by church law, because of the circumstances of his death.

For his grave site, he requested "a very small, very plain headstone of Little Falls, or Belleville stone, with this inscription:

HENRY WILLIAM HERBERT
Of
England
Aged 51 years
Infelicissimus"[26]

Herbert was buried in the center of Mount Pleasant Cemetery, the same cemetery that adjoined the Cedars. Sadly, the grave marker he requested was not installed, and he was buried in an unmarked grave.

Many years later, an article titled "A Visit to 'The Cedars'" appeared in *Rod and Gun* magazine and pointed out to American sportsmen that Herbert's grave site was yet unmarked. This prompted an organization to do something to honor Herbert, and the Newark Herbert Association of New Jersey was immediately formed. On the eighteenth anniversary of his death, they placed a simple stone at his grave, "in strict conformity with his last wishes."[27]

Major George B. Halsted delivered an address and spoke of Henry William Herbert of England, the Frank Forester of America.

Throughout Herbert's career, there was unhappiness. He constantly quarreled with friends and associates, and in his mind he never received the recognition, respect, and admiration of his peers. Herbert was an important contributor to American sporting literature, and it was not until after his death that the recognition he longed for was realized and his fame increased.

Twenty years after his death, a writer in *Forest and Stream* recalled that in Herbert's day, men who wrote about field sports were "classed among the low and vulgar":

Thirty years ago, Henry W. Herbert (Frank Forester) stood out alone as champion of American field sports, and nobly did he do his work. With a combination of tact, energy, perseverance and patience, he succeeded in bringing the beauties of the ennobling pursuits of forest and stream before the people in such a thorough, convincing way, that a change came over the public mind regarding this subject, and to-day nearly every Four Corners has its sportsmen's club working in different ways to protect God's creatures from utter annihilation.[28]

In 1881, *Frank Forester's Sporting Scenes and Characters* was published in two volumes, edited by Fred C. Pond. A year later, the *Life and Writings of Frank Forester* appeared, also in two volumes; this work was edited by D. W. Judd. Perhaps more importantly, Forester's books continued to be in demand, going through many editions, and his work has been enjoyed by practically every generation of outdoorsmen. After his death, his sporting books continued to be printed in the 1860s, 1870s, and 1880s. Incredibly, his books also appeared in the next century, with works such as *The Warwick Woodlands* and *Fish and Fishing* being published in the 1920s, 1930s, 1970s, and into the 1990s, 150 years after his death!

Henry William Herbert's life was filled with tragedy. He is remembered, however, even today, as a gifted writer; his Frank Forester books have appealed to generations of outdoorsmen and -women, and they will continue to be American sporting classics. Through his writings, Americans learned about the sportsmanship of the field, especially hunting ethics, which he emphasized, along with conservation of our incredible wildlife populations.

When Herbert arrived on the shores of this country, public opinion toward outdoor sports was that they were not only a waste of time but the "first cousins to drunkenness and dissipation."[29] Years after the death of Herbert, it was recognized that he had spent the last twenty years of his life fiercely combating this prejudice: "And it is partly this, no doubt, that makes the memory of that remarkable man so exceedingly dear to American sportsmen, who now fish and shoot with impunity, and even with repute."[30]

"THE LARGEST TROUT IN THE WORLD"

Following the completion of the Newburgh and Cochecton Turnpike in 1808, White Lake, a deep, 288-acre body of water in Sullivan County, became a destination of early American trout fishermen. As early as 1811, Dr. John Lindsley operated a boardinghouse near the lake and took in a few summer visitors and fishing tourists.

Located in the town of Bethel, White Lake is spring fed; its waters are cold and reach depths of more than 80 feet in several places. The lake derives its name from the white sandy shores and bottom and the transparency of its water.

While fishermen were visiting its shores at a very early date, the lake's reputation was elevated when Charles Fenno Hoffman wrote of a 6-pound trout being caught in the winter of 1832. At the time, both the man and the fish were significant; Hoffman was emerging as one of New York's literati, and a 6-pound trout was unheard of. Hoffman—poet, essayist and novelist—was well-known and among those writers who fostered a national spirit in literature. Although he may not have been at the same level as Washington Irving, William Cullen Bryant, or James Fenimore Cooper, his name was associated with other Knickerbocker writers, such as Fitz-Greene Halleck, George P. Morris, and Nathaniel P. Willis.

In 1830, Hoffman became coeditor of the *New York American,* and two years later, editor of *Knickerbocker Magazine.* During the ensuing years, he held editorial positions on a number of prestigious magazines, including *American Monthly Magazine, Literary World,* and the *New York Mirror.* As an avid outdoorsman, Hoffman also contributed some of the finest sporting articles that appeared on the pages of the *Spirit of the Times. Spirit* editor William T. Porter once remarked of him, "Few have contributed more to the amount, or done more to elevate the character of American Sporting Literature."[31] In the years ahead, more and even larger trout would be taken from the waters of White Lake, but Hoffman's story would be recalled for more than half a century.

Kauneonga is the alleged Indian name for the lake, and it first appears in the writings of noted poet-fisherman Alfred B. Street. Kauneonga is said to be "descriptive of the shape of the lake which somewhat resembles the outstretched wings of a bird."[32]

Street fished the lake in the 1830s, and in 1835 the June issue of *American Monthly Magazine* praised its waters in a poem titled "White Lake."

In 1840, one of the largest trout to come out of White Lake was caught by Otto Gilpin, who landed the fish in the narrows of the lake; it weighed 7 pounds. Three years later, a trout fisherman from Newburgh named Belknap caught another huge trout that made area newspapers. In an article titled "Fine Trout—Finer Picture," the *Newburgh Gazette* reported on the giant fish, "an object of

Large brook trout. *American Game Fishes,* 1892.

universal admiration." The article stated that a brook trout weighing 7 pounds and 6 ounces could be seen at "Old Fatty's—the familiar cognomen of mine host of the Colden Street Hotel." The trout was taken to Charles Tice, a portrait painter, who transferred the proportions of "his fishship" to the canvas "in such admirable style as to deceive many a practiced eye into the belief, while gazing upon his picture, that it was the *fish* and not his *representation* they were looking at."[33]

Another early American angling writer who recognized White Lake's reputation as a producer of giant brook trout was John J. Brown. Some angling literature collectors believe Brown should be credited with the authorship of the first useful American book on angling, *The American Angler's Guide.* First published in 1845, Brown's guide included a section advising anglers of the best fishing grounds. Under "New York," he writes, "we find the well-known White Lake, where trout have been taken of seven and three-quarters pounds' weight."[34]

Actually, even larger trout were taken: on February 8, 1843, the *Republican Watchman* reported "an old settler" weighing 8 pounds and 14 ounces had been caught by Louis Platt; the huge fish measured 26 inches in length! It was believed at the time that White Lake produced the largest brook trout anywhere: "Until pike were put into the lake, it contained the largest trout in the world."[35]

Most likely, it was pickerel, not pike, that were placed in the lake. In an article titled "Giants Among the Trout," the *New York Times* of June 8, 1885, reported: "Fifty years ago the largest brook trout ever known were found in White Lake, Sullivan County." It went on to state that the large trout the lake had become famous for had continued to be taken from its waters until 1850. After that date, large brook trout were eliminated from its cold, deep waters because of the introduction of two predatory species: black bass and pickerel.

Pickerel, the article stated, were taken from Brink Pond, in Pike County, Pennsylvania, and placed in White Lake waters in 1835. Bass were introduced in 1843 when John B. Findley hired an Indian "to fetch a number of black bass from one of the Northern New-York lakes." The *Times* article ended by stating that the days of the giant brook trout were "but a memory."

"White Lake Tally-Ho." O. & W. Railroad "Summer Homes," 1887.

The stocking records of the New York State Fisheries Commission reveal that the first trout stocked in White Lake were rainbows; twenty thousand California mountain trout (rainbow) fingerlings were planted on July 7, 1882. Reports of anglers catching rainbows at the time were rare, though one was reportedly captured in 1887, several years after the initial stocking.

In 1891, the commission changed its stocking policy and initiated a program of stocking lake trout; that year, one hundred thousand fingerlings from the Cold Spring Harbor Hatchery were planted. One year later, the records of the hatchery at Caledonia show that another fifty thousand lake trout were sent to W. C. Kinne to be stocked in the waters of White Lake.

ALFRED B. STREET AND THE CALLICOON CREEK

While Henry Inman immortalized the trout fishing of Sullivan County on canvas, other pioneer trout fishermen did their best to praise the county's trout fishing and natural beauty through poetry. One of the first was Francis L. Waddell, who lived in Monticello in the 1830s and published a charming poem that appeared in the *American Turf Register and Sporting Magazine* in June 1835. The title is "Trout Fishing, Sullivan County, N.Y.," a part of which is as follows:

> Come wander with me to the hemlock hills,
> Where romance dwells by the laurelled rills;
> For the stag, in the balmy month of June,
> Cools his panting sides in the *Callicoon*,
> And the eagle kens the morning beam,
> As it glittering smiles on the silver stream,
> While there in the wild and silent wood,
> Where feet of the hunter scarce intrude,
> The speckled trout in frolicsome play
> Are sporting their mirthful holiday
> In thousands, crowd each limpid brook,
> Unheeding the sportsman's wily hook.
> What a treat with a line and rod to creep,
> When the finny tribe in the shadows sleep,
> By the sloping bank of the crystal tide,
> And cunningly in the long grass hide,
> Then wait till a large trout passes by,
> Or cautiously play the barbed fly;
> And when takes hold the foolish trout,
> With angler's triumph pull him out.

There was a time when the Callicoon Creek enjoyed a reputation equal to that of the Beaverkill and Willowemoc Creek. Its waters ran as pure and cold as any, and the stream's notoriety dated back to the earliest days of American trout fishing.

The Callicoon attracted trout-fishing tourists as early as the 1820s and 1830s and had such a dense hemlock forest (before the stream was exploited by tanneries and deforested by farmers) that William P. Hawes once described it as having "grim ravines" with "everlasting darkness."[36] One of the country's earliest outdoor writers, Hawes, a distinguished New York attorney, wrote under the fictitious name of J. Cypress Jr. and fished the Callicoon Creek at a very early date.

Hawes contributed regularly to some of the first issues of the *Spirit of the Times* and the *American Turf Register and Sporting Magazine* and, following his death, his friend Henry William Herbert (Frank Forester) edited and had published *Sporting Scenes and Sundry Sketches* (1842), a book of the writings of J. Cypress Jr.

Another who praised the streams of Sullivan County, and the Callicoon Creek in particular, was Alfred Billings Street (1811–1881). Street was considered to be among the best contributors of angling literature and poetry. He wrote several poems extolling the Callicoon Creek, and a poem titled "Angling" is the most quoted, having found a prominent place in angling history.

The poem is found in John J. Brown's *American Angler's Guide,* first published in 1845, and one of the earliest works of American angling literature. Fittingly, perhaps, the stanza appears beneath an illustration titled "Trout Fishing in Sullivan County":

Alfred B. Street. *Knickerbocker Gallery,* 1854.

> We break from the tree-groups: a glade deep with grass;
> The white clover's breath loads the sense as we pass;
> A sparkle-a-streak-a broad glitter is seen,—
> The bright Callikoon, through its thickets of green!
> We rush to the banks: its sweet music we hear;
> Its gush, dash, and gurgle all blent to the ear.
> No shadows are drawn by the cloud-covered sun;
> We plunge in the crystal, our sport has begun.
> Our line where that ripple shoots onward, we throw;
> It sweeps to the foam-spangled eddy below;
> A tremor, a pull, the trout upward is thrown,
> He swings to our basket,—the prize is our own.[37]

This stanza is also found in Genio C. Scott's *Fishing in American Waters* (1869) and in Charles Goodspeed's classic *Angling in America* (1939). Another popular poem by Street praising the Callicoon Creek is titled "The Callicoon in Autumn." It was published in the December issue of *American Monthly Magazine* in 1835.

Alfred Billings Street was born in Poughkeepsie, New York, and at the age of fourteen (in 1825), he and his family moved to Monticello, in Sullivan County. At the time, Street recalled, the region was sparsely settled; most of the land remained a primitive forest; wolves, bears, and mountain lions roamed the woodlands; and streams literally teemed with trout.

Growing up amid such an environment, Street developed a fascination with nature and a deep appreciation of outdoor life. During the 1820s and 1830s, he found a lifetime of adventure exploring with rod and gun the secluded lakes, ponds, streams, and rivers of Sullivan County.

After finishing his education, Street studied law and was admitted to the bar. He opened a law office in Monticello, and though he practiced law, it was of little interest to him; literature, especially poetry, is what he enjoyed, and he decided to pursue a literary career. He had begun writing poems at the age of eleven, and by the time he was fourteen, William Cullen Bryant published his poems in the *New York Evening Post* under the name Atticus.

Although he would go on to write books and articles for some of the best annuals and periodicals of the day, Alfred B. Street became famous as a poet. His poems often had outdoor themes, such as deer hunting, fowling, and fishing. He wrote poetry descriptive of the natural beauty he found in Sullivan County and included waterfalls, streams, rivers, and lakes. He wrote poems about White Lake, the Delaware and Mongaup rivers, and the Willowemoc and Callicoon creeks.

When he was twenty-two, in 1833, "The Falls of the Mongaup" was published in an issue of the *Knickerbocker*. The falls was located on the Mongaup River, south of Monticello, was approximately 80 feet high, and was considered to be the third-largest waterfall in New York. In the 1830s, this spectacular waterfall was a great attraction to tourists who visited the region; they picnicked and marveled at the visual display of water cascading over ledges of bedrock. Considered one of the greatest scenic attractions of Sullivan County, the famous Mongaup Falls was destroyed in the 1920s when the Rockland Light and Power Company constructed a dam for hydropower.

Street's "The Willowemoc" is a poem about the noted trout stream that appeared in *American Monthly Magazine* in 1838. His poetry was very popular and could be found in all of the better literary magazines; in addition to the *Knickerbocker* and *American Monthly Magazine,* his work also appeared in the *U.S. Democratic Review* and *Graham's Magazine.* Street's poems were also translated into German and were popular in England. Those poems usually found in anthologies include "The Gray Forest Eagle," "Lost Hunter," and "The Settler."

It is likely that no one before or since promoted Sullivan County more than Alfred B. Street. His literary career included many articles that featured the sublime landscape of the region: "Life in the Woods" appeared in *Columbian Magazine* (1847), "A Pic-Nic at White Lake" in *New York Illustrated* (1847), and "A Day or Two's Fishing in Pike Pond" (Kenoza Lake) in *Graham's Magazine* (also in 1847).

In addition to his poetic tributes to the Callicoon, Street paid homage to the stream in an article titled "A Day's Fishing in the Callikoon." The story was first published by William T. Porter in the *Spirit of the Times* in September 1845, and a month later, the same article appeared in *Graham's Magazine.*

The article is written in the style of the sentimental and romantic aspects of angling, and although it does not contain technical information, it is historically important because it was written when the sport of trout fishing was still in its infancy. Street relates how he and two companions traveled on foot over the old Newburgh and Cochecton Turnpike, followed wood trails and bridle paths, and finally, with only a blazed tree trail to lead them, found the Callicoon Creek.

He writes of hooking a 3-pound trout and of his disappointment when his line snapped and the big fish was free. The trout took their baited hooks with eagerness, supplying the trio with an ample number of fish, which they devour over an open fire cooked "woods fashion, on a stick." Street also writes of a falls, quite possibly the area known today as Falls Mills:

This spot is the metropolis of the Callikoon trout. They swarm here by the thousands. I myself have stood at the end of that great jagged pine lying in the water, near the foot of yon falling sheet of foam and caught scores.[38]

Callicoon Creek at Falls Mills. Ed Van Put.

He praises the natural beauty of Sullivan County and boasts of its trout fishing:

When we say it is a first-rate day for trouting we mean something, for in the populous streams of Sullivan the finny tribe inhabitants seem to have an uncontrollable hankering for the sauce pan, judging from the willingness they exhibit to be caught.[39]

In 1839, Alfred B. Street moved from Monticello to Albany, and though he again opened a law office, he continued writing poetry and increased his literary talents, producing a number of books. A few of the most popular were *The Burning of Schenectady* (1842), *The Poems of Alfred B. Street* (1845), *Frontenac* (1849), and *Woods and Waters* (1860).

A man of books, Street later became the librarian of the New York State Library in 1848 and held that position for almost twenty years. His notoriety has faded over the years; however, anyone who reads his work quickly realizes that he was a man who loved nature and the forest and streams of Sullivan County. He should be remembered as one of our pioneer trout fishers and an important contributor to American angling literature.

Another angler who recorded early experiences along the Callicoon was the noted author Charles Fenno Hoffman. After a fishing trip to the stream in the 1840s, he penned an article in the August 22, 1846 issue of the *Spirit of the Times* titled "A Fishing Frolic in Sullivan County." Hoffman tells of taking the steamboat "Eureka" from New York and then the Erie Railroad to Middletown, followed by a stagecoach to White Lake, where he lodged at the Lake House. His party dined on trout taken from the nearby stream that flowed out of White Lake.

The next day, they loaded up their rods and baggage and set out for "Roper's hard by the Callicoon." After a restful evening, the party, which now had increased to five rods, set out in the morning through the forest to the Callicoon Creek. Hoffman wrote of the group: "A picturesque-looking set we are, with our fishing-dresses and gear, a combination of Indian, 'whiteman' and Yankee-Doodle."

Charles Fenno Hoffman, by Henry Inman. *Graham's Magazine*, 1843.

The party reached the area where the two branches joined forming the Callicoon; three men went up the North Branch, and Hoffman and one other fished up the East Branch; they lunched at streamside after catching "scores" of trout. Over the next two days, the men fished the Mongaup as well as the Callicoon and ended up catching 450 trout, "*several* of which would weigh half a pound, and a *great many* a pound!"

Charles Lanman

"THE PICTURESQUE EXPLORER OF OUR COUNTRY"

Sullivan County was certainly the hub of trout-fishing activity at a very early date, and artist Henry Inman was an important contributor to American fly-fishing history, but another artist and pioneer trout fisherman named Charles Lanman was also making Catskill trout-fishing history.

Charles Lanman (1819–1895) was born in Monroe, Michigan, but at a very early age was sent to his grandfather's home in Washington, D.C., for his education. Upon finishing his schooling, he moved to New York City, where he began a career as a journalist, artist, traveler, and author.

He received a good education and wrote exceptionally well of his personal experiences, describing the fishing in areas of the country then unknown to most anglers. Between 1835 and 1845, he explored the eastern United States, including the Catskills, and as was his custom, he carried along his painting and sketching materials as well as his fishing rod.

Lanman was one of the first Americans to recognize the restorative effect fishing had on individuals who enjoyed the sport, and he was the first angling author to write in great detail about the wonderful trout fishing found in the Catskills in the 1830s and 1840s. He was fascinated by the region and sketched the mountains and their rugged grandeur and fished for trout in their remote recesses. Lanman wrote glowingly of the Catskills in articles and books, promoting their scenic wonders and trout fishing.

He began making his piscatorial pilgrimages to the famous Plattekill and Kaaterskill Cloves as early as the 1830s, and he wrote an article about the region in 1844 titled "South Peak Mountain" (Overlook Mountain) that appeared in the *Columbian Magazine*. He wrote of staying in a farmhouse at the foot of the Plattekill Clove and of exploring the clove: "I came into the country to study—to forget that busy world and give myself up entirely to the hallowing influence of nature, and oh, how many 'mysteries sublime' has she revealed to man in my journeyings among the dear, dear Catskills!"[1]

Trout fishing on the Plattekill. *Harper's New Monthly Magazine,* July 1854.

Lanman was the first to introduce the Plattekill Clove to the public, and he wrote of the many waterfalls, caverns, and chasms and of the wild scenery found along the Plattekill Creek as it plummeted 1,100 feet in just 2 miles. He wrote descriptively of Blue Bell Falls, the Black Chasm, Devils' Chamber, and Double Leap, which featured a seemingly bottomless pool that contained "a hermit trout that has laughed at the angler's skill for a score of years."[2]

The notoriety of the Catskills increased a year later, when *Letters from a Landscape Painter* (1845) was published, with its first chapter titled "Trouting Among the Catskills." Lanman again wrote of staying at a farmhouse near Plattekill Clove and of hiring a local hunter and woodsman named Peter Hummel to serve as his fishing guide.

Their first excursion into the mountains was to the upper reaches of the Saw Kill, a treacherous journey up and over Overlook Mountain, through an unbroken wilderness, with no paths to guide them. Lanman and Hummel traveled over steep mountainsides with falling rocks and reached the Saw Kill after a laborious three-hour trip. Although the trout they caught were considered small, they had success, basketing 150 brook trout that they distributed among the farmers they passed on their return trip.

While roaming through the Catskills, it was not unusual for Lanman to request dinner at farmhouses that he passed along the way, and it was during these times that he gleaned information as to where the best trout fishing could be found. On one occasion, he learned of a stream called the Roaring Kill, a tributary of the upper Schoharie Creek, and when he fished this typical mountain stream, he found an abundance of trout and wrote of catching 160 natives from its rapid waters.

On another occasion, he fished the Schoharie Creek and located a large trout lying at the bottom of a pool near an area of clean white sand, where a spring entered the bed of the stream. Lanman was fascinated by the trout and watched it for a long time, admiring its beauty so visible in the transparent water. He contemplated the trout's repose and serene surroundings:

"He is so happy," thought I, "I will let him live." Presently, however, a beautiful fly lighted on the water, which the greedy hermit swallowed in a minute, and returned to his cool bed, with his conscience, as I fancied, not one whit troubled by what he had done.[3]

Plattekill, deep pool below a falls. Ed Van Put.

In *Letters from a Landscape Painter,* Lanman wrote of the natural splendor of the Catskills and that his most "unique and interesting adventure was a trip to Shue's Lake."* He made the journey with Peter Hummel and another local woodsman loaded down with axes, knapsacks, fishing tackle, gun, powder horn, and shot pouch. The trio climbed up the steep and rocky side of Overlook Mountain, over ledges and fallen trees, through ravines and underbrush, reaching the lake late in the day. They found shelter under a large overhanging ledge and went about the business of building a large fire and preparing their fishing gear:

> Eighty poles were then cut, to which we fastened our lines. The old canoe in the lake was bailed out, and, having baited our hooks with the small fish which we brought with us, we arranged the poles around the lake, in about seven feet of water. We then prepared and ate our supper, and awaited the coming on of night.[4]

As they sat around the fire, Peter Hummel told stories about the lake, which, he claimed, was named after a hunter named Shue, who had discovered it. Hummel told of catching a trout from its waters that weighed a little more than 5 pounds and of the many deer and rattlesnakes he had killed in the lake's vicinity.

---

*Shue's Lake is a 12.8-acre body of water on the border of Greene and Ulster counties known today as Echo Lake. The lake is also the source of the Saw Kill.

One of many waterfalls in the Plattekill Clove. Ed Van Put.

At nine o'clock they lit torches and checked their lines and, to Lanman's delight, they caught forty-one trout, which weighed between 1 and 2 pounds apiece. The men spent a restless night; they were awakened by the howl of wolves, owls, and barking foxes. Not being able to sleep soundly, they were able to check their lines throughout the night and by dawn had caught 102 trout, which averaged more than a pound apiece!

As a youngster, Lanman grew up hunting and fishing in Michigan Territory; he enjoyed everything about nature and all connections with the natural world. Surprisingly, he would go on to live most of his adult life in large eastern cities, first in New York and then in Washington, D.C.

Possessed with a passion for fishing and adventure, Charles Lanman traveled to other remote areas of the United States and Canada, exploring streams, rivers, ponds, and lakes. He fished these waters at a time when they were unspoiled, before they were defiled by pollution, before overfishing or any human activity. He visited these secluded areas of the country when travel was extremely difficult, traveling on foot, on horseback, or by canoe and writing, sketching, or painting as he went.

He was more than a proficient writer, being equally skilled with a brush as he was with the pen. In addition to being an author and amateur explorer, Lanman was a gifted artist who delighted in painting landscapes and nature studies. His adventure to Shue's Lake resulted in a painting titled *Shew's Lake at Sunset* (1844).

Lanman was refined, cultured, and popular in society, yet he pursued outdoor life and the wilderness when it was most primitive. He has been described as a "paradoxical mix of both the cosmopolitan gentleman and the frontiersman."[5] He was a scholarly angler, was familiar with the classic English angling books of his day, and possessed a substantial library. It has been written that he is "generally credited with being the author of the first book published in this country upon the subject of fishing as a pastime."[6]

Following his *Letters from a Landscape Painter,* Lanman wrote many books on fishing and travel. In 1848, *Adventures of an Angler in Canada, Nova Scotia and the United States* was published, which included a chapter on trout fishing in the Catskills. His Catskill exploits were also recounted in several other works, including *Haw-hoo-noo, or Records of a Tourist* (1850); *Adventures in the Wilds of North America* (1854); and *Adventures in the Wilds of the United States and British American Provinces* (1856). The latter work has a chapter titled "The Catskill Mountains" and received the praise of Washington Irving:

Charles Lanman. *Adventures of an Angler in Canada, Nova Scotia and the United States,* 1848.

> I anticipate great success therefore in your works on our American fishes, and on Angling which I trust will give us still further scenes and Adventures on our great internal waters; depicted with the freshness and graphic skill of your present volumes. In fact the adventurous life of the Angler amidst our wild scenery on our vast lakes and Rivers must furnish a striking contrast to the quiet loiterings of the English Angler. . . .[7]

In addition to his trout-fishing exploits, Lanman achieved notoriety as one of this country's earliest salmon fishermen. He wrote about Atlantic salmon fishing in books and periodicals in the 1840s.

He was an accomplished artist and exhibited his landscapes at the prestigious National Academy of Design in New York City as early as 1840; in 1846, he became an associate member and exhibited his work there for more than forty years. Many of his paintings were reminiscent of his love of fishing, and he often included a fisherman as part of the scenery. A few of his landscapes included such titles as *Trouting on the Upper Hudson, N.Y.; On the Ausable, N.Y.; On the Raquette, N.Y.;* and *Salmon Fishing in Canada.*

Along with his art and writing, Charles Lanman also had a distinguished career in public service. In 1849, he went to Washington as the librarian of the War Department, and the following year he became the private secretary of Daniel Webster, who, at the time, was secretary of state. He and the famous statesman often fished the celebrated Little Falls on the Potomac together for "rock fish or bass." They would begin their fishing day at four in the morning and end before the public offices were opened; Webster "took pleasure in congratulating himself with the thought that he had not robbed the government of any of its demands upon his time."[8]

During his Washington years, Lanman continued to write and paint, and was known for his skill with a fly rod. In time he would author thirty-two books and numerous articles, many on fishing. Charles Lanman has been hailed as "the undisputed pioneer of American angling literature,"[9] and during the 1840s and 1850s, his books and articles introduced the Catskills to a national and international audience. In a letter dated March 2, 1857, the great American author Washington Irving stated:

I look upon your work as a vade mecum to the American lover of the picturesque and romantic unfolding to him the wilderness of beauties and the varieties of adventurous life to be found in our great chains of mountains and systems of lakes and rivers. You are in fact the picturesque explorer of our country.[10]

It has been written that Charles Lanman "is an embodiment of what is expressed in the simple words *fishing tourist*.[11] In the days when he fished the Catskills, Lanman was more than just a fishing tourist—he was an early explorer and trail blazer for the countless trout fishermen who would come after him.

4

The 1840s

"... A GREAT HAUNT FOR SPORTSMEN;" TOURISTS INCREASE—
FISHERIES DECLINE; and THE FAMOUS STONY CLOVE

The 1840s and 1850s brought a period of significant change to both the fisheries and the forest landscape. These were decades of increasing numbers of trout fishermen and a rapidly declining brook trout population. The exploitation of the fisheries was the result of anglers removing excessive amounts of fish at the same time a streamside industry was destroying large numbers of trout, stream habitat, and water quality. This lethal combination of destruction was occurring on all the major trout streams in the Catskills.

The number of trout fishermen visiting the Catskills during the 1840s increased steadily; this was due in part to the glowing commentary about trout fishing found on the pages of the *American Turf Register and Sporting Magazine* and the *Spirit of the Times*. Many of the fishing tourists were city dwellers who were anxious to trade the heat, dust, din, and routine for the open spaciousness of the mountains and the pleasure, freedom, and excitement trout fishing had to offer.

At the time, America had more ardent devotees of the rod and gun than any other nation in the world. Recreational hunting and fishing was growing at a continuous rate, and ever-improving transportation enabled sportsmen to enjoy outdoor recreation more frequently. However, it was still unpopular, and even looked down upon, to write about field sports in the first half of the nineteenth century.

Henry William Herbert was compelled to write under the pseudonym of Frank Forester; his friend, William P. Hawes, wrote under the name of J. Cypress Jr. When Hawes contributed hunting and fishing articles to the *Spirit of the Times,* it was under the strictest code of secrecy. He lived in constant fear that he would be discovered as a writer of genre sporting sketches and lose his position as a highly respected New York City lawyer. Changes were occurring, though, and several books on angling were published by American writers in the 1840s that promoted Catskill trout fishing.

It was in 1845 that John J. Brown, a New York City tackle dealer who operated a shop on Fulton Street called the Angler's Depot, produced his pocket-sized manual titled *The American Angler's Guide.* Brown, at the time, relied upon various works published in England. He did, however, take issue with some English writers who believed there were no fly fishers in America: "There are hundreds of good fly anglers, and many that can throw a fly with the most experienced of Europe."[1]

The *American Angler's Guide* was very popular and went through several editions. It included information on various species of fish, tackle, angling techniques, and favorite fishing locations. Brown advised readers to "fish the Beaver Kill, the Mongaup, the Willewemack, and other kindred streams."[2]

It was also in the 1840s that Charles Lanman produced his books, *Letters from a Landscape Painter* and *Adventures of an Angler in Canada, Nova Scotia and the United States,* both of which promoted Catskill fishing.

The number of trout being removed by angling, however, in these early years was difficult to comprehend. Because of the difficulty of travel and the wildness of the region, most fishermen preferred to fish with others, in groups or in parties. Catches by individuals numbered at times in the hundreds, and it was common for a party of anglers to take hundreds—or even more than a thousand—trout in a single day, depending on their number and length of stay.

Once stagecoach travel was available in Delaware County and trout fishermen began traveling into the interior of the Catskills, one of the earliest destinations was the Hendrick Hudson House in Roxbury. The inn opened its doors as early as 1798 and was a frequent rendezvous of fishermen by the 1830s. By the 1840s, visitors found accommodations improved beyond what was expected in such an "uncultivated" region.

One fishing tourist visiting upper East Branch praised the Hendrick Hudson House in a letter to the *Ulster Republican* in the fall of 1846 and claimed the inn exceeded expectations: "There is a fine fall of pure mountain water within view of the Hotel where you can resort and have a bath which far surpasses any shower bath." And he enjoyed the excellent trout fishing " . . . and for trout, you have an abundance—a fine stream running within 100 yards of the Hotel. You can catch as many as you wish."[3]

By 1848, the New York and Erie Railroad skirted the western Catskills and followed the upper Delaware River through the borders of Sullivan and Delaware counties. The railroad provided not only swifter transportation to and from New York, but made the trout streams of the Delaware watershed and Sullivan and Delaware counties accessible to outlying cities with rail lines connected to New York. Trout-fishing tourists now came from as far away as Kentucky, Maryland, Pennsylvania, Virginia, and other eastern states.

When the Erie first opened, the popular Knickerbocker writer Nathaniel P. Willis traveled the railway on a "scenery-hunt." In the summer of 1849, he took the train to Deposit on the West Branch of the Delaware River, and then traveled by stagecoach over rough mountain roads another 20 miles along the stream to the village of Walton. Willis was a worldly traveler; he likened the West Branch of the Delaware to the Rhine and raved about its scenery. He breakfasted on trout and commented on Walton's "numberless brooks," that were "primitively full of trout."

He described the village as being the "cup" of a water lily being folded in by mountains, and he joked about being told that there was so much land here that some of it had to be placed "on edge." But he did not joke about the scenery, writing "but these upright mountain-sides are so regularly overlapped, each half-hidden by another, that the horizon, scollopped by the summits upon the sky, is like nothing so much as the beautiful thing I speak of—the rim of the water-lily's cup when half-blown."[4]

Willis found a special beauty about Walton that he admired, noting that the meadows were outlined with sugar maples like English parks, and the area had an "old country look" rather than

Trout fishing. *Frank Forester's Fish and Fishing of the United States and British Provinces of North America*, 1849.

the "raw" look of most American landscapes. He found the scenery incomparable, but stated "this West Branch of the Delaware is the Rhine of our country."[5]

Willis described the valley as being a mile wide with a hundred fertile farms and meadows, with trout streams flowing through them. He breakfasted on their trout and compared them with the famous Avon, in England, and he was astonished to learn that such productive trout waters were often nameless. He wrote of the vast wilderness surrounding Walton and likened it to "an unvisited island of culture in a sea of forest."[6]

Willis departed from Walton on horseback and rode over the summit and down along the Cadosia Creek. He did not fish, but his companions did, and he reported on their success: "Of course we had loitered at will, and our two companions, who had cut poles and fished as they came along, arrived, an hour after us, with a hundred trout strung upon birch rods. When the plank road is finished through here, for another summer's use, this bright brook, so overrunning with this delicious fish, will be a great haunt for sportsmen."[7] Willis recognized that trout fishing was an important activity for tourists traveling the new rail line, and he was correct in his assessment; the number of trout fishermen visiting the region did increase, as fishing tourists now had easier access from cities up and down the East Coast.

With the opening of the railroad, the *Spirit of the Times* informed its readership: "Beaver Kill, flowing into the Pepacton branch of the Delaware, formerly reached after a fatiguing journey via Newburgh and Monticello, is now easy of access, being within six hours of Chehocton (Hancock), the most beautiful village on the line of the Erie road."[8]

Most Erie passengers disembarked at Callicoon, Hankins, or Hancock, and those who did not fish the nearby Callicoon Creek were met by buckboards from various resorts or boardinghouses that were developing along the Beaverkill and Willowemoc Creek. The roads from the railroad stations were extremely bad, and travel was so uncomfortable and tiring that once they reached their destination, anxious fishing parties often stayed for days or weeks before returning.

During this period, the public roamed freely over the land, hunting, trapping, and fishing the many lakes, ponds, and streams throughout the Catskills, very much as the Indian had done. Even though the almost two million acres of the Hardenbergh Patent had been divided into fifty-two "Great Lots" and then subdivided as early as 1751, the Catskills remained sparsely settled until well after the Revolutionary War and the Declaration of Peace in 1783. The vast majority of the land was still owned by a relatively few absentee landlords, the majority of whom had never even seen their holdings. These tracts were vast areas of wild, mountainous, unbroken forest, and as such, it was difficult, if not impossible, to prohibit their use by the public.

Some lakes or ponds were known for the size of the brook trout they produced, whereas others developed a reputation for the incredible numbers of trout they contained. Those noted for large trout included White Lake and Long Pond (Tennanah Lake)* in Sullivan County and Big Pond and Russell Pond (Trout Pond)** in Delaware County. On the Ulster and Greene county border, there was Shue's Lake (Echo Lake)***; also in Ulster County, there were Sand Pond and Furlough Lake.

BALSAM LAKE

Of all the lakes and ponds located in the Catskills, the most famous and prolific is Balsam Lake. The lake was never known to have produced trout of large size; its reputation was built upon the incredible numbers of trout that fishermen removed from its waters. Even though it was remote, and travel in and out difficult, fishermen raided the lake's trout population in winter as well as summer and removed hundreds and, at times, even thousands of trout on a single visit.

---

*In 1894, the *Republican Watchman* reported that the lake had been renamed Tennanah Lake, allegedly the Indian name for Long Pond.

**The Beers Atlas of Delaware County (1869) depicts Russell Pond as Trout Pond, which is the name it is known by today.

***By 1880, Shue's Lake was renamed Echo Lake; see Evers, *The Catskills: From Wilderness to Woodstock*, 535.

A fairly shallow, coldwater lake of approximately 20 acres, Balsam Lake is located deep in the forest at the extreme headwaters of the Beaverkill. In the early days of settlement, men visited the lake in winter, cut holes through the ice, and netted barrels of trout, which they shared with their neighbors.

From the time Balsam Lake was discovered, it had been a favorite haunt of sportsmen. Not only did the lake have a bountiful supply of trout, but the area around it was populated by a large number of deer, many of which found their way to markets in Kingston. At the rear of the lake was a large sandbar that was frequented by deer at night. Visitors made dugout canoes from trees, and, with a torch placed to both hide behind and illuminate the shore, killed several deer in one night.

During the 1840s, reports of the trout fishing at Balsam Lake appeared frequently in the weekly newspapers in and about the Catskill region. They generally described the rugged, mountainous landscape, the difficulty of travel, and the phenomenal number of trout caught and kept by anglers. The majority of those who made raids on Balsam Lake came from within the Catskills or from the larger communities outside its borders, such as Kingston, Ellenville, and Rondout. Quite often their goal was not merely to have a good time and catch trout, but to collect and take home a supply of fish that would serve as food in the months ahead.

The *Spirit of the Times* reported on a group of six fishermen who had traveled from Prattsville to the head of Mill Brook, where they had spent the night after taking some three hundred trout from the stream. The following day, the party hiked over the mountain to Balsam Lake and set up

A native brook trout. Ed Van Put.

a camp at a crude shanty along the shoreline. They fished the lake until noon, and then tried the nearby Beaverkill, where they caught another three hundred trout. Sated by their success, the men returned to the lake, built a watch fire, enjoyed a strong cup of coffee with dinner, and strolled down to the lakeshore, where they reclined on a mossy bank:

> No sound of human toil broke the stillness, nor a habitation met the eye, while the large trees that skirted the lake seemed like sentinels keeping faithful vigil over the murmuring waves. Soon after we returned, and rolled our self in a blanket, with our feet to the fire, slept till rosy light broke o'er the world of woods.[9]

The party left the next morning, traveling back down the mountains to Mill Brook. Once they reached the stream, they again began fishing, filling their baskets, until they reached the house where they had previously spent the night. After dinner, they fished in the vicinity of their host, with each angler averaging more than fifty large trout. In two days of fishing, the party of six managed to catch 1,306 "fine trout," most of which were "pickled for home consumption."

Balsam Lake surrounded by mountains. Ed Van Put.

Even though fishermen visited the wilderness retreat at all seasons of the year, these incursions appeared to have little effect on Balsam Lake's trout population. The first visitors to these waters, which are far from any roads, experienced great hardship, traveling the last several miles on foot through a wilderness.

One story illustrating the perils and primitive nature of such a trip appeared in the *Rondout Courier.* After abandoning their sleigh and a drive of 14 miles into the woods, five Rondout sportsmen, "allured by traditional stories of Balsam Lake," started on foot for the fishing ground:

> The route was over three dreaded mountain ridges, trackless, precipitous, clothed in dense forest, and snow some three feet deep on the heights, and a trifle less in the gorges, ravines and valleys. To add to their toil, a crust had formed on the snow some two feet deep and on this was a dry powdered snow of a foot, and the wayfarers broke through the crust at every step. Four hours of wearisome effort brought them to Balsam Lake, an inconsiderable pond lying hemmed in by the feet of three or four mountains. Here a fire was built, and holes cut in the ice. The trout were abundant, biting at anything, a bit of white rag answering as well as the best bait, and, so eager were the fish, when one was drawn out others jumped out of the water in unsuccessful pursuit of the line.[10]

Hunters and fishermen made camp for days, even weeks, along the shores of Balsam Lake. Upon arriving, they usually made rafts to fish from or made dugout canoes by hollowing out a large tree. Bonfires ostensibly made to provide light and warmth also illuminated the woods and kept away panthers or mountain lions and other wild animals that were common to the upper Beaverkill:

> Soon after we started our watch fires, we retired for the night; but our rest was soon broken by a shriek from the midst of the forest, which greatly alarmed us; for we soon became aware of the near approach to our camp of some of the wild beasts that infect these woods.[11]

Men from towns and cities hired guides, who were acquainted with forest life. They came to Balsam Lake to live in the style of backwoodsmen, and once there, they were often joined by men who *were* backwoodsmen. Gentlemen-sportsmen met and mingled with tough characters: dead-shot mountaineer market hunters. The lake was a rendezvous for men of vastly different backgrounds and social standings; yet, in the confines of the forest, they joined company and shared campfires. Their love for the outdoors brought them together, and they sang songs and feasted on a hindquarter of venison and delicious trout. As fires burned low, the men exchanged woods lore and told tales of bears, wolves, and panthers.

It was also along the upper Beaverkill that James and Hannah Murdock were catering to early trout fishermen who found their way up the valley to explore the fishing. Known to sportsmen simply as "Murdock's," this resort was located several miles downstream of Beaverkill Falls and a little more than a mile upstream of Shin Creek.

James Murdock had come to the Beaverkill Valley in 1835, when it truly was a wilderness. A wealthy New York "gentleman" had just constructed a beautiful Gothic cottage along the Beaverkill for an invalid relative, and Murdock took the position to care for the man. As part of his employment, Murdock was given the privilege of hosting a limited number of anglers.

Following the death of the owner, Murdock purchased the property and operated what early trout fishermen viewed as first-class accommodations and *the* place to stay when fishing the upper Beaverkill. Guests not only enjoyed good food and good fishing, but were treated to picnics at Beaverkill Falls, nature walks, and moonlight rides.

Formerly Murdock's on the Beaverkill. Ed Van Put.

"JUDGE" FITCH: A FLY-FISHING PIONEER

Just north of Balsam Lake is the source of Mill Brook, a very productive and historic trout stream. In the 1840s, when brook trout were the only species present, Mill Brook was well known for its excellent fishing. The only accommodations were found with local farmers.

One of the first and finest trout fishermen to fish Mill Brook was Fitz-James Fitch. Fitch named and popularized a fly known as the Beaverkill in the 1840s, and he did so while fishing a deep pool at the base of a waterfall on Mill Brook. The Beaverkill was one of the first trout flies tied in America and was named by Fitch in 1846[12] or 1850.[13]

Fitch, who had not yet acquired the notoriety that he would in later years, was fishing with a couple of friends. The fishing was poor until he tied on a fly from his fly book that was unknown to him. He began taking trout almost immediately, and the fly was so killing that within an hour, he reeled in thirty-two native trout weighing between 4 ounces and a pound.

He shared a couple of the flies with his companions, who also did well with them. When they were finished for the day, Fitch salvaged the best of the flies that were used and took them to Harry Pritchard, the famous New York fly tier, and requested three dozen like it. The pattern is a modification of an unknown English fly that Fitch found in his fly book. Pritchard tied the pattern anew, and Fitch decided to name the fly after his favorite stream: the Beaverkill.

Years later, in an article on trout fishing in the Catskills, Fitch reminisced about Mill Brook and recalled another day he had fished in the 1840s. On this occasion, he caught more than thirty brook trout in two hours of fishing, and these fish were said to average, "by actual weight" one-half pound apiece! A half-pound (or 8-ounce) trout is a fish of about 11 inches in length, a good average size for native brook trout by today's standards and a measure of the quality of the fishing found in Mill Brook in these early prestocking years.

Fitz-James Fitch (1817–1896), a native of Delhi in Delaware County, was also one of the first to fish the upper Beaverkill. Fitch was educated at Delaware Academy, and in 1838, he entered the Delhi law office of Amasa & Amasa J. Parker. He was admitted to the bar in 1843 and moved to Prattsville, in Greene County, where he began his law practice. Eleven years later, he moved to Catskill, and in 1855, Fitch was appointed county judge and surrogate, a position he held for several years. The title "Judge" stayed with him and was used respectfully for the rest of his life.

Judge Fitch was a highly regarded fly fisher, a distance caster, and rod maker. He was respected by his peers as being "courtly, precise, considerate, and observant of all the little amenities of social life; he was withal a loyal friend and charming companion."[14] He was an expert on Catskill trout fishing and was familiar with all the major streams; he fished the Rondout, Dry Brook, Mill Brook, and the Neversink and Beaverkill with regularity, and he wrote of his fishing experiences in magazines and sporting journals.

Judge Fitch first came to the Beaverkill in 1838, accompanied by William Adams of New York and John Smedburgh of Prattsville. Adams and Smedburgh were Catskill veterans who taught Fitch how to fish with the fly, and they became best of friends. This trio made the journey with a team of three-year-old horses that belonged to Smedburgh, and they repeated the trip every year, with the same pair of horses, for twenty-one years. They always started out on the 24th of May and would stay ten days, always at Murdock's. They were gentlemen of the old school: "[N]one of them was ever known to utter a profane or coarse word, to fish on Sunday, to travel in or out on Sunday, and although abundantly supplied they were never known to offer a single drop of liquor to any one, even a guest."[15]

Under the pen name of Fitz, Judge Fitch often contributed fly-fishing and rod-making articles to

Fitz-James Fitch. *Catskill Rivers*, 1983.

fishing journals such as the *American Angler, Shooting and Fishing,* and *Forest and Stream,* and to newspapers in New York and the Catskills.

He is credited with inventing the creel, with its familiar shoulder strap and waistband, a creation most welcomed by the anglers of his generation. Previously they had struggled with cumbersome baskets, which were carried laboriously by a single strap over the shoulder, and they rocked back and forth with the casting motion. The Judge came up with the idea in the summer of 1859 while staying at Murdock's on the Beaverkill.

Judge Fitch kept accurate accounts of his fishing experiences for fifty consecutive years. He recorded every trout he caught during this period, even those he returned to the stream. He started keeping records in 1845, the year he caught the least number of trout: ninety-one. His best year was during the Civil War in 1863, when he caught 1,089. After the first five years, all of the trout he caught were on flies. Two years before his death in Prattsville, in 1896, he had caught a remarkable 28,478 trout!

In 1870, the Judge had moved from Catskill to New York City and, after practicing law in the city for several years, his health began to fail from overwork. His physician told him medicine would not cure him and advised that he should return to the Catskill Mountains that he loved and go into the woods and stay there; he needed outdoor exercise and fresh air to recover.

He took the doctor's advice and returned to Prattsville and, as soon as it became warm enough, he made a trip to the town of Denning, where he had fished many times. He constructed a small shanty along the West Branch of the Neversink, did his own cooking, and spent a part of each season living in the woods and fishing the West Branch.

Although it may appear the Judge was a victim of "fishing for count," he knew there was more to fishing than catching fish, and wrote in an article titled "Fishing—A Healthful Pastime": "There are many things besides catching fish that give pleasure to the fisher; vigorous, healthful exercise in the open air and usually in the midst of beautiful scenery. He should keep his eyes open and see everything worthy of admiration the waterfall, the landscape, the towering mountain and the pretty, tiny flowers at his feet."[16]

Though he improved upon the means with which to carry one's catch away from the stream, he was known and hailed as a trout fisherman who, very early on, released more trout than he kept, and he advocated that others do the same. He wrote about releasing undersized trout before there were size limits and encouraged catch and release in the 1880s, at a time when the idea was not practiced by many: "I look with great pleasure and pride upon my trout scores. . . . But I look with more pleasure and pride upon the figures which tell me of the number of those trout that were put back in the stream."[17]

From the detailed records kept in his diary, we are able to glean some idea of the population and size of the trout he and other pioneer anglers found in the Beaverkill before the introduction of hatchery-raised trout, when it yet contained its "original" strain of brook trout. Writing about the Beaverkill in the 1840s and 1850s, Fitch recalled "when one hundred 'saving' trout per day, weighing from fifteen to twenty pounds, was considered but the average sport."

In order to obtain some idea of how large these trout were on the average, we can use the maximum weight of 20 pounds, or 320 ounces, and realize that the average weight of the fish is 3.2 ounces. The conversion length of a trout weighing 3.2 ounces is approximately 8½ inches.

More accurately, perhaps, Fitch writes of a day when the sport was "exceptionally good" toward the end of May 1859. He recorded: "I had scored, as memoranda made at the time shows, 121 trout, having thrown back perhaps half that number of 'small fry.' The weight of those saved was twenty-five and a half pounds."[18]

On this exceptional day, the total weight in ounces is 408, with the average weight of the 121 fish being 3.4 ounces, or a trout again measuring approximately 8½ inches in length. An 8½-inch brook trout is not a large fish, but it is respectable; it should be remembered that this was the average length of 121 trout.

Being a pioneer trout fisherman, Fitch sampled the Catskills when it was special, when its trout were naïve, inexperienced, and possibly as numerous and unsuspecting as they would ever be again. In his time, he saw the depletion of trout populations and the introduction of domestic trout. In his writing, he urged all anglers to keep records of their catch, recommending they record the number of trout released and those kept, and even to weigh those removed from the stream. His idea was to monitor the success or failure of the fishery and to be in a better position to estimate trout populations.

Fitch was constantly writing about the wasteful habit of keeping fingerlings and other small trout: "[A]ll smaller ones must be carefully taken from the hook, so as to inflict the least possible pain and injury, and placed—not tossed or thrown—back into the stream."[19] He had argued against this practice since the 1860s and practiced what he preached, stating that he had released 8,952 trout during the years 1845 to 1886.

THE TANNERS

Tanneries were operating in Greene County along the Kaaterskill and Schoharie Creeks at least as early as 1817; one of the largest was built by Zadock Pratt along the Schoharie in 1824. By 1827, there were twenty-three tanneries operating along the streams of Greene County alone, and they were producing more leather than the rest of the state combined.

After the 1830s, the leather-tanning industry expanded as tanners competed to remove the vast, though limited, supply of hemlock trees found throughout the Catskills. The bark of the hemlock was a major component in the process of making leather from the hides of animals such as sheep, cows, and horses.

Tanners depended on hemlock and a good supply of water, and streams provided inexpensive waterpower as well as the large amounts of fresh water needed for the various stages of the tanning process. Streams were also convenient for ridding the tannery of its abundant supply of unwanted wastes, which were simply discharged into the nearby waterway.

From the onset, it was deemed more practical to construct tanneries in the Catskills and cart the hides in and out of the forest than to haul the bark out. At first, hides were brought up the Hudson River by sloop, then taken overland by wagon with horses or oxen.

In general, tannery workers lived in the woods, near the trees, in crude huts or shanties during the bark-peeling season, which was usually from May 15 to August 15 (but a mild winter could cause the season to begin in April). There were loggers who felled the trees; peelers who stripped off the bark; and teamsters who hauled the bark back to the tannery in winter on sleds and drays:

Life during the bark season was one continual camping out. For the Army was ever on the march, pursuing the disappearing hemlock, and in most cases, the bark peelers lived in log houses or hemlock shanties built for temporary use. . . .

Mosquitoes and gnats were thick, and smudge fires had to be kept up all night to make sleep possible. The men slept in bunks on the floor of the loft, almost suffocated by smoke in order that the insect pests might be kept away.[20]

Unhairing the hide and tan-yard.
One Hundred Years' Progress of the United States, 1870.

The hemlock bark was ground and then transferred to a leach house, where it was mixed with boiling water and kept for about a week; then the liquor was pumped to the tan yard as needed. Hides were first placed in vats in the beam house and left for several days; then they were removed, pounded until soft, and split down the middle into sides. The hides were then taken to sweat pits, where they were limed or sweated for five to eight days, depending on temperature. The smell from the sweat pits was horrible, and the ammonia emanating from them made the eyes sting badly.

If the hair on the hides could be rubbed off with the thumb, they were ready to be milled or pounded. Fleshers then proceeded to remove hair and scrape the hides clean; they were then treated to open the pores so that the leather would tan. The next step was to place the hides in a series of curing vats containing ooze made from bark and water. As the hides progressed through the vats, they were subjected to solutions of increasing strength.

Because large quantities of clean water were needed to control the tannic acid, the vats were often sunk in the ground next to the stream. When the tanning process was complete, the hides were put in a loft to dry, then treated with fish oil and rehung to dry, and lastly, treated with tanner's oil. The man who applied the fish oil had the worst-smelling job of all.

The tanneries were a dreadfully smelly business; the sap or slime on the hemlock bark would ferment and sour, and fish oil, animal hair, and the decaying flesh removed from the hides fouled the air. Curing vats, with their concoctions of tanbark and lime, were regularly emptied directly into the streams, killing thousands of trout and polluting the waters downstream.

Competition for the giant hemlocks was great, and as each tannery depended on the bark for survival, trees were cut down anywhere they could be reached. Those found along streams were felled across them, from one bank to the other, and the trunks and branches were left in the water. This exposed the stream to sunlight, obstructed the flow, and caused erosion. Hemlocks hundreds of years old were destroyed only for their bark; the remainder of the tree was left to rot in the forest. As the trees became scarce in Greene County, tanners moved into Ulster, then Sullivan and Delaware counties.

Tanneries were constructed on every major trout stream in the Catskills, and they had a negative impact on trout populations for more than fifty years. There were but a few along the Beaverkill, Willowemoc, and Neversink, but other streams suffered greatly from their effluents and forest destruction. There were as many

Over the beam and hide-splitting machine.
One Hundred Years' Progress of the United States, 1870.

as twenty-five tanneries operating in the Schoharie Creek watershed and approximately sixteen along the Esopus Creek and its tributaries. Along the main Esopus, there were no less than eight tanneries between Pine Hill and the hamlet of Shokan; the first was constructed in 1831.

The tanning industry peaked in the production of sole leather during the period from 1856 to 1873; this was especially true in Sullivan County and during the years of the Civil War. After the war, prices fell and exports were slow to recover; however, many tanneries went out of business for the sole reason that the supply of hemlocks was exhausted. This, more than any other reason, brought about the fall of the industry, and by 1885, there was hardly a tannery operating. The tanners were so complete in their destruction of the hemlocks that many believed the giant evergreens would never return. Today, a little more than a hundred years after the industry closed its doors, mature groves of hemlock trees are again found throughout the Catskills.

All over the Catskills, the tanner was destroying the pristine environment found along trout streams; the dumping of tannery wastes was outrageous and illegal. The industry was one of greed, waste, thoughtlessness, and wanton destruction, with a complete disregard for the natural beauty of the region. It is incomprehensible today to even imagine depositing such wastes into a clear mountain stream and destroying the waters downstream:

Everywhere along the streams rose the long ungainly buildings, and the water that formerly flowed like liquid glass over its pebbly bed now ran red as blood, and foul with lime, and ill-savored "leach," while the ground bark collected in pools and sifted in among the gravel, driving the fish from their hiding places and destroying the spawning beds.[21]

By the 1840s, trout fishermen were united in their dislike of the tanneries and complained bitterly about how they plundered the countryside, killed the trout, and polluted the streams:

It destroys the beauty of many a fair landscape—discolors the once pure waters—and, what is worse than all, drives the fish from the streams! Think of the sacrilege! The bright-tinted trout offered up upon the ignoble altar of calf-skin, sheep-skin, and cow-skin.[22]

In an article titled "A Trip to Delaware," written for the *Kingston Democratic Journal* in 1849, a fisherman wrote that the tanning industry was despoiling the dense growth of hemlocks on the mountainsides, and he told of the many tanneries he had encountered on all of the main streams. In contemplating the fate of the trout, he applied his own beguiling logic:

One can hardly imagine where a market could be found for such immense quantities of leather, even if every body was bare foot. The exhausted liquor and bark from the vats has proved as fatal to the trout of the large streams, as rum and gunpowder to the Indians. In some places the water is dyed as with blood for miles, and the poor trout are either killed or driven into the fastnesses of the mountain brooks. Rather an astringent treatment for the swift and speckled denizens of the brook, but how can *I* pity them, after having just dined off a dozen or so! There's reason to all things, it is said, and I'm sure there is in trouting. It is capital sport, and requires a canny hand and a quick eye, and the fish that's caught may feel proud of dying a victim to the noble science of old Izaak Walton; but to be smothered in tan bark is quite another affair.[23]

Blossom Falls on the Esopus Creek. *Picturesque Ulster* 1896–1905, published by Hope Farm Press 1991.

Tanneries were having a profound affect on the brook trout populations of the Catskills, and perhaps no stream suffered from the abuses of this industry as did the Esopus Creek. The name *Esopus* is of Indian origin and is considered a composite of the word "Sepu, a river, and es or us, diminutive, hence 'a small river.'"[24] The word was modified into *Sopus*, or *Esopus*. In the days of Dutch settlement, it was known as the *Esopus Kill*.

The Esopus Creek has its source near Slide Mountain at an elevation of approximately 2,648 feet. It begins flowing in a general direction northerly for approximately 8½ miles through Big Indian Hollow, a steep and narrow valley, to the hamlet of Big Indian, where the stream is joined by Birch Creek, which enters from the northwest.

From its source, the Esopus makes a rapid descent, dropping in elevation approximately 169 feet per mile, producing three waterfalls along this stretch, each more beautiful than the other; the uppermost is Otter Falls, then Parker Falls and Blossom Falls. The stream's swift-moving waters constantly increase in volume with the additions of tributaries such as Little Peck Hollow, Elk Bushkill, McKenley Hollow, Hatchery Hollow, and Lost Clove.

After it is joined by Birch Creek, the Esopus turns and flows in a more easterly direction for about 5½ miles, running through the hamlets of Shandaken and Allaben. At Allaben, the Esopus changes course again, and flows southeasterly another 12 miles through Phoenicia, Mount Pleasant, Mount Tremper, Beechford, Cold Brook, and Boiceville, where today it enters the Ashokan reservoir.

From Big Indian to the reservoir, the Esopus is joined by a number of coldwater tributaries, the largest being Bushnellsville Creek (Deep Hollow), Broadstreet Hollow, Woodland Valley Stream, Stony Clove Creek, the Beaver Kill, and the Little Beaver Kill. The stream gradient from Big Indian to the reservoir is approximately 35 feet per mile.

Settlement in the Esopus Valley was early compared with other areas of the Catskills, perhaps because of its proximity to Kingston, which was settled in 1652, or the fact that a road that had been an Indian trail paralleled the Esopus Creek at least as early as 1765.

Trade between local Indians known as the Esopus and Europeans probably occurred as early as 1609, when Henry Hudson sailed up the Hudson River. Kingston became the hub of the fur trade, and the Indians each spring brought their furs, especially the highly prized beaver pelts, to trade for brass kettles, steel knives, blankets, firearms, and other items never seen before by the Esopus.

Eager for manufactured goods, the Indians quickly decimated the beaver population, which must have been significant in the Esopus Valley. Esopus tributaries, such as the Beaver Kill and Little Beaver Kill, were apparently named because of their abundance of the fur bearers. Catskill historian Alf Evers writes, "Beaver found conditions along the streams radiating from the Catskills to their liking. In 1609 beaver dams in countless numbers slowed the current of Catskill streams."[25]

Upper Esopus Creek. Ed Van Put.

Beaver not only slowed the current, but their dams often caused streams to take new courses. Their removal of hardwood trees for food, lodges, and dams along stream banks caused erosion and siltation, and possibly warmed water temperatures.

The road that passed through the Esopus Valley traveled to and over Pine Hill and into Delaware County. It was used by many of the settlers who cleared the forest and made small farms in the wilderness at Bishop's Falls before 1750, Mount Pleasant by 1763, Mount Tremper area in 1783, and Phoenicia in 1787. The road was improved in 1802 and became known as the Ulster and Delaware Turnpike; travel along the road was significant enough that there were no less than eight inns, taverns, and "publick houses" before 1814.

Tanners, too, came early to the Esopus Valley. The first tanneries were constructed in the 1830s, and by the 1850s, there were already eleven along the main stream and its tributaries, six of which were located upstream of Phoenicia. In addition to the tanneries, the watershed attracted scores of sawmills, tray mills, turning mills, and chair factories. This concentration of streamside industries dependent on forest resources was greater than anywhere else in the Catskills.

Tanneries spoiled the countryside, fouled the air, and polluted the waterways. The tannery discharges along the Esopus must indeed have had an impact on the fisheries; in an article titled "A Week in Shandaken" (1845), a writer commented on the stream:

> The waters of this never-failing stream which have rushed onward for centuries over its rocky channel—sometimes covered by the overhanging branches of trees which grew upon its banks, or obstructed by the decayed trunks of others which, through age or the settler's axe have fallen over it; this stream once abounding with the finest trout, has had its waters checked in their course to turn the wheel of the manufacturer. No less than seven tanneries beside White Lead Mills, an Iron Factory, and numerous Flouring and Saw-mills are to be found upon it.[26]

Much of the earliest trout-fishing history in the Esopus Valley centers on the Stony Clove Creek, which flows into the Esopus at Phoenicia. In the earliest days of Catskill trout fishing, the Stony Clove was more famous than the Esopus. The stream was cited as a unique area by Henry E. Dwight in his "Account of the Kaatskill Mountains," published in the *American Journal of Science and Arts* in 1820. Dwight did not mention trout fishing, though he wrote of the clove's grandeur and rugged terrain, and of the small lake with its floating vegetation that a man could walk upon.

Charles Lanman, the noted artist and author, was among the first to sample the Stony Clove's trout fishing and write about it. He fished these waters in the 1830s, and he claimed that the stream was already famous when he visited it; he wrote of his fishing experiences in *Letters from a Landscape Painter*. Lanman and two companions caught a total of seven hundred trout in a single day!

Many of the early visitors to the Stony Clove boarded at Milo Barber's. Milo Barber owned 90 acres along the east bank of the creek north of Phoenicia. He purchased the land in 1812 and began farming. Several years later, he acquired an additional 31 acres, lying between the Esopus and the mouth of the Stony Clove, and by the 1830s, he operated an inn that was popular with trout fishermen.

Stony Clove Notch. Ed Van Put.

The headwaters of the Stony Clove. Ed Van Put.

The *Catskill Democrat,* on May 29, 1844, reported that four fishermen from the village of Catskill visited the waters of Shandaken, fished the Stony Clove, and filled their baskets with 52 pounds of trout! They reported on the excellent accommodations at Barber's and claimed, "Any quantity of trout may be taken by those skilled in that delightful recreation, to say nothing of the healthful nature of such an exercise. To all who are fond of the 'sports of the field and flood' we say, visit Mr. Barber's."

A few years later, the *Kingston Democratic Journal,* on June 14, 1848, reported that a group of ten gentlemen from Catskill traveled to Shandaken, stayed at Milo Barber's, and in two days' fishing caught fourteen hundred to fifteen hundred trout! In addition to having an "admirable" day "and the trout exceedingly plenty," Milo Barber and his "obliging family, made it one of the most agreeable excursions imaginable."

STONY CLOVE.

The road through the Stony Clove. *Harper's New Monthly Magazine,* September 1883.

One month later, it was reported in a local newspaper that a fishing party who traveled to the Stony Clove near Barber's met with "indifferent success." Though the number of fishermen in the party was not revealed, it was stated that the men caught 300 trout, which they considered inadequate, because "poaching scamps had swept the kill with a net."

The Stony Clove was far from being fished out. Two years later, an article appeared in the *Spirit of the Times*, dated June 29, 1850, and titled "Successful Trout Fishing," which told of incredible catches. The story was written by a trout fisherman who visited the area and described the surroundings of the Stony Clove, stating that the Clove "lies *off from* all roads ordinarily traveled, and *on* a road, which no sane man, save bark peelers or trout killers, would ever think of traveling." The writer describes the precipitous mountainous terrain, and avows that the Stony Clove is the "wildest spot within five hundred miles of Gotham."

The men found accommodations with local residents and, "though no palaces," the "humble dwellings" sheltered a "kindly people" that did their best to make them comfortable. There were ten fishermen in the party, though the writer claimed "Five of us only made pretensions to skill." The party fished the Stony Clove and its nearby tributaries, and though half were novices, ". . . in one day's fishing our party killed *nineteen hundred and eighteen trout*. This I affirm, on the honor of a true disciple of good old Izaak. If it shall be disputed, I will wager a box, or a score of boxes, of the best Havanas, that I will pick five men who will repeat the feat, in twelve hours' fishing, on any day between the 1st of July and the 1st of November."

5

The 1850s

THE HUDSON RIVER SCHOOL; "HOUSELESS ANGLERS;" and A "DAM'D FOOL"

Nathaniel P. Willis's fine description of Walton and the trout-fishing potentials found along the West Branch of the Delaware River surely spurred additional fishing tourists to travel the Erie up the Delaware to explore both branches. By the 1850s, railway travel was available along both of the main waterways that provided access to the Catskills. Along the Hudson River, a railroad traveled up the west shore, and cities such as Kingston and Newburgh had trains running to New York City on a regular basis. Easier and swifter railway travel allowed fishing tourists from cities to reach these traditional routes to the Catskills in just a couple of hours.

The Hudson Valley was changing rapidly, and while trees and especially hemlocks were disappearing in the Catskills via sawmills and tanneries, wealthy landowners who were settling along the Hudson were already reversing this trend. Writing from his residence near Newburgh, author Willis, who wrote descriptively of American life, remarked:

> A class who can afford to let the trees grow is getting possession of the Hudson; and it is at least safe to rejoice in this, whatever one may preach as to the displacement of the laboring tiller of the soil by the luxurious idler. With the bare fields fast changing into wooded lawns, the rocky wastes into groves, the angular farm-houses into shaded villas, and the naked uplands into waving forests, our great thoroughfare will soon be seen (as it has not been for many years) in something like its natural beauty. It takes very handsome men and mountains to look well bald.[1]

Throughout the 1850s, native brook trout continued to be removed from Catskill streams in alarming numbers. In August 1850, a fishing correspondent to that earliest of sporting journals, the *Spirit of the Times,* contributed an article from Delhi along the West Branch titled "Trout Fishing in New York." The writer boasted of the excellent trout fishing he found around Delhi: "Night after night have fine strings of delicious hard brook-trout made their appearance in our midst." He and a companion fished a nearby tributary and, after catching a dozen or more trout in a half-hour, started a wood fire and enjoyed a streamside repose:

The trout were cleaned, stuck upon pronged sticks, and well salted, then held up to the coals until thoroughly roasted; not "done brown," but to a crisp, white. *They were discussed*; oh, how delicious! A pull at the brandy-flask, and we lighted a "Yarrow," and, with our heads on a bog, and our feet on a log. We both went a-dreaming.[2]

In these early days of settlement, it was not uncommon for a weekly newspaper to receive copies of papers from other parts of the Catskills, which they read, looking for items of interest for their own readers. During the trout-fishing season of 1856, the editor of the *Walton Blade* noted in his newspaper that the *Norwich Reporter,* from nearby Chenango County, claimed that two fishermen belonging to the "universal Smith family" from Norwich had caught between four hundred and five hundred nice trout in Trout Creek, a tributary of the West Branch of the Delaware, downstream of Walton.

The *Walton Blade* editor took exception to the other editor's story and stated: "pshaw, why Mr. *Reporter,* you are a verdant. A few of our Walton *Blades,* not long since, paid a visit to the Beaverkill, a tributary of the East Branch, and with only 'hook and line,' drew from their native element over sixteen hundred of the spotted trout, and such fish too, that Trout Creek can't begin with."[3]

Two weeks later, the editor of the *Blade* published a response to his comments that appeared in the *Norwich Reporter:* "Yes, but there is a mighty difference, Mr. Blade, between a couple of gentlemen strolling leisurely along a stream for five or six hours, and a half dozen professional anglers camping down upon the Beaverkill, for a week, fishing all the time for dear life, and allowing no intermission except for drink. Name your best man, and your stream, and your time, and we will turn out against him a SMITH, who will fish him into fits before two o'clock in the afternoon."

The *Walton Blade* editor accepted the challenge and stated, "send on the best of your 'Smiths'" and claimed that his "Delaware Blades" did not camp out for a week on the Beaverkill, and actually caught 1,709 trout in seven hours with hook and line! "Come on then ye Chenangonians, you'll find the Delawares ever ready. Name your day."[4]

There must have been some pretty good trout fishermen in nearby Greene County as well; the *Windham Journal* of July 1, 1858, reported that nine "gentlemen" from the village of Windham made a three-day fishing trip into Ulster County, most likely the upper Beaverkill, and returned with a "fine lot" of trout, catching fifteen hundred to sixteen hundred!

The upper Beaverkill in the 1850s was sparsely developed, and the few settlers who carved out a farm in the wilderness provided trout fishermen with lodging and a place to fish. For the most part, the landscape was still one of a vast unbroken forest; the roads were bad, and along the Beaverkill at certain times of the year—spring and fall—they were almost impassable. One newspaper reported that what was "sorely needed" in the region was a "Preacher, Justice of the Peace, and a Path Master."

Despite the difficulty of travel, fishermen found their way to the region. The forest was primeval, and wildlife such as wolves, wildcats, bears, and panthers or mountain lions were said to be common. Men who lived in cities or villages were not always comfortable in such a setting, even when they traveled in groups; although some tolerated living in the wilds in tents, most opted for the sparse accommodations provided by local farmers.

THE HUDSON RIVER SCHOOL

During the early 1800s, the Catskill Mountains played a dual role; they not only attracted our country's foremost trout fishermen, but also many of our first and finest landscape painters. The Catskills are renowned for fostering the Hudson River School of landscape painters who, according to art historian John K. Howat, were "the most popular school of serious painters that has ever existed on the American continent."[5] The term *Hudson River School* applies to a group of artists of more than one generation, predominantly from New York, who gained national attention as landscape painters during the period from 1825 to 1875.

These artists roamed the mountains seeking their superb natural beauty. They found inspiration in the varied magnificence of cascading waterfalls, deep ravines, and projecting rock outcroppings and recorded it on canvas. They traveled the fern-laden banks of Catskill streams with sketch pad, easel, and trout rod. The Kaaterskill was the favorite, but there was hardly a stream known for its trout fishing that escaped their canvas. Catskill historian Alf Evers writes that these artists "took to traveling the mountains with a paint brush in one hand and a trout rod in the other."[6] When the sketch pad was put aside, a fly rod often was the replacement, and several members of the school were among the earliest to sample trout streams when they were fundamentally pristine and undisturbed by human activities.

Artist fishing. *Adventures in the Wilds of the United States and British American Provinces*, 1856.

Their paintings encouraged tourists to visit the wilderness, and they helped Americans formulate an appreciation for nature and the natural scenic beauty of the forest, mountains, streams, waterfalls, and the geological features found among the many hollows and cloves of the Catskills.

The term *Hudson River School* may have applied to these artists because their paintings also included the Hudson River and its shores, but also perhaps because they maintained a method and technique similar to that of America's first popular landscape artist, Thomas Cole.

Another possible implication for the name may have been due to the fact that many of the artists lived or had studios along the Hudson River in places such as Catskill, Hudson, Rondout, and Newburgh. Though they painted in other parts of the Northeast, all, at one time or another, worked in the Catskills. Alf Evers has written that some "lovers of the Catskills" have pointed out that these artists first worked in the Catskills and painted there so often that it might be more appropriate to call them the Catskill Mountain School.

Kaaterskill Clove, formed by the course of the Kaaterskill Creek as it descends down through a series of spectacular waterfalls, could be considered the birthplace of the Hudson River School; and the small hamlet of Palenville, at the foot of the Clove, has been called "America's first art colony."

All of these artists had an inherent love of nature and were lured to the wild and primitive scenery of the Clove where "they approached nature with reverence and portrayed it with the detailed care of a naturalist."[7] Kaaterskill Falls became one of the most popular subjects, and a pilgrimage to the falls was a trip every Hudson River School painter had to make.

Along with Thomas Cole, Thomas Doughty and Asher B. Durand are recognized as being the founders of the school, and Doughty and Durand were among the first fishermen to sample the excellent trout fishing found in the Catskills.

Thomas Cole

Thomas Cole (1801–1848) visited the region in 1825, when the mountains were still a primeval wilderness, and he was the first to paint Kaaterskill Falls. Cole was so inspired by the region that he moved to the village of Catskill in 1827 and maintained a studio within sight of its mountain peaks. From there he regularly made hikes through the rugged cloves, climbed and camped on the mountaintops, and wandered through the forest seeking new vistas, hidden lakes, streams, and waterfalls.

Palenville. *Harper's New Monthly Magazine*, July 1854.

On these excursions he sketched, made notes on particular details, and contemplated the natural beauty he had found. Later, with brush and oils, he produced some of the finest landscapes ever seen. Cole was especially active in the fall, when the foliage was prime with all the magnificent colors that are found only in a hardwood forest. His autumnal landscapes were spectacular and well-received in this country and abroad. When they were first seen in England, with their brilliant colors of fiery reds, bright glowing oranges, and yellows, the paintings were regarded "as an extravagant, so unaware were foreigners of the brilliant freaks of the early frost this side of the water."[8]

Cole loved the fall, and in an essay that appeared in *American Monthly Magazine,* he wrote:

There is one season when the American forest surpasses all the world in gorgeousness—that is the autumnal;—then every hill and dale is riant in the luxury of color—every hue is there, from the liveliest green to the deepest purple—from the most golden yellow to the intensest crimson. The artist looks despairingly upon the glowing landscape, and in the old world his truest imitations of the American forest, at this season, are called falsely bright, and scenes in Fairy Land.[9]

Thomas Cole was not a fisherman; his biographer Louis Noble tells us that sports such as hunting and fishing did not fit in with the sensitive nature of his character. Though not a sportsman, he loved the natural world, especially the Catskills, with its streams, mountains, and woodlands, and when he began to witness the early disappearance of the forest, he became a pioneer in the protest of its destruction.

Another biographer, Matthew Baigell, states:

Cole hated the rapidity with which the wilderness was disappearing. Even during his initial visits to the Hudson River Valley in 1825, he had to endure the sight of burned-over fields, the sound of sawmills, and the stink of the tanneries and tanners' wagons. He increasingly disliked the strictly utilitarian manipulation of the land.

"Nothing is more disagreeable to me," he said, "than the sight of lands that are just clearing with their prostrate trees, black stumps burnt and deformed. All the native beauty of the forest taken away by the improving man. And alas, he replaces it with none of the beauties of Art."[10]

Thomas Doughty

Thomas Doughty (1793–1856), born in Philadelphia, was one of the first to specialize in landscapes in the United States and was said to be an inspiration to Thomas Cole. Doughty began exhibiting landscapes as early as 1816 at the Pennsylvania Academy of the Fine Arts, and he became a full-time professional painter in the city of Philadelphia in 1820. He was one of the first artists to paint landscapes exclusively, and in 1834 art historian William Dunlap stated, "Mr. Doughty has long stood in the first rank as a landscape painter—he was at one time the first and best in the country."[11]

Though he was born in Philadelphia, and his career began in that city, Doughty also took up residence in New York City and Newburgh. He made frequent trips to the Catskills and was among the earliest to sketch Kaaterskill Falls; this work can be seen in an engraving titled "Catskill Falls" in the *Atlantic Souvenir* in 1828.

Doughty was a fisherman, and his love for angling is often reflected in his paintings. Many include fishing in their titles or feature fishermen along a streamside land-

Thomas Doughty. *Graham's Magazine,* June 1854.

scape. Some of his works include *Fishing in the River* (1828), *The Fishing Party* (1829), *The Anglers* (1834), *Fishing, The Trout Brook, The Trout Pool, Trout Fisherman, The Fishing Pool* (1850), and *The Fisherman.*

Doughty worked and fished in the Catskills during the 1820s and 1830s, and although he sketched in the famous Kaaterskill Clove, he was also familiar with the wild regions of the upper branches of the Delaware River in Sullivan and Delaware counties, including the Beaverkill, which at the time was not considered to be a part of the Catskills.

Of his trout-fishing experiences, there is little information; however, he was quite familiar with the woods and waters of Sullivan County, where he painted some of his finest landscapes. His well-known painting, *The Anglers* (1834), is said to be a scene along a stream in the western Catskills, most likely Sullivan County, where he was a pioneer trout fisherman and sketched and painted until the 1850s. The painting *Fishing Party* inspired his friend and noted author and poet Nathaniel P. Willis to write:

> Come to the lake the shower is past
> And the bright sun is put at last,
> Come! Take your baskets and away,
> We'll to the rock for trout today.
> Our hooks are good; our flies are new,
> Our flexile lines are strong and true.[12]

Doughty was a self-taught artist who loved nature, hunting, and fishing. Between 1830 and 1832, he and his brother, John, published a monthly magazine titled the *Cabinet of Natural History and American Rural Sports.* The magazine is noted for containing the first colored sporting prints made in America. The majority of these prints were done by Thomas Doughty, and today the magazine is sought after by collectors and demands a high price.

Asher Brown Durand

Asher Brown Durand (1796–1886) was painting in the Catskills in the early 1830s, and from 1837 on he exhibited a great many landscapes. Durand was a friend of Thomas Cole's and, at times, accompanied Cole into the wilderness around the area of Kaaterskill Clove. Durand, however, searched for new scenery, new streams and waterfalls, and began exploring what was then known as the Shandaken Mountains, which included the Esopus Creek and its tributaries.

His excursions into other portions of the Catskills may have been influenced by his interest in trout fishing; trout fishermen are always eager to try new waters. During the 1830s, Durand was painting and fishing while staying at local inns and farmhouses, and was often accompanied by students "who might acquire painting and fishing skills simultaneously."[13]

After Cole's death in 1848, Asher B. Durand became the leader of American landscape painting and a dominant figure in the art circles of New York City. In the 1850s and 1860s, he made annual summer trips to the Catskills that usually included trout fishing, and in 1853 and 1854, he spent the entire summer in the town of Olive in the Esopus Valley.

Durand did a series of forest scenes in the famous Stony Clove and produced a great many paintings from in and around Shandaken and the Esopus Creek. A few of the titles include

Mountain and Stream; Catskill Mountains near Shandaken; View of the Shandaken Mountains; Shandaken; Ulster County, N.Y.; Trout Brook; Shandaken Mountains; Bushkill Creek; and *On the Esopus.* Durand painted at least four paintings titled *Esopus Creek* and one titled *The Sketcher: Landscape with Fisherman and Artist.*

Durand was said to be the first American to paint directly from nature, meaning that he prepared his palette at home and carried a portable easel and stool. Most of the early landscape painters made pencil sketches and took notes when in the field, and did their painting back in the studio. In 1841, the screw-top, collapsible tin tube was patented. This invention enabled artists to travel with portable paints, and more landscapers followed Durand's habit of painting outdoors.

Painting outdoors in the Catskills is not always a pleasant experience, and

ART AND ARTISTS OF AMERICA.

BY E. ANNA LEWIS.

ASHER BROWN DURAND.

Asher B. Durand. *Graham's Magazine,* June 1854.

although accommodations at local farmhouses were inexpensive, the food provisions were often less than what city men were accustomed to. In October 1848, Durand writes from Palenville:

> The Clove is rich in beautiful wildness beyond all we have met with heretofore. . . . With the exception of two days, the weather has been so cold that we have worked in overcoats and overshoes, and, in addition, have been obliged to have a constant fire alongside for an occasional warming, all of which I have endured, pretty well, with no worse effect than a slight cold. . . . I caught a fine trout which I ate for breakfast—the only decent one I have had since I came here; sour bread, salt pork, and ham being the staple commodities.[14]

During the 1850s, a second generation of the Hudson River School was establishing their own reputation by following in the footsteps of Cole, Doughty, and Durand. These included such noted artists as Frederic E. Church, Albert Bierstadt, Jasper F. Cropsey, Sanford R. Gifford, Jervis McEntee, T. Worthington Whittredge, John W. Casilear, Davis Johnson, George Inness, William Trost Richards, John F. Kensett, and William and James M. Hart.

Many members of the group were fishermen, but only Gifford, Whittredge, and McEntee left behind substantial records of their Catskill trout-fishing experiences, with much of what is learned coming from the diaries of Jervis McEntee.

That these artists were attracted to trout fishing is not surprising because trout fishers, too, have an inherent love of nature and recognize and appreciate the natural beauty found along streams. Throughout the history of American trout fishing, there have been a large number of artists who were fly fishermen. Thaddeus Norris, in his classic *American Angler's Book* (1864), tells of the "quiet joys" of fishing, and of the "solace and peace it brings to the harassed mind, or how it begets and fosters contentment and a love of nature."

The trio of Gifford, Whittredge, and McEntee often sketched and fished together, especially in Ulster, Delaware, and Sullivan counties. Angling for trout was a common pastime of these men, and although they achieved great fame for their art, written records of their fishing exploits are difficult to uncover. Accounts of their lives appear often in articles and in books that focus on their art and all that is relative to it. Their angling experiences mostly appear in diaries and letters that have been retained on microfilm and in special collections.

Thomas Worthington Whittredge

Worthington Whittredge (1820–1910), as he was more commonly known, was born in Ohio and spent his boyhood on a small farm along the Little Miami River near Springfield. Born in a log cabin, he learned to hunt, fish, and trap within the region of his home at a very early age, and often, on the coldest nights of winter, in the foulest weather, he left a warm bed and traveled miles to check his traps and be home by daylight to do farm chores. He developed an intense love of the natural world. Later in life, he believed these deep feelings toward nature and his early outdoor experiences led to his study of art.

Whittredge began as a portrait painter but then concentrated on landscape painting in 1844; in 1849, he went to Europe to study and stayed for ten years. It was there that he first met Sanford Gifford, and when he returned to the United States in 1859, he and Gifford maintained studios on Tenth Street in New York. They were a part of a close-knit circle that included Bierstadt, Church, and McEntee.

It may have been Gifford who first encouraged Whittredge to visit the Catskills. After spending so many years in Europe, with its seemingly manicured woodlands, he stated:

> I hid myself for months in the recesses of the Catskills. But how different was the scene before me from anything I had been looking at for many years! The forest was a mass of decaying logs and tangled brush wood, no peasants to pick up every vestige of fallen sticks to burn in their miserable huts, no well ordered forests, nothing but the primitive woods with their solemn silence reigning everywhere.[15]

For the rest of his life, the Catskills remained Whittredge's favorite locale, and it was there that he fished with other artists, including Sanford Gifford. The two remained close friends for almost thirty years; they both painted and visited Kaaterskill Falls many times.

Whittredge also painted in many of the same places that Asher B. Durand did, especially around Shokan and Shandaken. Perhaps, because he was even more of a fisherman, he ranged even further, sketching along Dry Brook, near Arkville and at the headwaters of the East Branch of the Delaware near Roxbury, in Delaware County.

Worthington Whittredge was considered among the best painters of the Hudson River School and he spent many days, both summer and fall, in the Catskills. His paintings often depict forest scenes with trout streams and a fisherman, or a grouse, or couple of deer—"harmonious scenes lit by soft sunlight sifting through dense foliage."[16]

Whittredge had the same intuition that hunters and fishermen have; he possessed special knowledge and was able to recognize good trout and wildlife habitat. He was a good observer; when he looked at a stream or woodland scene, he saw added beauty, added promise. He often included deer in his landscapes; a few are titled *Deer Watering, Moonlight Landscape with Deer,* and *Deer in an Autumn Landscape,* an especially beautiful painting.

Perhaps because he was attracted to trout fishing, many of his landscape titles coincide with trout streams: *Trout Fishing in the Catskills; Fly Fishing; Dry Brook, Arkville, Catskills; Along the Upper Delaware; The Brook in the Woods; A Forest Stream; Trout Brook in the Catskills; Along the Delaware; A Catskill Brook;* and *The Trout Pool.* Of the last painting, Whittredge's biographer, Anthony F. Janson, writes, "We experience a rush of pleasure on approaching the enchanting scene, with its dazzling sunlight and cool, moss-green shade. *The Trout Pool,* Whittredge seems to say, is paradise regained, not on God's terms but man's."[17]

The painting *Along the Delaware,* ca. 1875, is a classic Catskill trout scene. The title suggests the Delaware River; but the painting is undoubtedly the East Branch of the Delaware, in the vicinity of Dean's Corners (Arkville), where Whittredge, Gifford, and McEntee sketched in the fall of 1873. The East Branch has long been called the "Delaware" by natives of the region; perhaps because it was believed to be the source of the Delaware River. The three artists stayed at the house of Davis Elmendorf and sketched the picturesque scenery of the upper East Branch and its tributaries every day.

Worthington Whittredge achieved great fame as a landscape painter, and genre paintings by him are rare; however, one particular work, because of its fishing background, should be noted. In 1885 or 1886, Whittredge visited Balsam Lake, famous for its inexhaustible population of native brook trout. He fished the lake and the nearby Beaverkill as a guest of the Balsam Lake Club, which was founded in 1883.

Worthington Whittredge ca. 1864. Archives of American Art, Smithsonian Institution.

He recorded his visit with a painting titled *The Club House Sitting Room at Balsam Lake, Catskills.* The painting depicts a young woman sitting at a writing desk next to a large fireplace. The woman may well have been his daughter Effie, as the club register reveals that she accompanied Whittredge on other occasions. His last visit to Balsam Lake appears to have been on September 6, 1890, when he was the guest of club president Cornelius Van Brunt. The notation on the register states, "Mr. Whittredge visited the Lake for the purpose of making some sketches of it, and of the surrounding scenery. None of the members of the Club are here at this time, but the Lake with all its beauty is here, as of old, to welcome him."

Sanford Robinson Gifford

Sanford Robinson Gifford (1823–1880) was born in Saratoga County, and when he was just about a year old, his family moved to Hudson, within sight of the Catskill Mountains. In 1845, at the age of twenty-two, he moved to New York City to study art. At first Gifford painted portraits, but as with many artists, he soon realized he would rather paint landscapes. In a letter to O. B. Frothingham, he relates:

> During the summer of 1846 I made several pedestrian tours around the Catskill Mts. and the Berkshire Hills, and made a good many sketches from nature. These studies, together with the great admiration I felt for the works of Cole developed a strong interest in Landscape Art, and opened my eyes to a keener perception and more intelligent enjoyment of nature. Having once enjoyed the absolute freedom of the landscape painter's life I was unable to return to portrait painting.[18]

When he visited the Catskills in 1846, Gifford, like other members of the Hudson River School, was drawn to the wonders of Kaaterskill Clove and its spectacular beauty. He got to know the Kaaterskill Clove intimately and throughout his career painted at least one scene from the Clove area almost every year.

Gifford, like Thomas Cole before him, was concerned over the encroachment and the destruction of the Catskill forest. One painting by Gifford has been credited with having a profound impact on the American conservation movement. Titled *Hunter Mountain, Twilight*, painted in 1866, the landscape depicts a stump-littered clearing deep in the forest with Hunter Mountain in the background. In the center of the painting, a small stream, stripped of all its protective vegetation, meanders out of its banks aimlessly.

James W. Pinchot, a wealthy New York art collector and intimate friend of Sanford Gifford, purchased the work, and since the 1970s, a number of art historians have interpreted the painting as "a sober assessment, a possible rejection of the effects of human settlement in the wilderness."[19] The painting, with its scarred landscape and offensive tree stumps, had an effect on Pinchot; he too developed concern about the disappearing forest and became "through his friendship with a circle of Hudson River School painters, including Sanford Gifford—a passionate conservationist."[20]

James Pinchot helped found Yale University's School of Forestry and served as vice president of the American Forestry Association, founded in 1875. He encouraged his son, Gifford, whom he named after Sanford Gifford, to enter the field of forestry. Gifford Pinchot became a well-known conservationist during the early 1900s and was the head of the United States Forest Service under Theodore Roosevelt.

Sanford Gifford loved streamside or river scenery and explored the Esopus Creek, the West Kill, and Schoharie Creek, sketching and trout fishing. His first recorded fishing trip occurred on the West Kill in July 1849, where he and a group of friends captured three bushels of suckers and a 2-pound brook trout! In the fall he traveled to other areas of the Catskills, including the West Branch of the Delaware, the East Branch of the Delaware, and the lower Neversink.

Gifford was one of the first of the "second generation" of the Hudson River School to visit the western Catskills, and it was most likely that trout fishing lured him to the Delaware watershed. His sketch books reveal that he worked along the trout streams of Sullivan and Delaware counties, including the headwaters of the East Branch. He did many sketches along the main Delaware River, one of which was of the famous confluence of the East and West Branches at Hancock on September 3, 1849. The sketch appears to include a few anglers, and today's trout fishers, familiar with the pool, would recognize the location even though the work was done more than 150 years ago.

In the fall of 1851, Gifford traveled to Sullivan County and explored streams and mountain views. In early October, he sketched the *Forks of the Beaver Kill and Willaweemock.* That Gifford found his way to the forks is not surprising; even at this early date, it was already a famous rendezvous for trout fishermen. Known today as Junction Pool, it is one of the most famous pools in angling literature and was the subject of Inman's noted landscape, *Trout Fishing in Sullivan County, New York.* Gifford also sketched other popular trout streams, such as the Little Beaverkill, Mongaup, and Callicoon Creek.

Gifford, like Thomas Cole, preferred to carry a small pencil sketchbook that he could produce at a moment's notice, even while traveling, to capture "the fleeting effects of nature." Whittredge once stated that Gifford was "always suspicious that if he stopped too long to look in one direction the most beautiful thing of all might pass him by at his back; the eternal truth Gifford sought was rare beauty. . . ."[21]

In his *History of American Painting,* Samuel Isham states that Sanford Gifford turned "the usual painter's hobby of fishing into a passion." He went trouting in the spring, salmon fishing in the summer, and fished for striped bass in the autumn.

Gifford was familiar with all the great trout-fishing waters of the Catskills, including the Beaverkill, Esopus, Dry Brook, Mill Brook, West Kill, Schoharie, Callicoon, and Willowemoc creeks, as well as the upper Neversink.

Sanford Gifford 1868. The Metropolitan Museum of Art, David Hunter McAlpin Fund, 1952. (52.605).

A few of his paintings included titles such as *A Scene on Esopus Creek; A View on Kaaterskill Creek; Creek Scenery in Ulster Co., N.Y.; Schoharie Kill; The Delaware River; On Schoharie Kill;* and *Spruce Creek in Catskills.* Spruce Creek flows off the slope of North Mountain and adds its water to Kaaterskill Falls.

Gifford traveled to the famous Restigouche and the Miramichi, and was one of America's earliest salmon fishers; annually he spent a few weeks pursuing salmon with A. W. Craven and Henry Kirke Brown, the sculptor. In the fall, he fished for striped bass off Montauk and the Elizabeth Islands near Martha's Vineyard. In 1877, he wrote that he was having a "fishing summer":

> I have had a fishing summer. The early part of the season I was in the lower provinces of Canada salmon fishing, in which I had fair sport. The last three weeks I was on the St. Lawrence and on some lakes in the province of Ontario, fishing for black bass—a fish with which I had little acquaintance before. . . . I am now about to go to one of the Elizabeth Islands about thirty miles from New Bedford to make the acquaintance of the striped bass. . . .
>
> After that I am going with Church and McEntee to the wilderness of Maine, near Mt. Katahdin, to fish for trout. Nominally, we go sketching. So you see that at least for once in my life I am likely to have my fill of fishing.[22]

Whittredge once remarked of Gifford's fishing ability: "He outgrew me and all his artist friends as a fisherman."[23] While he explored new species and places to fish, his "home" waters remained in the Catskills, and upon Gifford's death in August 1880, Worthington Whittredge remarked:

> We are told that he was born in Saratoga County. As an artist, he was born in the Catskill Mountains. He loved them as he loved his mother, and he could not long stay away from either. No autumn came that he did not visit them, and for a long period of his life he went in summer to her and the Catskills as a boy goes to school.[24]

Gifford had a lifelong friendship with Jervis McEntee. They were traveling companions and often spent summers together. They fished and sketched, and in winter, in New York, they saw each other daily. McEntee may have been his closest friend.

Jervis McEntee

Jervis McEntee (1821–1891) was born in Rondout, New York, a Hudson River community that adjoins Kingston. His home was located on Chestnut Street and had a distant view of the Catskills. As a youngster, McEntee would pretend his father's attic was an artist's studio. At first he tried his hand at business, but by 1858, McEntee opened a studio in New York and turned to landscape painting. He had been a pupil of Frederic Church in the winter of 1850, in New York, when he was twenty-two. Throughout his career, he would spend much of the winters in New York and weekends and summers in Rondout and the Catskills.

McEntee traveled to the Catskills as soon as he had decided to become a landscape painter; in the fall of 1858 and 1859, he stayed and sketched around the Esopus Creek at Mount Tremper and along Catskill Creek at East Durham and Leeds. That his work was generally near trout streams is not surprising; McEntee had fished for trout since childhood. Throughout his adult life, he made extensive trips through the Catskills, sketching and fishing for trout. He must have been fairly adept in his use of a fly rod, as he even tried his hand at shad fishing in the Hudson with a fly as early as 1874.

As an artist, McEntee was best known for his fall and winter paintings, though he also painted scenes that revealed his love of trout streams and fishing, such as *Where the Trout Run, The Source of the Delaware, Along the Dry Brook Road,* and *A Stream in the Woods.*

He and Whittredge would get together regularly in the fall, and the two traveled the mountains sketching the autumnal foliage. Together they visited many places, including the Batavia Kill near Kelly Corners, the Beaver Kill, an Esopus tributary near Mount Pleasant, and every hidden little stream in between that provided the wild scenery they were looking for. Whittredge once remarked on McEntee's knowledge of the Catskills, "[H]e knew every nook and corner of them and every stepping-stone across their brooks."[25]

Jervis McEntee ca. 1867.
Napoleon Sarony, the Century Association.

It was trout streams that held a special attraction for McEntee. He not only fished many of the Catskill streams, but also recorded some of his experiences with Whittredge and Gifford in a diary. McEntee's diary refers to many trout-fishing trips: to Mill Brook and Furlough Lake, the Beaverkill and the Willowemoc, and the West Branch of the Neversink with Sanford Gifford. His favorite stream appears to have been the upper Rondout, which he visited many times, boarding at Smith's, 2 miles below Sundown, at Fuller's in Sundown, and at Griswold's, located between Sundown and Peekamoose.

McEntee sketched and fished along many of the Esopus tributaries, including Watson Hollow, Beaver Kill, Stony Clove, and Mink Hollow. He was especially fond of an area known as Lanesville, along the Stony Clove, where it joins Hollow Tree Brook. It was here that he made many of his sketches, which he later turned into the landscapes that brought him fame.

Jervis McEntee died at his family homestead on Chestnut Street in January 1891. His diary has been of great interest to art historians and scholars for many years, and although my focus was on his angling experiences, I am compelled to record his comments of Wednesday, September 30, 1876:

My salvation is in going on and improving my pictures and it is fear that I may not be able to do this that often causes me anxiety. There is great danger that a man in need of money will be induced to work for popular favor and so prevent him from following out his own ideas. An artist above all men should be free from money troubles and I think constantly of how I can order my life so as to be independent in this respect.[26]

FISHED TO DEATH

It was during the 1850s that reports circulated that the streams were being "fished to death," and that brook trout were decreasing in size, as well as in number. With the coming of the railroads and the increase in fishing tourists, a greater burden was placed on native trout populations. There was concern over the rapid rate at which trout were disappearing from the mountain streams, and *pot fishers* became a derogatory term for those fishermen who took excessive numbers of fish.

Local newspapers bear this out, as they reported incredible catches. The *Kingston Journal,* on June 20, 1855, published an account of a party of "gentlemen" who returned to Kingston the week before "from a fishing excursion to our mountain streams, having caught about 1,400 trout during their absence."

Two weeks later, on July 4, 1855, the same paper reported that a party of four men from Kingston journeyed to the streams of Shandaken bordering Sullivan County and fished for eight days, catching between seventeen hundred and eighteen hundred brook trout.

Three weeks later, on July 25, 1855, a writer in the *Ulster Republican,* who stayed near Stony Clove, laments, "This enchanting stream, in whose depths lurk the speckled trout, and whose ripples once murmured in rhythmical measure to some Indian name, now drives sawmills and is called some outlandish 'Bushkill.' Every valley, every 'clove' sends down its trout-haunted mountain streamlet. The trout are disappearing rapidly, however, and it will not be many years before there will be none worth fishing for. I have counted sixteen fishermen along the stream in one day since I have been here, the most of them from Kingston, each intent upon exterminating as many trout as possible."

While these were indeed dark days for the fishery, there were fishermen who were beginning to take a totally different approach to their favorite pastime.

THADDEUS NORRIS AND THE "HOUSELESS ANGLERS"

Thaddeus Norris (1811–1877) was an expert fisherman, rod maker, and writer and known in his day as the dean of American anglers. In 1864, he wrote *The American Angler's Book,* which contained information on various species of fish, tackle, and trout and salmon fishing, as well as fly tying and rod making. The book also included personal angling experiences and was extremely popular. Even today, many consider it the best of the old-time fishing books.

Though he lived in Philadelphia, Norris spent many days in the 1850s staying at the Boscobel (Darbee House) and fishing the Willowemoc and Beaverkill, experimenting with flies and fly-fishing techniques. By the 1850s, Chester Darbee, the son of Hannah Darbee, took over the Darbee House and renamed it the Boscobel. Chester furthered the reputation of the famous resort and became a well-known host to Beaverkill sportsmen. The Boscobel was a familiar site to trout fishers for more than a century.

In *The American Angler's Book,* Norris writes that in 1852, he and "a few brethren of the rod," some of whom had met for the first time on the Beaverkill, became "drawn towards each other by a love of the gentle art," and they agreed to form themselves into an association under the "unassuming name of the 'Houseless Anglers.'" The name was taken in "contradistinction of the old Fish-House clubs"—associations known for their dinners and social gatherings rather than their love of angling.

The Houseless Anglers' goals were not to be boastful about their fishing, but to follow the teachings of Izaak Walton—"that fishing, like virtue 'is its own reward.'"[27] Norris and his friends also vowed to limit their catches and not attempt to fill their creels, as well as to introduce this philosophy to others and repress any rivalry or competition on the stream.

All members were fly fishers, and they met regularly each season where the Beaverkill joined the Willowemoc. Their number never exceeded ten. "They were of various pursuits: amongst them were a few artists, professionally so, and two more who were merely amateurs."[28] Norris dedicated the popular *The American Angler's Book* to these companions, writing fondly of his experiences on the Beaverkill and of how much he enjoyed a tradition that he called the "Noonday Roast."

The proper necessities for a roast were bread, butter, salt, pepper, a few matches, and a bottle of claret or ale. Norris and his friends cooked their

Thaddeus Norris. *The American Angler's Book*, 1864.

trout over a wood fire along the stream bank. Once a fire was going, they collected flat stones for plates and placed them near it "to warm properly." For their roast, they selected the smallest trout: "[T]hose under nine inches are best; scour them well with sand, wash them clean, and open them, but allow no water to touch inside, as the blood and natural juices of the fish should be retained as far as possible; cut off the heads, score them (not too deeply), and pepper and salt them well inside and out."[29]

One or two branches of "sweet birch" were cut, with as many twigs on them for the number of trout to be roasted. A fish was placed on each twig, running the twig along the upper side of the backbone and then held to the fire. When the trout were done, they were placed on the hot stone and buttered while warm.

The day's fishing was discussed and stories were told of past and present trouting experiences. The camaraderie and the feast were memorable: "[I]f there *is* an objection to it, it is that one is never satisfied afterwards with the taste of trout cooked indoors."[30] The Noonday Roast was an institution to Norris, who described this break in fishing activity by stating "many pleasant hours have been passed under the dark sugar-maple or birch cooking, eating, smoking, chatting, sleeping, many a long story has been told, and perhaps occasionally a *long bow* drawn."[31]

"After the roast." *The American Angler's Book*, 1864.

Included in the group of the Houseless Anglers were Chester Darbee and Peter Stewart, a well-known local hunter, angler, and woodsman. William Morris Davis was the president, and artist members included Henry Kirke Brown and John Quincy Adams Ward, an apprentice of Brown's who would one day surpass Brown as an accomplished and famed sculptor. Other probable members included Sanford Gifford, the landscape painter, and possibly Thomas Doughty, fellow artist and member of the Hudson River School, who was also a friend of Brown's and who was known to be painting and fishing in Sullivan County during these years.

Henry Kirke Brown

Fly fishing has long been called the gentle art. There certainly is art in fly tying and fly casting, and because these activities are demanding and enjoyable, the sport has attracted those involved in the arts, be they painters, writers, poets, or sculptors. Henry Kirke Brown (1814–1886) was an artist who had a passion for fly fishing and was among our early trout fishermen.

Brown was born in Leyden, Massachusetts, and at the age of eighteen he apprenticed under a portrait painter in Boston named Chester Harding. Although he started his artistic career as a painter, Brown soon discovered he had a talent for sculpture. In 1842, he traveled to Italy to study, remaining there until 1846. Upon his return, he opened a studio in New York City. About 1850, Brown cast the first bronze statue in America, the figure of DeWitt Clinton for Greenwood Cemetery.

His reputation grew as he produced fine works in bronze and portrait busts of famous men, including his friend, William Cullen Bryant. Brown loved horses, and he owned some of the finest purebreds, which he used as models. He possessed great knowledge of a horse's anatomy and "was the first American to disclose the possibilities of dignity and power in the monumental bronze equestrian statue."[32]

Henry Kirke Brown ca. 1870. Brady's National Photographic Portrait Studio, http://en.wikipedia.org.

Brown became famous for producing equestrian statues, and his greatest work is said to be of George Washington, which was erected in New York's Union Square and unveiled on July 4, 1856.* This was the first important equestrian statue erected in America, and it was paid for by wealthy and patriotic citizens of New York. At the unveiling, the Reverend Dr. George W. Bethune, popular clergyman, poet, and scholar, gave an eloquent address and presented the statue to the country. It is currently the oldest sculpture in the New York City Parks' collection.

Among his principal works are the statues of Dr. George W. Bethune in Packer Institute, Brooklyn (1865); Lincoln in Prospect Park, Brooklyn; Lincoln in Union Square, New York City (1867–1868); and the equestrian statue of General Winfield Scott, which was executed by order of Congress (1871). Brown worked in Washington, D.C., for a number of years, completing statues of General Nathaniel Greene and four figures for National Statuary Hall: General Philip Kearney (bronze), Governor George Clinton (bronze), patriot Richard Stockton (marble), and General Nathaniel Greene (marble).

In 1851, Brown was elected to the National Academy of Design, and he made the acquaintance of many artists of the Hudson River School. Two of his closest friends were Sanford R. Gifford and sculptor John Quincy Adams Ward, who once was a student of Brown's.

Exactly when he began fly fishing or learned fly tying is not known, but it was most likely in the mid-1840s. An interesting

Brown's statue of Washington, Union Square, New York City.

letter written early in 1849 reveals he was an advanced fly maker and practiced the art of directly imitating natural flies at a time when it was rarely, if ever, practiced in America. What is fascinating about the letter is that it depicts a drawing by Brown of an adult mayfly, a fly that is generally imitated with a dry or floating imitation, a practice that was almost unheard of in this country at the time Brown penned his letter. The letter was written to his wife, Lydia, on May 19 and depicts drawings of a pair of adult mayflies that Brown numbered 1 and 2. He writes:

This morning for the first time in my life I saw the mayfly No. 2. I have just drawn from one before me and is totally correct. This morning have caught several, they vary in color, the one

---

*A replica of the Washington statue was erected at West Point in 1916.

before me is of a light yellowish drab—eyes green, scales or ribs are of a slightly darker drab almost a light brown, while others are of a grayish color. I have imitated two this morning very closely—wings of the lightest slate wing feather of the peacock, head and extension end of the tag of the slightest shade of green using a green silk for tying answers this purpose—the whisks at the tail of horse hair, or the whisks of a black cat as that varies with the color of the body. Threads of mohair twisted hard serves well for the body. No. 2 is just about the average size, No. 5 hook is large enough, No. 6 at the extreme. They might also be very nicely imitated with gut bodies as you have seen them made, but there is great objection to having anything protrude beyond the head especially if it is stiff for should the trout hit it with his nose it would prevent his taking the hook, you will find this all very useful of course.[33]

Brown's letter of May 19, 1849. Archives of American Art, Smithsonian Institution.

In a letter written in July of the same year, Brown's wife, Lydia, writes to a relative that she, too, is involved with fly fishing: "I intend to try my luck at it this year and Henry has bought me one of the prettiest little fly rods you ever saw—it is light & elastic as a whip."[34] She goes on to state that she and Brown have both learned to make flies.

During the 1850s, Brown fished the Beaverkill annually, and he did so often in the company of William Morris Davis and Thad Norris of Philadelphia. The trio corresponded with one another regularly during the year and planned and met each summer, usually in May or June, at the Boscobel.

In 1861, Brown and his wife moved to Newburgh, where he lived and worked for the next twenty-five years. The move brought him closer to the Catskills, and undoubtedly fishing excursions became more frequent. In addition to the Beaverkill, his letters reveal he also fished the upper Rondout Creek and the Willowemoc; in August 1870, Brown writes of fishing Sand Pond and the Willowemoc, where he and his party caught 135 trout.

In addition to trout fishing, Brown was an accomplished salmon fisherman and fished annually in Canada, with his usual companions being Sanford Gifford, Alfred Craven, and John Quincy Adams Ward, whom he always referred to as Quincy Ward. Craven, a close friend of Gifford's and an avid salmon fisher, was a well-known American engineer and commissioner of the Croton Water Board for the city of New York. He was known for building the large reservoir in Central Park and for his leadership in forming the American Society of Civil Engineers, of which he became the first president.

Brown was also known as a man of character and principles. He was highly respected and was said to possess noble qualities. He was an abolitionist. Before the Civil War, in 1856, Brown was invited to make a design for one of the pediments of the Capitol in Washington. His idea was a mixture of allegory and realism, and he chose a strong black man sitting on a bale of cotton to symbolize the South. An official in charge of the pediment refused to have "a negro represented." When Brown asked what better substitute could possibly represent the industry of the South, he received no answer.

He was determined to depict that the industry of the South was founded on slavery, and he got his chance once again when a new Capitol building was to be constructed by the state of South Carolina at Columbia. Brown was commissioned to make a sculpture that was to fill the principle pediment: "The 'genius' of South Carolina was seen standing in the center, with Liberty (!) on one side and Justice (!) on the other, and about her every occupation and trade by which the State was supported, was represented as carried on by negro slaves, and, in the whole group, only one white man, and he an overseer!"[35]

The committee in charge of the pediment complained to Brown that there were too many black figures. Brown replied:

> Why, what is your objection? Don't you believe in slavery? Isn't it right in your opinion? Isn't the Southern system of Society founded on it, and isn't all your industry carried out by slaves? You wouldn't thank me, would you, if I were to put white men in the place of these negroes? I have only done, in the matter, just what the Greeks would have done. What made their art vital? What keeps it alive? Why, its Reality, its truth to nature and to facts! Are you ashamed of your facts, that you won't let me represent them?[36]

Henry Kirke Brown's "logic prevailed," the committee withdrew the objections, and Brown continued with the work. Unfortunately, his sculpture was never realized, and three years of hard work was destroyed when the Union Army invaded South Carolina and fired upon the old state capitol building. One shell landed on Brown's studio, which caught fire, and the finished statues, casts, drawings, and much of Brown's possessions were ruined.

Henry Kirke Brown was an excellent fly fisherman who knew and loved the sport. His letters tell us that as a fly tier, he was well ahead of his time; he was innovative when most Americans were still dependent on English trout flies that were imitations of the natural insects found along English streams. And although he was known to pursue trout on the waters of Long Island and the Adirondacks, his favorite waters were in the Catskills.

THE NEVERSINK

As fishing tourists increased in the 1850s, they began finding their way to the upper Neversink with regularity, primarily to the East and West Branches. Quinlan's *History of Sullivan County* states that the first settlers called the stream *Narvasing* and that it was spelled *Nevisinck, Nevisink,* and *Naewersink*. Various translations of the word include "mad river," or "a continual running stream which *never sinks* into the ground so as to be dry in places." It is also said to mean "water between highlands."[37] The Indian name for the Neversink is said to be Mahackamack, meaning "always running."[38]

The Neversink River begins at the hamlet of Claryville in the town of Neversink, Sullivan County, where the East and West Branches of the Neversink join together, flowing from a region that in the early days of settlement was known as Upper Neversink. Both branches run through narrow valleys and because of their inhospitable terrain were, as was most of the town of Denning, settled later than other areas of the Catskills.

The West Branch of the Neversink begins on the north slope of Slide Mountain at an elevation of approximately 3,400 feet. The stream flows northwest for about a mile and then turns southwest; before making this turn, the West Branch flows within several hundred feet of the source of the Esopus Creek, which flows at right angles in the opposite direction.

The stream then travels parallel to, and never very far from, the West Branch Road, joining the East Branch at Claryville, a distance of approximately 12½ additional miles. The major tributaries of the West Branch enter its waters from the north or roadside; they include Biscuit Creek, High Falls Brook, Flat Brook, and Fall Brook.

The East Branch of the Neversink has its source deep in the forest, far from any road, at an elevation of approximately 3,000 feet. It flows from a hollow between Slide Mountain (4,180 feet) and Cornell Mountain (3,860 feet) and runs in a general direction southwesterly for about 13½ miles before joining the West Branch at Claryville. The stream travels through a dense forest for about 5 miles and is joined by one major tributary named Deer Shanty Brook before reaching any type of clearing or settlement; this is at the confluence of Tray Mill Brook and Flat Brook, the site of a former mill that produced wooden ladles, spoons, trays, scoops, and bowls.

Of the two branches, the West Branch has a slightly steeper gradient, falling on an average of 133 feet per mile compared with the East Branch's 104 feet per mile. The valley of the West Branch has long been known as Frost Valley and has a wild and rugged landscape that was a deterrent to early settlement. Both valleys are extremely narrow, all the way downstream to where they join at a place known early on as "the Forks." The ruggedness of the terrain, combined with a minimum amount of flat land, made the soil unsuitable for plowing or cultivation; farming, in general, was not practiced in either valley.

Headwaters of the West Branch of the Neversink. Ed Van Put.

Many of the earliest inhabitants of the upper Neversink were lumbermen and tanners. The first tannery appeared just downstream of the forks in 1848, near the hamlet of Claryville. A year later, another tannery was constructed along the East Branch at the hamlet of Dewittville, and a third, also along the East Branch, at the hamlet of Denning.

Sawmills, tray mills, and turning mills were constructed along both branches, beginning as early as 1838, and by 1875, *Beer's Atlas of Ulster County* depicted a dozen mills operating in the upper Neversink region. All of these mills required timber and were supplied with hardwoods often taken from locations that were easy to access (such as along streams). Mature hemlocks for the tanneries were removed wherever they grew in abundance.

Most of the inhabitants along the upper Neversink were tannery workers or settlers who barely scratched out a living from the difficult terrain. It has been written that every "male inhabitant" in the vicinity was "by right of birth and inheritance either a fisherman or hunter, and quite often both."

While some lived in wooden framed houses, most found shelter in log cabins or shanties, along streams. These early residents hunted and fished; not for sport, but out of necessity.

At Dewittville, on the East Branch, Bailey Beers was an innkeeper who was "known and beloved of many anglers."[39] Beers was a colorful character who opened a public house in 1864 and delighted sportsmen who visited his old-fashioned tavern with tales of bygone days when the region was first settled, especially with hunting and fishing stories. A backwoodsman, he had come to the

Early settler and fishing resort owner Bailey Beers.
Picturesque Ulster 1896–1905, published by
Hope Farm Press, 1991.

upper Neversink in the early 1800s and worked as a bark peeler, a lumberman, and anything that would help him eke out a living. Beers recalled, "We had pretty hard sort of grub in them times and durned few of the bark peelers saw fresh meat mor'n once or twice a year, less of a Sunday or a holiday some of the men dug out a woodchuck or caught a coon. There was plenty of deer around sure enough, but firearms wuz scarce, and cost a heap, so that most of the time we eat salt pork and trout."[40]

The earliest trout fisherman to write about the Neversink was Fitz-James Fitch. He had fished both branches and the main Neversink downstream of Claryville for nearly forty years, and he possibly caught more trout in its waters than anyone. He plied his skills as an angler on Catskill streams at a time when brook trout were inexperienced and more numerous than they ever would be again.

Fitch made his first trip to the East and West Branches in the summer of 1851, and he wrote of this experience years later in an article titled "Recollections of an Angler."[41]

While the fishing was not memorable, the trip through the dense forest to the streams was one he never forgot. Fitch learned of a trail of marked trees over the mountains and through the forest that led to the West Branch. He and two fishing companions decided to make the journey and made their ascent at the eastern end of the 12- to 15-mile trail. From the onset, it rained heavily, making travel over the rocky outcrops and fallen trees slippery and treacherous.

The trio was tired when they reached the summit; their backpacks had become increasingly heavier as they soaked up the rain. They were to follow the trail to a stream and follow the stream to a road and a tannery. They came to a stream but were unsure if it was the right one, and after following it a short way, decided to search again for the marked trees.

The men thought they were lost. Drenched and exhausted, they stopped beside a large hemlock where a campfire had previously burned. They reasoned it was made by another lost and weary traveler, and they were right—the bark was peeled on one side of the tree, and on the smooth surface was carved "J. N. L., 1849," and below it, "Another dam'd fool, 1850." The fishing party added yet a third line that stated, "Three more of the same sort, 1851."

Fitch and his companions spent the night in the woods, and the next day crossed another mountain and emerged on the East Branch. They traveled 6 more miles to their destination and then spent a week fishing both branches of the Neversink. The stream was swollen from the heavy rains, making fishing difficult. Fitch reported fair sport, and, although he did not report the number of trout caught, he did state that the party was successful in catching enough for breakfast and dinner and, at times, enough for a streamside lunch!

6

The 1860s

JOHN BURROUGHS: A CATSKILL LEGEND

During the 1860s, the number of fishing tourists visiting the region fell dramatically while the country was engaged in the Civil War (1861–1865). However, because of the war there was an increase in the production of leather from the many tanneries operating in the Catskills.

Pollution problems from tanneries, which had begun back in the 1830s, continued to plague the Esopus Creek, and the stream suffered from the detrimental effects for decades. The poor water quality of the Esopus was yet apparent in 1861. When the trustees of the city of Kingston were looking for an additional water supply and turned to the Esopus Creek, they found the stream "badly contaminated by the tanneries which were devouring the hemlock forests along the creek's upper waters."[1]

The Saw Kill, an Esopus tributary. Winslow Homer (*The Fishing Party*), *Appleton's Magazine*, October 1869.

Discharges from tanneries, sawmills, and other streamside industries undoubtedly contributed to the stream's lack of early angling history. The vast majority of trout-fishing experiences that were reported in fishing journals, sporting magazines, newspapers, and books written before 1870 generally took place on Esopus tributaries.

As previously mentioned, the Stony Clove was a great attraction to early trout fishermen and continued to be so in the 1860s. A popular fishing resort along the stream was Ed Lane's. Fishing parties arriving by stagecoach at Phoenicia were picked up by Lane and then taken 4 miles upstream into Greene County to his one-story farmhouse in Lanesville. Lanesville was a favorite destination of landscape painter Jervis McEntee, who often fished and sketched in the area around a tributary named Hollow Tree Brook.

Lane's house was a primitive dwelling, uncomfortable, with poor housekeeping, but it was not the comforts of home that anglers were looking for—it was trout fishing, and the nearby streams were noted for their great numbers of brook trout. As was the custom of other resorts frequented by fishermen, unusually large trout were often featured by drawing the outline of the fish caught by guests. At Lane's, the trout were drawn on the kitchen door, along with the size and weight, and the name of the angler who caught the prize.

The Reverend Charles Rockwell furthered the reputation of the Stony Clove in a book published in 1867 titled *The Catskill Mountains and the Region Around.* The Reverend described the Stony Clove as:

> . . . a wild mountain stream, abounding in trout, where sportsmen sojourn or encamp, for days, or a week or more at a time, single parties taking sometimes many hundreds of these delicious fish, leaving behind them but a poor chance for unskilled fishermen, who know nothing of the mysteries of fly fishing, and choice kinds of bait, and of strongly attractive aromatic oils, by which the shy and cunning fish are with much tact and art, lured from their dark retreats.[2]

Rockwell also wrote that "The principal places for trout fishing in the mountains are Stony Clove and Warner's Kill." Warner's Kill is a tributary of the Stony Clove, and Rockwell recalled that friends caught, in a few days' fishing, sixteen hundred trout, with fifty of the largest weighing 30 pounds! He also claimed that two fishermen from the same party took seven hundred trout in Warner's Kill in a single day's fishing.

The depletion of the native brook trout population continued into the 1860s, and the numbers of trout removed from Catskill streams by angling alone is astonishing by today's standards. Fishing reports in area newspapers appeared with less frequency than they did previously, before the Civil War, which occupied most of the news; however, whenever articles did appear relative to fishing, they continued to report incredible catches. The *Republican Watchman* of July 15, 1863, told of a party of fishermen who visited the upper Rondout and Neversink earlier in the month and in one week's fishing caught fifteen hundred trout.

A year later, the *Bloomville Mirror*, on June 28, reported that two fishermen from Delhi who journeyed to the Beaverkill and stayed at Murdock's took more than 110 trout per day. The men wrote of their experiences to the editor of the newspaper, stating, "[W]e kept a record of each days work, and the number caught by each, which gives the following result. . . . A grand total for the three and a half days, 776 trout."

Despite this type of onslaught, Catskill trout streams continued to produce good fishing. From the diary of the venerable Fitz-James Fitch, who fished the Neversink for nearly forty years, we are able to learn what the trout fishing was like along that stream during the war years, before the introduction of hatchery fish. His records enable us to look back and make note of the abundance of native trout, as well as examine their size with more than just speculation. In an article in the *American Angler*, dated March 1892, the Judge reminisces about the trout fishing he experienced on the main Neversink, below the junction of the East and West Branches, in the summer of 1863.

He wrote that on June 30, he fished from 5:30 A.M. until 5:00 P.M., during which time he caught 205 native brook trout and reported that he kept a 16-pound basket that contained sixty-one "beautiful trout." An estimate of the average weight of these fish is 0.262 pounds; using a conversion chart, we learn that the average size of these trout was approximately 8.9 inches to 9.4 inches.

The Judge did not fish the next day, but waited till evening. The date was July 1, and he recalled it was the day the battle of Gettysburg began, a battle he described as "the beginning of the end of the war." He started fishing near twilight and stayed out until 10:00 P.M., catching thirty-one trout that weighed a total of 11 pounds. The estimate of the average weight of these fish is 0.355 pounds, and the conversion to inches estimates these trout to average between 9.4 inches and 9.9 inches.*

The abundance of brook trout still found in the waters of the upper Neversink during the 1860s is yet apparent in another fishing trip that Fitch made, two years later, with his good friends and fellow trout fishers Charles G. Adams and Dr. Walter De Forest Day. The men traveled by steamboat, stagecoach, and buckboard to Claryville, arriving on May 22, 1865, and found comfortable lodgings.

At Claryville, on the main Neversink, Ellen Snyder, Judge Fitch's sister, took in a few fishing boarders. Her husband was part owner of the tannery below the forks, and her home overlooked the Neversink. Wilbur Lament, who was town supervisor and an agent for the Bushnell & Snyder tannery, also took in boarders.

Judge Fitch became a well-known figure along the streams of the upper Neversink, and his reputation as a trout fisherman with the backwoodsmen was one of admiration; there were few in the town of Denning who could not tell stories of the Judge's amazing success with a fly rod.

The trio found the streams swollen from recent rains, but began fishing the next morning, managing to catch thirty-eight trout between them. They all fished with flies and, over the next ten days, traveled up both branches and fished the main Neversink below the forks as well. The men recorded their catch each day, including the number of trout released; and at the end of their stay, they had caught a total of 1,535 native trout, keeping 904 and releasing 631!

The fly fishers averaged more than 150 trout each day of their stay. Many of the fish kept were eaten at breakfast and dinner, and at times along the stream for lunch. Some trout were shared with the local populace, and others were taken with the party when they left.

The largest brook trout reportedly caught along the Neversink during the 1860s was taken by an angler named Abram Mullennix, who, on July 23, 1864, caught a 2-pound, 10-ounce trout near Claryville.

The enthusiasm for trout fishing continued to grow and received an added boost from the publication of a number of books on angling, most notably Thaddeus Norris's *The American Angler's Book* (1864); two books by Robert Barnwell Roosevelt, titled *The Game Fish of the Northern States of America and British Provinces* (1862) and *Superior Fishing* (1865); and Genio C. Scott's *Fishing in American Waters* (1869).

---

*"Conversion of Mean Lengths of Length Classes to Weights in Pounds," Guidelines for Stocking Trout Streams in New York State, p 52. Robert Engstrom-Heg, September 1990 (DEC Publication).

It was also in the 1860s that the Catskills began receiving added notoriety from literary magazines through the pen of John Burroughs, a native of Delaware County.

JOHN BURROUGHS: A CATSKILL LEGEND

John Burroughs (1837–1921) enriched the lure and lore of trout fishing in the Catskills. Famous throughout America as a naturalist, poet, philosopher, and writer, Burroughs established the nature essay as an important literary form. In many of his earliest works, he wrote about Catskill trout fishing and extolled the native trout. He fished the mountain streams at a time when they contained only their original strain of brook trout, and his writings informed the public of the wonders of the region and the joy of trout fishing.

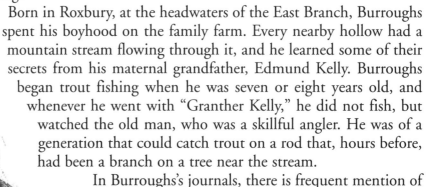

John Burroughs.
Scribner's Monthly, January 1877.

Born in Roxbury, at the headwaters of the East Branch, Burroughs spent his boyhood on the family farm. Every nearby hollow had a mountain stream flowing through it, and he learned some of their secrets from his maternal grandfather, Edmund Kelly. Burroughs began trout fishing when he was seven or eight years old, and whenever he went with "Granther Kelly," he did not fish, but watched the old man, who was a skillful angler. He was of a generation that could catch trout on a rod that, hours before, had been a branch on a tree near the stream.

In Burroughs's journals, there is frequent mention of fishing Meeker Hollow, Hardscrabble Creek, West Settlement Stream, and Montgomery Hollow, all tributaries of the upper East Branch of the Delaware; and Rose Brook, a tributary of the West Branch of the Delaware. These were his boyhood streams, and he was lured by them from morning till night. They often detained him on his way to and from school, and at times they held such promise that he skipped school to fish or swim, or both. On Sundays when fishing was not allowed, he carried a "fish-line" in his pocket and "cut a pole" in the woods:

Sometimes I returned with fish sometimes not. Father disapproved of the Sunday fishing, but he was human, and if I brought home several nice trout his reprimand wasn't severe. The trout appealed to him, and he never refused them as tainted flesh.[3]

From the hilltops near the farm, he could look off in the distance and see the summits of Graham, Doubletop, Slide, and Peekamoose, mountains that were the source of bigger streams that grew into rivers with names like Neversink, Esopus, Rondout, Willowemoc, and Beaverkill. No doubt as a boy he thought of fishing these waters, as even then, they were famous fishing grounds. The streams were, however, far off and not within walking distance, and in a wild region that was barely settled, that still contained bears, mountain lions, and a vast amount of unbroken wilderness.

Years later he reminisced, "From my native hills I could catch glimpses of the mountains in whose laps these creeks were cradled, but it was not till after many years, and after dwelling in a country where trout are not found, that I returned to pay my respects to them as an angler."[4]

As John Burroughs grew into adulthood, he did expand his angling experiences and made camping and fishing journeys into the distant mountains. In July 1860, at the age of twenty-three, he made his first camping trip with a friend, hiked to the source of the Beaverkill, and fished and camped at Balsam Lake. At the lake they fished with flies but were inexperienced and had trouble using them, until some men came along and showed them how.

As he visited these and other waters, he wrote of his experiences in a series of magazine articles. In July 1869, *Atlantic Monthly* published "Birch Browsings," a saga about a fascinating fishing expedition to Thomas Lake (Beecher Lake) made by Burroughs and a few friends in 1868. The lake was hidden in a dense forest between Alder and Balsam Lakes, at the headwaters of the Beaverkill, and the men had a difficult time finding it. The essay mentioned various trout streams found in the Catskills, the bird life, physical landscape, and natural beauty, and stated that "the great attraction however of this region is the brook trout with which the streams and lakes abound."

In 1870, Burroughs furthered the reputation of the Catskills when he wrote his delightful essay, "Speckled Trout." This classic work appeared in the October issue of *Atlantic Monthly*. "Speckled" was another common name for brook trout, and again he took his readers on a fishing journey through the Catskills that had occurred in June 1869. He provided readers with a vivid description of the wild scenery of the region and the delicate and graceful qualities of native trout.

Burroughs described taking a stagecoach to Big Indian, and he and his party traveled up Big Indian Hollow when he noted that "down low" the valley's log houses were being replaced by wooden-framed buildings; and, as he traveled up closer to Slide Mountain, people still lived in one-room log cabins. Burroughs commented on the difficulty of trying to subsist in the mountains: "People certainly lived close to the bone here, and no doubt gnawed it hard and I hope found the meat sweet, though there must have been precious little of it."[5]

The party fished the upper Esopus, and after sampling the main stream and finding few trout, tried the smaller tributaries and caught few there also: "We satisfied ourselves that there was precious little in the streams; for after tramping up and down the main branch and penetrating into the mountains where the smaller tributaries came down, we barely caught enough trout to afford a good smell for all."[6] Burroughs and his friends spent the night in a haymow over a stable, and in the morning they fished the streams again but had no better luck than the day before.

They then traveled over a trail past Slide Mountain to the head of the West Branch of the Neversink. During the 1860s, the average size of the brook trout found in the waters of the upper Neversink were said to be getting smaller, but they were still plentiful. Burroughs began fishing with flies but found it extremely difficult to cast because of streamside vegetation. He switched to worms, and he and a companion fished upstream while the others went down; by the time they rendezvoused with their friends, they had basketed nearly a hundred small trout.

The men encountered heavy rains and took shelter in an abandoned log house, where they spent the night. The next day they fished in the morning and took nearly three hundred trout before it began to rain again. This time they retreated to the remains of an old stable. It poured throughout the night, and the West Branch overflowed its banks, though the following day the weather cleared and it began receding. The party stayed another day and night, and on the last day hiked downstream to the mouth of Biscuit Creek, where they would spend their last night sleeping in a falling-down shanty.

The day before they left, Burroughs fished the West Branch upstream of Biscuit Creek for about a mile, using a trout's fin for bait. "Trout are real cannibals, and make no bones, and break none either, in lunching on each other" he wrote. Although the party ran into dismal weather, the abundant numbers of hungry trout they encountered brightened their spirits; he noted that Neversink trout were "small, but plenty eager."

A beautiful pool on the West Branch upstream of Biscuit Creek. Ed Van Put.

The party then traveled over mountain trails and through the forest to the head of the Beaverkill, where they set up their camp along the stream bank; Burroughs was designated to provide trout for supper and breakfast. As he fished the Beaverkill, he contemplated on its remoteness: "The solitude was perfect; and I felt that strangeness and insignificance which the civilized man must always feel when opposing himself to such a vast scene of silence and wildness. The trout were quite black, like all wood trout, and took the bait eagerly."

The following day they headed for Balsam Lake, and it was here that they had their greatest success. It was the first time they were able to use flies and not get tangled up in trees and underbrush; and during a thunderstorm, the trout went wild! Burroughs wrote of his success:

My fly was dragging, and as we were shooting over the water-grass which waved to and fro beneath the surface, two flame-finned beauties darted from the green depths and were instantly hooked. On this hint we backed water, took up a position with head to the wind, and for nearly an hour, amid the pouring rain and rattling thunder, the sport went on. I had on two flies, and usually both were snapped at the moment they touched the water. But the sport did not degenerate into wanton slaughter, for many were missed and many merely slapped the hook with their tails; and when we were a few short of a hundred, the blue sky shone out, and, drenched to the skin, we rowed leisurely back to camp.[7]

John Burroughs was a keen observer, an angler who took the time to look closely at his catch and appreciate the natural beauty of the native brook trout:

It pleased my eye so, that I would fain linger over them, arranging them in rows and studying the various hues and tints. They were of nearly a uniform size, rarely one over ten or under eight inches in length, and it seemed as if the hues of all the precious metals and stones were reflected from their sides.[8]

Another work by Burroughs that added to the notoriety of trout fishing in the Catskills was "A Bed of Boughs," which appeared in *Scribner's Magazine* in November 1877. This essay describes a remarkable trip he made to the upper Rondout Creek, upstream of Peekamoose Lake. He and a companion caught trout with great success, and after camping for a couple of days, traveled over mountains and through the forest to the East Branch of the Neversink, where they continued to catch trout.

Burroughs loved small mountain streams, and he loved to catch and eat native brook trout from them. On a camping and hiking trip to Slide Mountain, he described the headwaters of Woodland Valley Stream:

But the prettiest thing was the stream soliloquizing in such musical tones there amidst the moss-covered rocks and bowlders. How clean it looked, what purity! Civilization corrupts the stream as it corrupts the Indian. Only in such remote woods can you now see a brook in all its original freshness and beauty. Only the sea and the mountain forest brook are pure; all between is contaminated more or less by the work of man. An ideal trout brook was this, now hurrying, now loitering, now deepening around a great bowlder, now gliding evenly over a pavement of green-gray stone and pebbles; no sediment or stain of any kind, but white and sparkling as snow water, and nearly as cool. Indeed, the water of the Catskill region is the best in the world.[9]

John Burroughs wrote his first book in 1867 about his friend Walt Whitman, titled *Notes on Walt Whitman as Poet and Person.* He then produced a series of books on nature, some of which included the essays that pertained to his Catskill trout-fishing experiences. In 1871, he published *Wake-Robin,* a book that informed Americans of the fascinating world of birds; this was followed by *Winter Sunshine* in 1875 and *Birds and Poets* in 1877. His popular *Locusts and Wild Honey* appeared in 1879 and included "A Bed of Boughs" and "Speckled Trout." In 1881, Houghton, Mifflin published *Pepacton,* a book of essays, of which "Pepacton: A Summer Voyage," is the lead chapter.

Burroughs relates in the preface that he had "all the more pleasure" in naming his book *Pepacton* because it is the Indian name of his "native stream," and: "In its watershed I was born and passed my youth, and here on its banks my kindred sleep." The essay is about a float trip he makes down the East Branch of the Delaware River in a rowboat he made himself, a task he likened to: "Those fishermen who wind their own flies before they go a-fishing,—how they bring in the trout."

John Burroughs authored more than two dozen books; and they were, and still are, extremely popular, especially *Wake-Robin, Locusts and Wild Honey,* and *In the Catskills* (1910). He was a gentle man, and he had the ability to observe the natural world and transfer its wonders into words that readers enjoyed. His writings about trout fishing are original and stimulating, written by a sensitive man in love with his sport. His description of a trout fisherman is a classic:

> The fisherman has a harmless, preoccupied look; he is a kind of vagrant that nothing fears. He blends himself with the trees and the shadows. All his approaches are gentle and indirect. He times himself to the meandering, soliloquizing stream; he addresses himself to it as a lover to his mistress; he wooes it and stays with it till he knows its hidden secrets. Where it deepens his purpose deepens; where it is shallow he is indifferent. He knows how to interpret its every glance and dimple; its beauty haunts him for days.[10]

John Burroughs fished Catskill trout streams for nearly seventy-five years. And while his primary residence was a 9-acre fruit farm he acquired along the Hudson River in West Park, he spent part of every summer in the Catskills, either at the family farm or engaged in trout fishing. He enjoyed the scenery and activities along the majestic Hudson, but wrote that a small stream flowing past one's door had more attractions.

John Burroughs fished Catskill trout streams for nearly 75 years. *Cold Brook Gazette*, 1921.

He was considered an expert trout fisherman who fished with flies; but he was not a fly-fishing purist, and he opted for bait if conditions favored its use. He had the heart of a fisherman and was a writer with a unique style, possessing the ability to express the thoughts, observations, and emotions that are a part of angling.

He was especially fond of small mountain streams, and though he enjoyed exploring new streams and woods, he never outgrew his love for his boyhood streams near the farm in Roxbury. Throughout his life, he fished the same streams where he caught his first trout. It must have been a unique experience to know a stream, or streams, that intimately: not only to enjoy a day's fishing, but also to recall memories and reminiscences of other delightful days, at different ages, and to catch trout descended from those remembered from boyhood.

The sage of the Catskills recorded some of his trout-fishing experiences in journals and letters, and this enables us to get a glimpse of the trout fishing in the streams of his era. As he grew old and still fished, he would be filled with memories of other days; he dreamed along their meandering banks, and they refreshed him and made him feel young again. On May 4, 1878, at the age of forty-one, he writes "Willie & I went over to Meeker's Hollow fishing—the best day I have spent for a long time caught 10 lbs. of beautiful trout—103 in all. Three times as many as I ever caught there when a boy." The following year, May 12, 1879, "Went fishing over in Meeker Hollow, Frank with me—caught 55 nice trout. Very warm."

Meeker Hollow, a boyhood stream of John Burroughs. Ed Van Put.

An entry dated April 4, 1882: "Went a fishing along the old stream in the West Settlement; bright & early April weather; caught no fish but caught many memories of other days." And on May 3, 1883: "To Rose's brook with Curtiss fishing. Take 32 trout in the old stream of my boyhood." Another entry dated Monday May 11, 1891: "I go fishing up Montgomery Hollow, an old haunt of my boyhood. Take a fine string, nine of them from 9 to 10½ inches." All of these streams were, and still are, native brook trout waters.

Once, in 1887, Burroughs was invited by J. S. Van Cleef of the Balsam Lake Club to fish its waters. While there, he had the opportunity to look back at his beloved family dairy farm from the fire tower. He recorded in his journal: "Go with Mr. Van Cleef up to Balsam Lake & spend three days, a very agreeable time. Cool & delightful. Eat & sleep at a great rate; take about 50 trout from the lake in all, nearly as many casts for each trout as it takes bullets to kill a man in rear. On Sunday the 8th go to top of Balsam Mountain & get a glimpse of my native hills from the observatory there."

Burroughs also enjoyed fishing Woodland Valley Stream, known in his day as Snyder Hollow. He was especially fond of camping along its banks, particularly at the headwaters, along a route he used to climb Slide Mountain; he recorded visits he made in the 1880s and 1890s.

From his home at West Park he would take the train to Phoenicia and hike up through Woodland Valley. His journal entry in 1884, the same year rainbow trout were introduced into the stream, states: "Make camp Aug. 1st & take lots of trout. Play the old game of camping out & sleeping on hemlock boughs till Tuesday Aug. 5th. Have a good time, must try & write it up."

He returned the following year, and on June 10, 1885, he writes, "Today we pitch the tent in the old spot, & pass three delightful days there; plenty of trout, a cup of wild strawberries. Calculate that at least 10 Lbs. of trout are daily taken from the stream." Two years later, an entry dated May 24, 1887, informs us: "Went up Snyder Hollow, wife, Julian & I on the 18th. Stayed two days, trout scarce, 28 in all." And commenting on a trip to Woodland Valley in 1894 with his son Julian, he writes: "Took and ate about 90 trout from 5 to 10 inches. . . . A delicious time. Never had better."

Burroughs appreciated the pristine environment he found while trout fishing in places like Woodland Valley. If you happened to be on the stream in the 1890s and chanced to meet him, he would have been wearing a pair of rubber boots and a weathered, felt hat, decorated with some wet flies or hooks imbedded in the hat band. His attire was of subdued colors, blending with the natural landscape. If you talked with him, you would notice he was soft-spoken, and his eyes grayish, light-brown with a tinge of green. His hair was fine and wavy and, though he was a man in his fifties, he moved his slender frame along the boulder-strewn stream with grace and lightness to his step.

In his latter years, Burroughs befriended the Connells, who owned the Wintoon Lodge water, over on the West Branch of the Neversink. He first visited them in the summer of 1914 at the age of seventy-seven, and he returned each season until his death in 1921. As a young girl, Frank Connell recalled:

I often drove him to a likely spot, leaving him to walk home alone, gladly displaying his catch of speckled brookies—but oh, how much more he brought back! In one instance he brought back a rare flower, the *Habenarium Obiculata*, which he called the queen of the woods. His ever-seeing ear and eye were constantly noting bird nests, mosses, ferns, and best of all, bird songs.[11]

After a trip in 1917, at the age of eighty, Burroughs recorded in his journal: "The sweetness and charm of the place . . . Fish two hours;—take 9 trout—enough. . . . The soft murmur of the stream fills all the vale. It is like audible silence . . ."[12]

Another favorite fishing location of the aging Burroughs was DeBruce, along the Willowemoc, where he would stay with the Canfields on the Goff Road. Their rustic cabin was near the junction of the Mongaup and Willowemoc Creeks, and he undoubtedly fished the famous "junction pool," where the two streams come together. In a letter reminiscing about the trout fishing, he wrote: "Maybe we will walk and talk with the Willowemoc in June."[13]

Although he was enamored with the name *Willowemoc,* he had a decided preference for the Mongaup: "When fishing in the Willowemoc, the beauty of that lovely stream's lovely name enhanced for him its charm: 'Thy name casts a spell upon me, Willowemoc, Willowemoc!—but we take more trout from the Mongaup!'"[14]

John Burroughs wrote with a unique style and shared with the world his observations of rural life and nature. His writings endeared him to the American public, and by the turn of the twentieth century, he was considered the foremost among American nature writers. He was inspired by his love for the Catskills, their farmlands and mountain streams, and once while walking through the fields at Roxbury, he avowed: "Oh, my native hills! Will they ever mean to any one else what they have meant to me?"[15]

7

The 1870s

SMALLMOUTH BASS; "IF I WERE A TROUT"; and FISHING TOURISTS

At the end of the Civil War, an epidemic known as *railroad fever* had spread across America. Railroad construction became widespread, with new lines finding their way from populated areas and into the small secluded hamlets of the Catskills that bordered trout streams. Visions of great commercial activity and national expansion were on the minds of everyone; bankers, manufacturers, farmers, and resort owners dreamed of prosperity and profits.

Railroads brought the beautiful mountainous scenery of the region, with its fresh air and pure waters, to the threshold of the metropolis. With low travel rates, good railway accommodations, and inexpensive board, it was not long before the entire area became one vast summer resort. Now city dwellers could escape the heat and toil of their fast-paced lives and spend time in the country vacationing, much to the satisfaction of hillside farmers, boardinghouse owners, and hotel keepers.

The Rondout & Oswego Railroad began construction in

The first scheduled passenger service began on the Rondout & Oswego in 1870. *Gazetteer and Business Directory of Sullivan County*, 1872–73.

1869 with a rail line that started at Kingston and traveled up the Esopus Valley and over Pine Hill to Dean's Corners (Arkville). The railroad passed the mouths of many Esopus tributaries, and their exploitation was not only swift, but dramatic. Trout-fishing tourists, weekend visitors, and summer boarders now had improved transportation to the mountain streams, and this placed added stress on brook trout populations.

The first scheduled passenger service of the Rondout & Oswego began on May 2, 1870, and on June 1, the *Kingston Journal* advised its readers that the first trout ever shipped over the rail line arrived at their office. There were no laws prohibiting the sale of trout to markets at this time. The same paper, on July 13, reported that thousands of trout were being brought to Kingston since the railroad opened: "Several thousand speckled trout from the brooks of Shandaken, Olive and other sections of Ulster, have been brought to town of late. The Rondout & Oswego railroad cars transverse the trout districts of the county, and not only afford cheap travel for those who indulge in piscatorial sports, but also bring the fish to market in so short a space of time after being caught that they are nearly as hard and fresh as when first taken from the water."[1]

Coincidently, by this date many of the tanneries in the valley were closed, and the brook trout populations found in the upper Esopus and its tributaries, which had been plagued by tannery discharges, had been increasing. As tanneries closed in the watershed, trout fishing usually improved. However, reports by railroad users revealed that any increase in the trout population was now subject to being removed by hook and line in alarming numbers. For example, the Snyder tannery constructed along Woodland Valley Stream, then called Snyder's Hollow, closed in 1865, and it is apparent that the stream's trout population returned to its previous levels as seen in an article that appeared in the *Windham Journal* on July 25, 1872:

> A party from this place during last week visited Snyder's Hollow, in Ulster county, on a fishing excursion. They say they captured 670 of the speckled beauties, was out in a rain storm, got their clothing drenched, saw a Greeley and Brown flag, up in the Hollow, took "fishy" supper with a party of eighteen New Yorkers, and had a fine time in every respect.[2]

The waters of the upper Neversink were becoming extremely popular in the 1870s. Attracted by articles in sporting journals and the writings of John Burroughs, trout fishermen swarmed to its banks. Commenting on the popularity of the area during the season of 1874, the *Windham Journal* stated that every house and barn in the towns of Denning and Neversink was filled with trout fishermen, from all walks of business and professional life, and that they represented every section of the country.

Trout, though smaller, continued to be caught in great numbers, and experienced fishermen could still, in the early 1870s, catch a hundred trout in a day. On the West Branch of the Neversink, a favorite destination was the boardinghouse of sawmill operator William G. Satterlee.

His stretch of the stream was well known and was a favorite of Hudson River landscape painters Jervis McEntee and Sanford Gifford, who stayed and fished at Satterlee's. McEntee recorded in his diary a trip he made in June 1873. He and a friend took the train to Big Indian and walked from there over the mountain to Satterlee's: "We did not catch a great many fish but brought home about 40 nice ones."[3] He also recorded that the walk from Satterlee's back to Big Indian took about seven hours! The onslaught against the native trout population continued; this would be the last generation of the original wild stocks of brook trout. By the end of the decade, native trout would be infused with domestic brook trout raised in hatcheries. However, before this happened, another species of game fish was introduced that also had an impact on native fish populations.

Smallmouth bass were placed directly into the Delaware River near the city of Easton, Pennsylvania, and by the end of the decade, smallmouths had spread throughout the system: into the lower Beaverkill, the waters of the West Branch of the Delaware, and even the headwaters of the East Branch, at least as far as Arkville.

That piscatorial pioneer Thaddeus Norris was instrumental in introducing the species into the Delaware. Norris and a couple of friends raised money for the project in Easton and Philadelphia and stocked 450 smallmouth bass (taken from the Potomac) into the Delaware on October 26, 1870.

Norris spent about half the money raised and then applied the balance to stocking the Delaware with Atlantic salmon. The idea of stocking salmon in the Delaware River began as early as 1855 but was not realized until 1871, when Norris obtained a number of salmon eggs in Canada and sent them to Peter Christie's hatchery at Union Vale in Dutchess County. These fry, when hatched, were placed in the Bushkill, a Delaware tributary near Easton, Pennsylvania.

Salmon were planted again in 1872 and 1873, and from these stockings a number of fish returned and were caught in the main Delaware River. Fifteen or twenty grilse were taken in nets in 1875; nearly every year after, Atlantic salmon were taken in nets used for seining shad, one of the largest weighing 36 pounds! By 1879, reports of the anadromous fish were few, but this may have been due to the discontinuance of stocking Atlantic salmon after 1873.

THE RONDOUT CREEK

There is little recorded history of fishing tourists applying their skills along the upper Rondout Creek before the 1870s. One report in the *Ellenville Journal* dated June 12, 1869, tells of a "generous mess of beauties" being taken in the "Sundown Stream," a Rondout tributary. An item in the *Kingston Press* in July 1871 tells of a party of five who camped out for a week at the head of the Rondout in an abandoned bark peeler's shanty and caught between five hundred and six hundred trout.

In the spring of 1872, another Kingston newspaper reported on the escapades of a group of five fishermen who made a trip to the streams of Denning and brought back eight hundred trout and a black bear cub "as fat and handsome a young bruin as man ever saw."[4]

The *Ellenville Journal,* on August 13, 1874, also reported that a party of "New York gentlemen" fishing and camping at the headwaters of the Rondout for several days returned with "over 1,000 trout of large size."

The source of the Rondout Creek is a deep ravine between Rocky Mountain and Balsam Cap; the stream flow begins at an elevation of approximately 3,200 feet and runs in a general direction southwesterly about 3½ miles, cascading 1,500 feet before reaching the Peekamoose Road. The Rondout then parallels the road for the next 6½ miles, through a narrow valley best described as a mountain pass: Mountainsides rise sharply on each side with barely enough space for the stream and road. Evidence of rock slides are everywhere.

At the tiny hamlet of Sundown, the Rondout is joined by a stream once known as the East Branch of Rondout Creek, but is now called Sundown Creek. The name Sundown is derived from the narrowness of the valley; it is said that the sun's rays only shine between the mountains for a few hours each day. Downstream of Sundown the Rondout Creek increases in size, as does the landscape beside it, becoming large enough to be called a valley with open fields that are, or were, once farmed and used for pasturing livestock.

Major tributaries of the upper Rondout include Picket Brook, Buttermilk Falls Brook, Bear Hole Brook, Bull Run Brook, Sundown Creek, and Sugarloaf Brook. The stream flows out of the town of Denning, in Ulster County, and into the town of Neversink, in Sullivan County. From its source to Sugarloaf Brook, the Rondout drops more than 2,300 feet in elevation, averaging approximately 183 feet per mile!

The Rondout is a tributary of the Hudson River, and the name Rondout is derived from a fort, or redoubt, that was constructed in 1660 at its mouth on the Hudson River. The Dutch equivalent of the English word redoubt, meaning fort or stronghold, is *reduyt*. The early Dutch records of Wildwyck (Kingston) described the fort as *Ronduyt,* and the present form Rondout appeared as early as 1666.

Because of the rugged terrain—with its steep and rocky slopes, and soil unsuitable for tilling—there never were many settlers along the upper Rondout Creek. A local history pamphlet claims that a sawmill was constructed at the headwaters in 1838, at a place then called "the Devil's Pulpit,"[5] later "Peekamoose Gorge."[6] However, J. H. French's map of Ulster County, dated 1858, depicts no settlement past the farm of Albert Griswold, which was located approximately 2 miles upstream of Sundown, along the west side of the stream. In fact, the map shows a road only on the east side of the Rondout that ends on the opposite side of the stream from Griswold's; it also depicts only seven settlers living along the Rondout in the 10 miles upstream of Sundown.

A sawmill was constructed on the upper Rondout approximately 1½ miles upstream of the Gulf Hollow Stream (Peekamoose Lake), perhaps at the same location as the one in 1838, and a handful

Bridge over Peekamoose Gorge near Hill's mill. *Picturesque Ulster*, 1896–1905, published by Hope Farm Press, 1991.

of settlers constructed home sites in the area of Picket Brook, a Rondout tributary. Braving the wilderness, they cleared the forest and created pastures and apple orchards at an unusually high elevation. The sawmill was owned by Joseph Hill and had a 15-foot-high dam that created a great pool for trout, as well as a plunge pool below that was also excellent habitat for brook trout. Fishermen boarded at Hill's, and the Peekamoose Gorge was a favorite early fishing destination.

The stretch of water running from Picket Brook to the mill is best described by a fisherman who wrote about brook trout fishing in a Kingston newspaper:

> Above this the stream is somewhat smaller, but there is good fishing almost to the foot of the Peekamoose. In the canyon the water has worn out deep holes, almost like funnels, and the sides are so smooth that if a man falls in them, it is next to impossible for him to get out without help. There are not apt to be large trout in these holes, as they have no place to hide under projecting rocks, as below.[7]

The original road that traveled along the upper Rondout followed the stream up the steep slope of Peekamoose Mountain, then crossed over the Rondout at the sawmill and looped back downstream to the rim of Breath Hill. It then ran easterly, leading to Watson Hollow and West Shokan. In or about 1874, a new road was cleared to the headwaters of the Rondout, which went through a gulf or chasm.

Hill's sawmill, Peekamoose Gorge. *Picturesque Ulster* 1896–1905, published by Hope Farm Press, 1991.

The artist Jervis McEntee was especially fond of the upper Rondout. He was said to have sketched many beautiful scenes of the stream, and he also camped in the Peekamoose Gorge. When he fished the Rondout, he usually stayed at Griswold's, located between Sundown and Peekamoose; Griswold had cleared a small farm in the forest in 1844. McEntee traveled a couple of different routes to get there, though the most direct was to take the train from Rondout to Shokan, then travel up Watson Hollow through the notch at Peekamoose and down the Rondout Creek to Griswold's. The distance was approximately 28 miles, and it was always an eventful trip.

He recorded in his diary in August 1874 that he tried the new road, but found it very rocky. On one occasion, in the middle of June of the following year, McEntee and a friend left Rondout at 8:00 A.M. and did not arrive at Griswold's until 8:00 P.M. The journey, first by train, then by wagon, was interrupted because a forest fire had destroyed two bridges. The men had to lead the horse and carry the wagon over the charred bridges!

Two months later, McEntee again journeyed to Griswold's. This time he left Rondout at 7:30 A.M. and again took the train to Shokan. Instead of taking a horse and wagon, he and his fishing companion decided to walk through the notch and over the mountain. "It was a beautiful day with a fresh feeling in the air and we enjoyed the walk greatly. We carried lines with us and when we came to the Rondout we dug some bait and fished downstream for a mile or more where we could conveniently catch trout for supper."[8]

Most trout fishermen took the train from Kingston to West Shokan, and then hired a buckboard to travel up Watson Hollow through the narrow ravine, where they marveled at how the ice remained in some of the crevices between the rocks even in the hottest days of summer.

Closer to Sundown, several of the inhabitants along the upper Rondout also took in fishing tourists—most notably David B. Smith and Albert Griswold. Smith, who boarded trout fishermen from at least as early as the 1860s, was located 2 miles downstream of Sundown, and Griswold, 2 miles upstream. The cost of boarding at the homes of these early settlers was quite reasonable; in the summer of 1874, McEntee recorded in his diary that he and a friend had caught lots of trout while staying at Griswold's and that the charge for their stay of nearly three days, including care for their horse, was only $2.50. McEntee found the room and board to be comfortable and very inexpensive, and so he paid them $6.00.

The upper Rondout was also a favorite of naturalist John Burroughs, who fished the stream in the 1870s and 1880s. Burroughs was attracted to the wild scenery found along the Rondout and to the exciting adventures he experienced with his fishing rod. He was the first to write of its great natural beauty and of the abundant brook trout that its waters contained.

The first time Burroughs fished the Rondout, he camped in an old bark peeler's clearing near Picket Brook, in the gorge area upstream of Hill's Mill. He described Hill's Mill pond as being exceedingly clear and deceptive; the trout were so conspicuous that the pool seemed much shallower than the 10 or 12 feet it really was. He later wrote of his experiences in an article published in *Scribner's Magazine* in 1877 titled "A Bed of Boughs":

My eyes had never before beheld such beauty in a mountain stream. The water was almost as transparent as the air—was, indeed, like liquid air; and as it lay in these wells and pits enveloped in shadow, or lit up by a chance ray of the vertical sun, it was a perpetual feast to the eye,—so cool, so deep, so pure; every reach and pool like a vast spring.[9]

Burroughs found the Rondout's trout to be generally of small size, though abundant, rarely reaching a weight of more than a pound. He did, however, write of one large trout he hooked while sitting on a log that spanned the stream 10 or 15 feet above its waters. He knew he could not land the "noble" trout from his location, as his tackle was not strong enough to lift the fish that high over the water. He played the fish for ten minutes, and, when he thought it had tired, he cut his line and tied it to a finger and maneuvered himself closer to the water. Burroughs reached for the fish, and at his touch, the trout startled and the hook pulled free.

John Burroughs believed the Rondout was perhaps the most beautiful trout stream he had ever seen:

> If I were a trout, I should ascend every stream till I found the Rondout. It is the ideal brook. What homes these fish have, what retreats under the rocks, what paved or flagged courts and areas, what crystal depths where no net or snare can reach them!—no mud, no sediment, but here and there in the clefts and seams of the rock patches of white gravel,—spawning-beds ready-made.[10]

A favorite pool of Burroughs, and of most every angler who ever fished the stream, is the famous Blue Hole, a strikingly beautiful, 8- to 10-foot-deep plunge pool that is known to be the home of the largest trout in the stream. Burroughs loved the Rondout; his camping and trout-fishing adventures to its waters were among his most cherished memories. In the summer of 1880, he again camped for a week in the woods along the upper Rondout. He described his visit in his journal to that "beautiful stream" as one long picnic: "Trout and wild strawberries. Such a time as seldom comes to a man more than once in a lifetime."[11]

EAST BRANCH DELAWARE RIVER

Like the Esopus, much of the earliest trout-fishing history of the upper East Branch of the Delaware River centered on its tributaries, especially Mill Brook and Dry Brook. Trout fishermen journeyed to these waters in the 1840s. Thirty years later, as well as throughout the 1870s, they were still catching astonishing numbers of trout. The *Walton Chronicle,* in its "About the County" column of July 9, 1874, declared: "Over three thousand trout were taken out of Mill Brook last Saturday," and on May 29, 1879, the *Windham Journal* reported that parties of fishermen from Kingston took five hundred trout from the same stream.

The artist Sanford Gifford had visited the upper East Branch in 1849 and again in 1851; and he undoubtedly told his friends Worthington Whittredge and Jervis McEntee of the wonderful scenery and good trout fishing to be found there. McEntee, Gifford, and Whittredge stayed at Dean's in the early 1870s and fished Dry Brook. Dean's, at the time, was a popular stopover for trout fishermen.

McEntee also fished Mill Brook in the 1870s, often staying at Joe DeSilva's for a week at a time. McEntee, Gifford, and Whittredge were longtime friends, and in his diary, McEntee recorded several trips to Mill Brook, including an entry dated May 10, 1880, while he was again at De Silva's:

A law had been passed preventing fishing in Delaware Co. until the first of June but we had the privilege of fishing just over the line in Ulster Co. It was almost too early although on Tuesday we caught a number with the fly. On Wednesday we went to Furlow Lake but as we were there in the middle of the day we caught no fish.

Thursday we came home having had fine weather all the time.[12]

Jervis McEntee was known for his beautiful autumn and winter landscapes that were rich in color and Whittredge for his inspirational woodland interiors that often incorporated trout streams and their unequaled beauty. In his paintings, Whittredge also captured the pleasant serenity and promise known to trout fishers who idly explore mountain streams with the hope that just around the next bend will be a trout pool, larger and deeper, and holding more fish than the last.

Following the trout season, in late summer and fall, McEntee and Whittredge would return to the upper East Branch for their autumn sketching, staying weeks at a time, sketching streams, meadows, and forest scenes. They found the scenery around Dean's Corners (Arkville) exceptional, with scenery "as beautiful as anything could be." The two men were close friends, and the natural beauty of the area found its way into many of their paintings.

They both painted numerous Catskill scenes found along the upper East Branch and its tributaries. Whittredge sketched and fished along Dry Brook and the East Branch near Roxbury in the 1870s and 1880s. He captured the famous trout stream in a painting titled *Dry Brook, Arkville, Catskills*; and his paintings *Upper Delaware* (ca. 1875) and *Along the Delaware* (mid-1870s) are classic Catskill stream scenes; the latter portrays a fisherman walking along the bank and was undoubtedly sketched near Arkville.

The naturalist John Burroughs learned to fish along the small tributaries of the upper East Branch near the stream's source in the northeast corner of the town of Roxbury. The source of the East Branch of the Delaware begins in a narrow ravine at the base of Irish Mountain, with an elevation of only about 1,560 feet, significantly less than other Catskill streams (the Schoharie Creek begins at an elevation of 1,900 feet; the West Branch of the Delaware at 2,425 feet; the Esopus at 2,700 feet; the Rondout at 2,700 feet; the branches of the Neversink at 2,700 feet and 3,200 feet, respectively; the Beaverkill at 2,760 feet; and the Willowemoc at 2,900 feet).

The East Branch flows in a southerly direction, recruiting insignificant smaller tributaries for the first couple of miles. At approximately 5 miles from the source, the stream is joined by Trout Brook, Montgomery Hollow, and Hardscrabble Creek. As it flows through Roxbury, the East Branch is joined by Meeker Hollow and the West Settlement Stream. Bragg Hollow enters near the hamlet of Halcottville, and 2 miles downstream, the East Branch receives the waters of the Batavia Kill, the largest of these headwater tributaries.

At Arkville, the East Branch unites with the Bush Kill, which also adds a significant volume of water, making the East Branch a little river as it flows through the village of Margaretville, approximately 20 miles from its source. The gradient throughout these headwaters is far less than most Catskill streams, falling on an average of only 13 feet per mile in the first 21 miles; the Beaverkill drops approximately 65 feet per mile within a similar distance. The low gradient is appealing to beaver, and their past presence is evident by the ancient beaver meadows that are found throughout much of the headwaters.

A map in the Delaware County Clerk's Office, dated 1779, depicts the East Branch as "Pacatacans or Papakunk River." Another map, dated 1791, shows "Papakunk or Papacton."

John Burroughs maintained an intimate relationship with Meeker Hollow, Hardscrabble Creek, Montgomery Hollow, and the West Settlement Stream. Each stream is distinctively different, with its own characteristics, and they held a lifetime of memories for Burroughs.

He was seven or eight when he learned to fish on these waters, and he knew the riffles, the undercut banks, and the plunge pools below their waterfalls. On small streams he was an expert; he learned how to move quietly, in a stealthy manner, always upstream, and he enjoyed the excitement and expectations of the next pool or hole. Though eager, he learned patience and approached each new pool with a deliberate motion that would not alarm the trout, who always faced upstream in anticipation of drifting food.

Burroughs had great success on these, his boyhood streams, and catches of native brook trout recorded in his diaries reveal they held abundant numbers of trout. On days when he was joined by a companion, catches of between fifty and a hundred brook trout were not uncommon.

One summer, in the late 1870s, before the introduction of brown or rainbow trout into the watershed, John Burroughs embarked on a solo float trip down the East or Pepacton Branch, as it was also known at the time, an Indian name favored by Burroughs that was said to mean *marriage of the waters.*

He built a 12-foot, flat-bottom boat at Riverby, his home on the Hudson, and traveled with the boat by train to Arkville, in Delaware County. His plan was to travel down the East Branch from this mountain hamlet to Hancock, a distance he estimated at 50 miles.

He took along a couple of old blue army blankets, fishing tackle, raincoat and rubber boots, revolver, cooking utensils, and a stock of food. Arriving at the Arkville railway station, Burroughs, with the help of a young farmer, carried his craft the short distance to the nearby Bush Kill, which he thought was Dry Brook, a tributary of the Bush Kill, and began his voyage about 1 mile upstream of where the Bush Kill entered the East Branch. He fished as he floated downstream to his destination and caught enough native trout for his first campsite dinner. It is interesting to note that he also broke the second joint of his rod on a bass, most likely a smallmouth, before he reached the East Branch.

His trip may have been the first float-fishing trip down the East Branch, though fishing was not the primary reason for his adventure. Following the completion of his journey, the naturalist turned his float trip into a popular essay titled "Pepacton: A Summer Voyage" that was published in the August 1880 issue of *Atlantic Monthly.* The following year, Houghton, Mifflin published several of his nature essays into a book titled *Pepacton.*

FISHING TOURISTS

A second railroad, one that had an even greater impact on the trout populations of the Catskills, was actually started the year before the peacefulness of the Esopus was shattered by a chugging, spark-belching locomotive hauling carloads of passengers up that valley.

The New York & Oswego Midland Rail Road began laying track in June 1868 and ran from New York through Sullivan and Delaware counties, providing easy access to the Neversink,

Beaverkill, and Willowemoc on its way to Lake Ontario. Known simply as the Midland, the railroad officially was completed on July 9, 1873.

The Midland opened the door to a flood of anglers who could now travel to the western Catskills in a matter of hours and who could now commute regularly on weekends between New York City and the Beaverkill and Willowemoc.

Once railroads were established, more fishing articles began to appear in sporting journals and the major newspapers of New York City and New Jersey touting the excellent trout fishing found in the Catskills. Glowing reports were also written about the smaller tributaries, streams that were hardly known to most trout fishermen, which placed added pressure on the fisheries by exploiting the feeder or spawning streams.

Coincidentally, trout fishing in the 1870s became increasingly popular, being fueled by the publication in New York of *Forest and Stream*, a weekly journal devoted to fishing, hunting, and outdoor life in general. Started by Charles Hallock in 1873, *Forest and Stream* included the writings of many of the noted fishermen of the day, including Thad Norris, Seth Green, Fred Mather, Robert Barnwell Roosevelt, William C. Harris, Charles Lanman, Wakeman Holberton, and Sara McBride, the famous fly tier.

Subscriptions increased dramatically, and within a year, Hallock sold one-third interest to William C. Harris, who took over the business portion of the popular journal. The paper flourished.

Forest and Stream made its debut on August 14, 1873, and was soon informing its readership on the pleasures of trout fishing and how to use the new rail lines to reach the Beaverkill and Willowemoc:

> Frank Forester years ago sang the praises of the Willowemoc, and although its trout are not as abundant now as then, they are nevertheless numerous and often large. . . . By taking the 6 o'clock morning train of the Oswego Midland Railroad the angler can reach Morrston (Livingston Manor) at noon, distance one hundred and seventeen miles, enjoy the afternoon fishing, and fish all the next day until 3½ o'clock, when the train will bear him back to this city and land him at Cortland or Desbrosses street at 10½ o'clock, with his fish fresh and ready for the morning breakfast.[13]

Recognizing that trout fishing held a strong attraction for summer visitors, railroad officials began promoting trout fishing through advertisements in sporting magazines and journals. For many years, the Ontario & Western, which replaced the Midland, ran "hunters' and fishers' specials" with Pullman drawing-room cars that carried the names of the famous trout streams, such as Neversink, Willowemoc, and Beaverkill.

A writer for a New Jersey newspaper wrote that since the completion of the railroad, streams were being rapidly depleted of trout, and farmers were now charging $1.50 per day to fish. He cited the village of Neversink as being filled with fishermen and wrote that along the Beaverkill "may be found many of the celebrities of the country, statesmen, divines, politicians, etc., killing time in trying to kill trout."[14]

In the 1870s, the New York & Oswego Midland Rail Road published its first of annual booklets, advertising the "beautiful and picturesque scenery" among the mountains. Each season the railroad published 25,000 copies of *Summer Homes of the Midland* and distributed them in New York

City and New Jersey. They advertised, with wonderful descriptions, the mountain villages and their surroundings, including nearby attractions listing boardinghouses and resorts.

The booklets extolled the "primitive forests, and lakes and streams with trout" and the virtues of "healthful and pleasant retreats." They urged urban residents to escape from the exhausting and depressing heat of the city, and assured them that clubs of sportsmen were purchasing tracts of land and lakes at different points, and were doing "much to preserve the fish and game."

Every year the number of passengers increased, and in the spring it was common for the railroad to add a special car to accommodate trout fishermen "hastening to Sullivan County" for opening day.

In the early 1870s, incredible numbers of brook trout were still being removed from the upper Beaverkill, particularly by those fishermen staying at Murdock's, though many complained that the fish were becoming smaller. An item that appeared in the *Catskill Examiner* in August 1872 mentioned that a party of twenty fishermen captured fifteen hundred trout in a single day!

The removal of so many trout and the increase in the number of fishermen visiting Catskill streams did not go unnoticed; some local newspapers began making negative comments about overfishing. The *Prattsville News* reported that three beautiful trout were taken recently in the plunge pool at Devasego Falls, on the Schoharie Creek. The three brook trout averaged more than a pound and had an accumulated weight of 3 pounds and 10 ounces. The newspaper ended the item by stating, "Following the above announcement we presume the Falls will be at once 'whipped to death,' so as to preclude the possibility of propagation."[15]

Books that influenced trout fishing in the 1870s were *I Go A-Fishing,* by W. C. Prime (1873); *The Fishing Tourist,* by Charles Hallock (1873); *Pleasures of Angling,* by George Dawson (1876); and another by Hallock, *The Sportsman's Gazetteer* (1877), which included a directory to fishing resorts in the United States.

Writing about the state of Catskill trout fishing in 1876, Walter S. Allerton, a veteran fly fisher from New York who loved the mountain streams, gives some insight to what the fisheries were like at this time:

> I have fished the Beaverkill, the Neversink, the Big Indian, from where they were mere mountain springs that I could dam with a hand, and their eddies, holes, and shingly rifts are as familiar to me as the crossings of Broadway. Many streams there are where the trout are larger and more plenty, where the mountains tower more grandly upward, and the wilderness spreads in denser solitudes about, and I hope to make my summer camp on many such; but nowhere are there clearer, colder waters or more lovely valleys than amid the birch-clad Catskills, and many a veteran angler recalls, with a well-remembered thrill, his first cast on an Ulster or Sullivan trout brook.[16]

Allerton writes that the Neversink is the finest stream in the Catskills, though it is also the most persistently fished. Both the East and West Branches, he avows, "formerly contained an almost inexhaustible supply of fish; at present, however, it requires a long and patient day's work to fill even a small basket."[17]

He points out that the West Branch has two tributaries, Fall Brook and Biscuit Creek, that still contain large numbers of small trout, and that Biscuit Creek derives its name from the "biscuit" stones found in the stream bed.

He believes overfishing is to blame for the changes on the Neversink. "Some few years since, when I first fished this stream, a party of men, who drove over the mountain from the valley of the Esopus in three days' time, caught more than fifteen hundred trout, and they were only one of several dozen similar parties that season."[18]

Allerton concluded his fine article on the Catskills by stating: "Such is the best natural country in the State, and perhaps in the world, where every valley contains a river, and every river contains, or did contain, abundance of fish; the numbers that have been taken from its waters are beyond the power of computation, but they are rapidly becoming extinct, and there is no chance of their lasting many years longer unless the people can be compelled to desist from pursuing them in season and out, with all the appliances and means the ingenuity of man can invent for their destruction."[19]

That the sport of fly fishing was attracting even more followers is evidenced by the fact that the art of tying flies, which had been in the hands of professionals, was now being learned by individual fly fishers, and establishments that sold fly-tying materials began to make their appearance.

John Haily of New York City was said to be the first dealer in fly-tying materials in the United States.[20] His establishment was located at 320 Henry Street. In addition to selling materials to make flies, he also was a fly tier and sold flies. An advertisement placed in a March 1877 issue of *Forest and Stream* claimed he also gave lessons in the "art of dressing artificial flies." Haily is credited with creating the Royal Coachman in 1878, a pattern that at one time was the most popular trout fly in America. Haily varied the Coachman, a popular English fly, by adding a barred wood-duck tail and red floss in the center of the body.

Another dealer in fly-tying materials in New York in the 1870s was Sara J. McBride, who holds the distinction of being the first professional woman fly tier in America. McBride began tying flies with her father, John McBride, in upstate Mumford, New York, near Caledonia Creek. It's been written that you could tell a McBride fly from any other "and so could a trout." It was said that John McBride was very secretive about his profession and never allowed anyone in the room when he was tying. If a customer appeared at the door, he stopped tying and conducted all of his business on the front porch.

Sara McBride tied beautiful flies and developed a worldwide reputation. Supposedly, she never used a vise and tied everything in her hands. She was also fond of creating imitative trout flies from the natural insects. During the 1870s, her flies were in great demand, and she usually received a higher price for them than other professionals. She had few equals, and some veteran fly fishers believed Sara McBride was the best fly tier in the country.

She was known for more than her ability to dress flies; McBride promoted the idea of direct imitation of the natural insects found in the stream. She was the first—or, if not the first, one of the first—to write about fly-fishing entomology. In the spring of 1876, she wrote a series of articles in *Forest and Stream* titled "Metaphysics of Fly Fishing." The following spring she published another article, "Entomology for Fly Fishers," in the *Rod and Gun and American Sportsman*.

In 1876, Sara McBride traveled to England, Scotland, and Ireland and studied their fly-tying methods. Upon her return in 1878, she opened a shop at 889 Broadway in New York. In addition to selling materials, she sold flies, rods, reels, lines, and other fly-fishing paraphernalia. After a little more than a year in New York, Sara McBride returned to Mumford.

One of the earliest professional fly tiers in the Catskill region was William W. Cone, who lived in the hamlet of Masonville, Delaware County. Masonville is west of Trout Creek, between

Sidney on the Susquehanna River and Walton on the West Branch of the Delaware. Cone began tying flies in 1869 and, in addition to keeping a stock of flies, he sold leaders, lines, and other fishing equipment.

Cone's price list of trout flies printed for the season of 1884 listed sixty-six different flies; most were English patterns, but the list included several American flies, such as the Beaverkill, Seth Green, and General Hooker.

The introduction to Cone's list of flies states: "Dear Sir: Do you love the 'Gentle Art?' So do I. For 15 years I have tied trout flies for myself and others. Those who use them pronounce them strong and killing and come for more. I aim to furnish Anglers with the best fly for the least money and send out only my best work at a price that yields me but moderate wages."

Cone also took special orders and was familiar with what fly patterns were successful in New York and Pennsylvania. He told his customers he could tie any fly of any size, if he was provided a sample. And if a customer would let him know where they were fishing, he would select flies for them that "will be most likely to kill."

There is not a great deal of information known about William W. Cone; he fly fished for trout in nearby streams, especially Trout Creek, and the census of 1870 lists his age as fifty-three. At a time when most men listed their occupation as "farmer," and a few as "gentleman," he listed his as "hunter," a statement that indicates he may also have been a guide.

Outdoor recreation was growing, particularly the sport of trout fishing, which was illustrated in an article that appeared in an area newspaper:

The number of both City and Country who affect to be "trout fishers" is largely increased. It is said to be a rule in New York business circles that all applicants for positions of any kind, from that of bar-tender up through all grades of clerkships to a silent partnership, must be provided with a trout-pole, fly book and fish basket. No man or boy can "come the gorilla" in the stock exchange who doesn't own or can't borrow a German silver mounted fly pole. No law student can be admitted to the bar until he knows the difference between a "limerick" and an "Aberdeen," and owns a pair of hob-nailed "stogas." And the last time I was on the Beaverkill I encountered, rod in hand and creel on his back, a tailor's apprentice, fresh from Gotham, in a brand new suit of silver-grey corduroys! And in the country, the highway from boyhood to manliness leads through a trout-stream as certainly as through a cigar box. Hence the poor trout have next to no chance at all.[21]

The trout were disappearing, and it was only a matter of time until the free fishing enjoyed by everyone was doomed. Until then, the public continued to roam the countryside, camping and fishing freely wherever they chose.

Many believed that the railroads would be the end of trout fishing and the streams would never recover from this new onslaught of fishermen, who fished so persistently. With the coming of the railroads, new roads were built, and though they were crude and primitive, they generally followed streams, allowing further exploitation by anglers who visited the fishing grounds by wagon and camped streamside.

"Wagon fishermen," as they were known, carried the comforts and luxuries with them, bringing bedding, a good supply of food, a stove, and lanterns. They often found a comfortable place for their horses and made themselves at home. These men were not bound to any one place and lived right along the stream at all of the best fishing locations. When they depleted the trout in one area, they moved to another and worked the stream relentlessly.

There had been no stocking or planting of domestic trout by the New York State Fish Commission in the Catskills until 1876. Before this date, the native brook trout were of the original strain, but year by year overfishing reduced their average size and numbers. Trout populations had been dependent on the natural reproduction of the streams. Now, with more and more fishermen vying for fewer trout, competition developed the practice known as "fishing for count." Eager to best one another, anglers no longer kept only the larger "saving" trout but began keeping every fish, right down to the smallest fingerlings, and then they boasted of the number of trout they had taken.

Not surprisingly, there was a great deal of criticism directed toward this type of fishing in newspapers and sporting journals. Because of their relatively small size, trout were hauled from the stream by a "jerk of the wrist," which served to make quick work of the fish and did not disturb the water. Without laws to regulate an angler's success, the number of trout one angler could remove in a single day was extraordinary: "A party of five brought home 800 trout";[22] "A party of twenty captured 1,500 in a single day. . . . There have been by actual count over 2,000 fish in the cellar (at Murdock's on the Beaverkill) at one time."[23]

Newspapers throughout the Catskills continued to deplore the practice of fishing for count. The *Catskill Recorder,* on May 31, 1878, reported:

> 1,470 trout, weighing 120 pounds, were last week taken from the Beaverkill region by a couple of Saugerties butchering "sportsmen." These chaps could not possibly require this huge number of trout, and there should be some legal, since there is an absence of moral, force to prevent the wholesale slaughter of game fish to gratify the cruelty of certain men.[24]

Even though the area was but a few hours' travel from major population centers, the Catskills, except for the Adirondacks, were still the wildest and least-settled region of the state in the 1870s. Their mountainsides were steep and stony, and were not conducive to cultivation or settlement. Trout fishermen still encountered log cabins and the primitive life of the backwoods. Civilization barely touched the upper Beaverkill, and city dwellers longed to get away and experience a totally different way of life, be it for a weekend, several days, or the entire summer.

During the 1870s, one of the more celebrated trout fishermen to travel the banks of the Beaverkill was the actor Joseph Jefferson (1829–1905). Jefferson came from a family tied to the theater for three generations, and although his fame developed in 1858 when he was cast in the play *Our American Cousin,* it was his appearance in *Rip Van Winkle,* a morality play based on Washington Irving's story, that eventually made him one of America's best-loved figures.

Jefferson began playing Rip in 1866, and his performance was said to be masterful, "rare and precious," and one that mixed tears and laughter. *Rip Van Winkle* stood the test of time, and practically every child in this country was taken to see the play as part of their education. Jefferson immersed himself into Rip, and the role was seen as a "beautiful work of art." He bonded with his audiences so well that for years, the American public, out of respect and affection, refused to call him Joseph, and referred to him as Rip. The play never grew old, and four generations of Americans believed they personally knew Jefferson, and also believed they "knew him well."

Joe Jefferson was also an enthusiastic fisherman, and whenever he visited the Beaverkill, he usually stayed at Murdock's. When the trout were not taking the fly to his satisfaction, he traveled the stream banks, sketching the beauty of the landscape. He was a skilled artist and loved to paint almost as much as he did to fish. His work was exhibited at the Pennsylvania Academy as early as 1868 and at the National Academy in 1890.

Jefferson's popularity was huge; he was perhaps the most recognized name of the stage of his era. When he visited the Beaverkill, the word spread excitedly through the valley. When he was fishing, the "primitive inhabitants" of Shin Creek and Turnwood would leave the fields and woods to see him. They could not contain their excitement and would stand along the

The actor Joe Jefferson. *Rip Van Winkle as Played by Joseph Jefferson*, 1890.

stream bank or the nearby roadway asking him questions about Rip and about his dog Schneider. Obviously, this did, at times, interfere with his fishing, but Joe Jefferson was known for his good nature and friendly disposition.

He was an expert with the rod and fished the salt waters of Cape Cod and Florida, the salmon rivers of Canada, and Catskill trout streams. Upon his death in 1905, one obituary stated "his happiest days were spent perched near a stream, with a rod in his hand, and a whistle on his lips."[25]

With the depletion of native trout populations, fishing required more effort, greater skill, and finer tackle. Local anglers who lived along trout streams discovered they could no longer catch with hook and line all the trout they required. Many kept most of what they caught, and trout even less than 4 inches were often included in their catch. Some turned to nets, snares, set lines, and explosives, even using these distasteful methods when trout were on their spawning beds. This, it was said, was done to "spite the Yorkers," as all sportsmen were called. There were local anglers who held antagonistic views toward all things of the city and made conscientious efforts to ruin trout fishing.

PART 2

Reviving the Fisheries: 1870s–1960

8

Free Trout!

It was during the 1870s that the concept of replenishing streams with domestic trout was envisioned as a means of restoring trout populations, thereby improving the fishing. Once the idea was accepted, the business of hatching and raising trout developed quickly.

Observers of trout spawning determined early on that there was a tremendous loss of eggs when spawning fish deposited them in the streambed. Eggs were preyed upon by other fish and in some instances by the very fish that were spawning; and redds or nests were, at times, destroyed by freshets, flooding, and ice scouring. It was believed that if the eggs were protected artificially, there would be greater survival of the fry, and trout streams could be replenished with many more trout than nature could provide.

Fish culture in America began in 1853 when Dr. Theodatus Garlick and Professor H. A. Ackley of Cleveland, Ohio, succeeded in artificially propagating brook trout. Trout eggs were impregnated in the fall and hatched on January 22, 1854. Because of his pioneering efforts, Dr. Garlick, a physician and angler, has been dubbed the father of fish culture.[1]

Following Dr. Garlick's experiments, Stephen H. Ainsworth and Seth Green from upstate New York made great strides in the advancement of American trout propagation. After years of observing brook trout, Ainsworth, an avid fly fisher, constructed a fish farm with ponds in Ontario County and began hatching and breeding trout as early as 1859. His supply of water was inadequate to enter the business of marketing the fish, and he bred trout primarily for his own recreation and amusement.

Taking spawn. Fisheries, Game & Forest Commission Report, 1897.

Stephen H. Ainsworth. *Harper's New Monthly Magazine*, November 1868.

Ainsworth is credited with creating numerous inventions that furthered the field of fish culture, and his methods were followed by "all American pisciculturists."[2] His hatchery, located near West Bloomfield, New York, has been recognized as the first ever built in this country.

In 1862, the *Rochester Democrat and Chronicle* wrote a description of Ainsworth's operations, and the article apparently caught the attention of Seth Green (1817–1888), who lived in nearby Rochester. Green was born in the town of Irondequoit, was a commercial fisherman, and, at an early age, developed a reputation for his skill with a rifle and fishing rod.

His interest in artificially propagating trout developed while he was on a fishing excursion in Canada in 1837; he was 20 years old at the time and conceived the idea while observing salmon preparing to spawn. He climbed a nearby tree to get a better view and was astonished at the great loss of eggs consumed by brook trout, as well as by some of the very salmon that were spawning. Green watched the spawning activity for two days from his perch and concluded he would somehow try to find a way to preserve more eggs and thus create a situation in which there would be greater survival.

He visited Stephen Ainsworth and, shortly after, in 1864, traveled to Caledonia and purchased land along Caledonia Creek for the purpose of growing trout artificially. He asked Ainsworth to go into a partnership with him and teach him how to remove spawn and manage the trout eggs during the period of incubation. Ainsworth declined Green's offer, but told him he would gladly send business his way; he visited Caledonia several times to teach Green all aspects of the operation, including the care of the fish.

Seth Green went into the hatchery business in a big way. He constructed ponds, raceways, hatching boxes, troughs, and a hatching house. By 1866, he had an impressive facility; he had ponds with thousands of trout in them, one holding about nine thousand trout measuring between 9 and 20 inches. Ainsworth claimed that Green had caught every one of these trout with a fly from the adjoining Caledonia Creek. In a letter to the *New York Daily Tribune*, Ainsworth praised Green's establishment and wrote enthusiastically about one of the ponds: "Only think what a sight—9,000 such Trout all in the eye at once. What a gigantic and magnificent aquarium! I am certain that this is the largest and finest exhibition of Trout in America, and, probably, in the whole world."[3]

In the years ahead, Seth Green would put his ideas into practice and become the most famous and successful fish culturist in America, advancing fish breeding from inconsequential experiments to a financially profitable business.

When Green purchased a portion of Caledonia Creek near Mumford, New York, he used water from the stream and from the tremendous springs found on the property for the artificial propagation of fish. By 1868, he was operating the most extensive fish hatchery in America.

The first attempt at managing New York State's fisheries resources began with the formation of the Board of Commissioners of Fisheries in 1868. Chapter 285 of the Laws of 1868 authorized "an Act to appoint Commissioners of Fisheries for the State of New York." The first members of the commission were former governor Horatio Seymour, Robert Barnwell Roosevelt, and Seth Green.

Two years after its formation, the Fish Commission constructed a "hatching house" at Caledonia and named Seth Green as the superintendent. The site was leased from A. S. Collins, who had acquired the land from Green a few years earlier. At first, the hatching house was used only for the propagation of whitefish and salmon trout (lake trout).* But by 1874, the Fish Commission was notifying the public through news releases that live trout and salmon could be obtained at Caledonia, but only to those with suitable means of transportation—milk cans were suggested—and the fish could only be obtained during a period in February, from the 10th to the 26th.

Seth Green.
Harper's New Monthly Magazine, November 1868.

Seth Green believed depleted streams could again be made productive if they were stocked with hatchery-raised trout; during the mid-1870s, he promoted this idea in letters and articles to sporting journals and newspapers throughout the state. This type of promotion had an obvious appeal to members of the public and their political representatives in Albany.

The demand on brook trout for the "free distribution in public waters" became so great that the legislature in 1874 made an appropriation for the purchase of a site for a permanent state hatchery. Up until this date, the Fish Commission was still conducting the practical operations of its hatching house on leased premises, and at the time brook trout had not been hatched at public expense. The site chosen for the new hatchery was the very site where Green had started his original hatchery along Caledonia Creek; the purchase included about 6 acres, and a larger, more complete hatchery was constructed.

The ease with which trout eggs could be taken and fertilized, producing thousands of fry from a single pair of fish, was seen as an extremely exhilarating idea. In the annual report to the legislature for 1876, the Fish Commission noted: "The Caledonia establishment is now in a condition to supply all the eggs of brook trout, for which a demand is likely to be made in the future, by parties desirous of raising this delicious and profitable fish. It is therefore proposed to give to all such persons

---

*Green's services as a commissioner were discontinued when he took over the hatchery under the title of superintendent of fisheries, a title he held until his death in 1888.

as many of the young of these fish as they want. The benefit to the country will be in proportion to the number taken and as there is no limit to their production there need be none to their use."

It was stated that after February 15, 1876, the commission expected to have about one million brook trout for distribution. The fish could be picked up at Caledonia "free of expense" to all persons wishing to stock public streams and ponds in New York, or the fry would be sent anywhere, to parties paying the traveling expenses of a messenger to accompany the fry and deliver them safely.

From the outset, the Fish Commission focused its efforts and finances on fish propagation. Its plan was to replenish those streams throughout the state that had been depleted by overfishing and to stock them with domestic or hatchery-raised trout. In its report to the legislature for 1876, the commission stated:

> As is well known, there are thousands of small brooks and ponds crossing farms of our people, or running by their doors, and in some cases within the jurisdiction of a single ownership. The larger varieties of fish do not inhabit these waters, and they are too valuable for fish of a coarser class. They are in fact natural trout streams, but have become exhausted by over-fishing or neglect. Formerly, perhaps, they yielded a bountiful supply of valuable and delicious food; now they are entirely worthless. Their restoration should be no longer neglected, for the benefit which would result from the restocking of these waters would accrue to the people at large.[4]

Caledonia hatching house. New York State Fisheries Commission annual report, 1888.

Now, with these improvements and the ever-growing rail transportation, the commission was ready to meet the "urgent demands" of the public and replenish the state's trout waters. Caledonia was an excellent location for the distribution of hatchery fish; major railroad lines ran within a mile of the facility and connected with others that traveled to all sections of New York State.

Beginning in 1876, and for many years after, it became the commission's policy to issue an annual news release advising the public that trout could be had for free, by ordering them directly from Seth Green at Rochester. And every winter, newspapers throughout New York informed the public of when and how to order trout fry.

It was required that the recipient give a general description of the waters to be stocked, how many trout were desired, and an affidavit that the fish were placed in public waters. Unless the fish were picked up at Caledonia, the fry were shipped in tins, delivered by a messenger. In such cases, the person ordering the trout needed to give full instructions specifying which rail route to come by and who to notify for settlement, because it was expected that the messenger's expenses would be paid.

Applicants were cautioned to stock trout only in waters that would support them and to not overstock them with too many fish. In stocking the young brook trout, it was advised that they be placed in the headwaters and tributaries, and not in pools, along the main stream.

The number of brook trout stocked from the Caledonia hatchery increased each year: In 1874, seventy-five hundred fish were stocked, although in 1875, the year the hatchery was expanded, only twenty-five hundred were. In 1876, production leaped to more than a million (1,034,000); in 1877, 1,143,500; and in 1878, 1,368,000!

Records of the Caledonia hatchery reveal that some of these early plantings of hatchery brook trout did find their way into the Catskill region in 1876. The first stocking of trout from Caledonia placed directly into the waters of the Beaverkill appears to have occurred on February 16, when Charles Mead of Goshen placed twenty thousand fry in the area downstream of Shin Creek. On March 14, twenty thousand fry were sent to E. M. Cole of Greene County; and on March 16, I. Pruyn of Catskill received fifteen thousand trout fry and placed them in tributaries of Catskill Creek.

In addition to his success as a fish breeder, Green was known as one of America's finest fly fishermen; he was considered, at one time, to be the best fly caster in the country. He was winning casting tournaments as early as 1866 and won numerous casting championships from 1866 to 1878. He and fellow New Yorker Reuben (Rube) Wood of Syracuse were great competitors and dominated the single-handed fly-open contests. Green won in 1869, but in 1870 at Rochester, he would not enter the contest "as that would have kept out other casters who did not care to compete with him."[5]

In 1872, he won again, and Reuben Wood won in 1873, 1874, 1875, and 1876. Green won in 1878. Although the record appears to support a competitive balance between the two men, it appears Wood may have held a slight edge: "It is related that when ever Reuben (Rube) Wood cast in any event when Seth Green was entered he always had Seth cast first and then, because of his great affection for the older man he would never win from him. Neither would he let his younger brother Ira cast to beat Seth."[6]

In 1870, Green published a book titled *Trout Culture,* and in 1879, in collaboration with his lifelong friend Robert Barnwell Roosevelt, he expanded the work into *Fish Hatching and Fish Catching.* Green also wrote extensively on the subject of fish culture for newspapers and sporting journals; he was a regular contributor to the *American Angler,* a weekly journal devoted to fishing that was founded in 1881.

He also wrote a book titled *Home Fishing and Home Waters* (1888), and though he devoted most of his life to artificial propagation and stocking streams, he encouraged releasing trout. "Do not save any that are under six inches in length. In another year these will more than double their weight, and be fish worth taking. Do not act on the principle that if you do not take them, some one else will; but do your share manfully, and your good example will, without doubt, have its effect on others."[7]

****

It was in 1877 that the first public trout hatchery appeared in the Catskills in Greene County. Citizens in and around the village of Catskill formed a protective organization known as the Greene County Association for the Protection of Birds and Fish. Their goal was to ensure better enforcement of game laws, but they were also concerned with the loss of trout habitat and the destruction of trout streams in Greene County. They urged landowners along streams to preserve trees and streamside vegetation, and thus preserve the stream banks from erosion and keep the stream shaded and cool for trout. The group proposed paying a stipend for every shade tree planted along the stream.

The association also promoted the idea of placing old stumps and brush into the deeper pools of streams to provide shelter for trout and protect them from illegal netting, and they lobbied the Greene County Board of Supervisors to construct a trout hatchery to stock the streams of the county.

Believing that good trout fishing would bring additional tourists and lengthen the boarding season four to six weeks, the Board of Supervisors appointed a committee to look into the request. The idea was approved. In the fall of 1877, the committee contracted with the Hunter Steam Mill for lumber, and the building of the hatchery was under way.

A hatching house styled after the Caledonia facility was constructed on lands in Palenville owned by John Goodwin. The site, including springs and ponds, was leased from Goodwin, and A. W. Marks, who was recommended by Seth Green, became the superintendent. In December 1877, Marks traveled to Caledonia and received 135,000 brook trout and 30,000 lake trout eggs for the new facility. The Greene County trout hatchery produced approximately five hundred thousand trout annually until it ceased operations in 1884.

A year after the hatchery was constructed in Palenville, John N. Bennett of Stamford, in Delaware County, began hatching trout in his cellar with common pump water. By 1880, he was hatching upward of ten thousand brook trout by this method during the winter. Bennett made a trip to Caledonia and learned more about raising trout from Seth Green. When he returned, he constructed six rearing ponds and a hatching house, and produced brook trout up to weights of $1\frac{1}{2}$ to 2 pounds. Bennett provided trout for stocking the waters of the nearby West Branch of the Delaware and other local streams.

Before the advent of domestic trout, native brook trout were disappearing—in part as a result of overfishing, but perhaps even more so because of the loss of habitat. The clearing of the land and the development of mill-dams for water power and streamside industries—such as sawmills, tray mills, furniture factories, and tanneries—often resulted in the loss of trout habitat. Additionally, discharges by these industries at times raised water temperatures, lowered oxygen levels, polluted the water, killed fish, and made streams uninhabitable to native trout. Many now believed that trout fishing could be restored to its former levels only by the introduction of hatchery or domestic fish.

Railroads became eager participants in the Fish Commission's plan to restore the state's trout streams through stocking. They ordered their baggage men to carry cans of young fish and boxes of fish eggs and to assist anyone loading and unloading trout. Conductors were told to stop express trains at any stream and to plant fish, as long as they could do so without missing connections.

In addition to carrying cans of trout free of charge, the Ontario & Western, which ran through the heart of Sullivan County trout country, began stocking trout along its railway. Trout fishing was an asset to the railroad's passenger service, and officials determined that stocking was a necessity. Railroad records reveal that in 1878, twenty thousand trout were acquired, but in just a few years, the number grew dramatically. In 1884, 310,000 were stocked; in 1885, 460,000; and in 1886, 900,000!

Stocking trout was deemed so vital to the railroad that in 1890 the Ontario & Western constructed a special car designed strictly for transporting and distributing fish along the many miles of streams bordering its railway. However, not everyone looked upon the railroad as a blessing. The *Liberty Register,* as early as 1878, saw the railroad as a contributor to the problem of disappearing trout, stating that since the completion of the railroad, streams have become easy to access and were rapidly being depleted.

However, near the end of the decade, the Fish Commission began reporting to the legislature that, with rare exceptions, the raising and stocking of brook trout and planting them in "old worn-out" streams had, in many cases, "surpassed all expectations."

"THE TROUT OF THE PAST"

Private hatcheries appeared in many parts of the state and, in time, domestically raised brook trout found their way into New York's famed Fulton Fish Market, where they were marketed as brook trout—which, of course, they were. However, they did not measure up to the standards of the day when compared with trout taken in the wild that were also sold at the market, and the sensitive tastes of our forefathers were aroused. A writer for the *New York Sun* saw fit to expose their deficiencies in an article published in May 1880, titled "Fraudulent Trout":

> Among the present fictions is the general belief that from now through the season Fulton market will display on marble slabs, on ice, and even in live tanks, genuine brook trout. . . . There is nothing wild, or gamey, or brooky, or trouty about them. They are an artificial pond production, hand raised, liver fed, fat, flabby, and almost tasteless, and their tameness, as Selkirk puts it, is so shocking that a boy who perambulates the pond edge with his pan full of cold chopped liver can lift out the fish with his hands and throw them into the bucket or basket, to be carried to market.
>
> These tame and wholly artificial trout, thus bred and fed and fattened, are neither fish, nor flesh, nor good red herring, and the bigger and fatter they are the worse they are, the biggest and best ranking in insipidity with the common pond sucker. . . .
>
> While we highly approve of fish culture in general as a means of producing cheaply a greater abundance of solid food, of its sort, it is folly to suppose that the trout so raised will retain the wild, gamy flavor and delicacy that distinguishes the real and natural brook trout.[8]

At the same time that the New York State Fish Commission was embarking on its aggressive campaign to replenish the trout waters of the state, Charles Hallock, the astute editor of the weekly sporting journal *Forest and Stream,* commented that the science of fish culture was unable to rehabilitate those streams that had been altered by "civilization" and have produced nothing more than "a flabby and insipid counterfeit" of the native brook trout.

The Trout Display at the Fulton Fish Market, 1877. New York Public Library.

A beautiful Beaverkill brook trout. Ed Van Put.

Hallock, in a lengthy article titled "The Trout of the Past," lamented the passing of the native brook trout. In this December 11, 1879 issue of *Forest and Stream*, he remarked that the "wild mountain trout" have become "very nearly" extinct. He recounted how across the country brook trout were becoming scarce, and the fisheries were in a deplorable state.

He wrote that some would doubt his comments and stated that within the memory of "men not old," streams teemed with brook trout, and a hundred fish could easily be caught in a single day. He claimed that everywhere there are now streams that are almost barren, though only five years ago they were productive. And he asked veteran fishermen to visit their boyhood waters and see how many remain intact, and then they can challenge his position that "the trout of America is not essentially 'A Thing of the Past'." He asserted that brook trout, "beautiful representatives of a universal family" are now only found in abundance in the "almost inaccessible" isolated regions. Hallock asks: What happened to the great fishing?

He claimed there were others who "sensibly appreciate these truths" and recounted a letter he recently came across written by the Reverend Myron H. Reed, of Indianapolis, who agreed with Hallock's convictions:

> This is probably the last generation of trout fishers. The children will not be able to find any. Already there are well-trodden paths by every stream in Maine, in New York and in Michigan. I know of but one river in North America by the side of which you will find no paper collar or other evidence of civilization; it is the Nameless River. Not that trout will cease to be. They will be hatched by machinery, and raised in ponds, and fattened on chopped liver, and grow flabby and lose their spots. The trout of the restaurant will not cease to be. He is no more like the trout of the wild river than the fat and songless reed bird is like the bobolink. Gross feeding and easy pond-life enervate and deprave him.
>
> The trout that the children will know only by legend is the gold-sprinkled, living arrow of the wilderness—able to zig-zag up the cataract, able to loiter in the rapids—whose dainty meat is the glancing butterfly.[9]

Hallock wrote that hatchery trout "will amuse" newcomers to the sport and they will "titillate the uneducated palates of young men," but he painted a bleak picture of the future of trout fishing:

> . . . but he who would indulge the ecstatic pastime of which great pens have written and noble poets sunk, must fish *now*. Those to be born hereafter will never have the privilege of fishing for the trout as it was—the "trout of the past." It may be, possibly, that in some favored Caledonia creek, where the descendants of a master hand like Seth Green's hold perpetual watch and ward—whose waters have never been wholly depleted of their native stock since the beginning, and whose natural food both gods and men have permitted to grow upon its banks for their constant supply—it may be that some remnants of the ancient family will long be found in days to come, but they will be regarded as the relics of a Pompeii exhumed, or the strange golden creatures dug up from the ruins of the Aztec race.
>
> Let us not be supposed to discourage even the feeblest effort to cultivate fish-food; we have assiduously encouraged this industry from the beginning. But we may be pardoned for the tears we shed over the coming doom of a glorious race of aborigines, as graceful and wild as the native Indians themselves.[10]

"THE TROUT OF THE FUTURE"

No sooner had Seth Green begun the campaign to replenish the trout streams of New York with brook trout, when a new species of trout arrived at the newly constructed hatchery at Caledonia.

On April 8, 1875, the sporting journal *Forest and Stream* announced that ten boxes of "California brook trout" had arrived at the New York State hatching house at Caledonia. These trout eggs were a gift of the Acclimation Society of the Golden State and were said to be from fish similar to eastern brook trout in shape and flavor, but lacking the vermilion spots. It was also claimed that this shipment was the first ever to the eastern United States. In their year-end report, the Commissioners of Fisheries announced:

> Besides the trout indigenous to our waters, importations of the California brook trout have been received, with the intention of placing them in the waters of our State. This variety of trout is a much hardier fish, can be more easily handled, and every reason exists for the belief that it will thrive in our waters.
>
> On March 31, 1875, 1,800 of the eggs of this fish were received. Of these, we regret to say, a number had been spoilt during transportation, occasioned, no doubt, by an exposure to too high a temperature. Of the number that arrived safely, however, a fair percentage was hatched, and on January 7, 1876, there were 260 of them alive, looking fine and healthy, and about three inches long.[11]

Two years later, when these trout were three years old, Seth Green notified *Forest and Stream* in two separate letters that the California brook trout began to spawn on March 14, and he took forty thousand eggs from them. Green also reported that some streams were stocked with the newly hatched fry, and they were doing nicely, and that he retained a number of fry as future breeders.

The fry that were distributed were the first rainbow trout to be stocked into eastern waters, something Seth Green was very proud of. At this time the California brook trout were also being referred to as "California mountain trout." One of these stockings, and the first rainbows to be stocked in the Catskills, was received by A. S. Hopkins, of Catskill, New York. On August 29, 1878, he received 1,006 fry for the waters of Greene County, and some of these rainbows were stocked in the Kaaterskill Creek, both above and below the beautiful falls known as Fawn's Leap.

It was also in 1878 that "McCloud River trout" arrived at Caledonia; 150 trout fry were picked up at the California State Hatching Works at San Leandro and, of these, 113 survived the trip back and were said to be the first of this variety to arrive in the East. Hatchery records reveal that they arrived at Caledonia on May 16, 1878, about the same time that the original "California mountain trout" were three years old.

The first eggs of McCloud trout (seventy-two hundred) were received at Caledonia on March 26 of the following year; they were sent by J. B. Campbell, McCloud River, Baird, Shasta County, California. Of this shipment, Seth Green reported: "They feed well and are growing finely, and are equally as hardy as the California mountain trout, which they very much resemble. We have as yet deposited none in streams, but this season we expect more spawn when it is hoped a trial can be made."[12]

In the Eleventh Annual Report to the Legislature (1880) for the year ending 1879, Green reported that he now possessed two species of trout from California, the "mountain trout" and the "McCloud river trout." He stated that they were not quite as beautiful as native brook trout, but in flavor and taste just as equal, and they were hardier and easier to raise: "Of these the mountain trout has the finest game qualities, and the McCloud river trout attains the greatest size."[13] Green believed the two were separate species when, in fact, they are now both recognized as rainbow trout.

The report went on to say, slightly differently than previously reported by Seth Green, that in the spring of 1875, the Caledonia hatchery received five hundred eggs of the California mountain trout from Mr. Newell, of San Francisco. From these eggs, three hundred fry were hatched, and when they began to spawn three years later, in the spring of 1878, they weighed a pound apiece and numbered 275. From these adult trout, sixty-four thousand eggs (previously said to be forty thousand) were taken and, when hatched, were stocked around the state, with the exception of seventeen thousand that were retained by the hatchery.

The Fisheries Commission report for 1879 also commented on the ability of the California mountain trout to survive being caught and released. This was a concern to Green, because these trout would be spawning in the spring, during the open season, when anglers would be pursuing native brook trout.

Green saw the California mountain trout as a very rugged fish: "They are both amorous and quarrelsome, and during the spawning season have terrible battles. Before this is over they are cut and torn in a way that would seem to insure their death, and that would be fatal to brook trout. But they scarcely mind their injuries and are soon as well as ever. If they are

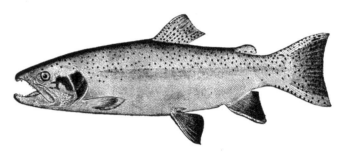

A large male rainbow trout. *Modern Fish Culture*, 1900.

not wounded in the gills by the hook so as to bleed, they will not be in the least injured and if caught while the angler is fishing for trout they may be returned to the water with the certainty of their living."[14]

Because they were known to withstand higher water temperatures, Seth Green believed the California trout were well suited for many streams and some of our larger rivers that never did hold many native brook trout. Brook trout were too delicate to reside in anything but the purest and coolest streams; poor forestry practices and the discharges of deleterious wastes by streamside industries, such as sawmills and tanneries, continued to destroy brook trout habitat.

In December 1880, Seth Green announced that he would be taking orders for California mountain trout from those wishing to stock public waters. At the beginning of the year, he calculated that he had 250 five-year-olds, 17,000 two-year-olds, and 34,000 one-year-olds. From these, he estimated he could produce in 1881 more than four million fry! By this date, sporting journals and fish culturists were also referring to the fish as *rainbow trout*.

At the beginning of the year, newspapers across the state carried a report by Green in which it was stated that he now had a large supply of California mountain trout. He considered these trout to be the "coming game fish of the eastern states" and boasted of their growth rates, how hard they fought when hooked, and that they would make the fishing tackle business "lively." Orders for the new trout poured into Caledonia, and more than 1,200,000 fry were distributed into New York's waters.

Several Catskill trout streams were among those stocked. On May 12, 1881, Ned Buntline provided rainbow fry for the streams around Stamford, and on June 24, J. D. Mayhew placed twenty-five thousand rainbows into the waters of the upper East Branch of the Delaware. On June 30, fifteen thousand rainbow fry were stocked around Hancock; and on the same day, Ed Sprague of Shin Creek (Lew Beach) stocked fifteen thousand into the upper Beaverkill and Shin Creek. A few days later, Montgomery Dodge of Westfield Flats (Roscoe) placed fifteen thousand rainbows in the lower Beaverkill.

In the fall, George W. Sears, the popular outdoor writer who used the pseudonym Nessmuk, wrote an article that was published in the *American Angler* about the decline of trout fishing. It was titled "The Exodus of the Trout," and Sears, like others, painted a bleak picture of the future of the native brook trout in America. "Salmo Fontinalis is becoming small by degrees, and deplorably scarce," he wrote in the November 19 article.

He claimed that it was "worse than useless" to restock the depleted waters, at least not on a scale to benefit "the great body of anglers." Wherever you go, he stated, "the trout are playing out." Sears blamed overfishing: "It is the constant, indefatigable working of the streams by skilled anglers, who turn out in brigades, supplemented by the granger, who takes his boys along in a lumber wagon, camps on the stream until he has *salted down* several butter tubs full of trout, and saves everything large enough to bite."

He also blamed human disturbances:

Now, on most of our streams the land has been cleared; the effect of which is, that each heavy rain converts the streams into muddy, raging torrents, foul with the droppings from cattle on a thousand hills, wherein no trout can thrive and breed for a length of time. Add to all this the log-drives and saw-mills, and I see not how the trout can be kept in stock, save in private waters where they can be carefully reared and provided for.

Does anybody know a practicable way of preserving the brook trout in free waters? I see none. True, we have many streams in a state of nature; but anglers increase as trout diminish; and such streams are infested by anglers from April to August, to an almost incredible extent, nearly all of whom basket anything more than four inches long.[15]

The only hope, Sears wrote, was to find a substitute for the brook trout, and he recommended the smallmouth bass.

Seth Green took notice of the article and responded with one of his own in the same publication on December 21, 1881. He agreed with Sears when he said, "the brook trout are bound to be exterminated before many years," and because of the same reasons given by Sears. However, Green replied that "great good" has been accomplished by restocking streams: "We have many waters in New York State which were entirely depleted a few years ago where good fishing can now be had, and the supply will be kept up many years longer than it would have been had not artificial propagation been a success."

Green's article was titled "The California Mountain Trout as a Substitute for the Eastern Brook Trout," and he did not agree with Sears that smallmouth bass were the answer. It was his opinion that the California mountain or rainbow trout would be an excellent replacement for the native trout: "Besides being hardy they are as gamy as the angler could desire. They are a fine table fish and grow to weigh from two to four pounds."

The New York State Fish Commission had begun to replenish the state's waters with rainbow trout. One of its first commissioners, the well-known angling author Robert Barnwell

Roosevelt, promoted their acceptance before a meeting of the New York Association for the Protection of Game:

> The complaint against them, said Mr. Roosevelt, is that they are too gamey—they smash light tackle with their tremendous rushes, and the angler must be especially prepared for them. They can be easily introduced into our trout streams, they will live where our trout will, and in some places where they will not. "They are the coming trout! They are perfection."[16]

Seth Green continued to promote the stocking of rainbows. He stated that his favorite trout was still the native brook trout, but, he claimed, they were being overfished in some streams and would not live in many others, either because of pollution or warm water temperatures. He argued that these streams could be made productive again with the introduction of the California trout. "Our trout are tender," he stated, and the rainbow is like a "bull-dog," as it can live in streams with 75-degree temperatures. Green was not sure if the rainbow trout could withstand tannery wastes or discharges, but he claimed if it does, "it will deserve to take the rank with the immortals."[17]

Over the next few years, rainbows found their way into many more Catskill trout streams; they were first stocked in the Willowemoc in 1882, when twenty-five thousand were placed in its waters, as well as in the Mongaup Creek. In July 1882, the Rondout and Sandburg Creeks were stocked with a shipment of twenty-five thousand fry; thirty-five thousand were distributed into the Neversink, Mongaup River, Kinne Brook, and Pleasant Lake.

Not all fisheries professionals agreed with Seth Green. Fred Mather, an equally noted fish culturist with the United States Commission of Fish and Fisheries, was not sold on the introduction of rainbows to eastern waters. When asked to comment on the fish, he said he had no personal experience with them but believed the state should be cautious and proceed slowly; as an imported species, they could totally displace a native one:

> I am not prepared to say much of the rainbow trout; I have watched it with interest in ponds, but do not know how it will agree in streams with the native. If it grows faster, it will get all the food and the native will suffer. In that case I am opposed to it. If it will live in streams where the native will not, then it may be a good thing.[18]

In spite of criticism, the stocking of rainbows continued. Another Catskill stream that received its first stocking of rainbows in the 1880s was the Esopus Creek, a Hudson River tributary that began in the Catskills, flowed easterly, and warmed considerably before reaching Saugerties on the Hudson.

Rainbows were first stocked in the Esopus watershed in June 1883. F. E. Whipple of the First National Bank of Poughkeepsie ordered ten thousand rainbows for Snyder Hollow (Woodland Valley Stream) and Ox Clove Creek, a tributary of the Stony Clove, upstream of Phoenicia. The trout were shipped to L. A. Chichester, who placed them in the streams.

The Callicoon Creek and its tributaries were stocked with fifteen thousand rainbows on May 12, 1885; the Schoharie Creek, East Kill, Kaaterskill, and Stony Clove and its tributaries received fifty thousand rainbow trout on May 24, 1886. From 1875 to the spring of 1884, an average of one million rainbow fry were stocked annually.

The stocking of rainbow trout had hardly taken place when doubts about the fish began to be heard. Reports to the Fish Commission claimed that rainbows were not readily found a year after their introduction into a stream. And it was feared that many fry were preyed upon when they were first stocked. Rainbows spawned in the spring; therefore, the fry were planted at a time when other fish were feeding greedily. In addition, it was rumored the fish were migratory and that when they reached a certain size, they moved.

Four years after they were introduced into the Beaverkill, the *American Angler* reported that rainbows were never caught in the Beaverkill where they were planted, but were found in the Delaware River, 75 miles downstream, in the deep water and large eddies, and that they were "quite plentiful."[19]

The *Walton Chronicle* gave credence to this statement when it reported that a boy fishing at Big Eddy (Narrowsburg) in the spring of 1884 "captured a California mountain trout that weighed over two pounds."[20]

Although rainbow trout were thought to have failed the expectations of the Fish Commission and Seth Green, there were signs near the end of the decade that there were streams where the fish had been stocked in which the species was doing exceptionally well. On some Catskill streams, wild populations were established that continue to the present day: primarily on the Esopus Creek and tributaries, Catskill Creek and tributaries, and the Delaware River and many of its tributaries.

When rainbows were stocked in the Esopus, the water quality was much improved over what it had been when tanneries were discharging their wastes throughout the watershed. By 1870, most of these streamside industries had closed, because the hemlock in the region had been expended and the tanners had moved on to those areas of the Catskills where the stately trees could still be found. And by 1886, Esopus water had become "less evil in smell and taste," so much so that the city of Kingston contemplated constructing a reservoir at Bishop's Falls.

Aerating the water of a milk can containing trout fry. *The Conservationist*, December–January 1964–65.

Before the stocking of rainbows, articles in newspapers and periodicals about Catskill trout fishing rarely mentioned the Esopus Creek; they usually advised trout fishermen to fish the Stony Clove, Mink Hollow Creek, Watson Hollow, and Snyder Hollow (Woodland Valley Stream). However, the Esopus Creek was an ideal stream in which to plant rainbows; it had all the criteria Seth Green outlined when he first announced that the fish was available for stocking.

On its way to Saugerties and eventually the Hudson, the Esopus picked up enough water from tributaries to be considered a river, and it included miles that were borderline trout water because of warm temperatures. Its watershed sustained massive abuses to its forest from sawmills and tanneries, and the stream had been heavily polluted by these activities, driving out brook trout that had inhabited portions of its waters.

After the initial stocking of rainbow trout fry in tributaries in 1883, rainbows were stocked directly into the Esopus Creek throughout its length. In the spring of 1884, W. Marsh, of Big Indian, received five thousand fry and placed them in the stream at Big Indian; in June of the same year, twenty-five thousand rainbow fry were stocked 15 miles downstream at Boiceville by M. H. Davis of that hamlet. In 1885, William E. Ripp of Saugerties stocked another thirty-six thousand fry in the Esopus and in the Plattekill Creek; and in June, Dr. H. R. Winter of Phoenicia added another fifty thousand fry to the Esopus near that village.

In the 1880s, Dr. H. R. Winter was considered the Izaak Walton of the Shandaken Valley. The doctor was an avid fly fisherman who maintained an office at the Tremper House. The hotel was large enough to accommodate hundreds of guests and was famous in its day for having "steam-heat, elevators, in-door plumbing and even a trout pond."

The doctor was known to recommend trout fishing to guests as a way of improving their health, both mentally and physically. He claimed trout fishing was found in beautiful places, with pure air and pure water, and as such would relieve the mental stress of business:

> Along the mountain streams are to be found the most romantic—the grandest—the most beautiful and picturesque scenes in nature during the summer months, when the foliage is in its brightest colors—numerous varieties of wild flowers—pure air to breathe, pure water to drink—the songs of birds, the music of the running waters—and, with the ever-changing variety of scenery, together with the excitement of trout-fishing, will make a person for the time forget he ever had any care, business or anxiety.[21]

Dr. Winter contributed a trout-fishing essay to the popular *Van Loan's Catskill Mountain Guide,* published in 1886. Titled "Trout Fishing in the Catskills," he urged fly fishermen to carry an assortment of flies so that they may exactly imitate the flies the trout are "jumping for." He included a list of flies that he recommended for Catskill streams; most were of English origin but were basically the standard patterns of the day.

The Esopus Creek was the one major trout stream in the Catskills that rainbow trout thrived in; they outcompeted brook trout for food and space, and grew to sizes never obtained by the native species. They quickly became the dominant species in those tributaries where they were placed, and following their introduction into the watershed, the trout fishing improved dramatically.

Three years after rainbows were introduced, two large trout were displayed in a tank at the railroad station at Big Indian, where they were the center of attention as visitors, gazing in awe, speculated as to how big they really were. Unfortunately, both died toward the end of the month, and, when weighed, were reported to be 1¾ pounds and 3 pounds, respectively!

Rainbows did exceptionally well in the Esopus. They grew rapidly, with some reaching weights of 3 and 4 pounds. They reproduced and spread throughout the system, especially in the lower section of the river, providing exciting fishing where there had been little or none before. In June 1887, four years after their introduction, rainbows were being caught as far downstream as Saugerties, near the mouth of the Hudson, and one "California mountain trout," weighing a pound, was found wedged in the mill race of the paper mill.

Trout fishing improved so noticeably along the stream that the *Kingston Daily Freeman,* on May 27, 1886, stated that as soon as farmers whose land bordered tributaries learned how good the fishing had become, they put up POSTED signs. This irritated the people living along the main stream, who also threatened to follow suit and prohibit fishing. The Esopus had escaped fishing clubs and the intensive posting that plagued other Catskill streams. Only one club was formed along the stream, and it was located so close to the source that its formation did not affect stream fishing.

In the June 16, 1887, issue of *Forest and Stream,* an article titled "A Catskill Mountain Club" announced that Judge Alton B. Parker and several other "prominent" men had formed a club and purchased 600 acres at the base of Slide Mountain. A log cabin was being constructed, and a dam was placed across a ravine that was the source of the Esopus Creek.

The club became known as the Winnisook Club. According to local lore, *Win-ni-sook* was the name of a legendary Indian who was 7 feet tall, very strong and muscular, and known as "Big Indian." Win-ni-sook fell in love with a settler's daughter named Gertrude Molyneaux, who, though she loved the warrior, married a man her parents approved of. It was said that he treated her badly, and Win-ni-sook continued to see the girl secretly, eventually convincing her to leave her husband.

This she did, and she spent several years living with the big Indian and members of his tribe. The husband vowed revenge, and after an Indian raid on the Dutch settlers to secure cattle, Win-ni-sook and members of his tribe were overtaken at the entrance to the valley now known as Big Indian.

Joe Bundy, the husband, saw his hated rival and placed a bullet near the heart of Win-ni-sook; dying from his wound, he hid in a hollow pine tree that stood nearby. Later, the woman he loved found him standing upright, but dead, inside the tree. She had Win-ni-sook buried at the base of the pine and lived with her children near the site until she, too, passed away.

In 1888, the log structure or cabin built by the club became known as Winnisook Lodge, and the lake formed by the dam was stocked with thirty thousand trout. In 1889, the Winnisook Club's capital stock was $3,000; shares were $200, and the stockholders were limited to fifteen. The majority of the club members came from Kingston; three were from Washington and the rest from various places in New York. Only one member had local ties, and that was Joseph H. Riseley from the nearby hamlet of Allaben in the town of Shandaken.

Over the next few years, several cottages were constructed by members around the lake, and in 1893, a new dam was constructed, forming a lake of approximately 6.37 acres. In time, Winnisook Lake developed a reputation for producing good brook trout fishing, with some trout weighing from 1 to nearly 2 pounds.

The Winnisook Club was as much a social club as it was a fishing club. Outings to the lake were popular by members and their families, especially on holidays, such as the Fourth of July. Members were also influential in state and national politics, especially within the Democratic Party, and over the years, Winnisook Lodge was visited by important men in the world of politics.

In 1896, the club was host to William Jennings Bryan while he was campaigning as the Democratic candidate for the presidency. His visit stirred great interest in and around the Catskill Mountains. Bryan had been campaigning in Dutchess County and was invited to Winnisook Lodge by James W. Hinkley, chairman of the Democratic National Committee. More than a thousand people gathered at Kingston Point to greet Bryan when he arrived, and the crowd cheered loudly until he began to speak, reported the *Kingston Argus.* Bryan and his wife were surrounded by enthusiastic admirers: "Women and girls begged flowers from her bouquet and one old man came in with a fishing rod as a present to her."[22]

The Bryans traveled by train up through the Esopus Valley on their way to Big Indian and Winnisook Lake. All along the route—Shokan, Mount Pleasant, Phoenicia, Allaben, Shandaken—at every station, the couple was greeted by supporters who had traveled miles over the mountains to see the candidate. Crowds both small and large were waiting to shake Bryan's hand and receive a button for their support. When the train arrived at Big Indian, there were several hundred people, and Bryan was almost lifted from the train. The reporter for the *Argus* wrote that the cheering echoed from the nearby hillsides and did not stop until Bryan spoke to the crowd.

William Jennings Bryan was not the only presidential candidate to visit Winnisook Lake. The club's first president, Alton Brooks Parker, who practiced law in Kingston and became a Supreme Court justice of New York and chief judge of the New York Court of Appeals, received the Democratic Party nomination for the U.S. presidency in 1904. Parker lost the election to Theodore Roosevelt.

9

The Preservationists

The first attempt at saving what remained of a rapidly declining fishery was the establishment of private fishing clubs and preserves, which posted their land against trout fishing. During the 1870s, and perhaps more than at any other time in their history, Catskill streams were being depleted of their native trout at an alarming rate; brook trout were decreasing in size as well as in numbers.

Some anglers blamed the declining trout population on the increasing number of fishermen, whereas others saw tanneries and other streamside industries as the cause of poorer fishing. The cutting of vast sections of the forest left stream banks devoid of trees and caused erosion, exposing the water to increased sunlight and warmer water temperatures.

These were years when trout populations were still dependent mostly on natural reproduction. The state hatchery at Caledonia was in its infancy, and even then, some knowledgeable fishermen thought restocking streams would fail.

There were not enough laws protecting streams, and the streams and the trout were, for the most part, subjected to overfishing, illegal fishing, pollution, and the loss of habitat. There were no state game wardens to enforce the few laws that protected fish. "The question of what to do with our trout fisheries; how to preserve the trout and prevent their entire extinction in our streams, is pressing itself upon the attention of many intelligent lovers both of the fish and the sport of taking them."[1]

One solution that was gaining in popularity among landowners and men who cared about the sport was the establishment of private, or posted, water. This was a drastic measure, and near the end of the 1860s, notices began to appear along streams advising trout fishermen that they were no longer welcome.

At the time, the formation of private fishing clubs was seen as an important step in the preservation of Catskills trout fishing. Clubs immediately reduced fishing pressure along streams by posting. They generally regulated the catch by restricting the method of angling to fly fishing only, imposing size limits, and reducing the number of trout that members could remove in a single day. Additionally, clubs employed a stream watcher or patrolman who not only prevented poaching, but, by his presence, further protected the fish from illegal methods of taking them, such as by netting, poisoning, and dynamiting.

In the Catskills, the first fishing preserve was established when a club was formed in 1868 along the headwaters of the Willowemoc Creek. Newspapers at the time reported that several sportsmen planned to create a trout preserve at Sand Pond for their use during the summer.

James Spencer Van Cleef, a prominent attorney from Poughkeepsie, purchased 143 acres, including Sand Pond, a 14½-acre body of water near the border of Ulster and Sullivan counties. Located deep in the forest, Sand Pond was famous for its large brook trout and was the frequent target of illegal netters.

Following the acquisition, Van Cleef took out an advertisement in local newspapers announcing his purchase and that fishing or trespassing at Sand Pond was prohibited under the penalty of the law. By 1870, he and several friends had obtained leases on Butternut Brook and approximately 4 miles of the upper Willowemoc, upstream of the tannery at DeBruce. These friends then purchased Sand Pond from Van Cleef and renamed it Lake "Willewemoc." This was followed by the purchase of Thomas Lake (Beecher Lake) and the famous Balsam Lake.

The group decided to call themselves the "Willewemoc" Club. Their membership was limited to twenty, and another Poughkeepsie attorney, Cornelius Van Brunt, was named president. In a letter to *Forest and Stream* dated March 19, 1874, Van Brunt informed readers that the club was formed not only to have a pleasant place to visit, but for the protection of the fish.

JAMES SPENCER VAN CLEEF

James Spencer Van Cleef.
The Courier, Poughkeepsie, New York.

James S. Van Cleef (1831–1901) was born in Athens, along the Hudson River just north of Catskill in Greene County. He was educated at Poughkeepsie, and like many of his Catskill trout-fishing companions, was a graduate of Rutgers University. Four years after graduation, he began practicing law in Poughkeepsie and became one of the city's most successful lawyers. Van Cleef was known as a serious trout fisherman, an early conservationist, and a leading member of the State Association for the Protection of Fish and Game.

Van Cleef worked diligently at preserving the trout fishing of the Catskills for more than thirty-five years. He not only was a founding member of the Willewemoc Club, but was also involved with the establishment of several other fishing clubs, including the Beaverkill Club, Balsam Lake Club, and the Sundown Fishing Club. For more than twenty-five years he wrote about stream conservation and the need to protect the fishing grounds, as well as fish and game law, on the pages of *Forest and Stream*.

Van Cleef was a pioneer in attempting to manage the fisheries of the Catskills, and though his work was accomplished on private waters, his goal was to preserve trout fishing. Van Cleef wrote articles and read papers before the American Fisheries Society, and an article titled "How to Restore Our Trout Streams" (1885) was one of the first published papers on channel restoration in the United States.

He recognized early on that deforestation, especially along stream banks, changed the "natural homes of the trout" and that the loss of trout habitat was the main cause of the dwindling trout populations. He was involved in the construction of artificial spawning beds at Sand Pond as early as 1878 and in the development of in-stream structures to improve habitat on the Rondout Creek (Sundown Fishing Club) as early as 1884.

Van Cleef believed strongly that until trout habitat was restored, it was useless to restock streams with trout. He stressed the importance of preserving wetlands and the negative effect that cutting of the forest had on a watershed.

He contributed fascinating reminiscences of the early years along the Beaverkill, and he wrote with reverence of the stream that was perhaps his favorite. His writing endeared him to those he never met, and he passed along to another generation the concept that trout streams were special and that their protection could not be taken for granted.

Van Cleef was an early Catskill Mountain trout fisherman known for his high ideals and sportsmanship. He was very active in the angling community and was a member of the National Rod and Reel Association, which held the famous fly-casting tournaments on Harlem Meer in Central Park.

A couple of years after the formation of the Willewemoc Club, Junius Gridley, Edward B. Mead, and Daniel B. Halstead of Brooklyn, and Robert Hunter of Englewood, New Jersey, spent the entire summer of 1872 boarding on the upper Beaverkill. The following year they constructed a small clubhouse about 1 mile upstream of Beaverkill Falls and became the parent group of an organization known as the Salmo Fontinalis Club.

The idea of prohibiting fishing began to spread, and POSTED notices started to appear on other waters, specifically the waters of Trout Brook, a tributary of the Beaverkill, in the town of Hancock. In the spring of 1872, an ad was placed in the local newspaper by Beals & Holcomb warning anglers that they were forbidden from fishing any streams or ponds on their premises.

By the summer of 1875, the banks of the East Branch of the Neversink were lined with POSTED signs prohibiting fishing on waters that had always been open to the public. The *Republican Watchman*, published in Monticello, reported that a portion of the stream ran through a wilderness, and that those doing the posting had better fence their land "before they attempt to keep the public from catching the trout that disport in the pellucid waters of this mountain stream."[2]

While the posting of streams began to occur at various locations throughout the Catskills, the majority of attempts at preserving trout fishing centered on the waters of the Beaverkill. In 1875, Royal Voorhess, a farmer who boarded trout fishermen and whose lands adjoined the stream, became concerned when his guests began bringing in fewer fish and were traveling further upstream to do so. Voorhess received a substantial portion of his income from trout fishermen, and he decided to do something to keep more trout in the stream.

Most farmers were reluctant to post their lands and prohibit fishing; they were concerned that they might incur the wrath of anglers who had always fished their waters, and they were afraid of retaliation. Voorhess believed something had to be done, and on July 1, 1875, he obtained leases along the Beaverkill from several adjoining landowners for the "exclusive rights of fishing, and preserving of the trout and other fish."

After obtaining the leases, Voorhess and several of his regular boarders filed a certificate of association and founded a society known as the Beaverkill Association: "The business of said society

POSTED sign on the Beaverkill. Ed Van Put.

shall be fishing and other lawful sporting purposes."[3] The leases and the certificate of association were filed in the Sullivan County Clerk's Office on September 9, 1875. This filing was the first of its kind in either Sullivan or Ulster counties, making the Beaverkill Association the first fishing club of record on the Beaverkill.

A couple of years later, two brothers from Brooklyn, by the name of Mead, constructed a boardinghouse that catered to fishing parties at Quaker Clearing on the upper Beaverkill. They owned approximately 1,000 acres and posted their water to prevent fishing to everyone except their guests.

Artist Jervis McEntee witnessed the changing times, and following a trip to Sullivan County in June 1877, he recorded in his diary:

On Tuesday Major Wilkinson and I went to the Willowemock and the BeaverKill on a fishing expedition, returning Saturday. We had a very pleasant time and found the country charming. We did not catch many trout but there are plenty there. The streams were low and yet we saw some fine trout caught while we were there. The good streams are being taken up by clubs now, and soon there will be no fishing except for those belonging to them.[4]

The relentless pursuit of brook trout on open waters continued, not only along streams but in lakes and ponds as well. In the summer of 1877, the *Ellenville Journal* spoke out against the undisciplined taking of trout from Balsam Lake. Even though the lake was remote and difficult to reach, men continually raided its trout population:

Every winter barrels of trout are scooped out with nets through holes cut in the ice on Balsam Lake and whose business is it? Parties of ten or a dozen campout for a week at a time on the shores of these secluded ponds; each one fired with the ambition to beat his fellows in the numbers of trout taken. Hence it is fish, from dawn to dusk, and everything that bites from two inches to twenty, must be kept and counted.[5]

During this same summer, stories regarding the excessive numbers of trout being taken were reported in Catskill newspapers. One told of two fishermen from Saugerties who caught 1,473 trout weighing a total of 120 pounds from the Beaverkill and Balsam Lake. And the other told of a party of "old Orange County sportsmen" who visited the Beaverkill the first week of June and stayed at Ed Sprague's near Shin Creek. There was no mention of how many were in the party, but the men arrived on a Monday evening and left on Saturday, having captured about 1,000 of the "speckled beauties."

This type of abuse of the fisheries, and the comments made by newspapers, did not escape the attention of the owners of Balsam Lake. The following year, Cornelius Van Brunt and James Van Cleef had the boats and rafts destroyed, posted the lake, and hired a watchman. In response, the *Kingston Freeman* told readers that Balsam Lake was now "guarded by a mountaineer with a big dog and a Springfield musket, it is not a popular place with the public generally."[6]

Beaverkill trout, at the time, were not faring well, and those most concerned over the trout fishing were veteran anglers who had fished the stream before its slide into mediocrity. One such fisherman was George Van Siclen, who was a founding member of the Willewemoc Club and an excellent trout fisherman. An example of his ability with the long rod occurred in 1877, when he caught three large trout at once in the waters of Sand Pond: The trio of fish measured 12, 13, and 16 inches! In addition, he was an expert fly caster who assisted in organizing some of the first casting tournaments in Central Park. He also wrote about the sport occasionally, contributing articles and letters to the *American Angler* and *Forest and Stream.*

George West Van Siclen.
The Holland Society Yearbook, 1888.

As did other members, Van Siclen hiked through the forest from Sand Pond 3 miles to fish the upper Beaverkill, a stream he had fished since the 1850s. He had witnessed the changes and was convinced that something needed to be done to halt overfishing. In 1878, after obtaining a lease and the cooperation of adjoining landowners, he and other members of the Willewemoc Club formed a new organization, known as the Beaverkill Club* and posted the stream.

Before the trout-fishing season of 1878, Van Siclen sent a lengthy letter dated March 23, 1878, to *Forest and Stream,* and a similar one was printed in various newspapers throughout the Catskills to make sure local anglers were notified of the posting. He requested that editors give his letter space before the opening of the trout-fishing season because it was of great interest to the fishermen where their newspaper circulated.

Van Siclen headed his letter "NO MORE TROUT FISHING IN THE UPPER BEAVERKILL," and he stated that the previous summer he had encountered three men on a buckboard who boasted of catching "over four hundred trout" which they kept in a "twelve-quart butter firkin." He claimed that all of the fish were less than 6 inches in length and that this type of activity was ruining trout fishing.

---

*The Beaverkill Club evolved into the Balsam Lake Club in 1883, and a year later, a clubhouse was erected on the lake, with the parent group of anglers being the same as those who founded the Willewemoc Club in 1868 and the Beaverkill Club in 1878. Cornelius Van Brunt, who had been the president of the Willewemoc Club, was elected as the first president of the Balsam Lake Club. Records of the Beaverkill Club in 1880 reveal that 1,364 brook trout were kept by members, having a total weight of 205¾ pounds. The average weight of those trout taken was 0.15 pound. A conversion table reveals that the average fish would have been approximately 7.5 to 7.9 inches.

He wrote that he had fished the Beaverkill since 1856 and that the trout fishing was deteriorating and he decided to do something to protect what remained of the fishery. He and several other landowners had joined together and posted the land and hired a patrolman to watch the stream. Van Siclen disliked the idea of preventing fishing that had been for so long free to all, but he emphasized that the trout fishing was ruined because of careless fishermen who killed all they caught.

The stretch of the Beaverkill Van Siclen referred to was practically all of the water upstream of Beaverkill Falls. There can be no doubt that the fisheries were in a deplorable state, and the public must have sensed the urgency, or at least recognized the need for Van Siclen's decision. There was no outcry, at least not in the press, nor were there any protest letters following the stream's closing.

One area newspaper, after publishing Van Siclen's letter, seemed to promote the idea of posting streams. On April 19, 1878, the *Hancock Herald* reported that there had been too much careless and destructive trout fishing, and urged stream owners to protect the fishery by closing them to all fishing. "We hope to soon see a general move in this direction from the present time until the streams are again stocked. Let our people think of this and take action."

Landowners over on the Callicoon Creek became alarmed over the increasing number of fishermen and of the trout being removed from its headwaters. After a meeting of the "Farmer's Club," a resolution was passed forbidding all fishing "except on one's own premises, without a permit." With few exceptions, Callicoon stream owners joined the club: "[T]rout-fishing now dances to the tune of a dollar and fifty cents a day."[7]

Over on the Neversink, several farmers began posting their lands against fishing, and one local newspaper called it "pure cussedness" and contemplated whether the stream posting was the result of "sports" from New York City and elsewhere that were looking to preserve the water to themselves.

In the beginning, confrontations over posting were inevitable, and one of the earliest occurred at the head of an Esopus Creek tributary called Bushnellsville Creek. An item in a local newspaper titled "Trout War" described how a party of "gentlemen" were assaulted, and warrants were issued to those who did the assaulting. A trial was held, and the "gentlemen" who were assaulted came out victorious; "the other party had to pay $20 for broken fish poles, blue eyes, skinned noses, and report says one chap swallowed his false teeth, but as he isn't dead yet or even suffering any inconveniences except for the absence of his grinders, the yarn is not credited."[8]

The Balsam Lake Club, established in 1883, went on to acquire 6 miles of the upper Beaverkill and more than 3,000 acres of wild forest by 1894. Club members enjoyed fishing the Beaverkill, but when stream flows were not conducive to good fishing, or a member simply wished to fish still waters, they cast their lines into Balsam Lake. The lake's bountiful supply of trout was replenished by a small stream that flowed into the north end. This stream offered ideal spawning habitat, and for generations, every fall, great numbers of brook trout entered the riffles to reproduce.

Balsam Lake's reputation was that its trout were always hungry, and even in the days of year-round fishing, they remained abundant no matter how many were removed. For years the trout maintained a size length of between 6 and 8 inches. One angler who began fishing the lake in 1845 discovered, nearly forty years later, that there was no "appreciable diminution in number and size of the trout in it. They are uniform in size, from three to five ounces."[9]

The same year the Balsam Lake Club was founded, Charles F. Orvis and A. Nelson Cheney published a collection of articles written by noted fly fishermen of the 1870s; the book was titled *Fishing with the Fly*. Club member George Van Siclen contributed an essay about a day on Balsam Lake, titled

"A Perfect Day." He reminds us that fishing clubs offered solitude, far from the clamor of the city, and with the worries of business but a distant memory. Van Siclen relates a scene worth repeating:

> Soon seated in my boat, I paddle to the shade of a tall, dark hemlock and rest there, lulled by the intense quiet. Ever and anon as I dreamily cast my ethereal fly, a thrill of pleasure electrifies me, as it is seized by a vigorous trout.
>   I have long classed trout with flowers and birds, and bright sunsets, and charming scenery, and beautiful women, as given for the rational enjoyment and delight of thoughtful men of aesthetic tastes.[10]

Fishing clubs were primarily formed because trout were becoming scarce, and those fishermen who had a desire to restore the sport to its former level saw no other method than creating fishing preserves. Clubs spread from the Willowemoc and Beaverkill to the beautiful Rondout Creek.

Posting came to the Rondout when the Peekamoose Fishing Club was formed in 1879. Within a few years, club fishermen would go on to control all of the best trout fishing, and for nearly a half century, the Rondout Creek remained private and posted, from its source downstream to where the stream is joined by Chestnut Creek.

The artist Jervis McEntee fished the Catskills for more than thirty years, and he witnessed many changes. In his diary entry dated July 21, 1884, he writes that fishing clubs were appearing on his beloved Rondout:

> We drove on down the valley which has changed but little since I was there last in 1876 and reached David Smiths almost 3 o'clock 8 miles from Wards cabin and two miles below the East Branch at Sundown. Found it a very comfortable place on my visits there. A club had leased the stream and they made this their headquarters. Mr. Smith was away from home superintending the building of a club house at Balsam Lake. We had dinner and spent the afternoon fishing, catching enough for dinner. Saturday we drove up to Sundown and sent the horse and wagon back by a man and fished the East Branch a short distance and the main stream back to Smiths catching 25 each mostly small ones.[11]

In August of the following year, McEntee fished the famed Peekamoose Gorge and recorded his experience in his diary. He wrote that a recent freshet had damaged Hill's Mill so badly that it was unable to operate. McEntee and a friend boarded at Hill's, and because the mill was down, he and the sawyer, George Hornbeck, decided to fish together. In the morning, the three men walked up the wood road to where Picket Brook entered the Rondout, then fished downstream, taking about fifty mostly small trout. What they did not eat for supper were cleaned and wrapped in newspapers, and packed in ice for the trip home.

The Peekamoose Fishing Club purchased 80 acres along the headwaters, and several leases from streamside landowners that included "All the right or privilege to fish or angle for brook trout in the manner and at times prescribed by law in and along the Rondout Creek."[12] The club's waters included approximately 6 miles of the stream, and its membership was never more than seven. Two of the club's most avid fishermen were John Quincy Adams Ward, the famous sculptor, and Anthony Weston Dimock, a well-known financier.

JOHN QUINCY ADAMS WARD

John Quincy Adams Ward (1830–1910) was born on the family farm in Urbana, Ohio. As a youngster, he enjoyed fishing, hunting, and creating clay models of men on horseback and of farm animals. As a teenager, he visited a sister who lived in Brooklyn, New York, and it was there that he began his life's work: At the age of nineteen, he became an apprentice of the eminent sculptor and fly fisherman Henry Kirke Brown.

John Quincy Adams Ward. *Harper's New Monthly Magazine*, June 1878.

Ward was an excellent student and assistant, and he and Brown quickly became close friends. Ward assisted Brown with his equestrian statue of George Washington, perhaps his finest work, and Brown showed his admiration for Ward by demanding that Ward's name be added to the base of the statue. Ward worked for Brown for seven years and eventually opened his own studio in New York in 1861.

During his years with Brown, he undoubtedly also learned about fly fishing, as Brown was an ardent fly fisher, and he influenced Ward in this area as well. During the 1850s, the two men often fished together in the Adirondacks, as well as on the trout streams of Sullivan County, including the Beaverkill, where they stayed at the Darbee House (or Boscobel, as it was also known).

Even after Ward opened his own studio, he and Brown remained close friends and made salmon-fishing trips together, along with landscape artist Sanford Gifford. It may even have been Brown who introduced Ward to the upper Rondout, as Brown was known to have stayed at David B. Smith's during the trout season in 1870 and 1872.

After opening his studio, Ward became one of this country's greatest sculptors and a leader in his field; for half a century he was known as the dean of American sculptors. "His style is imitative of no foreign school, but smacks of the man, of his American ideals, and American surroundings."[13] Naturalism was the dominant feature of Ward's work, and two of his earliest and best-known sculptures are titled *The Freedman* (1865) and *Indian Hunter* (1868), the latter a work that marked the turning point in Ward's career.

The Freedman is a bronze statue of a slave, seated, looking at the shackles from which he had been freed. *The Indian Hunter,* conceived in 1857, was the first work by an American to be placed in New York's Central Park. This sculpture depicts an Indian with a bow holding back a dog. Ward had visited the Dakotas and had studied American Indians in their natural surroundings, sketching and carefully detailing his subjects.

Ward made a bronze figure of Shakespeare (1872) for Central Park, as well as a bronze figure of a Civil War soldier for the 7th Regiment Memorial and a statue titled *The Pilgrim*. His work is evident all over New York City. There is a statue of William E. Dodge in Bryant Park and the Alexander Lyman Halley Monument in Washington Square Park. He also crafted the sculptural decoration for the pediment of the New York Stock Exchange.

In addition, Ward created the statue of George Washington on the steps of the Treasury Building on Wall Street (1883) and the famous Henry Ward Beecher monument (1891) that was erected in front of Borough Hall in Brooklyn. Upon the death of the famous clergyman in 1887, Ward was immediately summoned to make a death mask to be used in the preparation of the Beecher statue.

Ward's work included portrait busts, in bronze and marble, of many prominent individuals and equestrian statues of famous American generals. He knew and loved horses, and his equestrian statues were considered his best work. In the world of art, "Quincy" Ward was a prominent figure. He was one of the founders of the Metropolitan Museum of Art, where he served on the board of directors from 1870 until 1901.

Ward loved the Catskills and spent much of his time trout fishing, hiking, hunting, and horseback riding. He enjoyed working outdoors, making improvements to the landscape around Peekamoose, yet was sensitive to the wildness of the countryside.

The Indian Hunter. *Scribner's Magazine*, October 1902.

ANTHONY WESTON DIMOCK

Anthony Weston Dimock (1842–1918)—financier, author, sportsman, and outdoor photographer—was born in Yarmouth, Nova Scotia. Educated at Phillips Academy in Andover, Massachusetts, and Columbian University (now George Washington University), A. W. Dimock, as he was more commonly known, enjoyed a remarkable career on Wall Street. He became a member of the New York Stock Exchange at the age of twenty-one and dominated the gold market of America at the age of twenty-three.

By the time he was thirty, Dimock controlled the Bankers and Merchants Telegraph Company and was president of the Atlantic Mail and other steamship lines. At first he was a member of Marquand & Dimock, bankers and brokers, and later formed his own business, A. W. Dimock & Co. He became a millionaire and was known as the Napoleon of Wall Street.[14]

In the 1870s, while on a fishing trip to the Catskills, he discovered the Peekamoose area of the upper Rondout Creek, started buying land to preserve and protect it, and invited a few friends to join him in this endeavor. His purchase of land around his beloved Rondout included the famous Blue Hole and Dutchman's Hole.

A. W. Dimock. *Wall Street and the Wilds*, 1915.

Dimock was well known for his diverse occupations and for the genius he exhibited in them. However, it was his secret ambition, even at the height of his career, to live close to nature, in the wilds; to give up city life and hunt and fish and enjoy the outdoors. He viewed his holdings as a retreat: "From the first I spent all the time I could spare at the cabin and when burdens seemed greater than I could bear and there was no sleep for me in the city I had only to start for the woods and as the nearest station to the cabin was reached, and but ten miles of mountain road, ravine, and valley remained to be traveled my troubles fell away."[15]

At the height of his career, he left New York City to seek adventure in the West. He visited frontier army posts, hunted buffalo with Indians, and took pictures with a crude box camera. His pictures of elk and grizzly bears were said to be the first taken of big game in their natural environment. Dimock was among the first to carry a camera in the field, and he became a skilled outdoor photographer. He may also have been the first to publicly advocate substituting a camera for a gun; he did this as early as 1887.

Late in life he began writing for magazines such as *Scribner's, Harper's Weekly, Country Life,* and *Outing,* and he wrote several popular adventure books for boys. He is best known for writing sporting books, particularly those involving saltwater fishing. In addition to the Catskills, Dimock also spent time in Florida and became a pioneer saltwater fly fisherman; in 1908, *Outing* published his *Florida Enchantments,* a book he wrote with photographs taken by his son Julian.

He was one of the first to fish for tarpon, and in 1911 *Outing* published a book detailing his experiences titled *The Book of the Tarpon.* Considered a classic, this work was reprinted in 1912, 1915, 1926, 1990, and even in 2004. His last book was written at his home along the Rondout and is titled *Wall Street and the Wilds.* It is autobiographical and includes tales of his adventures in the stock market, as well as in the West. The final chapter is titled "The Happy Valley," a term he used to describe the upper Rondout and the Peekamoose area:

> The murmur of the stream is in my ear as I write, the towering cliff on its farther side hold my eyes, while at this instant a humming bird hovers among the flowering vines outside the opened window. Now my gaze wanders westward across the lawn, above the green of the nearby forest, to the bluish summit of the mountain beyond, and I realize why our friends exclaim with one voice: "No wonder you call it 'the Happy Valley!'"

Few of them know that we never so christened it, for it named itself. The words rose to the lips of so many that we came to feel that the name belonged, and so it stayed. The Spirit of the Valley gives to those who seek it the serenity of sages and the hearts of little children.[16]

A. W. Dimock knew many of the famous people of his day. He was friends with Henry Ward Beecher and his sister Harriet Beecher Stowe; he salmon fished with Joe Jefferson, the famous actor; and he was visited at Peekamoose by conservationist Gifford Pinchot and John Burroughs. When Burroughs visited Dimock, the sage of the Catskills told him he had not seen the Blue Hole in forty years, but he could go through the woods and straight to the famous pool, and he did, calling it "the loveliest spot in the Catskills."[17]

Dimock was a diverse fly fisherman. When in Florida, he sought to capture fish that ranged in the 50- to 150-pound class, and yet when he was on his home waters in the Catskills, he delighted in catching brook trout that rarely reached lengths of 10 inches or weighed more than a few ounces.

A year after he published *The Book of the Tarpon,* he spent a week fishing the Rondout with noted fly fisher Emlyn Gill, who wrote the first American book on dry-fly fishing, titled *Practical Dry-Fly Fishing* (1912). Gill taught Dimock how to use the floating fly, and the two men experimented with wet and dry flies, discovering that Rondout trout preferred the Whirling Dun to any other pattern. Emlyn Gill enjoyed the trip so much that he wrote an article titled "Dry-Fly Fishing with A. W. Dimock," which was published in *Field and Stream* in February 1913.

When the Peekamoose Fishing Club was formed, a log clubhouse was constructed with accommodations to sleep up to twenty. The spacious fireplace had a fieldstone hearth with a stone lintel over it and was inscribed THE CANTY HEARTH WHERE CRONIES MEET 1880.

Quincy Ward and A. W. Dimock spent their summers at the clubhouse and became close friends. The two men hiked the surrounding mountains and traveled up and down the Rondout with rods, broiling their brook trout over a wood fire on the rocky ledges of the beautiful mountain stream. Ward even carved a likeness of Dimock on an oaken stump next to the clubhouse as a reminder of their friendship.

For the first ten years, club members enjoyed their preserve and the camaraderie, peacefulness, and friendly relations that fishing clubs seem to foster. However, during the 1890s, the Peekamoose Fishing Club became infamous for a dispute between Ward and Dimock that took on epic proportions. For years, the two famous men made headlines in newspapers throughout the Catskill region and beyond. The *New York Times* and sporting journals and magazines reported on "The Peekamoose Row," "Dimock-Ward Feud," and "The Fishers Fall Out."

In the fall of 1891, the *Kingston Weekly Freeman* reported that the trouble began when Josiah W. Wentworth and his wife Cecile, a devout Catholic, built a chapel on the lands of the Peekamoose Fishing Club over a spring with alleged healing powers that flowed into the Rondout Creek.

Wentworth, a wealthy New Yorker, had acquired a large tract of land adjoining the club and constructed a rustic cabin called the Wigwam near the clubhouse in 1884. Though not a member, he was allowed to use club grounds, as he and Quincy Ward had developed a friendship.

Cecile Wentworth was a famous portraitist who was better known for her art in France than in America. She exhibited her paintings at the Paris Salon for many years, and her best-known work is a portrait of Pope Leo XII, which is in the Vatican Museum in Rome. Other noted paintings include portraits of Theodore Roosevelt, William Howard Taft, and General John J. Pershing, which is in the Versailles Museum. Her works can be found in the Metropolitan Museum of Art in New York City, the Corcoran Gallery in Washington, and other prominent museums.

Club members who were not Catholic disapproved of the construction of the chapel; and Ward, in a show of support for the Wentworths, decided to go to court to dissolve the Peekamoose Fishing Club. At the time, it was revealed that living club members included "James R. English of New Jersey, president; Louis E. Howard of Plainfield, N. J., vice-president; E. M. White, treasurer and secretary; John R. Hageman, Frank E. Simpson, A. W. Dimock and J. Q. A. Ward. Hageman is the president of the Metropolitan Life Insurance Company, and Simpson is a Boston millionaire."[18]

Three years later, the dispute was still in the headlines: "On a petition stating that he and Mr. Dimock were the only members of the club and that it is insolvent, Mr. Ward got an order last May for the appointment of a referee to determine whether the club should not be dissolved. Mr. Dimock moved before Justice Barrett recently to set the order aside, saying that there were seven members of the club and that it was in excellent financial condition."[19]

Ward obtained a court order to keep Dimock off club grounds, but this was later overturned. A couple of months later, the *New York Times* reported that the Peekamoose Fishing Club falling out "reached a very sensational climax a few days ago, when Mr. Ward and an officer, armed with a warrant of dispossession, forced Mr. Dimock and his family to vacate the premises."[20]

Even the popular sporting journal *Forest and Stream* reported on the matter on its editorial page:

> Personal quarrels, applications for a receivership, mandamuses, injunctions, evictions and trials for contempt of court make up the hopelessly tangled snarl of Peekamoose litigation. Where the merits of the case may lie is impossible for an outsider to determine; it is enough to know and to regret that a club of fishermen should have fallen into such unhappy ways. When lawsuits take the place of trout fishing, it is high time to reel up and separate and go each his own way.[21]

The battle between members of the Peekamoose Fishing Club continued, much to the delight of many Catskill natives and at least one editor of a Kingston newspaper. On September 12, 1896, the *Kingston Weekly Leader* ran a front-page story about the many disputes between club owners and the fishing public. The article stated that the *Leader* had chronicled for years the conflicts between fishermen who believed mountain streams should be free for all to fish and stream watchers hired by clubs. These confrontations at times included guns and clubs, which, in turn, resulted in arrests and litigation. "It is therefore somewhat refreshing to publish a falling out between club members, especially when they resort to guns and threaten to stock a private cemetery in the mountains. This has come to pass between members of the famous Peekamoose Fishing Club."

In the spring of 1897, several newspapers reported that Ward had won his legal fight with the other members of the fishing club and that the United States Circuit Court ordered the club to sell the 80 acres and fishing privileges owned by the Peekamoose Fishing Club. In the beginning of May, the club property was sold at auction. Ward and Dimock had representatives, and the bidding was quite spirited; in the end, Frank E. Simpson acquired the property, and it was stated that Simpson represented A. W. Dimock.

Two weeks later, a fire of suspicious origin totally destroyed the clubhouse and some small cottages on the grounds. The clubhouse had a studio and private apartments for members where photographic equipment, sporting trophies, and fishing and hunting gear were stored. Everything was lost.

It was not until the summer of 1899, nearly ten years later, that the newspapers wrote the final chapter on the celebrated Peekamoose Fishing Club case. The *Kingston Weekly Freeman* on August 17 reported that J. Q. A. Ward, the famous sculptor, had won; and that a deed had been filed in the Ulster County Clerk's Office transferring title to the land owned by the fishing club to Ward. It was stated that Simpson and Dimock had a falling out, and Simpson "has sold the place to Ward for $1." Simpson asserted that Dimock had promised to reorganize the club and bring in many new members. The *Freeman* closed by stating, "The club was considered to be hoodooed, and all sorts of disasters, estrangements, divorces and fistic encounters were attributed to the curse resting upon the place."[22]

At about the same time the Peekamoose Fishing Club was being formed, a second club began acquiring fishing leases from streamside landowners near the hamlet of Sundown and downstream to Chestnut Creek, a distance of 5 miles. In the summer of 1880, two members of the Sundown Fishing Club, Charles H. Post and George H. Hope, both of New York City, acquired a twenty-year lease on a stretch of the Rondout for the "exclusive rights of fishing and preserving and propagating trout."[23] This lease was later transferred into the name of the Sundown Fishing Club.

Over the next few years, the club purchased several more twenty-year leases that not only allowed fishing and the right to travel upstream and down along 2-foot and 10-foot easements, but included the "privilege also to build a breakwater and dam or dams for the purpose of making a pond or ponds for trout."[24] At this time, the concept of habitat or stream improvement was in its infancy and was not widely known or practiced. The Sundown Fishing Club was one of the first to practice stream improvement with in-stream structures and incorporate habitat improvements into their methods of improving the fishing.

In the 1890s, the club continued to obtain new leases and, at the same time, extended previous ones an additional twenty years. The Sundown Fishing Club controlled the water from Chestnut Creek near Eureka upstream into Ulster County above Sundown. When its earlier leases were extended, a clause was inserted that included the right to construct dams on tributaries for the purpose of making artificial spawning beds or to increase existing spawning opportunities for trout. The agreement stipulated that the dams could not be constructed as to raise the water above the adjoining banks, or to flood or injure the adjoining land. The club had the right to enter upon the land for the purpose of constructing, repairing, or maintaining such "dams or breakwaters & the pools connected thereby at all reasonable times and in such manner as not to injure the adjacent land or the crops thereon."[25]

In 1893, the Sundown Club acquired a 27-acre parcel of land that had formerly been a portion of the farm of David B. Smith. The land was downstream of Sundown and included a portion of the Rondout Creek and a trout pond. Earlier members stayed at those boardinghouses that took in fishing tourists, but now, after the construction of an attractive clubhouse, members dined and stayed at their own place.

The Sundown Fishing Club was limited to twenty members and included several avid trout fishers who were well known in the fly-fishing circles of their day. Acmon P. Van Gieson was the club president for many years; he was a veteran Catskill fly fisher who resided in Poughkeepsie, where he was the pastor of the First Reformed Church.

His knowledge of the region was vast enough that he was contacted to be a contributing correspondent to Mary Orvis Marbury's *Favorite Flies and Their Histories* (1892), a popular and important work about trout flies in America. Fly fishers around the country were asked to give their opinions on the best flies to use in their particular area. Van Gieson's favorite flies for fishing the Catskills were the Brown Hen, Coachman, and Yellow Professor. "I have found that when a cast made of these three will not take, nothing will take."[26]

Another noted member was James Spencer Van Cleef, expert fly fisher and conservationist. As a trout-stream preservationist, Van Cleef was a prominent figure in the fishing community.

In 1908, the club sold its 27-acre parcel to Frank L. Moore of Ellenville. Moore, a club member, continued to lease the fishing rights to Sundown Fishing Club until 1922, when it is believed the club disbanded.

POSTING AND OTHER RESTRICTIONS

The idea of posting streams was becoming more popular as year after year, ever-increasing numbers of fishermen continued to remove more and more trout from Catskill streams. They did so without restrictions, as there were few laws and no enforcement or protection for the fisheries. The only law

"A Sad Sight" (No Fishing Allowed). Fisheries, Game and Forest Commission Annual Report, 1898.

practiced was the "law of common decency," which was adhered to by those who considered themselves sportsmen: anglers who knew it was unwise to keep fingerlings and who kept, or killed, only a reasonable number of trout.

In New York State, fish and game laws are based on the premise that ownership of all fish and wildlife is vested in the state. This principle has been handed down from the common law of England, and although a statewide law restricting the use of seines was adopted as early as 1813, most laws were enacted to meet the specific needs of a particular locality. Many of these early fish and game laws were enacted by county government, through the board of supervisors; enforcement of them was the duty of all sheriffs, constables, and other police officers.

An example of this type of legislation occurred in 1849, when the counties of Sullivan and Delaware passed an amendment to the state law titled "An Act for the Preservation of Deer, Birds and Fish and the destruction of certain wild beasts." The amendments included two laws that affected fishing; one prohibited the use of the berry *Coculus indicus* or any other poisonous substance from being used to take or destroy fish, and the other prohibited the taking of trout between the first day of August and the first day of November. Under this act, any individual, or the "overseer of the poor," could sue the offender and recover all penalties that were imposed; the overseer of the poor had to use the money for the poor in the town where the crime had been committed.

Several years later, in 1857, the state legislature passed a bill relative to trout fishing that prohibited the taking of trout with anything other than a hook and line. A feature of this law, and of fish and game law in general, was that: "All penalties imposed by the act may be sued for and recovered, with the costs of such suit, before any Justice of the Peace in this State, by or in the name of any person making complaint thereof, one half of the fine imposed going to the complainant."

Known as the moiety system, it allowed any person to bring suit and recover one-half the fine. Though the system continued for many years, it was generally disliked by law enforcement officials.

The management of the state's fish and wildlife resources began with the formation of the Board of Commissioners of Fisheries in 1868. The legislation that established the commission was lobbied for by private initiative, mainly the New York Association for the Protection of Game, which later became the Sportsmen's Club of New York. The association was formed in 1844 and was said to be the first protective game organization in America.

In 1868, the state legislature passed a law prohibiting fishing on Sunday, and they were serious about the law's enforcement. A fine of $25 was to be imposed, or imprisonment in the county jail of the county where the offense was committed of not less than ten days for each offense.

The following year, the legislature passed an act to amend and consolidate several laws aimed to protect moose, deer, birds, and fish; and two years later, in 1871, changes were made in the law giving county boards of supervisors more authority to elect enforcement officers and impose regulations that were not included in the act, except in the case of deer, which the state continued to control. The board of supervisors provided for the election of game constables, who were nominated at town meetings, and these men had the same powers as civil constables.

The 1870s were a desperate period for Catskill trout fishing. Brook trout populations were declining, and although state and county levels of government continued to enact laws, there was little, or no, enforcement. Legislation was even proposed—and passed in the assembly—of an act that would have prohibited trout fishing in any waters of Delaware and Ulster counties and the town of Halcott in Greene County for two years. The law failed in the senate.

Laws restricting the number of trout that could be kept did not exist, and as trout populations diminished, so did the sizes of the fish found in the streams. Anglers kept trout of fingerling size, 3 or 4 inches, and many fishermen were outraged at this practice. The first attempt to prohibit the keeping of trout fingerlings, or young-of-the-year trout, appeared in 1876 when a law instituting a 5-inch size limit was passed by the Ulster County legislature. Many believed it was too little, too late.

The bill was introduced by James Murdock, supervisor of the town of Hardenbergh, who also owned and operated the famous fishing resort on the upper Beaverkill. Murdock certainly had firsthand knowledge of what was happening to the fisheries, and the legislation he proposed became known as the "Murdock trout bill."

Some people, at the time, saw the law as humorous and poked fun at it:

It certainly will be an amusing site to gaze at a squad of fishermen standing in the middle of a creek trying to measure such a slippery thing as a brook trout. Oh! Won't there be a deal of swearing, and won't Murdock be assigned to a hot place very often during the season? The law is no doubt a good one, and we suppose the best way to keep from infringing on it, is to know precisely how long a bait a 5 inch trout can take, and then, use the bait a little bit larger. A label might be attached to the hook—"No trout wanted that measured less than 5 inches."[27]

Others, the *Windham Journal* included, saw the need for increased legislation. In an article titled "Too Much Fishing," the newspaper reported:

A gentleman from the Town of Olive says hundreds of persons are on the streams fishing. That there must be a fisherman for nearly every pound of trout in that region. The whole country from the town of Olive towards the north and northwest is overrun with men and boys with trout poles on their shoulders, and not one in ten of them really catches a good big mess of fish. If some restricting law is not passed the streams will be virtually fished clean in a year or two. The trout now are very small.[28]

Further legislation was introduced to curtail trout fishing in the Catskills when the Greene County Board of Supervisors adopted an act in 1878 that stated "no person can catch or fish for 'speckled brook trout' or 'speckled river trout' except during the months of July and August, for a period of two years." Some hotel and resort owners took exception to the law, and in a letter to the *Catskill Recorder,* claimed that the law was unjust and would drive "all sporting men from N. Y., Phil., Boston and other places from our county."

Greene County streams did not receive the same amount of rainfall that other portions of the Catskills did, and some merchants wondered how many sportsmen from New York and other places would come to the mountain towns and spend their time and money after May and June, because those were the only months in the whole year that were good for trout fishing in that part of the Catskills.

Increasing concern over diminishing trout populations did bring about more restrictive laws, but enforcement of these laws, for the most part, continued to be nonexistent. Reports of trout being taken illegally with nets, spears, poisons, and explosives were common and were the cause of public outrage. There were few game constables appointed by counties; and sheriffs and other law enforcement officers were generally involved with what they considered more serious crime, and as a rule would not prosecute their friends and neighbors over fish and game violations.

There were game constables in those towns that chose to elect them; however, it was believed that "in most cases these officers, if not poachers themselves, were in the interest of poachers; the office was sought principally by those who wished to secure immunity for their own offending."[29] Laws protecting fish and wildlife were thought of as innovations of "natural rights," and until the rapid disappearance of fish and game awakened conservation-minded people, the laws were violated without penalty or punishment.

Anglers who were concerned over the fisheries were not deterred by the various laws in the different counties, but they were bothered by the lack of law enforcement. Most laws pertaining to fishing were enforced by clubs, societies, and individuals who took action because of public spirit or because the violation affected their personal interest or property.

10

The 1880s

"FIRESIDE FISHING"; "WHIPPERS OF THE CREEKS"; and "WAR ON THE NEVERSINK"

With the promise of trout streams being restocked and the formation of sportsmen's associations to enforce the laws protecting them, the outlook for the 1880s was one of optimism. It was claimed that Catskill streams would once again teem with speckled beauties, and although there were anglers who believed that there were still significant numbers of trout, most everyone agreed that the average size of the native species was greatly reduced from what it had been in the past.

The popularity of trout fishing in the 1880s is exemplified by the appearance of a new weekly journal devoted entirely to the world of fishing. Published in New York, the *American Angler* made its debut in the fall of 1881. Edited by William C. Harris, the newspaper was devoted to "fishing—brook, river, lake and sea—fishculture" and was immediately successful.

The 1880s were the first decade that the wild brook trout populations of the Catskills came under the influence of domestic brook trout. At this time, the science of fish culture was not sophisticated enough to determine what effect these introductions would have on the future of native stocks of fish, and trying to determine the size of the native brook trout before the introduction of domestic trout is not easy. From all accounts, the number of brook trout inhabiting the streams in our forefather's day was far greater than at present; and, as has been revealed, both the number and size of trout were steadily reduced.

The practice of "fishing for count" was still popular with some fishermen, and bragging about the number of trout caught was a habit that newspapers often criticized. The *Hancock Herald* was known to frown upon the custom, finding it unacceptable: "one of the fine 'messes' recently taken, over which the captor bragged, consisted of 150 trout—weight five pounds, an average of not much over half an ounce."[1]

But not everyone who fished the Catskills at this time was trying to outdo his brother angler or fish for count. Dr. Lyman Abbott, who succeeded the famous Henry Ward Beecher at Plymouth Congregational Church in Brooklyn, wrote of his experiences while on a fishing trip to the region. The noted clergyman traveled up the Esopus to Big Indian, and then over the mountain to the West Branch of the Neversink, and writing from High Falls Brook, he informed readers of the *Christian Union*:

THE
AMERICAN ANGLER.

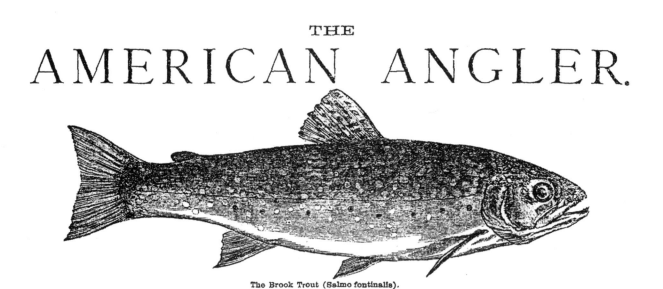

The Brook Trout (Salmo fontinalis).

DEVOTED TO FISHING—BROOK, RIVER, LAKE AND SEA—FISH CULTURE.

HREE DOLLARS A YEAR. }
NGLE COPIES TEN CENTS. }   NEW YORK, WEDNESDAY, DECEMBER 21, 1881.   { VOLUME I.
{ NUMBER 8;

On this particular trip we have had very good luck; nothing like the luck, it is true, that men have had in the past and are going to have in the future, but pretty good luck and a very good time. We have ridden fifteen miles on an extemporized buckboard; we have tramped up one stream to near its source, (Big Indian) and down another stream from near its source; (West Branch) we have seen some glorious scenery; we have had some glorious appetites, and at Smith's, on the Big Indian, and at William Satterlee's, on the Neversink, a first-rate opportunity to satisfy them; we have slept the sleep of the just and tired, and have eaten with a good conscience and a good digestion; each one of the party has *almost* caught a pound trout; and besides that, we really have caught all the trout we wanted to eat for breakfast . . .

Dr. Abbott also commented on why he fished, and his mode of travel:

Trout-fishing is simply an excuse for living for a week or a month in the woods; whether you bring home any trout or not is a secondary matter. You turn your back on civilization and conventionalism; you put on old clothes and are not anxious about the fit; you ride on an extemporized buckboard, made by long spring-boards extending from a front to a rear pair of wheels, and take more exercise in such a ride over a mountain road than gymnasium practice in a city would give you in a week.[2]

A buckboard along the West Branch of the Neversink.
The Woman Flyfishers Club, Autumn 1972.

For more than a half century, the Catskills had been famous for the plentiful number and size of its native brook trout. But during the 1880s, catches were reduced, and the sizes of the trout taken were often less than 4 inches, even when a 6-inch size limit was the law!

"Ben Bent," a fishing companion of Fitz-James Fitch, wrote an article for the *American Angler* lamenting the changes taking place in the Catskills. He recalled when the streams were filled with "the finest variety of home-bred mountain brook trout," and every one of them was a "natural trout stream." He blamed the "rural fish-hog" for the decline of the fisheries, and he pointed out the bitterness that existed between locals and "Yorkers": "The short-sighted, ignorant and combative countryman, with his silly antagonism against all things of the city citified, has conscientiously fostered the work of depletion and heroically contested all efforts at replenishing."[3]

The term *fireside fishing* or *stove fishing,* as well as *the reminiscent angler* appeared in print, as veteran trout fishers now sat around general stores, country inns, and taverns and complained about the fishing and the small sizes of the trout now found in the streams. Men who wistfully recalled the "good old days" reminisced, with "pipe and bowl," and remembered the beloved waters of their youth and the wonderful catches that were no longer possible. This would be the first generation of trout fishermen that, more than any other, could recall the "piscatorial glory" of the past.

Fireside fishing. *Sport with Gun and Rod in American Woods and Waters*, 1883.

Those "whippers of the creeks" who had not witnessed what the fishing had been like saw these tales of the past "as the wild and exaggerated inventions of antiquated anglers, who sought to hide their ignorance of advanced piscatorial skill and science by means of a prolific and elastic imagination."[4]

The level of enthusiasm for trout fishing during this decade, even when compared with modern times, is astonishing. It is understandable that every generation of trout fishers believes that *theirs* has more anglers and is more enthusiastic about the sport than those previous. But a review of a few newspaper items gleaned from library archives gives insight to the fervor that trout fishermen of an earlier era held for the sport.

On May 6, 1886, the editor of the *Hancock Herald* claimed that when the season opened, half the men in Hancock were on the trout streams! And although this no doubt was an exaggeration, the number of trout fishermen he encountered along Read Creek, a small tributary of the East Branch of the Delaware, was more accurate. The editor had a successful day and "took about thirty trout," but, he wrote, "there were not less than 20 fishermen on that creek during the day, some starting in before daylight in the morning."

The editor of the *Catskill Recorder* reminded readers that the open season for trout fishing was May 1. And Simon B. Champion, editor of the *Stamford Mirror,* replied: "No use of touching up a fisherman's memory, Brother Hall. They will be there, body and breeches, before May 1st. Fifteen fishermen to one trout is about the way it will average up." J. B. Hall, editor of the *Recorder,* responded: "We should say so! Why, hereabouts last spring the streams were lined with fishermen at 12 A.M. on May 1, and they actually fished by lantern-light, so eager were they to be in at the opening of the season."[5]

Three days after the trout season opened, Hall reported on a party of four men who traveled to the Shingle Kill, a tributary of Catskill Creek:

They arrived at sunrise, and found the stream literally lined with men and boys even at that early hour—Mr. Foote counted 8 men on the bank of the stream within a distance of 200 feet. Some of the "early birds" had lanterns with them. Notwithstanding that the streams were high and the fishermen were so numerous that they almost locked elbows, the Catskill party caught 60 or more nice trout.[6]

Trout fishermen continued to exploit the fishery by removing far more than was reasonable, and the large numbers of trout taken in a single day was incomprehensible. A report in the *Catskill Recorder* dated June 28, 1889, told of two men from Sullivan County who, in one day's fishing, caught 470 trout with a total weight of about 40 pounds. The newspaper made disparaging remarks about the "wholesale slaughter" and quoted the *New York Times* as stating:

> Is it any wonder that yearling fry are now all that can be caught in most of the streams, or that gentlemen anglers combine together and buy or lease the fishing privileges of streams. Where trout of decent size were once to be taken in fair numbers now only fry of 1½ oz. each can be found. Thanks be to our "trout hog" for the result. And the biggest hogs and more ruthless trout-catchers are the fellows who contribute nothing toward meeting the annual expense of stocking streams.[7]

****

The Ulster & Delaware Railroad traveled through the Esopus Valley and was so close to the stream that passengers could look out the car windows and view most of the Esopus all the way up to Big Indian. Criticism arose that the Esopus was too accessible and lacked the charm and quiet seclusion of other mountain streams. There were many farmhouses along the stream, and with the railroad paralleling one side and a major roadway along the other, the Esopus did lack the solitude of other Catskill trout streams.

In the past, many anglers seeking a more peaceful, or more primitive, fishing experience traveled up the Esopus Valley and sought out the headwaters of the Neversink, along the East and West Branches, an area that remained heavily forested with few dwellings. Because of the difficulty of travel and limited accommodations, fishermen generally camped along these streams for days or even weeks at a time. But the 1880s brought easier access to the East and West Branches; instead of traveling up Big Indian Hollow and over the mountains, fishermen now had easier access by traveling the New York & Ontario & Western Railroad,* which ran through Liberty, approximately 20 miles westerly of Claryville.

It was recognized that fishing tourists to the Neversink generally took the train from New York to Fallsburg or Liberty and that they were leaving considerable money in Sullivan County on their visits to these fishing grounds. This in turn caused the *Liberty Register* to warn farmers that they should stop fishing out of season and quit using nets and set lines.

Trout fishers had visited the West Branch of the Neversink for decades, and those who found camp life too uncomfortable stayed at Satterlee's. William Satterlee had good water and supplemented the income from his sawmill by taking in boarders. But with fishing clubs now established along the Beaverkill, Willowemoc, and Rondout, it was inevitable that he would be approached by fishermen wishing to preserve the upper Neversink.

These efforts to save the trout fishing began when the Neversink Club, which was formed in 1883, leased and posted all of the water from Satterlee's sawmill downstream to LeRoy's sawmill

---

*The Ontario & Western replaced the pioneer New York Oswego Midland Railroad.

near Flat Brook. This stretch of the West Branch was extremely popular with trout fishers; however, the club was intent on preserving the fishing and obtained leases from various streamside owners. The Neversink Club immediately regulated its members' trout fishing, setting a limit of twenty-five trout per day and imposing a size limit of 7 inches.

Membership in the club varied from three to five fishermen, with the most prominent members being Alfred Roe, president; Wakeman Holberton, secretary-treasurer; and Clarence M. Roof.

ALFRED ROE

Born in Ireland, Alfred Roe (1827–1898) immigrated to New York City and became a prominent New York attorney and sportsman. He was known as a staunch abolitionist before the Civil War, and he was a founder of the Union League Club, which had its origin in the abolition of slavery. Roe and other members of the Union League Club organized the first black regiment to join the Union Army and paid their expenses throughout the war.

"The Pleasures of Fly Fishing." *Outing Magazine*, June 1889.

WAKEMAN HOLBERTON

Wakeman Holberton (1839–1898)— sportsman, artist, author, and a native New Yorker—was perhaps the Neversink Club's most famous member. Throughout his adult life, Holberton was an avid fly tier and fly fisher, learning these skills as early as 1860 at the age of twenty-one. His passion for the sport was interrupted a year later when he enlisted in the Union Army as a second lieutenant and fought with the 72nd New York Volunteer Infantry in the Civil War.

After the war, he became involved with the fishing tackle business and owned and operated the Sportsmen's Emporium on Nassau Street in Manhattan. In addition to rods, reels, and other fishing paraphernalia, Holberton was also a representative for the celebrated McBride flies tied by John McBride and his daughter, Sara J., of Mumford, New York. Holberton had been an employee, at one time, of Abbey & Imbrie, a popular fishing tackle supplier located on Vesey Street; and, being a knowledgeable fly fisher, he was known to attract "the patronage of many of the very best anglers in the country."[8]

Holberton also pursued a painting career, primarily with fishing and hunting scenes as subjects. He lived in the woods along the shores of lakes and the banks of streams for weeks at a time, and traveled and fished many of the famous waters throughout the country. He became a fly-fishing expert on the Catskills, the Adirondacks, and the Yellowstone region of the West. And though he was primarily a trout fisherman, he was also an early proponent of catching bass on flies, which he first tried as early as 1862 and wrote about in *Forest and Stream.*

In his day, Holberton was among the best of American fly casters, and he handled a fly rod and artist's brush with equal skill. He competed at a Grand Anglers fly-casting tournament at Coney Island in 1881, and judges reported that he was "perfect in style and accuracy." As an artist, his paintings—*Speckled Trout, The Rise, Struggle,* and *The Death*—won great acclaim among the angling public.

He was very knowledgeable about trout flies, and he designed a number of patterns, the most popular being a fancy wet fly named the Holberton that some anglers called the Greenwood Lake. He was innovative and devised a style of tying known as the "Fluttering Fly," which was patented and eventually sold to Abbey & Imbrie. Basically, the fly was tied in the opposite direction from standard flies. It was fished by drawing it slowly through the water and stopping and starting the fly, which produced a fluttering motion to the wings that attracted trout and bass.

Holberton was well known in angling circles, and he fished and socialized with many of the leading anglers of his day, including Thaddeus Norris. He learned to roast a trout along the stream bank, and he described this special method in an article titled "That Big Trout," which appeared in *Outing Magazine* in June 1893. Holberton told readers to build a "dry wood" fire, and after the coals had died, take a half dozen trout, season them well, wrap them in a piece of buttered paper, then in a wet newspaper, and bury the bundle in the hot coals.

Though he traveled to the various trout regions of the United States, Holberton was most familiar with the Catskills. He often referred to the Beaverkill, Willowemoc, and Neversink in his articles, and it was obvious that he knew these streams as a veteran fly fisher. As an early conservationist, he wrote letters to the *New York Times* pleading for more enforcement of game laws and for the protection of the Adirondacks.

As an angling writer, he contributed articles to sporting journals and magazines throughout the 1880s and 1890s, generally writing about flies, fly tying, or fly fishing. He contributed to *Forest and Stream, Harper's Weekly,* the *American Angler,* and *Outing Magazine.* At times when he wrote for *Forest and Stream* about trout flies, he wrote under the nom de plume of Scarlet Ibis.

In general, he used his given name on magazine articles, such as "The Pleasures of Fly Fishing," "A Day on the Stream for Trout," "That Big Trout," and "Where to Go A-Fishing." His fishing and writing were diverse; he wrote of shad fishing on the Susquehanna, catching black bass on flies, and trout fishing in the Rocky Mountains in waters where he may have been the first to fish with flies.

The article titled "That Big Trout" was about a fishing trip to the Lycoming Creek, in north-central Pennsylvania, and of a large, 17½ inch, 2-pound brook trout! Holberton may have made that special trout the subject of a beautiful oil-on-canvas painting he completed in 1888 of a native brook trout and fly rod lying on the stream bank.

Holberton often wrote of the difficulty anglers experienced because they did not know the name of the fly, or flies, they had success with; and he was a strong proponent for standardizing American fly patterns. He argued that fly tiers were careless, kept altering old patterns when they reproduced or duplicated the flies, and caused some traditional patterns to appear with new names. Fly fishermen would, at times, place an order for a dozen Beaverkills, Professors, or Royal Coachmans and receive flies that were dissimilar to what another fly tier had made.

Holberton attempted to standardize fly patterns in 1882, and he did so by producing a linen-backed chart, 19 by 24 inches, on which he painted a watercolor showing a brook trout rising to a fly. Surrounding the trout in the form of a border were sixty-four fly patterns, numbered and named, that Holberton painted by hand. The chart was titled "Standard American Trout Flies," and fifty copies were made. Two years later, he produced a similar work when he painted a set of forty "Standard American Black Bass and Lake Flies."

In 1885, *Forest and Stream* announced that Charles F. Imbrie, of the famous Abbey & Imbrie fishing tackle house, was preparing an illustrated work that would help standardize trout, bass, and salmon flies. It was stated that Wakeman Holberton, "the celebrated fish artist and fly-tier" had "carefully drawn and colored over two hundred and eighty flies for this work in his careful manner."[9]

In 1887, Wakeman Holberton wrote *The Art of Angling*. The work included both fresh- and salt-water fishing, as well as how to fish for bass and trout. It also contained lists of flies that work best in the various parts of the United States as well as in Canada, and has a section on where to fish.

The book mentions the Neversink Club and the Neversink; and at the end, Holberton pens "Last Words," a thoughtful creed for sportsmen at a time when many anglers were still "fishing for count": "Do not catch or kill more fish or game than you can use; do not keep fingerlings, or fish for numbers, or descend to poaching in any shape; treat farmers civilly, and respect their rights; by so doing, you will find that your angling trips will be a joy forever."[10]

In 1889, the *New York Times* publicized another book by Holberton, "the well-known expert fly caster and artist." The book was a compilation of his fishing experiences, and these adventures were illustrated with sketches Holberton had made while on a lake or stream. The work was titled *Recollections of an Angler* and was praised by the *Times* for its "richness of illustration and ornamentation." And the reviewer claimed the book would be the "envy of all anglers who see it."

"Unfortunately, the public will not benefit," wrote the *Times* reviewer, "as there is only one copy of the book, and it was constructed simply for the author and his family—to recall the scenes of pleasant days with the trout and as a remembrance of mountain landscapes and views."[11]

Recollections of an Angler consisted of 101 pages and contained chapters telling the story of a single season's fishing trip to lakes and streams in the Adirondacks; Ralston, Pennsylvania; the Yellowstone region; and the Beaverkill in the Catskills. There are five full-page watercolors and forty-eight smaller watercolor pictures. "The scene is painted in water colors, the most killing fly decorates the page, and the camp fire at night is not forgotten. Besides the water colors there are 130 pen-and-ink sketches and drawings."[12]

CLARENCE M. ROOF

Clarence M. Roof (1842–1923) was the youngest of the trio and possibly the wealthiest. Born upstate in Cooperstown, New York, Roof and a boyhood friend formed an importing company known as Goode, Roof & Co., and moved from Cooperstown to New York City. The business imported and distributed pharmaceuticals, olive oils, wines, and other products from Europe.

As with the other two club members, Clarence Roof was an ardent fly fisher and, like Holberton, a skilled and expert fly caster. He, too, competed in casting tournaments, and at Madison Square Garden in 1897 he finished first in the single-handed long-distance trout fly-casting contest and third in the light rod single-handed fly-casting-for-distance contest. He also bested all casters in the obstacle fly-casting for accuracy and delicacy contest.

Clarence M. Roof (center). *Wintoon*, 1993.

THE NEVERSINK CLUB AND THE POSTING OF THE WEST BRANCH

Following the initial posting of the West Branch, Holberton stated in *Forest and Stream* that the rights of the Neversink Club seemed to have been respected, and that there was little, if any, poaching. This comment at the time seemed accurate; posting, in the beginning, did seem to be accepted by the public in general. However, as it grew in popularity and spread from one stream to another, posting began to be resented.

Through leases and purchases, clubmen were acquiring all of the best trout-fishing water in the Catskills. No stream posting angered the fishing public—and caused immense discontent among fishermen and landowners—more than the closing of the West Branch of the Neversink. Perhaps this was because the best water along the Rondout, Beaverkill, and Willowemoc was being controlled by fishing clubs, or because the West Branch was more accessible to a larger number of local trout fishermen. For years, the upper Neversink attracted fishing parties from the Esopus Valley and the Kingston-Rondout area, who traveled up Big Indian Hollow to the West Branch.

In March 1885, a Kingston newspaper carried an advertisement by the Neversink Club telling readers that the club had leased, for ten years, that portion of the West Branch of the Neversink lying between Satterlee's dam and LeRoy's mill "for private use and protection of the trout therein."[13] This announcement triggered a war of words and incidents involving fists, stones, guns, broken fishing poles, and broken bones that continued for years.

The conflict began with letters and editorials in local newspapers, then spread to national sporting journals. One of the most persistent and outspoken critics of the clubmen was Robert E. Best, a veteran Kingston fishermen who had fished the West Branch of the Neversink for many years. Best did not take kindly to the posting of his favorite stream! In a series of blistering letters, he argued that the leasing of the stream would destroy the summer boardinghouse business. Although the club leased the stream, it had no legal right to prohibit fishing, and he stated that he was going to continue to fish its waters. Best not only questioned the legality of leasing trout streams but also the very character of the men doing such an "un-American" deed:

> These migrating vagabonds hailing from New York, forming themselves into clubs, and leasing fishing streams for their selfish purposes, have been on the increase for some years. As a rule they spend but little or no money in the country where their nests exist, and where they have their drunken orgies, and sing their obscene songs. A few barrels of rum brought with them from New York, with what chickens they can steal from hen roosts, and the trout they can catch from the stream that has been stocked from the State hatcheries and placed there with Ulster County people's money, form the stock of summer substance.[14]

On April 9, *Forest and Stream* took notice of the Kingston newspaper articles and responded in a lengthy article of their own as to whether property owners have the right to lease or not. The sporting journal, on its editorial page, also took issue with Best's assessment of the clubmen and stated, "Knowing the high character of the gentlemen composing the Neversink Club, the Balsam Lake Club and the Willowemoc Club, most of whom are personal acquaintances, we regard the article written to the '*Freeman*' as a most vile slander."

For the next couple of weeks, Robert E. Best, the *Kingston Journal and Weekly Freeman,* and *Forest and Stream* exchanged criticisms on the pages of Kingston newspapers and the popular sporting journal. On April 16, the *Freeman* wrote of its concern over wealthy men from New York buying all the streams and singled out the Neversink Club in the town of Denning. It stated that the damage done to boardinghouses would be very great and that clubmen were never a benefit to the county. "They are an evil, for they teach the residents along the streams to drink whisky, and this is another reason why the feeling is growing so hot there against them."[15]

The most persistent argument put forth by those opposed to stream posting and private fishing preserves was that if the stream was stocked with trout by the Fish Commission, it should remain open to the public. Stocking, it was stated, brought the streams back to their original value as trout waters and was done at public expense. Therefore, it was reasoned, the trout in the streams were public property, and it should be illegal to post such waters and prevent the public from fishing them.

Stream owners agreed that the state owned the fish, even in their wild state; but they argued that they had the "right of property, and can exclude any person from trespassing upon their grounds for the purpose of fishing."[16] In effect, they granted that individuals had the legal right to catch state trout, as long as they did not trespass over private land to do so.

On April 23, the *Kingston Journal and Weekly Freeman* published an article by D. M. DeWitt, a Kingston attorney. DeWitt defended the club and stated that a group of gentlemen from Brooklyn and New York, who regularly fished the West Branch, became alarmed at the rapid decrease in the size and number of trout in the stream. The stream owners and farmers in the area were equally concerned and were anxious to halt the indiscriminate fishing, "but were afraid to incur their possible enmity." With this situation, the gentlemen formed the Neversink Club "with the cordial good will of the owners of the land."

DeWitt also stated as fact that "If a man own both banks he is *prima facie* (on first view) owner of the stream. If the banks are owned by different persons, each *prima facie* owns to the middle of the stream." He points out that the club "has bought from the owners of that portion of the river it occupies, not merely an exclusive privilege of fishing, not a mere lease, but the bed of the stream for a distance of 3½ miles. For that distance, whatever rights the owners had, the Neversink Club has purchased and now has—no more no less."

A week later, Best replied to DeWitt's article, disagreeing with him and insisting that because the stream was stocked with state trout it should be considered open water.

In a letter to the *American Angler*, Charles Hallock, founder of *Forest and Stream*, and at the time a most esteemed sportsman, stated his opinion on the rights of fishing clubs or individuals to have exclusive use of waters previously stocked at public expense. He believed that there was no need for either side of the dispute to be concerned, because in "due course" the "privileges of exclusiveness" along trout streams will be so insignificant "they will not be worth paying for."

Hallock was a strong supporter of the U.S. Fish Commission and the work of its commissioner, Professor Spencer F. Baird. In his letter, he pointed out that Professor Baird's policy had been not to recommend legislative action when dealing with fisheries problems, even though the Fish Commission had those powers. Instead, they had carried out the policy that it was better to expend public monies to make "fish so abundant that they can be caught without restriction and serve as cheap food for the people at large, rather than to expend a much larger sum in 'protecting' the fish, and in preventing the people from catching the few which still remain (or did remain) after a generation of improvidence."

Hallock declared "this is just the reverse of club logic," which he saw as making fishing available only to those who could afford it, as was the case in Europe. He believed that the actions of the clubs to preserve fishing by excluding public participation results in a "limited" effort compared with what the Fish Commission and its vast resources could accomplish:

When the victory rests, the individual or private club may hire fishing privileges, hold riparian prerogatives and cultivate fish which will cost them a dollar or ten dollars a pound to produce; they may wear the nobbiest outfits, and drink champagne at every meal; nobody will oppose or interfere. The impecunious or provident angler will not regard them with envy so long as he can have all the fish he wants for the catching of them elsewhere. Dude may stick to the tally-ho, but the progressive angler will prefer the railroad and the sleeping car.[17]

In a follow-up article a week later, Hallock wrote that in the future trout shall be so plentiful that "protective laws will be superfluous and that anglers shall enjoy the privilege of fishing without paying for it." This, he said, "will remove all dispute about riparian rights" and make clubs less desirable.

Following the posting by the Neversink Club, a number of incidents occurred between men hired to patrol the stream and trespassing fishermen. It was a general practice for "stream-watchers" to throw stones in the stream ahead of the poachers to discourage them by scaring the trout. At times the stones missed their mark and struck the poacher, who took off after the man hired to patrol. Fistfights began, and bruises and "duckings" in the stream were experienced by both sides. Revolvers and clubs were, at times, said to be brandished, and local anglers even threatened to stock the stream with black bass.

West Branch of the Neversink below Parker's. *Outing Magazine*, June 1889.

It was not only stream-watchers who incorporated the use of stones to chase away would-be poachers. Henry Van Dyke—clergyman, author—in his book *Little Rivers*, recalls " . . . and the Neversink, which flows through John Burroughs' country, and past one house in particular, perched on a high bluff, where a very dreadful old woman comes out and throws stones at 'city fellers fishin' through her land' (as if any one wanted to touch her land! It was the water that ran over it, you see, that carried the fish with it, and they were not hers at all.)"[18]

In April 1886, it was reported that at the third annual meeting of the Neversink Club, the club was "in a highly flourishing condition," and that the members would use every means to protect the stream from trespassers, because it now owned the property it formerly leased. This last statement was not quite correct; by the end of the trout-fishing season of 1885, club member Clarence M. Roof had purchased all of the water along the West Branch formerly owned by the Neversink Club. Roof also began construction of a lodge, which, upon completion the following year, he called Wintoon.

On July 10, 1886, the *American Angler* published an article titled "WAR ON THE NEVERSINK" and told of confrontations between stream-watchers and anglers who had fished the stream since boyhood. The locals accused the clubmen of fishing off club water in order to save the trout in their own waters, and that when anglers go on the club water they are accosted by stream-watchers who are "armed to the teeth to drive them off."

The article also stated there was another "circus" along the stream; a stream-watcher by the name of Parker started to drive men away, but the fishermen threw down their poles and attacked him. He ran away and returned, reinforced by his brother and two club members. "Every man threw off his coat. The fight took place in the water, the splashing, swearing and striking making a hideous din in the wilds of the Neversink."

Trouble continued into the next fishing season as Kingston papers reported, "Fights have been frequent of late, and the 'fishing war,' as it is called, is still in progress. The club reports it is impossible to get a jury to convict Denning residents who trespass."[19] By 1889, the Neversink Club had disbanded, and the burden of dealing with the annual confrontations with poachers fell to Clarence Roof, a problem he pursued with vigor and determination.

The added protection placed on the upper Neversink through posting and the stringent club regulations on size and catch limits must have had a positive effect on trout populations in the watershed. Walter S. Allerton, who had been critical of the declining trout fisheries in a Catskill article written in 1876, accompanied Judge Fitch on a successful trout-fishing sojourn to the Neversink in 1889.

On May 31, Judge Fitch and Chester A. Platner took a buckboard from Big Indian, up the hollow and over the mountain to Claryville, a distance of approximately 22 miles that took seven hours. They had reserved rooms at the judge's sister's house just downstream of the forks, and as always seemed to be the case when he fished the Neversink, the stream was high because of a freshet from recent heavy rains. The two men were joined by Reverend Charles G. Adams; however, the trio had to wait before fishing because of the high water.

They were finally able to get in the stream on Monday, June 3, but the water was still too high for good fly fishing; wanting trout for the table, they asked Platner to fish with bait, as the prospects of catching many trout on flies did not look good. Still, they managed to have a respectful outing, as the tally for the day was:

```
Platner saved 43 trout; threw back 35 = 78
Adams    "    14    "      "      "   29 = 43
Fitch    "    16    "      "      "   27 = 43
Total Catch . . . . . . . . . . . . . . . . . .164[20]
```

A few days after they arrived, the party was joined by Allerton, who, like Fitch, was an avid fly fisher who knew and wrote about the Catskills on occasion in sporting journals. The men did not fish on Sunday and lost five days due to the weather and flooding. Their total catch for six days of fishing was as follows:

Adams saved   53; threw back 167 = 220
Platner   "   99   "   "   140 = 239
Fitch   "   96   "   "   226 = 232
Allerton "   104   "   "   266 = 370
Total   352   799 = 1151[21]

Even with high-water conditions, Judge Fitch and his party averaged about 192 trout per day; with four men fishing, the average catch per person each day was approximately 48 trout!

In the summer of 1889, Kingston newspapers published a new advertisement warning against trespassing on the famous Satterlee stretch upstream of Clarence Roof. Martin R. Cook of Bayonne, New Jersey, had recently acquired a strip of land one rod wide (16½ feet) along both banks of the stream for more than a mile. Cook stated that this portion of the stream would be used as a private park for the propagation and protection of fish, birds, and game. A year later, Cook acquired additional land and owned all of the water from the mouth of Parker's Brook (Satterlee) upstream beyond Biscuit Brook, for approximately 2½ miles.

SALMON STOCKING

It was during the 1880s that the idea of stocking the Delaware River with salmon resurfaced. In the spring of 1883, between 225,000 and 250,000 Penobscot salmon, seven weeks old, were transported to the upper Delaware by a special "palace car" constructed for the purpose. These fish were sent by the U.S. Fish Commission to Hancock, where thirty-five cans of salmon fry were placed in the East Branch, with the remainder stocked in the West Branch around Deposit. The *Republican Watchman* reported on April 27, 1883 that the experiment was unsuccessful because the fry either died or were eaten by the immense numbers of "voracious bass which rule the waters of the Delaware."

However, reports of an occasional salmon once again made the pages of sporting journals. In the summer of 1888, the *American Angler* ran a story that a salmon weighing 17 pounds was caught running up the Delaware near the Camden Water Works in New Jersey. And a year later, *Forest and Stream* reported two salmon being taken, one by a Gloucester, New Jersey, fisherman who netted a 14-pounder.

In 1889, the New York Fish Commission obtained one hundred thousand Penobscot salmon eggs from the U.S. Fish Commission and had them hatched at Allentown, Pennsylvania. These fry were later distributed in the headwaters in Wayne, Sullivan, and Delaware counties.

11

A *Foreign Exchange;*
Game and Fish Protectors

As the knowledge of fish culture began to spread and hatcheries were constructed by states, the federal government, and private enterprise, the distribution of various species of fish via their ova (eggs) became a common practice. Fish that were not indigenous to one area were introduced: Shad went to the West Coast, and rainbow trout came east; brook and rainbow trout went to Europe, and European fish came to America.

These exchanges, at times, appeared to have been done on a whim, without much thought or science; and although some species did little harm or had no effect on natural fish populations, others had a major impact on native species. One of the most significant events, and one that shaped forever the trout fishing in the Catskills, was the introduction of brown trout from Europe.

A FOREIGN EXCHANGE

Seth Green had successfully shipped fish eggs across the Atlantic to England, but early attempts to transport trout from Germany to America were unsuccessful. "Bachforelle (trutta fario)" eggs were sent to the New York State hatching house at Caledonia as early as 1875 from the Huningen hatchery in Germany, the same year rainbows arrived from the West Coast. In April, twenty-five hundred eggs were received. Even though the eggs were packed in oval wooden boxes and wet moss, none survived the trip; when they arrived, they were found to be in a "horrible state of putrefaction."

A couple of years later, Professor Spencer F. Baird, commissioner of the United States Fish Commission, appointed Fred Mather to be in charge of foreign exchanges of eggs and fish. At this time, there were ongoing shipments of eggs of various fish with Germany, Holland, France, and England.

Fred Mather (1833–1900), like Seth Green, was an early fish culturist. Both men shared not only an interest in fisheries science but also a love of fly fishing. They were both involved with some of the first fly-casting tournaments, and they wrote about fish and fishing in books and sporting journals. Mather was among the earliest writers of *Forest and Stream* and was that journal's fishery editor for many years.

Mather was born in the Albany area of New York in 1833 and began his career as a fish culturist shortly after the Civil War, in which he had been a highly decorated soldier. Mather purchased a farm near Honeoye Falls, in upstate Monroe County, in 1868 and began raising trout artificially. He was esteemed in his profession and was a founding member of the American Fish Culturists' Association, which was contrived at a meeting in New York City on December 20, 1870. This association was the forerunner of the present-day American Fisheries Society.

Fred Mather preparing eggs for Europe. *Modern Fish Culture*, 1900.

When the U.S. Fish Commission was first formed, Mather was employed to hatch shad for the Potomac and Hudson rivers, and in 1874, he was sent to Germany with one hundred thousand shad eggs. Three years later, he was given the position of dealing with foreign exchanges. He traveled to Prussia, where he wrote to the editor of *Forest and Stream,* encouraging fish culturists in America to exchange eggs with a hatchery located in the upper Rhine Valley at the foot of the Black Forest, in Freiberg, southern Germany. Though he mentioned "the common trout of Europe (*Salmo fario*)," he encouraged Americans to import the "charr" or saibling (*Salmo salvelinus*), a fish he claimed was similar to our brook trout, though more brightly colored.

In 1880, Mather received a bronze medal at the World's Fishery Exposition in Berlin, where he was in charge of the American exhibit of fish culture and angling. When he returned from Europe, he was sent by Professor Baird to Roslyn, Long Island, to hatch salmon for stocking in the Hudson River. At this time Mather was also entrusted by Eugene G. Blackford of the New York State Fish Commission to select a site on Long Island for a fish hatchery. He recommended a site at Cold Spring Harbor, and when the facility was constructed in 1883 as a joint venture of the United States and the New York Fish Commission, Mather was its superintendent.

In December 1882, even before the hatchery was completed, Mather wrote to Professor Baird inquiring about the availability of eggs of grayling and the "European brook trout (Salmo fario)." Baird replied the next day that he had been offered trout eggs numerous times but had always turned them down, but he would contact Herr F. Von Behr, president of the Deutschen Fischerei Verein.

Professor Baird wrote to Von Behr, announcing that he was sending a shipment of lake trout, whitefish, and brook trout eggs, and ended his letter by stating "Mr. Mather is about starting a new hatchery on Long Island, near New York, in which he will do a great deal of work for the United States. He thinks he would like to have some eggs of the European trout. Can you send him some?"[1]

The Cold Spring Harbor hatchery began operations on January 1, 1883, and several weeks later, on February 28, Mather received eighty thousand brown trout eggs: sixty thousand "of a kind which grows large" and twenty thousand smaller eggs from tributaries of the upper Rhine. The shipment was sent by Von Behr and was from two different waters: The larger eggs came from trout inhabiting deep lakes and the smaller ones from mountain streams.

Many of the eggs had already hatched before they arrived, and the fry had perished, whereas other eggs were injured because of a lack of moisture. An announcement of their arrival in *Forest and Stream* brought requests for the new species, and on March 10, ten thousand of the large eggs and two thousand of the small were sent to Seth Green at Caledonia. On March 21, two thousand of the large eggs and three thousand of the small were shipped to Frank Clark, the superintendent of the U.S. Fish Commission hatchery at Northville, Michigan.

The eggs retained by Mather were placed in outdoor troughs with covers. Unfortunately, inquisitive visitors removed the covers at times, exposing the eggs to sunlight, which added to their mortality. The large-type eggs all perished within three to seven days after hatching. In the 1884 annual report of the New York Fish Commission, Mather wrote that only about eight hundred of the eggs from the upper Rhine lived and were placed in the ponds; these, too, proved to be a problem to Mather and his staff. When they were six months old, the fish were 6 inches in length, and in excellent condition:

> We were so proud of these fish that we often caught them to show visitors, and as often as we disturbed them we would find dead ones on the ground the next day.
> These specimens jumped out of the wooden rearing ponds, whose vertical walls project over a foot above the surface of the water. This fish seems to be given to this form of suicide, and it was only when their numbers had been severely thinned by it that we learned that they seemed prompted to it every time they were disturbed, either by putting in a net to catch specimens to show to visitors or at night by some animal swimming in the pond. In November, 1884, when they were a year and a half old, we removed them to a larger breeding pond, and the next morning the ground was covered with them, although this pond had banks a foot higher than those of the rearing ponds. At present not over fifty are left, and learning their habits has been expensive. I had no intimation of this habit from any of my European correspondents, and the fish differs in this respect from our own trout, which readily accepts capture and transfer.[2]

Fortunately for Mather, Von Behr sent another shipment of eggs, which were received on February 15, 1884; and on February 25, *Forest and Stream* reported on a shipment of trout eggs that came from England. The steamer Adriatic brought ten thousand "Salmo fario" eggs that were a gift of R. B. Marston, editor of the London *Fishing Gazette*. These were in three lots: Five thousand were marked "our best trout," three thousand were from the famous Itchen, and two thousand were from the Wey.

Brown trout had barely reached American shores when the debate over their merits began to appear on the pages of sporting journals. Some items were written by anglers who had fished in Europe, and they were convinced that the brown trout would be welcomed by all because they grew larger and were warier, gamier, and therefore superior to native brook trout.

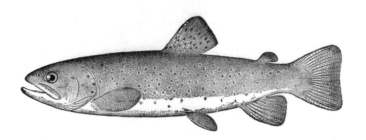

Brown trout. *Modern Fish Culture*, 1900.

One correspondent stated that English trout, as a rule, even in the best of streams, were not as abundant as trout were in American streams. By comparison, he said, they were pretty scarce; a basket of a dozen good-sized trout anywhere in Scotland or England could be considered good fishing. Another wrote that brook trout were easier to catch, took the fly more readily, and did not require the delicate approach that was practiced in England. "On many English streams the fish can only be taken with a dry fly, a practice unknown, so far as I know in America."

These comparisons annoyed American anglers who loved their native brook trout and in no way believed it inferior to any fish. When English authorities declared their trout was "only a charr," Americans took offense. One asked indignantly: "In what respect is a trout superior to a charr? Certainly the American charr is handsomer than the brook trout of Europe, as its crimson belly, at some seasons, makes it particularly beautiful, and its fine, almost invisible, scales give a softness to its skin that is not approached by S. fario."[3]

Secure in the knowledge that he now had sufficient stocks of the European trout, Mather, in May 1884, began placing forty thousand brown trout fry directly into the waters of New York in and around Long Island. The following spring, the hatchery expanded its stocking range and distributed 28,900 brown trout fry into the waters of Queens, Suffolk, Westchester, and Rockland counties.

Fred Mather believed brown trout were destined to become a favorite fish of American anglers. He had caught brown trout on flies in Europe, and he considered them to be the "gamiest" trout that he had ever taken on a rod. They grew faster and were equally as beautiful as native brook trout. In a letter to the *American Angler* published in their August 8, 1885, issue, he wrote: "I sincerely hope that the brown trout may be domesticated in America, for I believe that it is a fish that we will learn to love and one that will stay with us and not strike out for foreign parts, as the 'rainbow' has done in most waters."

Mather disagreed with Seth Green and the Fish Commission about the rainbow being the salvation of New York's trout waters; and in a paper read before the American Fishcultural Association he declared that the "brook trout of Europe" would be a better fish than the rainbow trout then being stocked in New York waters:

> I have suspected the so-called rainbow trout to be identical with the steelhead salmon, *S. gairdneri*, which is a migratory fish.
>
> We have been waiting and watching the habits of this alleged trout with great interest in order to learn if its habits might not show it to be, in some respect, different from the steelhead. The evidence of the Commission tends to show that it is a migratory fish and, if so, it may escape to the sea and be lost.
>
> The promise of the rainbow trout was that in it we had a quick growing fish, which was not as sensitive to warm water as our own "fontinalis," a desideratum which now promises to be filled by the brook trout of Europe, *Salmo fario*.[4]

In November 1885, both the Cold Spring Harbor and Caledonia hatcheries reported taking eggs from the brown trout that hatched from the original shipment received by Mather in the winter of 1883. Shortly after this announcement on the pages of *Forest and Stream,* W. L. Gilbert, who operated the Old Colony ponds at Plymouth, Massachusetts, wrote to the editor on January 7, 1886 claiming he had received, in February 1882, four thousand English trout eggs (*S. fario*).

These trout eggs arrived in America one year earlier than those sent to Mather at Cold Spring Harbor. Gilbert wrote that not more than thirty of the eggs survived the trip, and from these he managed to hatch about twenty-five good fry that he placed in a vacant pond. After one year, they were about 8 inches in length, and at the time of the letter, some of them weighed a pound or more. He stated that during the previous week, three trout had spawned, and he succeeded in obtaining three thousand eggs; he believed that these were the first "English trout eggs" ever taken in this country.

Forest and Stream would not confirm if Gilbert was the first to take spawn from brown trout in America, but Fred Mather, in the annual report to the New York State Fish Commission in 1886, confirmed that Gilbert did receive a small shipment of brown trout eggs, but he did not confirm the date.* At this time Fred Mather had begun to call the European brook trout "by the English name of 'brown trout.'"

The original eggs Fred Mather sent to Seth Green at the Caledonia hatchery arrived on March 12, and they arrived in fair condition, but "a little too advanced;" from the time they arrived until they hatched, 7,773 of the 12,000 had perished. Hatchery records reveal that the first stocking of brown trout fry from the Caledonia hatchery occurred in 1886, and that 116,000 fry were sent throughout the state, but only one shipment reached the Catskills. On March 30, four thousand fry were sent to E. D. Mayhew of Walton, Delaware County, to be placed in Spring Creek.

In the winter, the Fish Commission announced that it would have a limited number of "German trout" available next spring for stocking public waters. Applications must have been plentiful, as 307,000 brown trout were stocked into the waters of New York State, with 112,000 finding their way to the Catskills. Those streams planted with brown trout fry in 1887 included the Neversink, Beaverkill, Willowemoc and tributaries, the West Branch of the Delaware and tributaries, and the Kiskatom and Shingle Kill in Greene County.

In the spring of 1888, brown trout were placed in the Tremper Kill, a tributary of the East Branch of the Delaware; the East Branch of the Neversink; and the Vernooy Kill, a tributary of the Rondout Creek. On April 19, 1888, C. T. Conant of St. Remy, New York, stocked two thousand browns in the Esopus Creek.

Commenting on brown trout a year after their introduction to the waters of New York, Seth Green remarked that the success of the "German trout" was very favorable. And, he claimed, they were a "beautiful and gamy fish," and when prepared for the table were equal to any trout of this country. He did, however, have some concern over how the new species would interact with indigenous brook trout, and he took a cautious approach as to where the fish should be stocked.

---

*In a letter to *Shooting and Fishing* dated November 4, 1889, and published November 7, 1889, W. L. Gilbert, Plymouth, Massachusetts, took issue with a previous article that said Fred Mather was the first to receive brown trout eggs in this country. Gilbert stated he received, in January 1881, "a lot of brown trout eggs" from Guildford, Surrey, England. This date differs from the first claim by Gilbert but it does appear that he may have been the first to receive brown trout eggs that hatched in America.

Green thought that brown trout would thrive in the same waters as brook trout, but because they grew rapidly and to a larger size than native fish, he adopted the idea that they should not be placed in small streams containing native trout, "as there would not be sufficient food for them and in that case they would naturally reach that point of hunger where they would feed upon the brook trout."[5] Green saw the brown trout being planted only in the larger streams where there was more food and space for their bigger appetites.

As the reputation of the new species spread, American sporting journals and professional fish culturists debated about what to call the "brook trout of Europe." *Shooting and Fishing*, a weekly journal published in Boston, claimed the Caledonia hatchery was responsible for calling the fish "German trout," but mentioned that the last reports from Caledonia had switched to "European brown trout." The newspaper suggested shortening the name to "brown trout," the same name that the U.S. Fish Commission was using at the time.

This was followed by an editorial in *Forest and Stream* in November 1889 that suggested the fish be called the "Von Behr trout," after the person who sent the species to Mather in 1883. Two weeks later, *Shooting and Fishing* published another article on the subject, and it was mentioned that Monroe A. Green, superintendent of the Caledonia hatchery, believed the fish should be known as the "Mather trout" as "he ought to have great credit for introducing them."

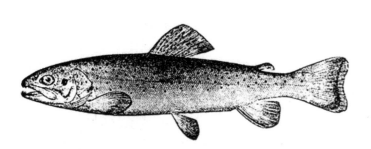

The "Von Behr or Brown trout." *Forest and Stream*, 1894.

Shooting and Fishing disagreed, stating that "brown trout" was the English name for the fish, and that it was short and more easily remembered than Von Behr or Mather: "Besides, according to Mr. Gilbert, the first brown trout that came to this country were not sent by Herr Von Behr and were not received by Mr. Mather."[6]

A short time later, *Forest and Stream* reported that Col. Marshall McDonald, then commissioner of the U.S. Fish Commission, proposed to name the species after Von Behr, and that in the future, all eggs and fry shipped from government establishments would be sent as "Von Behr trout."

Commissioner McDonald sent a letter to *Shooting and Fishing* claiming he did not intend to discredit the claims of Mr. Gilbert to having first introduced the European brook trout into this country, nor did he wish to detract from the credit of Mr. Mather. But he reiterated that Von Behr deserved recognition for the aid and cooperation of sending the European trout to America, and he declared that "Von Behr trout" was "well sounding," and not "too long." McDonald closed his letter: "I trust you will, in view of what I have stated, recognize the appropriateness of the name, and unite in making it current with all sportsmen."[7]

The name Von Behr never took hold, and for many years the "brook trout of Europe" was known as "German trout" or "German brown trout" and eventually by the name it is known today: brown trout.

GAME AND FISH PROTECTORS

At the beginning of the 1880s, the sporting public continued to lobby for adequate fish and game laws. There were complaints that laws changed too frequently, and before they were learned by outdoorsmen, they would be modified or superseded. It was difficult to remember the ever-changing clauses of the laws. Another reason for the confusion was the practice of having different laws pertaining to seasons and limits in adjoining counties. This caused unwitting violations, and to many sportsmen, this was worse than no law at all.

Another problem, and perhaps the more serious complaint, was the lack of enforcement, which, at the time, was dependent on clubs, associations, societies, and individuals who acted out of public spirit or monetary gain. Laws had provisions that allowed the informer to receive a portion of the penalty. This could cast suspicion on the person making the complaint and his mercenary motives, and allowed the offender the sympathy of being a persecuted man.

Local constables could not be depended on to prosecute friends and neighbors with laws that were seen as having no moral guilt attached. It was not until 1880 that professional law enforcement officers were appointed by the governor, given the power to enforce all laws protecting fish and game, and to arrest offenders. These men were salaried, with no share of penalties going into their pockets.

The governor appointed only eight game and fish protectors for the entire state. And they were selected without any geographical considerations: John I. Collett, of Cobleskill, Schoharie County, was the only officer in the entire Catskill region. Immediately, the appointments were met with criticism. Sportsmen declared that there were not enough officers and that they were not placed strategically so that they could do a good job. Large areas of the state—those with abundant fish and game resources—were left unprotected and at the mercy of the "poacher and trout thief."

These early game and fish protectors were charged with enforcing all statutes "for the preservation of moose, deer, birds and fish, or other game laws" in the name of the people of the state "against all offenders." The appointment of law enforcement professionals, if they performed their duties "conscientiously and without fear," was seen as a major advance by the sportsmen of New York.

Most of these men took care of those violations that came their way, but they had no supervision or accountability and performed their duties when and if they desired. That they did not do a more efficient job was not always the fault of the protectors; it was believed that because abuses of the laws protecting fish and game had occurred for so many years, enforcement of the law should be done on a gradual basis.

Three years later, Section 1 of Chapter 317 of the Laws of 1883 increased the number of game and fish protectors; Section 4 provided that they would come under the supervision of the commissioners of fisheries and that the commission would divide the state into districts, with each protector given his own territory. There was also greater accountability; each protector had to provide a monthly report giving an account of the suits he commenced, the disposition of the suits, the results of any that went to trial, and the circumstances of any not settled. No salary or travel expenses would be paid unless these reports were filed, and the protector in all respects faithfully performed his duties.

"Landing a double." J. H. Cocks, *Sport with Gun and Rod in American Woods and Waters*, 1883.

Section 2 stated that protectors were empowered to begin suits against violators in the name of the people. One half of the penalties recovered in civil actions over and above county and court expenses would go to the state, and the other half would go to the game protector, or to the individual bringing the suit.

Laws pertaining to fish and game were not readily accepted or respected by the public at this time, and these pioneer game protectors had a difficult time carrying out their duties. Many people still adhered to the belief that in America, the woods and streams were free, and laws limiting this freedom were looked upon with contempt: "The hatred entertained by the first settlers of this country toward the game and fish laws of the mother countries seems to be so deeply implanted that it has been transmitted through every successive generation to the present one with unabated force."[8]

Sometimes game protectors were ridiculed for not enforcing the law, and then mocked when they did—often on the front pages of newspapers. Some of the same editors, who lamented the deplorable conditions of trout streams, took issue when the lawbreakers were brought to justice, siding with the violators and claiming that they were poor victims, ignorant of the law. There was also great animosity toward game protectors over the fact that they received one half the fine, after expenses.

However, law enforcement did not become truly effective until Chapter 577 of the Laws of 1888, when the number of game and fish protectors was nearly doubled, and a chief game and fish protector was also appointed. During the 1880s, county governments continued to create laws protecting fish and game, and perhaps one of the most stringent ever enacted in the Catskills involved a popular trout stream that flowed through the town of Liberty, in Sullivan County.

In 1882, the Sullivan County Board of Supervisors passed "an Act for the preservation and protection of Brook trout in the Middle Mongaup River and its tributaries in the Town of Liberty, Sullivan County." Section 1 of the new law stated: "No person shall kill, or attempt to kill or catch any brook trout in the water of the Middle Mongaup River."[9] The stream was protected for three years, and a fine of twenty-five dollars was imposed for violating the law; one half of the penalties went to the complainant, one half to support the poor of the town.

Perhaps the most significant protection the trout populations of the Catskills received at this time was from the private fishing clubs that appeared along most of the best trout water on the Beaverkill, Willowemoc, Rondout, and upper Neversink. By the middle of the 1880s, the amount of trout fishing available to the public was limited to the lower portions of these celebrated streams, where water temperatures were often too warm, or marginal, to sustain numbers of native brook trout.

The leasing of streams and increase in posting caused a good deal of anticlub sentiment. Summer hotels that catered to the trout-fishing tourists in Sullivan and Ulster counties became very concerned over the matter and threatened to bring suit. They saw any loss of fishing tourists visiting the trout regions as vital to their survival; their living depended on the attractions that trout fishing provided to their area.

The resort owners grumbled that now a few men control "the great trout region" and they alone enjoy it with a few friends. They also argued that these streams were restocked by the state to their "old-time value" at public expense, and a few men should not be able to enjoy the benefits to the "exclusion of all others;" this they saw as "un-American, and unjust." It was said that the fish placed in the streams were public property, and the courts should be asked to decide if the streams could be closed to fishing.

Hotel owners urged others to join their effort, including boardinghouses and railroads. It was argued that streams were no longer "common property," and natives, who had lived within the "sound of their waters" for a half century, as well as city anglers, can now only fish them as "poachers."

A newspaper in Albany published a report questioning whether it was legal to have the state's "great fishing privileges" turned into a private corporation, or monopoly. "We want no corner on trout streams." It urged the legislature to interfere and to find the means to keep "the Gentle art of angling an entirely free privilege, open to all of our people."[10]

Outdoor publications, such as the *American Angler* and *Forest and Stream* joined in the fracas. One article questioned whether stream property owners even had the right to lease their fishing to clubs; another noted that the Fish Commission at times gave trout to owners of private waters, and did this action cause those waters to become public? It was claimed as fact that even well-stocked streams near cities soon became fished out when opened to the public and within a few years there was no fishing.

A correspondent, who was also a club member, responded to the criticism of the hotel owners:

> If the fishing in these streams would always remain as good as it was when the hotels were built and railways introduced into this section, their argument would be better, but unfortunately the reverse is the case. Four years ago I ceased fishing the Beaver Kill because it was utterly fished out, and for the first time fished in the Neversink River. I found there, as had been the case with the Beaver Kill and adjacent waters, the river almost devoid of fish; that parties from a distance were in the habit of visiting the streams with the apparent view of carrying away as many fish as possible, regardless of size, hiring small boys to increase the catch, and making use of other unsportsmanlike ways of depleting the streams. I have heard parties boast that they had carried away 1,100 fish (some of which were scarcely two inches long), the result of three days' fishing, besides all they ate.[11]

The correspondent stated that the Neversink Club limits the catch to twenty-five trout per day, and all trout must be 8 inches in length and taken with the fly. The goal of the club, he wrote, was to prevent excessive fishing, and he claimed that it was not the fault of the clubs that the streams were depleted of trout. It is the "thoughtless and indiscriminate slaughter" by the fishermen. He also argued that fishing clubs can exclude any person from trespassing upon their property for the purpose of fishing. "Granting that citizens have a right to catch State trout, I fail to find the authority that permits them to trespass upon private grounds."[12]

The battle of words over club rights continued for several years, and an article in the *American Angler* on November 5, 1887, by the esteemed editor William C. Harris gave further insight to the dilemma. Harris started out by writing, "The poetry of angling sings of freedom. The angler is free from care, the brook flows freely on its course, the free wind blows and the free bird carols in the forest." Harris explained that this sentiment is at the heart of the opposition to the stream protection practiced by private fishing clubs.

Men were annoyed to see posted notices along the streams they and their fathers were free to fish for so long. Harris wrote that while this is a natural sentiment, it is no more practical to leave all fishing waters free to everyone than it is to do away with fences and turn fields of crops back into "meadow-grazing lands" free for all. The value of good trout streams, he stated, has increased significantly, making it necessary to "lock the doors on the treasure."

"It is a fact," he wrote, that the angler who cannot afford the time and money to travel to distant areas must either own or lease his own water, or belong to one of the many clubs stocking and protecting streams. He warned that anglers, who in the past may have gotten permission from a farmer to fish, may find that next year the stream has been leased to a club, and the farmer's house is turned into a retreat: "We have nothing whatever to say for or against this system. We only point out a known fact and draw the plain conclusion that every angler who cares to provide for his enjoyment in years to come had better lose no time in securing some good angling privilege somewhere."

As angling clubs increased, a change came over public opinion regarding trout fishing as an accepted recreational outlet for those who worked behind a desk or in offices. Business or professional men were no longer looked down upon if they were seen on their way to the railroad station carrying fishing rods. The popularity of angling was now seen as a healthy pastime, and fishing tackle was seen as part of a gentlemen's equipment.

By the end of the 1880s, brown trout had been introduced to all of the major Catskill trout streams or their tributaries. They took over areas not used by brook trout and displaced and restricted native trout in others, driving them further into the headwaters or into small tributaries. But this took a few years, and the first year or two after brown trout were introduced, they were not heard from. One reason was that it took a year or two for them to grow large enough to be caught or to be of interest to fishermen. Their impact on the trout streams of the Catskills did not develop until the 1890s.

The 1880s still belonged to brook trout, and the policy of restocking streams continued to provide hope to anglers. But this revival was stymied, because by the end of the decade, virtually all of the best brook trout water was posted and private. By the late 1880s, the Willewemoc Club had left the upper Willowemoc and Sand Pond, and reestablished themselves firmly in the Beaverkill Valley.

A well-shaded stretch of the Willowemoc headwaters. Ed Van Put.

The club's leaving, however, did not create additional open water on the upper Willowemoc for very long. Almost immediately, Matt and Gil Decker, two brothers who ran a general store in the hamlet of Willowemoc and operated under the name of Matt Decker & Co., began acquiring and leasing some of the same waters.

Matt Decker established a fishing preserve and stocked it with trout he raised in ponds on his property. In addition, he purchased trout from private hatcheries. It was said that he had some of the best fishing in Sullivan County. He employed a stream-watcher, but poachers still managed to remove hundreds of trout. He then employed a second, and they patrolled the stream both day and night.

Decker added to his holdings in 1891 when he leased an additional 1,300 acres, and following an announcement that all poachers would be found and prosecuted to the fullest extent of the law, one unhappy correspondent retaliated by stating, "We have some people up here who would, if they could, control the air we breathe, the water we drink, and the sunshine, and wouldn't even allow the stars to twinkle without it brought money into their pockets."[13]

Those who supported Decker for establishing a preserve on the upper Willowemoc declared that the water had become a "butcher shop instead of a fishing ground," and that fishermen had "wantonly" destroyed the fishing. They believed the posting was justified and cited that only a year before, parties of fishermen from Liberty and Parksville caught six hundred trout, large and small, and depleted the stream; and that pools were dynamited; and that one group caught so many fish that they fed them to the hogs at the boardinghouse where they were staying.

THE UPPER EAST BRANCH

The headwaters of the East Branch of the Delaware were not affected by fishing clubs or posting in the 1880s, and at this time streams such as Dry Brook, Mill Brook, Tremper Kill, and Bush Kill were productive waters and were well known to trout fishermen.

In July 1883, the artists Jervis McEntee and Worthington Whittredge met at Dean's Corners (Arkville). They walked 3 miles to Kelly Corners to investigate the Batavia Kill, a productive trout stream that flows into the East Branch upstream of Margaretville. They liked the stream and the scenery enough to move their trunks the next day to a blacksmith's named George Best, who provided them with room and board. The two found enough to sketch along the stream that they stayed more than three weeks.

After he arrived at home, McEntee recorded in his diary that he left because he "fancied" Whittredge would rather be alone: "I am afraid Whittredge does not care for my companionship or perhaps for any and I don't think we were as congenial as when we were both younger."[14] After McEntee left, Whittredge traveled further up the East Branch to Montgomery Hollow Stream, a small spring-fed tributary that yet today flows over red shale ledges and forms a series of exceptionally pretty waterfalls, with trout pools of crystalline water and green velvet moss dripping with icy-cold spray.

Another popular tributary with trout fishers was a productive trout stream known as the Bush Kill, or Portertown Brook. Fitz-James Fitch, who promoted Catskill trout fishing through his writings for many years, referred to Portertown Brook as an "excellent trout stream" in an article on the

Catskills published May 16, 1889, in *Shooting and Fishing.* Fitch added that: "Thousands of trout are stolen from it annually by pot-fishermen, who find a ready sale for their *loot* at the fashionable summer hotels nearby."

Fitch also mentions that many trout are taken from the East Branch in the 7-mile stretch between Arkville and Lumberville, a small hamlet located at the mouth of Mill Brook.* He also writes that many large trout are caught annually along the East Branch upstream of Arkville to its source and that the village of Roxbury is near the best trout fishing. Early newspaper accounts reveal that brook trout weighing 1½ to 2 pounds were, at times, taken from the East Branch between Margaretville and Arkville.

As with other Catskill streams during the reign of brook trout, the number of trout taken by fishermen at times from the East Branch was also difficult to comprehend. A story in the *Walton Reporter* of August 15, 1885, tells of E. J. Thompson, who fished the East Branch at Arkville, taking 358 trout with him when he left the stream at dark, "the result of the day's sport."

Many fishermen at the time would agree that there was no "sport" in keeping such a large number of trout. Thompson was staying at the Locust House, a large summer resort that held up to eighty guests. He gave the trout to the owner, who cooked them the following morning and fed about one hundred people—and there were trout left. One of the trout weighed 2 pounds, and the next largest 1 pound, 14 ounces!

In September 1888, the *Roxbury Times,* a small Delaware County weekly, announced that Jay Gould traveled up the Ulster & Delaware railroad and made a trout-fishing trip to Furlough Lake, a famous trout pond located outside of Arkville, at the headwaters of Dry Brook.

The item was one sentence long and insignificant, except for the fact that Jay Gould (1836–1892) was one of America's most famous financiers, though some of his financial dealings were looked upon as scandalous. Within days of the announcement of Gould's fishing trip, the story found its way to the front page of the *American Angler,* the weekly fishing journal edited and managed by William C. Harris.

Harris made several stinging remarks in a column titled "A Blow To Angling."[15] Wrote Harris: "There can be no doubt that angling as a gentleman's pastime will suffer from the fact that Jay Gould has gone fishing in the Catskills." After lambasting Gould's character, and insisting his presence "can contaminate a mountain stream," Harris concluded by writing: "self-respecting anglers can easily avoid Roxbury till it shall again become a respectable resort for anglers."

Jay Gould was a Catskill native, born in the town of Roxbury, and at the age of twenty, he displayed his superior intellect by writing a fascinating history of the county in which he was born, titled *History of Delaware County* (1856). While only in his mid-twenties, Gould became a broker in railway stocks, and several years later was implicated, along with James Fisk, in a scandal, after the two men took control of the Erie Railroad. Gould became president, and he and Fisk were said

---

*About 1882, the hamlet of Lumberville had by petition changed its name to Arena. It was believed the new name would attract more summer visitors, as Lumberville sounded less refined. Why the name *Arena* was chosen is unclear, though some older residents said it was because of the mountains that surrounded the village that gave it the appearance of an arena. It was also stated that in the past, there were so many fights between lumberjacks or loggers, raftsmen, and villagers that Jack O'Conner, a local wit, "is said to have suggested the new name inasmuch as the village seemed to be the spot where the gladiators congregated to do battle." *Tuscarora Club's Forty-Year History,* 5–6.

to have "plundered" the Erie and manipulated the stock for their own interest. Public protest forced Gould out of the company and made him pay back $7.5 million dollars.

Gould also caused public outrage when a group of speculators he headed tried to corner the gold market, hoping to increase the price. This culminated in the financial panic known as "Black Friday," a day on which many Wall Street investors were ruined. Gould later obtained control of the Western Union Telegraph Company and the elevated railways in New York City, and was connected with many of the largest railway financial operations in the United States.

One year after Jay Gould's fishing trip to Furlough Lake, his son, George J. Gould, made a similar trout-fishing excursion, and by January 1890, newspapers were reporting that he had purchased the lake and 600 acres, along with a portion of Dry Brook, for a summer estate. George Gould constructed a log residence near the lake, encircled his property with barbed wire several feet high, and stocked his grounds with deer, elk, Jersey cows, and sheep. He built stables for his horses, kennels for his dogs, a hennery for his chickens, and a pigeon house for three hundred to four hundred pigeons. He also constructed a cottage for a gatekeeper and employed a large staff, including a gamekeeper. Today, more than one hundred years later, the Gould family still owns and maintains the family estate and additional acres. The landscape has been preserved in as natural a state as when it was acquired.

12

The 1890s

"AN ENEMY" OF "*FONTINALIS*"; THE IZAAK WALTONS OF WALTON;
THE END OF AN ERA; and ACID FACTORIES

Most of the major Catskill streams were stocked with brown trout in 1887. As previously stated, their appearance in the catches and creels of fishermen did not become apparent until 1889 or even 1890. And when brown trout did begin to make their presence known, there was immediate controversy and a difference of opinion over whether it was wise to have placed the fish in New York waters.

Throughout the 1890s, fears surfaced that because brown trout grew quicker and larger than brook trout, they would destroy the native fish. There was also criticism of the practice of indiscriminately stocking "foreign species" that the public was not fully informed about. Fuel was added to the controversy when an Englishman, living in this country, claimed on the pages of *Forest and Stream* that brown trout were "an enemy" of *"fontinalis"* and that it was wrong to introduce them into waters inhabited by brook trout. "When it grows large," he stated, it feeds totally on fish and "of course is a cannibal."

Following their introduction, brown trout thrived, especially in the lower sections of the Beaverkill, Willowemoc, and Neversink. In these larger waters, brown trout found an environment extremely beneficial to their growth and survival.

The lower sections were the most productive reaches on these streams, and the habitat was excellent: Pools were very large and deep, and riffles were rich in aquatic insects. Mayflies were abundant and, coupled with a large and varied minnow population, formed a wonderful food supply. Even more importantly, the water was generally too warm to support many native brook trout and therefore virtually free of competitive game fish. These circumstances not only ensured the success of the species, but allowed them to have a swift and dramatic impact on the fisheries.

Browns grew rapidly, and although some from the original stockings in 1887 may have been caught previously, the first reported catch in Catskill newspapers did not appear until May 1890. Irving W. Finch, a veteran Beaverkill angler, came into town with a "German trout" that measured 15¾ inches and weighed 1 pound, 9 ounces. This trout, a little more than three years of age, was one of the fry that traveled the train with "Gum" Dodge on his trip from the Caledonia hatchery.

Later that summer, an even larger trout was spotted living in Palen's millpond, which was located on a side channel of the Beaverkill, upstream of the Forks (or Junction Pool). It was said that every man in Rockland was after the big fish, but only "Gum" Dodge succeeded in hooking, and then losing, the trout.

Brown trout made a huge impact on the Beaverkill earlier than they did on other streams, and during the 1890s, no trout stream in the Catskills produced so many large browns. A few years after they were introduced, a reporter for the *New York Times*, in June 1891, stated that there were at least four large trout weighing more than 2½ pounds and another of more than 3 pounds caught in the Beaverkill, one being caught along the upper river near Lew Beach. He went on to report that near the junction of the Beaverkill and Willowemoc, there is "excellent" fishing for big trout, and he advised his readers to use bait, as there are "brown or German" trout present.

After the above report, a 2-pound, 11-ounce trout was captured downstream of Lew Beach, and another weighing 2½ pounds was taken at the old tannery dam at Beaverkill. The following summer, when the trout from the original stocking were in their fifth year of growth, E. J. Disbro of Rockland caught a trout measuring 24 inches and weighing 5 pounds, 10 ounces, at the covered bridge at Beaverkill.

That August, the Reverend Robert N. Josclyn, a resident of Minnesota vacationing on the Beaverkill, caught an enormous trout under the bridge at Craig-e-clare. This fish had been seen for years; after its capture weighed 6 pounds, 3 ounces; and was said to be a "California trout." Two years later, under the same bridge, Joseph Kelley caught another "California trout" that measured 23¾ inches and weighed 6 pounds. These trout were identified as rainbow trout, but their size makes one wonder if they were not misidentified and were actually brown trout.

The Beaverkill Covered Bridge Pool. Ed Van Put.

In August 1893, Jasper Barnhart of Beaverkill caught a 26-inch trout weighing 6 pounds at the Beaverkill covered bridge. Further upstream, Theodore Ingalsbe took a 22-inch trout that weighed 4 pounds, 1 ounce, on a no. 9 White Miller in Davidson's Eddy, just downstream of Lew Beach. A year later, the largest trout ever seen, a 32-inch, 8¾-pound brown, was found floating in the Beaverkill, not quite dead—the victim of a spear wound.

All over the Catskills, "German" trout were having an impact on the fisheries. It was common in the 1890s to read about large trout being caught, but they were not always identified as brown trout. It is believed that in the beginning many anglers were still unfamiliar with the fish but reported to local newspapers that they had caught "a trout." The size alone of the fish reported indicated they were not native brook trout. An example of this can be seen in the reports of the *Catskill Recorder* in the northeastern Catskills.

During the season of 1892, the newspaper wrote on May 13 that Florence Miller of New York City caught a trout in the "Schoharie kill" that weighed 3½ pounds on a 6-ounce rod, "a feat rarely accomplished by the most expert anglers," and her fishing companion caught a trout that measured 18½ inches and another measuring 14 inches. Two weeks later, the same paper reported that Harry Bloom caught a 22-inch trout that weighed 3½ pounds in the Kiskatom Creek. The Kiskatom had been stocked five years previously by Josephine Hopkins (Catskill, New York) with six thousand brown trout.

In June, the *Catskill Recorder* claimed that James W. Layman of Tannersville, fishing near the headwaters of the Schoharie, caught six trout that weighed a total of 10½ pounds; one measured 19½ inches, one 18½ inches, and another 17½ inches. No fish measured less than 13 inches in length. "This is perhaps the finest lot of trout ever taken in the Catskills. . . ."[1] On the same day, the paper reported that Thomas Deming of Jewett caught a trout in the Schoharie that measured 19 inches, and the next day caught another, that was 23 inches!

Trout fishing improved so much on the lower Beaverkill that articles praising that section of the river began to appear in sporting journals. One of the first was very descriptive and titled "How to Fish the Lower Beaverkill." The piece appeared in the *American Angler* in August 1893 and was written by S. K. Putnam, who gives explicit instructions on how to fish the water immediately downstream of Roscoe, from Junction Pool to East Branch. The author acknowledged that in the past, nearly everyone who visited the Beaverkill selected the upper river for their sport, but Putnam wrote that he wished to inform readers of the good fishing now found on the lower Beaverkill. He said that trout in the lower river would average much larger in size than those upstream and that "many of more than two pounds" were being taken from the "beautiful pools and grand rifts" below the junction of the Beaverkill and Willowemoc.

Seven years after the initial stocking of brown trout into the Beaverkill, an article appeared in the *New York Times* titled "Midsummer Beaverkill Fishing." Its author reported on the progress brown trout had made and on the difficulty Catskill fishermen were having in catching them, as ordinary trout tackle proved less than adequate:

Just now an unsolved problem of the Beaverkill, and, in fact, of the Willowemoc, is how to capture the large brown trout, *Salmo fario*, which, planted at Rockland, are now by migration and propagation up the river as far as Sprague's (Lew Beach), and vary in weight from ten to the ounce to ten pounds.

The European variety is piscivorous, and it preys on the American trout. A two pound brown trout caught the other day had dined on a quarter pound *Salvelinus*, and one of six pounds caught last year was digesting an eleven inch trout. An angler last month at Voorhess' hooked a brown trout of between four and five pounds, and at first the trout did not appear disposed to battle for liberty, but when it became convinced that the angler really meant it, it displayed its strength, and left with a leader and several yards of line, after breaking the angling wand in two places.[2]

While some trout fishermen were having trouble catching and landing the large trout, newspapers continued to report on many of the giant browns being taken, mostly in the Beaverkill. However, in 1894, J. D. W. M. ("Alphabet") Decker of Livingston Manor caught a "German trout" measuring 23 inches and weighing 6¾ pounds in the water of the lower Willowemoc Creek. The *New York Sun* reported that the trout had "defied" anglers for two years and had lived under the bridge near Decker's home: "No matter how he got the trout he has done a good thing, for it was a voracious cannibal, and waged a deadly warfare on the smaller trout in the brook."[3]

The following year, 1895, Joseph Kelley again caught a large trout in the Beaverkill, under Wagner's bridge at Craig-e-clare; this time Kelley's trout was identified as a brown that measured 23¾ inches and weighed 6 pounds, 15 ounces! Fishing downstream of Shin Creek, E. F. Davidson of Lew Beach caught a huge 28-inch, 7-pound, 5-ounce brown at Davidson & Wamsley's mill. Large brown trout were caught all through the 1890s, and although many were reported in local newspapers, there were possibly as many caught that had gone unreported.

Fishing at Sliter's dam on the Beaverkill, John Tompkins caught two trout weighing 3½ and 4½ pounds, respectively. A week later, Egbert Tripp of Turnwood caught on a "fly pole," under the same dam, a "German brown trout" weighing 4 pounds, 5 ounces, and a second enormous brown, 31 inches in length, weighing 10½ pounds!

One year later, another huge brown trout would make similar headlines. In June 1895, a large fish was again seen in Palen's millpond. The whole town heard of the big trout, and on the day it was decided to draw down the millpond and capture the fish, more than two hundred townspeople turned out. Workers from the new Beaverkill Hatchery, which had been constructed upstream, placed a net across the outlet, but somehow in the excitement, the big trout managed to leap over the net and escape into the raceway.

George Cochran, who had been standing on the bank, leaped into the raceway and succeeded in capturing the fish with his hands. It was immediately placed in a nail keg, and then transferred to a tank of water and taken to the nearby hatchery.

The giant brown trout measured 31 inches and weighed more than 9 pounds. It may have been a trout from the original stocking of 1887. At the hatchery, the fish was placed in a display tank, and in just a few days, several hundred visitors from all over the state came to view the great fish. In time, the trout succumbed to injuries it had received when captured and died. It was such a great specimen that the supervisor of the hatchery sent the trout to Rochester to be mounted, and upon its return, it was placed on exhibition at the Beaverkill Hatchery.*

While brown trout grew and multiplied, anglers were slow to praise or comment on them. This silence prompted the English editor R. B. Marston, who had gifted the Cold Spring Harbor hatchery with five thousand brown trout eggs, to wonder why so little was said about brown trout in American sporting papers: "The last report I heard was not quite so favorable as it might have been and I sincerely hope that our trout is not going to prove such a disappointment in America as the American brook trout has proved in England."[4]

---

*Apparently, when the Beaverkill Hatchery closed in 1904, the mounted trout was presented to the Palen family, whose heirs maintain a home alongside the historic gristmill. The magnificent brown trout is still there, on a dining-room wall, under a handsome glass dome, immortalized forever—just a stone's throw from the site where it captured the attention of an entire community. A tag on the mount reads: Brown or German Trout: Length—30½ inches, weight—9¼ pounds. Caught June 20, 1895.

It was not long before Americans did speak out about brown trout, and it was as Marston suspected; anglers began finding fault with the European import. It was feared that the rapid growth of brown trout in American waters was at the expense of the native brook trout, which they were eating and driving from the streams!

It was claimed that Americans were not fully informed about the European trout, and that in this country there was too much indiscriminate stocking. Some trout fishermen believed that there was no need to stock the fish and viewed their importation as a serious mistake. These sentiments began to spread, as the traditional large catches of native brook trout grew even scarcer, and many anglers attributed their empty creels to the voracious appetites of the German trout.

A 29-inch, 8-pound brown trout captured in Potick Creek, a tributary of Catskill Creek. *Dear Old Greene County,* 1915.

It became apparent that browns *were* competing with native trout for food, habitat, and spawning areas. In streams or stream sections, where the two species could coexist mostly because of water temperature, brown trout, by their aggressive behavior, replaced the native brook trout entirely. This was especially true on large portions of the Beaverkill and Willowemoc.

Reports began to surface in local newspapers that there were no longer "large catches of brook trout" in Sullivan County. The *New York Sun* believed the "Big fish" were depleting the streams:

No large catches of brook trout have reported this season by those fishermen who have hitherto successfully sought the speckled beauties in the streams of Sullivan county. The fishermen attributed their empty creels to the voracious appetites of the large German trout which were placed in the Beaverkill, Willowemoc, and other favorite Sullivan county fishing streams two or three years ago.[5]

With the opening of the trout season of 1897, the *Delaware Gazette* made the comment that it is "to be regretted," that "German brown and California trout" were ever introduced into our streams. The writer went on to say that they may grow faster and larger but they were unfit for "table use."

On May 17, 1897, an article appeared in the *New York Times* titled "Survey of the Once Famous Beaverkill—Places Where It Does Not Pay to Fish." The writer claimed that all that can be expected at the end of a day's fishing on the "once famous Beaverkill" is a "half a dozen small trout." His personal experience prompts him to tell readers not to believe the stories of fishing resort owners who claim that the Beaverkill is "full of trout."

He avows that the stream is "barren" from Beech Hill Brook downstream to Rockland, and he blames a freshet in 1895, but adds that even before then, the fishing from Lew Beach down to Rockland had been "but fair" at its best, in the past four or five years. He also cited pollution from a sawmill a mile below Lew Beach and the keeping of undersized trout by fishermen; and his article points the blame on brown trout as well:

> The brown trout—*S. fario*—problem is still unresolved. Will the European intruder eat up the native trout until they are extinct, or will careful stocking result in retaining both species? Fry stocking will not do it, and nothing but liming the entire river from the mill here to Rockland will eradicate the brown trout. Such a heroic remedy would result in ruining the Beaverkill as a trout stream for at least five years. Were yearling trout, or, still better, fish of eight inches used for stocking, as in the waters of the Blooming Grove Park Club, the native trout might still hold its own against its ferocious and ravenous cousins.[6]

The wisdom of stocking a fish that preyed upon their beloved brook trout was questioned by many, and enthusiasm for brown trout, what little there was, began to wane. In addition, browns were denounced as "logy and lazy," and it was said that they had inferior flavor when served at table. Comparisons between the species became more frequent, and it is not surprising that American anglers rallied to the defense of their own:

> In appearance the brown is scaly, flat, greenish-yellow, irregular in form, bad eye, homely overall. In the native the scales are invisible; he is gold and silver, round and symmetrical, and as beautiful an object as lavish nature produces. . . . As food, the flavor of the brown becomes "weedy" after the middle of May and is decidedly unpleasant to the taste, though early in the season he is not so bad. The native is sweet and delicious as long as the stream is up.[7]

Throughout the 1890s, large brown trout were being caught in sizes that were never imagined. Trout fishermen were, in fact, unaccustomed to catching such big fish, and more often than not these big trout smashed tackle and got away.

In May 1898, local papers reported that Alex Voorhess of Lew Beach caught a brown trout in the Beaverkill that weighed 5 pounds, 4 ounces. One of the most impressive catches of the day was made by William H. Mills, who stayed at Green's Hotel along the Beaverkill, on the Rockland Flats. In June 1899, Mills, fishing with minnows, caught four brown trout that tipped the scales at a total of 14 pounds, 9 ounces. His catch included fish that measured 19½ inches and weighed 3 pounds; 21 inches and weighed 3 pounds, 4 ounces; 21 inches and weighed 3 pounds, 4 ounces; and the largest, 25 inches, which weighed in at 5 pounds!

The stocking of brown trout was pivotal to trout fishing in the Catskills. Although they did reduce the native brook trout population dramatically, their introduction also created many more miles of trout-fishing water, as browns began inhabiting the stretches previously avoided by native brook trout because of water temperature. This amounted to added trout miles on the Beaverkill, Willowemoc, Neversink, Rondout, Esopus, Schoharie Creek, and the East and West Branches of the Delaware River.

BROWNS IN THE NEVERSINK

Stocking records from the state hatchery at Caledonia reveal that brown trout were first placed in the Neversink in March 1887. Four separate shipments of fry were sent to the village of Neversink; the first was received on March 22 by Newal T. Hodge, who placed ten thousand brown trout fry into Hodge and Conklin Brooks, small tributaries just northwest of the village and downstream of Nauvoo Brook.

The other three shipments arrived on March 30 and consisted of three lots of six thousand fry. These were sent to F. Dean, H. W. Dean, and N. J. Benson, who placed the browns in "wild meadow brooks," tributaries of the Neversink; Broom and Sharp Creeks; and Wolf and Hansen Brooks.

The Neversink below the village of Neversink. *The American Angler*, 1892.

In just a few years, browns were thriving in all of the large pools and lengthy riffles in and around the village of Neversink. The habitat was ideal for the new species, and with an abundance of aquatic insects and a plentiful minnow population, the food supply was excellent. Although brook trout did inhabit the water, their numbers and sizes provided little competition, and the browns grew rapidly and multiplied beyond expectations.

The water below the forks, where the East and West Branches joined, was not posted or owned by fishing clubs, and it was not long before trout fishermen were plying their skills downstream of, and even beyond, the village of Neversink. The word was being spread that the best trout fishing on the Neversink could now be found from Halls Mills downstream to 2 miles below the village, a distance of approximately 12 miles.

Theodore Gordon, the legendary Catskill fly fisher and journalist, caught his first brown trout in the Neversink in the summer of 1889. At the time, he was unaware that any trout other than native brook trout were in the stream. He had taken a few natives while fishing a single fly, a tiny Alder, and hooked a trout that was larger and fought with a little more determination. At first he was not sure what the fish was, and he believed he had caught a rare and unusual fish.

Intent on preserving the trout, Gordon placed it in his hat without even taking the fly from the fish's mouth, and ran as fast as possible to a little store attached to the hotel where he was staying. The storekeeper had a live-bait box in a raceway of water nearby, and the trout was gently placed in it, in the hope that it could be saved; unfortunately, the brown only lived a day or two.

Gordon later learned that brown trout had been planted in the river a few years earlier. He believed that the dates that browns were stocked were 1885 and 1886; however, stocking records reveal that the date was 1887.

The trout season of 1890 was a memorable one on the Neversink; brown trout were now three-year-olds and growing rapidly. The *Republican Watchman* of Monticello reported on June 7 that "The number of anglers who have churned the Neversink this year is unprecedentedly large, and more large trout have been captured than in many years past." The newspaper also claimed that fourteen-year-old Willie Dean of Neversink had caught "1,305 trout this spring!" A year later the teenager caught one of the first large brown trout to come out of the Neversink, a 2-pound "German trout," downstream of the Neversink Valley House.

In May 1891, a correspondent to the *New York Times* who lived in the city but was familiar with the Catskills advised readers to fish the Neversink, claiming that there was "no lack" of fishing grounds open to the public. Take the O. & W. to Fallsburg, he urged, and then the stage to Grahamsville 12 miles distant, and then a buckboard to Claryville. "A lover of trout fishing" he claimed, wanting to get away from "bricks and mortar," could fish for a week and have great sport between Claryville and the "Great Bend."

Until this date, the East Branch of the Neversink had been free of fishing clubs; however, in the summer of 1891, a club emerged in the area of Tray Mill Brook. Four men from Brooklyn purchased 560 acres and 2 miles of the East Branch, and formed the Hamilton Club. After a few seasons, a club member named Harrington Putnam bought out the other members and became the sole owner of the property.

Putnam was a prominent New York attorney who served for many years as a Supreme Court justice. He was known for his knowledge of admiralty law. Putnam expanded his holdings along the stream to more than 800 acres and occupied a seasonal residence on the banks of the East Branch known as Red Lodge.

It was also in 1894 that the water downstream of Clarence Roof's Wintoon Lodge, on the West Branch of the Neversink, was purchased and made into a fishing preserve. Rafael R. Govin of New York City acquired the last 1½ miles of the West Branch and an additional 1½ miles around the hamlet of Claryville, which included the lower portion of the East Branch and the main Neversink. Govin assembled hundreds of acres into an estate he called Tiverton.

Born in Cuba and educated at Columbia and Columbia Law School, Govin became a highly successful New York attorney, publisher, and financier. At one time, he owned several newspapers in Cuba, as well as papers in New York and Pennsylvania.

All during the 1890s, his upstream neighbor, Clarence Roof, continued to have trouble with poachers. Some men used nets and set lines, others fished at night; some were local, most were unknown; and in the summer of 1894, it was reported in a regional newspaper that one of Roof's night watchmen was hit over the head while patrolling!

The following year, an article appeared in

East Branch of the Neversink. Ed Van Put.

the *Pine Hill Sentinel* titled "The Denning Fish War," which told of the continuing conflicts between trout fishermen and fishing preserve owners, "both in the courts with law books as weapons and in the woods, where a physical warfare was waged with only the weapons furnished by nature. These battles have so multiplied that it seems as though there were a lawsuit or a fight for every fish in the brooks."[8] The paper went on to say that the problem was "especially lively," and in the courts, sentiment "favors the locals."

In order to get a fair decision in the courts, Roof began having trespass cases tried far from the town of Denning, where a jury made up of locals was apt to dismiss the charges or set a laughable fine, such as 6 cents! Cases began to be tried in far off Saugerties, Kingston, or Marbletown, and even if dismissed, they at least caused the defendants the hardship of traveling such great distances.

Another tactic Roof used to thwart the netting of trout was to place large quantities of brush, logs, and old stumps in the stream. He even tried a form of bribery: In the summer of 1899, the *Kingston Weekly Freeman*, on July 27, reported that Roof had long been annoyed with the residents of Denning who fished his private preserve and that there had been many confrontations, despite his hiring a large number of stream-watchers to patrol his water. "In pursuance of this he has just presented $100 to the ten school districts in the Town of Denning, coupled with the request that the residents refrain from further trespassing upon his stream."

Clarence Roof continued to add to his Wintoon preserve, assembling more than 3,000 acres and approximately 5 miles of the West Branch. He made many improvements to his extensive holdings and died at Wintoon Lodge in 1923.

By 1894, there were large browns in every pool along the Neversink, and Theodore Gordon estimated that they weighed from 1 to 6 pounds! The water in the Neversink was so clear that fishermen had no trouble in spotting the huge fish in pools with such colorful names as the Black Hole, Cat Pool, Red Rock Pool, and the Moody Hole. In just a few years, brown trout had become the dominant species.

Fishermen found it exasperating to see these immense trout lying, exposed at times, at the bottom of a pool and not be able to catch them. Individual trout became known for their abilities to elude anglers and yet remain in the same pool, year after year. But not all were as fortunate, and in the low flows of summer, trout were shot, snagged, or snared.

In one of his *Forest and Stream* columns, Theodore Gordon recalled seeing three trout, weighing between 2¾ and 5 pounds, being taken from a pool by two farmers using a wire snare: "I saw the men and two of the trout running as I passed up stream, but never dreamed that they could take the fish out of such a large body of water by snaring."[9]

In the summer of 1898, several papers reported on a "German" trout that was caught near Halls Mills that measured 26 inches and weighed 7½ pounds! The giant fish was caught by Charles Porter of Grahamsville, who sold the trout to a boarder at the Shield's House, where it was put on display and later resold at an even greater price.

BROWNS IN THE ESOPUS

Over on the Esopus Creek, rainbows were firmly established before the arrival of brown trout; but not everyone was enamored with the species, and for the same reasons fishermen disliked brown trout. After a fishing trip to Shandaken, Judge Alphonso T. Clearwater, state Supreme Court judge and noted Ulster County historian, informed the *Kingston Weekly Freeman* that he condemned the introduction of the California or rainbow trout. The judge claimed that they ate the fry of the native brook trout, and he feared that in time, rainbows would reduce the populations of brook trout—which they did.

Stocking records reveal that browns were first shipped from Caledonia for stocking in the Esopus Creek on April 19, 1888,

La Ment Hotel. *Picturesque Ulster*, 1896–1905, published by Hope Farm Press, 1991.

and C. T. Conant of St. Remy received two thousand brown trout fry. It was quite a few years after their introduction that browns received any mention in area newspapers. One of the first large brown trout to make headlines was a fish caught in 1899. In June of that year, the *Pine Hill Sentinel* mentioned a 24½-inch, 4-pound "German" brown trout that was caught in the raceway of Wey's mill at Big Indian. The large trout was taken to the La Ment Hotel, near the railroad station, and was put on exhibition. La Ment's was the headquarters for many fishermen who fished the waters around Big Indian.

BROWNS IN THE EAST AND WEST BRANCH

At first, the East and West Branches of the Delaware were not greatly affected by the introduction of brown trout. Both streams were overrun with smallmouth bass, but the West Branch held a number of rainbow trout that had established themselves with some success near the headwaters.

Rainbows had been introduced in the spring of 1881, five years earlier than browns. "California mountain trout" were placed in East Brook, in the village of Walton, and the following year, anglers reported catches of the new species that averaged about 6 inches in length. In the fall, a 9½-inch rainbow was captured when a mill pond was drained, and the trout was placed in an aquarium at the drug store, where most of the village took pleasure in watching this fascinating and strangely beautiful fish.

Over the next few years, rainbows did exceptionally well and were credited with improving the trout fishing. During the 1890s, large rainbows, some even in the 25-inch range, were caught from the West Branch, near Walton, Bloomville, Delhi, and Hamden. Two tributaries that acquired a reputation for holding large rainbows were Peak's Brook and Elk Creek; both streams were in the vicinity of Delhi.

Just as they had on the West Branch, some rainbows became established at an early date along the lower East Branch. State hatchery records reveal that two shipments of "California mountain trout" were ordered for the East Branch and its tributaries in 1881; on June 24, twenty-five thousand fry were sent to E. D. Mayhew, and on June 28, fifteen thousand were received by W. C. McNally of Hancock, who placed them in Spring Brook.

Some of the rainbows destined for Spring Brook may have been placed in Cadosia Creek; or, Spring Brook may have been another name for Cadosia Creek, as a year later the *Hancock Herald* reported that a trout fisherman was exhibiting a California mountain trout in town, which measured 7 inches, that he caught in Cadosia Creek.

Brown trout from the Caledonia hatchery were first sent to the waters of the East Branch in 1887, when E. Canfield of Middletown, New York, received ten thousand fry and placed them in Roods, Tyler, Russell, and East brooks. The following year, James Ballentine of Andes stocked brown trout in the waters of the upper East Branch, placing five thousand fry in the Tremper Kill and its tributaries.

At the time browns were introduced, the East Branch of the Delaware, from Hancock at the mouth all the way to Arkville, had become a bass fishery. Smallmouth bass multiplied rapidly and, much to the chagrin of some, displaced the pickerel population, a species that was popular with local anglers. The *Walton Reporter* on May 9, 1896, gave an example of just how common pickerel were in the East Branch. The newspaper told of George Miller of Downsville catching 21 pounds of pickerel, three of which had a total weight of 9 pounds!

While the East Branch at Arkville may have been colder than the preferred water temperatures of smallmouth bass, the species did much better from Downsville to Hancock, and bass dominated this stretch in the 1890s. Newspaper reports reveal large catches of bass, such as three fishermen catching 150 smallmouths at the village of East Branch in July 1895 and two anglers taking 50 pounds of bass near Fishs Eddy in September 1898.

Bass were so plentiful at the turn of the century that William C. Harris, editor of the *American Angler,* praised the fishery and made reference to how bass had displaced the "chub" that had previously dominated the pools and eddies on the lower East Branch. Writing in *The Basses Fresh-Water and Marine,* Harris states:

> At the junction of the east branch of the Delaware River and the Beaverkill, 150 miles from New York city, and all along the first-named water to Hancock, a distance of about twelve miles, some of the best fly-fishing for black bass in New York or any other State can be found. In this section there are scores of pools and long reaches where black bass swarm and rise freely to the fly, particularly in the early days of the season.[10]

Smallmouth bass, Louis Rhead illustration. *The Basses Fresh-Water and Marine,* 1905.

Perhaps because of the competition with smallmouth bass, it took brown trout longer to establish a viable population in the East Branch. On the Beaverkill and Willowemoc, where they had established themselves relatively quickly, browns did not have to compete with other species.

One advantage browns did have over bass was their preference for cooler water temperatures; the water temperatures of the East Branch, upstream of Downsville, were in their preferred range. This resulted in browns having a longer growing season, eventually reaching larger sizes more quickly than the bass. The transition began to take place as they slowly but surely became the dominant species in the upper East Branch.

In addition, brown trout spawned in tributaries, and their fry and fingerlings, so vulnerable to predation, were protected for a year or two before they descended downstream to the larger waters. Smallmouth bass, on the other hand, spawned in the main stream, and their young could be preyed upon by browns and a host of other predators.

THE IZAAK WALTONS OF WALTON

For many years, the hub of trout-fishing activity in the West Branch Valley was the village of Walton. This was due primarily to the fact that two excellent trout streams flowed on either side of the village; their cold waters also had a positive effect on the West Branch in the immediate area of Walton. One example of this is seen by a catch that Linus Crabb made in July 1875, when the *Walton Chronicle* stated that he had caught eleven brook trout, three of which were more than a pound, with a cumulative weight of 6½ pounds!

Both East and West Brooks flow in a general direction southerly before entering the West Branch; East Brook on the upriver—or east side—of Walton, and West Brook on the downriver, or west side. East Brook is approximately 10 miles in length, and West Brook flows about 8 miles. Even though both streams were altered significantly for manufacturing at an early date, they still maintained excellent trout populations for many years. F. W. Beers's atlas of the village of Walton in 1869 depicts a planing mill, another mill dam on East Brook, and a carding factory and tannery dam on West Brook.

Opening of the trout season. New York Public Library.

Newspaper accounts of the fishing, going back to the trout season of 1885, reveal that East Brook produced large numbers of trout in sizes that indicate good growth rates for a small stream. The *Walton Reporter* mentioned on May 30, 1885 one angler at the start of the season caught forty-two trout in East Brook that averaged 8 inches.

During the 1890s, the village of Walton boasted a significant number of trout fishermen, many of whom opened the season along the banks of East or West Brook. It is difficult to fully comprehend the degree of enthusiasm displayed for trout fishing by anglers then living in the vicinity of the village, but an example of its popularity, and what the opening day of the trout season was like during this period, is found on the front page of the *Walton Reporter* of May 2, 1891.

The editor claimed that on Thursday, the day before the season opened, there was such a run on fishing tackle that by nine o'clock there was hardly a "full outfit" left in any of the stores. On the morning of the trout opener, the streets of Walton were deserted, and East Brook was lined with fishermen: "It is safe to say that from seventy-five to one hundred Walton fishermen whipped the silvery waters of that stream."

One angler named Van Aken got up at three o'clock in the morning, certain that he would be the first on the stream, and before he traveled a half-mile, he encountered thirty fishermen at various pools along the brook! "He reeled up his line in disgust and went home."

Trout fishermen did begin to wander back into town by about 7:30 A.M. with stories, as well as fine catches, of trout. Some anglers reported taking as many as fifty fish, with the largest trout weighing in at over a pound.

It was also reported that Trout Creek, about 6 to 7 miles northwest of Walton, was "literally thronged," and landowners along the lower portion of the stream were charging $1.50 for the privilege of fishing.

One week after the above report, the *Walton Reporter,* on May 9, published a front-page article titled "Trouting at Trout Creek." This story was a description of opening day along the stream. It recalled how fishermen began to gather at the village of Trout Creek on Thursday to be on time for the Friday opening. "A number began fishing at midnight," and brought in a "fine mess."

The reporter stated, "The banks of the stream were black with fishermen, and the village literally swarmed with them." A barrel of trout was taken within 2 miles of the village, and Trout Creek was "thoroughly skinned." It was also stated that there was "hard feelings" between the farmers who charged for the privilege of fishing and those who did not.

THE END OF AN ERA

By the end of the 1890s, brown trout were firmly established in the streams and rivers of the Catskills. The reign of the brook trout had come to an end, and in the years ahead, trout fishermen would become familiar with brown and rainbow trout, which they would accept and value as game fish. However, it is doubtful that any generation of anglers would ever feel the same degree of affection and warm attachment as did those fishermen who knew the native brook trout.

The brook trout was a fish beloved by our pioneer fishermen, and it was the favorite fish of the old masters of American trout fishing. William C. Harris, author and editor of the *American Angler,* once declared: "We do not and can not wonder at their choice when we take this charr in hand and glance at its symmetrical form—a cleaver of the water—and the varied hues of its mellowed coloration, diffused in softness of tone over its entire body, with no jarring flash of color to mar its fullness of beauty."[11]

There is always speculation and discussion among trout fishermen about what the fishing was like in days of old, before domestic trout were introduced into our streams, lakes, and ponds. Then, as now, habitat often dictates how large a fish will grow, and brook trout between 15 to 20 inches, with weights of from 1 to 3 pounds, *were* taken on occasion, in the deeper pools generally formed by in-stream dams that were constructed for mills. These were rare fish; as a rule, any trout caught that weighed a pound or more made the newspapers, and not just locally, but in other parts of the region as well.

Walter S. Allerton, who fished and wrote about the Catskills in the days when only native brook trout were present, claimed that the largest trout he ever saw caught in Ulster or Sullivan counties weighed 4 pounds, 2 ounces. This was after the fish was kept in captivity with an unlimited supply of minnows to feed upon; the trout was originally caught in the Neversink and weighed, when captured, 3½ pounds. Allerton adds that such a fish was a rarity and that an average day's catch would not contain a trout larger than 12 inches.

Another veteran Catskill trout fisherman, James S. Van Cleef, who wrote often of the region and its fisheries, stated in a May 21, 1898 *Forest and Stream* article titled "Trout Waters and Trout Weights" that although trout in Catskill ponds "commonly" grew to a size of 2 to 3 pounds, those weighing more than a pound were not "very often" caught on a fly. There are large trout in some streams, he wrote, but they are usually found under a mill dam and seldom caught, except with bait.

Van Cleef recalled taking in one season, "about 1859," before he began using flies exclusively, three brook trout; two weighing 1 pound each, and one weighing 1 pound, 5 ounces. He also recalled Judge Fitch telling him that after fishing the Beaverkill for forty years, he had never taken a trout with a fly that would "tip the

A brook trout fisherman. *Outing Magazine*, July 1896.

scales" at 1 pound. But Fitch did, however, take "quite a number" of large trout, including one that weighed more than 2 pounds, on flies in the East Branch of the Delaware. This was in a "noted pool" that contained "many very large trout," located a mile or 2 above Margaretville.*

Native brook trout larger than 3 pounds were almost always caught in ponds or lakes. So rare were they, in fact, that for many years, P. T. Barnum offered a cash prize of $100 for any brook trout weighing 4 pounds, delivered alive and uninjured to the aquarium department of his New York museum.

---

*Quite possibly the junction of the East Branch of the Delaware and the Bush Kill.

One such trout was delivered to Barnum in the 1850s. Beaverkill fishing-resort owner James Murdock received a "great price" for a 5-pound, 2-ounce brook trout he captured in the pond known today as Big Pond, located near Turnwood.

Another even larger fish, and the largest brook trout ever reported from the Beaverkill valley, also came out of Big Pond. In June 1860, Charles Woodward of Andes caught a magnificent 24-inch trout weighing 6¼ pounds. Three years later, the *Republican Watchman* of December 23, 1863, reported that the week before, Woodward caught another trout weighing 5½ pounds. This trout supposedly was sold to P. T. Barnum for $75.

Appropriately enough, when the region was first surveyed in 1809, the pond was known as Trout Pond; it later became Big Trout Pond and finally, Big Pond. In the early days of settlement, the pond contained "large quantities" of trout; it was fed by large springs, and no streams flowed into it, but a good-sized stream flowed out. James Murdock owned Big Pond in the 1880s, and in 1881 he stocked the water with "black bass" he acquired from Seth Green, which remain present in the lake today.

Furlough Lake, in the town of Hardenbergh, was also rumored to have yielded a trout weighing 5 pounds that was taken to Barnum. However, one veteran Catskill fisherman who saw the trout exhibited in Barnum's aquarium estimated the fish to have weighed closer to 2½ pounds.

Another body of water that was well known for yielding large brook trout was Long Pond, now known as Tennanah Lake, in the town of Fremont, Sullivan County. In June 1861, the *Republican Watchman* reported on a "magnificent specimen" caught by David B. Beers that weighed 4¼ pounds!

In 1831, Benjamin Misner constructed a sawmill at the outlet of the pond that some referred to as Misner's Pond. The pond was stocked with trout well before there were even hatcheries to provide such a service. In 1833, Jacob and Benjamin Misner caught brook trout in Hankins Creek, Pise's Brook and other nearby streams, and placed them in Long Pond.

Whether the pond contained brook trout before this stocking is unknown, but for many years after, it produced large trout. Long Pond's reputation continued into the 1880s, and a newspaper account in the summer of 1885 told of Jerome Mille catching a 22-inch, 4½-pound brook trout.

Sand Pond was another body of water that enjoyed a reputation for producing large brook trout. Located at the headwaters of the Willowemoc in the town of Denning, anglers often took brook trout from its waters that weighed 2 to 3 pounds. A fishing party from Ellenville once, before the pond became private in the 1860s, caught a number of trout and graded them according to size: "the first thirty fish at the head of the line averaged two-and-a-half pounds each."

In 1868, James S. Van Cleef purchased the pond, and together with several fishing friends from Poughkeepsie formed the Willewemoc Club. The club immediately set about improving the fishing at Sand Pond, as there was only one stream flowing into it, and this was almost inaccessible to the trout, which were accustomed to spawning along the shoreline.

In 1870, at a time when habitat improvement was unheard of, the Willewemoc Club installed a spawning race (box) near the shore of the pond near the best springs. The idea was to improve spawning opportunities for the trout, and the method was successful. In 1877, new spawning beds were constructed, and hundreds of large brook trout were observed over them.

Members of the club recognized that the trout in Sand Pond were special and practiced an early form of catch and release. An early newspaper report described the practice:

The hook was successfully extracted and they were consigned to a wire creel, which was fastened to the stern of the boat. Taken ashore, the fish were transferred to a spring near the landing, where they were watched closely, and if one showed symptoms of any mortal hurt, he was forthwith dispatched for table use. The rest were put back into the pond, except such as might be needed on the "festal board." And thus the fish are caught over and over again affording abundant sport with no destructive waste.[12]

Sand Pond was eminent among Catskill trout ponds because of its sizable brook trout; fish measuring between 12 and 16 inches were common, and in 1872, the club recorded that the average-sized trout taken in the pond weighed 1 pound and the largest 2¼ pounds. Club member George W. Van Siclen made an unforgettable catch on May 29, 1877, when he hooked and landed three trout at one time. Van Siclen was using a leader with three flies composed of a Black Gnat, Coachman, and Montreal, and he managed to land fish measuring 16½, 12¼, and 10 inches!

Van Siclen was a scholarly fisherman, and in 1875, he edited and reprinted the first book on angling, which had been published in 1496 and written by Dame Juliana Berner. Titled *An American Edition of the Treatyse of Fysshynge Wyth an Angle,* the book was dedicated to the Willewemoc Club, and Van Siclen recalled the pleasant days deep in the forest:

> The present Willewemoc Club is not composed of Indians; nor is its club-house an Abbey, but a house of hemlock boards, with comfortable rooms; floors uncarpeted, except by the bedside; and a broad piazza, furnished with easy chairs, and overlooking a beautiful lake, full of trout; with an appanage of acres of woodland, and four miles of a fine trout stream.
>
> There I shall go when the apple trees are in bloom. And to please the congenial spirits of the modern monks who form the club, and the brethren of the angle through our land, is this little book reprinted.

One other body of water that yielded large brook trout in the Catskills was Lake Delaware in the town of Andes in Delaware County. Though privately owned by the Livingston family, posted, and patrolled, the lake was poached at times, and brook trout were taken that weighed between 2½ and 3¾ pounds.

In the early years, fishing writers and newspaper editors referred to the native trout as "speckled trout" or, more fondly and more often, "speckled beauties." Whichever name was used, the fact remained that the fish was greatly admired and was always held in high esteem:

> The speckled trout, that prince of the pure, cold, spring water brook or pond, like the sportsman who follows him, is in a class by himself. He is the aristocrat of fishes. Brainy and valiant, he is a delight from his capture to his place on the table.[13]

The brook trout's place on the table was revered, and an interesting facet of old-time fishermen is that many took an epicurean approach as to when they should be eaten. Most trout fishermen believed that there was a "season" when brook trout are "fit to eat." One indication was a measure of condition—when their heads were as small as to be disproportionate to the size of their bodies.

Fitz-James Fitch remarked: "It is not until the first of May, or thereabouts, that trout are fit to eat, and not until June that they are in perfect condition."[14] The general consensus among anglers was that brook trout were only in season in May and June and never eaten in late summer, fall, winter, or early spring.

Some men thought that the season for brook trout begins with spring floods, but others believed this was an error. "No man with a palate sufficiently delicate to distinguish between a 'red-wing' and a 'canvas back' will ever in our latitude covet a brook trout before the middle of May."[15]

Thaddeus Norris claimed that as fall spawning approaches, brook trout "fall off," in "flesh and flavor" which they do not regain until late spring. "In the streams of the forest however, they are seldom in season before the 10th of May."[16]

It was said that brook trout in the spring were weak, lean, and unwholesome, and were still recovering from fall spawning; and that until they restored their strength sufficiently to frequent the riffles of the streams they inhabited, they were not totally healthy or flavorful.

Some anglers believed that the trout were infested with parasites during the winter, which kept the trout in a weakened condition until warm weather appeared and the fish could rub the parasites from their bodies in the gravel. Those who ate trout in winter, or early spring, dined on "an unhealthy" fish, and the "offensive parasites."

Others believed that brook trout fed heavily on caddis larva in the early spring. "[T]he caddis fly enwraps itself in twigs and leaves, and as the trout swallows house and all, its flesh takes on a state of decayed vegetation."[17] It was not until the season advanced and better food was found that brook trout became "finely flavored."

Epicures of the past also insisted that the proper method to preserve the delicate flavor of brook trout necessitated dispatching the fish immediately. This was followed by placing the trout in damp moss, away from the sun and heat. Fish should be placed in the basket or creel so that they didn't touch each other and kept cool by frequent wetting; kept in this manner secured the "full delicacy of the trout."

Trout fishermen in the 1890s had reason to celebrate. Streams and rivers were beginning to recover from the abuses of the tanning industry, and the introduction of brown trout was seen by many fishermen as successful. However, just as the tanneries were permanently closing their doors, a new, larger, and even more destructive industry to streams and forests was developing in the Delaware watershed of the Western Catskills.

ACID FACTORIES

As with tanners, the wood chemical industry also exploited the forest, fouled the air, polluted the water, killed fish, and negatively affected trout streams. This new industry was the forerunner of today's chemical industry and can be characterized as the manufacturing of chemicals from wood by hardwood-distillation plants. They were known in the Catskills as "acid factories."

Acid factories required an abundance of hardwood, large quantities of fresh water to cool their distillation machinery, and unskilled labor to harvest the forest and work in the plant. And while the tanner laid waste to the hemlock, the wood chemical industry was less selective and cut down and used every species of hardwood tree. Thousands of acres of beech, birch, maple, oak, and chestnut were felled, cut, and split into 4-foot lengths. A single plant consumed up to thirty cords of wood in one day, and between five thousand and ten thousand cords each year. (One cord is a stack 4 × 4 × 8 feet).

Cordwood was placed in retorts, or ovens, and subjected to heat by a charcoal or coal fire. Approximately 60 percent of the wood was converted into a liquid called pyroligneous acid, from which wood alcohol, acetate of lime, and wood tars were obtained. Wood alcohol (methanol) was used as antifreeze and solvent. The rest of the wood was reduced to charcoal, which was removed and sold or used at the plant.

Clear-cutting by acid factories devastated mountainsides, speeded runoff from rains and melting snows, caused erosion, and sent sediment loads into streams that destroyed trout habitat, increased water temperatures, and had a negative impact on the fisheries and streams for years.

The first acid factory appeared near Hancock, in Delaware County, in 1876; two years later, a plant was constructed in Sullivan County on a tributary of Trout Brook, at a hamlet still known today as Acidalia. The industry grew rapidly, and at one time there were sixteen wood chemical plants operating in the Beaverkill watershed, with many being constructed in the 1890s.

From the onset, the wood chemical industry proved it was not compatible with trout streams or the environment, and the impact it had on the trout fisheries of the Catskills was catastrophic. Reports of fish kills immediately followed the construction of plants, and many fishermen believed acid factories caused more death and destruction to trout and streams than the tanneries and sawmills ever did. A dozen years after the first plant was constructed, a local newspaper declared that more trout were poisoned than caught in Hancock streams.

More than thirty plants were located in Delaware and Sullivan counties, primarily along the Beaverkill, Willowemoc, and the East and West Branches of the Delaware River. Acid factories were also located on the best spawning tributaries of these streams, including Spring Brook, Russell Brook, Horton Brook, and Trout Brook on the Beaverkill; and Sprague Brook, Cattail Brook, Hazel Brook, and Stewart Brook on the Willowemoc. On the East Branch, factories were constructed on Cadosia Creek, Fish Creek, Read Creek, Baxter Brook, Trout Brook, and Campbell Brook.

It was not just trout and streams that were the victims of the wood chemical industry; thousands of acres of forest lands were sacrificed, as woodchoppers marched

The acid factory at Livingston Manor on Cattail Brook. Courtesy Dan Myers, *The Wood Chemical Industry in the Delaware Valley*, 1986.

through, cutting virtually every tree greater than 3 inches in diameter. What they left behind looked like a wasteland, and the devastation caused by the clear-cutting did not go unnoticed. It was not just fishermen who saw the ugliness.

In one of the most remote and heavily forested areas at the head of the Willowemoc Creek, the correspondent to the Livingston Manor *Ensign* asked:

What will this country look like in ten years from now if the axe and saw, six steam saw mills and an acid factory continue on in their destruction of our beautiful forests? To see the hillsides denuded and laid bare by the woodsmen's axe spoiling the watersheds and drying up the streams and the damage done by freshets in time of heavy rains is a sad thing to many of us.[18]

And the editor of another county newspaper lamented on the same subject:

The forests of the Town of Rockland are disappearing into the acid factory retorts of that town like the water into a rat hole. Each factory is a whirlpool around which the forests are eddying in a constantly diminishing circle finally to forever disappear in its ever hungry vortex. . . . Surely the forests of Rockland cannot long service this careless demand.[19]

It was generally not profitable to haul wood great distances, and acid factories harvested their wood from nearby areas. When the wood supply was exhausted, some factories were dismantled and moved to another location, where wood was again abundant.

A denuded mountainside stripped by acid factory woodcutters.
Courtesy Dan Myers, *The Wood Chemical Industry in the Delaware Valley*, 1986.

Acid factory sites were often small communities within themselves. A site might contain horse barns, wagon sheds, blacksmiths, a woodworking shop, and company houses and a company store. Laborers at the plant were formed into three groups: factory men, teamsters, and woodchoppers. Factory men unloaded and piled the 4-foot logs, fed the retorts, and in some plants, sacked the charcoal. Teamsters brought the wood from the forest to the factory in drays or wagons. Woodchoppers downed the trees, cut them, and split them into cordwood. They used a 4½-pound double-bladed ax, entered the woods at dawn, and did not leave the mountainsides until dark, when they returned to the factory settlement.

One of the peak periods of employment was during World War I (1914–1918). Acetate of lime was used in the making of smokeless gunpowder, and there was a great demand for other products needed for the manufacture of explosives and for embalming.

Demand for the products of the wood chemical industry declined steadily as newer synthetic ones, equally good and cheaper to manufacture, came into existence. Plants began closing in the 1920s; others discontinued operations in the 1930s. The Livingston Manor plant shut down in 1943, and the plant at Hazel, along the Willowemoc, closed in 1945, as did the acid factory on Cadosia Creek. The last plant on the Beaverkill ceased operations in 1950, at Horton.

Fish kills occurred regularly downstream of virtually all acid factories and generally took place when streamside tar pits, or cesspools, overflowed or leached into nearby waters. These large pits or excavated holes were generally within 20 or 30 feet of the stream, were filled with residue wastes from pipes running from the buildings, and have been described as insoluble wood tar, known as "oil of smoke," a "mass of black, vile smelling liquid."

Fish kills were also the result of carelessness and incompetent laborers; valves were left open, and vats of acid, left unattended, overflowed into the stream. Some plants even discharged their lethal poisons directly into the stream on such a regular basis that they did not kill trout or other fish simply because there were no trout or any fish life located below them; their wastes kept the stream permanently depleted of all aquatic life.

Streams below acid factories reeked from their putrid discharges, and water samples taken near them often revealed that the stream was anoxic, containing zero oxygen! The bed of the stream was visibly unpleasant and usually possessed an active growth of slimy gray organic matter. The plant on Cadosia Creek had ruined the fishing from the mouth upstream 2 miles for years. The Conservation Department tested the water of Cadosia Creek in 1935 and found only 1 part per million dissolved oxygen; insect life was scarce, and tests with minnows revealed that severe stress was observed after 190 seconds and death within 16 minutes!

A new pollution law was adopted in 1892 and was used to halt sawdust being dumped into streams. It was believed to be stronger than previous laws that prohibited stream pollution, but before game and fish protectors began to enforce the law, they gave notice to all mills and factories and gave them time to correct any discharge problems.

All wood alcohol or acid factories produced slag, tar, lime, and acids that leached or ran directly into streams. Whenever streams were at low flow, the pollution was more noticeable. The new legislation did little to halt pollution, and most of those factories discharging into the pristine waters of trout streams continued to do so. Game protectors found it difficult to enforce laws of this nature.

Fish kills were the most obvious evidence that "deleterious or poisonous" substances were being dumped into the stream, but often by the time a game protector was notified, and drove the many miles by saddle horse or wagon to the site, the fish kill would be over, and the discharge long gone.

Those game protectors who did bring suit against acid factory owners met with stiff resistance. Factory owners were generally influential men who might ask, "Would you have us throw all these men out of work because we kill a few fish that some rich fisherman might otherwise catch?" Cases against acid factories sometimes took years, as they would repeatedly be knocked off the calendars. When they were tried, the fines were so small that owners continued doing business as usual; it was cheaper to run wastes into trout streams and kill fish than to remove the cause of the problem.

When action was taken against an acid factory for polluting Horton Brook, a tributary of the Beaverkill, in June 1893, the owners responded "that the bread and butter for their workmen is a far more important consideration than the matter of sport for anglers."[20] A faucet had been left on, and wood alcohol ran into the stream, killing hundreds of trout; the fine was only $50.

A couple of weeks later, an acid factory on Trout Brook, a tributary of the East Branch at Shinhopple, ran tar into the stream, killing all the trout below the plant and for a half mile downstream on the East Branch.

Letters deploring stream conditions in the vicinity of wood chemical plants appeared in local weekly newspapers and in national sporting journals. Acid factories affected streams for years, or for as long as they were operating; typical of the conditions along a trout stream that was burdened by an acid factory can be seen by the events that occurred along Spring Brook, a Beaverkill tributary.

The *Delaware Gazette* on August 22, 1894, reported that vats overflowed at the Spring Brook acid factory, and acid entered the stream, killing "a ton" of trout from 2 to 18 inches in length, all the way downstream to the Beaverkill. The *Roscoe-Rockland Review*, probably sympathetic to the factory owner, scoffed at the idea of "a ton" of trout, and stated it was more like 150 pounds, and in the mile and a half of stream that was affected, the number killed was only about 4,000 trout! The factory was fined $50, and this was considered "absurdly small."

A. Nelson Cheney, the state fish culturist, paid a visit to the Catskills and was appalled at the conditions he found along the Beaverkill in the area of Spring Brook. In an article titled "Trout and Acids," Cheney pointed out the importance of tourism to Sullivan, Delaware, and Ulster counties, and especially how trout fishers are attracted to these areas. And he let it be known that the state would discontinue stocking trout in any stream receiving acid factory wastes. He wrote:

> On a recent visit to the region of which I am writing, I found it infested with acid factories that were running their refuse into the streams and thus killing the fish. One of the factories was on Spring Brook, one mile from the point where it empties into the Beaverkill, and the brook is two miles above the State hatchery. I sent a man to procure some of the water and put a trout of known size into it and note the result. He reported that a 6-inch trout placed in the bucket of water lived four minutes, and when I saw the sample of water, I was surprised that the fish lived as long as it did.[21]

The problems associated with the acid factory on Spring Brook continued, and it was but a few years later that a veteran Beaverkill angler wrote to the local newspaper:

I saw and smelt something that made me feel very sad, namely, the condition of Spring Brook. . . . It was covered with some stuff from the acid factory, making it full of soapy bubbles, and on getting out the smell was very perceptible all along the main stream. Is there no way to stop it? There are few enough fish in the river now, and if this continues there will be less.[22]

It did continue, and six months later there were a lot less trout in the Beaverkill. At the peak of the spawning run, when adult trout moved up into Spring Brook from the main stream and commenced spawning, a chemical spill killed every trout below the factory. One man alone picked up twenty trout that weighed 20 pounds; and besides the many spawning adults, there were tens of thousands of trout eggs, either freshly deposited or still being carried by the trout, that also perished.

The following year a disgruntled fisherman, who spent a week fishing the Beaverkill in the Cooks Falls area, complained bitterly of his lack of success in the pages of *Forest and Stream*:

I caught a few California trout in the Russell brook about two miles above the Beaverkill River and ruined a pair of boots from the refuse of a wood alcohol factory that empties its chemical filth into, what otherwise has the natural condition for a good trout stream. The Beaverkill is a great stream for chubs, bass, wood alcohol and lemons.[23]

Streams held a low level of importance to the public in general during these years, and a number of Catskill trout streams had been the recipients of everything unpleasant or unwanted created by human activities. The least expensive and easiest way to be rid of garbage, creamery wastes, tannery wastes, acid factory refuse, sawdust, or effluents of sewerage treatment plants was to put them in streams. Streams were seen as waste disposal systems; whatever was discharged or dumped was carried away instantly or was displaced with the next flood or high water. What happened to these wastes, and what effect they had on the fish, water quality, stream, or even the people living downstream, was of little concern.

For more than seventy years (1878–1950), acid factories had a negative impact on the trout resources of the western Catskills. Because of the remoteness of some of the chemical plants, and the fact that during most of the year no one was on the streams, it can be assumed that many fish kills went unnoticed. Fish kills and the ruination of trout habitat were a large part of the history of the industry.

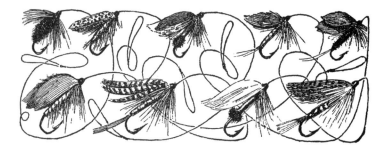

GEORGE W. COOPER, DEBRUCE FLY TIER

Until the late 1890s, Americans generally fished with English trout flies, which were not imitations of the aquatic insects found in this country. Most of the flies were imported, but even those tied here professionally were generally copied from English patterns. In the early years, the best tiers in New York and Philadelphia were former Englishmen and Irishmen.

It was not uncommon for American fly fishers, who did not know the name of an English pattern, to rename the fly; even the famous Beaverkill, a fly archetypally American, was of English origin. There were flies that were tied anew with alterations that also proved successful. An excellent example is the Royal Coachman. The fly is a modification of the famous English Coachman and was first tied in 1878 by John Haily of New York.

The first-tied standard American trout flies were wet-fly patterns, classified as "fancy flies." They became popular in the 1880s and employed various color combinations aimed at capturing the eye of the buyer. A few of the better-known patterns were named Allerton, Rube Wood, Holberton, Imbrie, General Hooker, and Seth Green, which was tied at least as early as 1872; as can be seen, the flies appealed not only to the eye, but to the vanity of anglers as well.

One of the most popular early wet flies was the Parmachene Belle, tied before 1885 specifically for the large brook trout then found in Maine. Flies tied for Adirondack waters were equally gay, brilliant patterns, and because these flies were not imitations of any natural aquatic insects, they were considered "lures." They were, nonetheless, effective at taking native brook trout, which seemed to have a preference for bright, gaudy flies.

The earliest professional fly tier of note in Sullivan County was a blacksmith from the hamlet of DeBruce, along the Willowemoc, by the name of George W. Cooper (1859–1932). Cooper was born in Napanoch, Ulster County, and when he was but an infant, his parents—Mathias and Elizabeth Cooper—traveled through the forest on a bridle path and settled at what is now DeBruce. The Coopers were one of the first families to settle in that area, when it was truly a wilderness.

In 1856, Cooper's grandfather had built a tannery for Hammond & Benedict; eventually, the settlement grew, and George Cooper became the village blacksmith. His shop was located along the Mongaup Creek, near where the Mongaup formed its famous junction with the Willowemoc.

As the hemlocks were depleted and the tanning industry closed its doors in the late 1880s, the citizens of DeBruce focused their attention on trout fishing and summer tourists. George Cooper enlarged his blacksmith shop into a post office and general store, in which, for many years, he sold trout flies, boots, and fishing tackle. His two sisters, Ada Cooper and

George W. Cooper. Courtesy of Jean Boyd.

Elizabeth Royce, became summer boardinghouse keepers. They owned and operated two of the best-known trout-fishing resorts on the Willowemoc: the Homestead and the Hearthstone Inn.

Cooper was an avid outdoorsman, a fine angler, and a fly tier. Exactly when he began tying commercially is not known; however, there is evidence that suggests he was tying in the 1870s. The rugged physical demands of a blacksmith do not seem to be compatible with the gentle hand needed to tie delicate trout flies; Cooper, though, had a reputation for being a skillful tier who raised his own hackle and possessed prized Rhode Island Reds.

His notoriety spread with the creation of the Female Beaverkill. This fly was a very popular early American pattern, and, although it is uncertain as to exactly when Cooper devised the fly, it was being used as early as 1913.

Today's imitationists believe that the fly George Cooper tied was created to imitate the female Hendrickson spinner (*Ephemerella invaria*), the most prolific fly hatch on the Beaverkill. Anyone who has fished the stream during this hatch can see the resemblance by noting the distinct yellow egg sac of the natural and can understand why Cooper added this feature to the fly.

NEW LAWS AND THE DIFFICULTY OF ENFORCING THEM

At this time, fish and game laws continued to be enacted by the boards of supervisors in the various counties until 1895, and then they became the duty of the state legislature. Conservationists, hunters, and fishermen saw this as a move in the right direction. In general, the open season for trout fishing in the Catskills began on May 1 and closed on August 31, with no fishing allowed on Sundays. This was a relatively short fishing season—about 106 days. The short season was in effect from the early 1870s until the 1920s and undoubtedly contributed to the trout fishing being as good as it was during this period.

Size limits may also have helped; in 1876, the Ulster County legislature passed the law known as Murdock's Trout Bill, which imposed a 5-inch size limit on trout. The size limit was expanded to 6 inches in 1885, and by the late 1930s had increased to 7 inches.

During the 1890s, Catskill streams were still being "fished to death," and another type of fisherman, known as "wagon fishermen," was having a negative effect on trout resources. These men traveled by wagon and camped along the stream. Supplied with a mattress and bedding, food, lantern, and stove, they made themselves at home. They dined and ate at streamside, and spared the expense of a boardinghouse or hotel room. They camped close to the best fishing places, and when one area was devoid of trout, they moved to another, working the streams relentlessly.

Laws limiting the number of trout that could be removed from a stream were nonexistent; only fishing clubs restricted anglers from participating in this wasteful practice. "Count-fishermen" were still doing their best to eliminate what was left of the original strain of native brook trout, and the editor of *Forest and Stream* wrote disapprovingly of the practice:

> But one thing is as clear as the sun at noontime. In this day, when the number of anglers is multiplying out of all proportion to the supply of fish, it behooves every person interested in fishing to frown down and discourage fishing for count in trout brooks. Something is out of gear, when two men can catch a thousand trout in four days and make a boast of their achievement. The first

thought that flashes through one's mind is that such trout fishermen are getting more than their share. One wonders what will be left for those who come along a little later. There is precious little satisfaction for the late comers in that old refrain, "You'd orter been here last week, two sports catched a thousand."[24]

The American system of sportsmanship, the editor stated, seems to have been founded on "bad sentiment" from the beginning: "He who would catch the most or slay the more than his fellows was the hero."

****

There were laws prohibiting sawmills from discharging sawdust into trout streams at least as early as 1879, but enforcement of pollution laws was difficult. They were generally unpopular with newspaper editors, politicians, businessmen, workers, and consumers, who saw anything that added to the cost of manufacturing as being an unnecessary nuisance. What were a few fish worth compared with the extra burden placed on the sawmill operator? Fishermen, however, believed the dumping of sawdust into the streams was the result of sheer laziness.

Fishermen witnessed the consequences of the unchecked degradation of stream habitat, but they were in a minority, and fishing was a pastime or a diversion from the world of earning money. And the Catskills was a region where economic struggle was common, and any law protecting fish over business was unpopular—not only with the businessman who was doing the polluting, but with the community in general as well. Streams were seen as conveyors of waste, and business was considered the primary necessity of life, not recreation.

In the Esopus Valley, there were many sawmills located along the Ulster & Delaware railroad and the Esopus Creek; and it was said that if the dumping of sawdust continued in the trout streams in Ulster County for much longer, the trout would entirely disappear. However, when sawmills in Big Indian, Shandaken, and Allaben were sued by the local game and fish protector in the summer of 1890, the cases kept being delayed in the courts, and they dragged on for years.

Fish and game law cases in Ulster County were deliberately knocked off the calendar, term after term. Game and fish protectors were constantly reminding sawmill owners who dumped their wastes into trout streams that they were in violation, and in the early 1890s, warnings were being issued that the practice needed to come to a halt. The editor of the *Walton Reporter*, in an editorial titled "Saw-Mills vs. Fish," disagreed with the "recent crackdown" on sawmills and stated that the law was "a stupid blunder" and needed to be changed; and, he claimed, sawdust was not harmful to trout. The editorial also said that even though he talked to many, the editor had yet to find anyone that said sawdust was "in any way destructive" to fish.

Sawmills generally constructed high dams that obstructed fish passage, and the sawdust they discharged into the stream often filled the pools below them. Trout fishermen claimed that the sawdust floated on the surface, ruining the fishing, but then sank to the bottom and destroyed trout habitat.

In 1892, the law was revised, and "Section 190. Polluting Streams" stated: "No dyestuffs, coal tar, refuse from gashouses, sawdust, shavings, tanbark, lime or other deleterious or poisonous substance, shall be thrown or allowed to run into any of the waters of the state, either private or public, in quantities destructive to the life of or disturbing the habits of fish inhabiting the same." Scores of letters were written to the chief game and fish protector, complaining that this law was being broken every day, and after giving a warning, sawmills all over the Catskills were finally cited for polluting streams with sawdust. In Greene County, several mill owners paid $100 fines, and the action taken in Sullivan County by protectors met with little resistance.

Fishing below a sawmill. Fisheries, Game & Forest Commission report, 1897.

FISH-HATCHING ESTABLISHMENTS

At about the same time that salmon were being stocked into Catskill trout streams, a bill was introduced in the state assembly and senate to establish a fish-hatching establishment near the headwaters of the Willowemoc Creek in Sullivan County. The idea behind the legislation was that Sullivan County, with its abundance of trout streams and lakes, would be better served by a hatchery located within its borders.

Another reason given was that the Ontario & Western Railroad traversed more than 40 miles of trout streams, and it would be an advantage to have a hatchery near the railroad. In 1890, the O. & W. had transported more than a million fry in Sullivan and Delaware counties, of which two hundred thousand were purchased and stocked by the railroad. At this time, all of the trout stocked in the region came from either Caledonia or the Cold Spring Harbor hatchery on Long Island.

A further incentive for developing a state hatchery in the Catskills was that the area was becoming a very popular summer resort. Streams teeming with trout would be an additional welcomed attraction to tourists and would therefore increase railroad passengers.

Shortly after the bill was introduced, articles began appearing in local newspapers urging the state to place the hatchery not on the Willowemoc, but in Roscoe, because of its closeness to the railroad station. The citizens of Roscoe and Rockland were willing to pay for the land selected, and the O. & W. would also contribute to the cost. The bill establishing the hatchery passed in the assembly, but was defeated in the senate.

A similar bill was passed the following year, but the governor used his veto power, claiming a new hatchery was unnecessary. Local politicians were determined to get a hatchery for Sullivan County, and the bill was reintroduced to the legislature again in 1893; this time, the governor signed it, with the location being decided by the Fish Commission.

In late August, officials of the Fish Commission visited the county in a private car of the O. & W. to search for a suitable hatchery site near Livingston Manor or Roscoe. They met with representatives of the two communities. In Roscoe, they looked at Darbee Brook, a low-gradient, springlike stream that flowed through Rockland. They found the water temperature to be 58 degrees Fahrenheit but believed the flow was not sufficient. The commissioners also looked at the Beaverkill, tested its waters at three locations, and found the stream "very satisfactory." The party then boarded the special car and traveled to Hancock, to the Junction Pool of the East and West Branches of the Delaware, "to fish for bass."

In November, it was announced that a hatchery would be constructed at the old Dodge sawmill, about 1½ miles from Rockland Station, with the water being taken from the Beaverkill, "the greatest trout stream in the world." The site included about 4½ acres and was on the border of Sullivan and Delaware counties. Local residents paid for the purchase of the land; and Fred Mather, superintendent of the Cold Spring Harbor hatchery, pronounced the site "excellent" in every way.

The new hatching house was completed the following July, but when the commissioners visited the new facility near the end of the month, they discovered that the Beaverkill's water temperature was 80 degrees Fahrenheit, when 60 degrees was the maximum temperature preferred when the site was chosen! The new hatchery used Beaverkill water, which was piped about 1,300 feet to the hatchery troughs. Herbert Annin, who had worked at Caledonia, became the superintendent, and the facility was named the Beaverkill Hatchery. In the winter of 1895, the new facility contained more than a million eggs; however, in the spring, a flood completely surrounded the hatching house and filled the troughs with sediment, killing a large number of trout and eggs.

In the annual report to the legislature, it was stated that the Beaverkill Hatchery was expected to produce nearly a million fry each year. But after the flood, Supervisor Annin was reluctant to send for more eggs, fearing that additional flooding could happen at any time and that it was "impracticable" to build breeding ponds at the hatchery. During the spring there was the danger of spring freshets, and during the summer, water temperatures remained "for weeks above the limit that would sustain trout life." "It is unfortunate that this hatchery was ever located where it is," said Annin, and he recommended moving it to another nearby location.

A couple of years after the hatchery opened, the superintendent claimed that he suspended operations for three months out of the year because of warm Beaverkill water temperatures, and he recommended closing the hatchery for five months out of the year. By 1898, the fish commissioners were harshly criticized for placing the Beaverkill Hatchery at this location and were reminded that local people advised them to construct it along Darbee Brook.

The following year, Annin said it was impossible to raise fingerlings, and the fry had to be removed by the middle of May because of the water temperatures "warming up so very fast" when hot weather arrived. The hatchery struggled along for the next few years, but ceased operations in 1902. The state leased the hatchery to private interests, who were also unsuccessful in raising trout.

Finally, in 1904, the commission conceded that it had made a mistake in building a hatchery at that location. Ten years after it opened, the governor announced that the Beaverkill Hatchery was

The Beaverkill Hatchery. New York Ontario & Western Railway Co., 1896.

being abandoned and signed a bill to permit its discontinuance. He presented the building to the citizens of Rockland, who used horses to move it across fields to a location along the main road, where it was for many years the home of the Rockland Hose Company.

Some saw the hatchery as a calamity from the start; they believed officials should have known better. The Beaverkill, they argued, is a good trout stream, but its flows and water temperatures were too erratic to serve a hatchery. Locals urged the state officials to choose Darbee Brook, and they chastised them for being so shortsighted. No one was more disappointed than the residents of Rockland and Roscoe; they had worked diligently to bring a fish hatchery to the area, trusting the facility would be a definite asset to the community. They had placed their faith in public officials to select a proper location and even put up their own money to acquire it.

Just before the closing, the state began looking for a suitable hatchery site in Delaware County. In 1898, money was appropriated for the Fisheries, Game and Forest Commission to establish a new facility. Investigations took place all over the county before officials decided on a location in Cold Spring Hollow along Whortleberry (Huckleberry) Brook, a tributary of the East Branch of the Delaware, just outside Margaretville.

The state purchased 35 acres, about 2 miles southeast of Margaretville, in the fall of 1901. Following hatchery construction in May 1902, Herbert Annin of the Beaverkill Hatchery became the superintendent. Known as the Margaretville Hatchery, the facility, in August, sent the first shipment of fifteen hundred brook trout to Walton. The hatchery raised fry for Catskill trout streams for many years; however, on June 8, 1933, the superintendent was told to close the hatchery by July 1 and to liberate all the trout as soon as possible.

The Margaretville hatching house. Ed Van Put.

A group of sportsmen traveled to Albany in an effort to keep it open, but in a letter in early June, Commissioner Osborne notified the local fish and game club, giving the reasons for the hatchery's closure. Osborne stated that the cold water of the Margaretville hatchery was suited for brook trout but not for other species. He also mentioned that throughout the state, the overwhelming majority of fishermen were demanding an increase in the numbers of legal-sized trout to be stocked, and there were no facilities at the hatchery for raising trout beyond fingerling size, nor could they be added.

The Margaretville hatchery's water was so cold that its trout eggs hatched later than those of any hatchery in the state, and it was difficult to get good growth on fingerling-sized fish.

Economics were also cited. The Margaretville hatchery was the only facility in the state that still kept a horse, even in 1933, to enable the foreman to travel to town in winter to get supplies and the mail.

No one was more involved in trout propagation in the Catskills than Julius G. "June" Smith. Where he learned his fish-breeding skills is not known, but he was said to be hatching trout eggs as early as 1884. Smith constructed several hatcheries and fishing resorts, beginning with Alder Lake, in the town of Hardenbergh, Ulster County. In 1889, he traded farms with Asahel Bryant, who owned Aulder Pond, a small and shallow body of water that flowed into the Beaverkill near Turnwood.

Smith had served in the Civil War with the Third New York Cavalry, and at the war's end, he became a fishing guide. A year after his purchase of Aulder Pond, he received financial assistance from Colonel Charles H. Odell, a wealthy Pittsburgh steel manufacturer who owned a stretch of the Beaverkill that included Beaverkill Falls. Smith constructed a fish hatchery and a dam, creating a larger and deeper body of water, and changed Aulder Pond into Alder Lake.

The new lake was stocked with trout taken from the Beaverkill, and on April 10, 1890, *Shooting and Fishing* reported that fifty thousand trout were also purchased from a hatchery in Rhode Island. Although thirty thousand perished on the trip, the rest were apparently stocked in Alder Lake. A hatching house was built below the dam, and at the rear of the lake, where spring feeders flowed, shallow ponds were made by building small dams and fishways that allowed spawning trout to enter from the lake. When the trout were in the ponds, they were netted and taken by buckboard back to the hatchery, where the ripe fish were stripped of their eggs and milt and returned to the lake. The fry were raised until they were large enough, and then they, too, were stocked in Alder Lake. As production increased, trout were sold, and even, on occasion, acquired by the state of New York.

In 1891, a corporation was formed called the Alder Lake Club, and a large clubhouse was built, along with a barn and icehouse. Membership was limited to forty, and most members came from the Kingston area. Samuel D. Coykendall, a millionaire railroad and steamboat company owner, was a well-known member of the club.

After June Smith left Alder Lake, he established the Orchard Lake Hatchery in 1894 at the headwaters of Sprague Brook, a Willowemoc Creek tributary. Smith became well known for his fisheries work, pioneering, at least locally, an industry that was becoming profitable and popular. The Orchard Lake Hatchery became the largest private hatchery in the county, selling more than a thousand dollars' worth of eggs and fry in 1895, with orders exceeding the supply produced in its second year of operation.

Orchard Lake was owned by Stoddard Hammond, a tanner and acid manufacturer, who enlarged the lake in 1896 and established the Orchard Lake Trout Preserve. The hatchery continued to sell trout to various parts of the state until about 1911 when the property, including Orchard Lake, was sold to the Orchard Lake Club, a group of about fifty New York City sportsmen.

June Smith also purchased land along a small stream in Liberty where he once again constructed a small lake and a hatchery that sold trout to various fishing clubs and landowners in Sullivan County. Smith was well known throughout the area for his expertise in raising trout, and he assisted others in constructing trout hatcheries.

Another early trout hatchery that was located in the Beaverkill watershed was built by Bruce Davidson of Lew Beach. Davidson's hatchery was built the same year he constructed Waneta Lake, in the town of Rockland, and turned it into a trout preserve. He took in boarders who enjoyed fishing and not only stocked his lake, but also sold trout commercially, at least until 1905.

One other private hatchery of note began operations during these years in the Esopus Valley. James Cruickshank of New York City developed a fish and game preserve on approximately 1,500 acres, about 1 mile from the Big Indian railroad station. A hatchery and rearing ponds were constructed in 1900, and the facility was known as the Big Indian Trout and Game Preserve; trout were sold for stocking to individuals and clubs. And an advertisement in a local newspaper in 1907 stated that fry and yearling brook trout were for sale, and "larger brook trout for the table."

SALMON IN THE CATSKILLS

The 1890s also saw the continuation of the stocking of Atlantic salmon into the waters of the Delaware watershed. The Pennsylvania Fish Commission placed sixty thousand Atlantic salmon fry in the West Branch of the Delaware, below Deposit, in 1890; and the smolts were reported to be quite numerous in the upper river for two years afterward. In 1891, three hundred thousand more salmon fry were stocked. The following year, the commission hatched 150,000 Penobscot salmon eggs at their Allentown hatchery and 150,000 at the Carry hatchery, and placed thirty cans of fry along the East Branch at City Brook and Read Creek, upstream of Hancock. Many of these fish were observed the year after they were introduced and before they departed for the sea.

In a personal letter to *Forest and Stream*, written in June 1895, Henry C. Ford, president of the Pennsylvania Fish Commission, stated that there was "quite a run" of Atlantic salmon up the Delaware River. Ford wrote that nearly every shad fishery from Fort Delaware to the Water Gap had taken salmon in their nets from 9 to 12 pounds. He believed that these fish were from the stockings made in 1890 and 1891, and claimed he knew of a hundred salmon taken between Gloucester and Port Jervis.

"The Salmon." *The American Angler's Book,* 1864.

By the summer of 1896, a 12-pound salmon was captured in the East Branch near Hancock, and this was the first salmon said to be caught upstream of Port Jervis. In the fall, the *New York Times* published a lengthy article on the number of salmon being caught in the upper Delaware River. On September 4, 1896, the *Times* reported that in the long and deep pools of the East and West Branches, "noble" salmon were seen leaping unexpectedly from the water "to the great wonder of the black bass fishers" around Walton on the West Branch, and the hamlet of East Branch, where the Beaverkill joins the East Branch of the Delaware.

Seven salmon were said to have been speared illegally by fishermen who were supposedly out for eels in Lakin's Eddy, on the East Branch, a couple of miles upstream of Hancock. One of these salmon, a 9-pound specimen, was shipped to Middletown, in Orange County, where it was examined by several ichthyologists and declared a salmon.

The article also revealed that two salmon were caught by fishermen on the West Branch; one taken in August, 5 miles downstream of Walton, and the other a half mile upstream of the village that measured 32 inches and weighed 10 pounds. A couple of weeks later, another Atlantic salmon was taken in an eel rack on the Beaverkill, a couple of miles upstream of where the Beaverkill joins the East Branch—this fish weighed 14 pounds! In all, five salmon were reportedly taken from the Beaverkill.

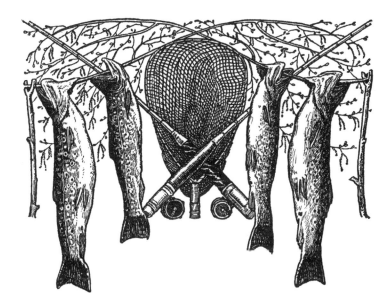

The impact that brown trout had on Catskill trout streams cannot be overstated; the fish reproduced and thrived in all of the lower river environments, those areas where silt and vegetative matter accumulated, where gradients were less steep, and where an abundance of aquatic insects could be found—particularly mayflies, including burrowers, as well as those that preferred slower water. Here, insect life was richer than upstream, where hatches were more varied but not as plentiful.

These waters were known as excellent producers of surface-riding mayflies; in a short time, every pool along the Neversink, Beaverkill, Rondout, East and West Branches of the Delaware, and the Willowemoc contained several large trout, and it was not unusual to see dozens of trout rising throughout their length. This coming together of brown trout and the magnificent mayfly hatches of the Catskills would alter forever the way fly fishers would cast their flies on Catskill streams and rivers.

The Willowemoc near DeBruce. Courtesy of Jean Boyd.

During the 1890s, trout fishing would change dramatically, as trout fishers of the day observed that floating flies were needed. This new era saw the adoption of the English practice of using dry or floating flies. A new type of fly fisher was emerging, and the Catskills would play a leading role in the development of dry-fly fishing in America.

13

*The Nascent Stages
of the Dry Fly in America*

Fishing with floating or dry flies had its origins in England during the first half of the nineteenth century. English fly-fishing historian John Waller Hills writes in his *A History of Fly Fishing for Trout* (1921) that the first mention of the "superiority" of a fly that floats on the surface over a fly that sinks occurred as early as 1800. And although the dry fly may have been used at this early date, Hills suggests that the invention of the dry fly was not complete until there was "intentional drying of the fly" (false casting).

This does not occur until 1851. Hills writes that from this date forward, the dry fly has a "continuous history." Its use, however, did not become common until 1860, and its practice was limited to a few rivers until Frederic M. Halford popularized the method in the 1880s.

Halford, an avid fly fisher, not only adopted the practice of dry-fly fishing but improved upon the method by solving technical difficulties, by contributing to the development of better tackle, and perhaps, most importantly, by creating better flies. Halford studied the aquatic insects of English chalk streams: waters that were low gradient and slow flowing, waters with stable flows and temperatures, waters with weed beds and flat glassy surfaces on which mayflies drifted, tempting brown trout to feed upon them. These were streams that received heavy fishing pressure, and the trout were unusually wary; fly fishermen did not wade or even enter the water, but cast from the stream banks at individual rising trout.

Halford became a militant advocate of the dry fly and wrote extensively of its use. He insisted on exact imitation of the natural insect and developed a series of dry flies to imitate the principle hatches found on the waters he fished, paying strict attention to form, size, and color. In 1886, he produced *Floating Flies and How to Dress Them,* and in 1889, *Dry-Fly Fishing in Theory and Practice.* With the publication of these two books, the popularity of dry-fly fishing soared and spread beyond England to other countries and, importantly, to the United States.

In this country, it has long been acknowledged by angling writers and historians that the first reference to fishing dry flies in America occurred on the Willowemoc Creek and appeared in Thaddeus Norris's *The American Angler's Book* (1864). As will be seen, the tactics depicted by Norris met Hills's criteria for dry-fly fishing: The flies were false cast for the purpose of "intentional drying of the fly":

If it could be accomplished, the great desideration would be, to keep the line wet and the flies dry. I have seen anglers succeed so well in their efforts to do this . . . by whipping the moisture from their flies, that the stretcher and dropper would fall so lightly, and remain so long on the surface, that a fish would rise and deliberately take the fly before it sank.

One instance of this kind is fresh in my memory: it occurred at a pool beneath the fall of a dam on the Williwemock, at a low stage of water—none running over. The fish were shy and refused every fly I offered them, when my friend put on a Grannom for a stretcher, and a minute Jenny Spinner for a dropper. His leader was of the finest gut and his flies fresh, and by cracking the moisture from them between each throw, he would lay them so lightly on the glassy surface, that a brace of Trout would take them at almost every cast, and before they sank or were drawn away. He had tied these flies and made his whip especially for his evening cast on this pool, and as the fish would not notice mine, I was obliged to content myself with landing his fish, which in a half hour counted several dozen. Here was an exemplification of the advantage of keeping one's flies dry . . .*

Fishing historian Charles Eliot Goodspeed also saw the importance and "historical interest" of what Norris had written, and states in his classic work *Angling in America:* "Norris's comments on 'upstream fishing or with the wind at one's back' and his remarks on drying the fly are the most important features of his work."[1]

Thaddeus Norris was an experienced trout fisherman, and his comments informed fly fishers of a very useful tactic. Undoubtedly, some did, occasionally, employ his lesson; however, many years passed before Americans would take dry-fly fishing seriously, and then not until the establishment of brown trout in American waters. When the dry fly was adopted as a primary method of fly fishing, it was the Catskills and the Willowemoc Creek in particular that played an important role in its development.

Fishing with floating or dry flies was not unknown to Americans at the time that Halford published his classic books, but as a fly-fishing tactic, its use was limited to a few of the more sophisticated, well-read fly fishermen who learned of the technique through English fishing literature or subscriptions to English sporting magazines and journals. In the early 1880s, dry-fly fishing articles did appear in American publications, even in newspapers, but they were rare, and when they did, they were usually republished English fly-fishing articles.

A few American fly fishers learned to fish the floating fly while visiting England and wrote of their experiences upon their return. One such article appeared in *Forest and Stream* on September 15, 1887. Written by Graydon Johnston and titled "Floating Fly-Fishing," Johnston described an experience he had fishing the dry fly in England on the river Wandle. A year later, *Shooting and Fishing* published an article titled "Dry Fly Fishing" by the fishing editor of the English publication *Land and Water.* The editor of the American publication stated on November 1, 1888 that the method was a "mode" of fishing popular and "perhaps necessary" on some English streams, "but little, however, in practice in America."

Brown trout had just been introduced and had not yet established themselves in American waters. American streams were still primarily brook trout waters when the dry fly was the rage in

---

*The experience described by Norris took place on the Willowemoc Creek near Cottage Street, in Roscoe, near the mouth of Stewart Brook, at the site of the old Cochran & Appley tannery dam.

A Catskill Trout-Fishing Sampler

Native brook trout (on moss)

Ancient beaver meadow—Beaverkill headwaters

Source of the Beaverkill

Plunge Pool on the East Branch of Callicoon Creek—Falls Mills

Callicoon Creek

Upper Willowemoc

Beautiful native brook trout

The Blue Hole on the Rondout Creek

Beaverkill covered bridge

Horton Bridge Pool on the Beaverkill

Junction Pool, where the Willowemoc and Beaverkill meet

Hamden Covered Bridge on the West Branch of the Delaware River

Meeker Hollow

East Branch of the Delaware River

Schoharie Creek

Habitat structures on the upper Beaverkill

Autumn brook trout

Halls Mills Covered Bridge on the Neversink

Falls Mills on the East Branch of Callicoon Creek

Some Typical Catskill Flies

Olive Quill tied by Theodore Gordon

Red Fox

Quill Gordon

Christian Red Body

Bivisible

Light Cahill tied by Winnie Dette

Red Quill

Royal Coachman tied
by Theodore Gordon

Hendrickson tied by Rube Cross

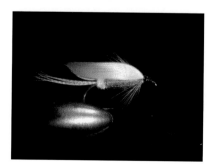

Female Beaverkill

Catskill

Royal Coachman wet fly

Bradley Special

Gray Drake tied
by Mahlon Davidson

Two-Feather Fly tied by Harry Darbee

Darbee Stone Fly tied by Harry Darbee

Brown and White Bucktail

Phoenicia Bucktail

Upper Esopus

An excellent condition rainbow

Esopus at Cold Brook Bridge

Buttermilk Falls Brook, a tributary of Rondout Creek

Pepacton Reservoir in the Catskill Mountains

Hunter Falls on the Willowemoc

Old Falls on the Neversink

A wild Beaverkill brown

West Branch of the Delaware River

Hardscrabble Creek brook trout

Stony Clove

Balsam Lake

Fall Brook, a Willowemoc tributary

A waterfall along the West Branch of the Neversink

Otter Pool on the West Branch of the Neversink

Headwaters of the West Branch of the Neversink

A Hewitt Dam on the East Branch of the Neversink

A waterfall in Plattekill Clove

Schoharie Creek near Hunter

A placid pool on Rondout Creek

The Schoharie barrier dam

Amongst the trout on the Delaware River

Rainbow trout from the East Branch of the Delaware

President Jimmy Carter at Dark Eddy on the Delaware River

"Home in the Woods"
Thomas Cole 1847

Brook trout illustration
Ellen Edmonson, New York State Conservation Department

"Trout Fishing in the Catskills"
T. Worthington Whittredge, c. 1868
Courtesy of the Reading Public Museum, Reading, Pennsylvania

"Trout Fishing in Sullivan County, New York"
Henry Inman c. 1841
Munson-Williams-Proctor Arts Institute
Museum of Art, Utica, New York, 83.14

England, and in this country, most Americans were slow to change their fly-fishing tactics; they fished with two or three wet flies, fishing them down and across. Fly fishermen of all nations tend to be traditionalists, and as long as brook trout remained abundant, there was no great need to adopt dry or floating flies.

It was also firmly believed that dry flies were suited to streams of low gradient; smooth, flowing waters, overfished waters, where the trout had grown wary because of constant fishing pressure. English doctrine also stated that the method involved fishing to individual rising trout with imitations that matched the natural insects the fish were feeding on. Brook trout seemed less sophisticated; generally, when they were feeding, they could be taken on bright or fancy flies that were not imitations of natural insects.

As of 1888, dry flies were still relatively unknown in America. That was the year *Forest and Stream* began publishing advertisements for English floating flies. William Mills & Son, of New York, advertised in February. In March, Kewell Bros. of San Francisco promoted floating flies; their ad stated "These flies are intended for use dry, a mode of angling that will no doubt soon find favor in this country, especially where the trout are educated and shy."

One correspondent even offered to give readers a free sample of Halford's flies. J. Harrington Keene, an Englishman living in upstate Cossayuna, Washington County, wrote to the editor of *Forest and Stream* and offered to give to anyone, upon request, a sample of English floating flies. Keene advised that he had learned to dry-fly fish in England and was familiar with the work and flies of Frederic Halford.

J. Harrington Keene was an avid fly fisherman, professional fly tier, and angling author who learned his skills along English trout streams and had in fact published a book on angling in that country as early as 1881. In 1886, he published another, titled *Fishing Tackle: Its Materials and Manufacture.*

In 1888, Keene produced *Fly-Fishing and Fly-Making*, a work that includes only a brief mention of floating fly fishing. The book was published in the United States, but it was basically English. Keene had only been in America since 1885 and had neither the experience nor the knowledge of trout fishing at the time to write a book on American fly-fishing methods and tactics.

In the second and expanded edition of *Fly-Fishing and Fly-Making* (1891), Keene includes a section titled "Floating Flies," in which he gives fly-tying instructions on how to make various types. However, unlike traditional English fly tiers who largely incorporated the use of fur and feathers, he was an ultra-imitationist who used various unconventional materials to imitate floating flies. He focuses on "Keene's New 'Scale' Wing" flies: patterns tied with detached bodies, legs made with "gut," and wings made from membrane taken from fish scales, cut and shaped, preferably taken from shad, buffalo fish, or tarpon.

Keene also used cork for the bodies of larger flies and tied "exact imitation" wings with gauze, which was drawn to shape, colored, and, after waterproofing, cut out in the shape of wings. Although both styles were innovative and somewhat lifelike, these flies were also lifeless. It is doubtful that they were successful along trout streams here or in England, and this may explain why they remained unpopular.

Keene devotes little of the book to dry-fly fishing instruction, and perhaps this is best explained by his comment: "[T]here is no general necessity for floating flies as yet in the rivers of this country."[2] Other than the mention of a few standard American wet-fly patterns, the book is relatively devoid of references to American trout fishing.

Keene's comment at the time seems correct, as some knowledgeable fly fishermen, who were aware of the dry fly, still believed that it was not necessary to fish with floating flies in America. A few thought that the method could only be adapted to pool areas and only when streams were low—in summer, when pools were reduced in flow to flat glassy surfaces, more like English chalk streams. Others simply thought wet flies on American trout streams were superior. William C. Harris, editor of the *American Angler,* mentioned the use of the dry fly in a fall issue of 1888: "Again, in this country down-stream fishing is followed as a rule; fishing up-stream is too laborious, hence impracticable for many anglers on nine-tenths of our trout waters which are swift-rushing brooks; moreover, a floating fly on such streams would not seem so attractive as one danced deftly across the current with judgment and skill."[3]

When he arrived in America, Keene began writing fishing articles for several sporting publications, including the *American Angler* and the *American Field.* Although he contributed articles over an extended period of time, his writings were never popular or appreciated by the majority of American fly fishers. One reason given was that Americans doubted his information, and his writings were biased by constant references to English fly-fishing methods that many Americans believed were significantly different from their own. Keene was looked upon as an Englishman writing about English fly-fishing techniques, and as such, his contributions to the development of dry-fly fishing in America were not significant.

Fly Fishing and Fly Making was reprinted in 1891, 1893, and again in 1898, and although the trend toward the use of dry flies was beginning to turn, these later editions continued to state that there was still no general need for dry flies in America. This was inaccurate. By these dates, brown trout were well established, and Americans were indeed moving in the direction of the dry fly.

At the time of Keene's death in 1907, it was written that "he never received the appreciation that his work deserved," and, "On the stream he was a patient and skillful angler, but it is said by the few who knew him well that he never quite became reconciled to American trout and American trout streams."[4] This last comment may further explain why Americans did not look upon his work more seriously.

Several years after his death, Keene's wife, Anna, was tying quality trout flies professionally from her home in Queens, New York. An article about women who tied artificial flies professionally appeared in *Forest and Stream* in September 1911. It reported that her flies were "superb, especially those made for dry-fly fishing."

One of the first Americans to adopt the dry fly as a primary method of fly fishing was Theodore Gordon (1854–1915). Gordon was one of this country's most knowledgeable fly fishermen, and he was pivotal to dry-fly fishing and the development of American dry flies. Theodore Gordon was the connection between traditional English dry-fly methods and the adoption of the dry fly to American waters.

He was an ardent and expert fly caster, fly tier, and journalist, and in fact was familiar with English fly-fishing tradition and its angling literature, both historic and contemporary. Gordon was also one of those rare individuals who was both a good angler and a good writer; his writing was modest and unpretentious. He not only subscribed to the famous London *Fishing Gazette,* but beginning in 1890, he contributed articles to it as well.

Gordon was born in Pittsburgh, Pennsylvania, on September 18, 1854, and as a boy he learned to fly fish along the trout streams of Pennsylvania. He began trout fishing in the Catskills as a young man in the 1870s; he knew the region when its streams contained only native brook trout. He had spent three weeks there one summer in the 1870s, fishing along the Stony Clove, a few miles above Phoenicia. In a letter to a friend, he recalled that the trout were very small; however, one day he located two large brook trout in a deep pool below a small dam. He estimated the larger of the two to weigh about a pound and the other half that weight. On the day of his discovery, he was joined by a cousin who lived near Newburgh, and Gordon led him to the pool, giving him the opportunity to try for the large trout. On the very first cast, the cousin caught the larger of the two: "It was a real beauty for so small a stream, beautifully colored and quite fat."[5]

It was in the Catskills that Theodore Gordon spent a large part of his life, fishing and writing about the Beaverkill, Esopus, Willowemoc, and Neversink. These were the streams where he experimented with dry flies and from where he wrote so many of his articles, sharing with readers his personal experiences along his favorite streams and his love of the Catskills.

From 1891 until his death in 1915, Gordon contributed articles to the *Fishing Gazette* and *Forest and Stream,* writing extensively about trout fishing in the Catskills, especially Sullivan County, where he spent the last ten years of his life. Exactly when he began fishing in the region is not known; however, he claimed to have fished the Willowemoc as early as 1877 and the Neversink in the late 1880s. His columns in *Forest and Stream* were often titled "Sullivan County Notes," "On the Neversink," "On the Beaverkill,"

Theodore Gordon at age 31. *New York Herald Tribune*, 1964.

and "Little Talks about Fly Fishing." Gordon understood Catskill trout streams better than anyone of his generation; he lived along the mountain streams and witnessed the seasonal changes, and how they affected the rivers and streams.

Gordon was as knowledgeable a fly fisherman as anyone of his era. He wrote primarily about the habits of trout, tackle, flies, methods, and tactics. He was an excellent observer of the natural world, and he wrote intelligently. His work was admired, and he was known as a fly-fishing authority throughout America and Great Britain.

Importantly, Gordon was a prolific letter writer, who corresponded and formed friendships with England's most well-known fly fishermen, including Frederic M. Halford; R. B. Marston, editor of the *Fishing Gazette*; and G. E. M. Skues, author of the popular *Minor Tactics of the Chalk Stream* (1910) and other books.

Theodore Gordon shared his American fly-fishing experiences and ideas with his British counterparts, and it was this exchange of information between these celebrated fly fishermen that was pivotal to the adoption of the dry fly to American waters. Gordon caught his first brown trout in 1889, and it was about this time that he became fascinated with the dry fly. He had read Halford's books and was influenced by them, and he wrote to Halford asking what flies he could recommend for him to use on American trout streams.

In February 1890, Halford replied that he was unfamiliar with the genera and species of the natural flies of American streams, and he decided to send Gordon a selection of his patterns to choose from. He also urged Gordon to collect natural flies and send them to him, and he would try to imitate those. R. B. Marston also sent Gordon a selection of the best English floating flies, and both men urged Gordon to select those patterns that would work best on American waters.

As Gordon became fascinated with the dry fly, he fished on the surface, even, at times, when he recognized that a wet or sunken fly would work better. For a few years, he carried fifteen dozen of the best English dry flies, trying them whenever he noticed a good trout rising. He had adopted the English tradition of casting only to trout rising to natural insects, and though he found the English rod and line unnecessarily heavy, he did take a few trout. He then began to lose his enthusiasm for dry-fly fishing until an incident occurred that renewed his interest. Years later, he reminisced in an article in *Forest and Stream*:

> I had been fishing the rapids up stream with two flies when I came upon a fine reach of smooth, gliding waters, and sat down at the tail end to smoke a pipe and rest. While sitting there I spotted three good trout rising at the lower end of the pool, and taking off the stretcher fly, replaced it with a small floater. I did not bother to remove the dropper, which happened to be a favorite fly of my own tying. Changing the tail fly occupied a few minutes and in approaching the fish I naturally kept the flies in the air by a series of false casts. These dried the dropper so much that it floated quite as well as the orthodox dry fly, and the result was that all three trout rose at it and were killed one after another. It seemed that they moved out of position to get it, and passed by the tail fly. This was an eye opener. It showed that a good wet fly pattern, if properly dressed with sufficient hackle was also a good dry fly pattern, and that my own flies could be made to float well. This gave me a great start and added interest to the floating fly.[6]

From this time on, Gordon realized he need not depend on English dry flies. With his interest renewed, he persisted and pioneered methods that brought the dry fly to the forefront of American fly fishing. By 1890, Gordon was experimenting and tying imitations of the natural insects he found along Catskill streams, and he began creating some of the first purely American dry flies that were, and are, accepted as standard fly patterns. His success did not go unnoticed; the editor of *Forest and Stream* reported in November 1890:

> Mr. Theodore Gordon is one of the most thorough fly-fishermen we have ever had the pleasure to meet. He believes what is worth doing at all is worth doing well, so he pays attention to all the little details that go to making a good angler; and above all, will not use bait under any circumstances. He would as soon shoot a quail on the ground. He thinks that we are all wrong on the subject of artificial flies, and believes we ought to discard various foreign fancy patterns, and copy our own natural insects and flies as closely as possible. He carries out his theory in practice. On the Neversink last season no one brought in better baskets of trout than Mr. Gordon, whether they used fly or bait.[7]

Standard American flies at this time were basically "fancy flies," colorful wet fly patterns tied to attract native brook trout. With the introduction of brown trout and floating flies, Americans began to look more seriously at imitating the natural aquatic insects found along their streams. Another example of this new philosophy appeared the following spring in the *New York Times* in an article titled "Trout in the Neversink," which depicted the success of another Neversink fly fisher who, after catching and releasing a small trout, reports:

> Your luck, beginning in a small way, however, does not stay at small beginnings, for before you have gone many steps you are rewarded by a good sized, lusty trout, who gives battle for all he is worth. This is what you came for, so give him his way for a time, but be sure that you land him eventually. There is an overhanging bush under which you see a big fish jumping. He takes no notice of your flies. You therefore put on another trio and try him with one after another, only to be maddened by having your trout disregard them utterly, while, with a slap of his tail in derision, he takes the natural fly close to your clumsy lure. Finally, you make up your mind that you will take him at all hazards. You then proceed to catch one of those at which he jumps, and, selecting one from your book which nearly resembles it, apply it. Shorten your line until it is just long enough to reach him, enough so that he will not see you, and the next time his nose appears above water toss it into his open mouth. He gasps with astonishment—one of his last gasps—for he is outwitted, hooked securely, and your triumph is great. There he lies in the bottom of your basket, a very beauty, not quite a pound, long, slim, with brilliant spots. . . .
>
> It is wise to catch some of the ephemera so that you may model your next flies upon them; for if you are a true sportsman you undoubtedly manufacture your own flies. "Imitate nature" is your maxim, and thus be as wily as the game is wary. . . .
>
> A WOMAN[8]

Theodore Gordon and friend on the Neversink, ca. 1912. Courtesy Catskill Fly Fishing Center.

It is unfortunate that the sportswoman who wrote the article did not reveal her name; she was clever and obviously an experienced fly fisher, and though she does not mention her use of the dry fly, her descriptions reveal that this was the method she was using.

During the 1890s, the use of the dry fly was spreading, and some of our most noted and influential fly fishers—such as Theodore Gordon, Charles F. Orvis, and A. Nelson Cheney—began to write and inform others of the value of floating flies, urging them to add the method to their fly-fishing repertoire. Gordon not only wrote about using the dry fly, but was giving talks at fishing club dinners on dry-fly fishing at least as early as 1897. Cheney, an authority on fish and fishing, began using dry flies in 1894 and used his column "Angling Notes" in *Forest and Stream* to inform readers of his success. However, at the end of the decade, the majority of American fly fishers were still devoted to the wet fly.

One of the first American books to mention the dry fly was *Favorite Flies and Their Histories* by Mary Orvis Marbury, published in 1892. The book depicts a color plate of fifteen English dry flies and mentions Halford's *Floating Flies, and How to Dress Them.* It also contains lengthy quotes from Halford, but makes no mention of the dry fly being used in America. The book does state that on hard-fished streams, Americans are paying more attention to finer leaders, smaller flies, and flies that imitate the natural insects.

Also in 1892, Rand, McNally & Co. published *American Game Fishes,* a book edited by George O. Shields that included chapters written on various species by A. N. Cheney, Charles Hallock, Fred Mather, and many others, including a chapter titled "Fishing-Tackle, and How to Make It," which was written by J. Harrington Keene. Along with instructions on how to make rods, leaders, etc., information is provided on how to tie artificial flies, accompanied by two very attractive color plates of flies, presumably tied by Keene. Although dry-fly fishing is mentioned only briefly in one sentence, there are included, among the patterns depicted, a few floating flies.

Keene identifies one interesting mayfly pattern with a detached or extended body as Straw Floater and an even better-looking imitation known as Double-Winged Red Spinner. Both are tied English style, heavily hackled, with wings and hackle slanted toward the tail of the fly. Keene's instructions include how to fold hackle and tie double-divided wings, a practice inherent to English trout flies. Also depicted is his Cork-Bodied Floating Fly, a pattern using cork as the material for the body.

Perhaps two of the most interesting floating flies are a novel pair of detached-body mayfly patterns that are tied with horsehair for legs, with a body and wings shaped from the membrane of a tarpon scale. These flies are realistic looking, but have an overall hard, lifeless appearance that does not work well for trout flies. Keene boasts of their lifelike appearance and avows that they are almost indestructible; he claims that is the reason tackle makers are reluctant to manufacture them.

Writing on the merits of the dry fly in *Forest and Stream* in 1898, angling author and fish culturist Fred Mather stated: "In America as far as I know dry fly-fishing is not practiced: it is a modern use of the fly which is said to be killing where the trout are wary and discriminating."[9] Following a brief description of dry-fly fishing, Mather goes on to write: "Somehow the dry fly has not tempted me to try it. It looks like hard work to little purpose, and where I fish there seems to be no necessity for it."[10] Mather's comments were probably echoed by most American trout fishermen at this time.

It would be ten years before the next book of note mentioned the use of floating or dry flies. In 1902, William C. Harris, former editor of the *American Angler,* described dry-fly fishing in

Salmon and Trout, a book in which Dean Sage contributes information on salmon and Harris on trout. In a chapter titled "Methods of Fishing for Trout," Harris devoted less than two pages to its use, and one-half page of the two is devoted to a quote from an English writer. Harris writes: "Fishing with a dry fly is more in use in England (with one fly only) where the streams are somewhat sluggish, than in America, although a few of our experienced anglers have practiced it for many years."[11]

Flies tied by Keene including two samples of "Keene's new scale wing" patterns, a Yellow May Fly, top, third from left, and Dark Dun (o). *American Game Fishes,* 1892.

Several years later, Edward Breck, in *The Way of the Woods* (1908), includes a section of several pages devoted to the dry fly. He gives a good description of dry-fly fishing as it is practiced in England, where he learned the method, and he mentions that English flies are tied as exact imitations of the natural flies that the trout are found feeding on. He also writes that this type of fishing is the "highest development of the art of angling." At the end of the section on dry-fly fishing, Breck recommended several English books on dry-fly fishing.

Also in 1908, *Outing Magazine* in its July issue published an article titled "How to Use A Dry Fly" by artist-angler Louis Rhead. Rhead was a frequent visitor to the Beaverkill and Willowemoc area where he spent days, weeks, and entire summers fishing and experimenting with flies. His article claims that dry-fly fishing is not practiced by many Americans, and he indicates that the time to fish dry flies are July and August, when streams are very low and clear. He gives an accurate description of the tactic, writes that it is not a practical method on "rapid" streams, and recommends Halford's *Dry Fly Fishing in Theory and Practice.*

Though the use of the dry fly in America before 1900 was tenuous, it was continuous; and the Catskills, and particularly the Willowemoc, were conspicuous in its development. Two of the most important books on dry-fly fishing were written by fly fishers who stayed at DeBruce and learned their skills along the Willowemoc.

George M. L. La Branche. *Forest and Stream,* October 20, 1906.

Preceding a book on dry-fly fishing, George M. L. La Branche (1875–1961) wrote a lengthy article titled "The Evolution of a Dry Fly Fisherman" that appeared in the magazine *Recreation* in July 1909. The article gives a description of dry-fly fishing along with photographs of dry flies and related gear, and in it La Branche reminisces about an incident that occurred in 1899 along the Willowemoc when he first began using the dry fly.

La Branche was spending the second half of May at DeBruce, fishing every day with two or three wet flies, with varying success. He fished every evening for an hour or two in the long pool that was formed at the junction of the Mongaup and Willowemoc creeks. The pool was alive with rising trout, but La Branche had difficulty taking these obviously feeding fish.

In his book of wet flies, he carried an article he had removed from an English angling journal that described dry-fly fishing. La Branche read and reread the information, and noted that two points were important: one was to cast "lightly" upstream of the rising trout, and the other was to let the fly float downstream without drag. He also realized that he had no flies that resembled the description of an English dry fly and no flies that resembled an imitation of natural insects.

La Branche saw that on the English dry flies, the hackle and wings were tied almost at right angles to the hook, not "down wing" or parallel to the hook, as were his wet-fly patterns. He selected a #10 Beaverkill and Queen of the Waters, doctored these wet flies by forcing the wings into an upright position with tying thread, and by stroking the hackle fibers made "a very presentable dry fly." He tested the fly in a glass of water and was satisfied at the way it floated.

La Branche fishing the Willowemoc Creek. *Recreation Magazine*, July 1909.

In the evening, he returned to the junction pool and tied on the Beaverkill. On the very first cast, he rose and hooked a rainbow trout; on the second cast, he hooked another good rainbow; and in quick succession, he caught three nice rainbows and one brook trout, all more than a foot in length, the largest 14 inches! The La Branche article went on to give technical advice on how to fish dry flies, with the author stating that he had his "greatest success" on the Beaverkill and Neversink. Years later, the article was cited as an important contribution to the development of dry-fly fishing in America.

Dry-fly fishing continued to have few advocates. Most fly fishers still believed that the method was not suited to American waters and that it was meant to be used only on slow, clear placid streams with smooth or flat surfaces. And others were waiting for someone to identify American trout stream insects and create fly patterns like Halford had done in England.

One other fly fisherman who contributed greatly to the use of the dry fly in America was Emlyn M. Gill (1861–1918). Beginning in 1911, Gill wrote a series of introductory articles that appeared in *Forest and Stream* titled "Practical Dry Fly-Fishing for Beginners"; the last of the series was published in 1912. At the time Gill began his series, he was quoted as stating that one of the largest New York fishing tackle dealers, and one of the few that carried a stock of dry flies for several years, told him that "there were not more than a hundred 'real' dry-fly fishermen in the United States."

On June 9, 1912, the *New York Times* published a lengthy article titled "Veteran Angler Urges Dry Fly Fishing in America." Dry-fly fishing was still relatively unknown, and the opening sentence asked, "What is dry-fly fishing?," referring to it as "the English method of catching trout."

The writer stated that men like Emlyn Gill were making determined efforts to introduce more Americans to dry-fly fishing, and that in the last year or two there were significant advances in this direction. Gill was quoted throughout the article, and he gave his opinion on techniques, what flies to use, and where and when it was best to use them. He deviated from the English purists and told readers not to wait for rising trout, but to adopt a policy of "fishing the stream" and "fishing the rise."

It was also in 1912 that Emlyn Gill produced the first American book devoted to the use of the dry fly. Just as Thaddeus Norris had enshrined the Willowemoc with his reference to early dry-fly fishing along the stream as early as 1864, so too would Gill in his work titled *Practical Dry-Fly Fishing*. Gill began using dry flies in 1905 or 1906, learning his skills along the Willowemoc Creek. He tended to stay and fish at the same places George La Branche did and especially enjoyed the water around DeBruce. Gill wrote fondly of his Willowemoc experiences and modified dry-fly fishing to fit the circumstances that he encountered. In his introduction, he acknowledged that his friend George La Branche was one of the very best of all-around American anglers and the most expert of American dry-fly fishermen with whom he fished.

Emlyn M. Gill. *New York Times*, June 9, 1912.

Practical Dry-Fly Fishing is a book filled with good advice. Gill gave concise and accurate information, even recommending that fly fishers carry a small "bug net" to collect and copy natural flies with a similar imitation. He also makes an impassioned plea to trout fishers, writing that they should think about the trout they are catching, and he recommended releasing trout: "He alone deserves the title of sportsman who returns carefully to the water all trout that he does not need for food; as soon as the fish is taken into the net, all the sport to be had with that particular fish is over, and when killed and put into the creel it has become simply *meat*."[12]

Emlyn Gill's book awakened interest in dry-fly fishing, and at the time of its appearance, *Field & Stream* published a lengthy series of articles by George La Branche titled "The Dry Fly in America." La Branche wrote of his experiences and his favorite flies, tackle, and methods, including one he called "creating a hatch." His theory was that by repeatedly casting with "precision and delicacy" in the same location in an area where a trout could be expected, a trout, even if not feeding, would take up a position in the line of drift of the artificial fly; then it would only be a matter of time before the trout took the fly.

La Branche began the series of articles by paying homage to his favorite pool, the site where he cast his first dry fly so many years previous:

> The Junction Pool, the meeting of the waters of the Willowemoc and Mongaup, a beautiful spot, and one famous among fly fishers to me, it is the loveliest water in the whole world, not alone because it is beautiful, not because it holds many fine fish, nor because I have taken many fine fish from it; but on this very water, though it has changed in character since that day many years ago, I rose my first fish to a floating fly.[13]

A year after *Practical Dry-Fly Fishing,* the second American book on fishing with a dry fly appeared when Outing Publishing Company produced *Fishing with Floating Flies* by Samuel G. Camp. The book included chapters on how, when, and where to use the dry fly, as well as chapters on equipment, flies, casting, and entomology.

But even in 1913, the majority of Americans were still not using the dry fly as an everyday method of fly fishing, and some saw it as a passing fancy. A reporter for the *New York Times* on July 6 commented: "In more than one store experienced salesmen openly branded dry-fly fishing as a fad destined to pass quickly." However, the same writer saw things differently; in an article titled "New York's Foreign Trout Lured by Foreign Tackle," he recognized the connection between the brown trout that were now inhabiting all Catskill trout streams and the necessity of the dry fly:

> To the brown trout, when all is said, must be credited much of the recently growing fancy for British dry fly methods by American brook fishermen. New Yorkers, some of them grudgingly, have led the movement, because the brown trout were first imported to the State; anglers elsewhere have begun to follow suit, especially in the few other States which have planted the foreign species.
> All of which is not surprising. The astonishing feature of the changed trouting conditions is that the American tackle dealer seems bent on discouraging the dry fly.[14]

Finally, in 1914, Charles Scribner's Sons published the book that influenced many Americans to take a closer look at the method and adopt the dry fly in earnest. George M. L. La Branche, who had written about the dry fly for many years, presented his thoughts, philosophies, and tactics into an excellent manual titled *The Dry Fly and Fast Water.*

La Branche was familiar with trout streams all over the Catskills, and he knew the waters of the Callicoon, Beaverkill, Neversink, and Kaaterskill Creek, but it was the Willowemoc that was most special to him and along its banks that he honed his dry-fly fishing skills.

When he first began fishing with dries, La Branche, as did others, would only fish to rising trout in pools on the smooth, slow-flowing waters of which he believed Frederic Halford would approve. As he gained experience, he realized that dry flies could also be used with success in riffles, in pockets behind boulders, or, for that matter, anywhere on the stream. However, being influenced by English writers who insisted dry flies could not be used on mountain streams, he was not comfortable in doing so: "It seemed to me that by continuing to use the dry fly on them I was profaning the creed of authority and inviting the wrath of his gods upon my head."[15]

Fortunately, he continued to fish the dry fly on Catskill streams and abandoned the idea of fishing only to rising fish, and it was the knowledge and experience he gained in doing so that led to the success of his popular book. Commenting on *The Dry Fly and Fast Water,* Theodore Gordon, who knew La Branche intimately, stated:

> I know Mr. La Branche by reputation, and his ideals are high. He fishes the floating fly only, and kills a few of the largest trout. All the rest are returned to the water.
>   His point of view is original, and there is not a dull page in this book. He has no great faith in the imitation of the natural insects and gives a very short list of artificial flies.[16]

La Branche was a true presentationist who believed he could fish through the entire season with just a few fly patterns. He saw little value in exact imitation and proved to American anglers that they need not be locked to English traditions. In *The Dry Fly and Fast Water,* he gave the dressing for eight different flies, although he stated he rarely used more than six; if he were forced to do so, however, he claimed he could get along with only one: the Whirling Dun.

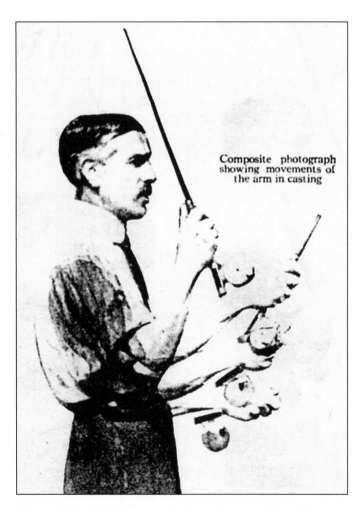

George M. L. La Branche casting form. Photo by Roger B. Whitman, *Country Life,* 1921.

La Branche was an excellent trout fisherman who prided himself on fly-casting accuracy and presentation. After a fishing trip to a famous chalk stream in England, an article appeared in the London *Fishing Gazette* that praised his casting skills: "His flies go where he wishes them to go and act as he directs them when they get there. Briefly, Mr. La Branche is a very beautiful fisherman."[17]

Theodore Gordon, Emlyn Gill, and George La Branche were among the pioneers of American dry-fly fishing, and through their writings, they encouraged others. However, it was Gordon who led the way and had the greatest impact by developing some of the first purely American dry flies.

It was not long after his death that Theodore Gordon began receiving the credit he deserved for his contributions to American dry-fly fishing. In 1931, Dr.

Edgar Burke revealed the respect he had for Gordon in his excellent book titled *American Dry Flies and How to Tie Them.* On the first page, Dr. Burke writes:

> When we say that Theodore Gordon was the "father of dry fly fishing in America" the statement must not be taken to mean that he *invented* fishing with floating flies. Such a claim, if made, is easily disproved. English anglers used dry flies before his birth (September 18th, 1854, at Pittsburgh, Pa.) but, so far as is known, he was the first American dry fly fisher. He was also a skillful fly tyer, who taught his art to a whole school of successors, some of whom are still practicing his teachings in the Catskills.
>
> Animated by Gordon's success, these men began upstream fishing with floating flies and their example gradually spread until, from this small nucleus, there developed the present day cult of devotees of the dry fly in America.[18]

14

The Catskill School

Theodore Gordon first learned to fish for trout along a number of the fine streams of Pennsylvania. He spent his teenage years in trout country and, like most youngsters, he first learned to catch trout on worms. He was quite successful in doing so, with the exception of one stretch of stream that flowed slowly through a meadow. This portion contained weed beds and lots of trout that Gordon could not interest with worms or other baits.

On one particular day, he happened upon a fly fisherman whom he recognized as a well-known sportsman. The man was impeccably dressed, his equipment was the very best, and he was fishing the meadow stretch where Gordon had difficulty catching trout. The youngster saw that the man was catching a great many trout; and when he departed, he decided to walk home beside the smartly dressed fly fisher. The veteran shared his knowledge with Gordon and gave him one of the artificial flies he killed his fish with.

This experience changed Theodore Gordon, and he resolved to become a fly fisherman. He spliced various portions of old rods together and made his first fly rod, and the following weekend, he went out and caught twenty-two trout on the fly that the friendly man had given him.

At the age of thirteen, Gordon studied the *American Angler's Book*. From Norris, he learned the fundamentals of fly tying. In the beginning, and for many years, he tied flies in his hands, and it was not until he became interested in dry flies, at the age of thirty-five or thirty-six, that he switched to a vise.

When Gordon began tying dry flies, he was greatly bothered by the lack of American dry-fly patterns, and he urged others to copy the natural flies they found along streams. English flies did not imitate American aquatic insects, nor did their imitations float well on Catskill trout streams; they were overly dressed and tied with soft hackles. After Gordon had read the works of Frederic Halford, he read everything available pertaining to tying flies. He dissected English floating flies tied by Holland in order to learn how English fly tiers tied on their wings. Some of these flies he purchased directly from England, and others were sent to him by R. B. Marston.

The flies Halford sent to Gordon as samples were tied with soft hackles, and although they may have floated adequately on the slow-flowing waters of English chalk streams, they did not float well on the surface film of Catskill trout streams. Gordon recognized that dry flies needed stiffer hackles to float on streams of rapid descent; instead of using soft hackles, he substituted feathers from roosters, and he tied them at right angles to the hook so that they would float better.

He imitated nature whenever possible and tied flies that looked natural in size and color. Gordon studied the aquatic life found in Catskill streams, and he maintained an interest in creating flies that were suited to American waters. In an article that appeared in the *New York Times* in the summer of 1900, a reporter wrote from the Beaverkill that "Anglers who are interested in the entomology of fly fishing will be glad to know that Theodore Gordon, the famous amateur fly tyer, is at Hornbeck's, at Rockland, for the season. His studies will no doubt have interesting and valuable results."[1]

Gordon was meticulous about the quality of the dry-fly hackle he used and was diligent in selecting the exact shades to match the fly he was imitating. He was a firm believer in the excellent qualities found in blue dun hackle—light, medium and dark—and he had friends raise roosters for him so that he could obtain the best hackle. Gordon preferred stiff rooster hackles tied sparsely on the hook, with just enough hackle to float the fly, believing that this was better than the English practice of tying both hen and rooster feathers on the same fly:

> I must confess that using hens' hackles in front of cocks' hackles for floating flies does not satisfy me. I much prefer the latter by itself, when it is to be had of good quality. I fancy that Duns with just enough hackle to float well kill better than those dressed with two or more, and having a bushy appearance. A few stiffish hairs support the fly as well as many soft ones, and the fly cocks much better.[2]

Gordon tied a fly he called a Golden Brown Spinner at least as early as 1902. As it is mentioned in the *Fishing Gazette* by R. B. Marston that year, the fly is tied with wood duck wings, badger hackle, and golden body with wood duck tail. The pattern became known as the Gordon, and became popular in the early 1900s, when the famous New York tackle dealer William Mills & Son tied and sold them to their customers.

However, it is the Quill Gordon, a classic American dry fly, that is most associated with Theodore Gordon. The origin of the Quill Gordon appears to be 1903. In 1912, Gordon wrote a chapter on American trout fishing for an English book edited by Sir Herbert Maxwell, titled *Fishing at Home and Abroad*. In the book, Gordon gives a description of the fly, and states "This fly has been in use nine years, so had proved itself."

Gordon tied and used Quill Gordons in various shades—light, medium, and dark blue dun—in two or three different sizes. He was even particular about the shades of the peacock quill he used to make the bodies, using both light and dark, and he usually varnished the body before winding the quill. He often used the different shades of Quill Gordons to match what was on the water, and he tied the same fly at times using pale blue dun wool instead of quill.

There were times when Gordon tied his wood duck wings without splitting them, but more often they were split and divided. Preston Jennings, author and fly-fishing entomologist, who produced the first serious book on matching artificials to the natural flies trout feed upon, believed Gordon was the first to tie upright, split-wing dry flies with the flank feathers of mallard or wood duck.

Catskill fly tier Harry Darbee had a collection of Theodore Gordon dry flies. He did not display them, or even speak about them very often, as they were precious; I know they were one of his favorite possessions. Harry maintained a lifelong love of trout flies and possessed a wealth of information on their manufacture. He was a wonderful conversationalist who—on rare occasions, late in the evening when no more customers were in his front-room fly shop and the talk had turned to Theodore Gordon—would enter the "feather room" and return with a special box.

It was a silver metal box with trays of flies tied by Gordon. Harry treated them like hidden Rembrandts, and the first observation was that the Quill Gordons varied in color. Another feature that I remember was that the tails on the flies were upturned fibers of wood duck flank feathers. Their appearance was more realistic as mayfly imitations but lent little support to the fly when riding the surface film.

The Quill Gordon and Gordon *were* two of the first purely American dry flies. At some point in his life, Gordon began tying professionally and began selling flies through mail order or personal contact. The high quality of the dry flies he tied by cannot be overstated, and those who purchased and fished with his flies are the best to judge Gordon's workmanship.

Guy R. Jenkins, who corresponded with Theodore Gordon and also purchased flies from him, reminisced about his dry flies:

> In the early days Mr. Gordon was the only source in this country of an Honest-to-God dry fly, except the English flies in some few tackle stores. I cannot emphasize too strongly that flies tied by him on eyed hooks, as far back at least as the middle '90s, were as delicate in construction, as stiff in hackle, and practically as varied in pattern, as flies of the finest tiers today. They were not just a first step—a crude beginning of the art in America—but the fully formed and finished product.[3]

Another noted fly fisherman commenting on his fly-tying abilities was George La Branche: "I think Mr. Gordon was, perhaps, the greatest student of fly fishing in this country, and without exception the best flytier I have ever known."[4]

In England, Gordon's dry flies were looked upon with admiration. Following the death of Theodore Gordon, R. B. Marston, the editor of the English *Fishing Gazette* wrote: "He was I believe, the first American angler to take up, if not dry-fly fishing, at any rate the making of floating flies, according to our best authorities, Halford, 'Val Conson,' (Skues), etc. and he made excellent flies with which I have often done well on our British waters."[5]

Gordon spent the last ten years of his life as a full-time resident of Sullivan County. He hunted grouse and woodcock in the fall, and fished in the spring and summer. He found the harsh Catskill winters unbearable at times, but like many who enjoy the outdoors, he was fond of walking the woods whenever there was a fresh snow and reading the tracks of the various forms of wildlife that passed by. He would stay for weeks at a time along the rivers he loved—the Beaverkill, Willowemoc, and the Esopus—but he made the Neversink the area of his primary residence.

Theodore Gordon was constantly creating different floating flies. He experimented and changed patterns, styles of wings, and body types, and was particularly intrigued with the many shades of natural blue dun. His Gordon and Quill Gordon were extremely popular during his lifetime. The Quill Gordon is, in fact, still considered to be a standard dry fly and is used by many.

In 1912, Gordon tied a fly with wings of gray mallard wing quill, blue dun hackle, a body of blue-gray dubbing with fine gold tinsel ribbing, and a tail of gray hackle fibers. It is a good imitation of the various blue-gray flies that appear on the surface in the early part of the trout-fishing season. He named the fly the La Branche after his friend George La Branche.

One fly pattern that was an enigma to Theodore Gordon was the Royal Coachman. He knew it was a successful pattern, but he could not rationalize its success. He was always puzzled by the fly, and thought that its appearance, with its peacock herl body and bright red floss, red-brown hackle and white wings, was so conspicuous on the water that it should frighten trout.

He called it a lure and believed it represented a glorified ant. However, Gordon has been credited with creating a variation of the fly that became extremely popular, and was known as the Fan-Wing Royal Coachman. William Bayard Sturgis, in his fine book *Fly-tying* (1940), writes that in the spring of 1909, Theodore Gordon sent a fly order to Leslie Petrie of New York City. Included in the order were some additional patterns not requested by Petrie. This was a custom of Gordon's. One of the patterns was a Royal Coachman, tied on a #14 hook, with fan wings of wood duck breast feathers. Sturgis goes on to say that the fly is on display in the Gordon collection at the Anglers' Club of New York.

Gordon spent the greater part of the last thirty-five years of his life on or near the famous trout streams of Sullivan County: the Beaverkill, Willowemoc, Esopus, and Neversink. And he, more than anyone, popularized the trout fishing along these streams through his writings in *Forest and Stream*. Gordon was familiar not only with the larger waters, but was knowledgeable about the smaller tributaries as well.

During the last three years of Theodore Gordon's life, he boarded at the farmhouse of Anson Knight, who owned 61 acres along the right bank of the Neversink, just downstream of the covered bridge leading to the village of Neversink. It was here that Gordon died, near the river he loved, in 1915.

At the time of his death, his peers considered him to be not only an expert fly fisherman but also the most proficient fly tier in the United States. He was a popular fishing journalist and was known as an authority on fly fishing, not only in this country but in England as well.

Gordon was loved by those who knew him, as well as by readers who had never met him but were familiar with his writings in *Forest and Stream*. The sporting journal published several letters shortly after his death that paid tribute to Gordon. One admirer named Davies sent an interesting letter that appeared in the October issue. It not only praised Gordon but also stated his appreciation of the knowledge he gleaned from Gordon's articles. In closing, he stated:

I am happy to say that I did not make the mistake of waiting until Gordon's death to express my appreciation of his value. In *Forest and Stream* in 1913, I acknowledged my indebtedness. It has been a long established fad of mine to give my flowers to friends while they live to enjoy their fragrance and beauty, which I think is far preferable to piling floral wreaths upon a cold grave.

So, Farewell, Brother Gordon. Our admiration and affection goes with him, and when on the streams he loved so well and with such skill portrayed the "gentle art," we will think of him—
"As in a happier mead,
Where fish are ever on the teed.
When skies are fresh and fields are green,
And never dust nor smoke is seen,

No news sheets, nor subscription-lists,
Nor merchants, nor philanthropists.
For there the waters fall and flow
By fragrant banks, and still below
The great three-pounders rise and take
The 'Palmer,' 'Alder,' 'Dun' or 'Drake,
Now by that stream, if there you be,
I prithee keep a place for me."
CHARLES D. DAVIES

Theodore Gordon's remains were taken by train from Liberty to New York City, where he was interred in a vault (No. 26) in Marble Cemetery. The small one-half acre cemetery is located between Second and Third Avenues, and Second and Third Streets, not far from Washington Square Park. Interestingly, or curiously, this old and obscure cemetery is also the final resting place of two other expert fly fishers who plied their skills along Catskill trout streams.

William Adams and John G. Smedburgh were pioneer Catskill trout fishermen and were the brothers-in-law of the renowned Judge Fitz-James Fitch. The trio fished the Beaverkill every year, beginning in the 1830s, for more than twenty years, visiting those special waters each year with the same team of horses. The remains of both men were interred in the 1870s, and Judge Fitch reminisced about the two, who were also his best friends. In *The American Angler* in March 1892, he stated that the cemetery, at that time, was "almost forgotten."

Just a few years after the death of Theodore Gordon, a very popular book written by George Parker Holden, titled *Streamcraft* (1919), informed readers that flies tied in the style of Theodore Gordon could still be acquired: "While no one may fill Theodore Gordon's unique place as a writer specially beloved of all American anglers, the reader may be interested to learn that flies tied in the exquisite Gordon fashion are still obtainable from Gordon's friend and neighbor, Mr. H. B. Christian of Neversink, N. Y. Mr. Roy Steenrod of Liberty, N. Y., likewise is familiar with the patterns . . ."[6]

Streamcraft was the first book to acknowledge the important relationship between Theodore Gordon and Frederic Halford, and the development of the dry fly in America. It was also the first book to mention the Quill Gordon and Golden Spinner, or Gordon.

During his years in the Catskills, Theodore Gordon socialized with several local outdoorsmen who shared his interest in hunting and fishing. He not only fished and hunted with Bruce LeRoy, but boarded with him at times. Bruce was a farmer who maintained roosters for Gordon's use in fly tying. Their friendship appears to have been important and perhaps dates further back than any others, as Bruce LeRoy named a son who was born in 1891 after Gordon: Theodore Gordon LeRoy.

Gordon also fished with Roy Steenrod (1882–1977), who lived in Liberty and was employed at the post office. Their friendship began in 1904, when he met Steenrod while mailing fly orders to customers; at times, especially in the winter, he boarded in Liberty at the Liberty House.

Another of his fishing companions was Herman Christian (1880–1973), who lived in Neversink and had a reputation as an excellent trout fisherman, particularly when it came to catching large trout.

Gordon did not view the tying of dry flies as a particularly difficult task. He had learned from books and by taking apart the flies of others, a logical practice of anyone desiring to understand how a fly was made. His view was that anyone could learn to tie a fly and that fly tying was a "minor art and depends on color sense and experience."[7] He was also generous with his fly patterns. When William Mills & Son had difficulty tying Quill Gordons, he sent them a sample to duplicate, as well as other patterns; they then imitated his style of making dry flies.

The fly-tying skills acquired by Theodore Gordon were passed on to both Christian and Steenrod, but in different ways. Christian insisted he did not learn directly from Gordon, and though he often visited him, he never saw Gordon tie a fly. Christian learned on his own, primarily as others had done, by taking flies apart, including, undoubtedly, some of Gordon's, as he often gave Christian flies to use.

Steenrod did learn directly from Gordon, whom he visited a couple of days a week, either to fish, or sit and talk, or tie flies. The two men also corresponded frequently, and Gordon supplied Roy with materials, hooks, and flies to use as samples.

A third fly tier who claimed to have learned directly from Theodore Gordon was Reuben R. Cross (1896–1958), a Neversink native who also tied in the style of Gordon. He followed the path of his teacher and became a professional known for his delicate style of dry flies.

By the 1920s, these Catskill natives were being recognized for their distinct method of tying and creating American dry flies. Artist and fly fisher Louis Rhead, in an article written in *Forest and Stream* in November 1922 and titled "The Evolution of the Trout Fly," stated that Americans were "just going over the top wave of the dry fly craze," and that the majority of expert anglers were still using Halford's English patterns, even though they did not imitate American trout stream insects.

Rhead also wrote that in the Neversink region of the Catskills, "a small school of expert fly dressers" had formed under the leadership of the late Theodore Gordon. He mentioned that several patterns of flies are made, but the most popular is the Quill Gordon: "They are beautifully tied and would do credit to English artisans. Several experts have told me they are most effective in rising trout."[8]

In the years ahead, this "school" would increase in number and include many of the most famous fly-tying professionals this country had ever produced. They became known particularly for their skill in tying a style of dry fly that originated with Theodore Gordon known as "Catskill."

Theodore Gordon developed a purely American style of tying dry or floating flies. According to legendary fly tier Harry Darbee, Gordon changed the anatomy of the dry fly by setting his wings with the butts facing toward the rear of the fly and by winding the hackle at right angles to the hook shank. He also used nonabsorbent materials and tied his flies sparsely hackled.

ROY G. STEENROD

Roy Steenrod was born in the Sullivan County town of Liberty, located approximately 5 miles east of the village of Neversink. As a youngster, he fished for trout in the streams near his home, catching his first trout in the small brook that flowed through the middle of town.

He began using dry or floating flies in 1906, shortly after meeting Theodore Gordon. Gordon considered Roy a very good fly fisherman, and it was not until the winter of 1914 that Gordon began to teach him how to tie dry flies. Gordon gave Steenrod his first vise and nurtured Roy's passion for fly tying, a passion he maintained for the rest of his life.

Two years after learning to tie dry flies, Roy Steenrod developed a floating pattern of his own that not only equaled the popularity of the Quill Gordon, but surpassed it. The fly, known as the Hendrickson, was tied to imitate one of the early and prolific mayfly hatches on the Beaverkill.

One of Steenrod's favorite fishing companions was Albert Everett Hendrickson, a New York businessman affiliated with steamship lines and the U. S. Trucking Corporation. Hendrickson had been a customer of Theodore Gordon's. Shortly after Gordon died, he came to Liberty to meet Steenrod and ask Roy to tie flies for him. The two became lifelong friends and fished together all over the Catskills, including on the Esopus, Neversink, Willowemoc, and Beaverkill.

These were the years that the dry fly was becoming increasingly popular, and on a fishing trip with Hendrickson to the Beaverkill, Steenrod first tied his famous dry fly:

> One day in 1916, while we were fishing the Beaverkill below the Junction Pool at Roscoe, a hatch of flies came on. We had never seen the fish rise so freely for any fly as they did this hatch. I caught one of the flies and put it into my fly box, and after lunch that day at Ferdon's I tied some patterns of the fly as nearly as I could. We took fish with that fly day in and day out, and for years it proved to be a killer and is so today. One day, while sitting on the bank of the stream perhaps two years after I had tied the first patterns, the matter was brought up as to what I would call or name the fly. Looking at A. E., the best friend a person could ever wish to have, I said "the fly is the Hendrickson." I saw at once that A. E. was pleased.[9]

The Hendrickson, as first tied by Roy Steenrod, was tied with a body of several shades of fur from a red fox; and following the habit of Theodore Gordon, it was tied to match the color of the natural fly then on the water by blending the fur. The wings were wood duck flank feathers, as was the tail. The tail was tied similar to the way Gordon tied his tails; two or three fibers tied upright in the best imitation of the natural mayfly. In time, Roy changed the tail to the same shade of natural blue dun as the hackle.

Though his Hendrickson was a direct imitation of a natural mayfly, Steenrod believed that fly fishing was 90 percent presentation. Gordon would not use a Royal Coachman dry fly, but it was a part of Roy's fly-fishing tactics. Early on, he tied the fly in the fan-wing style, and later, he used the hair-wing Royal Coachman.

Steenrod often advised fly fishers that when there is a good hatch of flies on the water, and the trout are feeding heavily, yet you are unable to take fish on the nearest imitation, go in the opposite direction and put on a Royal Coachman. He was successful with this method many times.

One of Roy's favorite streams was the North Branch Callicoon Creek, a tributary of the Callicoon Creek. When he fished the stream in the 1920s and 1930s, there were several mill dams along the stream: "with deep dark pools below and all had many rainbows and browns 18–20 inches, boy what fishing and the stretches between mills produced many 12 inch and over trout."*

Roy Steenrod became involved with regional conservation efforts. In 1919, he became a founding member of the Liberty Rod & Gun Club and was its first vice president. Through the club, he lobbied state officials on a variety of conservation issues; among them, better stocking policies and a public fishing program.

---

*Steenrod's unpublished personal notes.

Perhaps influenced by Gordon's conservation ethics and teachings, or a desire to be more directly involved with conservation and fish and wildlife, Roy Steenrod became a fish and game protector for the New York State Conservation Commission in 1927. The area he patrolled and was responsible for was one of the Catskills' prime fishing regions and included the Neversink, Beaverkill, and Willowemoc.

Game Protector Roy Steenrod, front row, far right. New York State
Conservation Department Annual Report, 1929.

Roy Steenrod became a prominent enforcement officer known for his fairness in dealing with those who violated fish and game laws. Not all were criminals; there were years of his tenure that included the era of the Great Depression, when many did not have the means to put food on the table through employment and entered woods or stream going beyond the legal bounds of the law. Roy became known for his dedication to duty, but also for his compassion and common-sense approach to law enforcement. This quality, combined with his fame as one of Sullivan County's most famous fly fishermen, made Steenrod an asset to the Conservation Commission, which was still struggling for an identity and public acceptance.

In 1952, when he reached the age of seventy, Roy was forced to retire under a statutory age limit. In just a few weeks, Sullivan County sportsmen and friends went out and found the largest place they could to hold a dinner and pay tribute to a man that they held in great respect. More than two hundred people attended the event. Harry Darbee, a friend of Steenrod's, was fond of stating that half of those in attendance were adversaries that Roy had arrested!

An outstanding quality of the man was that he greatly enjoyed teaching others the skills he had for tying trout flies—especially children, whom he taught by the hundreds at Boy Scout camps, as well as at the DeBruce Conservation Camp. For nearly fifty years, he had been involved with scouting, and he received the Silver Beaver award for his services. Following his retirement, Roy began teaching at the DeBruce Conservation Camp on a regular basis, giving instruction on woodcraft, hunter safety, fly casting, and fly tying. He taught until he was eighty-five years old. Some of the very youngsters in whom he instilled conservation ethics would become fish and wildlife biologists and environmental conservation officers.

Roy Steenrod was an asset to his community. He was a civic leader, a scout leader, a conservationist, and a public servant who was admired by many. When he retired as a fish and game protector, he was replaced by the equally competent Burton R. Lindsley.

Roy Steenrod at Theodore Gordon's fly-tying vise.
Courtesy Charlotte Steenrod.

Talking about the event years later, Burt's wife, Betty, recalled being on Main Street in Liberty one day, and the couple saw the highly respected Steenrod pass by in uniform. Burt looked at Betty and told her, "I want to be just like him."

HERMAN CHRISTIAN

Herman Christian was born in Eureka, a small hamlet located at the mouth of Chestnut Creek where it entered the Rondout Creek. He fished for trout as a youngster, and in 1891, when he was nine years old, made his first trip to the Neversink, a river he would become well associated with. He traveled from Eureka with two fishermen and camped on the banks of the Big Bend Pool, one of the most famous pools on the Neversink.

In 1896, at the age of fourteen, he caught his first large trout on a set line. It was a 19½-inch, 2-pound, 8-ounce fish, and he promptly sold it for 50 cents. When he turned fifteen or sixteen, in about 1897 or 1898, he began using flies. It was not until 1906 that he met Theodore Gordon. He knew of the great fly tier and wanted to get some of Gordon's flies. Bruce LeRoy advised Herman that a good way to meet Gordon and make a favorable impression was to bring him some quality fly-tying hackle. The two not only struck up a friendship, but also fished together and exchanged thoughts on trout and trout-fishing tactics. Gordon began to give some of his flies to the younger man.

When Christian could not get as many flies from Gordon as he wanted or needed, he began tying his own. He learned by taking apart and then retying Gordon's flies a year or two before Gordon died, in 1913 or 1914. Nonetheless, Gordon, in a roundabout way, passed his skills on to Herman Christian.

Christian generally tied most of the fly in his hands, tying on the wings, tail, and body without a vise. He then finished off the fly by placing it in a vise and winding the hackle in a unique figure-eight style. In just a few years, he had learned the craft well enough to have photographs of a few of his dry flies, including a Quill Gordon and a bass fly known as the Christian Special, featured in George Parker Holden's popular book *Streamcraft*.

During the 1920s, Herman created a pair of dry flies that were popular locally. Both patterns had wood duck flank feathers for wings and dark blue dun hackle and tails. One had a red floss body and was ribbed with peacock quill with equal segments of the floss showing. The other had an olive-green body and was also ribbed with peacock quill.

Christian tied flies professionally for fifty years, and although he tied exceptionally well, it was his skill as a trout fisherman that made him famous, especially in the Catskills. For years he maintained a reputation for finding, and then catching, large trout; and it is doubtful that anyone caught as many big fish as did Herman Christian. He enjoyed fishing with dry flies during the day, but this skill was overshadowed by his reputation with wet flies at night, usually two or three flies tied on a #6 or #8 hook. Christian's favorite dry fly was a #11 Quill Gordon; English hook sizes, at the time, came in odd numbers as well as even.

Christian was so successful at taking big trout that some anglers questioned how it was possible. In a letter to Roy Steenrod in 1915, Theodore Gordon gave his opinion on how he thought Christian accomplished his unique feats: "Christian is also a great expert, and has more patience and perseverance than any other man I ever met. This is the secret of his big fish. That and going for them *at the correct time.* I think he deserves the big trout he catches and am glad to see them when he brings them to me to show."[10]

In 1911, Christian took first place in the *Field & Stream* fishing contest by catching a 5-pound, 11-ounce brook trout, which he captured in the Neversink in a pool about a half mile upstream of Woodbourne. He had hooked a brown of about 8 inches and was reeling the fish in, when it was grabbed by a large fish and then let go. Christian stood still, and the big trout came to within 10 feet of him, and then retreated to the side of a large rock.

He rested the fish for about an hour by fishing the tail of the pool, and then, crossing the stream, he tied on a #10 Wickham's Fancy. By crossing the stream, Christian was shielded from the trout by a large boulder, and he commenced casting; on the second cast, the trout took the fly, and the battle began.

Christian believed the trout was a brown until he saw it up close, and then was surprised to find that it was a giant brook trout measuring 21½ inches in length, with a 12½-inch girth, and weighing 5 pounds, 6 ounces! (The editor of *Field & Stream* allowed 5 ounces for shrinkage.) The prize catch was caught on a 10-foot Chubb rod that weighed 7 ounces. Christian ended his account by stating: "If any of you fellows who read *Field & Stream* like trying your luck in the Neversink for a day or two come and see me. We have the fish."[11]

Two years later, Christian caught another 6-pound, 12-ounce monster brook trout on a home-made fly from Sand Pond, at the headwaters of the Willowemoc Creek. When the New York State Conservation Department compiled its original list of record fish in 1941, biologist Cecil Heacox of the Rochester office determined that Herman Christian's catch qualified as the official state record.

The following year, 1914, Herman Christian took second place in the *Field & Stream* contest with a 5-pound, 13-ounce brown trout he caught in the Neversink at Big Bend Pool on a #8 Pig's Wool fly. And this feat was followed by catching a 29½-inch brown trout a mile upstream of the village of Neversink that weighed 8 pounds, 4 ounces. The great fish was taken at night on a #6 Dun Fly: dun hackle, dun muskrat or seal's fur, with a dun hackle palmered, and wood duck wings. In 1918, at Bradley's Rock Pool on the Neversink, Christian caught a 25-inch brown trout that weighed 7 pounds.

There are no permanent records of all the large trout Herman Christian caught in his lifetime, only newspaper or magazine accounts of those fish that he entered in contests or were mentioned in books. In 1933, Christian walked into Whit Wells's sport shop in Liberty with a pair of brown trout that he took out of the Neversink, which weighed more than 14 pounds! The larger was 7½ pounds and measured 26 inches! The following year, he placed second in the big fish contest held by the *New York Herald Tribune* with another monster brown trout he caught in the East Branch of the Delaware, which weighed 8 pounds, 6 ounces and measured 26 inches!

Herman Christian spent the greater part of his life near the Neversink, living on Schumway Road, not very far from the famous Big Bend Pool. Schumway Road traveled through a mostly uninhabited area and looped around to a point near the covered bridge at Claryville. Christian purchased the property in 1919, acquiring 315 acres that included the stretch of the Neversink and Big Bend Pool. He immediately sold the river frontage and 299 acres to Edward R. Hewitt, who was assembling a large portion of the lower Neversink.

Some years ago, I went looking for Christian's house. By this time, a good portion of Schumway Road had been abandoned when the city of New York acquired significant acreage around Neversink reservoir. I found an old foundation, the remains of a small chicken house, and the usual evidence associated with an abandoned home site: old fencing, lilacs, and daffodils.

In order to confirm my findings, I talked with Burt Lindsley, the conservation officer who had replaced Roy Steenrod. I knew Burt would know every back road, as well as most of the hunters and fishermen in his region. He assured me that the place I had found at the end of Schumway Road was Christian's house. He recalled that on the side of the simple wooden-framed dwelling were nailed the skeletal heads of many large trout and that there was a well-worn foot path running down to Big Bend Pool.

When Burt knew Christian in the early 1950s, he was living a reclusive life. Christian was in his early seventies, living alone, and had developed a reputation as being cantankerous. He maintained a garden, fished, hunted, trapped, and guided. As far back as the 1925 census, his occupation was listed as "guide." He was an excellent woodsman, hunter, and trapper who enjoyed living close to the land, and for most of his life, he earned a simple living tying trout flies, trapping, and guiding fishermen.

Christian's house. *The Anglers' Club Bulletin*, 1950.

Burt mentioned that as you entered the front door, there were steps with a door to the left that Christian used as his fly-tying room. He believed Herman lived only in this room and that it included a large couch that he would sleep on. While patrolling the backwoods roads looking for "deerjackers," Burt would often stop for a visit. Christian always had a pot of very strong coffee on the stove, which he made by just tossing the grounds in boiling water. He recalled that no matter how late it was at night, Christian was awake and tying flies; he never seemed to sleep!

Burt received complaints about Christian—not unusual when someone has a reputation for being a successful hunter or fisherman—but he never caught him violating the law. Christian, in conversations, did confess to some misdeeds, but Burt stated that he would always talk in the past tense, that "he knew or did things, law-breaking things, but that was a long time ago."

Herman Christian died days after his ninety-third birthday in Delhi, Delaware County. His funeral was held in Liberty, and burial was at the Rural Cemetery in Grahamsville, in the town of Neversink. The cemetery lies along the Chestnut Creek, just upstream from where he was born at Eureka, which is now covered by the waters of the Rondout reservoir.

REUBEN R. CROSS

"Rube" Cross was born just outside the village of Neversink, on the family farm on Mutton Hill. He grew up at a time when the beautiful Neversink Valley, and the river running through it, was a

Christian with a Payne rod given to him by Gordon. *The Anglers' Club Bulletin*, 1950.

trout fisherman's paradise. That he became a gifted fly tier is not surprising, because the village of Neversink, in those days, was a hub of trout-fishing activity. Once brown trout had established themselves in the lower Neversink, fishing tourists flocked to the village and set up headquarters in such places as the Neversink Inn, Little River Lodge, Herron's, Neversink Lodge, and a host of other boardinghouses and farmhouses that welcomed trout fishermen.

From whom—or how—Rube Cross learned to tie flies has always been a bit of a controversy. He claimed on many occasions to have learned from Theodore Gordon and stated so to fly-fishing historian John McDonald (*The Complete Fly Fisherman,* 1947). "Cross told me he had learned to tie flies from Gordon. Gordon was his mentor. Roy Steenrod later doubted the literalness of that but I remember Cross as forthright and a witty denuder of pretension."[12]

Before McDonald's interview, Cross had told Harold Smedley (*Fly Patterns and Their Origins,* 1943) that he knew Theodore Gordon and, early on, had obtained a few of his flies and copied them until he perfected Gordon's style.

In his own book, *Tying American Trout Lures,* written in 1936, Rube Cross proves he was familiar with the flies of Theodore Gordon when he writes: "The late Theodore Gordon used wire on his Gordon Quill for effect only, giving its body a bronze shade which is characteristic of some of the natural insects."[13] And in his second book on fly tying, written four years later and titled *Fur, Feathers and Steel,* Cross stated: "Theodore Gordon, whom I well remember, did much to popularize the dry fly in America. He tied his own flies and was quite jealous of his art."[14]

What complicates the issue even further is an article on Cross that appeared in *Outdoor Life,* written by Edwin Teale in December 1934, titled "Reuben R. Cross: Dry Flies from a Kitchen Workshop." In the article, Cross states that he began fishing with dry flies, and tying them, when he was eighteen (1914), and that he learned through trial and error and copying standard dry flies. He does not mention Theodore Gordon.

To find what is correct is sometimes difficult, but what is certain is that Cross was familiar with Gordon's flies. He lived in the right place to have known Gordon, and he stated that he obtained Gordon's flies and copied them. This he did unquestionably.

Roy Steenrod doubted that Cross learned from Gordon, and Herman Christian was adamant that Cross did not, stating that Cross did not even know Gordon and that he was just a boy when Gordon died in 1915. Rube, however, would have been eighteen or nineteen years old at that time, and was certainly old enough to have learned from Gordon before his death.

Like most boys growing up in the sparsely populated, mountainous area of the Catskills, Rube learned to hunt, fish, and trap at a very early age. He caught his first trout at the age of five and shot his first deer when he was fifteen. Natives then, and even today, tend to judge a man by how well he gets along in the woods. Rube knew the streams, the deer trails, the forest, and the mountaintop ponds. He loved the woods, trout fishing, and small-town country life. However, the Catskills were never an easy place to make a living, and as was often the case with young men, Cross left the farm for city life.

He traveled to New Jersey and found employment, but did not stay away for long. He returned for visits and sometimes stayed longer; then it was off to New York City for a while, return, and leave again. Even as a young man, Rube was popular in his home village of Neversink; when he was away, the people of Neversink missed him as much as he missed the country. Comments appeared in the *Liberty Register* on his comings and goings:

August 29, 1919: "Rube Cross is out of a job again. His boss refused to obey orders, so he quit."

June 4, 1920: "The guessing contest is over. We now know who will run the casino this summer. Rube Cross is the 'bimbo' whose smiling face will adorn the sody fountain."

September 9, 1921: "Rube Cross has taken the job as manager of Taylor's turning mill."

March 31, 1922: "Reuben Cross is working for Rob Broden."

November 1, 1923: "We sincerely hope that Rube Cross, who is spending the winter in New Jersey, will pay us a visit occasionally, as his presence at social functions put plenty of 'pep' into the entertainments."

January 24, 1924: "Reuben Cross arrived in town last week looking as big and husky as a plate of cornbeef and cabbage."

February 21, 1924: "Reuben Cross motored up from New York last Thursday and was given a rousing reception by his former buddies. The bankroll which 'Rube' brought with him was so large that no grey-hound could jump over it."

And finally Rube Cross came home to stay:

April 30, 1925: "Mr. & Mrs. Reuben Cross, of New York arrived in town Monday. They expect to rent rooms here. The river was lined with fishermen Sunday."

Rube Cross with a prize rooster. *Outdoor Life*, 1934.

It was in the summer of 1925 that Rube returned to Neversink. The census records for that year reveal that he lived on Hollow Road and that his occupation was "Maker (Trout flies)." He became known as a perfectionist, tying dry flies with an exactness few could duplicate, and it was not long before he developed a reputation for making quality dry flies.

In a few years, Rube Cross became the most celebrated fly tier in America, and he tied in the traditional style of the Catskill School that started with Theodore Gordon. A Cross-tied fly had perfectly matched wings; incredibly stiff, evenly wound hackle; a finely tapered body; and a tail of the stiffest hackle possible. The fly had a generally sparse appearance and was tied to float in the surface film just like a natural insect.

It is difficult to believe that Rube Cross did not learn his tying skills from Theodore Gordon; there were too many similarities between the way they both went about tying flies and the flies that they produced. Like Gordon, Cross raised his own roosters in order to obtain the best-quality hackle, keeping at times thirty or more that he crossbred to obtain the elusive blue dun shades. And also like Gordon, he was a strong believer in the appeal of blue dun hackle on dry flies: "There is no doubt that the lighter and darker shades of blue dun are the most effective shades of hackle used to dress artificial flies for the taking of trout in the northeastern states."[15]

And like Gordon, Cross was very particular about the stiffness of the hackle he used in tying flies; he believed hackle was the most important part of a dry fly. Before winding the hackle, he stroked the fibers toward the butt of the feather to determine if it was acceptable. He used a clothespin to keep tension on his tying thread and finished off his flies with half-hitches rather than a whip finish. Cross used fine wire at times over his quill-bodied flies, and he also cocked his tails slightly up from the hook shank, methods that were also used Gordon.

During the 1930s, Rube Cross was the premier fly tier in the country, annually demonstrating his skills in tackle shops and before large crowds at the National Sportsmen's Show in New York. Cross was a big man. He was 6 feet, 2 inches tall; solidly built, weighing more than 200 pounds; and he had the hands of a lumberjack. But he captivated audiences as he created delicate and elegant trout flies. Magically, his fingers united gossamer thread with dainty feathers and frail quills onto a hook in a manner trout, too, found fascinating.

How good were Cross-tied flies? Eugene Connett commented on them in his trout-fishing classic, *Any Luck?*, published in 1933. Connett writes: "When we come to consider the best dry fly patterns, I can say without hesitation that the most *killing* fly is the quill Gordon, properly tied—as Reuben Cross ties it."[16] Connett also claimed that he considered Rube Cross "the best professional fly tier of dry flies in America."[17]

Cross tended to tie the standard fly patterns of the day, such as the Quill Gordon, Hendrickson, Dark and Light Cahill, Ginger Quill, Royal Coachman, Honey Dun, Catskill, and Leadwing Coachman. He was known to use only the best materials and never deviate, even slightly, from the standard dressing. When he ran out of quality dry-fly hackle, he would not substitute, nor would he ever use a slightly different shade of hackle than the one called for—even though most fishermen would not know the difference.

Cross did create a few flies of his own. Perhaps the best known was a fly called the Cross Special, a dry fly tied in the classic Catskill style. In fact, the fly was a "cross" between the Quill Gordon and the Light Cahill. He first tied the fly because those two patterns were the best and most pop-

Frank Berner, Liberty, New York, with a 5-pound brown caught on a Cross Special. *American Fly Tier*, 1941.

ular in the Catskills. Cross put the Light Cahill body on the Quill Gordon, and the fly was instantly productive.

A fly that is still used today by trout fishermen everywhere is the Hair-Wing Royal Coachman. Al McClane, the longtime editor of *Field & Stream,* in his popular work *The Practical Fly Fisherman* (1953), credits Rube Cross with creating the switch from fan wings to hair wings: "In 1930, Reuben Cross of Neversink, New York, was asked to dress some Royals for L. Q. Quackenbush of the Beaverkill Trout Club, using a substitute for the fragile white mandarin breast feathers. Reub asked his supplier for any part of an animal with stiff, kinky, white hair. All the dealer could find was a half-dozen impala tails, but they were exactly suited to the task."[18]

In 1936, Reuben R. Cross became the first professional fly tier to have published a book on fly tying. Cross revealed to all his methods, tips, and secrets in a handy little volume titled *Tying American Trout Lures.* The book was a giant step in the advancement of American fly tying, and experts and novices alike were treated to advanced techniques by a master fly tier. *Tying American Trout Lures* also gave tips on raising roosters for quality hackle, including how to breed chickens of certain colors to get the natural blue dun shades necessary to tie many of the Catskill dry-fly patterns.

Rube Cross maintained a lifelong love of history, at least for local or regional history. He loved the Catskills and the simple, quiet life of the mountains, and he at times contributed articles of historic nature to local newspapers. His interest in history may have been inherent, as he proudly told listeners that his ancestors on his mother's side came to America in 1630 and that his paternal great-grandfather fought the British in 1812, then married a "Mohawk Indian squaw" and settled in the Catskills, clearing the land along the Neversink Valley on Mutton Hill.

In October 1938, at the age of forty-two, Rube Cross moved out of the Neversink Valley forever. As early as the 1920s, unconfirmed reports circulated that a large dam was to be built on the Neversink, and in 1929, newspapers confirmed that a dam would be constructed when engineers hit bedrock about 1 mile downstream of the village of Neversink. By 1935, rumors went through the village that those residents with relatives buried in the cemetery were being asked to move the bodies, as they would soon be flooded.

Dramatic changes were going to take place: Homes, businesses, farms, and all properties were being appropriated in preparation for the building of a water supply reservoir for the city of New York. It was clear that the community and the river Cross loved would be destroyed. Rube didn't wait to see the destruction, and so he moved over to the Beaverkill at Lew Beach.

In addition to continuing his career as a professional fly tier, Cross also began writing magazine articles, mostly on fly tying, for such publications as *Field & Stream, Outdoor Life, Country Life,* and *American Fly-Tier.* And it was while living in Lew Beach that he also produced a second instructional book on fly tying titled *Fur, Feathers and Steel* in 1940.

At first Cross and his wife, Bessie, lived at the Beaverkill Trout Club. They later took up residence along the Shin Creek Road in a two-story house next to the Methodist Church. Rube settled nicely into the social life of a hamlet that, although smaller than his hometown of Neversink, was nonetheless similar in many ways. Everyone knew and saw each other daily, and shared the experiences of simple country life. Rube Cross was well liked for his sense of humor, wit, and ability to tell stories; he was boisterous, sensitive, and generous.

On a summer evening in May 1941, a tragic fire destroyed his home and everything in it. Fond of local history, Rube had collected a number of artifacts and memorabilia associated with the Catskills; his home was described as a "veritable museum" in the newspapers that announced the tragic fire. Inside were a prized book collection, old guns and swords, Indian artifacts, antiques and irreplaceable manuscripts, and, of course, all of his fly-tying materials and supplies. And although there was insurance on the house he was renting, there was none on the contents.

Friends and neighbors came to his aid, and perhaps even more importantly, customers and other fly tiers as well, who donated materials so that he could get back into business. Many years later, Al McClane recalled this difficult time: "The attitude of the purist toward his fly dresser is one of remarkable devotion. When the home of Reub Cross burned in Lew Beach back in 1941, his frenzied followers took up a collection to put him back in business, for the balding, corrosive, caustic-tongued wit of the Beaverkill tied trout flies like no other man. And there were those who couldn't fish without flies made the Cross way."[19]

Rube Cross made every effort to pass along his knowledge of fly tying. He tied before thousands at sportsmen's shows and tackle shops, and wrote articles and two books on the subject that eventually were republished in one volume, titled *The Complete Fly Tier*, in 1950.

Rube stayed in the Beaverkill Valley for another year or two, but then moved to Rhode Island. His reason for leaving may have been the fire—the devastating loss of all his personal belongings and those things important to him that he had accumulated during a lifetime of tying flies. Then again, he could also have been lured, like others during the war, to the attractive pay of working in a defense plant. He landed a job in a wire factory in Pawtucket, though he continued to tie flies professionally and appear at sportsmen's shows.

Even after the war, Rube Cross did not return to the Catskills, as he had always done in the past. He chose to spend his remaining years in Providence, where he died on November 4, 1958, at the age of sixty-two. His spirit will always be in the mountain communities where he was born and where he was the standard-bearer, for a while, for the school of Catskill fly tiers that began with Theodore Gordon.

Years after Cross's death, Al McClane remembered visiting Rube to learn more about tying flies: "A huge man, half poet, half mountain lion, he was generous to a fault. His dill-pickle-sized fingers spun the most beautiful flies I will ever see."[20] Al had been fifteen years old at the time, and Rube wrote an inscription in Al's copy of *Tying American Trout Lures*:

To My Young Friend
I dreamed,
That I again my native hills had found
The mossy rocks, the valley, and the
Stream that used to hold me captive
To the sound.
And that I was a boy again.
(Anon)
Reuben R. Cross
Jan. 3, 1937

15

The 1900s

"FORAY OF THE MANHATTANESE"; and "FISHOMOBILING"

By 1900, trout fishing in the Catskills had changed. Trout fishermen were learning how to catch brown trout on dry flies, and many believed that the new species furnished more sport. Although the number of trout caught in a single day was far less than in the past, a growing number of fly fishermen favored catching the larger trout.

However, as the new century approached, once again the Catskills' fishery was threatened, this time by a massive water-supply plan that included damming and diverting the water of every major trout stream to New York City.

In the spring of 1899, there were rumors that the Esopus Creek might be impounded and used for a New York City water-supply reservoir. One Kingston newspaper told of a dam being constructed at the base of the Big Indian Valley in the town of Shandaken. The entire valley lying between the mountains would be flooded, and the report claimed that there appeared to be no benefit to the county if the reservoir was built. The story ended by stating: "It certainly would not enhance the beauty of the scenery of the Catskills and it would not add to its popularity as a summer resort."[1]

In the fall of 1903, newspaper reports claimed that New York City was now looking to build a huge artificial lake by constructing a large dam, again on the Esopus Creek, at the famous Bishop's Falls. In addition, a 13-mile tunnel would be constructed that would take water from the Schoharie Creek and send it down the Esopus to the new reservoir. Hundreds of farms and villages would be flooded, and approximately 14 miles of the Ulster & Delaware railroad would have to be moved or be inundated.

Two years later, the state legislature passed, and the governor signed, Chapter 724 of the Laws of 1905. Originally known as the Catskill Water Act, this was amended and reenacted as the Water Supply Act of 1905. The law vested the city with broad powers to find and develop new sources of water for New York and permitted the city to acquire land in the Catskills for a water supply. Also in 1905, the New York City Board of Estimate approved the construction of a Catskill water-supply system.

In November, the *Ellenville Journal* published an article titled "Gobbling Up the Streams" and reported that New York City had formulated a plan to remove additional water supplies from the Catskill mountain region. A map was filed in the Ulster County Clerk's Office at Kingston, which revealed that New York City proposed to remove all of the water from the Esopus Creek and the tributaries that flowed from the north into both the Esopus and the Rondout Creeks, including the Lackawack, or upper Rondout.

The paper also stated that a large dam was proposed on the Rondout Creek, upstream of Honk Falls, which would take "every drop of water" from that stream! The *Journal* was definitely opposed to the idea and ended its article with a superfluous statement:

> The JOURNAL has held all along and still believes that no living man is capable of estimating the damage likely to result to the material interests of western Ulster from this foray of the Manhattanese upon our mountain streams. No impending event has offered greater menace since the days when the Tories and redskins were on the warpath for pillage and murder.[2]

Before New York City acquired lands and rights for the construction of the reservoir in the Esopus Valley, the State Water Supply Commission, which was created by the legislature, held the first of a series of public hearings at Kingston. There was standing room only, and Judge Alphonso Clearwater, esteemed historian and a man known for his distinguished public service, led the opposition against the construction of the reservoir.

The judge represented the Ulster & Delaware Railroad, banks, businesses, and several large landowners. He argued vehemently that the city was given too much power to arbitrarily disrupt whole communities and a way of life, and that the hearings were unconstitutional. Others argued that the people in the Catskills did not want the reservoir, and boardinghouse owners would be greatly affected financially by its construction.

In the end, the State Water Supply Commission ruled in favor of the dam builders, and the city of New York now had the right, under the law, to force farmers to sell the land their ancestors had cleared and to acquire homesteads, businesses, mills, general stores, hotels, railroads, churches, and everything else associated with village life.

Local people quickly developed animosity toward the city, especially after they were portrayed in New York newspapers as country bumpkins. Soon, those living where the reservoir was to be built were harassed by surveyors and others, who trespassed on their lands, behaved rudely, cut down trees, and destroyed stone fences in preparation of the new reservoir.

Anger toward New Yorkers continued to surface, even though many had been their summer boarders. "New York people, it was said, were arrogant Sabbath-breaking and ignorant barbarians who believed that the people north of their city line existed only for the convenience or profit of New York."[3]

Before the construction of the dam, and before the valley was flooded, Winfield T. Sherwood wrote a lengthy and informative twelve-part series of articles that appeared in *Forest and Stream* describing a camping and fishing trip he and a few friends made to the Esopus Creek. The men spent more than a month in the spring and camped along the river at the mouth of the Bushkill, near the village of West Shokan.

The articles were a popular chronicle of the group's adventures trout fishing, exploring tributaries, camp life, their meeting with bear hunters, interesting and colorful villagers, and the retelling of camp yarns.

Sherwood described the natural beauty and tranquillity of the valley, and the wonderful nature of the people who lived along the river. He wrote of how their passing of the day was often marked by the tinkling of cowbells as the cows were gathered for milking, or the chime of the school bell, or the movement of a familiar train that ran through the village, or the closing whistle of a sawmill.

The campers caught browns and rainbows, large and small, fished the famous pool below Boice's house in the evening and the riffle at the Dugway, and they were frustrated by the large brown trout that lay stationary at the bottom of the pool under the bridge across the Bushkill!

In his series, Sherwood disguised the village of West Shokan by calling it Unasego. On closing, he paid tribute to the area and referenced nearby High Point and Tice Teneyck mountains:

> To those who have followed the preceding chapters, it may be of interest to know that when the present plans of the water commissioners of the City of New York are executed the entire section of which I write will be a vast artificial lake. Upon the completion of the great Ashokan dam the rifts will one by one be stifled by the rising flood, and their music cease—for a time. Fish will swim where the pine path now winds, and water-grasses wave where the campfire burned. The beautiful village which I have called Unasego must move back, excepting Mr. Cushman and the old bear hunter; but High Point will not move back, and Tice Teneyck will remain to mirror its beautiful sides in the pool which men have made.[4]

Construction of the "Ashokan" reservoir began in 1907, and when it was completed, nine villages or hamlets—including Brown's Station, Olive City, Ashton, Broadhead's Bridge, West Hurley, Glenford, Shokan, West Shokan, and Boiceville—were destroyed. Approximately 2,000 people were relocated; and 504 houses and farms, 10 churches, 10 schools, and 2,637 bodies from 32 cemeteries were removed.

In a letter to Roy Steenrod during the winter of 1915, Theodore Gordon wrote:

> I wish that I could find some old photographs of the country about where the Shokan lake will be. I used to consider it, where the mountains spread apart, one of the most beautiful sections of the Catskills. It will be all a waste until they cover the devastated country with water, turning it into a large lake.[5]

New York City acquired a total of 15,222 acres, of which 9,500 were cleared of all trees, brush, and every trace of man or beast. Perhaps the site of this massive clearing is best described by Elizabeth Burroughs Kelley, daughter of Julian Burroughs and granddaughter of John Burroughs:

> There were great changes even in the mountains, in John's Catskills. A great lake had been added, blotting out landmarks and eradicating whole villages. Shortly before the water had been brought into the area, Julian had driven his family through it—a land of such devastation that it haunted the children for a long time afterward. Not a building had been left standing, every tree had been cut down, every object that could be picked up had been carried away; and then all those acres had been burnt over. All that could be seen was a blackened, desolate land extending for miles, completely barren like something out of a nightmare.[6]

IN THE VALLEY OF THE EAST BRANCH

The undisciplined slaughter of trout that had continued along Dry Brook in the 1890s must have had an influence on George Gould, son of Jay Gould, who had purchased Furlough Lake in 1890. By the summer of 1894, Gould increased his holdings to approximately 2,300 acres; three years later, newspapers reported he had purchased an additional 2,658 acres. By the trout season of 1898, through ownership or leases from various landowners, he controlled approximately 4 miles of stream and, in time, added to these holdings until he had acquired almost all of Dry Brook.

Gould's forest home was made from hand-hewn logs of hemlock, logged on the property, with the bark left on the logs to give them a more rustic appearance; the building was once described as a "veritable palace of logs." In addition to the lodge, a barn and two servant's cottages were also constructed, as well as a milk house, large hennery, and dog kennels. Furlow Lodge, as it was known, was connected with the Ulster & Delaware Rail Road by telegraph and telephone. In addition to the usual livestock of cows, oxen, and horses, George Gould raised pheasants, elk, and deer and owned a variety of sporting dogs.

Shortly after Gould's acquisitions along Dry Brook, individuals began to purchase sections of Mill Brook for the purpose of preserving the trout fishing along that famous stream. By 1901, a fishing club known as the Tuscarora Club was formed, and its members engaged in an active program of buying and leasing stream sections from landowners who were tired of poachers.

Ultimately, the club purchased the land of Joe De Silva, who had boarded trout fishermen for so many years. They constructed a clubhouse and eventually controlled almost the entire Mill Brook. The Tuscarora Club included some very fine fly fishers. Two of the best known in the early years were Edward R. Hewitt, author of several books on fly fishing, and Henry Ingraham, author of *American Trout Streams* (1926). The two men were friends who shared an intense desire to learn everything about trout, streams, fisheries science, and ways to improve trout fishing.

Ingraham's *American Trout Streams* is a guide to stream management and one of the first of its kind written by a serious-thinking trout fisherman, one who wanted to know more than just what flies a trout may take or when was the best time to go fishing. The book included chapters on stream ecology, pollution, trout foods, spawning, stocking, disease, and habitat improvement.

Henry Ingraham challenged the methods or attempts to improve the trout fishing of his day. He argued that millions and billions of trout fry are stocked "to no purpose" because of the lack of "exact knowledge" as to how, where, and when to stock, and whether there is protection or food for the trout when they are stocked. He believed that stocking could never replace natural reproduction. He was critical of stocking the same waters with different species and of how little was known about the fisheries. Ingraham was a strong advocate of taking a biological approach to trout fishing and claimed that some waters would never be self-sustaining trout streams.

Ingraham recommended tougher laws to protect fish and pleaded for increasing the size limit to 8 or 9 inches instead of 6 or 7 inches. He based his argument on the fact that 6- or 7-inch trout will not spawn, as they are still immature. He believed that trout should not be thought of as a "food fish." "The trout is primarily a sportsman's fish. His value is aesthetic and recreational. Laws should be passed based on this theory."[7] Ingraham strongly opposed deforestation and urged the Tuscarora Club to acquire land surrounding the watershed of Mill Brook and replant thousands of trees.

The new club promised adjoining landowners that they would replenish the stream by stocking trout, post the waters, and keep out poachers by patrolling. Some of their tactics aimed at thwarting poachers did get the attention of the locals. One newspaper reported: "The 'Bear Trap' signs posted on the grounds of the Tuscarora Club does not seem to scare the boys very much—the trout seems to float down the stream just the same."[8]

The Tuscarora Club became incorporated in 1902, and by 1946, it controlled 7 miles of the stream. The natural scenery along Mill Brook is spectacular. The stream has at least eight pools from 8 to 15 feet deep—deep enough to hold the largest trout. Mill Brook flows through two gorges of bedrock and contains ledge-rock pools and waterfalls unequaled anywhere in the Catskills. Two waterfalls are impassable to fish and are estimated to be 15 to 20 feet high; below the lower, larger falls is a plunge pool approximately 50 feet wide and 15 to 20 feet deep. In the judgment of knowledgeable Catskill trout fishermen, Mill Brook is the most beautiful trout stream in the Catskills!

Falls along Mill Brook fished by Fitz-James Fitch in the 1840s.
Tuscarora Club's Forty-Year History, 1941.

PUBLIC WATERS

Entering the twentieth century, the same old argument continued of whether a stream could become posted and private once it had been stocked with trout from the state fish hatchery. When streams were first stocked, they were, for the most part, free to everyone; and when trout were planted in those streams, the public benefited from the stocking. Although not public waters in the strictest sense (they flowed through private lands), they were public waters for all intents and purposes because the public had "unrestrained" access and use of them for trout fishing.

As angling grew in popularity, fishing privileges grew in value, and trout streams that had always been free became posted. In fact, they became what they had always been legally: private waters.

All that the Fish Commission required when ordering fish was an affidavit that the trout would be placed in public waters. Frequently, those persons ordering and stocking the trout were not stream owners, nor did they have permission of the owners to stock fish. Yet, "free fishing" advocates insisted on fishing the entire stream on the grounds that the stream had been stocked at public expense.

In the spring of 1900, a bill was introduced to the legislature by a state senator from Brooklyn. The legislation basically stated that waters stocked since April 17, 1896, would be open to the public for fishing, and that it would be the duty of the fish commissioner to keep such waters open to the public. The writer of the article questioned how a stream could be made an open stream just because state trout fry were stocked in the headwaters, 20 or 40 miles away?

James S. Van Cleef, the attorney from Poughkeepsie, who was a leading member of the State Association for the Protection of Fish and Game and an authority on fish and game laws, published a lengthy letter to the editor of *Forest and Stream.* The subject of the letter was the perplexing problem of "Public Waters."

Van Cleef begins by writing that it is a fact that all of the trout that are furnished by the state are stocked in private waters, not public waters:

> All small lakes, ponds and nearly all the streams of this State are essentially private waters and not public in any sense of the term, and they cannot be made public by any legislative act or any declaration of the Commissioners of Fisheries. The rights of riparian owners are fixed and certain, and they are vested rights incident to the ownership of the fee.[9]

Van Cleef declared that he had asked the commissioners to define what they meant by public waters, but they had never done so. He said that all they had ever required when stocking fish had been an affidavit by the applicant that the fish would be stocked in public waters. The result, stated Van Cleef, was that private streams had been stocked all over the state, and fish were furnished by the state on the pretense that they were public streams, and very often by individuals who did not own lands along the stream:

> The result has been that many of our finest streams have been practically destroyed by stocking through acts of trespass to which the State has really been a party, and it is a grave question whether a claim for these injuries to the rights of riparian owners could not be successfully made to the Court of Claims of this State.[10]

Van Cleef pointed out that a serious result of this liberal stocking policy had been the claim that because a stream was stocked at some point, this made the waters public. And, he said, this had resulted in the "worst elements in the neighborhood" insisting on fishing the entire stream because the waters had been made public, thus depriving riparian owners of their "exclusive right of fishery."

During the 1903 season, Catskill newspapers published many articles regarding the public's right to fish in streams that had been stocked at public expense. This led to optimism that the Beaverkill would become an open stream and available to all for fishing. Rumors spread through the angling community, and the hopes of many were fortified by a letter published in the press from J. W. Pond, chief protector of the Forest, Fish and Game Commission.

The *Catskill Mountain News* declared "Chief Game Protector Pond Says All May Wade and Fish in the Beaverkill." Chief Pond contended that waters stocked with fish at state expense since April 1896 were open to public fishing, regardless of posting. He claimed that one could not trespass over lands that were posted, but if you could wade the stream without crossing land, you had the right to fish. Pond was citing Section 212, Chapter 319 of the Laws of 1896.

This letter only added more confusion to an already bewildered fishing public; however, a case that was heard in the appellate division concerning trespass, for the purpose of fishing, went a long way to solving the rights of landowners. On July 11, 1903, *Forest and Stream* published the full text of the opinion of a suit brought by William Rockefeller against Oliver Lamora.

Several decisions of the lower courts favored Lamora and were based on the premise that the state had stocked the waters. This was not accepted by the higher court, as there was no evidence that the stream had been stocked with the consent of the owner, and it was stated that in the course of nature, these fish might pass into the waters of the preserve. The law that stated waters had to remain open was repealed.

It was claimed that the owner or lessee of lands possess the exclusive right of fishery in the water flowing through the land, and they have the right whether they own 50,000 acres or 1 acre. "A Lamora has no more right to fish without leave on the property of a Rockefeller than a Rockefeller has to fish on the property of a Lamora."

The editor summed up his article by writing: "The farmer's exclusive right to fish in his meadow brook is a right as clearly, definitely and inalienably vested as is his exclusive right to mow the meadow hay. This is a common law right, and may be invaded neither by individual trespasser nor by legislative statute without due recompense."

Along the upper Beaverkill, the Hardenbergh correspondent to the *Roscoe-Rockland Review* expressed his own thoughts on the subject:

> It is almost time to hear the fish question argued. The natives will drop in at the post offices, grocery stores and blacksmith shops and each speak their little piece. The "free" fishing men will contend that God made the fish for everyone, and that the "club" men cannot stop them if they get in the stream and do no damage to crops or fences, also that the State has stocked the streams for years at the expense of the tax payers of the State of New York. On the other hand the anti-fisherman will state that they live in free America a God-loving country, where the rights of all are protected, where men can purchase property and if they do not choose to open it to the public they have a perfect right to keep off trespassers; that the State has not stocked the upper Beaverkill and it does not effect their rights that the lower part of the Beaverkill was not stocked by the State. If by chance some of those so called "free fishing" men should have willed to them property with trout stream attached would they open it to the public? Or would they hunt around for a rich clubman and sell it for a fancy price?[11]

It was said that on the Beaverkill, farmers were charging 25 or 50 cents to fish over them, but some anglers refused to pay and got into arguments with the farmers. This caused some farmers not to let anyone fish, and they even threatened to shoot. One streamside landowner near Turnwood not only hired a stream-watcher to patrol, but placed an "ugly" three-year-old bull along the stream. The bull had killed a horse the previous fall, and the correspondent from Hardenbergh declared that if anyone intended to fish there this summer without permission, they had better run "when they hear the bull bellow" because it had been turned "loose on the island."

In the East Branch Valley, the misfortunes of two fishermen from Downsville were reported in the *Walton Reporter*. The men were fishing along Terry Clove, a tributary of Coles Clove, which ran into the East Branch upstream of Downsville. They were quietly "whipping" the stream for trout when, out of nowhere, a farmer with a big dog and a double-barreled shot gun came in sight.

The men expected trouble and immediately decided to "break for safety," but the dog was in close pursuit. Just as one of the "unlucky sports" stumbled over a stone wall, the dog "got him" by the seat of his pants and would not let go!

The farmer concentrated on the second fisherman, who was racing through a field of oats, and yelled "halt;" and when the fisherman continued, he fired with both barrels! The gun was loaded with bird shot, and the distance so great that it had no more effect on the fisherman than "rice on a wedding couple," but the fisherman stopped anyway.

The two hapless anglers were allowed to depart and were informed that two Walton fishermen had cleaned out the stream of trout the day before. "Fishermen will do well to avoid this section of Terry Clove for a few days."[12]

A common practice when fishing in the Catskills was to have one's catch taken to the kitchen of the hotel or boardinghouse where one was staying and have it prepared for breakfast or dinner. If the fisherman kept more trout than he needed, it was also expected that he would share this special meal with other guests, who were perhaps not as fortunate or maybe did not even fish. One local newspaper published an entertaining story of a "gentleman" who was not so generous:

> Last week a gentleman boarding at one of our leading hotels in town, who is a great lover of trout, thought he would avail himself of a basket of beautiful trout offered for sale by some apparently lucky fisherman. He examined several of the speckled beauties lying on top, and was heard to remark that no one else would get a taste of them. Shortly after sending the basket with contents into the kitchen, it was found to contain only 3 or 4 trout on top, the rest being suckers. The gentleman got very much excited, and several bad words escaped his lips, he was assured by observants that suckers are easily caught.[13]

BROWN TROUT VERSUS BROOK TROUT

In the early 1900s, and a little more than a dozen years after the introduction of brown trout into Catskill streams, the European import was still controversial and was disliked by a great many Americans. They saw the fish as a menace and deplored its practice of eating brook trout.

By 1900, so few applications for brown trout fry were received that the state was forced to adopt a new policy regarding the fish. The number of breeding brown trout kept at the hatcheries was reduced, as well as the production of eggs and fry. Sportsmen were intent on not placing brown trout in their favorite native trout streams and instead ordered brook trout fry.

By 1907, Commissioner George M. Bowers of the U.S. Bureau of Fisheries in Washington, D.C., informed readers of *Forest and Stream* that the federal government not only cut back but totally stopped raising and distributing brown trout in the United States. Commissioner Bowers's reason for this discontinuance was due to the fact that "this trout attains a larger growth than the native trout and is more cannibalistic." He also stated that in streams where brown trout had been introduced, the brook trout either disappeared or became very scarce, and he claimed that "in no instance" did brown trout prove superior "to the native trout of this country."[14]

The editor of *Forest and Stream* disagreed with this decision, and in an editorial stated:

The increase in size and numbers of the brook trout in eastern streams, through restocking is too slow. The presence of a few brown trout is welcomed by all who cast the fly, for in the waters where they are increasing there is fair sport now where there was little or none a few years ago, and there are few men who would not rather take one of the big fellows than a score of native trout that barely exceed the legal minimum length.[15]

Brown trout had many detractors, but angling journalist Theodore Gordon strongly defended the species:

I honor the sentiment which inspires the lover of the native fish, but I remember what the fishing was in the old days before brown trout were introduced, and what it is at the present time. The trout were numerous, but the average size was very small. . . . The first time I fished the Willowemoc, thirty years ago, one could take many trout, but a large proportion were smaller than I would now care to basket. It was the same on the Beaverkill and Neversink. We did not have nearly as many battles with sizable trout as we do nowadays. We never killed any two or three pound fish or had occasional sight or touch of monsters that thrilled our nerves with wild excitement.

It is natural and patriotic to exaggerate the fine qualities of our own trout and to remember with delight our early fly fishing experiences, but for the man who prefers a reasonable number of fairly large trout to many little ones the sport is better, upon the whole, in this part of New York than it was in the days of "fontinalis" only.[16]

Some anglers disliked brown trout simply because they were more difficult to catch. A. Nelson Cheney, an avid fly fisher and columnist for *Forest and Stream,* urged Americans to change their tactics and use smaller flies and finer leaders for daytime fishing. He wrote "fish fine and far off," and he urged readers to adopt the tactic of dry-fly fishing.

Cheney was also in charge of fisheries for the state. He decreased the number of brown and rainbow trout that were being stocked, and increased the number of brook trout. This policy was due mostly to the fact that in recent years, the public had ceased ordering brown or rainbow trout; therefore, the demand for brook trout had increased.

After reporting on a 5½-pound brown trout caught on a bucktail in Junction Pool, a reporter for the *New York Times,* who was staying along the Beaverkill in 1900, also wrote on June 24 that there was a good deal of discussion in the evenings at the various fishing resorts on the future of the "German or European trout." He wrote that some anglers dislike brown trout because they prey on "American trout," and will soon make them extinct. It was said to be common to see brown trout chasing brook trout and that violators of the law prohibiting set lines often used small brook trout for bait to lure the large browns.

This dim view of the native trout's future was shared a year later by a writer for the *New York Sun* in an April 26, 1901 article, who denounced brown trout, claiming that veteran sportsmen believe that in five years there will be no brook trout in the best streams of Sullivan County. The writer called brown trout an "imported cheat" and a "greedy cannibal," and claimed that some of the fishing preserves where browns are present would "give any price" if they could be rid of them.

Other newspapers also attacked the fish, and the state, declaring that the Fish Commission had followed a policy that fishermen desire size above all else, called for the immediate halt to the stocking of brown trout before all the brook trout were consumed or a race of hybrids created "inferior to either parent."

The argument for or against browns continued and found its way into two angling books published in 1902: *Salmon and Trout,* by Dean Sage and others; and *The Speckled Brook Trout,* edited by Louis Rhead.

William C. Harris, angling expert and founder of the *American Angler,* contributed a chapter titled "The Trouts of America" for the Sage book and declared that the brown trout has "lost popularity" among trout fishermen. Harris claimed that the reason that brown trout grew rapidly, to large size, was because they preyed on smaller trout, and he stated that they never should have been placed in streams inhabited by native brook trout where they "ravage at will on *fontinalis.*" He believed that the stocking of brown trout should be discontinued and that fishing clubs and landowners should use every means possible to destroy brown trout if they were introduced into waters inhabited by natives.

Benjamin Kent, a veteran Beaverkill trout fisherman, contributed a chapter titled "An Angler's Notes on the Beaverkill" for the work compiled by Louis Rhead. Kent recalled that after brown trout were introduced into the Beaverkill, they came on with a "rush" and multiplied so rapidly that they now outnumbered brook trout. Kent compared the two species:

> In appearance the brown is scaly, flat, greenish-yellow, irregular in form, bad eye, homely over all. In the native the scales are invisible; he is gold and silver, round and symmetrical, and as beautiful an object as lavish nature produces. In a sporting way, the brown rushes at a fly and impales himself and then holds back hard and dies limp and wilted . . .[17]

A large Beaverkill brown trout. Ed Van Put.

Kent writes that the native fights harder; and when netted, still resists, and keeps on "fighting and kicking to the bitter end." He claimed that brown trout after the middle of May become "weedy," and "unpleasant to the taste," and that brook trout are sweet and delicious, "as long as the stream is up." Kent sums up his opinion on brown trout by stating "they are here to stay and will remain as long as there are trout in the stream."

Brown trout did multiply and spread rapidly

on the Beaverkill, but Beaverkill Falls was impassable, and browns were prevented from reaching the uppermost portions of the stream. By 1896, the Balsam Lake Club had acquired more than 6 miles of the Beaverkill and prided itself on the fact that up until 1906, no brown trout had ever reached its waters. But on May 14, 1906, a club member brought in a "German Brown" measuring 11¼ inches and weighing 8 ounces! There was shock among the club members and a feeling of disbelief and helplessness. In July, the club secretary caught three browns, and on the same day, another member took three more, with one fish measuring 14¼ inches and weighing 14 ounces. Years later, club members reversed their attitude toward brown trout and claimed that browns were "a blessing" to the stream.

Another fishing club that took pride in not having brown trout in its upper waters was the Tuscarora Club, which was located on Mill Brook, a tributary of the East Branch of the Delaware. The club also had a natural waterfalls barrier to brown trout migration, and although they stocked browns, they never placed them above the falls. Having a stream in which only native brook trout were found was unique, and older club members instilled a prejudice against brown trout to new members that lasted for years. In a book titled *Tuscarora Club's Forty-Year History*, we learn that browns were an "unwelcomed intruder to be eradicated whenever and wherever possible." Catching brown trout was likened to hooking a pickerel when fishing for bass.

In the early days of the club, when its waters contained only native brook trout, a fish 9 or 10 inches in length "commanded respect," but 11- or 12-inch trout were not considered rare; even a few in the 13-inch range were taken now and then. For years, the club water above the falls was never stocked with anything but brook trout, and the older members believed that it should stay like a sanctuary for "their beloved Fontinalis;" they despised brown trout and referred to them as "European invaders."

Over the years, members did notice that although there were significant quantities of brook trout above the falls, they seemed to be getting smaller, and it was rare for anyone to catch one longer than 7 or 8 inches. The club requested Edward R. Hewitt—a knowledgeable fish culturist, author, and fly fisher—to look at their upper water to determine why no large brook trout were present.

Hewitt claimed that the upper section would never produce large brook trout because it was overcrowded. The upper water would gradually rise in temperature as a result of "deforestation," and in severe droughts, it would be difficult for brook trout to exist. He recommended stocking brown trout, and this divided the club. One member stated frankly that brown trout were "a pest and to Hell with it." After considerable discussion, however, club members voted to stock the upper waters with browns.

Proponents of the brown trout claimed streams that were once famous for their brook trout were "fished out," but they were once again furnishing good fishing because of the introduction of brown trout. It was reasoned that it was better to have browns, even if they were "not equal" to native brook trout, than to have no trout at all.

These advocates of brown trout were also of the opinion that it was better to catch two or three large browns than a basket of small brook trout. A sporting journal editor claimed that most men would rather take "one of the big fellows" than a host of natives that would barely be of legal size.

Writing from Sullivan County on the opening day of the 1907 season, fishing journalist Theodore Gordon commented on brown trout and recalled the years immediately after they were introduced. He told readers that from 1894 to about 1900, there were a great many brown trout that grew to enormous size, but now trout that big are very scarce.

Gordon loved the European import, and he favored stocking them. He had fished Catskill trout streams for thirty years, and it was his opinion that the fishing was better for the past fifteen years than when there were only native trout. He argued that it might be fun to catch hundreds of tiny trout on a fly, but it is "not sport in the true sense." Writing from the Beaverkill in the summer of 1906, Gordon claimed that the majority of fish now caught in the Beaverkill are brown trout and that the average size is "certainly" larger than the native trout.

Gordon mentioned that the largest brook trout he ever saw was taken from the Neversink in 1898, and it measured 16 inches. Because browns were stocked, many fly fishers had enjoyed "a fight that thrilled the nerves," taking browns up to 3 pounds and even larger. Gordon believed that there was a great deal of prejudice against brown trout, and he often spoke out in their favor, declaring that they were necessary to give the "best results" then found in Catskill streams.

He wrote that the Esopus was greatly affected by the stocking of browns and claimed that before their introduction, there was a large population of rainbows in the stream, but rainbow trout had decreased dramatically in size and numbers. This, in his opinion, was unfortunate, because it was a stream that rainbows had thrived in.

IN THE ESOPUS VALLEY

With browns now inhabiting the waters around Big Indian, fishermen who stayed at La Ment's were often treated to seeing catches of trout as they had never seen before. On July 14, 1900, the *Kingston Weekly Leader* told its readers that guests at La Ment Hotel were astonished when Henry Wait, who fished in front of the hotel, returned after two hours with six trout weighing 13 pounds! Though Wait was eager to exhibit the fish, he would not show anyone the fly that he caught them on. Those staying at the popular fishing resort referred to the fly as "Wait's unknown."

Brown trout had not only taken over this portion of the Esopus, but were attaining sizes never reached by brook or rainbow trout. In 1902, Gordon wrote on the pages of *Forest and Stream* of a monster brown trout that made his home under the railroad bridge abutment at Big Indian:

> Nearly every one has heard of the big fish that had its home in the abutment of a bridge near Big Indian Station in the Catskills. We have been favored with many estimates of the weight of this fish from 4 to 7 pounds mostly, and have had notice of his death many times, recently that he had been shot. We have often watched this fish when out of his hole, and can bear witness that he was an ugly, black, big headed brute. There were other fish there, however, one not so large, but a real beauty.[18]

On May 14, 1904, the *Kingston Weekly Leader* reported that Miles Parker of Slide Mountain had taken six "German brown trout" within a mile of Big Indian station. The trout were weighed by the railroad station agent and totaled 7½ pounds! A few years later, in another column on the pages of *Forest and Stream,* Gordon again reminisced about the giant brown under the railroad abutment:

The Big Indian 7-pounder lived in the same small pool for four years at least, but this trout had a hole in the abutment of a bridge into which he returned when disturbed, and out of which he could not be poked. At last a scoundrel shot the old fellow with a rifle. It was very amusing to watch the behavior of strangers when they caught sight of that trout. Some men would go wild with excitement and longing. They would put off for their rods, miles perhaps, and return in haste; they had little doubt of taking the great fish in a minute. If still in position when they returned, the first cast of fly or bait sent the shy monster to his den. In four or five years of residence, he was hooked four times.[19]

At one time Gordon believed the Big Indian portion of the Esopus was the "most prolific trout stream in the country."[20] He had great success using an imitation he tied and called the Esopus Fly. This pattern imitated a large yellow mayfly found on that stream, and although it is mentioned in letters, its dressing remains unknown, other than it was tied with a very pale yellow wool body.

Brown trout also began appearing downstream. A favorite haven for big fish was the Green Deep, a long deep pool located just downstream of Broadstreet Hollow or what some called Forest Valley. Browns spread to the lower Esopus, below Phoenicia, but rainbow trout were still the more dominant species, at least downstream to a point below Bishop's Falls, where they could be seen at times jumping in the huge, deep pool at the base of the falls. A historic gristmill was situated beside the waterfalls, along with a stone house constructed by Jacob Bishop in 1796.

Theodore Gordon wrote in the *Fishing Gazette* of the miller

Bishop's Falls, a great pool for large trout. *Picturesque Ulster*, 1896–1905, published by Hope Farm Press, 1991.

baiting a hook with a hellgrammite and lowering it from a mill window into the deep and foamy pool. He immediately hooked an 18-inch rainbow trout, which he was able to haul about 50 feet to his room within the mill.

The brown trout population was increasing rapidly, and browns were growing larger than rainbows ever had. Esopus rainbows, while still abundant, were decreasing in numbers and size. Commenting on the subject in *Forest and Stream*, Theodore Gordon claimed that rainbows of 1½ to 2½ pounds were getting scarce in 1906.

THE NEVERSINK

By 1900, the Neversink River, especially the water upstream and down of the village, had become a trout fisherman's paradise, and in the spring, when the hatches were in full swing, the large pools were filled with rising brown trout. The river was being fished more than in the past. Fortunately, brown trout continued to extend their range and were now inhabiting the Neversink all the way downstream to Old Falls, a distance of approximately 20 miles below the forks.

The year 1900 was a fantastic year for trout fishing, and large trout were being caught all through the fishing season up and down the river. On April 28, the *Walton Reporter* told of a huge brown—26 inches, weighing 5 pounds, 15 ounces—taken from the deep pool below the Old Falls bridge. The trout was known to have eluded fishermen for more than two years and, though hooked several times, it had not been landed until S. H. Palmer, of Passaic, New Jersey, caught the giant trout.

In June, several newspapers reported that Eli Garritt took a brown 26 inches in length that weighed 6 pounds, 2 ounces. Garritt, it was stated, had taken eighteen trout since opening day between 2 pounds, 6 ounces and 6 pounds, 2 ounces! Also in June, the Reverend C. L. Chapman of Camden, Ohio, caught a 24½-inch trout that weighed 4½ pounds. A month later, the *Republican Watchman* reported that Elsworth LeRoy took a 25-inch brown that weighed more than 6 pounds.

Yet not everyone was happy with the trout imported from Europe and how well it was doing in the Neversink. An article that appeared in the *Kingston Weekly Leader* on June 1, 1901, titled "Trout Yarns" had plenty to say:

> The *Republican Watchman* says Mr. Van Gaasbeek of Kingston caught 81 trout in the Neversink, some of the fish weighing 3 pounds. It seems to be an ordinary thing now to catch a 3 pound trout. They are not, however, the lively original trout of the Catskill stream, but are imported trout which are logy and lazy and act as though they wanted to be hooked out. The original Catskill mountain spring trout is a fighter, and when one is caught on a hook it makes every pound of its weight in pulling, fighting capacity, three times that of the foreign trout.[21]

There were men, however, who developed a reputation for their ability to capture the large browns that now inhabited the Neversink. Gordon's friend and fishing companion, Herman Christian, was certainly a fly fisher who worked at finding—then catching—big browns. Another who earned the title of a piscatorial sharp was Eli Garritt, who lived near the Neversink in the hamlet of Woodbourne, about 5 miles downstream of the village of Neversink.

The census of 1892 listed Garritt's age at thirty-five and his occupation as "sportsman." Even before the stocking of brown trout, he was making extraordinary catches of native brook trout and finding his way into area newspapers. The *Ellenville Journal* on May 15, 1885, reported: "Eli Garritt, the Woodbourne fisherman brought to town on Tuesday a very handsome basket of trout, one exceeding a pound in weight, and 23 of them weighing 14 pounds."

With the establishment of brown trout, Garritt took to guiding, but still found time to indulge in his favorite pastime. He consistently took browns from the Neversink for more than forty years.

Every year stories of large browns taken from the lower waters appeared in area newspapers. Many in excess of 5 and 6 pounds came from the Neversink downstream of the village of Neversink, at Hasbrouck, Woodbourne, and the deep pool at Old Falls.

There had been boardinghouses in Neversink that catered to trout fishermen when the stream contained only native brook trout; now with brown trout virtually at their front door, business was better than ever. In 1907, a Neversink correspondent to the *Ellenville Journal* reported on August 1, "Neversink has within the last three years leaped into a popular summer resort. Fishing is splendid, and social life is at its height here."

How popular the river was with trout fishermen can be seen by a comment made by Theodore Gordon in his fishing column, dated June 27, 1909: "Last Saturday afternoon there were thirty men on about two miles and a half of the stream. I met ten of them, and hearing that twenty more were coming down upon me, confined my attentions to one long pool, until they began to appear at the top. Then discretion seemed the better part of valor, and I fled, through soaking wet bushes, homeward."[22]

ON THE RONDOUT

While trout fishing on the upper Rondout Creek was controlled by private trout-fishing clubs throughout the greater part of the nineteenth century, the lower section was, for the most part, open to public fishing—that is, from Lowe's Corners downstream to the hamlet of Lackawack. This stretch was also known as the Lackawack Stream.

Within these 7 miles of the Rondout there are only two tributaries of any size that can be considered trout streams: Chestnut Creek, which entered at the hamlet of Eureka, and Trout Creek, which came in near Montela. The Chestnut Creek was well known as a stream that produced "run-up" fishing; whenever there was a spring freshet, large brown trout from the lower Rondout would follow the roily water, enter the Chestnut, and travel upstream through the village of Eureka.

In the era of the brook or speckled trout, this section of the Rondout had limited trout-fishing opportunities. Although brook trout could be caught in the vicinity of the tributary mouths, the lower Rondout was limited because of flow and warm water temperatures.

Records from the Caledonia hatchery show that rainbows were introduced in 1882 when twenty-five thousand "California mountain trout" were placed in the Sandburg and Rondout Creeks. By the fall of 1884, reports of 2-pound rainbows appeared in local newspapers, and the species provided good trout fishing until the early 1890s.

Brown trout arrived in 1888. The annual report of the Commissioners of Fisheries for that year reveals that four thousand fry were shipped to the Vernooy Kill, a tributary of the lower Rondout. These appear to be the first brown trout stocked in the watershed, and eventually they became the dominant species, perhaps because of the discontinuance of rainbow stocking or because of their more aggressive nature.

As with the East Branch of the Delaware, good brown trout fishing came later to the Rondout than on other Catskill streams such as the Beaverkill, Neversink, and Willowemoc. But, when they became established, the fish grew large and provided good trout fishing in a lower river section that previously had only limited opportunities. In the early 1900s, catches of 3- to 5-pound browns were not unusual, and trout of even larger size were taken.

A couple of examples of the sizes of these early brown trout were found in the fading pages of the old *Ellenville Journal*. On August 12, 1909, the newspaper reported that a large brown was caught by a boy named Van Wagener; the fish measured 24 inches and weighed more than 5 pounds. The trout was caught near Eureka and was given to P. H. Mitchell of the Mitchell House, where it was displayed before it was taken to Ellenville to be photographed. A year later, on April 20, 1910, the *Journal* mentioned an even larger trout: a 25-inch brown caught by Newton Phillips, taken at Lackawack.

THE WEST BRANCH OF THE DELAWARE

The West Branch of the Delaware River was known in the earliest days of settlement as the Mohawk branch of the Delaware. The Indian name for the river was Oquago. Its source is in Schoharie County in a small hollow between Mount Jefferson and Mine Hill, in the town of Jefferson, at an elevation of approximately 2,425 feet.

After flowing a little more than a mile, the stream enters Stamford reservoir, then passes through Utsayantha Lake and the village of Stamford. The stream elevation drops approximately 700 hundred feet during the first 5 miles, averaging about 140 feet per mile.

Leaving Stamford, the West Branch flows approximately 40 miles through the hamlets and villages of Hobart, South Kortright, Bloomville, Delhi, Hamden, and Walton before reaching New York City's Cannonsville reservoir. Major tributaries include Town Brook, Lake Brook, Elk Creek, Steele Brook, the Little Delaware River, Peak's Brook, Platner Brook, and Bagley Brook.

Throughout this stretch of the West Branch, the stream is basically low gradient, dropping in elevation approximately 14 feet per mile as it slowly meanders through a wide valley by Catskill standards. Practically the entire valley is devoted to agriculture; there are hardly any forest lands along the valley floor; and crops, fields, and pasture line both sides of the stream with a thin strip of vegetation along the banks.

Mature trees and brush follow the stream's course, but in many lengthy stretches, there is no vegetation, and the stream is exposed to sunlight and bank erosion. Dairy farms are found along the entire length of the stream, and often hillsides adjoining the West Branch are also cleared for agricultural purposes.

At Delhi, the Little Delaware River enters the West Branch. From this point downstream, the West Branch is large enough to be called a river. The flow is increased significantly, yet there are many braided channels. Cold water enters the West Branch from a myriad of tributaries throughout its length but especially around the village of Walton, where East and West Brooks and Pines Brook enter.

By the late 1890s, the trout-fishing mania that had a hold on Walton continued into the twentieth century. The *Walton Reporter,* in 1900, once again gave a synopsis of what the village was like on the first opening day of the new century. The paper informed readers that villagers were driving in all directions long before daylight, and as usual, East Brook was a favorite destination of Waltonians.

These following reports that appeared in the *Walton Reporter* in the early 1900s illustrate how important trout fishing was to the village of Walton and its residents: The front page of the paper on April 19, 1902, had an entire column devoted to opening day. The story featured a caption that stated that an army of fishermen made "big catches of trout" and "something less than two hundred" trout fishermen made their way to the streams around Walton: "Some of the more ambitious didn't go to bed at all and so were saved the trouble of waking."

As usual, the favorite fishing ground was East Brook, and it was estimated that a thousand trout were taken from its waters. George Seaman took fifty-one at the headwaters, and Dan Roe took nearly as many. Reverend Robert Knapp took a trout that weighed a pound and several others almost as large; another angler caught an unspecified number with one fish weighing more than a pound.

Several anglers filled their creels or baskets; one woke at two in the morning and fished until noon the next day, catching sixteen nice trout. Two fishermen caught 103 trout but would not tell anyone where they caught them.

Arthur Webster was one of the first successful anglers to come into town with his catch. He showed off twenty trout, two of which measured about 12 inches. A great many trout fishers brought in good catches, some from surrounding streams, and the trout were "unusually large and fine."

On opening day in 1903, a significant number of trout fishermen were out, despite the cold and disagreeable weather. Al Tiffany made the best catch, taking thirty-six "good ones" from East Brook. Ray Morrow fishing the same stream took eighteen trout. Mert Loomis and Dan McLean started up East Brook in the middle of the night and "froze," but they did manage to catch a few trout.

The following season (1904) found the same type of weather conditions, and yet the East and West Brooks were lined with fishermen. Clair Seeley began fishing the headwaters of East Brook at dawn and managed to take a dozen "fine trout" with several weighing 1¼ pounds. On the second day of the season, the weather was better, and many anglers took good baskets of trout.

On opening day in April 1905, Arthur Courtney and Ira Robinson took fifty-six "fine trout" along East Brook, and another angler caught forty-nine in West Brook and Carrs Brook. A couple of days later, Clair Seeley caught thirty-eight trout in East Brook; only three were less than 9 inches, and the largest measured 12 inches.

"Fishin' Time Is Here" was one of the headlines of the *Walton Reporter* on April 21, 1906. Streams were high and muddy, and air temperatures were cold, but nothing seemed to dampen the enthusiasm of Walton trout fishers: "many got out of bed at one or two o'clock in the morning and started for the fishing ground." As usual, East Brook was the favorite destination, though Will Arnold took eleven "good ones" in West Brook.

The front page of the *Walton Reporter* of April 20, 1907, ran an opening day article and claimed that everyone who had ever fished was out with their rod Tuesday morning. Old men and boys were crowding the streams, and East and West Brooks were "whipped" from morning to night. A favorite location was Borden's Pond near the railroad station; between 150 and 200 "fine trout" were taken from the pond, the largest being a 2-pounder! The newspaper claimed that there were more trout caught on Tuesday than on any previous opening day, despite the inclement weather.

WILLIAM "BILL" KEENER: "CHAMPION FISHERMAN"

In the summer of 1900, there was great concern along the Beaverkill when smallmouth bass began showing up in the lower river in numbers and sizes that had not been seen before. Two Roscoe anglers fishing the lower river at the beginning of July caught fifteen bass weighing between one-half to 1 pound.

Bass were reported as far upstream as the Palen mill, about one-half mile upstream of Junction Pool. This could have been the result of a drought that reduced the flow and warmed water temperatures, thereby influencing migration.

Some saw bass as a threat to the existing trout population and expressed their concerns, arguing that there was no sense "dumping" trout into these waters only to have them eaten by the bass. The sporting editor of a local newspaper claimed that the state did not stock the Beaverkill downstream of its junction with the Willowemoc, and that all trout were placed between Rockland and Lew Beach, upstream of Junction Pool.

At this time, the lower Beaverkill, or what many called the Big River, continued to produce exceptionally large brown trout. Expert fisherman and proprietor of the famous Roscoe House, William Keener, caught a fine 25½-inch brown in Ferdon's Eddy that weighed 5½ pounds in the first week of June. Ferdon's Eddy is the first pool downstream of Junction Pool and was a favorite of anglers because it always held large trout. The following summer, almost to the day, in the same pool, I. W. Finch of Roscoe caught a large 26-inch brown that weighed 6½ pounds!

The stream was producing many trout in the range of 10 to 15 inches, as well as an occasional big fish between 20 and 25 inches. Trout fishermen had never caught trout in the sizes or weights that now appeared to be common up and down the Beaverkill. This was also true along the Willowemoc, and in June 1900, Howard Fredenburgh of Livingston Manor caught what may have been the largest trout ever in that stream when he landed a 29-inch brown that weighed 7½ pounds!

Nearly every season after 1900, there were newspaper reports that told of browns being caught that weighed 4, 5, or 6 pounds. But one of the largest was a brown trout taken by E. F. Davidson of Lew Beach, who, in August 1908, caught an "old rounder" that measured 29 inches and weighed 7½ pounds!

One fish that was anything but common made its debut in a local newspaper on November 7, 1903. The Cooks Falls correspondent to the *Walton Reporter* informed readers that a "German trout" measuring 38 inches and weighing nearly 15 pounds was found dead in the Beaverkill near Cooks Falls. The monster trout was weighed and measured at Leighton's store, and many people saw it.

The huge fish caused quite a stir up and down the valley, and newspapers from outside the region also told of its incredible size. No doubt there were some who did not believe the report. One fisherman in particular was John Wilkin from Middletown in Orange County. In an article about the big fish in *Forest and Stream* on January 9, 1904, Wilkin wrote that when he heard the report he thought it was a "whopping lie," and wrote to his friend "Bill" Keener, "genial proprietor" of the Roscoe House. Keener replied:

I can tell you all about the big trout. I am the first one who saw it after the two small boys found it. On November 1 I was down the track about three miles below here and met the boys coming down with the trout strung on a cane, carting it between them. I measured it, and it was plumb 3 feet 2 inches long. They took it down to Cook's Falls and it weighed 14¾ pounds. It was very poor; if it had been fat it would have weighed 20 pounds at least. This is no fish story. Lots of people saw it. It was a German brown trout. It was found down by the old stone mill between here and Cook's Falls. The time of the high water last month it ran up a little spring brook between the track and river; when the water went down it could not get back, and I suppose starved to death. I don't think it was dead when the boys found it, but the boys were afraid of the law and said they found it dead. I had a hound dog with me and the trout's head was as large as the dog's. It does not appear possible that there could have been such a fish in the river, but it is true.

Wm. Keener

The first fly fisherman to establish a reputation for catching large brown trout along the "lower" or "big" Beaverkill was a Delaware County native named William Keener (1849–1926). Born in Andes, Keener came to Westfield Flats (Roscoe) as a child and spent the rest of his days living near the Beaverkill.

He grew up along the river and was as familiar with it as any man; he knew all of its pools and riffles, and the favorite haunts of trout. He had a complete understanding of how trout adapted to the seasonal variations of flows and water temperatures, he was knowledgeable about the great fly hatches, and he learned when and where to fish. From the 1890s until the 1920s, his name appeared often in newspapers, sporting journals, and books on trout fishing.

Newspapers referred to "Bill" Keener as a "champion fisherman" or an "expert fisherman," and there is no doubt that he was the most famous fly fisherman of his day on the Beaverkill. He was also the proprietor of the Roscoe House, a trout fisherman's rendezvous, located near the railroad station. In addition to enjoying his Irish wit and humor, fishing tourists sought his advice on trout, flies, and where to fish. "Fishing for count" was finally on the way out, and the next generation of anglers would measure their success in inches and pounds, not in the number of trout they had caught.

Keener's Roscoe House. Ed Van Put.

One can only imagine the conversations that took place at the bar of the Roscoe House, discussing the huge brown trout that now inhabited many of the pools along the lower Beaverkill. Bill Keener was said to be a quiet man, preferring to listen to others; he was not one to give advice unless he was asked, but when asked for an opinion, he would give it in a direct manner and with few words, "often to the discomfort of wiseacres and always to the pleasure of those who knew him."[23]

One of Bill Keener's friends was the noted artist and angling author Louis Rhead. "He swears awful at times," wrote Rhead of Keener. "You see at a glance his [Irish] ancestry, and though born in the Catskills as his father before him, he was the fiercest 'Home Ruler' for the 'Old Sod' I ever met or heard of."[24] Keener obtained great fame as a fly fisher, in part because of the writings of Louis Rhead, who wrote of his exploits in magazines and books.

One of the most unique catches Keener ever made was at a time when he and Rhead were fishing Junction Pool. Keener was fishing his usual cast of two wet flies and hooked and landed a 3-pound, 9-ounce brown trout and a 4-pound smallmouth bass! The brown had taken the dropper, and the bass the end fly. Catching two fish at once using this method was not unusual, but catching two fish as large as these—and the fact that one was a bass—was extremely rare. Though the two species often inhabit the same water, they do prefer to feed at different water temperatures.

Bill Keener was a celebrity along the Beaverkill. Generations of trout fishermen had come to know and appreciate his contributions to the region, from directing the stocking of fry and fingerlings to dispensing information and the wisdom he had secured in years of trout fishing. Fishermen who stayed at the Roscoe House saw him as an amiable host who ran his hotel on the principle "of a home and not a mere hotel."

When Bill Keener died in the summer of 1924, Dr. William Bruette, editor of *Forest and Stream,* printed an obituary on the editorial page, which was edged in black. Dr. Bruette claimed Keener was a "sportsman of the finest type" known everywhere as the best trout and bass fisherman in the Catskills, and that his customers enjoyed hearing his "quips and sallies" on those who bragged and boasted of their fishing abilities:

> His own nature was the very opposite, modest in the extreme, generous, charitable, and possessed of a very winning manner to his intimate friends of whom he had many. The thousands of anglers who now enjoy the fine fishing of the Beaverkill and Willowemoc are much indebted to Mr. Keener, who has for many years upheld the best traditions of the craft and used uncommon sense in properly stocking the streams, by placing the young fish in situations where they had ample food and quick growth. No angler in the entire state of New York was better known and none was more esteemed.[25]

"FISHOMOBILING"

Another significant event that occurred at the turn of the twentieth century was the development of the automobile: a form of travel that greatly shortened the distance between fishermen and trout streams. The first automobile seen along the Beaverkill was during the trout season of 1902. Mass production of the new method of transportation began in 1901, and that year there were approximately eight thousand automobiles in the United States. A dozen years later, ownership leaped to 1,194,261!

The automobile created "day-trippers," a new group of trout fishermen who could now spend hours on the stream and return home in a single day. "Motorcars" reached the fishing grounds more quickly and thereby allowed anglers to spend more time in the water. And they changed the way people fished for trout; if fishing was poor in one area, they simply piled back in the car and drove from pool to pool, or from stream to stream. Fishermen no longer had to plan ahead for a few days' fishing at local resorts, and it was believed that the automobile would surely be the end of trout fishing.

"Fishomobiling." *Field & Stream*, April 1909.

Shortly after the introduction of automobile travel, advertisements and articles appeared in outdoor magazines fostering the use of motor cars for trout fishing. One idea that was promoted was "Fishomobiling," a term used to describe camping with an automobile. Even Ezra H. Fitch, president of Abercrombie & Fitch, wrote about a fishing trip that he and four others—including Lou Darling, a noted fly caster and fisherman—made to the Esopus Creek in the spring of 1909. The party camped along the stream in the area of Big Indian, and although the overall success was not very great, Darling managed to take a 6½-pound brown!

The men camped in "real automobile tents" designed for automobilists by Abercrombie & Fitch Co., slept in "automobile sleeping bags," and dined on an "automobile table," all items that could be purchased at the famous retail store.

When automobile fishermen began showing up along trout streams, one of the biggest complaints against them was that many fished on Sunday. Not everyone obeyed this law, which had been enacted as early as 1853, but the majority of anglers did and complained bitterly when the law was violated.

The general feeling among the local population was that the law prohibiting fishing on Sundays was being broken more than ever by "motor parties" of city fishermen. This caused locals to become indignant, and they viewed this practice as disrespectful of their religious convictions, which added to the mistrust between the two cultures.

Fishing on a Sunday was considered "Sabbath breaking," which was a misdemeanor, according to Section 2142 of the Penal Law. A fine of not less than $5 or more than $10 was imposed, with the fines doubled if charged for the second time, even if not convicted on the first offense! Residents of Ulster and Sullivan counties became enraged when day-trippers came on Sundays and spent the whole day fishing, returning with "fine strings" of trout. They encouraged constables to arrest the offenders and fine them.

A correspondent from the town of Denning, along the upper Neversink, complained in the local press about ". . . auto parties, load after load, from Kingston, Napanoch, Ellenville, New York, Newburgh, Middletown and, in fact, many other places too numerous to mention, who come to our peaceful valley Sunday after Sunday to fish and practice legal shooting?"[26] After further complaining that many who fish are men of wealth, who are not ticketed, he ended his letter by saying, "It is a most disgraceful thing to witness Sunday after Sunday," many of these men are "drunken rowdies" who endanger the lives of others as they speed along the roads and "are in no fit condition to drive their cars on these outings."[27]

"Real automobile tents." *Field & Stream*, April 1909.

The law prohibiting fishing on Sunday continued for many years, well into the 1920s. Eventually, however, such blue laws were eliminated, and fishing on Sunday became an accepted practice.

16

1910–1920

EDWARD R. HEWITT, "RIVER OF OUR DREAMS," and LOUIS RHEAD

By 1913, work on the Ashokan reservoir was about completed, and in September, the gates of the dam were closed and the huge (8,315-acre) reservoir began filling. On June 14, 1914, work on the dams and dikes was finished, and one year later, Esopus Creek water was flowing through the Catskill Aqueduct on its way to New York City. Approximately 6 miles of the Esopus and one-half mile of the Bushkill were flooded by the new reservoir.

In December 1916, *Forest and Stream* published an article titled "Good Fishing Near Large Cities." The piece was written by Theodore Gordon before he passed away and was taken from the manuscript library of the sporting journal. Gordon wrote about a subject "near to his heart," the "fishing of the future," particularly public fishing.

The article cited the good trout fishing found in England and Wales on publicly owned water-supply reservoirs that serviced nearby cities. These waters were stocked and regulated with size and daily fish limits and open to the public for a small annual fee. Gordon urged that the new Ashokan reservoir follow this example and be opened for public fishing.

He also advised that there would be no need to stock Ashokan, as the lake would automatically stock itself, and the trout would grow rapidly. The Esopus, he claimed, was one of our best trout streams, and he recalled having "great sport" with rainbow and brown trout from the present dam site upstream to the beginning of the new reservoir. He urged that the lake be managed as a trout fishery and not be stocked with pickerel or bass.

Gordon wrote that the lake would give an excellent opportunity to the "every day hard-working man" who could travel up from the city for a day's fishing, be provided with recreation, and be treated to beautiful scenery with air that is pure and "bracing." He emphasized the need to provide public fishing, stating: "The small-salaried man and the workman can take a day off now and then, and the value of the fish taken will, by supplying his family with a perfect food fish, defray the cost of his railway and fishing tickets."

Gordon ended the article by writing: "I have had my share of sport, probably far more than I was justly entitled to, and I can not avoid thinking of the young anglers and others who so long for a little good trout fishing."[1]

Shortly after Theodore Gordon's article, a catastrophic fish kill occurred along the Esopus Creek from Phoenicia downstream to the new reservoir. Newspaper accounts in October 1917 told of hundreds of trout, and by some estimates "a ton of trout," being killed during a three-day period when the city of New York pumped chemicals into the stream in an attempt to "purify" the Esopus above the reservoir.

The city had erected a "plant" on the land of Thomas McGrath near the railroad station at Phoenicia "for the purpose of having a station from which purifying substances might be pumped into the waters of the Esopus Creek."[2] The pumping had started on a Friday, and upon seeing hundreds of dead trout soon after it had begun, the next day State Forester Jay H. Simpson told city officials to stop the further use of the chemicals. However, chemicals were released again on Saturday evening, and by Sunday, the number of dead trout had increased by hundreds more. Trout were found lying at the bottom of the pools for miles below Phoenicia, ranging in size from fingerlings to fish more than 20 inches in length!

"LET'S KEEP OUR STREAMS OPEN!"

No one at this time could foresee that the "splendid" fishing found along the Neversink was doomed, and splendid it was. In the fall of 1914, John G. Wilkin of Middletown, New York, wrote to Tarleton H. Bean, the state fish culturist, and stated that during the season that had just passed,

The Neversink, ca. 1918. *Streamcraft*, 1919.

he had caught some "nice browns" on the Neversink at the "Pines." Wilkin was being modest, as he had caught the following: one fish weighing 6¼ pounds, two of 4½ pounds, one of 4 pounds, one of 3 pounds, and several weighing about a pound each. All of these trout were caught on a fly between 8:00 P.M. and midnight!

The first event that greatly affected the trout fishing surfaced in the summer of 1919, when local newspapers began reporting that someone was attempting to purchase the Neversink from Halls Mills bridge, about 2 miles downstream of the forks, all the way down to the covered bridge in the village of Neversink.

This was prime trout-fishing water that included the famous Big Bend Pool and a major stretch of the river that had always been open to public fishing. This was the very water made popular with fishing tourists, who read of the beautiful Neversink and its brown trout through the writings of Theodore Gordon on the pages of *Forest and Stream*. By the end of May, the *Liberty Register* reported: "City residents blessed with money and desirous of having something good all to themselves are buying up the Neversink River between Bradley and Claryville, it is said, with the intent to post it and keep it for themselves alone."[3]

It was argued that the Neversink had been stocked annually by local fishermen, that "People will not come here if there is no place to fish," and "Next year, if all the streams are posted, the hundreds of fishermen who have been coming here, will go elsewhere, and the columns of publicity which resulted from their visits will follow them. Let's keep our streams open!"[4]

It soon became known that wealthy industrialist, Edward R. Hewitt, was purchasing as much of the Neversink as he could. Hewitt was fifty-three years old at the time, and his first purchase included the famous Big Bend Pool and nearly 300 acres. Deeds recorded in the Sullivan County Clerk's Office reveal that on June 24, 1919, Herman Christian purchased 315 acres along the Neversink that included the Big Bend; on the very same day, he sold all of the riverfront property and practically all of the land to Hewitt. Christian retained 16 acres, being that portion lying south of Schumway Road. Hewitt went on to purchase approximately 2,800 acres and about 4 miles of prime trout water.

EDWARD RINGWOOD HEWITT

Edward R. Hewitt (1866–1956) caught his first fish while he was still wearing dresses. He was fishing the stream that ran through the family estate at Ringwood Manor in northern New Jersey. A stableman had dug a worm that his nurse baited on a hook, and young Hewitt, fishing from a bridge, lowered the bait into the stream. He promptly hooked a good-sized chub and let out a yell, swinging the fish up onto the bridge; he pounced on it and soiled his dress, as the chub had bled from swallowing the hook. The nurse, in a huff, hurried the boy off to the house to clean him up.

Hewitt never forgot the incident; he was four or five years old at the time and felt like a hero when he proudly showed the catch to his mother. A couple of years later, he began fishing with an uncle who taught him the fundamentals of trout fishing; at the age of eight, he caught his first trout. From that day on, he developed a passion for trout fishing that stayed with him for the rest of his life.

Edward R. Hewitt was born at Ringwood Manor. He was the son of wealthy industrialist Abram Hewitt, a former mayor of New York City, and the grandson of Peter Cooper, famed inventor of Jell-O, industrialist, and philanthropist who founded Cooper Union for the Advancement of Science and Art in New York.

Following graduation from Princeton and the University of Berlin, Hewitt first worked as an inventor, developing a one-cylinder automobile that was marketed in England. He later formed the Hewitt Motor Company in New York and turned his attention to truck engines. He designed an engine that was adopted by Mack Trucks, and his company was later taken over by International Motor Company.

It's not clear when Hewitt began to fish in the Catskills, but he fished the Neversink at least as early as 1881; he was fifteen years old at the time and was already a skilled wet-fly fisherman. He caught his first brown trout in the late 1880s on the lower Neversink, in the large pools found near Hasbrouck, where Wynkoop Brook enters the river. He must have been smitten with the charms of the river, as he returned many times to fish the Neversink, at times as a guest of Clarence Roof, who controlled most of the best water on the West Branch.

A year after his purchase, Hewitt wrote to the local newspaper that he had bought the land and the Neversink for a "private country place" where he could relax and stated, "I also feared that it might be secured by someone who would post it and close the fishing on this beautiful stream."[5] Hewitt's letter was preceded by a headline that stated "Neversink Waters Will Not Be Closed." This was certainly good news for the residents of Neversink and the nearby village of Liberty, where visiting trout fishermen were an economic asset; they arrived by rail and often stayed in the villages while fishing the river.

Although he kept the water open, there were some restrictions imposed by Hewitt. He stated that these waters should no longer be looked upon as open water to the public, where everyone could trespass through his property. He would allow only residents of Sullivan County to fish—with a fly, anytime during daylight hours, during the open season—and they could keep no more than twenty trout per day. His invitation specifically excluded hotel visitors and summer boarders.

Hewitt's generosity lasted three years. Before the opening of the trout season of 1923, he wrote to area newspapers stating that he was forced to close the Neversink because the fishermen of Sullivan County did not cooperate with his restrictions and were not sportsmen enough to use his preserve without abusing the privilege he gave them.

Hewitt claimed that the stream was subject to one violation after another. The second year it was opened, it was poisoned several times, and the last year it was not only poisoned, but dynamite was used in all the large pools. He said that he had removed six setlines from Big Bend Pool and that he had no choice but to close the stream. Hewitt warned that the Neversink would be patrolled by a watchman, and violators would be arrested. Permits could be obtained from the watchman, but they would only be issued to known sportsmen and only to residents of Sullivan County.

An editorial in the *Liberty Register* praised Hewitt for keeping the Neversink open after he had purchased the river: "Here is one man who bought property along a good trout stream and threw it open to the natives."[6] The editor went on to condemn the type of individuals who would "indulge in a flagrant discourtesy" and stated that it was unfortunate that true sportsmen had to pay the price for others' misdeeds.

The following week, a letter to the editor appeared, written by a native of Neversink that outlined the local sportsmen's view of Hewitt's posting of the Neversink:

You state that "he threw that part of the stream which was his property open to whoever wished to fish it, etc.", Mr. Hewitt could not open the stream, for it had been open from time memorial. It is also a question whether any of the large local trout streams can be legally posted. So far, persons with money have assumed the right because no individual angler has felt that he could afford to fight the case up through the courts for a decision.

So far as the Neversink is concerned, beginning a short distance below the Hall's Mill Bridge, property owners for generations have recognized that the stream bed is state ground. Most deeds cover only the bank of the stream.[7]

It was also argued that native trout fishermen "made" the fishery by stocking millions of trout over the past forty years and that it was the fishing that induced Hewitt to buy the property. The writer stated that city sportsmen post to keep the fishing for themselves and their friends, and to enjoy what locals had created.

Over the next couple of years, the dispute with local trout fishermen quieted down, and Hewitt began taking steps to improve the fishing on his water. And although he would fish for trout and salmon all over Europe and North America, the Neversink became his home waters.

Hewitt did more than just fish the stream; he set out to learn everything about its trout and was determined to improve his fishing. As a chemist, he studied the effects that carbonic acid, temperature, and oxygen had on trout growth and survival. He learned to read trout scales under a microscope and aged individual trout; he studied their anatomy, vision, habitat, growth rates, spawning, predators, preferred foods, habitat, and life expectancy. Hewitt did all these things when the field of fisheries management was in its infancy. He had a habit of breaking with tradition and was always searching for new ways or methods. He was an innovator and never totally accepted established ideas. He did not like to accept ideas as fact without experimenting himself.

Hewitt constructed a hatchery on his Neversink property and became a fish culturist. In the process, he visited hatcheries all over the East Coast to learn about trout-raising methods and growth rates. He experimented with trout diets and studied the livers of trout, their cholesterol, and the effects that various vitamins had on them. As an ardent student of chemistry, Hewitt maintained a laboratory in his home for his entire life.

Edward R. Hewitt. *Seventeen Famous Outdoorsmen,* 1929.

After noticing that there were areas along the stream where trout were never found, he built his own flow meter and studied water velocities at various depths. He learned that trout had preferred currents and that the current flowing over gravel where the stones were less than 2 inches in diameter had the same speed down to the streambed. When the stones were about the size of one's head or larger, the current was slower because of the eddy currents from the stones; there might be 6 inches of slowed-down water even when the surface was flowing at a much greater pace.

In 1926, Hewitt revealed much of his findings in a book published by Charles Scribner's Sons titled *Telling on the Trout.* The book also included a chapter on trout vision. Photography was another of Hewitt's passions, and he did a great deal of experimenting with underwater cameras to learn what floating flies looked like to the trout.

As early as 1929, Edward R. Hewitt was working at making his Neversink fishery as productive as he possibly could. He conducted a tagging program on his water to study trout movement, mortality, and their physical condition. He learned that only a few of the large brown trout that he stocked survived the winter. This, he determined, was because they lost weight shortly after planting and went into the fall in poor condition.

In 1930, he tried the same experiment with large domestic brook trout. He stocked 225 fish, of which it was determined that 100 were caught. One trout traveled 8 miles downstream and another 7 miles upstream of where they were planted. Hewitt learned that brook trout did better than browns, and in a letter to the *Liberty Register,* he stated that he would continue these experiments until he got a better understanding of their meaning.

He also recognized that raising trout in hatcheries had become an established industry, but little work had been done to improve conditions for trout by creating better stream habitat. Hewitt believed that it was wiser to spend money on the stream rather than stocking more fish; good habitat, he reasoned, would automatically result in more catchable-sized trout.

In the 1920s, he began building low "log wire dam" structures at properly selected sites. These were designed to raise the water upstream by 1 to 2 feet and create a plunge pool on the downstream side. They were built in series in those parts of the stream that contained shallow riffles: sections that were often too wide and too thin, areas that did not hold many trout. He believed that the plunge pools were the most important function of the structure as they provided daytime hiding places; in the evening, adult trout left these sanctuaries and cruised the pool in search of food.

Hewitt insisted that whatever type of structure was constructed, it should provide an undermined area in the plunge pool. His dams provided good fishing even in the middle of summer, when the stream experienced low-water conditions. He believed that pools 2 or 3 feet deep were better than one much deeper and that a "fishing dam" was more difficult to construct than an engineered one.

Hewitt found that trout wintered well under such a structure, and this resulted in many more large fish available at the beginning of the season. His fish dams were near imitations of structures created by beaver; Hewitt used logs, sticks, brush, and gravel. Though high enough to raise the pool area upstream approximately 2 feet, his dams maintained a low profile so that ice would go over the structure without causing damage.

While he was engaged in the process of making his own water more productive, he generously shared his knowledge by publishing his findings in a series of articles and several books relative to his improving the trout fishery of his water on the Neversink.

In 1930, he wrote an article for *Forest and Stream* titled "Stocking in 1929," with a subtitle, "How to Improve Conditions on Your Trout Stream." The title was a bit misleading, as the essay was about constructing in-stream structures aimed at improving trout habitat. Hewitt gave explicit instructions on how to build the structure, as well as the cost, and why structures were necessary to improve the fisheries. He viewed improving trout habitat as essential to good fishery management.

"A fine trout pool made by a log wire dam in the Neversink where only a shallow rapid existed before."
Better Trout Streams, 1931.

Hewitt had owned his Neversink water for twelve years and had done extensive work to improve the holding water and carrying capacity of the stream. Some of the in-stream structures were experimental; if they failed, he set out anew and tried again. In 1931, Charles Scribner's Sons published his *Better Trout Streams*.

He wrote the book to pass on to others the things that he had learned. Years later, he recalled that *Better Trout Streams* was the first book on improving trout waters and that it was instrumental in improving trout habitat across the country. Hewitt stated: "I feel that in focusing public attention on the environment of trout in streams, I performed a real service to my fellow fishermen."[8] Hewitt's name is attached to a low-head type of dam built of logs and planks that is still constructed today; "Hewitt dams" create a plunge pool on the downstream side of the structure but do not generally raise the water significantly on the upstream side.

The use of in-stream structures to create or improve trout habitat is an accepted practice of fisheries management. In the United States, the history of this methodology can be traced back to the pioneering efforts of Catskill fishing clubs and individuals such as James S. Van Cleef and Edward R. Hewitt. In-stream structures developed in the Catskills have formed the foundation for structures still being used today.

Better Trout Streams contained more than information on how to construct in-stream structures; it included information on aging trout by scale reading, water chemistry, aquatic insects, trout growth, and feeding and raising trout, along with stocking results.

A pair of log and flat stone pool structures on the upper Beaverkill. Ed Van Put.

Throughout the 1930s, Hewitt continued to write articles, especially for *Field & Stream,* such as "The Condition of Trout in Streams" (1932), an article describing the physical conditions of trout fed different diets and his observations on the stocking of large hatchery trout. In "Better Trout Fishing" (1933), he describes the needs of trout—food, temperature, shelter—and advised readers to get involved with stream or habitat improvement. He wrote of ways to create habitat by using a team of horses and urged trout fishermen to contact him directly: "I will be glad to correspond with anyone desiring to improve a stream and will do what I can to help in the way of advice, as I am most interested in promoting the cause of better fishing for everyone."9

In 1934, Hewitt wrote "Wintering Trout Streams" and mentioned being troubled as to why hatchery trout lose weight immediately after stocking. He firmly believed that Catskill trout, hatchery and wild, moved downstream after spawning, even when good deep pools existed along the upper river sections.

Hewitt had a habit of carrying a small piece of mosquito netting and would seine the stream to determine what trout were feeding on. This practice led to his becoming an influential figure and early proponent of nymph and midge fishing on American waters. He promoted his ideas on nymph fishing through articles in sporting journals at a time when fly fishermen used either dry flies or wet flies. And he pioneered the use of extra long leaders with very fine tippets for nymph and midge fishing.

He also developed a method that eliminated the shininess of leaders by soaking them in a solution of silver nitrate, then developing them like a photographic negative; the leaders were made dark and nonreflective.

In 1933, he wrote an article titled "Midge and Nymph Fly-Fishing" that appeared in *Field & Stream* in March. This was quickly followed by another, in June, titled "More About Nymph Fly Fishing." Hewitt strongly urged the use of midges fished below the surface, and he gave excellent advice on midge fishing at a time when fishing with #22 flies and fine tippets was practically unheard of.

Hewitt did more than write articles about what he was learning along

A Hewitt-type dam on the East Branch of the Neversink, the only habitat in a shallow and wide stretch of water. Ed Van Put.

his Neversink waters. During the 1930s, a series of handbooks appeared with titles such as *Hewitt's Handbook of Fly Fishing* (1933), *Hewitt's Handbook of Stream Improvement* (1934), *Hewitt's Nymph Fly Fishing* (1934), and *Hewitt's Handbook of Trout Raising And Stocking* (1935). These handbooks often had a small pamphlet that accompanied them; basically, this was a catalog for purchasing a number of fly-fishing items sold by Hewitt. Titled "Hewitt Trout Fishing Specialties," they contained items such as flies, leaders, line grease, leader soak, "Hewitt Opaque stained leaders," and "Hewitt Balanced Trout Feed."

In Hewitt's later years, he ran his Neversink Camp as a fishing club where fly fishers could come and try their skills for a fee. Some of the best-known fly fishers in the country fished his waters, and most, at one time or another, encountered Mr. Hewitt, who held court for these visitors at his old farmhouse, giving advice, arguing, teaching, boasting, criticizing, and demonstrating his techniques. He often caught trout when others had difficulty. He knew his water, the trout, and the fly hatches from years of study. He was extremely opinionated and did not hesitate to tell visitors that they were doing things all wrong.

In addition to pioneering nymph fishing, Hewitt created a fly known as the Neversink Skater. This was a dry fly tied on a #16 hook with large, usually light ginger hackle, tied with a diameter of about 2 inches; there was no tail. The fly was so lightweight and was made with such stiff hackle that Hewitt fished the fly by skittering it across the surface. He took plenty of large trout with this method, and he developed a reputation of doing so during low-water conditions.

Perhaps the best-known fly that he created, and his personal favorite, was the Brown Bivisible. It is not known when the fly was first tied, but the Bivisible is mentioned in his book *Telling on the Trout,* which was published in 1926. In the 1930s, the Bivisible was possibly the most popular dry fly in the country; fly tiers and fly shops had trouble keeping it in stock.

The Brown Bivisible is made with brown hackle tied palmer down the length of the hook and is finished off with a few turns of white hackle. Hewitt created the fly for fishing dry in fast water; it was called Bivisible, he stated, because: "The white wisp enables the angler to see the fly readily hence the name I gave it—Bivisible because I can see it and the trout can see it."[10]

Edward R. Hewitt was an excellent fly fisherman who developed a reputation as being one of the best of his generation. He was intelligent and inventive, and he possessed a burning curiosity to know everything about trout. He began using the dry fly in about 1905; on the day he did, he came to the conclusion that the leader was the most important aspect of dry-fly fishing. Later, he would also avow that the size of the fly was more important than the color or the design. And like his close friend George La Branche, he was not a believer in strict imitation:

> Each stream, of course, has flies which are more suitable to it but I find that if I have Quill Gordons, and Hendricksons and an assortment of Bivisibles of various sizes, I can generally get about as many trout as any one will get. I, of course, carry many other patterns, mostly to amuse myself in seeing whether one fly is any better than another, but really I do not catch any more fish with this lot of flies than I would with only a few patterns.[11]

Hewitt fished other Catskill streams, such as the Callicoon Creek, the Beaverkill, and Mill Brook. He was a member of a small club along the upper Willowemoc. He and George La Branche and four others owned a stretch of the stream where Fir Brook enters the Willowemoc, just upstream of the hamlet of Willowemoc. The club was formed in 1929 and was known as the Willowemoc Fishing Club, Inc. It dissolved in 1937. Although the property was sold, Hewitt and La Branche retained life rights to fish the water.

He also fished the upper Rondout and was fond of telling about the time he was visiting his friend Anthony Dimock, who owned a stretch of the stream. Dimock, over tea, mentioned that in thirty years, none of his guests were ever able to take a trout out of the Blue Hole in clear, low water and that he would like to see if Hewitt could do so. Never one to walk away from a challenge, Hewitt removed a rod from his vehicle, and he and Dimock walked to the famous pool.

Hewitt had fished the Blue Hole several times in the past and knew it was a difficult place to catch a trout when the water was low. He described the pool as being about 70 feet across and perhaps 10 to 15 feet deep, with the water plunging into it after cascading over two giant broken rocks. The stream exited the pool at the far corner of a bar of fine gravel.

Recognizing that a cast into the middle of the pool would only alarm the trout, Hewitt took a position downstream about 50 feet from the gravel bar. He cast into the placid pool, placing his line and most of the leader on the gravel bar, with only a foot or so of the leader and fly landing in the water. After the fly had rested a moment, he moved it cautiously; immediately a trout came up from the depths and took the fly. He guided the fish out with a steady pull over the gravel to where he was standing, without disturbing the pool. Hewitt proceeded to catch fifteen trout between 8 and 10 inches, proving to Dimock that his reputation as an extraordinary fly fisherman was deservedly earned.

The famous Blue Hole with a gravel bar visible on the right. Ed Van Put.

Another of Hewitt's plans to improve the fishing in the Neversink was to stock salmon into the river. He caused a sensation in the spring of 1935 when he announced that he was planning to introduce salmon from Norway into the waters of his camp on the Neversink. He was the guest speaker at a Liberty Rod & Gun Club dinner and made the announcement following a showing of a film on how a dry fly looked to a trout from below the surface.

Hewitt imported eggs of Norwegian Blege salmon, a landlocked variety that did well in rapid-flowing water. The eggs of about two thousand were hatched at his Neversink facility and had grown to approximately a pound apiece. Just before their being placed in the river, the hatchery was broken into one night, and most of the salmon were stolen. Hewitt did manage to salvage about fifty salmon, and he stocked these into the Neversink; at a later date, three were reportedly taken on flies.

Throughout the 1920s, 1930s, and 1940s, Edward R. Hewitt was the acknowledged "dean of American fly fishing." His contemporaries in the fishing community always referred to him as Mr. Hewitt. This was done not because of age, but out of respect for a man who possessed so much knowledge and had made significant contributions to the world of fly fishing. Hewitt made you think. This fact was not lost on Lee Wulff. Wulff also became one of this country's most famous fly fishermen, and he believed that Edward R. Hewitt's role in American fly fishing was greater than Theodore Gordon's:

Gordon came first. He wrote well, fished hard and often. He pioneered with dry flies in America. But it was Hewitt who shocked us, broke with tradition and made us think of the larger scope of trout flies.

Hewitt worked on trout-raising and stream improvement. He tested foods; he studied temperatures. He built dams that aerated the water and gave big trout suitable hiding places. "Hewitt" dams, where the stream falls over an extended wooden barrier, are still common in the Catskills, and a tribute to his inventive mind.[12]

Lee Wulff "loved and respected the 'old man.'" He admired the fact that Hewitt often broke with tradition, and that his "thinking was free and open." Those of us who were fortunate to know Lee understand this admiration; there was a lot of Ed Hewitt in Lee Wulff.

Hewitt's removal of 4 miles of the Neversink certainly changed the habits of those anglers who had fished this portion of the river for years, and his posting placed more fishing pressure on the remaining open waters. And it was not too many years later that trout fishermen and the very families that had cleared and settled the land began to hear rumors of an even greater threat—not only to the river, but to their very existence in the Neversink Valley.

At first, rumors circulated in the winter of 1920 that a large dam was going to be constructed at the Big Bend, flooding the valley above. In 1921, the Board of Water Supply of the city of New York was asked to find new sources of water, and by 1928, the city's Board of Estimate had approved the construction of additional water supply reservoirs.

In 1922, the *Sullivan County Review* reported that every few weeks some portion of the region receives "a fright" when a party of engineers of the New York City Board of Water Supply comes into an area and begins to survey and map valleys and streams. They tell the worried villagers that they have no information as to why they are there, other than that they were "ordered" to make the survey. Following their departure, rumors were rampant about what farms, properties, and villages would be under water. Sadly, several villages along the Neversink were visited.

In 1925, the states of New York, New Jersey, and Pennsylvania formed the Delaware River Treaty Commission and agreed to share the waters of the Delaware River. This tristate treaty paved the way for the city to construct dams on tributaries of the Delaware River, including the Neversink, for water supply. At first, the city seemed focused on building a huge dam in the vicinity of Cuddebackville and flooding the Neversink Valley upstream to Wurtsboro.

However, a few years later, news reports announced to the people of Neversink that engineers drilling in preparation of a city reservoir had struck bedrock about a mile below the village. One headline stated "Dam Would Flood Neversink Village," letting the people of Neversink know that their homes would be "under many feet of water."

"RIVER OF OUR DREAMS"

Another well-known fly fisherman living along the Neversink in the glory days of the famous river was William A. Chandler (1883–1974). Chandler moved to the small hamlet of Bittersweet, just upstream of the village of Neversink, in 1916.

He preferred fishing dry flies and used them almost exclusively. He was a good fly tier and tied his own flies because he was not satisfied with those imported from England or sold over the counter in the United States. He experimented with dry flies at a time when dry-fly fishing was relatively unknown to most fly fishermen. Chandler firmly believed that wings were the most important part of the fly, and he added extra fibers to tails. The standard at the time was two or three fibers, and Chandler used six or eight.

He limited his favorite fly patterns to four, generally tied them on the model perfect hook straight-tapered shank with a turned-down eye, and preferred using hook sizes 11, 13, 15, and 17.

One of these patterns—and one that he may have been responsible for originating—is the Bradley Special, a Catskill-style dry fly named after William A. Bradley, one-time member of the Beaverkill Trout Club. Chandler and Bradley experimented with a pattern that would float well in fast water. "The result is a fly dressed with brownish Mallard wings, rough red brown fur body, medium red hackle and tail. This pattern has proven excellent all season under general conditions."[13] Later, the pattern evolved into a dressing with a body of blue-gray fur from the back of a red squirrel, spun on a double strand of red silk, and tied to expose a little of the red silk. The wings were also changed to mallard flank feathers.

Chandler's second favorite fly is a Light Cahill, a standard dry-fly pattern devised near the turn of the twentieth century, the origin of which can be traced to the trout streams of the Catskills. The creation of the fly has been placed with either Theodore Gordon or William A. Chandler. A closer look at the pattern Gordon tied reveals that his Light Cahill is dissimilar to the Light Cahill pattern made popular by Chandler, which is the fly that contemporary trout fishermen are most familiar with.

Gordon shaded or lightened a fly known as the Cahill* by changing the hackle from dark red to light brown; he stated in one of his columns that it was also tied with a body of pale blue dubbing. In a letter to G. E. M. Skues in 1912, Gordon wrote: "The Light Cahill does well when a pale blue is on the water and is one of the standard patterns, dark and light and dressed in several sizes."[14]

Clearly the fly Gordon refers to is of a bluish tone and not the Light Cahill that Chandler tied; Chandler's fly is tied in the classic Catskill style, with drake mandarin or wood duck flank feathers for wings, a trim body of light cream-colored fur from the belly of a red fox, and light ginger cock's hackle for the tail and hackle (originally the tail was wood duck flank feathers). Fly-fishing entomologists believe that this pattern is an excellent imitation of the pale cream or yellow *Stenonema* mayflies.

Roy Steenrod, who knew both Gordon and Chandler, claimed that William Chandler should get the credit for tying the first Light Cahill. As to exactly when he originated the fly is not known; however, a *New York Times* article published in 1920 featuring the Light Cahill states that it was a few years previous, which would place the date at or about 1916 or 1918.

Of the fly, Chandler, in the *Angler's Club Bulletin* in April 1923, writes that he modified a Light Cahill tied by Theodore Gordon: "The only change that I made is to use a lighter colored hackle and increase the number of Wood Duck tail whisks. This is also a good general pattern and especially so during the evening, bad light conditions, and when the Light Olives and Yellow Duns are on the water."

His third fly was the Quill Gordon, and Chandler wrote that this fly was very effective when hatches of "medium dark olive duns" were on the water. The fourth fly he selected was a Fan-Wing Royal Coachman, a fly that Chandler stated was created by Theodore Gordon. He rarely used the

---

*A dark fly with wood duck wings, dark blue-dun (muskrat fur) body, and dark red hackle and tail. The first mention of the Cahill I have been able to find was in an article by Wakeman Holberton in *Forest and Stream* in 1882, in which he lists the Cahill with "flies that proved most killing" (March 9, 1882, 110).

fly, but did so occasionally late in the evening, when poor visibility prevented him from seeing the Light Cahill.

William Chandler was raised on a farm across the Hudson from Albany, in Rensselaer. As a young man, he was fortunate to find employment that incorporated the skills and knowledge he possessed as a fly fisherman. He first worked as the manager of a Troy, New York, sporting goods store. He then moved to New York and became a fishing tackle specialist on the staff of Abercrombie & Fitch; later, he was an associate of William Mills & Son.

Chandler became familiar with Catskill trout streams and developed a friendship with Theodore Gordon. He fell in love with the Neversink and dreamed of living in a place where he could just walk out his door and be on the river. Soon he and his wife, Martha, began thinking about leaving city life and settling in the beautiful valley with the river flowing through it.

William Chandler on left. Ed Van Put collection.

They made their move in 1916 and began by operating a small fishing resort, immediately making plans to purchase it the following year. Known as Neversink Lodge, the property consisted of 12 acres and was located on the west side of the Neversink, just upstream of the village in an area known as Bittersweet.

Bill greatly enjoyed being able to look at the river every day, to see firsthand the daily changes taking place and all of the mayfly, caddis, and stonefly hatches. He loved being able to walk to the water in a matter of minutes and to look for rises in the large, deep pools of the river as it flowed past his door. He could now spend more time than ever along the Neversink. Living along its banks enabled him, even if for only an hour or so, to walk across the road and cast a fly to a rising trout.

He and Martha enjoyed hosting trout fishermen, with the "tackle talk" at the table: the stories of big trout caught and of the ones that got away. They were always meeting new people, and yet they had a number of regulars who fished the Neversink every summer. There were fly fishers from the city who were notified by wire or telephone as soon as the hatches started and trout began to feed on the surface. The Chandlers worked as a team, and it was Bill who enjoyed a reputation in the kitchen for his pancakes and sausages.

Bill Chandler also got involved in his community. He was elected a town justice, then supervisor of the town of Neversink. Concerned about the future of trout fishing, he began organizing sportsmen and was a charter member of Neversink Rod and Gun Club, the Liberty Rod and Gun Club, and one of the few members of the Anglers' Club of New York who hailed from Sullivan County.

Neversink Lodge. Courtesy Robert H. Wood.

It was through the Liberty Rod and Gun Club in the 1930s that he and Roy Steenrod lobbied for a state public fishing rights program. In 1933, at a time when there was an increase in posted water along the Neversink, he and his friend Judge Foster of Liberty purchased a half mile of the river and kept it open to public fishing.

Recognizing the need for a greater sportsman's voice on matters related to fish and game, he worked to create a more powerful and effective organization, uniting the various clubs scattered throughout Sullivan County. On December 10, 1936, Bill Chandler became the first president of the Sullivan County Federation of Sportsmen's Clubs. As president, he fought for better trout-stocking policies for Catskill streams and the need for a hatchery in Sullivan County.

Chandler's lobbying efforts eventually led to the acquisition of the Catskill Mountain Hatchery at DeBruce in the town of Rockland and to the state's eventual development of a public fishing rights program. In 1937, Chandler was elected to the state legislature as an assemblyman, and as such, he continued to be active in conservation matters.

William Chandler. *Liberty Register.*

Though he had a fondness for the upper Willowemoc and the Beaverkill in the area of the covered bridge campgrounds, his favorite stream remained the Neversink. Bill Chandler loved the entire Neversink Valley and knew it intimately. He was familiar with both the East and West Branches, their long flat pools and bottleneck riffles, and he knew the names of the wildflowers, ferns, and forest trees found along streamside banks.

The Chandlers too, were victims of the New York City Board of Water Supply; their fishing resort and home was condemned, along with hundreds of others, and was to be burned and bulldozed to make way for the proposed Neversink Reservoir. They did not leave as others had done, but stayed until their home was taken by the city, just before reservoir construction. Then they moved to Liberty, where they spent most of their remaining years; Martha passed away in January 1974, and Bill in December of the same year. They are buried side by side in the tiny Claryville Cemetery alongside a small white, green-shuttered church with a steeple fittingly adorned (for a streamside house of worship) with a handsome trout weather vane. The location of their final resting place must have been chosen judiciously, as the cemetery is the closest to the waters of the Neversink. It lies across the road from the forks, where the East and West Branch join to form their beloved river; in fact, the sound of flowing water distinctly penetrates the solitude of their final resting place.

The Neversink that we knew with the wild life, birds and flowers is gone. It has been taken for a thirsty horde in a far off city. For us, the sun has set to rise no more on the River of Our Dreams.
—William A. Chandler

BROWNS IN THE RONDOUT

After 1900, the trout fishing along the lower Rondout Creek improved significantly, mostly as a result of the introduction of brown trout. However, the fishery and the people living in the valley faced the same dire consequences as those living in the valley of the Neversink.

One of the strangest catches on the Rondout occurred 1911. On April 13, the Montela correspondent to the *Sullivan County Review* told the story of John Hamilton, head sawyer of the water-powered sawmill near Montela. Hamilton was about to saw a red oak log that had been underwater in the mill pond; the center of the log had been hollow, and after squaring it off, he began removing inch boards until he noticed a flash of something through the thin veneer.

Hamilton stopped sawing and looked closer at the object and discovered an immense brown trout wedged tightly in the hole. With his knife he cut away some more of the thin wood and the huge trout fell into his hands: "It is presumed the trout had been accustomed to lying in the hollow log and becoming frightened when the log was taken from the water had tried to go out forwards instead of backwards, pushing itself so far into the hole as to become helpless." The giant brown measured 27½ inches and weighed 7 pounds!

In the summer of 1912, the *Ellenville Journal* mentioned two other large browns taken from the Rondout. On July 17, Calvin Van Wagner, of Eureka, captured a brown that measured 26 inches and weighed 6½ pounds. And on August 8, John H. Divine, an excellent fly fisherman from Ellenville, caught a 23-inch brown that weighed a little more than 4 pounds; this trout was taken to the Lackawack House where it was put on exhibition.

The following season, the *Ellenville Journal,* on June 26, 1913, reported that John H. Divine caught a monster brown from the Rondout. The great trout was a real "sockdollager" that measured 27 inches and weighed 6 pounds, 3 ounces! The fish was taken to the brewery in Ellenville, where it was placed on ice, before being sent to New York to be mounted.

Divine's huge trout made the pages of *Forest and Stream* and was mentioned in Theodore Gordon's column of July 19, 1913. Gordon wrote that he had met John Divine along the Neversink and that he was having success with the wary browns of that esteemed waterway. Divine was an expert fisherman, and he informed Gordon that his favorite pattern was a dark gray-hackled fly, with a red tail, and that he had used the fly successfully on large trout and for evening fishing.

One other example of how well brown trout were flourishing in the waters of the lower Rondout was a fish caught by Robert McConnell and reported in the *Journal* on June 11, 1914. McConnell's giant brown was on exhibition at the Wagner House; it measured 26 inches and weighed in at 6¼ pounds.

The Lackawack House catered to trout fishermen, and reports by guests fishing the lower Rondout were common in local newspapers during the trouting season. On May 18, 1916, the *Ellenville Journal* reported on the success of two visiting doctors from Paterson, New Jersey: "They are guests at the Lackawack House, and fishing the stream within a half mile either way of the house came in with sixteen beauties that tipped the scale at just 16 pounds. There are seventeen guests at the Lackawack House at present."[15]

The Rondout is where Cecil Heacox caught his first trout. Little did he realize the significance of his catch.* He spent his boyhood years in Napanoch, a small hamlet along the Rondout Creek, downstream of Ellenville. This section of the Rondout was not trout water, but as a youngster, he heard tales of trout being caught in the coldwater or upper part of the stream above the falls at Honk Lake.

Cecil's father was a country doctor in the days when doctors traveled great distances through the mountains by horse and buggy. As a youngster, he pestered his father to allow him to accompany him when he made house calls along the upper Rondout.

---

*Cecil Heacox would go on to a career in conservation and become a pioneer fisheries biologist and the first district fisheries manager for the Southern District, which included the entire Catskills along with Rondout Creek.

When the day came that Cecil was allowed to travel with his father, he was taken to Lackawack and dropped off at Sheeley's Hotel so that he would have a place to go to should his father be late in coming back. The boy walked to the nearby stream and began fishing; his father had loaned him an Abbey & Imbrie bamboo fly rod and a Hawkeye reel, "a pretty fancy outfit for a boy who had never fished for trout."

Fate or destiny must have been at work that summer day, for the inexperienced seven-year-old hooked—then hauled out of the water—a trout that weighed nearly a pound! Pouncing on the fish, Cecil was unaware of what he had caught until a patron from Sheeley's bar told him he had captured a "German brown." The words "German brown" caused his "heart to skip a beat." The year was 1910, and for a youngster fishing for trout for the very first time, catching a brown trout was special. The event and the fish left a lifetime impression on the boy. Sixty-four years later, and after a successful career in fisheries, Cecil Heacox reminisced on catching that first trout in a book he authored, titled *The Compleat Brown Trout*.

The wonderful brown trout fishing along the lower Rondout Creek did not last. Rumors of a dam in the valley had persisted ever since the state legislature passed the Water Supply Act of 1905, and again when New York City surveyors were working in the Rondout Valley in 1907. The reality

Rondout reservoir and the flooded Rondout Valley. Ed Van Put.

of a dam being constructed between Eureka and Lackawack finally surfaced in 1931, when the Supreme Court gave its approval for New York City to remove 440 million gallons of water per day from the Delaware watershed.

Once approval to tap the Delaware was made, the city announced a three-stage plan: first, to develop the Rondout and Neversink reservoirs; second, to construct a dam and reservoir on the East Branch of the Delaware River; and third, to impound the Beaverkill, Willowemoc, and Little Delaware River. Because development of the Beaverkill, Willowemoc, and Little Delaware as water supplies would exceed what the Supreme Court said the city could remove, the city had to return to the Supreme Court for approval.

In 1936, area newspapers began reporting that New York City would be taking title to the condemned lands in the valley as soon as the commissioners of appraisal were appointed and sworn in. Seven miles of the Rondout Creek—including the hamlets of Lackawack, Montela, and Eureka—would disappear, and twelve hundred people would be evicted from their homes. Some of the older families had lived on farms in the valley for more than one hundred years. Even a half-century later, the grandchildren of those forced to leave the valley would tell stories of how their grandparents watched New York City workers burn down their homes.

Work on the dam located near the village of Lackawack began in August 1939 but was halted because of World War II. In 1946, the project was reactivated; the dam was completed in 1951.

LOUIS RHEAD

One of the more colorful characters fishing the Catskills near the turn of the twentieth century was an Englishman named Louis John Rhead (1857–1926). Rhead came to the United States in the 1880s. He achieved great fame as an illustrator of books and magazines, and worked as art manager with his brother, Frederick, at D. Appleton & Co., Publishers. The two illustrated a number of books together under the name the Brothers Rhead.

Louis Rhead also painted in oils and watercolors, and exhibited his art in England and America. He won a gold medal in Boston in 1895 for artistic posters and another in St. Louis at the Exposition of 1904. Many of the books he illustrated were juvenile classics, such as *Robin Hood, Swiss Family Robinson, Gulliver's Travels, King Arthur and His Knights, Treasure Island,* and *Kidnapped.* His work was so popular that it is still found in books published today.

Rhead began fishing in 1888 or 1890, and he soon developed a passion for trout fishing. Exactly when he began fishing in the Catskills is uncertain, but by 1900, he was a regular, and his favorite streams were the Beaverkill and Willowemoc. When he fished the Willowemoc, he often stayed at the Hearthstone Inn in De Bruce, which was hosted by Elizabeth Royce and located near the famed junction of the Mongaup and Willowemoc Creeks. The inn was known for catering to fishermen, serving 4 o'clock breakfasts and dinners as late as 9 o'clock.

In addition to his art, Rhead became a prolific writer of fishing articles and books on fishing; he also created the artwork for many of the covers of *Forest and Stream* when it became a monthly magazine. While fishing the Beaverkill, he was a familiar guest of the Roscoe House and the Campbell Inn. He stayed at the Campbell Inn for the greater part of the 1901 fishing season and collected material for *The Speckled Brook Trout,* a book that was edited and illustrated by Rhead and

Louis Rhead fishing Junction Pool on the Beaverkill. Archives of American Art, Courtesy Chas. Scribner's Sons.

contained essays written by many of the noted trout fishermen of the day, including Charles Hallock, William C. Harris, and A. Nelson Cheney. A few of the excellent illustrations included are of the Beaverkill, the Willowemoc, and the Mongaup Creek.

Rhead fished the upper Willowemoc and Beaverkill, but his favorite water was the lower Beaverkill, or big river, because of the variety it offered. He especially enjoyed the water between Cooks Falls and the hamlet of East Branch, where he caught brook, brown, and rainbow trout, as well as chub and bass.

In the early 1900s, Rhead wrote a number of fishing articles for *Outing Magazine* on subjects such as the best flies for brook trout, worm fishing for brook trout, and dry-fly fishing.

After the publication of *The Speckled Brook Trout*, Rhead edited another book titled *The Basses Fresh-Water and Marine*, which was published in 1905. Beautifully illustrated by Rhead, the book has a fascinating cover: front and back (not dust jacket) are the sides of a large striped bass. Tarleton H. Bean, state fish culturist, and William C. Harris, editor of the *American Angler*, contribute most of the text, but Rhead adds a few chapters of his own, including one titled "Bass in the Beaverkill."

In 1908, he produced *The Book of Fish and Fishing*. He wrote glowingly of the trout streams of Ulster, Sullivan, and Delaware counties; and of the Beaverkill and Willowemoc; and how he and his friend, William C. Harris, enjoyed fishing the upper Willowemoc from the hamlet of Willowemoc downstream to the village of De Bruce, catching "many a good trout."

During the summer of 1911, Rhead rendezvoused at the Roscoe House with George La Branche (who was still developing his dry-fly techniques on the upper Willowemoc) and Dr. Tarleton H. Bean. Rhead and Bean visited the Beaverkill between Roscoe and the hamlet of Beaverkill, and La Branche and Rhead fished along the lower river.

Both La Branche and Bean must have developed a special relationship with Louis Rhead; in 1916, when he produced his most noted work, *American Trout-Stream Insects,* he paid tribute to his friends. On the frontispiece is a fine drawing of George La Branche dry-fly fishing, possibly on the Willowemoc; the book is dedicated to Tarleton Bean. *American Trout-Stream Insects* has been hailed by some as "the first American work on trout stream insects"[16] and by others as "America's first angling entomology."[17]

Before publication of the book, Rhead had spent three years studying and collecting aquatic insects along the Beaverkill. A strong proponent of the theory of exact imitation, he wrote a seven-part series published in *Field & Stream* in 1914 titled "The Entomology of American Trout Streams."

At the time, *American Trout-Stream Insects* was the only book dealing with American aquatic insect life. However, the plates of natural flies depicted in the book, though finely drawn, are not identified in a scientific manner and are given names Rhead devised, such as "Shiny-Tail," "Chocolate," "Spot-Wing," and "Purple Drake."

There has also been criticism over the fact that he did not include dressings of the artificial flies that are in the book, even though he went on to design almost one hundred different flies. It appears that Rhead deliberately excluded the dressings in an attempt to control their manufacture and sales. His "nature flies," as he called them, were sold only from his home and through the New York City firm of William Mills & Son, which had the exclusive rights to make and sell the flies. Rhead also promoted the flies in fishing articles he wrote for *Forest and Stream,* and advised his readers that they could obtain them by writing to the editor of the magazine.

American Trout-Stream Insects was not this country's first entomology; it was, however, the first book devoted to the theory of exact imitation. Louis Rhead was a strong believer in direct imitation, and he tied his flies as true copies of the naturals he found along the Beaverkill. He dubbed the standard flies of his day "fancy flies," and he believed that they were useless: "If an exact copy of the natural insect is offered to the fish—even if that natural insect is not in flight—it is sure to entice and lure a trout more readily than a fancy fly."[18] How ironic it is that not even one of the many flies he designed and promoted are known to trout fishermen today, and many of the flies he dubbed as "useless" are still in use.

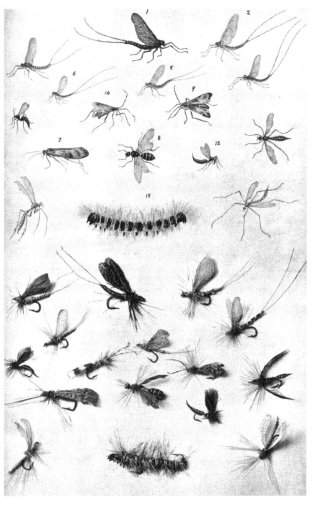

Flies for the month of August and their imitations. *American Trout-Stream Insects,* 1916.

Although some of his ideas may appear naïve, Louis Rhead was an innovative and knowledge-able fly fisherman. In May 1922, in a *Forest and Stream* article, he wrote about fishing a nymph as a dry fly, a sophisticated technique at the time. And that same year, he developed what may have been one of the earliest fly-fishing schools when he and English fly caster Fred G. Shaw began a "School for Fishermen" in Brooklyn. Shaw taught casting; Rhead, trout habits, food, tactics, and equipment.

In many of his articles on trout fishing, Rhead was always discovering new flies that were "more killing;" his writing was not modest, and he had no qualms about making boastful claims about the flies he invented. He created "nature flies," "metal bodied flies," "shining fly minnows," and so on. In this way, he was similar to fellow countryman J. Harrington Keene, who also tried to promote the special flies he created that were "different" and "better than the rest."

Louis Rhead fished the Beaverkill for more than twenty-five years. He knew its riffles and pools, and those who knew him claimed he fell under its spell and that he loved the Beaverkill. Although he was of the old school that usually fished with two or even three wet flies, he did become a dry-fly fisherman. It has been said that he was a beautiful caster: that he was graceful, his casting was effortless, and he was a joy to watch. One who fished with Rhead and reminisced about his fly-fishing abilities was William Schaldach, artist and angling writer:

> Louis Rhead had a great devotion to the natural-imitation theory, and he tied lifelike replicas of crawfish, hellgrammites, nymphs and adult flies. He would fish these diligently, day after day, and the empty creel with which he often returned never dampened his spirits. Anglers called him a luckless fisherman and kidded him unmercifully; but usually, when things were at their worst, he would show up with a brownie or rainbow of prodigious size and silently slay his critics.[19]

ON THE ESOPUS

In the early part of the century, success along the lower Esopus—a big, burly-type of stream, with lots of fast water and large boulders—was very dependent on water temperatures; and until rainbow trout were introduced, there was little fly fishing in this lower portion. The stream channel was wide, with a great deal of erosion along its stream banks. Trees were not large enough to adequately shade the widened waters, and as the season progressed, the fishing became unpredictable.

By summer, or late June, temperatures would begin to rise, and trout fishing was poor or very limited. There were also times when large numbers of rainbows were known to run up into the cooler tributaries in August, especially on the Bushkill, after a rain.

However, when water temperatures were favorable in the spring, the lower Esopus could pro-vide exciting fishing for large trout. In an article featured in the English *Fishing Gazette* dated June 1, 1912, Theodore Gordon wrote of his friend, Dr. W. E. Halsey, who fished the lower Esopus on May 2 and 3, and caught thirty-five trout between 14 and 18 inches.

Writing about the impact that rainbow trout had on the trout-fishing resources of the Catskills, Gordon commented that the rainbow was a success, "affords the best sport," and "is game to the backbone, and rises freely at natural and artificial flies." Gordon made these comments in a chapter titled "American Trout Fishing," published in England in a book titled *Fishing at Home and Abroad* (1913) by Sir Herbert Maxwell.

Gordon wrote that if brown and rainbow trout could be maintained in the same waters, fly fishermen would have good sport: "These conditions existed for a time in the Esopus in Ulster Co.

N. Y. The rainbows were very numerous many years ago and a fair number were taken this year (1912) up to one pound and a half. This shows they have maintained themselves to a certain extent. Allowing for the differences in coloration, many of them resemble a small fresh-run salmon, with small heads and beautifully proportioned, plump bodies."

The stocking of rainbow and brown trout had created fishing opportunities along many more miles of the Esopus than when the stream contained only native brook trout. With more trout water available, fishing tourists increased accordingly, as the stream was easily accessible by train. The railroad followed the Esopus up through the valley and stopped at stations such as Brown's Station, West Shokan, Boiceville, Cold Brook, Mt. Pleasant, Phoenicia, and Big Indian.

The Esopus became a popular destination of fishermen, and fishing pressure could be heavy at times; it was not unusual to see a fisherman every half-mile from Cold Brook upstream to Big Indian, with the greater concentration at the last mentioned station. Some anglers would start at one railroad station, such as Cold Brook or West Shokan, and if the fishing was poor, they would board the train and move upstream, perhaps stopping at one or two places until they found better fishing. Because of the convenience, there were also fishermen who would take the train upstream to the next station and fish back downstream.

One of the earliest dry-fly fishermen to fish the Esopus Creek was Art Neu, an excellent trout fisherman who owned a sporting goods store in Newark, New Jersey. Art was well known for his fly-casting abilities, and as a member of the famous Newark Bait and Fly Casting Club, he became a national fly-casting champion. He and other club members—such as Jack Schwinn, Lou Darling, and outdoor writer Ken Lockwood—were regular visitors to the Catskills, plying their talents along the Beaverkill, Willowemoc, Neversink, and the Esopus, which, before the completion of the Shandaken tunnel, was a favorite.

A year after the Ashokan reservoir was filled, Neu had an unforgettable day just upstream of where the Esopus joined the new reservoir. His party had been on the stream for a week; the water was high and the fishing unspectacular. On June 14, 1916, he walked down to the last pool before the reservoir, then known as the Miller Pool. His partners, who were fishing upstream, met with only fair success; but Neu found rising trout, and for about an hour, he was amid a number of large feeding fish.

He fished a dry fly for that hour, and although he released several small trout, he kept five browns that measured 15 inches, 17 inches, 19 inches, 21 inches, and 24 inches (the largest weighed 4 pounds)! Art Neu loved the Esopus and considered it among the finest trout streams he ever fished; but when the Shandaken tunnel was completed in 1924, the flows from it were so radical and inconsistent that he and other trout fishermen looked elsewhere. They stopped fishing the stream and moved over to the Beaverkill.

Another early dry-fly fisherman who was associated with the Esopus Creek near the turn of the twentieth century was Louis S. Darling (1874–1917). In his day, Darling was known as one of this country's best fly casters and for his fishing abilities and outdoor articles. At one time, he was in the employ of Abercrombie & Fitch and was considered an expert trout fisherman. He could cast with either hand, and, like his friend Art Neu, he was also a noted member of the Newark Bait and Fly Casting Club.* He competed in casting tournaments for many years and was the national dry-fly casting champion in 1916.

---

*"The club is the oldest scientific angling and casting club in the east and one of the oldest in the nation." Club history, *www.newarkbaitandflycastingclub.org/.*

Louis S. Darling. *The American Angler*, 1917.

Lou Darling was an early proponent of dry-fly fishing, and although he fished other Catskill trout streams, the Esopus was his favorite. He fished, and sometimes camped, along the stream for twenty-five years, from 1892 to 1917. His favorite stretch was the water between Shandaken and Big Indian, but he also wrote that huge trout and good sport could be had on the lower Esopus.

Darling is credited with creating, in 1910, a popular early dry-fly pattern known as the Catskill, a fly that was fashioned from two of his favorite trout flies: the Cahill and the Oak. He took the wings of the Cahill and the body of the Oak and combined those features into the Catskill. He claimed, "Wood-duck wing and orange body will take trout anywhere."[20] The pattern was a favorite of Theodore Gordon's, who tied many of the flies for customers and for his own use. The pattern is as follows: wings—wood duck flank feathers, split and divided; body—orange wool; hackle—light brown; and tail—wood duck flank fibers.

Upon Darling's death in 1917, his friend Art Neu wrote, "The old Esopus River, in Ulster County, New York, which he had fished and loved for twenty-five years, and which he had written about in verse and prose, will not seem the same with his sober, bearded face missing when the camp fire glows."[21]

17

The 1920s

A STATE RECORD BROWN TROUT; THE BEST OF TIMES;
and DR. EMMELINE MOORE

The new Ashokan Reservoir provided brown and rainbow trout with plenty of space and abundant food. In the summer, when Ashokan stratified, trout could seek out preferred cooler water temperatures and—coupled with adequate oxygen and a food supply of plankton and minnows—they grew rapidly. When these trout matured, most of them traveled up the Esopus and its tributaries before spawning; browns in the fall, rainbows in late fall and early spring.

Work on the second stage of the Catskill system had begun in 1917. This involved impounding the Schoharie Creek by constructing a dam at the hamlet of Gilboa in Schoharie County and creating a 1,500-acre reservoir. The waters of the Schoharie were then to be diverted to the Esopus Creek through an 18.2-mile tunnel; known as the Shandaken tunnel, it was, at the time, the longest in the world. The Schoharie watershed drained 314 square miles and, added to the Ashokan reservoir, made the total water supply for the Catskill aqueduct 571 square miles.

The tunnel project took seven years to complete and formally opened on February 9, 1924. The dam across the Schoharie was not

Shandaken Tunnel or Portal. Ed Van Put.

completed at this time, but its waters were diverted by the use of a small temporary dam. Shortly after 9:00 A.M., waters from the Schoharie Creek began flowing into the Esopus at the tiny hamlet of Allaben. While a number of city officials stood nearby, the American flag was raised. Formalities and speeches were offered by prominent men who were involved with the construction work.

Two years before the tunnel's completion, it was estimated that New Yorkers were using 109 gallons of water per person per day! Even with this new abundance of water added to the Ashokan reservoir, it was estimated that the city would have an adequate supply of water only until 1935, a span of eleven years. In the meantime, the city of New York was already in the process of looking for an additional source of water in the Catskills, where it was claimed that there was an inexhaustible supply.

The dam at Gilboa, on the Schoharie Creek, took 4 years to complete. The new reservoir began filling on July 25, 1926. The reservoir would eventually completely cover the former village of Gilboa, which the city had condemned; 1,330 bodies were exhumed and relocated, and 500 people were displaced along with their homes, barns, farms, businesses, church, and every aspect of village life.

Schoharie Creek. Ed Van Put.

It was rumored that some Gilboa residents who refused to vacate their homes were burned out by authorities while they were off visiting neighbors. In October 1925, fire destroyed many of the buildings of the village, including homes, stores, a church, and a hotel. At this time, the buildings were owned by the city but were being rented, and the occupants had not received final eviction notices. It was believed that the fires were set deliberately to prevent New York City from capitalizing on a deal with a movie company that wanted to film the village being consumed by fire. The official explanation was that a rubbish fire was left unattended and caused the destruction. By the end of the year, city workers burned the remaining buildings.

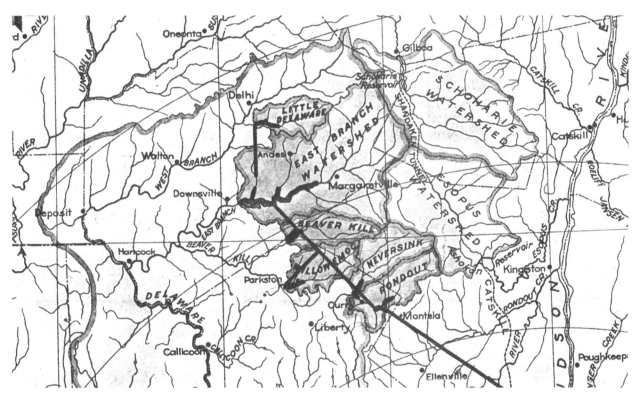

A map depicting New York City reservoirs on every major trout stream in the Catskills, ca. 1927. Ed Van Put.

The new Schoharie reservoir was approximately 5 miles in length, with depths of between 50 to 120 feet. The *Walton Reporter* commented on the reservoir's completion in a front-page article on July 31, 1926: "Soon the farms of the Schoharie valley and the streets of Gilboa will be sleeping under many feet of water, and in a few years, all to be remembered by an uninterested public will be that somewhere in the Catskills, some few hundred people gave up their homes that New York City's thirsting millions might drink."

THE ESOPUS CREEK

During the early 1920s, catches of rainbows and browns weighing 4 to 7 pounds were occasionally reported; but in general, the sizes of Esopus Creek trout did not appear to change dramatically. An article published in the *Cold Brook Gazette* in May 1921 gives an example of what the trout fishing was like a few years after the Ashokan reservoir was filled, but before the tunnel began delivering cold water to the Esopus. A fly fisherman named R. F. Auger wrote that he had been fishing the Esopus practically every weekend since 1916, and for the past three seasons he carefully recorded each trout he caught, what fly the fish was taken on, and where the trout was caught.

In April 1919, Auger caught forty-two trout, and none was larger than 11 inches. In April 1920, eighteen trout were taken, and a trout measuring 11½ inches was the largest. In April 1921, 114 trout were caught, with many measuring between 11 and 13 inches. It was stated that the most killing fly in 1919 was the Queen of the Waters; in 1920, the Female Beaverkill; and in 1921, a Blue Quill.

Auger adds that all of the trout were taken on dry flies, and more than 50 percent were returned to the water unharmed: "I have always kept well above Phoenicia until Decoration Day—to Big Indian in high water and then later down to Cold Brook."[1]

More big-fish stories have emanated from the waters of the Esopus than any other Catskill river; some appear factual, others maybe not. In February 1923, an article appeared in *Outing Magazine* titled "Rudolph King of the Esopus." The story was written by William C. Morris Wiley about a giant brown trout that makes his home in the beautiful pool opposite the Phoenicia garage. At the head of the pool, along the south bank, is a huge boulder approximately 10 feet high and 20 feet wide, and alongside this particular rock lives "Rudolph." Everyone around Phoenicia knew about Rudolph, as the great trout had become a legend and had lived in the same location for seven years.

The author informs his readers that if they were to visit the boulder in July or August, when the stream is low, and climb on top and look directly down into the water, "you can see him." He writes that there is a wheel from a surrey with the hub and spokes knocked out lying on the stream bottom, and the trout lies inside the wheel with its nose almost touching one side, while his tail fans the other. Wiley goes on to state that the enormous brown is 36 inches in length—and he knows this to be correct, because he measured the diameter of a similar wheel!

The monster brown had been hooked by the author while he was fishing a wet fly, one day when the water was a little discolored. The trout took a #8 yellow Pig's Wool Fly, but it escaped by running downstream, breaking a heavy leader. For several years, Wiley had fished the Esopus for at least thirty days, devoting two early mornings before daybreak and two nights trying flies, minnows, and worms on the giant trout, but with no success. Once he even "shingled a mouse": floated a live mouse on a piece of wooden shingle down the stream and, when in position, slid the mouse off the shingle so it had to swim directly over the big trout. But Rudolph would have none of it!

He tried spinners, spinners with flies, and bucktails, but all was for naught. Occasionally, Rudolph was hooked, but Wiley says he had chosen his home wisely. Just downstream of his pool, the stream takes a sharp bend and has a heavy current and a series of rapids littered with large boulders—giving him lots of opportunities to escape.

Another large trout that made news in 1923 was caught by T. E. Spencer at the Chimney Hole (Miller Pool) and Ashokan reservoir. This giant brown weighed 19 pounds, 14 ounces! No measurement of its length seems to have been recorded, but in the August 1946 issue of the *Conservationist,* an official publication of the New York State Conservation Department, Spencer's fish is listed under "Brown Trout" as one of "New York State's record game fish." It states: "19 lbs. 14 oz., taken by T. E. Spencer in 1923 from the mouth of the Esopus River at Ashokan Reservoir."

A few years later, in 1926, the *Liberty Register* ran a front-page story about another enormous brown trout that lived in Excelsior Pool on the Esopus. The story first appeared in New York papers and told of a monster brown that had eluded trout fishermen for years. The trout met its demise in January when the mill pond on the stream was drained. The brown trout measured 42 inches, had a jaw spread of 19 inches, and weighed a whopping 27 pounds and 3 ounces!

The newspaper went on to say that "R. C. Smith, of Phoenicia, N.Y. prominent trout angler and deputy game warden, who related the story, personally saw the trout measured and weighed and stands behind the authenticity of the tale."[2]

T. E. Spencer with his state record brown trout. *Forest and Stream,* 1924.

BROWNS IN THE EAST BRANCH

Shortly after the turn of the twentieth century, brown trout weighing 4 to 5 pounds began showing up in the catches of fishermen along the upper East Branch, especially in the area between Arena and Arkville. In 1900, a brown trout measuring 24½ inches in length and weighing 6¾ pounds was taken from the Tremper Kill, and by 1910, large brown trout were also caught in Dry Brook, Mill Brook, Vly Creek, and the East Branch, as far upstream as Roxbury. There were still plenty of bass in the river, but by the 1920s, bass fishermen were, on occasion, surprised when a monster brown grabbed their bait and took off downstream into the rapids faster than the angler could follow.

Newspaper accounts disclose that in the 1920s, brown trout were growing larger and inhabiting more of the upper East Branch, and that anglers fishing in tributaries were also catching browns much larger than the native brook trout they were accustomed to. The fishery was changing. This fact is apparent in the comments made by the Downsville correspondent to the *Sullivan*

County Review in 1926: "The recurrent question usually heard after the trout season has closed 'Why aren't there as many bass and pickerel in the river as there used to be?' is again current."[3]

It was not only bass fishermen who were concerned about changing fish populations; trout fishermen, too, were upset by the takeover by brown trout of the better brook trout streams in the watershed. Writing in the *Walton Reporter* on September 11, 1926, Rev. William Tatlock, an ardent trout fisher, expressed his concerns after catching a couple of browns in one of his favorite streams, Falls Clove Brook.

Falls Clove Brook was well known for its excellent brook trout fishing, and was supposedly free of "German browns" because of an impassable waterfall located near the mouth. The reverend was dismayed as to how the browns traveled through the falls when he fished there during the 1924 season: "The streams containing native trout only are becoming so rare that every true lover of the native will hope that the aliens have gained no considerable foothold in Falls Clove."

Large brown trout were now found in virtually all the deep pools and eddies along the upper East Branch. Although some were caught by local fishermen and reported to area newspapers, it is obvious that many were not. By no means do the fish reported represent all of the large trout removed from local waters; many fishermen shied away from publicity, preferring to keep their favorite stream out of the public eye. In either case, we should be grateful to those fishermen who did report their catch, as they left behind a historic record of their fishing that gives insight to a fishery that otherwise might not be known.

In September 1924, a skilled trout fisherman named Niles Fairbairn, who lived outside of Margaretville, caught a brown trout that measured 23 inches and weighed 5 pounds, 3 ounces. A few years later, Fairbairn captured the attention of Margaretville residents when he brought into town one of the first really big trout ever seen in the county. In August 1929, Fairbairn placed a 26¾-inch brown weighing 6 pounds, 10 ounces in the window of the Bussy Store on Main Street.

"German Brown Trout, 6 lb., 10 oz., 26¼ inches caught by Niles G. Fairbairn." Courtesy Dave Budin, Del-Sports, Margaretville, N.Y.

EAST AND WEST BROOKS

The trout-fishing mania that usually gripped Walton was alive and well in the 1920s. As usual, good trout fishing was found along East and West Brooks that entered the West Branch in the village. On opening day in 1923, the *Walton Reporter* stated in its April 14 issue that the West Brook was lined with fishermen and that Barney Wallace caught an 18-inch brown at the mill dam on the East Brook; the trout was exhibited in the Reynolds & Stebbins window. Two years later, on April 11, the newspaper reported that "as usual East Brook was the chief Mecca of the followers of Izaak Walton" and practically every farmhouse had one or more cars parked nearby. One farmer estimated that more than fifty automobiles containing trout fishermen passed his farm on opening day.

Fishing along East Brook, Lorin Wakeman took forty-four; Sheldon Wakeman, thirty-two; Harry Pettis, thirty-six; A. E. Woollett, thirty-three; and Sears and Howard Brown took about ninety trout between them. Women, too, participated in opening day activities; "Mrs. H. L. Griffin" took nine "beauties" in East Brook, Wauneta Munn caught ten, Fanny Walker caught three, and Ruby Taylor took one. Freda Brown went out with her father, Sears, and caught a "nice mess" in the West Brook.

The trout opener of 1928 was a memorable day. The *Walton Reporter* of April 14 stated that long before daylight, local fishermen were traveling by automobile up and down East Brook; those who wandered off the paved road soon found themselves bogged down in the mire that comes with

Checking undersized trout. *The Country Gentleman,* 1924.

spring trout fishing. "Mrs. Herbert Griffin" of nearby Mundale, known for her incredible opening-day catches, took thirty-six "nice trout" by 10:30 A.M. from a small tributary of East Brook. Albert Jones caught thirty-two in East Brook, and Theodore Seely and Graydon Dutcher each caught twenty-six trout. J. B. Townsend landed twenty-one, and A. E. Woollett caught thirty-eight trout before 10 o'clock in the lower portion of East Brook. A few weeks later, Gerald Rode took a 19½-inch trout that weighed more than 3 pounds on the Sines farm on East Brook.

The opening of the 1929 season began on April 13, and the *Reporter* claimed that streams were high because of a storm, but in spite of the adverse conditions, Mike Lurenze caught his limit of twenty-five trout in East Brook, Harry France took eighteen, and his brother Vernon another seventeen. Basil Steadman took sixteen trout, and Earl Thomas creeled twenty-five speckled beauties.

Mrs. H. L. Griffin, "always the champion fisherwoman," captured seventeen good-sized trout from upper East Brook. "Mrs. Griffin says she has fished in every kind of weather and has waded through snow banks to get her line into the brook, but this year had the experience of killing two snakes while out fishing."[4]

HAIL TO THE BEAVERKILL AND WILLOWEMOC

The largest reported trout to come out of the Beaverkill in the 1920s was a 27-inch brown weighing more than 8 pounds, taken by Fred Shaver of Turnwood. The giant fish was caught on the upper Beaverkill, downstream of Beaverkill Falls. The largest brown captured in the Willowemoc Creek measured 24¾ inches and weighed 6¼ pounds. Al Romer of Livingston Manor caught the fish in Decker's Eddy, a bend pool that changes at times, but always manages to maintain significant depth and to hold a big fish or two.

It was in 1923 that DeBruce blacksmith and fly tier George Cooper sold his general store and post office to Mahlon Davidson. Davidson, like Cooper, was a fly tier and a Catskill native from the Lew Beach area, on the upper Beaverkill. He hunted, trapped, and fished and was one of the last to make solid wooden rods of bilberry and shadbush (Juneberry).

The store was a popular meeting place for fishermen who wanted to know what flies were hatching, or which flies to use and where were the best places to fish, while they visited DeBruce and fished the Willowemoc and Mongaup creeks. In addition to general merchandise, Davidson sold some fishing tackle and trout flies. Like Cooper, he raised his own roosters for dry-fly hackle, mostly red and blue duns, and is credited with creating a dry fly known as the Davidson Special in the 1920s. It was tied similarly to the Light Cahill, but had a body of fox fur, dyed pale green, from the bark of willows.

Davidson's store was a short walk from the Hunter Road bridge, which spanned the Willowemoc. In June 1934, he took a 26-inch brown trout under the bridge on a #8 Hendrickson wet fly!

BROWN TROUT VERSUS BROOK TROUT: THE DEBATE CONTINUES

During the early 1920s, fishermen and the State Conservation Commission were still concerned about the effect brown trout were having on the trout streams of the state. The Conservation

DeBruce store and post office. Courtesy Emerson Bouton.

Commission continued to advise anglers who ordered brown trout from the hatcheries to keep the foreign trout out of brook trout streams. Actually, by this date, brown trout had been stocked in so many streams all over New York that it was impossible to prevent them from migrating anywhere they wanted to, barring impassable barriers.

The public was being advised that brown trout would "exterminate" the more "delicate" brook trout; and some of the applications the commission received for stocking browns were held until an investigation by an expert of the Conservation Commission could determine whether there was "still hope" of preserving the native brook trout fishing, or if stream conditions were such that it was better to stock brown trout.

Sportsmen were told to avoid stocking brown and brook trout in the same waters, as this was deemed a serious problem. "The German brown trout will not harmonize with the native species and after the introduction of the foreign species it is but a short time before they gain complete ascendancy and dominate the water to the eventual extermination of the native brook trout which is considered by sportsmen preeminently the better fish."[5]

In these instances, the Conservation Commission, at times, requested that a petition be signed by twenty-five "leading citizens or game clubs" of the vicinity, testifying that it is "futile" and a "waste" of fish to continue to stock brook trout in the stream. By 1926, it was announced that brown trout were becoming more popular with sportsmen, and because of the increasing demand for the fish, hatcheries were once again increasing production of fry and fingerlings.

This statement was undoubtedly correct, and in May 1926, William J. Schaldach, writer and artist, published a thought-provoking article in which he also claimed that fishermen's attitudes toward brown trout were finally beginning to swing in favor of the species. He recalled that when browns were first introduced, there was not a lot of enthusiasm for the fish, mostly because of their aggressive behavior toward native brook trout, but there was also doubt about the future of our trout streams once browns became established.

Schaldach questioned whether there was even a need, at the time, to introduce brown trout into American waters. However, he gave a synopsis of the events affecting trout streams and of the important role brown trout would play in the future of trout fishing.

He wrote about how deforestation had degraded streams by robbing them of their shade and increasing their water temperatures. And of how removing trees along the banks increased erosion, which in turn caused streambeds to become laden with more sediment than normal, destroying trout habitat.

He cited the indiscriminate habit of our culture to dump wastes into trout streams, and he recalled how "tan liquor" and refuse from creameries, acid factories, and sawmills polluted once-clean water, further damaging streams. He claimed that streams that once held "natives" now contained brown trout or no fish at all. Schaldach wrote that fishermen blamed the loss of brook trout entirely on the aggressiveness of browns, "carefully" avoided their own responsibility, and looked the other way when trout habitat and the water quality of trout streams was being destroyed.

Schaldach summed up his essay by saying that the brown trout is a "welcome" immigrant, but that those streams that still contain only native brook trout should be treasured and guarded carefully. However, where conditions are not favorable to brook trout, he writes, we should stock brown trout and "let us cease calling him the 'German' trout or 'European' trout, for he is now an American citizen, and a most desirable one."[6]

THE BEST OF TIMES

Improved roads and automobiles increased the number of trout fishermen who were now motoring to and from the famous Beaverkill. During the 1920s, a large following of regulars were fishing the lower river every weekend, developing a familiarity and love for its waters not readily found on other streams. The most loyal disciples were fly fishermen, who knew that the Beaverkill was special and that its lengthy, deep pools, abundant fly hatches, and eager-to-rise trout offered classic dry-fly fishing.

It was a new era in fly fishing. The popularity of the dry fly had by now passed that of the wet fly, and many fly fishers believed it was the best of times:

> It was a time of changing tactics, steadily improving tackle, and greater experimentation with dry flies. A new breed of Beaverkill angler advanced the sport of dry-fly fishing by becoming familiar with the river's major fly hatches, learning where and when the best trout fed, and determining

Driving along the Beaverkill at Painter's Bend. New York State Conservation Department Annual Report, 1929.

which flies should be used to take them. Many of these Beaverkill regulars recognized their fishing as unique and developed an intimate relationship with the river that was to last a lifetime.[7]

These were glorious years for the Beaverkill. During this era, there were many fishermen who were writers of angling books, magazines, sporting journals, and outdoor columns for newspapers, as well as colorful characters, fly tiers, storytellers, fishing guides, and fly-fishing experts. They mingled on verandas; in front of spacious fireplaces at the Campbell Inn, Roscoe House, and Rockland House; or at Frank Keener's Antrim Lodge, which enjoyed a special relationship with angling writers.

Behind the bar at the Antrim was a huge mounted brown trout, with several others lining the walls. The bar was known as "Keener's Pool," not just because it was such a favorite watering hole of fishermen, who often stood two and three deep waiting for a drink, but also because of the fabulous tales that were told of big trout that were caught or lost, or of fish that no one could catch that haunted a certain pool. All fishermen and many locals knew that the largest trout in the Beaverkill were caught in Keener's Pool.

During the 1920s and 1930s, many of the biggest names in sporting or angling literature were casting their flies on the surface waters of pools that their writings would enshrine, such as Barnhart's, Hendrickson's, Ferdon's, and Mountain Pool; men such as John Taintor Foote, Louis Rhead, Eugene V. Connett III, George La Branche, Corey Ford, William Schaldach, Ray Holland, and Alfred W. Miller (Sparse Grey Hackle.)

Eugene V. Connett III (1891–1969) was an avid fly fisher who spent many days along the Beaverkill and Willowemoc. He contributed fishing articles to sporting journals and magazines at least as early as 1916, when he promoted dry-fly fishing on the pages of *Forest and Stream*. Connett also contributed to *Field & Stream, Country Life*, the *American Angler,* and the *Sportsman,* and he wrote several books on fishing, the most popular being *Any Luck?* Published in 1933, *Any Luck?* included fishing tactics, equipment, casting, flies, and personal experiences, and a chapter titled "The Willowemoc, New York."

Connett was a frequent visitor to DeBruce, and he writes of staying at comfortable inns and fishing the upper Willowemoc and lower Beaverkill. In the chapter on flies, he highly praised Rube Cross and Catskill dry flies and claims that in twenty years of dry-fly fishing, the Quill Gordon has been the most "continuously successful" fly on brown trout waters.

Connett is best remembered as the founder, in 1926, of Derrydale Press, the premier American publisher of sporting books. Derrydale specialized in printing limited editions of books on angling, shooting, and other field sports. The first title to carry the Derrydale imprint was a book written by Connett in 1927, titled *Magic Hours Wherein We Cast a Fly Here and There.* Books published by Derrydale Press are still highly valued, especially with collectors, who pay several hundred dollars and more for copies.

Ray Holland was the editor-in-chief of *Field & Stream* and was, at times, accompanied on fishing trips by John Taintor Foote (1881–1950), who purchased property near the famous Covered Bridge Pool at Beaverkill in 1926. Foote was an ardent sportsman and greatly enjoyed upland bird shooting and trout fishing. By profession, he was an author, and a good one: He contributed humorous short stories and articles to publications such as *Colliers, American Magazine,* the *Saturday Evening Post* and *Field & Stream.* In addition, he was a playwright and a successful Hollywood screenwriter, especially for movies about horses, such as *Kentucky* and *Sea-Biscuit.*

John Taintor Foote wrote seventeen books, several of which were very popular with fly fishermen, including his classic *The Wedding Gift: A Fishing Story* (1924), *Fatal Gesture* (1933), *Broadway Angler* (1937), and *Anglers All* (1947). Although his fishing stories are characterized as fiction, he would include comments about the Catskills, Sullivan County, the Beaverkill, and the Esopus, places that he knew and fished. His books have stood the test of time and are still being reprinted for a new generation to enjoy.

Alfred W. Miller (1892–1983) wrote under the pseudonym Sparse Grey Hackle. For many years, he contributed fishing articles to sporting magazines, such as *Outdoor Life, Sports Illustrated,* and the *Anglers' Club Bulletin,* of which he was also the editor. In addition, Sparse contributed articles to several of New York's leading newspapers as a guest contributor for Ray Camp, Don Stillman, and *New York Times* Pulitzer Prize–winner Walter W. "Red" Smith. Sparse not only filled in for Red, but at times they spent weekends "matching wits" with trout along the Neversink.

Sparse was fascinated by the Catskills. He fished its storied streams, especially the Beaverkill and Willowemoc, for many years. He wrote of personal experiences, but he also preserved Catskill history, interviewing and writing about Herman Christian and Roy Steenrod, and their relationship with Theodore Gordon, in his still-popular *Fishless Days, Angling Nights.*

Corey Ford (1902–1969) was an outdoor writer and humorist for more than thirty years. He contributed articles to a variety of magazines, such as *Colliers,* the *Saturday Evening Post, Vanity Fair,* and the *New Yorker,* but he is perhaps best remembered for his association with *Field & Stream* and the humorous column he wrote monthly, dubbed "Minutes of the Lower Forty."

Ford was a friend of Ted Townsend, the famous game warden from Westchester County. Townsend taught Ford how to fish a floating fly and introduced him to the Beaverkill in the 1920s. Townsend was an expert with the dry fly; he tied his own flies and carried a butterfly net to capture the natural flies he found along the stream. He packed a large sewing basket containing fly-tying materials, and at streamside, he studied the naturals he caught and tied imitations of them. Barnhart's was his favorite pool, and Ted was commonly seen sitting on the stream bank tying a dry fly, fussing with the color so that it matched the natural that was coming off the water.

Townsend and Ford often stayed at Ed Ferdon's River View Inn, which overlooked the Beaverkill, just downstream of Roscoe. Corey Ford learned to fish a dry fly at Barnhart's Pool and wrote about the "friendly boarding house" and all the great pools along the Beaverkill in an article titled "Profile of a Trout Stream."

Years later, he would recall the pleasant times he spent along the Beaverkill in a memorable article titled "The Best-Loved Trout Stream of Them All." He wrote warmly of his days along the stream and spoke for many when he stated: "A great trout stream like the Beaverkill is a legend, a fly book filled with memories, a part of the lives of all the devoted anglers, living or dead, who ever held a taut line in its current."[8]

During the 1920s, William J. Schaldach (1896–1982) was one of America's best-known artist/outdoor writers, and through his articles and artwork, he contributed significantly to the lore of the Beaverkill. Schaldach fished the stream for the first time in 1922, and from then until 1934, he spent from two weeks to three months of every fishing season in the Roscoe area. Having spent so much time on the Beaverkill, he got to know its waters intimately, and whenever he wrote about the famous river, he did so with warmth and admiration.

Bill Schaldach came to New York in 1919. During the day, he sold tackle for a sporting goods firm, and at night, he studied art. At first he began fishing for trout in the nearby streams of Westchester County, primarily the East and West Branches of the Croton River.

During these years he met and became friends with a group of sportsmen that included the well-known game protector Ted Townsend, who had a reputation for being an excellent dry-fly fisherman, and Les Petrie, an above-average trout fisherman who tied "exquisite" dry flies. Townsend and Petrie were regulars on the Beaverkill, and it was not long before Schaldach was joining them. He, too, became enamored with the river.

Schaldach began writing and illustrating for *Forest and Stream*, the highly respected sporting magazine, in the early 1920s; he later became an associate editor with *Field & Stream* when the two magazines merged. At *Field & Stream,* he worked with Ray Holland, who promoted him to managing editor when Schaldach was still in his twenties. He became an associate editor and wrote about hunting, fishing, and conservation, and he penned a regular fishing column. Occasionally, he employed his artistic skills and contributed a cover for the magazine.

In 1944, Schaldach authored *Currents & Eddies,* a book that featured his beautiful artwork and his reminiscences of the Beaverkill. In a chapter titled "The Bountiful Beaverkill," he gives a fine description of all of the famous pools downstream of Roscoe and recalls the "remarkable sport" he enjoyed there, referring to the 1920s and the 1930s as the "golden era."

Schaldach also contributed articles to magazines such as *Esquire, Outdoor Life, True,* and *American Forests.* He illustrated many books and published a few of his own, notably *Fish by Schaldach* (1937), *Coverts & Casts* (1943), *Currents & Eddies* (1944), *Upland Gunning* (1946), and

The Wind on Your Cheek (1972). As an artist, he was a watercolorist and pen-and-ink illustrator. His art is distinctive, and many of his works were scenes along the Beaverkill, where he often sketched at places like Barnhart's or Hendrickson's, pools he often fished when he put down his pencil. One of his most beautiful watercolors is a painting of a brook trout titled *Trout Rising to a Fly* as it appears in *William Schaldach: Artist Author Sportsman*.

In *Currents & Eddies*, Schaldach writes of "Pop" Robbins, whom he fished with many times, and describes as the "dean of the Beaverkill." Richard D. "Pop" Robbins (1863–1937) was a wealthy broker from Brooklyn who began fishing the stream on weekends and vacations, when it contained only native brook trout.

When the Fly Fishers Club of Brooklyn was formed in 1895, Robbins was a founding member. He enjoyed fishing their club water, which was located on the upper Beaverkill between Roscoe and the hamlet of Beaverkill. Poor health and dwindling finances forced Robbins into early retirement. He settled in Roscoe and became a guide on the waters he had fished during better times. He opted to spend his remaining days living near the Beaverkill, and he adopted a more simple life, renting a room in a boardinghouse a short distance from Junction Pool. Pop also worked at odd jobs and eked out a living that included waiting on tables as well as guiding trout fishermen.

Knowledgeable and kindhearted, he passed on his fly-fishing knowledge to more than one generation of fly fishers, fly tiers, and angling writers. He was especially popular with the young beginner fly fisherman, who fondly called him Pop and listened to his every word about trout, flies, tackle, and the methods he used along a river he loved.

Robbins fished the Beaverkill, which he called the grandest trout river on earth, for half a century and was known as a fine gentleman and a great angler. He had fished the Beaverkill before and after the introduction of brown trout, and there was never any hesitance on his part over whether the fish was good or bad; he saw brown trout as the "salvation" of the Beaverkill, especially because of its habit of surface feeding, which required the practice of dry-fly fishing.

Pop adopted the tactic early, but also being innovative, he fished a combination wet and dry fly that was said to be deadly. He would tie a tiny wet fly on the tippet and a Bivisible on a dropper about 18 inches above it, letting the flies drift naturally in the current and using the dry fly as a strike indicator.

After coming to Roscoe, the physical ailments that reversed his fortunes and lifestyle worsened, and he became crippled with arthritis. The joints of his hands and feet grew grossly swollen, and his fingers became fixed in distorted positions. He found it difficult to perform even simple tasks. Although he could hardly get around, he never stopped fishing his beloved Beaverkill.

He had to force his fly rod into his twisted hand, but his gnarled fingers would not allow him to tie on a fly. In his last years, he often sat along the banks of Ferdon's or the Forks (Junction Pool) and patiently waited for someone to come along and tie on a fly, usually a big Bivisible or Fan-Wing, something he could still see on the mirrored surface of the big river.

Even though he was in constant pain, Pop Robbins never lost his kind and generous disposition. Before he died, in the winter of 1937, he expressed a desire to be buried in the cemetery overlooking the junction of the Willowemoc and Beaverkill, "so I can look up the Willowemoc, down the Big Beaverkill and across to the Little River."[9] His wish was carried out, but for many years he lay buried in an unmarked grave.

In 1953, a small group of Beaverkill regulars who could not stand to be away from the river very long began to meet, each year, during the winter in Roscoe, just to be near the Beaverkill. The group called themselves the Angler's Reunion Club, and they met each January for three days at the Antrim Lodge. They dined and reminisced about the past season, the fly hatches, new fly rods, and old friends who were no longer with them. The men were "dedicated to conservation and protection of the historic Beaverkill."[10]

Over the years, the annual pilgrimage to the Antrim drew noted wildlife photographers, artists, outdoor writers, nationally known angling authors, fly-fishing experts, and fly tiers. In 1956, eighty members convened at the Antrim, and a small group visited the River View Cemetery to pay homage to Pop Robbins. A wreath was placed at his grave site, and a poem was read in memory of this long-forgotten friend of the Beaverkill. That day they decided to start a fund for a proper headstone to mark the site.

The group fulfilled its promise. On an open hillside is a headstone etched with a leaping trout chasing a mayfly and the inscription DICK "POP" ROBBINS, 1863–1937. If indeed Pop Robbins's spirit can look down upon these great waters, then he has seen countless trout fishers who, like he, have been lured and charmed by the waters of the Beaverkill.

MANAGING THE FISHERIES

The demand on trout resources had always been greater than streams could naturally produce. Even when, in the late 1870s, the Fish Commission began to replenish streams with domestic or hatchery-raised fish, fishing pressure continued to be greater than the trout populations of Catskill streams—or, for that matter, streams throughout the state—could withstand.

The stocking of streams by applications from individuals, farmers, sportsmen, resort owners, landowners, or anyone desiring trout fry or fingerlings continued into the 1920s. There was no charge for the trout; applicants only need agree to receive the cans of fish and arrange for their distribution. For a half-century, this system stayed in effect with little or no thought as to where the trout were being stocked or to the ecology of the streams the fish were planted in.

There was growing concern, however, about the efficiency of the practice, and news releases were issued warning sportsmen against planting trout in streams that contained pickerel, bass, or walleye. Trout were, at times, simply dumped in the nearest stream when transportation to their destination was too difficult.

It was recognized that some waters received too many fish, whereas others received too few. There was growing concern that trout were being placed in streams where there was no knowledge of the stream's biology or rate of reproduction.

In the early years, there was little progress toward monitoring or supervising streams that were receiving hatchery trout. And it was widely held that "Nature" was not as efficient as man in hatching and rearing trout, and that young-of-the-year fish of all species would survive almost everywhere in practically any quantity.

It was believed that there were enough trout being produced for replenishing the streams, but that many were being wasted through improper stocking, as trout were often placed in unproductive or unsuitable waters. There were also streams that were heavily stocked that had self-maintaining wild trout populations; the added fish did not necessarily improve the fishing, but could make it even worse. The old practice of streams being stocked by individuals who simply applied for trout and dumped them into a stream was deemed a serious problem.

During the 1920s and 1930s, the Conservation Department placed greater emphasis on the "scientific planting" of trout; it was believed that this was the only way to achieve the best results. The department began an education campaign, issuing publications that instructed individuals on how to stock fish and stating that it was not the number of trout stocked that was important, but rather, how and where they were planted.

The Conservation Department also urged fish and game clubs and associations to get involved with stocking, as they believed that there would be better cooperation with groups of organized sportsmen than individuals, and they sent "experts" out to speak to clubs on the proper methods of stocking.

An example of the cooperation between sportsmen and the department surfaced on August 23, 1930, when the fish car *Adirondack,* with 180 cans of brown trout fingerlings aboard, was in a train wreck about 14 miles from Kingston. The derailment would have proved fatal to the trout were it not for the assistance of Ulster County sportsmen.

Charles Finch, secretary of the Ulster County Fish and Game Association, and Fred Housman, president of the Phoenicia Fish and Game Association, were notified and came to the aid of the fish. With members of their clubs and other volunteers, the trout were removed from the wreck and distributed into suitable waters of Ulster County.

One of the advancements made toward better stocking practices was the use of trucks by the hatcheries. Some streams were far from railroad communication and were best reached by this method. Trout carried on the trucks were stocked by department employees who were more knowledgeable about water temperatures, oxygen, and pH.

New York State has a proud and lengthy history in the field of fish culture and fisheries management. The first attempt made to manage New York's fisheries resources was in 1868, with the formation of the Board of Commissioners of Fisheries. Chapter 285 of the Laws of 1868 authorized "an Act to appoint Commissioners of Fisheries for the State of New York," and Seth Green, Robert Barnwell Roosevelt, and Horatio Seymour were the first members.

The practice of hatching and raising trout began in New York State as early as 1859, when Stephen Ainsworth began breeding trout near West Bloomfield in upstate Ontario County. A few years later, Seth Green made great advances in fish propagation at his hatchery along Caledonia Creek and became the most successful fish culturist in America.

Other notable men with international reputations in fish culture who were associated with the New York State Fish Commission were A. Nelson Cheney (1846–1901) and Tarleton H. Bean (1846–1916). Green, Cheney, and Bean wrote extensively for sporting magazines and journals, primarily on fish culture, and in so doing, informed the public on the problems and successes associated with fisheries resources.

Cheney was a passionate angler who, in 1895, was selected to fill the position of state fish culturist. An authority on fish and fishing, he was an early contributor to the popular journal *Forest and Stream,* of which he was the fishing editor for about nine years, writing a column titled "Angling Notes." In addition to his many articles, he coauthored, with his close friend Charles F. Orvis, *Fishing with the Fly* (1883), a collection of fishing stories by noted anglers. A seemingly timeless work, the book was republished more than a hundred years later, in 1986.

Tarleton H. Bean became state fish culturist in 1906 and held the position until his death in 1916. Like Cheney, he too enjoyed the respect of his peers as an authority on fish, and he contributed greatly to American ichthyology. A prolific writer, Bean was a frequent contributor to *Forest and Stream,* and he published *Food and Game Fishes of New York* (1902) and *Catalogue of the Fishes of New York* (1903). Before being employed by New York State, Tarleton Bean was the first curator of fishes for the Smithsonian Institute; he also worked for the U.S. Fish Commission for several years.

In these early years, much of the focus of the Fish Commission was on propagation, building hatcheries, raising trout, and replenishing streams. A more comprehensive approach to the problem of a declining trout population and the ever-increasing demand for better trout fishing did not occur until the 1920s, and New York State was at the forefront of a more scientific approach to managing the fisheries.

DR. EMMELINE MOORE

During these years in which fisheries management in America would make great strides, the New York State fisheries program was led by a highly capable scientist, Emmeline Moore (1872–1963). Emmeline Moore was born and raised on a farm in Batavia, Genesee County, in western New York. Even as a child, she showed interest in natural history and the flora and fauna of nearby wetlands; as a young adult, she earned a B.A. from Cornell University and a year later she received an M.A. from Wellesley. In 1914, she studied under noted fish culturist George Embody at Cornell, where she earned her Ph.D.

In April 1926, the state legislature appropriated $15,000 from the conservation fund to be used by the Conservation Commission to begin a program of biological surveys of all of the watersheds throughout the state "to determine the most practical methods of increasing fish production."

The Conservation Commission began the

Dr. Emmeline Moore. The American Fisheries Society.

surveys of the different watersheds throughout the state in 1926, with scientists hired from universities to carry out the work. Moore headed the landmark fisheries research and management program. The fieldwork included temperature, volume of flow, habitat evaluation, quantitative food studies, fish-population estimates, and, among other things, evaluation of stocking policies. The purposes of the surveys were "to determine the most practical methods of increasing fish production."[11]

Moore began her career with the commission in 1920 and was New York's first investigator-biologist in fish culture. She was truly a pioneer and was one of the first to enter the field of biological research. Her leadership in a program aimed at increasing the productivity of the Lake George fishery led to her appointment as chief aquatic biologist and director of the New York State Biological Surveys.

The science of fisheries management was in its infancy. One of the most important objectives of the biological surveys was to develop an improved stocking policy for hatchery-reared fish based on field studies of each body of water and to acquire essential information that would lead to better management of the state's fisheries resources.

The surveys provided valuable data, a kind of blueprint for a long-term fisheries program. The unit responsible for the scientific investigations of the watersheds was known as the Bureau of Biological Survey.

The fieldwork included collecting various biological and physical data relative to fish production, such as distribution and abundance, water chemistry, pollution, temperature, volume of flow, habitat evaluation, quantitative food studies, and the effects of disease.

After a watershed was surveyed, stocking decisions were made based on the scientific study of the individual character and conditions of the stream, including temperatures, food supply, existing fish population, growth rates, reproduction, pollution, and other data relative to conditions

Dr. Emmeline Moore, seated in the middle of the second row, and her staff.
New York State Conservation Department Annual Report, 1929.

affecting fish life. An inventory was taken of all species present, and the data that was collected established historical baseline information that is still useful today.

Between 1926 and 1939, New York State conducted the most comprehensive scientific surveys of any state's water resources, and Dr. Moore supervised and edited all fourteen watershed reports. She is credited with forming a bond with many universities and colleges around the country by hiring and encouraging numbers of students and faculty to collect summer data on these watershed investigations. She also managed to publish technical papers on fish culture and fish diseases, and in 1927, she became the first woman president of the American Fisheries Society.

The staff in the field consisted of scientists under the direction of Moore, who was selected to supervise the surveys after a search of the United States and Canada. "[S]he was the best qualified individual long before 'women's lib.' She had impeccable credentials in science," recalled Cecil Heacox, in his *The Education of an Outdoorsman*. He described Moore as "a prim gray-haired lady of awesome dignity."[12]

At a time when women professionals were unheard of, Dr. Moore served as chief aquatic biologist for the Conservation Department, which was superseded by the Conservation Commission from 1932 until 1944. In addition to setting the standards for a professional fisheries staff, she established regional fisheries districts. The purpose of the districts was to maintain closer contact with anglers and "their problems" and to meet the need for closer contact with specific watersheds and their changing environments.

Every year, from the time the biological surveys were initiated in 1926, colored plates were made of the fishes of New York State. The first of these paintings were the work of the artist Ellen Edmonson, who traveled in the field, skillfully captured the scientific detail and natural colors of the fish, and reproduced them with "accuracy and distinction."

Moore saw the addition of the color reproductions as a highly important contribution to the survey reports and claimed that they enhanced the reports and aided educationally in the identification of fish species."

Hugh Chrisp, an equally talented artist, also contributed

Artist Ellen Edmonson at work in the field. Biological Survey of the Champlain Watershed, 1929.

to the collection. Upon completion of the surveys, these "reproductions of freshwater species" were to be assembled into "an illustrated work" titled *The Fishes of New York State:* "a volume for which there is real need in advancing information of our native species of fishes," stated Moore.[13] These color plates, though painted more than seventy-five years ago, are still being used by New York State for fish identification and educational purposes.

There were no fisheries biologists in government before 1926; the New York State Conservation Commission and the biological surveys became a training ground for fisheries scientists. In addition to Emmeline Moore, who became nationally famous for editing and directing the watershed surveys, many of those working on the biological surveys would go on to make significant contributions to the field of fisheries science and management. Among the many who became well known in their field of study were George C. Embody, Albert S. Hazzard, James G. Needham, John R. Greeley, Paul R. Needham, and Karl F. Lagler.

Known as the dean of American ichthyologists in the 1930s, Dr. George Embody began his work in fish culture and fishery biology at Cornell in 1911. He became the university's first professor of fisheries science and is recognized as one of the earliest leaders in fisheries ecology. Embody is remembered as a pioneer in fish culture, in trout field studies, and for his work in fish population harvest and dynamics.

Dr. James Needham was appointed professor of limnology at Cornell in 1906 and was one of the most respected and revered biologists at the university. Needham's principal interest was in the aquatic insects of streams. He and his son, Dr. Paul R. Needham, who also taught at Cornell and worked on the surveys, produced *A Guide to the Study of Fresh-Water Biology* (1938). The work was an indispensable textbook for students of limnology.

James Needham authored or coauthored more than a dozen books. He, along with Embody, assisted Paul Needham with advice and criticism on his manuscript *Trout Streams* (1938). This book is a classic guide, containing important and reliable information on trout, trout foods, and stream biology, and discusses fisheries research and management.

Albert S. Hazzard received his Ph.D. at Cornell in 1931 and worked as an associate aquatic biologist with the U.S. Bureau of Fisheries. In 1935, he became chief fisheries biologist and director of the Institute for Fisheries Research, Michigan Department of Conservation, a position he held until 1955. Following his career at Michigan, he became an assistant executive director of the Pennsylvania Fish Commission (1955–1963).

Dr. Hazzard was a strong proponent of stream or habitat improvement structures and was the author of numerous scientific papers and *Natural History of Fishes, Ecology of Fishes,* and *Fish Management Methods.* He is best known as an advocate of catch-and-release (no-kill) trout fishing. Long before the idea was accepted or became popular, as early as 1952, he proposed, "[C]atch all the trout you can but don't kill them; put them back."[14] At the time, this option as a fisheries management regulation to improve the fishing was unheard of, and his suggestion was "deemed beyond belief."

John R. Greeley was an instructor in zoology at Cornell at the time he participated in his first survey in 1926. In the early 1930s, he was with the Michigan Institute for Fisheries Research, but returned to New York to participate in other watershed surveys. While with the Michigan Department of Conservation, he coauthored *Methods for the Improvement of Michigan Trout Streams* (1932). In time, his career took him back to New York and to the Conservation Department. Dr. Greeley eventually held the same position as Dr. Moore: chief aquatic biologist.

Karl Lagler worked on the 1935 survey of the Delaware and Susquehanna watersheds, which included most of the streams in the western Catskills. After receiving his M.S. at Cornell in 1936, he went to the University of Michigan and received his Ph.D. (zoology) in 1940. In addition to being employed by the New York State Conservation Department, he served as a research associate for the Institute for Fisheries Research, Michigan Department of Conservation, and was chairman of the Department of Fisheries at Michigan for many years. His *Freshwater Fishery Biology* (1952) is considered a classic text and reference book for students, teachers, and fisheries professionals and has been reprinted numerous times.

The biological surveys were a landmark undertaking and were the first step to better manage the state's fisheries resources. Investigations included many of the biological and physical factors associated with fish production, such as water temperature studies, water chemical tests, and depth, flow, pool, and shade conditions. Also appraised were the distribution of fish species, their abundance, the adaptability of introduced species, quantitative food studies, aquatic vegetation and plankton, and the presence of diseases.

The surveys recommended the size, species, and number of trout to be stocked. This annoyed some anglers, especially those who preferred the old method of stocking unlimited trout on top of existing populations. The surveys helped to eliminate the stocking of harmful species. They reduced the number of trout stocked in streams with wild populations; increased the efficiency of stocking by recommending species, numbers, and sizes to be stocked; and enabled hatcheries to better plan their production by using simplified stocking distribution procedures rather than the application system.

The biological surveys replaced the philosophy that the more trout stocked in the stream, the better the fishing. They placed a more scientific emphasis on trout management, providing a more thorough knowledge of the fisheries resources. Stocking policies were now aimed at a stream's carrying capacity and angling pressure; waters too warm to support a trout fishery were not stocked. Fisheries biologists began looking at the trout's environment and what it took to make or sustain wild trout populations. New York State was the first state to make an inventory of its fisheries resources, and the program served as a blueprint for other states.

The 1930s

THE CATSKILL STYLE: THE NEXT GENERATION

Toward the end of the 1920s, a second generation of Catskill School fly tiers was forming in a vacant room over a movie house in Roscoe. Walter Dette (1907–1994) and Harry Darbee (1906–1983) knew little about tying trout flies, but they were young men and eager to learn. Walt was twenty-two and Harry, a year younger.

Perhaps they were inspired by the stir that the fishing season brought to town, or maybe they saw the demand for dry flies that accompanied fishing tourists. These were the years that artist/author Bill Schaldach described as the "golden era," and Roscoe was a hub of trout-fishing activity. Located along the banks of two famous trout streams, the quiet little village came alive during the summer months, when swarms of fishing tourists converged upon its fishing resorts and boardinghouses.

Railway travel in the mid-1920s was decreasing because of improved roads and bus travel, but the O. & W. still ran the Mountain Limited, the Roscoe Express, and Saturday and Sunday Specials. It was a common sight to see eager passengers disembark at the railroad station carrying a suitcase in one hand and a fly-rod case and creel in the other.

Many more fishermen now traveled improved roadways by automobile and filled the town on weekends. All over Roscoe, fishing was a topic for discussion: in eateries, taverns and stores, the barbershop, bank, and post office. Even farmers who boarded fishermen were not exempt from having an opinion about how good or bad the fishing was and which flies were best for taking brown trout.

Walt Dette and Harry Darbee were best friends since the seventh grade. They hunted and fished together and started out, like most boys, fishing with worms in small streams for native brook trout. As they grew older, they changed tactics and switched from worms and grasshoppers on tributaries to wet and dry flies on the "Big Beaverkill." They developed a life-long love of trout flies and fly fishing.

Harry learned to fly fish by tagging along with local experts, especially Pop Robbins, who took a liking to Harry and thought of him as a "fishing son." The old man taught him about the Beaverkill, the habits of its trout, and an appreciation for the river's ecology.

Walt learned about fly fishing on his own. He watched men practicing casting on the lawn of the Roscoe House and those who stood waist deep in Cairns, Barnhart's, or Ferdon's floating dry flies to rising trout. He learned by watching others. Both young men were friends with Corey Ford, and they often fished with the outdoor writer along the Willowemoc, where it flowed through Roscoe. Years later, in a memorable article titled "The Best-Loved Trout Stream of Them All," Ford reminisced about the 1920s and recalled: "I can still see Walt splashing across the rapids in dungarees and high leather boots—he always scorned waders, and would wallow through water up to his waist in the most frigid weather—and casting one or another of his homemade flies accurately into the jaws of a rising trout."[1]

In 1927, Walt and Harry decided to enter the professional world of fly tying and rented space above the movie theater in Roscoe. They were joined by Winifred Ferdon (1909–1998), who was dating Walt. Winnie was the daughter of Edwin and Mary Ferdon, who owned and operated the River View Inn, a popular fishing resort overlooking the Beaverkill, just downstream of Junction Pool. Winnie did not know any more about tying flies than Walt or Harry, but she grew up around trout fishermen, and she did know something about fly fishing.

The trio learned to tie by taking apart the flies of Rube Cross, who was, at the time, the most well-known fly tier in the country. They sat at a work bench in front of a bay window over the theater. Walt would carefully unwind each turn of thread, and Harry and Winnie took notes. Then they would each try their hand at tying a fly. They learned well enough to sell some flies, and they made a few dollars rewinding fly rods. However, their careers as professional fly tiers did not last, and each went out and pursued other interests, but only for a short while.

Walt and Winnie married, and she took a job at the bank; Walt was working at the drug store. Harry became a short-order cook, and he trapped, guided fishermen, and dug ginseng. He even left the Catskills for awhile and became a traveling salesman.

After awhile, the Dettes moved to the River View Inn and helped in its operations. They tied flies and sold them to inn guests from a display case set up by Winnie's father. Their first catalog was produced in 1929 and was titled "Dry Flies, W. C. Dette, Roscoe, N. Y." In 1931, they took over the inn, but the Great Depression had an effect on its business, and they closed the place the following summer.

Employment in the Catskills was never easy, and Walt and Winnie decided to tie flies professionally on a full-time basis. In 1933, they received a letter from Harry Darbee, asking if he could join them in their fly-tying venture, and once more the trio was reunited in the business of fly making.

This time their adventure proved more successful. They tied retail and took special orders. They also tied large orders of flies wholesale for sporting goods dealers. At one point, they decided they needed someone to sort hackle in order to speed up their production, so in the spring of 1934, on the recommendation of Pop Robbins, they hired Elsie Bivins (1912–1980), the daughter of the woman who rented Pop his room in Roscoe.

Elsie became proficient at sorting hackle, and she asked Harry to teach her to tie flies. A romance ensued, and soon after learning to tie, she and Harry were married. Shortly thereafter, Harry Darbee ended the partnership with the Dettes, having decided that he and Elsie would now share their talents under the name of E. B. & H. A. Darbee.

Walt and Winnie Dette, ca. 1940s. Mary Dette Clark.

THE DETTES

The Dettes furthered their reputation as fly tiers, and in 1937, they tied at the National Sportsman's Show at New York's Grand Central Palace. Every year, thousands of outdoors men and women attended the show, and audiences stood three and four deep to watch the Dettes tie their favorite trout patterns.

Walt Dette was a perfectionist. He was precise with his proportions, especially about the length of the hackle on his dry flies. His Catskill-style dries were tied, some said, better than Rube Cross's. Walt was disciplined about fly proportions, and each of his flies were exact duplicates of the other; he tied with a consistency rarely seen in other tiers.

After a couple of years, the Dettes' business was successful enough that they no longer tied wholesale for dealers; in fact, they hired two or three additional fly tiers. This was the only time Walt and Winnie were dependent on fly tying as their sole source of income.

In 1939, Winnie returned to her job at the bank, and a couple of years later, Walt went to the city to work in a defense plant. After the war, he found employment as a carpenter and then was hired by the New York City Board of Water Supply. Although they both found full-time employment elsewhere, the Dettes never stopped tying flies professionally.

They had a fly shop in the Esso gas station on Route 17 just outside of Roscoe, and they continued to sell their flies there until 1955, when they moved their operations to a room in front of their home on Cottage Street. They sold their flies retail and took special mail orders from all across the country. Many of their walk-in customers were fly-fishing regulars whom they had known for years and who only fished with their flies. The most popular patterns tied were Hendricksons, Quill Gordons, and Light Cahills, as well as Hair-Wing and Fan-Wing Royal Coachmans.

The Dettes tied in the traditional Catskill style and required large amounts of good-quality natural blue dun hackle. This was always difficult to obtain and necessitated their keeping a small flock of roosters and hens at the rear of their home. Throughout the years, they created and recreated various fly patterns for their customers, the most popular being the Coffin Fly, which Walt developed with Ted Townsend in 1929. The fly is tied to imitate the large Green Drake spinner found along the Beaverkill in early June. It was originally tied with a body of white polar bear fur, wings with black hackle tips, yellow badger hackle, and a tail of wood duck flank feathers.

Throughout their lives, Walt and Winnie were recognized as premier fly tiers; their work was featured in many outdoor magazines, newspapers, and books on angling. An excellent example of

Mary Dette Clark. Courtesy Barbara Jaffe.

their fly-tying skills can be found in A. J. McClane's *The Practical Fly Fisherman,* published in 1953. Featured are color plates of dry flies, wet flies, nymphs, streamers, and bucktails tied in their exquisite style.

Today, the tradition of tying "Dette flies" is carried on by their daughter, Mary Dette Clark. Mary, like her mother before her, was born in the River View Inn overlooking the Beaverkill. She grew up listening to trout-fishing conversations and was surrounded by fly-tying hooks, feathers, and furs, and she watched her parents tie flies and greet customers with information on water temperatures, stream conditions, and which flies were hatching.

Mary learned to tie at a young age, but did not tie flies seriously until she was about twenty-three years of age. At first she tied from her home on Long Island and mailed flies to her parents, who placed them in the display cases of their shop.

Following the death of her parents, Mary continues to operate the business founded so many years before by Walt and Winnie. She ties practically year-round, living in Roscoe during the summer months, but preferring to spend the winters in the more hospitable climate of Long Island. Mary follows the tradition of tying Catskill-style dry flies—such as Quill Gordons, Red Quills, and Hendricksons—and she ties custom orders. Like her father, she is a perfectionist and has a following of regular customers who will only fish with her meticulously tied trout flies.

E. B. AND H. A. DARBEE

When the Darbees began tying flies professionally, they did so under the name of E. B. & H. A. Darbee. There was a stipulation in the dissolved partnership agreement that Harry had with the Dettes that stated that if Harry went into the fly-tying business, he could not do so in Roscoe; so the newlyweds moved to nearby Livingston Manor.

Harry was born in Roscoe on April 7, 1906. That he had an interest in fly fishing and fly tying is not surprising; his ancestors were among the earliest to settle along the "Great Beaver Kill," in the 1790s and were the first to cater to the earliest fishing tourists. His great-uncle was Chester Darbee, friend and angling companion of Thad Norris, Henry Kirke Brown, and others who participated in the "Noonday Roast," as mentioned in Norris's *American Angler's Book.* The Darbees owned the land bordering the famous Forks, or Junction Pool, and the small stream that empties into the grand pool is named Darbee Brook.

Harry had a lifetime love of the natural world. This was no doubt inspired by John Burroughs, whom he met as a youngster when Harry's family lived briefly in West Park, not too far from Burroughs's home. Harry became friendly with the famous naturalist, joined him on nature walks, and was fascinated by his knowledge of the region's flora and fauna. Harry had great respect for Burroughs, and throughout his life, one of his prized possessions was a book Burroughs gave him on his birthday, titled *American Boy's Book of Bugs, Butterflies and Beetles.*

While his family lived at West Park, Harry spent his summers at his grandfather's house in Lew Beach, where the Beaverkill is joined by Shin Creek. He caught his first trout in Shin Creek, a stream he always said contained the prettiest wild brown trout in the Catskills. The Darbees moved back to Roscoe when Harry was ten years old, and his interest in trout fishing and the outdoors intensified.

Elsie Bivins was born in the town of Neversink, far up in the headwaters of the Willowemoc, in a region that was sparsely settled but popular with trout fishermen. She also came from a family involved with trout fishing: Her parents owned and operated a trout-fishing preserve that was a part of the water leased by the Willowemoc Club, the first fishing club in the Catskills. Elsie's parents boarded fishermen, and their water was known to Theodore Gordon and all who took their fly fishing seriously.

In the early days, the majority of flies tied by the Darbees were sold wholesale to dealers at two thirds the retail price. Most of these flies were bucktails and wet flies. Years later, Harry recalled one order that was for eight hundred dozen wet flies! The work was tiring and tedious; they often tied a gross of a single pattern, but by the time they finished the pattern, they had it mastered.

Harry had great hands for tying flies; they were small and fine and well suited to the delicate tasks associated with fly tying. Elsie possessed a sharp eye for color and quality hackle selection, and they both could wing a fly as quickly and expertly as anyone. The Darbees became accomplished professionals, experts with feathers, furs, and fly proportions. They continued improving their skills, becoming among the best of their trade.[2]

During the 1930s, the price of dry flies increased, and the Darbees began specializing in floating flies. Harry had taken apart the flies of Herman Christian, Rube Cross, Roy Steenrod, and even the legendary Theodore Gordon; he and Elsie tied in the traditional Catskill style. And their first printed catalog emphasized: "The dry flies listed in this catalog are the finest flies possible to produce and are dressed after the manner made famous by the late Theodore Gordon; who paid especial attention to tying the fly so it would balance on the water in the position of a natural insect."

The Darbees began tying dry flies on odd-numbered hooks. Almost everyone tied in sizes 10, 12, 14, and 16, but their flies were tied on hook sizes 11, 13, and 15. "People knew there was something different about my flies," Harry told angling writer Al McClane, "but they couldn't quite figure it out. It was a good gimmick."[3]

The Darbees also developed a reputation for tying various patterns of deer-hair-bodied dry flies; their flies were uniformly dense and evenly shaped. These were flies tied by spinning deer hair on the hook shank, then trimming them down, leaving a full-bodied appearance. The hair, being hollow, allowed them to float extremely well in fast water or in the riffles at the heads of pools. They worked as a team when they produced these patterns; Harry tied on the tail and spun the bodies, using deer, caribou, or bighorn sheep, and Elsie did the trimming. After a number were accumulated, they both tied on wings and hackle, and customers found it difficult, if not impossible, to tell their flies apart.

Harry and Elsie were meticulous with their proportions, and they were particular about the color and quality of the hackle they used in tying traditional Catskill-style dry flies, such as Quill Gordons, Hendricksons, Red Quills, and Light Cahills. And like Rube Cross, they never deviated, even slightly, when tying Catskill patterns. Their beautifully tied flies enhanced their reputation, and fly fishermen began seeking out Darbee-tied flies. Like the Dettes and Rube Cross, they, too, developed a following of loyal customers who wanted only their flies:

Elsie and Harry Darbee, ca. 1940s. Courtesy of Judie Darbee Smith.

One of our biggest customers was Joseph P. Knapp, chairman of Crowell-Collier Publishing Company. He owned 4½ miles of the Beaverkill, leased a stretch of the Natashquan in Labrador, and fished all over the world. I remember one day while he was picking up an order of flies, Knapp said, "It takes a lot of flies to make a living. If the time comes when you and Elsie don't have orders, my friends and I will take all you can tie." We thought that was the kindest thing anyone had ever said to us, especially in the depths of the Depression, but we were able to make ends meet without having to take advantage of his offer.[4]

During the late 1930s and early 1940s, the Darbees lived along the upper Beaverkill between Turnwood and Lew Beach. They then moved to Beaverkill and occupied the old post office in the spring of 1943. That fall, Harry was drafted into the U.S. Navy at the age of thirty-seven. Elsie moved to Roscoe and stayed with her mother, and continued to tie special mail orders from customers.

At the end of the war, in 1946, the Darbees acquired a house a short walk from the Willowemoc, about midway between Roscoe and Livingston Manor. They set up a fly shop at the front of the house and sold flies, fly-tying materials, rods, lines, books, and everything required of fly fishermen.

They refused to use dyed or bleached hackle when they tied Catskill-style dry flies; nor would they use furs that were tanned, preferring raw furs with their natural oils left in the hides. Harry was a big believer in natural blue dun hackle, and he was convinced that flies tied with natural dun, with its various tones and hues, reflected light in a unique way and therefore better deceived the fish. The Darbees always kept chickens and raised a large number of dun roosters of various shades, always trying to improve the quality of the hackle.

Harry and Elsie loved what they did. Their lives revolved around fly tying, fly fishing, and trout fishermen; their way of life allowed them to be together every day. They never seemed to be able to fill all of their customers' orders for flies, and almost all the flies they sold in their shop were tied by others who tied wholesale for them.

There were times when Harry would sneak away to go fishing, and sometimes Elsie would join him on an outing to the East Branch or lower Beaverkill. But otherwise, Elsie was always at her fly-tying table, and regular visitors knew that she tied far more than Harry. It was a treat to watch her place perfectly matched wood duck wings on a dry fly. One could only marvel at her abilities. When asked to perform the task slowly so that you could watch her every move, in order to learn her secret, she would do so, but no amount of watching or practicing could duplicate her skill.

Elsie took care of business. She had to, as Harry would at times give away more in one day than he sold. Making money was not part of his agenda—it just was not important to him. He had a special kindness not found in most men. Walt Dette, too, was graced with that same special quality, and it is not surprising that they were lifelong friends.

Elsie tied the majority of special orders, and Harry tended to the needs of customers. He would inform visitors about where to fish and what flies were hatching, and give advice on fly-fishing techniques. Harry was a conservationist; interspersed with his wisdom and anecdotal stories, he would preach that rivers and streams needed protection, especially from road and dam builders, gravel removers, and polluters.

The Darbees passed along a message to everyone they met that if you fished, you needed to be aware of and involved in protecting trout and their habitat, and that this was an endless fight. Fishermen had to get involved because there were always forces trying to destroy streams and their water quality.

The fly-tying skills of Harry and Elsie Darbee have been recognized by their peers and by all those involved in fly fishing. Their overall contribution to the sport is immeasurable; they and their fly-tying skills have been featured in numerous magazine and newspaper articles, as well as in more than seventy-five books on fishing and fly tying.

Harry Darbee created a few trout flies, and one of the earliest, a pattern first tied in the 1930s, is a dry-fly pattern known as Darbee's Green Egg Sac, which developed into a fly known as the Shad Fly. The pattern was used to imitate the prolific hatch of caddis that appeared on the Beaverkill each year, at about the same time shad arrived at the headwaters of the Delaware River.

Harry enjoyed tying flies with deer hair, and one of the most notable flies he is associated with is the Rat-Faced McDougal, a high-floating dry fly that is tied with a tail of ginger hackle fibers, a clipped tannish-gray deer-hair body, cream grizzly hackle tips for wings, and ginger hackle, usually in sizes 12 and 14. Harry certainly popularized the Rat-Faced McDougal, but it appears that Percy Jennings—a member of the Bush Kill Club, which is located on the Bush Kill, a Neversink tributary—is the creator of the pattern. Jennings, an avid fly fisherman and fly tier, tied the fly at least as early as 1937.

Jennings had purchased a few deer-hair bodied dry flies from Harry that he called the Straw May. The Darbees tied several patterns of this style on long-shank hooks, and in Harry's words, the fly "resembled a cross between a deer hair bass bug and an over-dressed trout fly." Jennings took the Straw May flies and altered them slightly, and tied them on smaller, regular dry-fly hooks. He tied two types: one had a "tail brown buck tail, body light grey buck tail, wings cream colored, or white with dark center, hackle points, and ginger hackle; the other pattern had a tail of brown buck tail, body dark grey buck tail, wings barred Plymouth rock hackle points, and hackle from a Rhode Island red rooster."[5]

An unusual deer-hair–bodied fly that Harry created is the Darbee's Stonefly, a large floating pattern tied to imitate the large stoneflies found along the Delaware River. The fly was featured in a June 1964 *Field & Stream* article written by A. J. McClane, titled "Best Flies for Big Trout." Harry tied the stonefly on a #10 3XL hook. He tied a small bunch of brown deer hair for the tail, gray caribou dyed yellow and trimmed rather flat for the body, two rusty-dun hackles slightly longer than the body and "laid down flat," and a small bunch of brown deer hair to form a collar, as in a Muddler Minnow.

Harry also discovered a unique style of dry fly that has been written about in magazines and books known as the Two-Feather Fly. The Two-Feather Fly was an attempt to create an ultralight dry fly to imitate the large mayflies that hatch along the lower Beaverkill, East Branch, and Delaware rivers. Standard imitations were usually tied on large hooks, sizes 8 and 10, and they were heavy and required heavier tippets of 3X or 4X. They usually landed on the water too heavily. Harry wanted a fly that was the right size, but without the bulk and weight; a fly that would land on the water softly and could be fished with a lighter tippet.

He developed a method of making a realistic detached-body fly, which required only two feathers; one was used for the tail, body, and wings, and the other for the hackle. He tied this fly on a short-shank hook and typically used flank feathers from a mallard, wood duck, or teal. By snipping out the center of the tip of the feather, he fashioned the tail; then, by stroking the fibers forward and adding a drop of cement to hold them in shape, he produced the body, which was then tied to the hook shank. The remaining portion of the feather was used for the wings. A stiff, dry-fly quality hackle was added in the conventional manner to make the fly buoyant.

The fly was practically weightless, and when cast, it landed on the water as softly and as delicately as a natural. A Two-Feather Fly floats on the surface film with grace and beauty; it looks like a real mayfly, and its silhouette or shape is very realistic. On the flat surfaces of slow-flowing pools, where trout are often wary of conventional dry flies, the Two-Feather Fly is a killing imitation.

The Two-Feather Fly was written about by A. J. McClane in *Field & Stream* in October 1960 and was also featured in an English book by John Veniard titled *Fly Tying Problems* (1970). The popularity of the fly was short-lived, which is surprising, perhaps because its style was against tradition. However, it may someday resurface; it is easy to tie, lightweight, lifelike, and fishes well in flat, glassy water.

The Darbees' fly shop was more than a place to buy trout flies; it was a place where fly fishers gathered to discuss trout fishing, their successes, or lack thereof; to gripe or boast; and to meet friends. United by fly fishing, men and women, generally of diverse backgrounds, conversed and shared angling experiences. There were wealthy clubmen and city firemen, state troopers and truck drivers, the unemployed and corporate CEOs. Bob Boyle, a friend of the Darbees and a *Sports Illustrated* editor and writer, once described the shop as follows:

It serves as a gathering in or out of season, for anglers, local characters, fishery biologists, curious tourists and wandering oddballs who come to hear Darbee hold forth on all sorts of subjects, often until dawn. The atmosphere is Cannery Row, out of Abercrombie & Fitch.[6]

ALONG THE BEAVERKILL

During the 1930s, large brown trout continued to be taken in the Beaverkill. On May 8, 1930, the *Liberty Register* reported that Ira Decker of Kerhonkson took a 23½-inch trout that weighed 5 pounds, 11 ounces on a wet fly near Lew Beach. However, the biggest trout taken in many years was brought into town ten days later by Arthur Tyler of Livingston Manor, who showed off a 30-inch brown trout that weighed 10 pounds! Tyler claimed he took the monster fish on a "light stone dry fly," but the *Liberty Register* reported that there were plenty of doubters. Veteran Beaverkill anglers refused to believe that a trout of this magnitude would succumb to a floating fly.

The trout had been seen several times along the Beaverkill and was said to be blind and injured. A rumor circulated that Tyler may have found the trout dead or dying and that he did not catch the fish as was suggested. Either way, the great fish was sent to a New York taxidermist, and when it returned, it was placed on the wall of the lobby of the Roscoe House.

Several other large brown trout made the pages of the same newspaper. In May 1933, Leo Lane of Liberty, Sullivan County, caught a huge 6-pound brown measuring 24½ inches on a Squirrel Tail fly tied by Rube Cross; the trout was caught at Lew Beach and had an 8-inch trout in its stomach! The outline of Lane's big fish (see opposite page) made the side of the Burke house (formerly Murdock's). Tracing the outline of large trout on the outside of fishing resorts was practiced in the Catskills at least as early as 1841.

In early May 1935, Charles Volke of Roscoe took a 25-inch, 5½-pound brown at Ferdon's Eddy, just downstream of Junction Pool. The following season, William Sandstrom of Highland Falls had a great day fishing in Barnhart's Pool with a bucktail, taking a 25½-inch brown trout that weighed 6 pounds and eight other trout measuring between 12 and 14 inches! In June 1937, local expert Ed Young of Liberty took an equally large 25½-inch brown that weighed 6¼ pounds from the Beaverkill, near Horton.

UP THE WILLOWEMOC

It was in the 1930s that another club appeared along the upper Willowemoc. This club was somewhat different than all others that were formed in the Catskills in that its membership was made up entirely of women. The Woman Flyfishers Club became incorporated in 1932, but did not have a clubhouse until 1937, when it leased one along the Willowemoc Creek.

The property that the club rented was the old fishing resort formerly owned by Elsie Darbee's parents. It included a mile of the Willowemoc and 265 acres, with "good grouse cover." The club also leased three additional miles of the water downstream, through the courtesy of the Willowemoc Fishing Club, of which La Branche and Hewitt were members; and they hired the man with the reputation of being the best poacher in the valley to be their stream-watcher and "guardian."

The outline of Lane's large trout on the Bourke house above Lew Beach. Judy Van Put.

There were eight founding members, but the Women Flyfishers Club increased in numbers rapidly, reaching fifty-two by 1939. From the onset, these were women who fly fished and were good at it. Members fished their waters with their families and with each other, but they especially enjoyed annual club outings, where they got together and shared meals, camaraderie, their love of fly fishing, and participated in a casting and fishing contest.

First club house. *The Woman Flyfishers Club* Fortieth Anniversary issue, autumn 1972.

The club stayed on the upper Willowemoc for ten years. In 1948, they moved to the upper Rondout and leased a 2-mile stretch of water around Sundown. Although the stream was posted, it seemed as though every time a member arrived, they ran into poachers. The club stayed for two years and then left because of the "smallness of the water" and the fact that there "were poachers at every bend." In 1950, the Woman Flyfishers Club moved to the West Branch of the Neversink, leasing a small, but comfortable clubhouse and 2 miles of stream from Wintoon Waters, part of the former Clarence Roof property.

Although the Catskills were the Woman Flyfishers Club's home waters, club members traveled all over the world in their pursuit of game fish; they did so when travel was difficult and hazardous, and accommodations lacked the comforts and the conveniences we experience today. Some members were married to men who were avid fly fishers, and along with their husbands, they owned unique stretches of private water along Catskill trout streams. Although they may have roughed it at times, members also had some remarkable and memorable outings, especially along the Beaverkill and on the waters of Margaret and Joseph Knapp.

The Knapp water was located between Lew Beach and Turnwood and was a favorite of early members, not only because of the fine fishing, but because of their midday luncheons, which were "fabulous." The Knapps entertained their guests by dining at streamside, at an opening in the woods, on a long lace-covered table with "nine silver champagne coolers." A whole salmon was flown in from Canada, and dinner would include "2 roasts of beef."

The Woman Flyfishers Club remains along the West Branch of the Neversink, and their membership still includes some of the best, most talented, and experienced fly fishers in the country.

AMERICA FINALLY GETS A FLY-FISHING ENTOMOLOGY

Even with the growing use of dry flies and the almost yearly creation of new floating fly patterns, very few fly fishers were interested in fly-fishing entomology or of the concept of exact imitation. Theodore Gordon had a strong interest, possibly because he had a connection to Halford and other English fly fishers who believed in the theory, as did Louis Rhead, who was English and did make a crude attempt to identify natural insects he found along Catskill streams with imitations he devised.

But in general, Americans, during the first thirty or forty years of using the dry fly, cared little about exact imitation or entomology. Fly hatches of aquatic insects were rarely written about or mentioned in fishing articles featured in outdoor magazines or, for that matter, in books published about fly fishing. The consensus was that flies had to be "near enough" in color, size, and shape or silhouette, and that accurate casting and presentation were the most important components to successful dry-fly fishing.

It was not until the mid-1930s that a book featuring a correlation between the natural insects and dry-fly imitations finally arrived. It is true that some of the standard dry-fly patterns then in use *were* imitations of natural fly hatches, but until Preston Jennings produced *A Book of Trout Flies,* the average fly fisherman knew little about entomology.

Preston J. Jennings (1893–1962) was the first American to write a book accurately identifying the major fly hatches found along trout streams and connect them with artificial flies. The book was published in 1935 by the Derrydale Press in a limited edition of 850 copies.

A Book of Trout Flies focuses on Catskill trout streams. Preston Jennings was an avid fly fisherman who had a great deal of experience along the mountain streams; and although he did collect samples of the natural flies, he also received assistance in gathering specimens from fellow fly fishermen Roy Steenrod and Art Flick. Jennings gathered data for several years, from 1933 to 1935, with collections being made along the Neversink, Esopus, Schoharie, Beaverkill, and the East Branch of the Delaware River.

As a fly tier, he was excellent and well-qualified to create fly patterns that best imitated the natural insects found along trout streams. Jennings created some superb imitations of natural insects that were included in his book, but he also recognized that some of the standard flies trout fishermen were using at the time were already imitations of important hatches. He included them in his work as well, such as the Quill Gordon, Light Cahill, Hendrickson, and a few others that he believed matched hatches. Two flies that have become standards in the Catskills that were created by Jennings are the Grey Fox and the American March Brown.

Jennings's work was an inspiration to others, and he set the standards they would follow. Jennings took a scientific approach to fly fishing, and *A Book of Trout Flies* became a fly-fishing classic that is still used by trout fishers today.

ART FLICK

Arthur B. Flick (1904–1985) was born in New York City, and it was there that he became interested in fishing. He was a teenager when he began fishing for tommy cod in the Hudson River off the pier at 133rd Street.

His first opportunity to fish for trout came when his parents, in 1919, purchased a small country inn deep in the Catskills, near the tiny hamlet of West Kill in the Schoharie Creek watershed. He was fifteen years old at the time, and he started out, like most youngsters, fishing with worms. His success was limited, but he learned about the habits of trout, the type of water they preferred, where they fed, and how to approach the stream cautiously.

Art Flick. Photo by Terry Ireland. Courtesy Catskill Fly Fishing Center & Museum.

Two years later, Flick moved to Kingston, a small city on the fringe of the Catskills, close enough to the Esopus Creek that he began fishing the stream whenever he had the opportunity. At about this time, he met an experienced fly fisherman who convinced him that he would get more enjoyment out of trout fishing if he fished with flies. Art's satisfaction increased dramatically once he switched, and he never forgot the man's kindness.

It was in 1934, at the age of thirty, that he moved to West Kill and took over his parents' Westkill Tavern—an attractive, neatly kept, small wooden-framed hotel located on the north side of Deep Notch, the narrow pass that separates the Esopus and Schoharie watersheds. Flick wanted to turn the resort into a haven for trout fishermen and grouse hunters.

Over the years, Flick became an authority on fly fishing and was a major contributor to the history of the sport, especially in the Catskills, where he spent most of his life. From the beginning, he got involved with conservation, through local fish and game clubs, county and state conservation groups, and any organization he believed was working toward improving and preserving the outdoor sports he loved. He not only joined organizations but became a leader in the battle to protect our hunting and fishing heritage.

He became a member of the Conservation Commissioners Advisory Council and the State Conservation Council, and as early as 1949, he contributed an article to the New York State *Conservationist* titled "Zone the trout Fisherman?" Flick proposed the idea that some streams should be restricted to fly fishing only.

Channelizing the Esopus near Big Indian; making a stream look like a road.
Survey of the Lower Hudson Watershed, 1936.

He believed that the only way that trout fishing on public waters could be maintained was by instituting special fishing regulations that restricted fishing methods, thereby providing the trout more protection. Stocking more trout was not the answer. "There is very little satisfaction in catching stocked fish fresh from the hatchery, from the standpoint of either food or sport." He argued that they could not be compared with fish that were in the stream for a "decent length of time."

Flick criticized fisheries professionals for not being more progressive with regulations restricting the methods by which anglers could fish for trout, and he asked why a portion of a few streams could not be restricted to the use of artificial, unweighted flies. He urged that 20 percent of a stream be set aside for fly fishing only, and the result would be that the entire stream would benefit. He claimed that in those areas limited to fly fishing only, the daily limit could be reduced to half, and the trout should have a size limit of 10 inches.

In the early 1960s, he urged the Conservation Department to adopt legislation establishing special regulations on the Schoharie Creek, and in 1962, the first "fish for fun" or "no-kill" stretch in the state was established on the Schoharie along 1.4 miles of stream.

Over the years, Art Flick wrote numerous articles for outdoor and conservation magazines. In an article titled "Must We Rape Our Streams?" that appeared in *Trout* in the Autumn 1974 issue, he wrote about the destruction of stream habitat by highway departments. In the past, it was common to put their heavy equipment into streams under the guise of being "experts" in flood control. It is hard to comprehend how men who build roads could believe that they knew anything about stream hydraulics or flood control. Their ignorance was obvious; when they removed their bulldozers, they usually left the stream looking exactly like a road.

One of the earliest visitors to the Westkill Tavern was Preston Jennings, who at the time was involved in writing his classic *A Book of Trout Flies*. Jennings and Flick developed a friendship that included fishing together, and Jennings asked Flick to collect specimens for him of the aquatic insects that the trout were feeding on. In doing so, Flick also took a greater interest in stream entomology and approached his fishing with the idea of matching artificial flies to the naturals that were hatching.

Another visitor to Westkill Tavern was outdoor writer Raymond R. Camp. Camp urged Flick to write his own fly-fishing entomology. It took some prodding, but Flick began collecting on his own. For three years—1936, 1937, and 1938—he spent the entire trout season collecting specimens along the Schoharie Creek and did very little fishing. He wanted accurate records of the emergence dates of the important fly hatches and did not want to miss a species. He wrote a prelude to his own book on the major fly hatches in the Catskills in an article titled "The Natural Insects of the Schoharie River" that was published in the *Anglers' Club Bulletin* in February 1941.

In 1947, Flick authored a pocket-sized manual titled *Streamside Guide to Naturals and Their Imitations*. The book was very successful, and practically every fly fisherman owned a copy. It identified the principal hatches found in the Catskills and either gave the pattern that best imitated the natural, such as the Quill Gordon or Hendrickson, or gave a dressing for an artificial fly that would work best when the natural was on the water. Some patterns followed the advice of Jennings in his book and included Jennings's American March Brown and Grey Fox, but Flick also created several patterns of his own.

Streamside Guide was and still is an extremely popular book with trout fishermen everywhere; it was in great demand during the years that it was out of print, with some very high prices being paid for used editions. Finally, in 1969, with a lot of help from author and editor Nick Lyons, Crown Publishers Inc. reprinted the book under the title of *New Streamside Guide.* Sales were incredible, eventually topping the 150,000 mark. In 1972, Flick edited a book titled *Art Flick's Master Fly-Tying Guide,* a work also published by Crown, featuring the tying of various fly patterns by well-known fly fishermen.

Although Art Flick was not a commercial fly tier, he tried his hand at raising roosters for hackle, and he tied a beautiful fly in the Catskill style. Preston Jennings helped Flick with his fly tying and introduced him to dun hackle; he taught Art the difference between a good fly and a poorly tied fly. Years later, Flick told Cecil Heacox that the greatest compliment he ever received as a fly tier was when Jennings told him: "We have now reached a point where the pupil is doing a better job than the teacher."[7]

In the late 1970s, Flick became involved in an organization known as Catskill Waters, which was formed with the single goal of forcing New York City to improve water releases downstream of several of their reservoirs. Meetings were held in the Antrim Lodge in Roscoe and generally lasted for hours. Flick would attend, even though it meant three hours of driving over backcountry roads, which at times were covered with snow. He was in his seventies at the time, and he rarely missed a meeting; he knew his support was important, and if the aim was to improve Catskill trout fishing, he was in favor of it.

Because his name had been associated with many different fly patterns over the years, I wrote to Flick in 1984 and asked what flies he created and in what year he first tied them. In typical Art Flick fashion, he answered me immediately, probably that very day. Art's friend Nick Lyons used to joke that Art must have had a typewriter set up in the tiny West Kill post office.

Flick wrote that recalling dates was difficult, as there was little reason at the time to record them, and he did not wish to guess; however, he replied:

> Flies I feel I can honestly say I originated are: Red Quill; Early Brown Stone (wet); Stone Fly Creeper (wet); March Brown Nymph; Hendrickson Nymph; Isonychia Nymph; Black Nose Dace.
> I would feel guilty claiming to have originated the variants, for originally, I believe they were tied by Preston Jennings, at least the Grey Fox and Dun, but his patterns were tied with gold bodies, in the main. I changed to quills on the Grey Fox Variant, Dun Variant. The Cream Variant I believe is mine and I believe the Small Dun Variant with the olive body is mine, to use when the Blue Wing Olive flies are emerging. I'm reluctant to claim to be the originator of any pattern unless I'm absolutely sure, Ed. Unfortunately, I never kept track of dates, never dreaming there would be any need for them, so sorry I can't help you with that request Ed.[8]

Art Flick was a man whom everyone admired; he was a dedicated conservationist who watched over his beloved Schoharie Creek in every way possible. It is difficult to find anyone as dedicated to protecting a stream as he was the Schoharie. His name and the stream were so interwoven that the mention of one immediately inferred the other.

One of his rituals was the planting of willows. Each spring he would receive a couple of hundred from the Conservation Department and plant them to stabilize stream banks devoid of vegetation or in areas damaged by floods. One of my favorite anecdotal stories about his dedication to the stream's ecology is told by his friend and Schoharie regular J. Michael Migel. Mike relates how one year after Quill Gordons on the Schoharie had been scarce, Art worried about their survival and literally took matters into his own hands: "On a cold day in April, when it was too cold for them to get off the water he picked them up by the handful, warmed them with his breath, and carried them safely to streamside brush where they could rest and then mate."[9]

Art Flick was a fine gentleman who contributed greatly to the sport of fly fishing. Throughout his life, he was an active conservationist who was always willing to help and participate in any cause that improved trout fishing. The next time you tie on a Red Quill or a Cream Variant, stop and think for a moment of Art Flick, not because he created the pattern, but because he was someone who cared about, and made a difference, in the sport you are enjoying today.

Schoharie Creek downstream of Hunter Mountain. Ed Van Put.

SCHOHARIE CREEK

The name *Schoharie* is said to be a Mohawk Indian name, meaning "floating driftwood." The stream begins near the head of the Plattekill Clove at the base of Indian Head Mountain, in the town of Hunter, Greene County. The elevation is approximately 1,900 feet, and the Schoharie flows in a general direction northwesterly and northerly for approximately 27 miles before reaching

Schoharie reservoir. Along its course, it flows through the hamlets of Hunter, Jewett Center, Lexington, and Prattsville, and recruits tributaries such as the Roaring Kill, Gooseberry Creek, East Kill, West Kill, Little West Kill, Batavia Kill, and Huntersfield Creek.

In 1934, New York State's Bureau of Biological Survey published its investigation of the Mohawk-Hudson watershed. The work included the Schoharie Creek and was the first fisheries investigation in the Catskills. The report stated that the construction of the Gilboa dam and New York City's Schoharie reservoir had almost ruined one of the best fishing streams in the region.

Before the construction of the reservoir, Devasego Falls was a natural barrier that separated the trout and bass populations of the Schoharie Creek; trout inhabited the water above the falls, and smallmouth bass, which were abundant, occupied the stream below the falls. Dam construction on the Schoharie backed up the water and flooded Devasego Falls and automatically allowed small-mouth bass to enter the upper Schoharie Creek and do great harm to the trout fishing.

Bass multiplied rapidly and inhabited the Schoharie at least as far upstream as the village of Hunter. At the time of the report, it was claimed that a barrier dam constructed in the area of Prattsville would have little value, because the stream was now infested with bass and they had taken up permanent residence in the Schoharie Creek. It was concluded that a barrier dam should have been constructed before the reservoir was built!

The survey also recognized that the warm water temperatures of the Schoharie Creek in dry years could be a problem to the fisheries, and the stream above the reservoir had a "natural tendency to heavy flooding," which had been worsened by deforestation in the valley.

The barrier dam on the Schoharie Creek. Ed Van Put.

In the summer of 1938, the *Roxbury Times* announced that Civilian Conservation Corps (CCC) workers were scheduled to erect a barrier dam at Prattsville to prevent "black bass" from migrating out of the reservoir and "eating trout in the upper Schoharie Creek." The following year, a fisheries investigation by the Bureau of Fish Culture revealed that the Schoharie and its tributaries—including the Batavia Kill, East Kill, and West Kill, along with many smaller tributaries—were at their lowest level in ten years. Water temperatures in these streams were reported to be 84 degrees, which resulted in the death of many brown trout between 7 and 10 inches in length. In addition, thousands of small bass between 1½ to 2½ inches also perished because of high water temperatures and low water.

OVER ON THE EAST BRANCH

As tackle improved and anglers learned how to catch the monster browns found in the East Branch of the Delaware, more large trout found their way into area newspapers. A year after Niles Fairbairn's giant 6-pound, 10-ounce brown made headlines, Russell Todd caught a beauty that

The Old Stone Schoolhouse Pool below Margaretville. Ed Van Put.

tipped the scales at 7½ pounds and measured 26 inches. Todd's trophy fish was caught in July 1930 near Dunraven and won a prize in *Field & Stream's* national fishing contest.

The following year, on August 7, 1931, the *Roxbury Times* reported that the largest trout ever taken was caught at Hall's Bridge near Arena. A "city" fisherman camped in the area hooked a small chub on a spinner that was seized by a brown that measured 30 inches and weighed 10 pounds. A regular landing net was deemed too small for the fish, and a minnow seine was used to capture the giant trout.

In 1933, Roy Place of Margaretville brought into town a brown trout measuring 27 inches and weighing 6½ pounds that he caught in his favorite pool between Arena and the village. This large trout was displayed in the window at the L. Bussy & Co. store and attracted so many people for the day that it "almost rivaled the Commencement exercises of the local high school."[10]

The following season, James Martin caught a 26-inch brown that weighed in at 5 pounds at the iron bridge near Arena, and in August 1936, the *Catskill Mountain News* wrote of Velie DuMond of Arkville catching a 25-inch, 5½-pound brown trout in the East Branch. On a summer evening in July 1939, George Merritt of Margaretville was fishing the "swimming hole" near the village from a row boat and hooked a huge trout on a #4 Black Gnat. George leaped out of the boat and successfully landed a 26-inch "German brown" that weighed 6 pounds, 5 ounces!

During the 1920s and 1930s, big brown trout inhabited all of the large pools and eddies of the upper East Branch, and places like Fuller's Flat, Tishmacher's, and Keener's Flat became well-known destinations of trout fishermen. The water between Margaretville and Pepacton, especially around the hamlets of Arena, Union Grove, and Shavertown, were becoming famous for the number of large trout they produced each season.

This notoriety did not escape the notice of Herman Christian, the great Catskill fisherman who caught so many large trout along the Neversink. Herman was no stranger to the excellent trout fishing found in the East Branch Valley, and although the Neversink was where he established his reputation, he fished the East Branch often. His favorite water was from Rock Eddy to Shavertown; Rock Eddy was a great pool between two bends in the river about 2 miles upstream of Pepacton. Herman took a brown trout measuring 26 inches and weighing 8 pounds, 6 ounces—an exceptionally heavy trout for its length.

The Biological Survey of 1935 of the Delaware watershed reported on the fisheries of the East Branch as well as its tributaries. This pioneer study examined the river from its mouth at Hancock to its source above Roxbury. Fisheries biologists claimed that the East Branch was "undoubtedly one of the most productive fishing streams in the State,"[11] even though the stream was heavily fished. However, they also cited the lack of streamside vegetation, trees, and brush along sections of the river that did not provide adequate shade and caused unnecessary warming, thereby limiting trout production.

Poor farming practices were mainly responsible for the loss of trout habitat on the East Branch. Bottomland or flat land along rivers and streams in mountainous areas is always the most desirable; the cutting of trees along stream banks to get the most pasture and allowing cattle to graze up to the bank led to the loss of all vegetation. Cattle were often free to enter the stream at any location to obtain water. This led to trampling and collapsing the exposed banks, and erosion, once started, became difficult to control and resulted in warmer water temperatures.

Lack of shade and vegetation caused erosion and warming along the East Branch. *A Biological Survey of the Delaware and Susquehanna Watersheds*, 1935.

The survey stated that bass and pickerel were reportedly smaller than they were in the past and that this may have been due to the reduction of young shad, which served as forage food for these species. Shad no longer migrated into the East Branch in the same numbers they had previously. The smaller size of bass and pickerel may also have been caused by the competition or predation of pike-perch (walleye) that had been introduced into the system and were now found from Pepacton downstream to Hancock.

The report analyzed the fisheries and recommended stocking policies based on the different species found along the East Branch. Biologists claimed that the stream contained warmwater fishes almost exclusively from the mouth at Hancock upstream to the Beaverkill, though a few trout were reported being caught annually in the riffles and in spring holes. They recommended stocking bass only in this section, but also expressed doubt as to its effectiveness, because of the abundance of young bass and the natural spawning that already took place. Young-of-the-year smallmouths were found to be numerous in all of their fish collections.

From the Beaverkill upstream to Clausen Brook, which is approximately 2 miles past Harvard, the study found that a fair number of trout were taken, but the East Branch was still mainly inhabited by bass, pickerel, and pike-perch, and they advised against stocking trout.

The section from Clausen Brook upstream past Shinhopple, Corbett, Downsville, and Pepacton to the mouth of Lower Beech Hill Brook was a stretch in which brown trout were taken regularly in fast water and in spring holes: "The ordinary pools, however, are inhabited almost exclusively by warm-water fishes."[12] Stocking legal-sized brown and rainbow trout was recommended, and it was stated that they should be placed in spring holes and fast water areas: "Losses will undoubtedly occur even under the most favorable conditions, but to place large numbers of hatchery-reared fish in the long still pools which are inhabited by pickerel, pike-perch and bass would be an unjustifiably wasteful policy."[13]

The Biological Survey claimed that the best trout water along the East Branch was found between Lower Beech Hill Brook, about 1 mile downstream of Shavertown, and the Batavia Kill, 6½ miles upstream. It was reasoned that this section had the steepest gradient and therefore a "consistently fast flow" that appeared to favor trout over the warm-water species present in the East Branch. Biologists concluded that the good conditions found on many of the tributaries were responsible for maintaining the East Branch as a trout stream.

They also declared that a couple of the larger trout streams flowing into the East Branch suffered badly from the removal of streamside vegetation that, in turn, caused erosion, loss of habitat, and warming, mainly on the Tremper Kill and Plattekill. Mill Brook was seen as one of the best natural trout streams in the region, with the Bush Kill also being ranked as a very pro-

Fishing for smallmouth below Downsville.
A Survey of the Delaware and Susquehanna Watersheds, 1935.

ductive and heavily fished stream. Dry Brook exhibited good water temperatures, habitat, and food production, all of the natural requirements that contribute to making a first-class trout stream.

The survey team completed pollution studies in 1934–1935 and determined that the source of pollution was from sewage, milk and milk products, tanneries, slaughter houses, and acid factories; all had an effect on trout stream production.

Perhaps the most blatant example of a polluted trout stream was at the Kerry Company wood chemical factory along Cadosia Creek, a tributary of the East Branch just upstream of Hancock. The plant constructed tar pits along the banks, which overflowed and leached into Cadosia Creek, destroying the stream bottom. Tests downstream of the last tar pit revealed only 0.1 part per million of dissolved oxygen, compared with 9.0 parts per million above the plant.

Hardly any bottom life existed in the polluted section. A test conducted with a live cage of minnows placed in the area revealed severe stress in only 190 seconds and death in 16 minutes! The conclusion of the report was that this type of pollution was caused purely by neglect and could be eliminated with proper disposal of factory wastes.

In the watershed, at the time, there were many creameries and milk-shipping plants, and although most were nonpolluting, some had serious water-quality problems. The effluent from washing and spillage often reached the streams, and when large amounts of milk accumulated in a slow-moving waterway, it formed concentrated pools that fermented and depleted oxygen from the stream.

Milk plants used large amounts of wash water, and even plants with filtering systems or septic tanks would become overloaded and would discharge unwanted wastes into nearby trout streams. Investigators stated that the extreme headwaters of the East Branch originated in a polluted bed caused by the creamery at Grand Gorge. Other milk and milk-product pollution was found above Hubbell Corners, Margaretville, and Pepacton.

One of the earliest angling authors to write about the fisheries of the East Branch was John Alden Knight (1890–1966). Knight fished the upper East Branch regularly in the 1930s for both smallmouth bass and trout, and related his experiences in a book titled *The Theory and Technique of Fresh Water Angling* (1940). He was a member of the school of anglers who used bucktails along the larger trout waters with great success, and the East Branch was one of the streams in which he learned of the allure that minnow imitations had on big fish. Bucktails were the rage in the 1920s and 1930s, and Knight wrote of a particular method that used two bucktails on the same leader—a deadly rig unique to the Catskills.

Knight wrote several books on fishing, as well as numerous magazine articles. He was said to be the first nationally syndicated hunting and fishing columnist. Perhaps, however, he is best known for developing the Solunar theory and tables: a forecast of the daily feeding times of fish and wildlife.

NILES FAIRBAIRN

During the 1930s, the Margaretville Rod & Gun Club had a membership of more than three hundred sportsmen. Founded in January 1933, it was the largest club in the Delaware County Federation of Sportsmen's Clubs (by the early 1950s, membership grew to more than six hundred, making the club the largest in the state). One of the club's most noted trout fishermen was Niles Fairbairn.

Niles G. Fairbairn (1886–1965) was born in Seager—not really a village, or even a hamlet, but a place where a few houses came together along the narrow Dry Brook Valley in the town of Hardenbergh, Ulster County. From an early age, Fairbairn was an exceptional hunter, trapper, and trout fisherman. In a region known for outdoorsmen, he developed a reputation as an excellent woodsman and guide. For many years, he was employed by the New York State Conservation Department as a trapper, handling nuisance bear and beaver complaints, and trapping foxes as part of a rabies control program.

As a trout fisherman, Niles Fairbairn had a special talent for catching large fish, especially at night, on flies he tied himself. He may not have owned expensive or fancy tackle, nor was he sophisticated about the theories of fly imitation and presentation, but he was a very good trout fisherman.

His exploits with a fly rod began in 1929, when he took second place in the *Field & Stream* fishing contest and won a cash prize of $75 for catching one of the largest brown trout in the United States. Using a fly of his own creation, Fairbairn caught the huge 26¾-inch brown mentioned previously, which weighed 6 pounds, 10 ounces!

In the summer of 1935, Fairbairn received further notoriety when he taught the famous Helen Keller to fly fish. This extraordinary woman was known throughout the world for her ability to overcome being deaf and blind. While staying for several weeks in the Dry Brook Valley, she wished to try her hand at fly fishing. Fairbairn taught her how to cast a fly rod, and on the very first cast, she caught a small brook trout. Her next fish was much larger, and the battle between trout and angler lasted more than ten minutes. In all, three trout were taken, and Helen Keller described her experience as "the thrill of my life."[14] Years later, Hollywood would make a movie about her life, titled *The Miracle Worker* (1962). It starred Patty Duke, who won an Oscar portraying Helen Keller.

Following his years as a state trapper, Niles Fairbairn became the superintendent of the department's Conservation Education Camp at DeBruce. At the camp, youngsters were taught outdoor skills, conservation ethics, fly tying, and fly fishing. They were also entertained by the assortment of wildlife kept about by Fairbairn. There was a pet opossum, an occasional bobcat kitten, and a porcupine that would climb up his leg and sit on his lap. Niles usually went about the camp followed by a spotted fawn.

Over the years, Fairbairn went on to catch many large trout, and although he never succeeded in topping his prize-winning brown, he came close. He had a reputation for catching brown trout more than 5 pounds, and it was claimed that he only fished on moonless nights, with a #6 black fly. In June 1950, the *Catskill Mountain News* reported that Niles caught fourteen trout that month between 16 and 24½ inches, with the largest weighing 5¾ pounds!

Niles Fairbairn with a 6-pound, 8-ounce brown.
Liberty Register, 1957.

While working at DeBruce on a moonless summer night in 1955, Fairbairn caught a 24½-inch brown that weighed 6½ pounds! He caught the huge trout at ten o'clock at night on a deer-hair mouse in Red Rock Pool on the Willowemoc Creek near DeBruce.

Niles Fairbairn possessed a unique talent for handling and training wildlife—in particular, bobcats, foxes, porcupines, and otters. He trained porcupines to sit up and eat from a dish, sit on his lap, climb on his shoulder, and nibble on his ear! He assisted magazines such as *Life* in obtaining wildlife photographs, and in 1959, he was hired by Walt Disney as an advisor and animal trainer in

the making of a nature film titled *Flash, the Teenage Otter,* a Disney classic movie that can still be seen or rented today.

Fairbairn retired from the Conservation Department in 1957 and soon became the resident caretaker and counselor of the Boy Scout reservation at Alder Lake. He continued to teach youngsters to enjoy and appreciate the outdoors. Along with his thrilling and imaginative stories of wildlife and his ability to handle animals, he endeared himself to many of the scouts who spent part of their summers in the Catskills.

A. J. MCCLANE

Niles Fairbairn received notoriety that spread beyond the Catskills, but the most famous trout fisherman to learn and ply his fly-fishing skills in the Margaretville region was Albert Jules McClane (1922–1991). Though Al was not born in Delaware County, he spent a significant portion of his youth in the Margaretville-Arkville area, and it was in this region of the Catskills that he learned to fish and developed a desire to pursue a career in fisheries and fishing journalism. For nearly fifty years, he contributed articles on fishing, adding greatly to the lore of the Catskills. He wrote often about the Neversink, Beaverkill, Esopus, East Branch, and main Delaware River, and he informed readers about the remarkable fly fishermen and fly tiers found in the Catskills, bringing their notoriety to a national audience.

His official byline was A. J. McClane, and it was the most familiar and respected name in the world of angling journalism. A prolific writer, Al sold his first article when he was only seventeen years of age; titled "Bouncing for Trout," he sold the piece in 1939 to *Outdoor Life*.

Although his career as a writer began with *Outdoor Life*, A. J. McClane is best known for his longtime association as the fishing editor of *Field & Stream*. He traveled and sampled fishing all over the globe. He fished in the best places, with many of the greatest fly casters and fly fishermen in the world, as well as statesmen, generals, princes, kings, and Hollywood stars, and he shared these angling experiences with a loyal readership.

A. J. McClane on the upper Beaverkill. *Fishing with McClane*, 1975. Francis Davis photo.

McClane was a sophisticated, polished master angler who enjoyed a reputation with international credentials. He was extremely knowledgeable about fish, fishing, fly tying, and fly casting, and he was a superb writer. His advice was flawless, and when he passed along information on techniques, you could be sure that he had used them and that they were proven. He wrote unpretentiously and was a master of metaphors, using words that were not only original, but that made you pause and admire his abilities as a writer.

A. J. McClane wrote about the trout fishing he found in other countries, yet throughout his lifetime, he never forgot his Catskill roots. It was here that he learned to fish for trout, and his writings included reminiscences of Delaware County and of the upper East Branch and its tributaries.

In October 1967, *Field & Stream* published what many believe is a fine example of Al's work. The essay, titled "Song of the Angler," is about why people fish, and McClane writes an unforgettable story in reply to a philosophical question that is not always easy to answer. In the piece, he recalls his boyhood days:

> Have you ever noticed how often anglers tend to share their good fortune? I have seen this happen many times among perfect strangers who simply meet on a stream. I remember a man who, after landing a beautiful rainbow trout below the Fair Ground Bridge on the East Branch of the Delaware, turned to a bug-eyed kid holding a 98-cent telescopic fly rod, and snipping the March Brown pattern off his leader gave it to the boy. "See what you can do with it, son." That's all he said. I was that boy and I can't tie a March Brown on my leader today without blessing my Good Samaritan.

McClane came to the Catskills in 1935 as a thirteen-year-old; he and a friend had hitchhiked to the mountains from Brooklyn. These were the years of the Great Depression, and the two boys were looking for summer work near Arkville. They met Basil Van Kleeck, a dairy farmer from Rider Hollow, a tributary of Dry Brook, who offered them room and board. McClane recognized that the area was central to some of the best trout fishing in the Catskills, and for several years afterward, he spent summers in the Margaretville-Arkville area, working on farms, as a lineman for the Jenkinstown Power and Light Company, and a variety of other summer jobs.

Margaretville was home to a number of veteran anglers at the time, most of whom fished the waters of the upper East Branch below the village, where the river meandered its way through flat and fertile farmlands. This was "big water," with large deep pools and eddies and lengthy insect-rich riffles and runs.

During these teenage years, McClane met and fished with many of the great anglers in and around Margaretville, such as Ray Neidig, Dan Todd, Mike Lurenze, John Alden Knight, and Doc Faulkner. This was trout country, and these fly fishermen were his mentors; Al was just a kid at the time, but was allowed to "tag along."

Ray Neidig was a professional fly tier and an avid night fisherman who lived in Union Grove, where the Barkaboom Stream entered the East Branch. Dan Todd (1881–1952) was an extraordinary fisherman who was born along Dry Brook. He was raised on a farm, but he preferred village life; as a young man, he became the station agent first at Arkville, then at Margaretville railroad stations.

Al McClane maintained a close relationship with Dan Todd, who, in addition to being an avid fly fisher, tied flies and was an expert in a valley known for its trout fishing. Todd was in his early fifties at the time and an active outdoorsman; he was secretary of the Margaretville Rod & Gun Club and was a respected member of his community.

McClaine revealed his talents as a fly fisherman early in life. In April 1936, at the age of fourteen, he was fishing the East Branch on a day when the stream was high and the weather cold and snowy. He was using a nymph, and after landing several trout, hooked into a monster brown too big for his net. After a lengthy battle, he beached the fish in a snow bank and then proudly paraded it ". . . by way of the lumberyard, the butcher shop, the drugstore, and the ill-named Palace Hotel, making sure everybody in town saw the fish. Dan Todd weighed it at the railroad station—7 pounds, 2 ounces, not an adult trophy for the East Branch in those days, since fresh mounts in double figures to 15 pounds or more hung glassy-eyed on every saloon wall."[15]

McClane and Todd fished together often, not only on the East Branch but on other streams in the area, such as the Delaware, West Branch, and Esopus. Todd was a veteran fly fisher who not only taught the youngster fly-fishing tactics, but also about stream life and the relationship between aquatic insects and trout. Todd was knowledgeable about all of the major fly hatches; he not only studied their behavior, but collected samples and preserved them in formalin. His collection of nymphs and adult flies was kept at his office at the Margaretville railroad station, where he was the telegraph operator and stationmaster.

McClane recalled that he and Todd would ride the tracks paralleling the river on a handcar, enjoying an excellent view of the East Branch. When a number of swallows or cedar waxwings were found feeding over the stream surface, they stopped, put their rods together, and started fishing. Years later, as an established fishing journalist, McClane would call upon these boyhood experiences and write about Dan Todd and his other mentors, passing along the fishing tips he learned from them.

Todd tied imitations of nymphs in the early 1930s at a time when their use by fly fishermen was still relatively unknown; he and McClane also worked at tying fly patterns that imitated the minnows they found in bass and trout stomachs. McClane became skilled with streamers and bucktails along the East Branch, and he developed a fondness for them that stayed with him for the rest of his life. He often stated that the years fishing with Dan Todd were some of the best years of his angling career:

> Both the East Branch and the Esopus were tremendous producers in those days with 5 to 7 pound brown trout not unusual for somebody who knew the water. Despite the abundant daytime hatches of caddis and mayflies, the largest trout, and some of these were in the 10 pound class, were invariably taken at night on big wet fly patterns.[16]

McClane considered the East Branch from Shinhopple to Hancock, and the main Delaware from Hancock to Port Jervis, to be some of the greatest smallmouth water in the country. He also caught smallmouths while fishing for trout on the waters between Arena and Shavertown, but they were less common in the late 1930s; the water was more famous for the size of the browns that the river produced.

A. J. McClane knew all of the best places to fish in the Catskills. He was familiar with the waters of the Neversink, Beaverkill, Willowemoc, and Schoharie Creek, and once took a 6-pound male rainbow on a black marabou streamer at Five Arch Bridge on the Esopus. He fished smaller streams as well, such as Basket Creek, Stony Clove, and Beecher Brook, but he had very fond memories of a small tributary of Dry Brook named Rider Hollow.

He became familiar with Rider Hollow the first summer he came to the Catskills. Working on the Van Kleecks' farm, he got to know the stream and its native brook trout intimately, and this experience contributed to his interest in fish and fishing. In 1939, he entered Cornell University and majored in fisheries. He also worked at the experimental hatchery at Ithaca and participated in all of the fieldwork expected of a future biologist, including backpacking trout fingerlings into Finger Lakes tributaries and studying trout migration.

Following a stint in the U.S. Army during World War II, during which he received the Bronze Star and Purple Heart, McClane joined the staff at *Field & Stream* in 1947. His writing spanned half a century, and he enjoyed an enviable career as a fishing journalist and a savant of fish cookery. He also wrote for *Esquire, Life,* and *Gourmet* magazines.

Al McClane wrote many books on fishing. Popular works include *McClane's Game Fish of North America* (1984) and *McClane's Angling World* (1986). Although *McClane's New Standard Fishing Encyclopedia* (1965) sold more than one million copies, his *Practical Fly Fisherman* (1953) is considered a fly-fishing classic. Al McClane was also an authority on fish cookery, and he wrote a best seller in 1977 titled *The Encyclopedia of Fish Cookery.*

PUBLIC FISHING RIGHTS AND STOCKING LARGER TROUT

During the 1930s, great strides were made in the field of fisheries management, and the Conservation Department was fortunate to have the services of not only Dr. Emmeline Moore, but a commissioner named Lithgow Osborne (1892–1980) of Auburn, Cayuga County.

Osborne was a fly fisherman, and perhaps this contributed to his enthusiasm for pursuing ways to improve trout fishing. One thing is certain: He had a major impact on the entire department, and during his tenure, fisheries management leaped into the twentieth century, with New York State at the forefront of managing its trout resources. "Commissioner Osborne put an imprint on the whole department. Ahead of his time, he was aware of conservation's broader environmental aspects and its future significance."[17]

Under his leadership, the Conservation Department improved and expanded its fisheries management programs, and developed a public fishing rights program that allowed the state to purchase permanent fishing easements on the privately owned trout streams of New York. Without this program, the lengthy stretches of public fishing along the Beaverkill and Willowemoc—or, for that matter, along any of the popular Catskill trout streams today—would not exist.

After Edward R. Hewitt purchased and posted miles of the Neversink, water that had been open for so many years and stocked by local sportsmen, there was great concern among trout fishermen that more streams would become private and posted. The amount of water along streams that was open to the public was shrinking yearly, and, fearing greater losses, members of twenty rod and gun clubs, representing five thousand sportsmen from four counties, joined forces to pursue a public fishing program.

Lithgow Osborne. http://www.cayuganet.org.

Their concerns over posting were aired at a meeting in Middletown, Orange County, in the winter of 1923. Sullivan County was well represented by the Liberty Rod & Gun Club, and its president, Roy Steenrod. Steenrod suggested that the group form an alliance, with the idea that sportsmen would be better represented. This was done, and bylaws were adopted: "A bill was drawn up at the meeting, to be introduced at this session in Albany, asking that $1,000,000 be set aside for a purchase of streams, lakes and land in this section," reported the *Sullivan County Democrat*.[18]

That the Liberty Rod & Gun Club was at the forefront of this request is not surprising; the club's membership felt the loss of the Neversink personally, and they were equally concerned over other Sullivan County trout streams. Could the lower Beaverkill and Willowemoc become posted? Would there be public trout fishing in the future?

The bill was unsuccessful. A couple of years later, the Liberty Rod & Gun Club announced that it would attempt to purchase narrow strips of land along the Beaverkill, Willowemoc, and Neversink in an effort to keep them from becoming posted. Most likely, this idea did not materialize because of the expense of such a project.

When the Conservation Department published its report to the legislature in 1933, it acknowledged a growing posting problem:

> While we are better situated in respect to lake fishing, the anglers for trout slowly but with ever increasing numbers are being excluded from large sections of our finest streams. Good stream fishing will always be most difficult to maintain by reason of the limited number of suitable streams in each region, the seasonal changes in volume and temperature of water, and the comparative ease with which landowners can post them. . . .
>
> Assuming the State had a far greater supply of funds to carry on. What then? It could greatly expand the foregoing services. It could buy strips of land on either side and under large sections of our principal trout streams and develop them to carry greater numbers of larger fish.[19]

It was not until 1935, however, under the leadership of Commissioner Osborne, that a program of purchasing public fishing easements on privately owned streams became a reality. The legislature that year allocated $100,000 from the Conservation Fund for the acquisition of "fishing rights and approaches thereto by purchase or lease." The acquisition was for "the sole and exclusive

An early public fishing easement sign along the Beaverkill. Ed Van Put.

right, privilege and easement of occupying and using at all times hereafter as a fishing ground and for no other purpose, for the use and benefit of the public."*

Briefly, public fishing rights easements enabled the public to fish and wade in the stream, and walk along the banks. They also allowed the department to improve the stream with the installation of in-stream and bank stabilization structures, and protect stream banks by planting trees or shrubs. In addition, the easement enabled the department to post the stream with signs informing the public that they have the right to fish along the easement.

The Conservation Department's policy for the purchase of public fishing easements stated that streams needed to be of "sufficiently large size," with "continuous flow" in summer to withstand heavy fishing pressure. It was also desired that they be streams recommended by the Biological Survey and capable of supporting brook, brown, or rainbow trout and be streams where a minimum of 15 miles of contiguous waters could be acquired.

The commissioner announced that the department would not acquire public fishing easements in the Catskills, because it would be far more expensive than anywhere else. However, two years

---

*The first public fishing acquisition in New York State was also in 1935 when James N. Rosenberg and John D. Shattuck gave as a gift 2.76 miles of fishing rights and 33.09 acres along the Bouquet River in the Adirondacks to the Conservation Department.

later, after securing additional funding, Commissioner Osborne revealed that negotiations were under way with landowners along the Beaverkill and Willowemoc. Speaking at the annual dinner of the Liberty Rod & Gun Club, Osborne gave the news that area sportsmen had waited so long to hear: The first public fishing rights agreement acquired in the Beaverkill watershed was signed along the Willowemoc in 1936.

The success of the public fishing rights program was dependent on the willingness of landowners to sell their fishing rights, and by the end of 1938, the department had purchased 9.70 miles along the Schoharie, 8.42 miles along the Beaverkill, and 4.90 miles on the Willowemoc Creek.

Historical marker at Hazel Bridge Pool on the Willowemoc Creek. Ed Van Put.

Also under Osborne's tenure, a significant discovery occurred in 1939 when an electrical method of collecting wild trout in streams was developed by David C. Haskill of the Lake George hatchery at Gansevoort. By using a portable generator of approximately 500-watt capacity, capable of delivering 110 or 220 volt alternating current, biologists were now able to sample trout populations in streams more accurately and better determine their productivity.

Fish were temporarily stunned by electricity and were collected with long-handled nets and placed in holding cages, where they recovered quickly. Fisheries biologists were now able to estimate wild trout populations, determine if trout were reproducing in the stream by collecting fry or fingerlings, sample year classes or ages of the fish, and note the physical condition of the trout. From these data, determinations could be made of the health of the stream and how, or if, the stream should be stocked. This was seen as a significant step to better fisheries management; most streams could now be sampled with greater accuracy. Previously, samples were collected using nets or seines that were entirely unsatisfactory. Trout escaped quickly out the area being netted, and the irregular stream bottoms made capture difficult.

Another significant event during Osborne's years as the commissioner was the tremendous expansion of the duties of the Conservation Department, one of which included overseeing the Civilian Conservation Corps. The CCC was formed in 1933 by the federal government. Thousands of young unemployed men from urban areas enrolled in a "peacetime army" devoted to battling erosion and restoring declining timber resources. These were the years of the Great Depression, and "Roosevelt's Tree Army" planted millions of trees and eagerly worked on forestry and fish and game projects.

The Bureau of Biological Survey was directly responsible for the stream improvement projects. Fisheries projects included stream improvement on trout streams along state-owned lands. This work attempted to create better habitat, mostly in the form of pools, with in-stream structures such as log and stone dams, and bank stabilization with log cribbing, deflectors, and the planting of trees. The trees also provided shade. In the Catskills, CCC work occurred along the Schoharie Creek and its tributaries—the Catskill Creek, the Beaverkill, and Willowemoc Creek—as early as 1934.

Before 1930, stream improvement was conducted mostly on private water; however, the CCC provided inexpensive labor, and stream improvement projects would expand in a few years "from a small region in New York to a massive nationwide effort."[20]

In the 1920s, the use of trucks aided significantly the stocking of trout streams; trout were stocked by employees of the department, who had experience and knowledge about changing water temperatures and were familiar with where to place fry or fingerlings in the streams. In 1930, a total of 9,116,909 trout were stocked in New York State; of this number, only 6,328 were yearlings or adults (more than 7–8 inches). This number is less than one tenth of 1 percent of the total number of trout stocked, as 99.9% were fry or fingerlings. During the years from 1920 to 1930, there were, on average, 9,901,411 brook, brown, and rainbow trout stocked throughout New York State. Although there was an increase of yearling/adult trout stocked in 1928 and 1929, 99.98% of all of the trout stocked during this ten-year period were still fry or fingerlings.

As the number of trout fishermen increased, the need to restock became greater; by 1934, however, there was more emphasis on stocking larger trout instead of fingerlings. This was seen as progress within the Conservation Department, "meeting the hearty approval of all sportsmen."[21] Policy within the department was beginning to change, and the Bureau of Fish Culture began changing its stocking policy during the 1934 season, increasing the production of yearling trout—trout in the 6- to 9-inch range—to 3.5% of the total number of trout stocked in New York waters:

> In the past several years it has been the policy of the Bureau to hold many trout through the winter, putting them out in the following spring as yearlings of legal size. That better sport should result for the angler is obvious; and many letters received from sportsmen during 1935 show that this has been the case throughout the State generally.
>
> It is now planned to hold, through their first winter, at least as many fish as existing funds will allow. In this way, and only in this way, can good fishing be maintained for the growing army of fishermen.[22]

By 1936, the department was looking for ways to cut expenses at trout hatcheries, and the use of dry feeds was "generally introduced." These dry foods were mixtures of fish meal, cottonseed meal, dried milk, buttermilk, and salmon egg meal, and were far less expensive than the fresh meat that had been in use from the time hatcheries first produced domestic trout. The goal of the Cortland Experimental hatchery was to discover diets that resulted in healthier and faster-growing fish at the lowest possible cost.

The 1937 report repeated the claim that "one of the ways to meet the demands of anglers is to stock larger trout." However, it was pointed out that there would be higher costs associated with keeping trout in the hatcheries longer, and this increased the danger of fish diseases, as ponds were filled with trout for more months of the year.

The report to the legislature went on to say: "As fishing has become heavier and heavier with the growth of population, and as the automobile and good roads have made more and more waters easily accessible to anglers, the number of fish put out has had to be increased." The department at this time also instituted its plan to stock the streams with the assistance of the sportsmen's federations; this system helped to prevent the overlapping of stocking activities by the various clubs and led to a fairer distribution of the fish. Fish distribution was improved as trucks were now equipped with oxygen supplies and were capable of carrying greater numbers of trout.

By 1938, the Bureau of Fish Culture announced that it had made advances in the science of fish culture, citing, "Careful selection of brood stock, the introduction of new and better diets, together with the 'feeding chart,' which furnishes a definite basis for the efficient utilization of feeds, have had a pronounced influence on hatchery production."[23]

It was claimed that for the past couple of years, the most important problem in the hatcheries was the development of "cheap yet satisfactory" fish food. Dry meals and frozen marine fish were used with varying degrees of success, and dry-meal diets were excellent in some hatcheries, but in a few caused high mortality and poor growth. Experiments continued with a mixture of dry feed and some meats, but it was found that if the water was used over and over in a long series of ponds, then the meat and fish diet was superior.

PROBLEMS WITH THE PORTAL AFFECT THE ESOPUS

When Schoharie reservoir was completed in 1926, flows through the Shandaken tunnel increased significantly. The carrying capacity of the tunnel was 600 million gallons per day, and the added volume to the natural flow of the stream profoundly affected the Esopus Creek. Such huge amounts of water entering the Esopus, along with the water temperature fluctuations associated with the flows, disrupted the complex relationships between the aquatic insect communities and other organisms, including plankton and minnow species, which trout required as a food supply.

The high flows coming out of the Shandaken tunnel made the Esopus, downstream, practically unfishable. The fishing was ruined, not solely because of the high water, but also by the highly discolored and turbid Schoharie water, which gave the Esopus an overall muddy appearance all the way to the reservoir, 12 miles downstream!

Trout fishermen complained bitterly, and by 1930, the New York City Board of Water Supply made some concessions to the fishermen by lowering the flows from the tunnel on weekends. On Friday afternoons, the Shandaken tunnel would cease flowing, and the Esopus would return to its natural levels, but on Sunday evenings, a full tunnel flow would commence and be maintained throughout the week:

> Anyone can readily tell whether or not water from Gilboa Dam runs through Esopus Creek by observing the color of the stream. Clear water means that the tunnel is closed: the Esopus has its natural color. Any inflow from the Gilboa Dam, however, completely alters the character of the Esopus. The current then takes on a turbid appearance, distinctly yellowish, due to the fact that Gilboa Dam drains a region of clay soils unmistakable in color.[24]

How much the change in the releases affected fishing is not easy to measure, but during the summer of 1932, Rudolph De Silva of Boiceville caught a monster "German brown" in the Esopus in the vicinity of Cold Brook. De Silva caught the large brown on a minnow using a 4½-ounce fly rod. The trout measured 29 inches and weighed nearly 8 pounds! The fish was taken to Kingston and was entered in a couple of fishing contests that were held at sporting goods stores.

It is unknown how long these concessions by the city were performed, but in 1935, the issue of poor fishing resurfaced in local newspapers. The *Walton Reporter* on April 12 published an article that stated that the city of New York has agreed to regulate the flows from the Shandaken tunnel during the trout fishing season "in order that the Esopus Creek may again present good trout fishing to the many anglers who used to swarm this popular trout stream from the headwaters of the Ashokan reservoir to Shandaken."

The article claimed that for some time, sportsmen have been trying to get the city to stop the high flows that occur when excessive amounts of water are released from Schoharie reservoir during the week. Boardinghouse owners, it was stated, have lost a considerable amount of business because of the poor fishing. And it was said that for awhile, the city did close the tunnel on weekends, but the high flows during the week caused the fish to inhabit areas that were "high and dry" when the flows were shut off:

> The Phoenicia Fish and Game association this spring hit on a plan which probably will work out to the advantage of all concerned. The city has agreed to maintain the flow through the Shandaken tunnel at an even rate. This flow will be about a half flow at all times. By so doing the height of the stream will be maintained to give good fishing and at the same time the city will be able to deliver sufficient water from the Gilboa reservoir to the Ashokan reservoir.[25]

After the opening of the Shandaken tunnel in 1924, the Esopus Creek, downstream to the reservoir, was kept in a near constant state of discoloration; how muddy the water appeared was generally a result of how much flow was coming out of the tunnel. The turbidity and high flows caused some trout fishermen to change their tactics when fishing downstream of the tunnel.

Preston Jennings, the noted fly fisherman and author of *A Book of Trout Flies* (1935), believed that the use of bucktails, flies that imitate minnows, became popular in the Catskills after the Shandaken tunnel began flowing into the Esopus and kept it in "an almost constant roily state by the introduction of the clay-laden water from the Schoharie."[26] Jennings wrote that the first of these flies that came to his attention was called the Esopus Bucktail.

Bucktails are generally used in spring when streams are high and discolored from runoff of melting snow or rains. They are bright flies and are designed to get the fish's attention. The Esopus Bucktail was originated by William Mills & Son of New York City and had a reputation for catching large brown trout. The pattern is as follows:

Head: Black.
Tail: Of bright red bucktail, cut off sharply, one third as long as the wing. A good sized bunch of bucktail is used to give the effect of a paintbrush when cut off.

Body: Medium gold or silver tinsel. The body is first filled in with wool to enlarge it before adding the tinsel. This fat body is designed to give a large, shiny area. Regular-length hooks are used so that the body and the tail are of the same length.

Wing: In any of the following color combinations: black over white bucktail; brown over white bucktail; red over white bucktail. The wing is one-half longer than the body and tail combined. It is raised to an angle of 45 degrees from the body to show the body more clearly and to give more action in the water. The wing is rather fully dressed.[27]

Another pattern equally as popular in the 1920s and 1930s that was used on the Esopus between the tunnel and the reservoir is the Phoenicia Bucktail. This fly is an adaptation of the famous Black Ghost that was first tied in 1927. It is the same, except that it is ribbed with gold tinsel instead of silver and has a tail of a double section of dark yellow wool and no throat hackle. The dressing is as follows:

Head: Black.
Tail: Double section of dark yellow wool.
Body: Black silk, dressed heavy and tapered at both ends.
Ribbing: Gold tinsel.
Wing: White bucktail.
Cheeks: Jungle cock (optional).

A third pattern, known as the Brown and White Bucktail, is mentioned in Ray Bergman's classic *Trout,* first published in 1938. Bergman writes that the fly was originally tied for use on the Esopus Creek. He gives the dressing as follows:

Head: Black.
Body: Silver tinsel.
Hackle: Crimson.
Tail: Crimson.
Wing: Brown bucktail topping white bucktail.[28]

****

In 1936, the waters of the Lower Hudson River, including the Esopus Creek and its tributaries, were studied by the Bureau of Biological Survey. The survey established a baseline of information that future biologists would use to develop a better fisheries program. It was believed that basic studies of aquatic biology were a prerequisite of determining a proper stocking policy, but the program went beyond improving the way fish were stocked.

They investigated the growth rates of fish, the results of overstocking, and water quality, as well as which conditions might be affecting wild populations and stream improvement. It was recognized that improving the fisheries depended on regulating catch rates and improving habitat or environmental conditions.

The Biological Survey served as advisor for stream improvement projects on state lands, and this work was carried out by using CCC labor. Work in the Esopus Valley commenced in 1934–1935, when a series of small stream improvement dams were constructed on Ox Clove Brook, a tributary of the Stony Clove near Phoenicia.

The stream, before the structures, held mostly native brook trout and had lengthy stretches of shallow water that provided poor habitat for adult trout, especially in low water. Pools were constructed by using logs with board facing. The structures that were made were basically pool diggers; they scoured a pool on the downstream side of the structure but also raised and slowed the water levels upstream.

"Stream improvement" was a relatively new program of fisheries management, and the work along Ox Clove Brook was some of the

Stream improvement pool along Ox Clove Brook. Survey of the Lower Hudson Watershed, 1936.

first developed on public lands in the Catskills. The Biological Survey evaluated the project and found that deep scour holes were made below the structures, but sediment (gravel) had filled in a number of pools upstream. However, in doing so, spawning habitat was created, and the trout found it very desirable.

The survey crew observed spawning in the fall and discovered that these sites were used more than the unimproved extreme headwaters, which were filled with large stones and water that was too shallow. The following June, the crew seined some of the pools above the structures and found an abundance of wild trout. They also seined the plunge pools:

Seining of one scour pool below a dam yielded 14 trout, three of which were over the 6-inch legal size limit. As the pool was only approximately 15 by 20 feet, with unsuitably shallow water immediately below, the population of trout appeared to be large in relation to the area bottom. Check of other pools indicated trout to be equally numerous wherever depths were suitable. Unimproved areas had young trout but few fish of legal size. This stream is heavily fished and many of the largest trout are removed by anglers.[29]

When the Esopus was surveyed in 1936, fisheries scientists commented on the effect that the Shandaken tunnel was having on the stream. They stated that the tunnel was responsible for turbidity, for the introduction of warmwater species such as "small-mouthed bass and pike-perch," and for the sudden fluctuations in volume and stream temperature.

The warmwater species competed and preyed on trout, and thereby limited trout production. The sudden lowering of the stream level regularly left some fish "high and dry," resulting in mortality; and although trout were able to withstand temperature changes, it was stated that when temperature changes were as much as 11 degrees in just a few minutes, that "Apparently trout are able to tolerate these changes, but they are certainly abnormal and probably physiologically injurious to some extent."[30] It was also claimed that the turbidity resulted in a "mechanical coating" of the streambed, which was injurious to the aquatic insect population, and the change of light penetration also affected productivity to some degree:

> The average cooling of the water during the summer and addition to the volume are evident benefits. To take advantage of these favorable features, and to ameliorate some of the injurious conditions it is evident that any steps possible toward regulation of the Gilboa water more evenly through the season will be to the advantage of fishing.
>
> A definite conclusion as to whether the total effect of the addition of Gilboa water has been beneficial to trout fishing or otherwise is impossible to make from the information obtainable in one season's survey. Other factors, as for example, recent floods and over-fishing, obscure the issue. Certainly small trout are common in this part of the river, although not as abundant as in the reaches above the tunnel entrance. Despite unfavorable factors this stream system still has unusually good natural advantages for trout and will maintain excellent fishing under a reasonable fishing load.
>
> Temperatures just above the tunnel entrance run notably higher than below except of course during periods when the Gilboa water is shut off. Apparently these temperatures ordinarily do not exceed the toleration point for brown trout; in fact it seems probable that these higher temperatures are favorable to the growth of brown and rainbow trout and thus increase the productivity of this water. Trout of these species from a size of 6 to 10 inches are abundant, but larger specimens appear rare. It is evident that this water as in the section below is excessively fished. Ideal stocking would include fish above 10 inches in length. Brook trout are encountered fairly commonly in this stream above Oliverea, but as fishing is mainly for brown and rainbow trout they only are recommended for stocking.
>
> Criticism of the fishing in this stream is mainly that fish above the 12-inch size are becoming relatively rare as compared with a few years ago. The one obvious explanation of course is over-fishing. Two possible corrections to this condition are evident: limitations of the catch and proper stocking. Stocking of Esopus Creek has been regular and occasionally quite heavy but it has been almost entirely with fingerling fish.[31]

Another favorable benefit of the Shandaken tunnel not mentioned in the 1936 survey is that in winter, the added flow from the tunnel kept the Esopus free of ice. Other Catskill streams freeze over and have significant amounts of ice, including "anchor" ice, but the Esopus below the tunnel is generally ice-free, having the appearance in winter of a giant spring creek. The damage caused by ice jams scouring the streambeds and banks with their destructive movements downstream are a phenomenon that the Esopus escapes.

Stocking records for the ten years (1926–1935) before the Biological Survey indicate that the Esopus Creek received 119,535 brown trout; 19,050 rainbow trout; 6,500 brook trout; and 4,000 "steelhead trout," with an additional 11,000 steelhead being placed in tributaries. The average number of trout of all species stocked each year during this period was approximately 14,900; the vast majority, if not all, of these stocked fish were fingerlings or fry.

The negative problems associated with the Shandaken tunnel and the Esopus continued. When the city poured water down from the Schoharie, the stream was extremely difficult to fish, and the unpleasant appearance of muddy water and high flows turned fishermen away.

The turbidity problem was compounded by the fact that most streams in the Esopus watershed also had clay deposits along their banks, similar to the Schoharie. At times, stream courses would move or shift into one of these deposits, causing the tributary to become discolored, similar to the water flowing from the tunnel. Some tributaries, such as the Stony Clove or Woodland Valley Stream, would run turbid for days, months, and even years, either until the clay was eroded away, the stream again took a new course, or the clay soil was covered by gravel or other stream sediments.

It is a premise that a trout's environment includes streams with clean, transparent water, water so pure and cold that if need be, one could pause and drink it. Many trout fishermen, especially fly fishermen, were disappointed by the appearance of the Esopus, and the high flows and discoloration turned them toward other waters. Outdoor writers and angling authors, too, tended to ignore the stream, and compared with other Catskill trout streams, the Esopus, for many years, received far less publicity and recognition.

RAY SMITH

The best-known fly tier that ever lived in the Esopus Valley was Raymond C. Smith (1900–1975). Ray lived in Mt. Tremper, along the Little Beaverkill, an Esopus tributary, about 5 miles downstream of Phoenicia. In addition to being an excellent fly tier, Ray was an expert trout fisherman known for his casting and guiding skills. In the 1930s, he sometimes directed trout-fishing trips for organizations, including the New York Athletic Club.

He tied flies professionally and sold many of his creations through Folkerts Brothers in Phoenicia. Their store on Main Street was considered the unofficial headquarters of Esopus trout fishermen and was the place where information on local trout fishing and which flies were working was dispensed freely. Additionally, visitors could buy almost anything, as the store contained a soda fountain and sold newspapers, gifts, hunting and fishing equipment, and licenses. They had a great inventory of trout flies, mostly tied by Ray Smith. The store's window was filled with a variety of items, but fly fishermen could not walk past that array of beautiful flies arranged in an oval display: the handiwork of Ray Smith.

Ray was born in Chichester, just north of Phoenicia, along the famous Stony Clove. He displayed his talents at fly fishing as a young man with his ability to cast a fly and compete with the best in a valley known for its trout fishing. When the Phoenicia Fish & Game Association held casting tournaments, it was usually Ray and his brother Floyd who walked off with most of the prizes.

Ray Smith with a large Esopus brown. Courtesy of the Phoenicia Library Association.

Ray Smith was known to favor fishing with three wet flies at one time, but the fly he is best remembered for is a dry pattern he popularized known as the Red Fox. The pattern is tied in the traditional Catskill style, with wood duck flank feathers for wings and tail, a body of red fox and rabbit fur blended, and light straw color hackle from a buff leghorn rooster. Ray believed that the fly was first tied by Weatherbys of Englewood around 1900 and was called the Modified Cahill. Ray claimed that the Red Fox was best when fished after May 15 and worked well on browns as well as rainbows. The Red Fox was extremely popular along the Esopus for many years and can still be found in the fly boxes of Esopus fly fishermen.

Another favorite floating fly of Ray Smith's was the Ginger Quill, dressed "light and sparse." He tied the pattern in sizes 14 to 18, and he believed that it fished better in the late afternoon, especially on bright sunny days or on windy days on smooth or flat water. Ray tied the Ginger Quill with wings of slate hackle points, tail of light straw hackle, body of stripped peacock eye ribbed with copper wire, and hackle of buff Minorca rooster, tied sparse.

Ray, like other famous Catskill fly tiers, gave fly-tying demonstrations of his techniques in New York City, notably at Abercrombie & Fitch and at Macy's department store. He had a reputation of being a fine guide, and his clients included some well-known personalities of the day, including Fred Allen, the popular radio personality of the 1930s and 1940s, and George Herman "Babe" Ruth, who fished the Bush Kill and the Esopus in the spring of 1938.

WEST BRANCH OF THE DELAWARE RIVER AND MIKE LURENZE

When the trout season opened in 1930, stream conditions were far from ideal; the night before opening day was bitter cold, and those who arrived along the trout streams in early morning found that ice had formed along the edges of many of the pools. Streams in general were also low but clear, and the trout were wary. Despite these adverse conditions, limits of twenty-five trout were still taken by experienced anglers, and the popularity of trout fishing along East and West Brook continued.

Local newspapers reported that Mike Lurenze of Walton traveled up river to Bloomville and caught his limit in the West Branch; that Harry France, "Walton's expert fly fisherman," caught twenty-five trout in East Brook on flies; Albert Jones caught nineteen up East Brook; and Fred Conklin captured eighteen along West Brook.

A few weeks into the season, the *Walton Reporter* commented that the trout fishing in the streams in the vicinity of the village was changing: "Walton streams, which have always been noted for their fine native brook trout fishing, are fast becoming infested with the German brown trout. If the number of brown trout is allowed to increase to any great extent a native trout in Walton streams will soon be a rarity."[32]

The warning appeared to be sincere, as the following season the newspaper reported that although catches were small, the trout captured were of good size: "The prize offered by J. E. Wood & Son for the largest trout displayed in their window Saturday was won by Abram Delameter of Hamden, who brought in a 15-inch fish. Sears Brown had on display at Wood's a mess of about ten trout, the two largest being brown trout 14 inches in length."[33] The newspaper also reported that Basil Stedman caught ten or eleven large trout from lower East and West Brooks, and proposed that these trout had run up from the West Branch.

In April 1934, the *Roxbury Times* wrote that Leon Moore of Walton caught a 3-pound "German brown trout" along East Brook near the junction of

West Branch of the Delaware River upstream of Hamden. Ed Van Put.

the West Branch. Brown trout, however, did not thrive in the West Branch, or at least not as well as they did on other Catskill rivers. There is little evidence in newspaper accounts of their being caught by anglers during the late 1890s or even in the first decade of the 1900s.

In 1899, Norman Howland of Walton took a brown measuring nearly 2 feet in length that weighed 4½ pounds from East Brook, but there was some confusion at the time as to which species the trout was, because browns were still unfamiliar to most fishermen. There were other trout reported being caught in sizes that were obviously too large to be native brook trout, but there was no distinction as to whether they were browns or rainbows.

The West Branch population of brown trout was certainly not as great as was found along the East Branch during the 1920s and 1930s; nor did brown trout caught between Walton and Stamford match up to the size of those taken in the East Branch.

The 1934 trout season was a good one, and the *Walton Reporter* reported two exceptional catches. In July, while fishing the West Branch around Delancey, Clifford MacFarlane of Walton captured three large trout; the largest was a brown that measured 23½ inches and weighed 3 pounds, 15 ounces. MacFarlane took two other browns that measured 17½ and 18 inches, and the total weight of the three fish was 9 pounds. Just before MacFarlane's catch, Mike Lurenze had taken a 23-inch trout along with two others, with a total weight of 10 pounds.

Mike Lurenze at his fly-tying vise.
Walton Reporter, 1938.

Two of the largest trout in the archives of the *Walton Reporter* between 1885 and 1941 were caught in the Hamden area of the West Branch. In August 1929, Marshall Thomson of Hawley's Station took a "German brown" on a Beaverkill fly that measured 26 inches and weighed approximately 6 pounds, 15 ounces. And in July 1940, Atwood Crook of Hamden caught a "German brown" measuring 28½ inches that weighed 7 pounds, 14 ounces. Crook took his monster brown on a #6 Black Prince wet fly that was tied by Mike Lurenze, who had taken a 5½-pound brown the week before!

During the 1930s, Mike Lurenze was not only an excellent fly fisherman, he was an equally skilled professional fly tier. He began tying trout flies in 1931 after he was unsuccessful in trying to buy a specific pattern that he thought would catch trout in local waters. He soon realized that his own creations were better than those he could purchase, and it was not long before his friends and fishing companions began asking him to tie for them. Lurenze started tying wet flies, and as he gained experience, he graduated to dries, nymphs, streamers, and bucktails. As his reputation grew, he took special orders, and his business expanded to receiving orders from all over the United States. Even though the spring was his busiest time of the year, he recognized that the skills he had learned could make him self-employed on a year-round basis.

In the spring of 1938, Lurenze opened a "quite swanky" shop above the J. J. Newberry store in Walton. He was tying trout flies in the Walton area for many years. Exactly when he stopped tying or left the area is unknown, but he was exhibiting his skills at Walton High School in the late 1940s.

A SURVEY OF THE WEST BRANCH

The 1935 Biological Survey of the Delaware River watershed found the West Branch of the Delaware to be shallower and warmer, and to have slightly less flow than did the East Branch. Because of these environmental factors, biologists believed that the stream did not have much water that was favorable to trout, and because of the smaller volume of water and the lack of adequate habitat, "it is also less favorable for warm-water fishes."

Bass were found in the stream several miles upstream of Delhi, and the Biological Survey recommended a limited stocking of legal-sized brown trout in the stretch of water between Chambers Hollow, 3½ miles upstream of Walton, to just upstream of Bloomville. "This planting should be done in the fall or spring because temperatures are unfavorably high in summer."

The West Branch was found to contain sections that were polluted by slaughterhouse wastes and by wastes from milk by-products. Approximately 2 miles were deemed polluted and unsuitable for stocking; however, above the pollution, the stocking of brown trout was recommended to the stream's source.

THE NEVERSINK AND PARKER FOOTE

By the 1930s, it was no longer an issue of where the reservoir would be constructed, but when, and news reports beginning in the summer of 1931 indicated that it would be soon. That year, the United States Supreme Court allowed the city of New York to remove 440 million gallons of water a day from the Delaware River system. This action was the result of New Jersey seeking to prohibit, through the courts, the city from using water from the Delaware River. Now the way was clear for New York to begin construction of reservoirs on the East Branch of the Delaware and on the Neversink.

In 1935, the Bureau of Biological Survey did fieldwork along the Neversink with the intent to develop a more scientific stocking policy and a program of better fisheries management. These fisheries scientists determined that the Neversink was "excellent for brown trout" from the dam at Fallsburg to the confluence of the East and West Branches. It was stated that there were mainly three limiting factors "(1) a below average insect food production; (2) competition for the food by the tolerant and abundant chubs or fallfish and (3) very heavy fishing."[34] The survey also noted that fallfish and suckers were overabundant between Fallsburg and the confluence of the two branches, and claimed that they were a nuisance to anglers, and limited trout production.*

Speaking at a dinner at the Lenape Hotel in Liberty in the spring of 1937, Conservation Commissioner Lithgow Osborne stated that New York City reservoirs need not destroy any of Sullivan County's famous trout streams other than that portion of them that would be inundated. Sportsmen had let the commissioner know that they were concerned that reservoir construction would destroy major portions of the county's trout fishing.

---

*In a letter to G.E.M. Skues (England), Theodore Gordon in 1912 stated: "Some idiot put chub above the Falls of the Neversink and they have multiplied and worked their way up into all the large pools. A perfect nuisance." *The Complete Fly Fisherman*, 434.

The commissioner also claimed that his department had proposed the building of barrier dams upstream of the reservoirs to prevent warmwater species from traveling upstream to compete with trout. The state would also move quickly to acquire public fishing rights or easements to make up for the stream mileage that was lost to fishermen because of reservoir construction.

The state of New York was not successful in acquiring public fishing rights along the Neversink or its East and West Branches above the Neversink reservoir. Almost all of these waters were private and remain so. Although most have changed ownership, what remains of the Hewitt water is still maintained by members of his family.

The heirs of Clarence Roof continue to own Wintoon Lodge and approximately 5 miles of the beautiful West Branch and surrounding forest lands. For more than a century, the family has been a good steward of the land, maintaining and preserving a pristine wilderness environment, aesthetically even more pleasing than when Clarence Roof began to acquire the property back in 1885.

During the 1930s, the Neversink was still a hub of trout-fishing activity. The village contained a number of fly tiers, fishing guides, establishments, and boardinghouses that catered to the needs of fly fishermen. Trout fishermen continued to ply their skills in and around the village and to fish the famous pools along the river, especially the Black Hole, a favorite meeting place of anglers.

The Black Hole was located at Hewitt's lower property line and the beginning of the open water; it was a long, deep, and dark pool. It was *the* place trout fishers would pause after fishing upstream, and it was not unusual to find twenty or more anglers lining the banks. The pool was a social rendezvous where a fly fisher could converse with the brethren and tell how he'd fared. Good catches were shown off, and big trout were fawned over. Methods and ideas were exchanged, and opinions on which flies to use were usually a part of the conversation.

But the inevitable loss of the community and the beautiful river running through it was too much for some to ponder each day, and it was not surprising when Rube Cross, a Neversink native, left the valley. He was not the first to leave ahead of the destruction New York City had planned for the Neversink. Cross left for the Beaverkill in 1938, following the course of a close friend and fellow fly tier, Parker Foote. Foote also looked to the river and its famed trout fishing for a living, and he decided the year before to abandon the valley and relocate to Connecticut.

Parker Foote was not a local; he moved to the area from New Hampshire in about 1930. It was probably at this time that he and Cross became friends. They not only fished together, but shared fly-tying materials and undoubtedly each other's thoughts on trout flies and fly tying as well.

Foote was known as a very good fly caster and fly fisher. He guided, repaired fishing rods, and operated—but did not own—a fishing resort known as Little River Lodge. During the off-season, he was known to travel to New York and give casting demonstrations before sportsmen and at the same time, pick up orders for flies.

He tied professionally and had a reputation for tying excellent flies. His fly shop, like that of most Catskill fly tiers, was in his home: a small cottage next to the larger boardinghouse that accommodated hunters as well as trout fishermen. The décor, as might be expected of an outdoorsman, was quite rustic, with rods, rifles, and shotguns on the walls, as well as sporting prints, mounted deer heads, and large trout that Foote had captured in the nearby Neversink.

He tied the traditional Catskill patterns: Quill Gordon, Light Cahill, Hendrickson, and a variety of Bivisibles. And like all Catskill fly tiers, he had high standards for dry-fly hackle and was never satisfied with what he was able to procure for color or in the quality of stiffness necessary to float a dry fly. The best hackles usually came from roosters at least two years old, and although many more people kept chickens then than today, no one but a fly tier kept a rooster that long!

Foote was personally acquainted with the feathers he used when tying dry flies, and he treated them with high esteem, labeling individual cigar boxes with inscriptions of the names of the roosters they were taken from. "John Henry Hackle" referred to a badger-colored bird. "George" was a bantam that was cream colored and just right for Light Cahills. There was "Avery," the big New Hampshire Red, and "Rube Cross Blue," an obvious reference to one of Cross's special dun-colored roosters.

Foote returned to the Neversink on occasion for visits. Eventually he left Connecticut for his native New Hampshire, where he spent his final years along the Baker River, a river said to be similar to the Neversink.

At the end of 1939, lawyers for New York City filed maps in the Sullivan County Clerk's Office depicting what properties the city intended to take through condemnation. The *Liberty Register* on January 4, 1940, advised readers that this was the first step that set in motion the legal process for evacuating the people from the land. The second step was for the court to appoint a board of commissioners to award damages for the properties taken. As soon as the oaths of office of the commissioners were filed in the courthouse, the title to the properties on the map automatically belonged to the city.

On January 11, 1940, the editor of the *Liberty Register* lamented on the fate of the Neversink:

> Few residents of Sullivan County will be able to contemplate the flooding of this particular section of the Neversink valley without a gnawing regret. With the eventual disappearance of one of the most beautiful reaches of the beautiful Neversink will vanish a part of the lives of many people who knew the scene but transitorily. Let us not overlook, however, those from whom this reservoir will take a more real part of their lives—those who live there now where their ancestors reared quaint cabins in the midst of virgin forests. A chapter in their family's history is to be closed, and forever. These people, in a sense, are to be cast homeless upon the world, uprooted from spots hallowed by generations of working, struggling forebears.[35]

The city of New York moved quickly, and some people living in the village were notified that they had to be out of their homes by July 7, 1940. Construction began that year on new roads and bridges needed to facilitate the construction of the 7-mile-long reservoir. The Neversink reservoir project required the condemnation of 6,149 acres, with 340 residents and 259 buildings. Included were productive agricultural land, mills, stores, houses, hotels, bowling alley, farms, garages, a church, and cemeteries. By the fall of 1942, any buildings that remained, including the old church, were completely leveled; even the concrete trout ponds of Hewitt's were destroyed and hauled away. Work on the reservoir was then halted because of World War II.

19

The 1940s and 1950s

A CHANGE IN POLICY; "GIVE NATURE A CHANCE";
THOSE RESERVOIRS!; and SALMON IN THE NEVERSINK

In January 1940, Commissioner Lithgow Osborne announced that he was seeking a dramatic decrease in the length of the trout season because of the drought during the summer of 1939. He even contemplated closing it entirely. Osborne suggested that the season begin on May 1 and end on August 1; in addition, he desired to lower the daily limit from fifteen trout to eight.

At the end of the month, the *Catskill Mountain News* declared that "many of us will not understand the reason back of this recommendation in that fish may be replaced by stocking from the hatcheries." However, the editor also recalled that the many weeks of dry weather took a heavy toll on trout in the small streams. The article went on to say, "It may be the better part of wisdom to restrict the take the coming season in order that nature may have opportunity to restore, supplemented by restocking from the Conservation Department hatcheries."[1] But the commissioner's daring idea, no matter how practical, was not readily accepted by the trout-fishing public.

In May, Commissioner Osborne visited Sullivan County as the guest speaker at the Liberty Rod and Gun Club's annual dinner. He had visited the county several times, and being a fly fisher, he undoubtedly enjoyed coming to Liberty, as this particular club had among its membership some of the most noted names in the fly-fishing world, including Roy Steenrod, George Cooper, William Chandler, and Rube Cross.

At the dinner, the commissioner spoke of the future of trout fishing, and he promoted the idea that better fisheries management, not more stocking, was necessary to improve the sport. This was a dramatic departure from practices of the past. Osborne then presented an eight-point program aimed "to improve fishing and to preserve natural fishing."[2] He stated that trout were stocked for years, yet fishing did not improve, and he claimed that stricter regulations placed on the angler were the key to making trout fishing better. He reminded his audience that the year before he had urged a radical decrease in the length of the season as well as a reduced creel limit, citing the need to build up wild trout populations.

His speech focused on restoring a wild-trout fishery, and he pleaded with the sportsmen to "give nature a chance." He stressed that "nature" could bring wild populations back if enough "seed stock" were left in the stream at the end of the fishing season, and that the department was already spending more money on trout propagation than could be justified. Osborne also claimed that natural reproduction (wild trout) still outproduced artificial propagation—"that is a basic fact"—and he again stressed the need for "seed stock" at the end of the season.

Stocking more trout, unless coordinated with "other measures," he claimed, offered a temporary success, but in the long run was expensive and unsatisfactory. The answer was better fish management and reduced catch rates or limits. At the end of his speech, Osborne stated that it was now necessary to reverse the trend, as "we are heading straight for the complete triumph of the liver-fed hatchery-reared trout."

He told his listeners to consider his recommendations and to understand that the old methods were not working. He claimed that if the department did not impose stricter regulations, those streams that naturally produce trout "won't produce any trout worth mentioning." He concluded his speech by saying, "I appeal to you who have such a great interest in real trout-fishing to help me not let this happen."[3]

Commissioner Osborne's eight-point program included the following:

1. Create regulations designed to keep more trout in the stream so there can be "seed stock;" impose a shorter season and smaller creel limit.
2. Increase slightly the number of trout stocked in accordance with "anglers' fair share of the unexpended balance in the Conservation Fund."
3. Halt any increase in the number of legal-sized trout (adults) stocked, especially in streams "suitable for natural growth of fry and fingerlings."
4. Increase the Conservation Department's supervision of trout-stream stocking to make it more effective.
5. Increase and broaden research, and experiment to determine better hatchery methods and stocking practices, including what species should be stocked, in what streams, how many, and what sizes. Above all else, determine what happens to hatchery trout after stocking and why.
6. Continue to purchase public fishing rights.
7. Continue a program of stream improvement on state-owned waters.
8. Establish an antipollution unit with a mobile field lab and two trained biologists.

Days after he presented his ideas, the *Liberty Register* stated in an editorial that the sportsmen of Sullivan County disagreed with the commissioner. They believed that not enough trout were stocked and the Conservation Department should halt "further experimentation" and place even more trout in the streams!

The comment made by Commissioner Osborne regarding what happens to hatchery trout after stocking, and why, had been a riddle to fishermen and biologists for years. Two years earlier, the New York State Conservation Council proposed this same question for discussion by a group of experts at the council's convention in Syracuse.

The conclusion was that there seemed to be no one answer. A few of the reasons that were put forth were that many trout are caught, some are killed by other fish and predators, and some die from insufficient oxygen or lack of food. Writing in the *Herald Tribune,* outdoor writer Don Stillman said that Edward R. Hewitt, an authority on streams and raising trout, claimed that laboratory examinations he conducted revealed that hatchery trout often die because of fatty degeneration of the heart or kidneys, perhaps a result of rapid growth under artificial conditions. Stillman went on to say that the panel of experts agreed that a great deal of scientific work was still necessary "to learn the many obscure secrets which may contribute to the puzzle."[4]

With the outbreak of World War II, there was a sharp reduction of Conservation Department activities. Many employees left for the service, either through enlistment or because of the Selective Service Act, and others left to work in defense factories to help with the war effort. Labor became scarce, as did the gasoline that was used to stock fish. Fish food, especially meat, was in short supply. Many hatcheries were forced to underfeed their trout; in some instances, there were periods when fish were not even fed. However, by 1943, dry food was proving to be very successful, and trout were showing good growth with lower mortality than fish fed straight meat.

When the trout season opened in April 1945, the war was not yet over, and the Conservation Department issued a news release stating "Release One Trout on Opening Day." Acting Conservation Commissioner Vic Skiff declared:

> No matter how good the day no fisherman can put his whole heart in that first wetting of the line until the rest of the boys are back again. One thing we CAN do to help will be for each successful angler to return one trout to the water on the opening day—one trout with the wish that it will grow and take another fishermen's lure some day—a veteran's. There's more to this than merely a gesture of remembrance, it would represent a genuine individual contribution to the goal of better fishing when the boys come home.[5]

In the beginning, the state stocked only fry. Then it was believed that fingerlings would improve trout fishing, but near the end of the war, fish culturists were becoming convinced that legal-sized trout were the answer to the "better fishing problem." In 1944–1945, both fingerlings and yearling trout were being stocked, and the stated goal was to get "the most stocking benefit at the most economical cost."

Writing in the April/May 1950 issue of the New York State *Conservationist,* C. W. Greene, senior aquatic biologist with the Conservation Department, discussed the complexities of stocking fingerlings or yearling (legal-sized) trout. One reason given for stocking yearlings was that on heavily fished trout streams, stocking legal-sized fish could immediately replace those removed, and that by stocking trout 6 inches or larger, many of the hazards or dangers from predators and competition with other small fish were avoided.

However, it was also noted that hatchery-reared legal-sized trout were relatively short-lived when placed in a wild stream environment, and it became obvious that "one-season" trout were not going to develop into the larger trout that anglers preferred. Greene pointed out that "the most extensive stocking, numerically," was still with fingerlings. And he stated that experiments with marked fingerlings demonstrated the success of fingerling stocking: "Efficiency of such stocking can be very high because of low cost of hatchery production and the high rate of return, by weight, to the angler. Also, when these trout reach angling size they are practically wild."[6]

HAIL TO THE BEAVERKILL

The number of large brown trout—fish more than 5 pounds—reportedly caught in the Beaverkill after the war was greatly reduced. Newspaper reports of trout even more than 4 pounds were rare, but the largest was a monster brown caught at Junction Pool on May 26, 1949, by Howard Lindsley of Livingston Manor. Lindsley's huge fish tipped the scales at 8 pounds, 2½ ounces and measured 27 inches in length with a 15-inch girth!

Many years later, I interviewed Howard, and he told me that he caught the brown on a night crawler. The water was "just right"—a local term dating back to the 1880s and used by trout fishermen in the Catskills. It means the river was just beginning to rise and discolor from rain, marking the time when big trout leave their hiding places and begin to feed heavily. This is a common Catskill term that I have heard and seen in print in local newspapers many times. Lindsley's large trout is the last fish of this size reportedly taken from the Beaverkill; large trout have been caught, but nothing has approached the size of his 8-pound, 2½-ounce brown.

Howard Lindsley with an 8-pound, 2½-oz. brown trout. Ed Van Put collection.

An interesting aside on the front page of the *Livingston Manor Times* in 1948 told a story of a rather unusual weekend fishing trip that may have been the first of its kind. The newspaper related that Terence Horsley of Hale Cheshire, England, flew here from England on Friday, went fly fishing in the Neversink on Saturday, the Beaverkill on Sunday, and then returned to London by plane on Monday.

Horsley, an editor with a London newspaper, authored books on angling and aviation. An expert pilot, he flew 1,100 hours during the war while with the Royal Air Force. Horsley was here to collect material and photographs for an article on trout fishing in America for the *Saturday Evening Post*. He was a guest of the Beaverkill Trout Club, and he claimed that there were few trout streams in the world "comparable to the Beaverkill." He reported that he had caught and released fifty trout while fishing the two streams: "Must say you've the clearest streams in the world—the clearest water—so trout fishing's the most difficult I've come across. Capital sport though. Capital."[7]

THOSE RESERVOIRS!

In 1927, the New York City Board of Estimate had approved plans to construct six additional reservoirs, and every major trout stream in the Catskills was to be dammed and have their waters diverted through a series of tunnels to New York. The people of the Catskills and the thousands of fishing tourists who visited the region annually were stunned! It was estimated that construction would be completed by 1939 and that 600 million gallons of water per day would come from the Delaware River drainage. The loss of so many miles of good trout fishing to be inundated by impounded water was incomprehensible to trout fishermen.

The city's plan hit a snag, however, when the state of New Jersey went before the Supreme Court of the United States to prohibit New York State and New York City from removing 600 million gallons per day from the Delaware River system. New Jersey contended that these withdrawals would seriously impact navigation, waterpower, sanitary conditions, industrial use, agriculture, municipal water supplies, recreation, and the oyster and shad fisheries. Pennsylvania joined with New Jersey and became a party to the suit.

On May 25, 1931, the Supreme Court decreed that the city of New York was limited to withdrawing 440 million gallons of water per day. The court also required that a minimum flow be maintained at a point on the Delaware River downstream of Port Jervis and noted that New York would be permitted to petition the court for more water in the future.

This ruling limited the number of reservoirs that the city could construct. The Neversink would remove 105 million gallons per day and the East Branch, at Pepacton, 335 million gallons per day. The construction of the Rondout reservoir was not affected by the ruling, as its waters flowed into the Hudson River. Litigation and the Great Depression did affect construction, and work on the additional reservoirs did not begin until 1937.

Plans to construct a dam on the Beaverkill and Willowemoc were then reviewed, and the city planned to return to the United States Supreme Court to request that the 440 million gallons of water per day be increased to 540 million gallons. Work on these two reservoirs was to begin in the early 1940s.

World War II put a hold on all reservoir construction, but at the end of the war, in 1947, Board of Water Supply engineers once again turned their attention to the famous Sullivan County trout streams and began drilling test holes. In January 1948, the *Liberty Register* reported borings for the new dams on the Willowemoc, about a mile above Livingston Manor, and on the Beaverkill at Jersey Brook, just upstream of the hamlet of Beaverkill. These reservoirs, the newspaper declared, will be located "in the heart of the best trout fishing in all the Eastern United States."

It was rumored that test borings in the Beaverkill Valley failed to locate bedrock at a satisfactory site. This was encouraging to Beaverkill anglers, who did not want to lose any portion of their favorite trout stream. One newspaper editor stated that fishermen may "breathe a little easier" also knowing that the city would need to return to the Supreme Court to reopen the case for additional water.

One year later, the Liberty Rod and Gun Club adopted a resolution for the legislature that was designed to prevent New York City from taking the Beaverkill. Members did not believe that it would alter the plans of the city, but wanted to go on record as being opposed to destroying the famous fishery:

> Whereas, in order to satisfy the demands of the unmetered water consumers in the City of New York, the Board of Water Supply of that city, with the consent of the State of New York, has taken extensive areas of Sullivan and adjoining counties, including some of the county's best loved recreation spots; and has also reserved for this narrow use many miles of the Neversink River; and
>
> Whereas, it is obvious that these enormous appropriations of land and waters will not be sufficient for more than a few years, and the city of New York is already working on the development of the resources of the East Branch of the Delaware, and is contemplatively viewing the Willowemoc and Beaverkill River basins; and
>
> Whereas, these areas and these waters are world-famed among sportsmen and naturalists, and have in the past been trodden and written upon affectionately by some of the mighty figures in these fields; and
>
> Whereas, recreation and simple outdoor sports are recognized as being not without value to the people of this state, and are, in addition a necessary source of livelihood to business interests and employees within the affected areas.[8]

The resolution was resolved with the statement that an amendment to the Water Supply Act should be made, preventing New York City "from taking from our recreational treasury the wealth of the Beaverkill stream, that the said stream may be left inviolate for the primary and principal use to which its beauty and perfection dedicate it—the recreation of the people of this and other states."[9]

Another powerful conservation organization that lobbied against a dam on the Beaverkill or Willowemoc was the Beaverkill-Willowemoc Rod & Gun Club. This group of sportsmen had a membership of more than one thousand—the largest in Sullivan County. Fly tier Harry Darbee was, at various times, president, conservation chairman, and editor of its informative newsletter, *Voice of the Beamoc;* Elsie Darbee served as secretary and treasurer.

The Beamoc, as the club became known, lobbied hard for legislation that prohibited any municipality from constructing a dam for water-supply purposes on the Beaverkill or Willowemoc. A bill was passed by the legislature, but was vetoed by Governor Thomas E. Dewey. Later in the year, trout fishermen everywhere rejoiced when it was learned that New York City had revised its plans, and instead of damming the Beaverkill or Willowemoc, it was now focused on the West Branch of the Delaware River.

At a hearing held in Delhi, in Delaware County, conducted by the Conservation Department's Water Power and Control Commission on the proposed construction of a dam on the West Branch of the Delaware, representatives of the city of New York officially stated that the city was no longer interested in the development of the Little Delaware, the Beaverkill or the Willowemoc as sources of water supply. Following this announcement, it was reported in the *Conservationist* that this was seen as an important victory for fishermen. "And they can rejoice, in the fact that the Little Delaware, the Beaverkill and the Willowemoc will be preserved for trout fishing."[10]

New York City also agreed to a plan for constructing barrier dams, at its cost, to protect the fishing in tributary streams flowing into the reservoirs, wherever such dams could be built on city property. Fishermen were greatly concerned for the streams flowing into the reservoirs; they feared that they would they be invaded by warmwater predator species that would inhabit the new impoundments.

In November 1950, the Water Power and Control Commission granted approval for the construction of the Cannonsville reservoir, contingent upon the United States Supreme Court's modification of the 440-million-gallons-per-day restriction. In June 1954, this amount was increased to 800 million gallons per day.

Organized sportsmen were delighted that they did not lose the free-flowing waters of the Beaverkill and Willowemoc. Their opposition to the construction of dams on these streams, and the fact that the city had decided to go elsewhere for their additional water, was seen as a reason to celebrate. Modern anglers were learning that there was strength in numbers and that they had a voice. Other battles to protect the fishery resources of the Catskills would follow, but at the time, this was seen as a major victory.

FOCUS ON THE ESOPUS

The original gates that allowed the waters from the Schoharie reservoir to enter the Shandaken tunnel operated best at full capacity, thereby causing many of the problems associated with the heavy flows down the Esopus Creek. At some point in the 1940s, changes were made to the gates that allowed them to operate at partial openings, and this reduced flows. Although this was done for better operational efficiency, the change reduced the negative impact to the existing fish populations and improved angling conditions.

Despite the turbidity and the problems associated with it, the Esopus continued to be a prolific trout stream. In the 1940s and 1950s, the stream developed a reputation for pro-

The Esopus Creek at the mouth of the Beaver Kill. Ed Van Put.

ducing large rainbow trout in the spring. Rainbows that had migrated to the Ashokan reservoir grew exceptionally well and returned to the Esopus to spawn. Many were caught in the smaller tributaries, such as the Stony Clove, Woodland Valley Stream, Bushnellsville Creek, and Broadstreet Hollow, in the high flows of April and early May.

A rainbow in excellent condition. Ed Van Put.

An example of the success that trout fishermen could have when braving the high flows of spring is illustrated in a copy of the *Townsman*, published in Grahamsville. The weekly newsletter of May 5, 1948, reported that James Correll of Walden, New York, caught three rainbows in the Esopus measuring 18¾, 20, and 20½ inches. One week later, the *Townsman* stated that Ted and Joe Jadick, also of Walden, caught rainbows measuring 16, 18, 20, 20, 21, and 23 inches.

The *Catskill Mountain News* gives another example of the type of fishing that rainbows migrating from the reservoir produced. On April 14, 1950, the paper reported that Robert Krein caught a 20-inch rainbow in the Esopus, Charles Osborne a 20½-inch rainbow in the Chichester Stream (Stony Clove), and Julian Jankowsky a 20¼-inch rainbow in the Esopus.

Large brown trout also continued to be taken from the stream. The *Townsman* of May 5, 1948 also told of a "monster" trout being taken at Five Arches Bridge: Merlin Yerks, of Walden, caught a 27¾-inch brown that weighed 8 pounds, 7 ounces. And the *Catskill Mountain News* of September 1, 1950, reported that Floyd Smith, brother of Ray Smith, "expert Catskill mountain fisherman," landed a 27-inch brown trout weighing 6 pounds in the "Lanesville Stream" (Stony Clove).

Five Arches Bridge on the Esopus Creek. Ed Van Put collection.

****

During the 1950s, the Conservation Department conducted extensive studies of the principal trout streams in the Catskills. The work was accomplished for a variety of reasons, including how to best manage the fisheries that would be affected by the reservoirs.

In 1950 and 1951, the Southern Fisheries District of the Conservation Department conducted fisheries investigations in the Esopus watershed. The fieldwork was carried out to get an estimate of the existing trout population and to measure the amount of natural reproduction of rainbow, brown, and brook trout. It was believed that the information collected also would be useful in the management plan for the new reservoirs then being constructed on the Rondout, Neversink, and East Branch of the Delaware River.

Along the Esopus, a total of fifty-two widely separated sample sections were electrofished. However, no studies were conducted below the tunnel portal because of the depth of the stream and the swiftness of the water. The investigation revealed one of the most abundant trout populations ever discovered by conducting this type of survey. Trout outnumbered nontrout species, a situation rarely encountered except at the extreme headwaters of a few streams inhabited by brook trout.

Upstream of the portal it appeared that rainbows smaller than legal size were absorbing most of the stream's productivity, but they did not contribute many legal fish to provide angler satisfaction, especially after the large spawning rainbows returned to the reservoir. The study also revealed that there were twice as many legal-sized brown trout as there were legal-sized rainbow trout, yet total counts showed three times as many rainbows as browns.

The report that followed stated that when New York City completed Ashokan Reservoir, and for some years after, brown trout were the dominant species in both the reservoir and the Esopus itself. It was claimed, however, that in recent years, because of the liberal stocking of rainbow trout, a run of rainbows comparable to the annual spring spawning migration in the Finger Lakes had developed.

After the 1950 fieldwork, the Esopus watershed experienced two major floods, and it was desirable to resurvey in 1951 to assess flood damage to fish and stream habitat. Fish collections were made on the Bush Kill, Little Beaver Kill, Beaver Kill, Stony Clove, Woodland Valley Stream, Broadstreet Hollow, Birch Creek, and Bushnellsville Creek. In addition, tributaries of these streams were sampled, as well as smaller tributaries to the Esopus.

The survey revealed two important facts regarding the trout population of the Esopus Creek and its tributaries. The first was that trout populations were greater than nontrout populations; this was rare in New York State waters and occurred, it was stated, only where "environmental conditions are exceptionally well suited to trout production."[11] The second finding was that rainbow trout were the most dominant trout in the watershed; this fact differed from the 1936 survey. The biological survey in 1936 found that brown trout were much more numerous than rainbows, and brook trout were the least common.

Biologists found that fingerling rainbow trout were the most abundant age group collected. The report went on to say that in the spring, large adult rainbows run out of Ashokan reservoir and dominate the stream population. These trout, however, furnished a limited amount of fishing, because as soon as the rainbows were finished spawning, they returned to the reservoir. It was also stated that rainbows between 7 and 12 inches made up the majority of fishermen's summer catch.

The total number of trout collected in the two-year study was 10,046; of this number, approximately 95 percent were wild trout and 6,877 (68.5%) were fingerlings. Of the total number of trout collected, 7,185 (71.5%) were rainbow trout, 2,382 (23.7%) were brown trout, and 479 (4.8%) were brook trout. It can be seen that native brook trout were becoming rare in the watershed; however, it was claimed that brook trout were more abundant in the headwaters of some streams than collections indicated.

The trout population of the Esopus was great but consisted of small fish, mostly yearlings in the 5- to 7-inch range. However, in the spring, large rainbows entered the stream, coming from the Ashokan reservoir to spawn. Some of these trout, after spawning, found pools to their liking and stayed in the river long enough to be caught. Although the Esopus contained an abundance of small trout, as well as some that were very large, the trout in the 10- to 15-inch range were almost absent, either because of overfishing or the fact that they stayed in the reservoir because of immaturity.

These detailed studies on the Esopus and other Catskill streams continued for several years, and they provided valuable data on the various fish populations: "Although the great increase in fishing pressure and other encroachments associated with an expanding human population and contracting fish environment show their influence, the Catskill trout streams still provide some very satisfactory angling."[12] A summary of the fish populations in the streams is given below.

FISH POPULATIONS IN CATSKILL TROUT STREAMS

STREAM SYSTEM	Year Studied	No. 300' Sections Studied	Total No. Fish	No. Brown Trout	No. Brook Trout	No. Rainbow Trout	Total No. Trout	Est. No. Trout Per Mile	Est. No. Legal Trout Per Mile
Beaver Kill......	1953	43	4,604	945	305	130	1,380	563	220
Delaware River (East Branch)..	1952	76	13,618	987	809	149	1,945	454	145
Neversink River..	1951	51	958	127	447	.....	574	197	35
Esopus..........	1950	52	9,556	1,597	367	3,983	5,947	2,006	140
Rondout........	1950	46	7,429	201	915	31	1,147	438	66

OLD BESS

In May 1955, another storied monster brown trout made the front page of local newspapers. Like "Rudolph," this trout also resided near Phoenicia. For four or five years, a huge trout known as "Old Bess" haunted the waters of Mother's Pool. Located about 1 mile below the famous fishing town, Mother's Pool flowed close to Old Route 28 at the base of Mount Tremper. The pool was a favorite of large trout, and its easy access from the highway also made it a favorite of generations of trout fishermen.

Many of the regulars who visited Folkerts or Elmer's Diner and swapped stories and fly patterns knew where the big trout resided, but no one was clever enough to figure out how to catch her. Old Bess gained a reputation as a wily adversary and was deemed warier than all other trout: too large, too strong, and considered uncatchable. She had been hooked, but not landed, and once the word spread about town, Old Bess became a legend.

However, on April 29, 1955, at about 2:30 in the afternoon, Old Bess met her match when she grabbed a small minnow attached to the end of the line of a veteran trout fisher named Larry Decker.

Ed Gilligan, the rod and gun columnist with the *New York Herald Tribune,* broke the story on May 1. He reported that Lawrence M. Decker, a building painter and decorator from Goshen, New York, caught the 9½-pound trout known as Old Bess. Gilligan wrote that the huge fish had defied anglers for years, and although it was known where the trout was, no one could catch it. After the big trout was landed, it was taken to Folkerts, where it was measured and weighed. The trout was in excellent condition and nicely colored; its length was 30¾ inches, and it weighed 9½ pounds!

When Larry Decker caught Old Bess, he was using a two-piece Payne bamboo fly rod given to him years before by Jim Payne, the famous rod maker. He was also using a Shakespeare automatic fly reel rigged with 6-pound-test monofilament line, and he fished with minnows using seven small split shot—not six or eight, but exactly seven.

Decker began the day by catching a 20-inch brown trout at the head of Mother's Pool near a large rock. He fished his way down, got about halfway, and walked back to the head of the pool. Then he hooked one of the largest rainbows he had ever seen and fought the leaping fish until the hook pulled out.

He returned to the head of the pool for the third time and was standing about 40 feet downstream of the large rock when Old Bess struck his minnow. Decker immediately knew he had a large trout by the way the fish moved and tugged. The trout went to the depths of the pool and sulked, then slowly began making its way downstream. After a half-hour battle, Decker found that the fish had taken him halfway down Mother's Pool. He could feel the strength of the big fish and began to worry about landing it in a net; he knew this would be difficult.

Mother's Pool, Esopus Creek. Ed Van Put.

Other fishermen fishing downstream noticed the great bend in the Payne rod, and one angler decided that Decker needed help. When the fisherman who wished to assist saw the great size of the trout, he "stood motionless with wonder." At one point, he managed to slip his net under the trout, but when he lifted it, the net was only big enough to hold the giant trout's tail. The fish bulled its way out of the net and swam off with renewed strength. The helpful angler again tried to net Old Bess, but was once more unsuccessful. Decker thanked the man and told him that the fish was not ready for the net.

Larry Decker with "Old Bess."
Courtesy of the Phoenicia Library Association.

After an hour-long battle, Decker maneuvered himself below the trout and placed his own net carefully under Old Bess. The net's deep bag was filled with the giant fish, and Decker waded toward shore with his spectacular catch.

Ed Gilligan was fishing on the Esopus. He did so often, and he was about a mile downstream, just behind Hoffman's Diner. He had just switched from wet flies to dries when he heard horns honking along the highway. He didn't know what the commotion was about, but when he left the stream, Gilligan traveled up to Folkerts, which was crowded with other anglers who had heard the news. Larry Decker allowed the fabled trout to "lie in state" in the freezer at Folkerts, where Old Bess was viewed by hundreds of envious anglers.

Gilligan, who wrote about the fish in several of his columns, once stated that an angler with a deep sense of public spirit even quit his job in order to devote more time to get Old Bess out of the Esopus. He reasoned that Old Bess was eating her weight in hatchery trout every day for about ten years. And because it cost the Conservation Department about $1.65 a pound to raise hatchery trout, Old Bess was costing sportsmen $3,650 each year!

****

After the construction of the Shandaken tunnel, the Esopus Creek was a frustrating and perplexing place to fish. Trout fishermen never knew what to expect when they visited the stream; its flows and the amount of turbidity were unpredictable, even from one day to the next. At times the level of the stream and its discoloration appeared as if a dam had just burst; the next day, flows could be low and clear.

Paul O'Neil. Photo by George Silk. *Life*, August 28, 1970.

Yet some men have had such memorable days on the stream that they would fish no other, taking the bad days along with the good. The Esopus has a following of devoted trout fishermen who know its moods and idiosyncrasies and accept them—though, at times, grudgingly.

Just about everyone who has ever read Paul O'Neil's classic essay, "In Praise of Trout—and Also Me" agrees that it is the best profile of the Esopus ever written. O'Neil maintained a summer residence along Woodland Valley Stream and plied his skills with a fly rod along his home waters and the Esopus for many years. An excellent writer, his work was featured in such classic American magazines as *Collier's*, the *Saturday Evening Post*, and *Life*.

"In Praise of Trout—and Also Me" first appeared in the May 8, 1964, issue of *Life*. Two years later, it was reprinted in a book titled *American Trout Fishing*, which was published to commemorate the fiftieth anniversary of the death of Theodore Gordon. The book included a select number of articles penned by noted angling writers Lee Wulff, A. J. McClane, Ernest Schwiebert, Roderick Haig-Brown, Dana Lamb, Sparse Grey Hackle, and Arnold Gingrich. Even among these elite author/anglers, O'Neil's piece was one of the best, and his writing endeared him to a host of fly fishers.

CATSKILL MOUNTAIN FISH HATCHERY

About 1917, Robertson S. Ward, a wealthy sportsman from Newark, New Jersey, established a trout hatchery along the Willowemoc Creek, downstream of the hamlet of DeBruce. Known as the Willowemoc Creek Hatchery, the facility was moved to another location, probably because the water was colder: to the Mongaup Creek, about a half-mile upstream of DeBruce, in 1922. Along with the hatchery, Ward constructed a rustic fishing lodge, which he used as a summer residence.

Ward raised trout more as a hobby than as a moneymaking enterprise. He kept the name Willowemoc Creek Hatchery and employed a hatchery manager and all the latest scientific techniques in raising trout. The hatchery was profitable.

Mostly brown trout were raised, and every couple of years, eggs were purchased from new sources to prevent inbreeding. The hatchery sold trout all across the state: to local private fishing clubs, to sportsmen's organizations that stocked public waters, and even to the state of Pennsylvania.

When Robertson Ward died in 1932, organized sportsmen's clubs, along with resort and hotel owners, began lobbying politicians to have the state purchase the hatchery. Local newspapers joined the effort and lent their support and influence. It was argued that ever-increasing fishing pressure was depleting the famous trout streams of Sullivan County, forcing local sportsmen to stock area streams at their own expense while trout from the Willowemoc Creek Hatchery were being shipped out of state to Pennsylvania.

Two years after Ward's death, there were rumors that the state of New York was interested in acquiring the land containing the famous Toad Basin Spring, which was located upstream of Ward's hatchery. In 1935, the Biological Survey of the Delaware and Susquehanna watersheds examined Toad Basin Spring and noted its possibility as a water supply for a hatchery.

The spring was one of the largest and best in the entire watershed; its water temperature in winter was 44.5 degrees Fahrenheit, and it never rose more than half a degree in summer. At that time, however, the rumor proved to be false, and the state continued to stock Sullivan County streams with trout from the Rome, New York, hatchery, 150 miles away.

The scarcity of labor, fish food, gasoline, and materials during World War II caused the Willowemoc Creek Hatchery to close, and the property was put on the real estate market. Finally, on July 16, 1946, the Conservation Department purchased the Ward property, including all the hatchery equipment. In addition, 243 acres were acquired that included Toad Basin Spring, bringing the total purchase to 335 acres.

The ponds of the Ward hatchery continued to be used by the Conservation Department for the purpose of raising fingerlings in 1947 and 1948, but work on an entirely new, modern hatchery began in April 1948, about a half-mile upstream of the Ward facility. Known as the Catskill Mountain Fish Hatchery, the new building included a meat-grinding room, a food-storage room, a garage, an office, a laboratory and workshop, and hatching troughs. Outside, twenty concrete rearing ponds were constructed, measuring 15 feet wide and 50 feet long.

At the same time the new hatchery was being constructed, the Division of Conservation Education was busy renovating the original Ward buildings, and they began operating a summer conservation education camp for boys. Youngsters were taught by department experts, and their lessons included forestry, fish and game management, soil conservation, outdoor photography, fly tying, fly casting, and shooting.

The Catskill Mountain Fish Hatchery began operations in the fall of 1949 and proved to be a great asset to the Catskills, providing quicker and cheaper transportation, a staff familiar with Catskill streams and the problems associated with them, and trout raised in the same waters in which they would later be placed.

"THIS VALLEY IS DOOMED!": THE EAST BRANCH OF THE DELAWARE RIVER

Large trout continued to inhabit the East Branch of the Delaware River well into the 1940s, and local newspapers published the stories of successful trout fishers. In May 1940, the *Catskill Mountain News* reported that C. L. McFee caught a 22-inch, 3¼-pound brown near Margaretville, and in July the paper told of another brown measuring 24 inches and weighing 5 pounds, caught by J. A. Brundage in the Creamery Pool.

A couple of years later, three more large browns were taken in the Margaretville area. In May 1943, George Fairbairn took a 5-pound, 6-ounce brown near the Stone Schoolhouse Pool; Earl Jenkins caught a 4½-pound brown above the cemetery; and Nelson Graham caught another big trout above the playground that measured 24 inches and weighed 4 pounds, 4 ounces.

In July, the *Downsville News* reported that for several weeks, a very large trout was seen in the "swimming hole" downstream of Margaretville. The big fish then moved upstream and was making the north side of the long pool in front of the old D&N railroad station its new home. "The big fellow has daily admirers; he refuses all offers of food by the hook method. Some say the fish will weigh over six pounds."[13]

Another report in the *Downsville News* dated June 22, 1944, reprinted an item from the *Hancock Herald* and depicts how diverse the fishing was in June along the lower East Branch, within the village limits of Hancock. The article stated that Lloyd Nichols, of Hancock, waded into the East Branch and landed a 15-inch rainbow trout and two legal-sized smallmouth bass. Nichols returned the bass, as the season had not opened; a few casts later, he hooked and landed another 15-inch rainbow and another smallmouth. Following a brief period of inactivity, he then landed a nice 17½-inch brown trout. Nichols completed the week by catching, a few days later, five walleyed pike weighing between 3 and 5 pounds.

The East Branch at the railroad station at Margaretville.
N. Y. O. & W. Railroad "Summer Homes," 1908.

By the middle of August, the same newspaper reported that the bass fishing in the East Branch, from Downsville downstream to the main Delaware River, was excellent. Walleye fishing was also good; however, it was reported that the rivers were "working," and it was the time of the year when anglers complained about "particles of foreign matter in the water."[14] The West Branch of the Delaware was the hardest hit by these annual "patches of scum" on the water's surface, and some fishermen claimed it was impossible to cast a line or fish under these conditions.

Larger browns were taken from the East Branch in the second half of the decade. The Margaretville newspaper reported that in 1945, two huge browns were caught in the same week: Velie DuMond caught one measuring 27 inches that weighed 8 pounds, and Ray Neidig took another weighing 6 pounds that measured 24½ inches!

An example of what the fisheries were like on an opening day of the season can be found on the pages of the *Catskill Mountain News* on April 19, 1946. Though the air temperature was cold, just 24 degrees at 6:00 A.M., it rose significantly when the sun began to shine. Stream conditions were good, and the usual snow water found on most opening days was absent; snow on nearby mountainsides had disappeared in early March. Stream levels were lower than normal, being compared with the low flows found in July.

Many of the trout fishermen lining the East Branch and its tributaries had traveled from other parts of New York or from New Jersey, Pennsylvania, or other states. The news report stated that many fishermen in the good pools along the East Branch fished without waders and claimed that hundreds of fishermen took thousands of trout. A count made at 8:00 A.M. along the Bush Kill revealed twenty-seven fishermen between Clovesville and Arkville, and it was estimated that only half were seen because some areas were not visible from the highway along the 3-mile stretch.

A great number of anglers caught their limit, and the largest trout was a monster brown measuring 27 inches and weighing between 7 and 8 pounds, caught in Fuller Pool, downstream of Arena. Game Protector Bryan Burgin of Margaretville reported no serious violations and said that he counted hundreds of fishermen along the streams he patrolled.

The following season, Cecil Fuller of Corbett caught a "German Brown trout" weighing 6 pounds near Union Grove, and Fred Titus made the front page of the *Liberty Register* on April 24, 1947, with a 24-inch brown weighing 4¾ pounds. Many of the largest trout were caught in the vicinity of Shavertown. In 1948, Dominago Andrea took a brown that measured 26 inches and weighed 7 pounds, 2 ounces; and in 1951, Ray Winner captured another East Branch beauty measuring 27 inches that weighed 6 pounds!

People living in the beautiful valley of the East Branch were threatened by the construction of a reservoir as early as 1909, when surveyors were working along the river. At the time, not many gave credence to the rumors that New York City was seeking additional water and was preparing to construct a dam that would displace hundreds of people. Many years passed, and even though the city constructed a huge reservoir at Ashokan and another on the Schoharie Creek, it was incomprehensible that New York could possibly need so much additional water.

People became more uneasy about their way of life and the future of their communities after the Supreme Court agreement of 1931 gave New York City the right to remove water from the Delaware watershed. However, the Great Depression put the project on hold in the 1930s, as did World War II in the 1940s, and even though the city had announced that the project would go forward following the Depression, so many years had passed that some believed the reservoir would never be built.

Construction did begin in 1947, and the name of the project was the Downsville-Pepacton Dam and Reservoir. The taking of private land for public use by the power of eminent domain also began the same year, and when it was completed, everything familiar to generations of Catskill natives was gone forever.

Residents such as Amanda Fletcher, who owned the general store in Shavertown, found a cloth proclamation issued by the State Supreme Court nailed to one of her trees. It stated that New York City was going to build a dam and a reservoir, and that all the land in the area would be purchased by the city through condemnation. This was how the city spread the news throughout the valley!

The East Branch Valley contained four villages: Pepacton, Shavertown, Union Grove, and Arena. In between these communities were many beautiful farms, along the fertile river flats. In the Catskills, flat or bottomland is at a premium, and the valley of the East Branch contained some of the best land for agriculture.

The valley was broader than most and contained more cows than people. A railroad followed the river, and the landscape was dotted with open fields and wildflowers, pasture, grassy crops, and scenic views. The railroad brought tourists, some of whom came for the fishing, others to get away from city life. Tourists stayed at the hotels, boardinghouses, and farmhouses. An example of a popular resort was the Norris Homestead in Shavertown. It was advertised as a modern farmhouse and boasted that a feature of staying at the farmhouse was "Norris Eddy," noted for its fine bass and other fish.

During reservoir construction, the *New York Daily News* published a three-part series in 1952 titled "This Valley Is Doomed!" The series was sensitively written by Joe Martin and Kermit

Jardiker, who visited the region and interviewed many of the residents who were being forced to leave their homes. The articles described how the reservoir was having such a negative impact on Catskill residents and compared the 200-foot-high dam being constructed to a headstone for the entire valley.

The reporters told a moving story of one resident named Mary Thain who, at the time, was forty-five years of age and lived in Shavertown in a nine-room house overlooking the East Branch. They had heard rumors that Mary had a "most remarkable window" overlooking the river and that when she knocked on this window, fish began to rise! They visited her home and found a "slender, graceful woman" who assured them that this was true.

Mary demonstrated by rapping on the glass, and in an instant, fish began making little swirls as they broke the surface film of the stream. They were hungry, and whenever Mary rapped on the window, she followed up by feeding them small pieces of bread she tossed from her porch.

When she was asked what she would miss when the reservoir was completed and everything—including her home—was under water, Mary stated that she would miss the fish and many other things, including her family: "I've got more than 100 relatives scattered through the valley. Now we'll really be scattered. You can't get a new home just where you want it."

Once construction started in the valley, people were divided into two opposing groups: the locals or natives on one side, and the men who came there to work on the project on the other. In spite of this conflict, Mary Fletcher met Edward Thain, who was a construction worker, and they fell in love and were married:

> Her friends felt no sense of betrayal over the marriage. As far as the valley was concerned, Mary Thain can do no wrong. The valley loves her and there is concrete evidence of it.
>
> During World War II, she enlisted as an Army nurse. She was restless then, tired of the valley, but after she had spent almost five years on the battlefronts of the Pacific, the valley tugged. She dreamt of it often. In particular, she thought of a certain white house by the river. She didn't own it, but she had envied those who had.
>
> When she returned home, someone mentioned that the house was up for sale. She managed to scrape together $2,500, a pathetically small sum for such a property. The house faces not only the river but Main St. as well, and there is also a charming garden. At twice $2,500, the property would have been a tempting bargain.
>
> But when the word got around that Mary wanted the place, not a single one of the valley people put in a bid, and Mary got the house of her dreams.
>
> Now it will be destroyed. You can't outbid the city.[15]

By the time all of the land was condemned, a total of 13,384 acres were acquired by New York City, and 947 people were forced to leave their homes, farms, stores, churches, schools, garages, hotels, taverns, sawmills, and villages. Cemeteries were also removed, including 2,371 grave sites, the oldest dating back to 1792.

Some of the houses and barns were resold and moved to nearby lands not condemned by the city. Those that remained were burned, along with any other buildings standing. The entire valley, roads, bridges, stone walls, and 22 miles of the East Branch were inundated by the new reservoir that began filling on September 15, 1954.

"JULIUS CAESAR" AND NEVERSINK SALMON SUCCESS

In the fall of 1946, area newspapers reported that work on the Neversink dam had been renewed. It was several years before the dam was completed, but on June 4, 1953, the reservoir began filling. Following the Neversink reservoir's completion, it was announced that New York City would discharge a minimum of ten million gallons per day to the river below the dam during the summer period and three million gallons per day during the winter. These releases were ordered the year before the reservoir started filling and were made "to prevent harm to boating and fishing."[16]

That the releases were inadequate could be seen almost immediately, as trout fishermen found large brown trout concentrated in the low flows below the dam. The *Livingston Manor Times* on June 25, 1953, reported, "Fishermen are having a field day in the Neversink river, due to the lowering of the stream by closing of the outlet at the Neversink dam by the New York City Board of Water Supply, thus confusing the fish in deep pockets." The newspaper went on to report on two fishermen, who took five trout weighing a total of 16 pounds, 4 ounces. Two of the trout were browns that weighed more than 4 pounds!

****

"Julius Caesar" and Frank Hovey Roof Connell. *Wintoon*, 1993.

It was along waters of Wintoon — the estate formerly owned by Clarence Roof on the West Branch of the Neversink—in the late 1950s that another legendary Catskill brown trout, by the name of "Julius Caesar," resided under a rocky ledge in a place known as Otter Pool. Whether the great fish spent part of its life in the reservoir is unknown, but it was seen at Otter Pool and was fished over for a couple of years with an assortment of flies—wets, dries, nymphs, and streamers— to no avail.

Before Julius Caesar ruled the West Branch, the largest trout taken along Wintoon waters had tipped the scales at 4 pounds. When the mighty Caesar's reign ended, he weighed 10½ pounds and measured 31 inches! The great trout was a fearsome specimen, displaying a 15½-inch girth and a huge hooked jaw.

A trout as large as Julius Caesar could live anywhere he desired in the West Branch of the Neversink, and why the fish chose Otter Pool will never be known—

there are larger and deeper pools on the stream. Perhaps the answer lies in the words of Kim Connell, who knew the stream as intimately as anyone. Connell spent a major portion of his life exploring, learning, studying, and enjoying Wintoon. He knew the trails made by man or deer, every waterfall, wild apple tree, riffle, and pool:

> Otter is dark and feels subterranean because of the shadows cast by the bower of overhanging hemlock trees. It's as if the river passes through a grotto. On the far side watery stalactites drip from a spring that flows into the middle of the pool, which is long but narrow and deep. The river whispers profundities as it slides into the cavern of hemlocks, and Julius Caesar's last words can be heard in the eddy near the head of the pool where the river circles back on itself. Out in the depths, the wisdom of all the stones the river has passed over is hidden under the bedrock shelf that juts out into the belly of the pool. This forms a cave within a cave. Under that shelf Julius Caesar lived like a prehistoric king, a beast the likes of which the river may never see again.[17]

****

In 1950, in preparation of the construction of the new reservoir, the city of New York appropriated 1,315 acres and about half of the Neversink that was owned by Edward R. Hewitt. Following the construction of the reservoir, Hewitt, now in his late eighties, was still determined to have salmon fishing in the Neversink.

In a letter to the *Liberty Register* published on June 9, 1955, he stated that salmon fishing would soon be a possibility in Sullivan County. He told readers that at his urging, the Conservation Department had stocked the new reservoir the previous fall with fifteen hundred landlocked salmon. These fish averaged 5½ inches in length and were placed in the reservoir on September 13, 1954.

Hewitt also announced that the state had trouble getting salmon and that he had purchased from the Kincardine Fisheries, Ardgay, Ross-shire, Scotland, ten thousand eyed Atlantic salmon eggs. These eggs arrived at Idlewild (John F. Kennedy) airport, and Cecil Heacox of the Conservation Department made arrangements to have the eggs picked up by a hatchery truck and taken to the Catskill Mountain Hatchery at DeBruce.

The eggs were hatched at DeBruce, and the unfed fry were planted in the Neversink near Halls Mills Bridge by the Conservation Department. Ed Hewitt gave explicit instructions that the fry be planted—as soon as their egg sacs were absorbed—in gravel sections upstream of the reservoir.

In August 1955, Hewitt again wrote the newspaper stating that four salmon had been caught in the Neversink River and reservoir within the past year. The fish weighed 1¾ pounds to 2¼ pounds, and Hewitt was convinced that these salmon were progeny of the Norwegian salmon he initially stocked many years before.

The following year, 1956, Hewitt purchased another ten thousand Atlantic salmon eggs from Scotland, and like the previous shipment, these were received and hatched at the state hatchery at DeBruce and were also stocked in the Neversink.

Edward R. Hewitt died at the age of ninety in February 1957, but before he passed away, the final shipment of Scottish salmon were received; they were stocked in the Neversink the following April. The *Livingston Manor Times* reported on the event: "These Atlantic Salmon, a legacy from the late Edward R. Hewitt to the People of the State of New York, were purchased by Mr. Hewitt in Scotland as eggs, and hatched at the Catskill Fish Hatchery operated by the Conservation Department, which directed the stocking. This was the third and final planting in the great experiment to establish Atlantic Salmon in the Neversink."[18]

Hewitt's "great experiment" proved unsuccessful. However, about a dozen years after the last stocking of salmon, New York State Conservation Department fisheries biologist William H. Kelly decided to try again. Kelly did a survey of the reservoir. He completed temperature and chemical analyses, studied existing vegetation and thermal stratification, and sampled plankton and existing fish populations, including forage species that would serve as food for the salmon.

Bill Kelly with a brace of Neversink salmon. Courtesy of Drew Kelly.

It was determined that a forage species needed to be introduced, and Kelly decided on rainbow smelt, which were obtained from Blue Mountain Lake in the Adirondacks. Approximately two and a half million smelt eggs were spread on wooden trays lined with burlap, and these were placed along the shoreline of the reservoir, in Black Joe Brook and Dry Brook, in the spring of 1971.

Between 1973 and 1975, a total of thirteen thousand 5- to 7-inch salmon smolts of "sea-run" stocks were introduced into the reservoir. In the fall of 1975, four thousand 3.1-inch fingerling salmon from landlocked freshwater stocks in the Adirondacks were planted in the West Branch of the Neversink upstream of the reservoir. One year later, 15,200 fingerlings averaging 1.2 inches were also placed in the West Branch. A follow-up survey of the stream revealed that the West Branch was a suitable salmon nursery.

In May 1979, the first reported Atlantic salmon was caught by an angler fishing from shore. The fish was one from the fall stocking of 1975; it measured 20 inches and weighed 3½ pounds. The program of stocking salmon in the Neversink Reservoir continues to the present day, and it is a legacy of Bill Kelly's, who was persistent in his desire to establish a salmon fishery in the Neversink Reservoir. Kelly's interest in fisheries went beyond his professional occupation; over the years, he earned a reputation in the Catskills as being a skilled and knowledgeable fly fisherman, and he was equally as proud of his profession as he was of his accomplishments with the long rod.

20

Addendum

The lore of the Catskills can be found on the pages of countless articles that have appeared in newspapers, magazines, journals, and books on trout fishing. It is a rare fly fisher who has not read of the region's storied streams, their pools and riffles, and of the legendary fly fishermen who contributed to trout-fishing history.

Today, Catskill streams and rivers remain a favorite destination, and waters such as the Beaverkill, Willowemoc, and Esopus still have the allure to draw fly fishers from across the country. Some come as if on a pilgrimage to fish these streams steeped in history and tradition. They wish to wade in the waters and cast their flies in the same currents as the great anglers of an earlier age: anglers who tied to their leaders two or three wet flies with names like Queen of the Waters, Scarlet Ibis, and Coachman, then danced them down and across the current, near the surface, and attracted speckled trout in numbers that are incomprehensible today.

Some travel long distances to fish these hallowed waters, but the majority of fly fishers found in the Catskills live within a two-hour drive, coming from the greater New York City metropolitan area, which includes New York City, northern New Jersey, southwestern Connecticut, northeastern Pennsylvania, and the southern tier of New York State. This represents the largest metropolitan area in the United States, with a total population of 21,923,089 as of 2005—nearly twenty-two million people!

Following World War II (1939–1945), there was a great increase in the number of trout fishermen that was due perhaps to a greater focus on outdoor recreation and more leisure time. The spinning rod was created during this period, which produced scores of instant anglers and placed added fishing pressure on Catskill trout streams. Previously, even those who fished with bait most likely used a fly rod and, because of the difficulty of casting bait, needed to get close to their quarry by wading. Spin fishermen, however, could now cast across the entire stream with a worm or small lure and did not need to enter the water; they could cover more of the stream in far less time.

The need to restrict anglers became increasingly obvious in the 1960s, as reduced limits did not always obtain the results necessary to improve the fishing to the level fishermen were demanding. The idea proposed by Dr. Albert Hazzard back in the early 1950s of "catch all the trout

Electrofishing survey along a Catskill trout stream. R. Rehbaum.
The Conservationist, March/April 1986.

you can but don't keep them; put them back," began to be accepted as an alternative regulation aimed at improving trout fishing.

Twenty-five years after Commissioner Osborne recommended stricter regulations be placed on trout fishermen, fisheries professionals began doing exactly that, at least on some Catskill streams.

In 1962, the first "no-kill" or "fish-for-fun" area was established along 1.4 miles of the Schoharie Creek. The regulation stated that all trout should be returned to the water unharmed;

single-hooked lures were required. However, this regulation was removed after a few years because it did not achieve the results fisheries biologists had expected. It was believed that the Schoharie contained too many competing species, such as white suckers and smallmouth bass.

In 1965, "no-kill" regulations were again adopted, although this time along the lower Beaverkill in Delaware County. The special fishing area began at the county line and ran downstream approximately 2.5 miles, and included many of the historic pools so popular with fly fishermen. The regulation stated that all trout were to be returned to the water unharmed. Because the "no-kill" area was so successful on the Beaverkill, it was instituted along a stretch of the lower Willowemoc in 1969. These stretches of the two streams became the favorite of many, so much so that by the mid-1970s, the amount of "no-kill" water along these streams was increased to 8 miles. These special regulations are still in effect; trout in these sections grow and hold over, despite being hooked many times during the fishing season.

The "no-kill" areas contain excellent populations of trout throughout the fishing season. Because they hold so many trout and offer excellent fly hatches, they have been "learning centers" for beginning fly fishers, who have honed their skills along the Beaverkill and Willowemoc, casting to rising trout.

In the "days of old," trout fishermen generally fished from April 1 to about the Fourth of July, when streams became low, at times warm, and the trout were scarce and difficult to catch. Today, with so many trout found in the "no-kill" stretches, fishermen have changed their tactics, using finer leaders and smaller flies, and continue fishing through the low-flow period of midsummer. Trout-fishing activity increases dramatically along the Beaverkill and Willowemoc in the fall, as this water is open year-round. It is not unusual to see fishermen in the "no-kill" areas on sunny days, even in the dead of winter.

****

No single event affected streams and rivers in the Catskills more than the construction of New York City water supply reservoirs. Their development destroyed nearly 50 miles of trout streams: 7 miles of the Rondout, 7 miles of the Neversink, 22 miles of the East Branch of the Delaware River, 5 miles of the Schoharie, and 6½ miles of the Esopus Creek.

The Rondout reservoir was put into service in 1953, the Neversink in 1954, and Pepacton (East Branch) in 1955. That same year, work began on the Cannonsville reservoir, located downstream of Walton on the West Branch of the Delaware River. Cannonsville was the last New York City reservoir to be constructed in the Catskills; it was completed in 1967.

Although reservoir construction eliminated stream fishing, the man-made "lakes" did create an excellent trout fishery. All of these reservoirs offer exceptional trout fishing; browns in the 10-, 15-, and even 20-pound range are caught in the Pepacton reservoir, and rainbows up to 10 pounds are taken from Ashokan. The Neversink contains brown trout as well as salmon; the Rondout, lake trout and browns. Large browns can also be caught in Cannonsville, and Schoharie Reservoir is known for its walleye fishing. The six reservoirs cover a surface area of approximately 23,044 acres; Ashokan is the largest at 8,055 acres, followed by Pepacton with 5,696 acres, the smallest being the Schoharie with 1,112 acres, and the Neversink with 1,461 acres.

All of the reservoirs are open to public fishing upon obtaining a free-access permit from New York City; permits can also be obtained to place a rowboat on individual reservoirs for the purpose of fishing. Pepacton and Ashokan are the most popular with trout fishermen, who fish from shore or keep a boat on the reservoir. Night fishing from boats, using lanterns that attract schools of baitfish, is a common practice. Large trout are lured to these baitfish; at times, boats are so plentiful on Pepacton that in the black of night, they resemble fireflies bobbing on the reservoir's surface.

The habitat of the streams below each of the reservoirs has changed significantly: Ashokan, Rondout, and Schoharie because of the lack of water releases; and Cannonsville, Pepacton, and Neversink because of beneficial coldwater releases discharged from the bottom of the reservoir dams. Below the Neversink reservoir, there are approximately 15 miles of water affected by these releases; the East Branch is affected for 32.6 miles, and the West Branch for 17.3 miles. After reservoir construction, smallmouth bass and fallfish populations decreased, and trout populations increased to higher levels. Coldwater releases not only affected bass populations, but drastically reduced a favorite food of smallmouth, the dobsonfly (hellgrammite).

Since the advent of coldwater releases below New York City reservoirs, the region has also been given a second season. As natural stream levels begin to decline and flows and fly hatches are reduced, the lower Neversink and the East Branch (and West Branch) of the Delaware are often flowing at higher levels, with cooler water temperatures and summertime hatches that offer challenging fishing for larger trout.

****

Changes to the flows below the reservoirs are the direct result of the efforts of a coalition of sportsmen, conservationists, and fishing organizations. In the summer of 1976, a small but potent group fought the bureaucracy of the largest city hall in America and walked away with a victory some have hailed as the greatest Catskill environmental battle in New York's history. The fight was led by a determined coalition of trout fishermen known as Catskill Waters, and their goal was to change the way New York City released waters into the rivers below its reservoirs.

From the time the Shandaken tunnel began operation in 1924, trout fishermen had a love-hate relationship with the "portal" and its discharges of cold but turbid water flowing into the Esopus Creek. The practice of New York City operating the tunnel with inconsistently high and low flows was viewed as being detrimental to the fishery. High flows generally caused so much turbidity that trout fishermen were turned away from the stream; other times, flows were shut off so rapidly that fish perished from being stranded in side channels and small pools of water. These problems emanated from a system in which water was taken from one reservoir and sent to another. It should have been easy to resolve, yet it persisted for a half century because the city refused to alter its practice.

Major flow problems existed below all of the city's impoundments. Downstream of the Neversink and Pepacton reservoirs, stream flows were woefully inadequate, and the releases along the West Branch and Delaware Rivers were similar to the Esopus: too great on some days and too little on others. This resulted in rapid water-temperature and stream-level changes, at times in a matter of hours, stressing fish and causing mortality. After Cannonsville reservoir was completed in 1964, it was not uncommon for water temperatures below the dam to rise from 50 or 60 degrees Fahrenheit into the 80s, then recede back to the 50s or 60s a few days later.

When water temperatures rose above 78 degrees for a few days, trout concentrated off tributary mouths or in spring holes; they did so because they were in distress. On the Delaware, this led to additional problems; at these times, the trout often became infested with an external parasite known as *Argulus*, or fish louse. These parasitic copepods suck out the fish's body fluids; when they break the skin, they cause intense irritation and wounds that can become infected by other organisms.

Under most circumstances, *Argulus* does no great harm, but when trout become concentrated because of high water temperatures, they become heavily infested, which can lead to their death. How many browns and rainbows perished under these circumstances is unknown, but it was not unusual to see sores or *Argulus* on trout after they had spent time concentrated off a tributary.

One event that proved to be pivotal in changing the way that New York City released water from its Catskill reservoirs occurred in the summer of 1972. In July, water temperatures along the Delaware River reached 86 degrees, and thousands of trout concentrated at the mouths of tributary streams. These fish were stacked side by side like cordwood, hundreds pressed together—a mass of trout—their noses tight to the colder tributary water, which acted like a life support system.

During this period, New York State Department of Environmental Conservation Fisheries Biologist Tony Bonavist began documenting the unnatural conditions that existed on the Delaware. Tony recorded water temperatures and oxygen levels, and took photographs of the large concentrations of trout located at the tributary mouths. Before this occurrence, no DEC official had witnessed or recorded the perilous circumstances the "wild" trout fishery was faced with as a result of the inadequate water releases.

Two years later, in 1974, the Esopus Creek was the site of a large fish kill after the Shandaken tunnel was closed abruptly, leaving thousands of trout stranded. Ed Ostapczuk, president of the Catskill Mountain chapter of Trout Unlimited, began supplying DEC Commissioner James Biggane with information regarding the mismanagement of the Esopus by New York City.

Clipboard in hand, Fisheries Technician Ed Van Put is surrounded by a dark mass of trout
off a Delaware River tributary (1972). Courtesy of Tony Bonavist.

In November, Commissioner Biggane issued a news release and cited "massive fish kills" on the Esopus, stating, "We have tried to work out on a voluntary basis with the city solutions to the problems caused by inadequate releases, but it is apparent that this approach has not worked." He pledged "appropriate legal action to assure adequate releases from New York City's Catskill area reservoirs to preserve fisheries in the Esopus, Neversink, the East and West Branches of the Delaware and the main stem of the Delaware. The public has a right to be protected against such irresponsible actions as the abrupt closing of the Shandaken portal, which resulted in killing tens of thousands of fish." He directed the matter to the attorney general's office. Ostapczuk also got the attention of the attorney general's office, and there was talk of drawing up a lawsuit against New York City.

During the winter of 1974–75, a group of about twenty-five sportsmen (many of whom were members of fishing organizations), DEC officials, and Peter N. Skinner and Cyril Moore of the attorney general's environmental protection unit, were brought together at the Antrim Lodge in Roscoe by Frank Mele of Woodstock. Frank, an avid fly fisher, musician, and novelist, urged the saving of the blue ribbon waters of the Catskills. Mele had never been involved in any conservation disputes, but he approached the issue of reservoir releases with determination and extreme devotion. He invited organized sportsmen from several counties to join forces and form a coalition with one goal: to improve the water releases downstream of the New York City reservoirs. It was claimed that the city could increase its releases and give "true" conservation releases to the rivers—and still satisfy its drinking-water demands.

Phil Chase—science teacher, fly fisher, conservationist, and popular outdoor columnist with the *Times Herald Record* of Middletown—was perhaps the group's most knowledgeable individual on the complex reservoir release problem. Phil had been writing about the inadequate water releases on the Neversink for many years. He was a lone voice educating sportsmen, prodding them to get involved and force New York City to own up to the destruction it was causing to Catskill rivers. At the meeting at the Antrim Lodge, slides were shown depicting low stream flows and trout concentrated off tributary mouths.

Monthly meetings began to be held at the Antrim Lodge, and a committee was formed known as the Citizen's Steering Committee for Reservoir Management. Its role was to plan action for organizing documentary material and coordinate the work with groups that had been working independently. The committee hoped that the attorney general's office could negotiate with New York City for written, legal contracts regulating future water releases.

In June 1975, Phil Chase wrote in his column that Representative Maurice Hinchey of Saugerties had introduced a bill in the assembly on March 4 that would give the state the power to regulate water releases from the reservoirs into the streams below them "in order to protect and enhance the recreational use of those rivers." A similar bill was introduced in the senate, and "great support" was given to both bills by U.S. Representative Matthew F. McHugh of Ithaca, who sent a representative to many of the meetings at the Antrim.

The bill in the senate was sponsored by Senator Jay Rolison, Poughkeepsie, and was a direct outgrowth of the Temporary State Commission on the Water Supply Needs of Southeastern New York. His bill stated that the lack of water-release regulations "resulted in the virtual destruction of certain streams below impoundments by limiting or eliminating other legitimate uses of these waters." It authorized the DEC to establish downstream release schedules below the reservoirs, and Hinchey's bill did the same. At this time, it was claimed that relations between the city and Catskill residents were viewed as "poor" and were "characterized by hostility."

At the Antrim's June meeting, it was reported that negotiations between the attorney general's office, the DEC, and the city had proved futile. And it was stated that the city was reneging on negotiations for test releases that were to be carried out by Doug Sheppard, DEC supervising aquatic biologist, so that a computerized model could be established that would protect Catskill streams.

Frank Mele blamed a major portion of the problem on new DEC commissioner, Ogden Reid, who had not answered letters. Mele called Reid "rude" and "discourteous" and stated that he had done nothing at the administrative level to negotiate with the city. Mele urged that letters be sent to the governor asking for Reid's removal. He also suggested a tighter unification of the concerned organizations and suggested renaming the Citizen's Steering Committee. "This would be a clearing house for all organizations and perhaps be entitled Catskill Coalition of Environmental Protection." He told members to be prepared to form the coalition at the July meeting.

As a member of the original Citizen's Steering Committee, John Hoeko of Fleischmanns had sent Commissioner Reid a letter in April in which Hoeko cited the city's mismanagement of releases. He pointed to the "documented fish kills, degradation of warm and cold water fisheries, catastrophic flood potential and severe economic loss to the Catskills." He urged the DEC to work with the attorney general's office to facilitate litigation, and he prodded the commissioner to attend the next meeting at the Antrim Lodge.

At the July meeting, the Citizen's Steering Committee name was changed, and Catskill Waters was founded. Its goals were to work with the DEC to get New York City to release water out of Cannonsville more gradually, to reduce water temperature fluctuations, to increase the flow to the Neversink from ten million gallons per day to fifty million gallons per day, to increase the flow from Pepacton to sixty million gallons per day, and to stabilize the flow from the Shandaken tunnel.

John Hoeko was elected president of the newly formed Catskill Waters. The dynamic twenty-six-year-old was described as "an aggressive, competent young man who, with the rest of the organization, is determined to save the rivers." Frank Mele was elected vice president; Ed Ostapczuk became secretary-treasurer; and Phil Chase, Art Flick, Alan Fried, and Phil Neish, directors. Hoeko brought in speakers from the DEC, local politicians, and eventually, even Commissioner Ogden Reid. Support by the DEC grew as Ogden Reid became a staunch ally of Catskill Waters, giving their cause the highest priority. DEC engineers and chiefs of bureaus picked up the battle for the rivers as representatives of the steering committee journeyed to Albany to intensify the pressure.

In August 1975, a fish kill occurred along the East Branch of the Delaware River below Downsville. An article in the *Oneonta Star* on August 15 stated that the attorney general's office cited "possible litigation" against the city and reaffirmed the Justice Department's commitment to former DEC Commissioner James Biggane's orders: to take the city to court if negotiations failed.

Catskill Waters sent out a news release stating that the DEC had an excellent management plan for increasing water releases called "The Alternate Release Proposal." However, the problem lay in the actual implementation of the plan. It was demanded that the DEC become more aggressive and pursue a litigious route to make the agreement binding with the city. Hoeko called New York City's past actions with the releases "environmental genocide" and urged stronger action.

In October, Assemblyman Maurice Hinchey journeyed to the Antrim Lodge and spoke at the meeting of Catskill Waters. The group was inspired by Hinchey's enthusiasm and let him know that they appreciated his introducing a bill that could be vital to the future of Catskill trout streams.

By the spring of 1976, Ogden Reid was being praised for his strong support. Reid had started out badly with Catskill Waters, but many believed this was because he was being kept out of the loop and was not receiving their information. Once he did, the group believed he showed great leadership and good insight on state problems. Reid came to Sullivan County and spoke about the need for proper releases, and he described the current release schedule as a desecration, stating that it would no longer be tolerated; Phil Chase praised him for his great leadership.

Just as Reid was proving himself to be invaluable to Catskill Waters, he was suddenly forced to resign. On May 2, 1976, the *Times Herald Record* praised Reid on its editorial page: "Ogden R. Reid was, we suspect, a victim of his own integrity. He took seriously his sworn responsibilities as commissioner of environmental conservation, to protect the environment, and that's probably what did him in." Reid had ordered an investigation into General Electric's discharge of PCBs into the Hudson River, and he had supported Catskill Waters in their fight to get proper reservoir releases.

It was also in May that a fund-raising banquet was held at King's Catering House in Livingston Manor to benefit Catskill Waters so it could continue to battle for adequate releases. Author/editor

Nick Lyons was the emcee, and Robert H. Boyle, author/Hudson River activist, was the guest speaker. The event was an overwhelming success and was highlighted by the unexpected entry of Ogden Reid, who had recently been asked to step down as DEC commissioner. Reid was treated to a standing ovation as he made his way into the dining room filled with Catskill Waters supporters.

In May 1976, three legislative hearings were held on water releases at Binghamton, Boiceville, and Monticello. Testimony by sportsmen, politicians, environmentalists, and state agencies was given in support of passing the water release bill. John Hoeko reported that "In Albany the legislation is moving well that would place the DEC in charge of managing the reservoirs." It had passed in the senate by a vote of 44 to 9, and there was optimism it would pass in the assembly as well. Political action for legislation intensified, and Hoeko lobbied hard for the bill's passage. On June 28, 1976, the *Times Herald Record* headline exclaimed boldly "Catskill water flow bill wins by 1-vote margin." The newspaper credited Maurice Hinchey and Representative Jean Amatucci of Huguenot, the proposal's sponsors in the assembly, for leading a "lengthy and heated debate against New York City legislators who tried to kill the bill." Amatucci and Hinchey had earlier argued for the bill to be released from the assembly ways and means committee, where it had been stalled.

Much to the chagrin of Catskill Waters, a month after the legislation was passed, Governor Hugh Carey claimed he would veto the bill. Congressman Matt McHugh's office contacted Assistant Secretary of the Interior for Fish and Wildlife Nathaniel Reed. Reed sent a telegram to Governor Carey, telling him that he supported the legislation, and he urged him to sign it. Carey signed the river's bill into law.

Pete Skinner of the attorney general's office was "invaluable to the success" of Catskill Waters, yet he gave much of the credit to the passage of the legislation to John Hoeko, who virtually lived in the offices of legislators. "People will never know just how much they owe John," reported Phil Chase in his *Times Herald Record* column of August 1, 1976.

No sooner had the Catskill Waters battle ended when Ed Ostapczuk found himself in the middle of another major conflict that threatened the Esopus Creek. This involved the politically influential New York Power Authority and was known as the Prattsville Pumped Storage Project.

The Prattsville project called for the construction of a storage reservoir above the Schoharie reservoir. Water from Schoharie was to be pumped to the storage facility and returned, generating power by flowing through turbines on the way back. It was claimed by those opposed to the project that this would have kept silt in the Schoharie reservoir in a constant state of suspension and eliminate its essential stratification. The result would be an increase in turbidity and an end to the cold-water regime that flowed through the portal and into the Esopus Creek, thereby having a significant detrimental effect on the trout fishery.

In July 1976, Ostapczuk helped organize a coalition of fishing and environmental organizations to defeat the pumped storage project. A group was formed on September 28, 1979, and became known as the Esopus Legal Defense Fund, with the four major contributors being the Catskill Center for Conservation and Development, Theodore Gordon Flyfishers, Trout Unlimited, and the Phoenicia Fish and Game Association. By the time this battle was over, the organization would spend nearly a quarter of a million dollars in legal and consulting fees.

Ostapczuk was involved in the Prattsville project for twelve years, and the general consensus was that it would have destroyed the Esopus fishery. He credits DEC Region 4 Senior Aquatic

Biologist Kay Sanford, whose report on the proposed project alerted sportsmen of the impact the project would have: "This sounded the alarm for all anglers of the Esopus Creek."

The Prattsville Project was opposed by the DEC, the Environmental Protection Agency, the U.S. Fish and Wildlife Service, and organized sportsmen; and after a costly ten-year legal battle before New York's highest courts, the New York Power Authority, on May 19, 1987, withdrew its proposal. The defeat of the project was seen as the most important environmental victory of the 1980s, and many credit Ed Ostapczuk for his involvement. In addition to his being active in various conservation efforts, Ed somehow found the time to become one of the finest trout fishermen in the Catskills.

****

A few years before Catskill fly tier Elsie Darbee passed away, she began to promote the idea of establishing a museum in the area of the Beaverkill and Willowemoc dedicated to preserving the history of fly fishing in the Catskills. In 1978, a small group of local men and women began meeting to perpetuate the idea and elected Elsie as president, a position she held until her death in 1980. In 1981, the group became known as the Catskill Fly Fishing Center, and Dr. Alan Fried of Livingston Manor became the president. Under Dr. Fried's leadership, the organization grew and established its first home in the old movie theater in Roscoe, the same building where Walt and Winnie Dette and Harry Darbee had begun tying trout flies years before.

Through donations and a constantly growing membership, the Catskill Fly Fishing Center purchased a permanent site along the Willowemoc Creek, downstream of Livingston Manor. The 35-acre property included an old farmhouse, a barn, and a half-mile of the Willowemoc Creek. Shortly after the purchase, a building fund was established to construct a professional museum that would include a research library, archival storage, and a display area.

The center received significant support and a financial boost in September 1984, when former President Jimmy Carter and First Lady Rosalynn Carter accepted its invitation to come and fish the Catskills. The Carters stayed at the Beaverkill Valley Inn and spent five days fishing the Beaverkill and Delaware rivers. An avid fly fisherman, President Carter desired to aid the center, and in the hours between those he spent trout fishing, he gave freely of his

President Jimmy Carter playing a rainbow trout at Dark Eddy on the Delaware. Ed Van Put.

time, attending a number of public appearances and a formal fund-raising dinner that was extremely successful in helping the center raise funds for their project.

A year after the Carters' visit, Paul Volcker, chairman of the Federal Reserve and enthusiastic fly fisherman, contributed his notoriety by hosting a fund-raising event that also greatly aided the Catskill Fly Fishing Center. These benefits were crucial in providing funding for the center's goal.

In May 1995, the Catskill Fly Fishing Center and Museum opened its doors and introduced the public to a climate-controlled, state-of-the-art, 4,000-square-foot modern museum, which would eventually include a research library and videos, environmental information concerning streams and rivers, and an area for fly tying and rod building.

The museum features exhibits showing artifacts from anglers and fly tiers who contributed to the history of Catskill fly fishing. Visitors can see a Theodore Gordon dry fly; discover what Lee Wulff's fly-tying desk looked like; watch and hear master fly tier Poul Jorgensen as he tied at his vise; and compare dry flies tied by Rube Cross and a host of men and woman who contributed to the sport of trout fishing in the Catskills.

Coda

An important feature of the Catskills is the Catskill Park. The park is not a park in the normal definition of the word, but denotes a geographical boundary often referred to as the "blue line." It covers portions of Delaware, Greene, Sullivan, and Ulster counties. The Catskill Park encompasses approximately 705,000 acres and is a mixture of public and private lands.

Most of the mountainous tracts are inside the blue line, and the average summit is approximately 3,100 feet, with ninety-eight peaks being higher than 3,000 feet above sea level and thirty-four mountains being 3,500 feet or more. The two highest are Slide Mountain at 4,180 feet and Hunter Mountain, at 4,040 feet. Almost as high are Black Dome Mountain at 3,990 feet and Thomas Cole Mountain at 3,945 feet.

The public lands that are owned by the state of New York within the park are known as the Catskill Forest Preserve. They are protected as wild forestlands; their timber may not be sold, removed, or destroyed, and the land retains a wilderness character. These lands belong to the People of the State of New York, and they are used freely for hiking, cross-country skiing, camping, trapping, hunting, fishing, and other recreational activities.

Since its creation in 1885, the forest preserve has grown from 34,000 acres to nearly 300,000 acres of "forever wild" forestlands. These lands are important to preserving the integrity of the mountain landscape, as well as the water quality of the region's water-supply reservoirs and trout streams.

New York City is also a large holder of protected lands in the Catskills. The city owns 34,000 acres of "buffer" land around its six reservoirs located within the Catskill Park. In addition, the city has an ongoing land acquisition program aimed at protecting and enhancing its water supply. In 1993, the Environmental Protection Agency issued New York City a waiver of the required filtration (required to guard drinking water against microbial contamination) of its surface water supplies. This requirement was waived on the condition that the city would take certain steps to "maintain and protect" its Catskill "drinking water quality." One of those steps is the Watershed Land Acquisition Program, aimed at preserving environmentally sensitive lands affecting its reservoirs, such as streams, wetlands, floodplains, stream corridors, and forest and agricultural lands.

Presently, New York City is required to solicit the owners of at least 355,000 acres of land. The goal is to purchase fee title or conservation easements on lands that would protect and maintain high water quality. As of June 2004, the city had purchased nearly 35,000 acres in fee and an additional 6,000 acres under conservation easements.

In order to protect the pristine character and preserve the water quality of the Catskill region, it is important that the state and city continue their acquisition programs. The region is sensitive to large-scale development, and preservation is the only sure way to protect the land and its environment.

Because of its proximity to the New York metropolitan area, the availability of large parcels of land, and the anticipation of gambling casinos, the Catskill region today is attractive to great numbers of resort and seasonal home developers. New York State continues to add to its Catskill holdings, preserving and protecting highly sensitive lands with steep slopes and thin soils from ill-conceived development.

New York State often receives assistance with its acquisition programs from nonprofit land conservation organizations, such as the Catskill Center for Conservation and Development, the Nature Conservancy, the Trust for Public Land, and Open Space Institute. At times, gifts are given in the form of property or easements, but often these organizations will provide aid in acquiring land that the state is interested in purchasing. The process of purchasing lands by New York State is often lengthy and can result in the loss of a critical sale. This process can be facilitated by a nonprofit organization, which can purchase the property more quickly and hold it for the eventual resale to the state.

The most active in land acquisition in the Catskills has been Open Space Institute. The organization recognizes the importance of protecting the region and has been working diligently to preserve key or sensitive areas. Since the 1970s, OSI has been responsible for protecting more than 20,000 acres in the Catskills. Recently, OSI partnered with the Trust for Public Land and conveyed a 5,000-acre parcel to the Catskill Forest Preserve, the largest addition in more than a century.

On April 1, 2004, the opening day of the trout season, Governor George Pataki commemorated the 100th anniversary of the Catskill Park by announcing the preservation of more than a mile of the Willowemoc Creek and 240 acres bordering the famous trout stream. This stretch once belonged to the Willewemoc Club, the first fishing club founded in the Catskills, and later was the home of the Woman Flyfishers Club. The acquisition of more than a mile of the Willowemoc may prove to be the largest single purchase of prime trout water in the Catskills. This historic and significant purchase also came about through the efforts of the nonprofit Open Space Institute.

****

Flooding has become a major issue of great concern to private landowners and communities in the Catskill region. Over the past ten years, floods have increased in size and frequency. During this period, there have been six major flood events that have resulted in significant damage to stream habitat, property, and infrastructure.

Streams and rivers in the Catskills have historically flooded their surrounding landscape; it is a natural process. The steep and stony mountainsides, with their lack of permeable soils, induce rapid runoff; waterways rise quickly, and sediment—including clay, sand, silt, and an unsorted mixture of rocks and gravel—travels downstream. As trees mature, their added weight to the stream bank makes them more susceptible to the process, and it is inevitable that they, too, will join the mass of eroded materials moving downstream in the rapid waters. Erosion is evident on all streams, and it is these continuing actions that reshape the mountainous landscape.

These violent acts of nature have been witnessed from the earliest days of settlement, and local history is often measured by the various floods written about or recalled by residents. One of the first floods to be recorded during these early days was known as the "pumpkin flood" or "pumpkin freshet." The event occurred in the fall, before the pumpkins had been harvested. The water rose in the night and inundated the fields around Arkville and Margaretville. So quickly had the stream risen that the river was covered with pumpkins.

Floodplains are vital to Catskill streams. During periods of high water, when streams are allowed to overflow their banks, the velocity from the high water is reduced, thereby causing less stream-bank erosion, as well as a lesser amount of gravel, sediment, and debris that would otherwise move downstream.

Unfortunately, during periods when no flooding has occurred, there has been encroachment and construction in the floodplain by seasonal and permanent residents, and by infrastructure, such as roads, culverts, and bridges. In mountain communities, roads generally parallel streams out of convenience, as the valley floor (created by the stream) has the lowest gradient, making road construction easier. Gravel for the roads was often taken from the streambed. These activities robbed streams of their natural floodplains and caused conflict between streams and the people who live along them.

To get an idea of the frequency and size of recent floods, I gleaned the surface water records of peak stream flows from the gauging station at Cooks Falls on the lower Beaverkill. In the ninety-two years of record keeping, the flow at Cooks Falls peaked above 20,000 cubic feet per second (cfs) fifteen times. In the first fifty-five years (1914–1969) of record keeping, this occurred only five times, or an average of once every eleven years. During the next thirty-six years (1970–2006), the Beaverkill peaked above 20,000 cfs every 3.6 years; in the last ten years (1996–2006) in the Beaverkill watershed, there have been six major flood events: a flood approximately every 1.65 years!

The size or volume of the flood waters also has increased significantly during the period of record. Previously, the highest peak flow at Cooks Falls was 31,600 cfs in March 1951. In the past ten years, that was exceeded five times: on January 19, 1996, at 42,900 cfs; on December 17, 2000, at 34,400 cfs; on September 18, 2004, at 42,100 cfs; on April 3, 2005, at 50,800 cfs; and on June 28, 2006, at 62,400 cfs. The past two floods have recorded flows never seen before in the history of keeping flow records at Cooks Falls.

Streams in the Catskills are a powerful, unpredictable force. Yet after every flood, there is a movement to "clean out the streams," as there are still those who have the misguided belief that these streams can be manipulated and that channelizing streams of rapid descent by bulldozing, straightening, deepening, widening, and removing gravel will reduce flooding.

The Stream Protection Law began in 1965. Before its passage, it was common practice for highway departments to bulldoze streams under the guise of "flood control" and use the gravel for road construction. Many Catskill natives remember that time and still believe that "cleaning out the streams" will alleviate flooding. The reality is that the work performed in the past often *increased* flooding. When this work occurs, not only is habitat destroyed, but streams actually cause more damage because of the indiscriminate, haphazard, and thoughtless bulldozing. When gravel is removed from the bed of the stream, the velocity of the water is increased greatly and causes additional flood damage to property owners downstream. In addition, the stream will replace the gravel that was removed by eroding the banks upstream of the work area, causing damage to property owners upstream as well.

Many people affected by flooding want to do *something*, whether or not it is the correct approach; and although there are laws—both federal and state—that protect Catskill streams, and permits needed before any disturbance to the bed or banks can take place, there continue to be, in some areas of the region, unpermitted damaging stream disturbances following flooding. This is of great concern to fishermen, environmentalists, and state and federal officials involved in administering stream protection laws, as well as to landowners whose properties are affected by careless stream work.

Jack Isaacs, a Department of Environmental Conservation fisheries biologist, has had the daunting task of protecting Catskill streams for more than twenty-five years. A veteran of many floods, he points out that after a flood, people want to blame and punish the streams. His approach has been to educate with meetings, slide presentations, and instruction. Isaacs has spent countless hours with earth-moving contractors, highway supervisors, engineers, and public officials, convincing them that channelizing causes great harm, and the less disturbance to the stream, the better.

One solution to flooding problems that is gaining acceptance is a buyout: the purchase of properties that have been flooded, and removal of those structures that were allowed to have been constructed in the floodplain. Following the 1996 flood, the city of New York, to protect its water supply and restore the floodplain, purchased a number of properties in the Margaretville area that were located along the banks of the East Branch Delaware River and repeatedly flooded. Other communities along Catskill streams have followed suit and have been successful in obtaining grant monies to buy out and remove structures that were built in the floodplain.

Flooding in the Catskills will continue, and the way that local communities deal with the problem is even more important today than in the past. Careful attention needs to be paid to development and to the protection of wetlands and floodplain areas.

****

Trout populations in Catskill streams are constantly changing because of a variety of environmental and human factors. However, even today, it is difficult to find a stream that does not contain native brook trout. Their size and abundance is determined by food, habitat, and the absence or presence of competitive species, primarily brown or rainbow trout. On streams such as the Beaverkill and Willowemoc, it is still possible to venture up to the headwaters on public (New York State Forest Preserve) land and catch twenty or more brook trout in an hour's fishing; and there still remain trout streams in the Catskills where an angler can catch a hundred trout in a day's fishing! These are streams in which brook trout are the primary species present, and their sizes rarely exceed 8 to 9 inches; typically, they range in size from 4 to 7 inches. When a stream is impounded by a beaver dam, the size of the brook trout can increase dramatically because of the added volume of the ponded water and the additional food supply. Under these circumstances, native brook trout of 12 inches are not uncommon.

Brown trout remain common throughout the Catskills. They can outcompete brook trout for food, space, and habitat and can withstand higher water temperatures than those preferred by brook trout. There are still good numbers of browns in the 20- to 24-inch range found in most of the larger trout streams, especially where streams are affected by the coldwater releases from New York City reservoirs. However, the huge brown trout that inhabited the major streams or rivers before the mid-1940s are not as abundant as in the past. Today, if a trout is caught that weighs more than 5 pounds, chances are that it inhabited one of the city reservoirs for a portion of its life.

Rainbow trout in the Catskills are the dominant species in only a few streams. Nevertheless, in recent years, there appear to be changes occurring in the fish population of the Beaverkill watershed, and the once-dominant role of brown trout is being challenged by rainbows. The stocking of rainbow trout had preceded browns by several years, but they had not established themselves in a wild state, except in the main Delaware River and the lower East Branch of the Delaware.

After brown trout were introduced into the Beaverkill in the late 1880s, they virtually took possession of the stream, especially in the larger, lower river section where they have reigned for more than a century. Before 1986, any rainbow trout that were caught in the lower Beaverkill were generally fish that were stocked by one of the fishing clubs located along the upper reaches. Since then, however, wild rainbows, large and small, are being caught with some regularity along the lower Beaverkill and at least as far upstream as Spring Brook at the upper end of the Rockland flats.

It appears that rainbows have been moving up through the Beaverkill system, possibly from the East Branch of the Delaware River, and they now inhabit many of the tributaries (nursery streams) of the lower Beaverkill. And undoubtedly they will continue to multiply and extend their range even further upstream. Whether this will be seen as something positive or negative with today's trout fishermen remains to be seen, but they are adding wild trout to the stream. It will be interesting to see if, in the future, they increase in numbers to the point that they become more abundant than browns or maintain a population of equal numbers.

Endnotes

Full listing of publication information for shortened endnotes appears in the Bibliography.

PART ONE
FONTINALIS: PRE-1800s TO 1870s

Chapter 1

1. Myers, *The Catskills: Painters, Writers, and Tourists in the Mountains 1820–1895*, 35.
2. Myers, *The Catskills*, 34.
3. Irving, "The Catskill Mountains," *The Literary World* (November 1, 1851), 350.
4. Senectutus, "Early American Fly Fishing Literature," *The Anglers' Club Bulletin* (October 1954), 4.
5. Irving, *The Sketch Book of Geoffrey Crayon, Gent.*, 347.
6. Goodspeed, *Angling in America*, 74.
7. Burnaby, *Travels through the Middle Settlements in North America in the Years 1759 and 1760*, 117–118.
8. Gould, *History of Delaware County*, 155–156.
9. Nathaniel P. Willis, *New Mirror* (September 9, 1843).
10. James Pierce, "A Memoir on the Catskill Mountains with Notices of their Topography, Scenery, Mineralogy, Zoology, Economical Resources, &c." *American Journal of Science and Arts* (1823, vol. VI), 92.
11. Rockwell, *The Catskill Mountains and the Region Around*, 134.
12. Smith, *The Inland Fishes of New York State*, 234.
13. *The People's Press* [Kingston] (August 29, 1861), 1.

14. Lanman, *HAW-ho-noo or Record of a Tourist,* 57.
15. *Liberty Register* (April 6, 1923), 2.
16. *Spirit of the Times* (July 21, 1838), 180.
17. *American National Biography,* 719.

Chapter 2

1. George W. Van Siclen, *Forest and Stream* (May 6, 1880), 175.
2. Alice D. Palen, *Liberty Register* (April 6, 1923), 2.
3. *American Turf Register and Sporting Magazine* (August 1838), 369.
4. Dunn, Esther C. "Inman's Portrait of Wordsworth," *Scribner's Magazine* (February 1920), 252.
5. Inman, Henry. "The Fisher Boy," *The Atlantic Souvenir* (1830), 251.
6. Quoted in Picton, Thomas. "Old Time Disciples of Rod and Gun," *The Rod and Gun* (February 12, 1876), 313.
7. Ibid.
8. Ibid.
9. Quoted in "Henry Inman", *Bulletin of the American Art-Union* (August 1850), 71.
10. *Spirit of the Times* (April 6, 1844), 61.
11. Huntington, *A General View of the Fine Arts, Critical and Historical,* 284.
12. *Spirit of the Times* (January 24, 1846), 561.
13. *Spirit of the Times* (March 18, 1843), 67.
14. Quoted in Wildwood, *Frank Forester's Sporting Scenes and Characters,* 45–46.
15. Judd, *Life and Writing of Frank Forester,* 69.
16. *Spirit of the Times* (April 9, 1881), 229.
17. *Spirit of the Times* (April 23, 1881), 282.
18. "Americans at Play," *The Living Age,* from *Macmillan's Magazine* (July 24, 1897), 259.
19. *New York Times* (July 20, 1858), 4.
20. Judd, *Life and Writings of Frank Forester,* 70.
21. Herbert, "Trout and Trout-Fishing," *Graham's Magazine* (May 1851), 394.
22. Wildwood, ed., *Frank Forester's Sporting Scenes and Characters,* 15–16.
23. *New York Times* (May 18, 1858), 1.
24. Ibid.
25. Ibid.
26. Ibid.
27. Wildwood, *Frank Forester's Sporting Scenes and Characters,* 36–37.
28. *Forest and Stream* (February 8, 1877), 7.
29. "Americans at Play," *Macmillan's,* 259–260.
30. Ibid.
31. *Spirit of the Times* (April 9, 1842), 63.
32. Quinlan, *History of Sullivan County,* 117.
33. *Newburgh Gazette* (March 1, 1843), 2.

34. Brown, *The American Angler's Guide* (1849 ed.), 412.
35. Quinlan, *History of Sullivan County*, 136.
36. Quoted in Forester, *Sporting Scenes and Sundry Sketches*, 112.
37. Street, *The Poems of Alfred B. Street*, vol. 1, 209–212.
38. Street, "A Day's Fishing in the Callikoon," *Graham's Magazine* (October 1845), 155–159.
39. Ibid.

Chapter 3

1. Charles Lanman, "South Peak Mountain," *The Columbian Magazine* (1844, vol. 1), 279.
2. Lanman, "South Peak Mountain," 282.
3. Lanman, *Letters from a Landscape Painter*, 5.
4. Lanman, *Letters*, 12–13.
5. Harry Frederick Orchard, *Charles Lanman Landscape and Nature Studies*, ii.
6. *Forest and Stream* (March 21, 1896), 238.
7. Letter to Lanman from Irving, *The Complete Works of Washington Irving*, 156.
8. Lanman, *Private Life of Daniel Webster*, 99–100.
9. *Forest and Stream* (July 7, 1887), 517.
10. Letter to Lanman from Irving, *The Complete Works of Washington Irving*, 609.
11. *Forest and Stream* (March 16, 1895), 201.

Chapter 4

1. Quoted in Wetzel, *American Fishing Books*, 36.
2. Brown, *The American Angler's Guide* (1849 ed.), 413.
3. *Ulster Republican* (September 2, 1846).
4. Willis, *Hurry-Graphs; or Sketches of Scenery, Celebrities and Society, Taken From Life*, 73.
5. Willis, *Hurry-Graphs*, 76.
6. Willis, *Hurry-Graphs*, 73.
7. Willis, *Hurry-Graphs*, 80.
8. *Spirit of the Times* (June 22, 1850), 2.
9. *Spirit of the Times* (September 18, 1847), 352.
10. *Rondout Courier* (February 11, 1853), 2.
11. *Bloomville Mirror* (July 27, 1858), 2.
12. Sturgis, *Fly Tying*, 104.
13. Smedley, *Fly Patterns and Their Origins*, 11.
14. *Forest and Stream* (December 12, 1896), 471.
15. J. S. Van Cleef, *Forest and Stream* (March 16, 1901), 209.
16. Fitz-James Fitch, "Fishing—A Healthful Pastime," *The American Angler* (July 24, 1886), 1.
17. Fitz-James Fitch, "A Trouting Outing," *Shooting and Fishing* (August 22, 1889), 326.

18. Fitz-James Fitch, "Basket Straps, Shoes, Etc.," *The American Angler* (April 22, 1882), 259.
19. Fitz-James Fitch, "Fishing—A Healthful Pastime," *American Agriculturist* (June 1886), 259.
20. Haring, *Our Catskill Mountains,* 102–103.
21. *Republican Watchman* (February 8, 1878), 4.
22. T. Addison Richards, "The Catskills," *Harper's New Monthly Magazine* (July 1854), 153.
23. *Kingston Democratic Journal* (September 12, 1849), 2.
24. *Kingston Weekly Freeman* (August 6, 1904), 4.
25. Evers, *The Catskills: From Wilderness to Woodstock,* 20.
26. *Ulster Republican* (January 22, 1845), 1.

Chapter 5

1. Willis, *Out-Doors at Idlewild,* 47.
2. *Spirit of the Times* (August 10, 1850), 296.
3. *Walton Blade* (May 27, 1856), 3.
4. *Walton Blade* (June 10, 1856), 3.
5. Howat, *The Hudson River and Its Painters,* 69.
6. Evers, *The Catskills: From Wilderness to Woodstock,* 397.
7. Howat, *The Hudson River and Its Painters,* 15.
8. *Catskill Examiner* (April 21, 1877), 3.
9. Cole, "American Scenery," *American Monthly Magazine* (January 1836), 10.
10. Baigell, *Thomas Cole,* 22.
11. Dunlap, *History of the Rise and Progress of the Arts of Design in the United States,* 381.
12. Quoted in Howard N. Doughty, unpublished manuscript, New-York Historical Society, 77.
13. Evers, *The Catskills: From Wilderness to Woodstock,* 397.
14. John Durand, *The Life and Times of A. B. Durand,* 185–186.
15. John I. H. Baur, ed. *The Autobiography of Worthington Whittredge 1820–1910,* 42.
16. Ibid.
17. Janson, *Worthington Whittredge,* 110.
18. Archives of American Art, microfilm reel D10.
19. *American Paradise: The World of the Hudson River School,* 230.
20. Kirk Johnson, *New York Times* (June 7, 2001), B1.
21. Weiss, *Poetic Landscape,* 165–166.
22. Quoted in Cikovsky, *Sanford Robinson Gifford,* 345–346.
23. Quoted in Baur, *The Autobiography of Worthington Whittredge,* 60.
24. Baur, *The Autobiography of Worthington Whittredge,* 59.
25. Quoted in Phillips and Weintraub, *Charmed Places,* 81.
26. *McEntee & Company,* 38.
27. Norris, *The American Angler's Guide,* 490.
28. Ibid.
29. Ibid.
30. Ibid., 499.

31. Ibid., 497.
32. Johnson, ed., *Dictionary of American Biography,* 123–124.
33. Brown, Henry Kirke Brown Papers, microfilm reels 2770, 2771.
34. Brown, Henry Kirke Brown Papers, Archives of American Art, microfilm rolls 2770, 2772.
35. *Newburgh Daily Journal* (August 7, 1886), 3.
36. Ibid.
37. Quinlan, *History of Sullivan County,* 456.
38. *Republican Watchman* (February 23, 1883), 4.
39. Walter S. Allerton, "Notes of the Catskill Range," *Forest and Stream* (December 14, 1876), 289.
40. Quoted in DeLisser, *Picturesque Ulster,* 155–156.
41. *Catskill Recorder* (December 15, 1866), 1.

Chapter 6

1. Evers, *The Catskills: From Wilderness to Woodstock,* 590.
2. Rockwell, *The Catskill Mountains and the Region Around,* 329.
3. Quoted in Johnson, *John Burroughs Talks,* 37–38.
4. Burroughs, *In the Catskills,* 195–196.
5. Burroughs, "Speckled Trout," *Atlantic Monthly* (October 1870), 430.
6. Ibid.
7. Ibid., 439.
8. Ibid.
9. Burroughs, "The Heart of the Southern Catskill," *The Century* (August 1888), 612.
10. Quoted in Orvis and Cheney, *Fishing with the Fly* (1968 ed.), 144.
11. *The Woman Flyfisher's Club, Fortieth Anniversary 1932–1972,* vol. XIX (Autumn 1972).
12. Quoted in Barrus, *The Life and Letters of John Burroughs,* 255.
13. Ibid., 107.
14. Ibid., 13.
15. Ibid., 3.

Chapter 7

1. *Kingston Journal* (July 13, 1870), 4.
2. *Windham Journal* (July 25, 1872), 3.
3. Jervis McEntee Diary, June 3, 1873, Archives of American Art, microfilm rolls, D180, D9, D30, 4707.
4. *Kingston Daily Freeman* (May 27, 1872), 4.
5. Erts, *Denning History Pamphlet,* 1975.
6. DeLisser, *Picturesque Ulster,* 152.
7. *Kingston Weekly Freeman and Journal* (June 10, 1886), 4.

8. Jervis McEntee Diary, Archives of American Art, microfilm rolls D180, D9, D30, 4707.
9. Burroughs, "A Bed of Boughs," *Scribner's Magazine* (November 1877), 68–69.
10. Ibid., 69.
11. Burroughs Journal entry, June 25, 1880, Vassar Library Collection.
12. Jervis McEntee Diary, Archives of American Art, microfilm rolls D180, D9, D30, 4707.
13. *Forest and Stream* (July 9, 1874), 346.
14. *Liberty Register* (June 7, 1878), 3.
15. *Catskill Examiner* (August 3, 1872), 3.
16. Walter S. Allerton, "Notes of the Catskill Range," *Forest and Stream* (December 14, 1876), 290.
17. Ibid., 289.
18. Ibid.
19. Ibid., 290.
20. Smedley, *Fly Patterns and Their Origins*, 136.
21. The Rev. Dr. E. W. Bently, *Ellenville Journal* (July 20, 1877), 1.
22. *Kingston Journal* (May 29, 1872), 3.
23. *Ellenville Journal* (August 3, 1872), 1.
24. *Catskill Examiner* (August 3, 1872), 3.
25. Quoted in Jefferson, *The Autobiography of Joseph Jefferson,* p. xiii.

PART TWO
REVIVING THE FISHERIES: 1870s–1960s

Chapter 8

1. Cheney, "A Synopsis of the History of Fish Culture," *Fisheries, Game and Forest Commission Report 1897,* 192.
2. William F. G. Shanks, "Fish-Culture in America," *Harper's New Monthly Magazine* (November 1868), 735.
3. Stephen H. Ainsworth, letter to the *New York Daily Tribune* (January 25, 1866), 9.
4. New York State Fisheries Commission Annual Report, 1876, 17.
5. *Who's Who and What's What in Fly and Bait Casting in the United States,* 4.
6. Ibid., 6.
7. Green, *Home Fishing and Home Waters,* 36–37.
8. *Republican Watchman* (May 21, 1880), 3. (Copied from the *New York Sun*).
9. *Forest and Stream* (December 11, 1879), 890.
10. *Forest and Stream* (December 11, 1879), 890.
11. New York State Fisheries Commission Annual Report, 1876, 18–19.
12. Quoted in New York State Fisheries Commission Annual Report, 1880, 45.

13. Ibid., 5.
14. Ibid., 6.
15. Nessmuk, "The Exodus of the Trout," *The American Angler* (November 19, 1881).
16. *Forest and Stream* (December 22, 1881), 411.
17. Quoted in New York State Fisheries Commission Annual Report, 1882, 18.
18. *Forest and Stream* (April 27, 1882), 250.
19. *The American Angler* (July 4, 1885), 7.
20. *Walton Reporter* (April 3, 1884), 4.
21. H. R. Winter, "Trout Fishing in the Catskills," *Van Loan's Catskill Mountain Guide*, 126.
22. *The Kingston Argus* (August 26, 1896) 4.

Chapter 9

1. *Ellenville Journal* (July 29, 1877), 3.
2. *Republican Watchman* (June 9, 1875), 3.
3. Misc. Book No. 2, Sullivan County Clerk's Office, 603.
4. Jervis McEntee Diary, Archives of American Art, Smithsonian Institution, microfilm rolls D180, D9, D30, 4707.
5. *Ellenville Journal* (July 20, 1878), 1.
6. *Kingston Weekly Freeman and Journal* (May 2, 1879), 1.
7. *Republican Watchman* (May 17, 1878), 4.
8. *Kingston Weekly Freeman and Journal* (May 23, 1879), 4.
9. *Kingston Weekly Leader* (June 7, 1889), 7.
10. George Van Siclen, "A Perfect Day," in Orvis and Cheney, eds., *Fishing with the Fly*, 237.
11. McEntee Diary, July 21, 1884, Archives of American Art, microfilm rolls, D180, D9, D30, 4707.
12. Liber 238, page 275, Ulster County Clerk's Office.
13. *New York Times* (May 2, 1910), 9.
14. Gill, "Dry-Fly Fishing with A. W. Dimock," *Field and Stream* (February 1913), 1095.
15. Dimock, *Wall Street and the Wilds*, 385–386.
16. Ibid., 469.
17. Ibid., 468.
18. *Kingston Weekly Freeman and Journal* (October 4, 1891), 5.
19. *Kingston Daily Freeman* (July 26, 1894), 7.
20. *New York Times* (September 23, 1894), 1.
21. "Peekamoose Troubles," *Forest and Stream* (October 27, 1894), 353.
22. *Kingston Weekly Freeman and Journal* (August 17, 1899), 6.
23. Liber 82, page 575, Sullivan County Clerk's Office, August 24, 1880.
24. Liber 86, page 187, Sullivan County Clerk's Office, April 5, 1884.
25. Misc. Book, page 303, Sullivan County Clerk's Office, November 26, 1890.
26. Quoted in Marbury, *Favorite Flies and Their Histories*, 170.
27. *Kingston Weekly Freeman and Journal* (January 26, 1876), 4.

28. *Windham Journal* (June 14, 1877), 3.
29. New York State Fisheries Commission Annual Report, 1886, 22.

Chapter 10

1. *Hancock Herald* (June 3, 1880), 3. (Using a conversion chart, the average size of these trout was between 4.0 and 4.9 inches.)
2. *Kingston Weekly Freeman and Journal* (June 4, 1880), 5.
3. Ben Bent, "Trouting Near New York—The Neversink and Streams of the Catskills," *The American Angler* (June 23, 1888), 390.
4. *Hancock Herald* (May 27, 1886), 3.
5. *Catskill Recorder* (March 29, 1889), 3.
6. *Catskill Recorder* (May 3, 1889), 3.
7. Quoted in *Catskill Recorder* (June 28, 1889), 3.
8. Theodore Gordon, letter to Roy Steenrod, in McDonald, *The Complete Fly Fisherman*, 513.
9. "Nomenclature of Artificial Flies," *Forest and Stream* (March 5, 1885), 109.
10. Holberton, *The Art of Angling*, 53.
11. *New York Times* (February 24, 1889), 16.
12. Ibid.
13. *Kingston Argus* (March 18, 1885), 5.
14. Quoted in *Kingston Journal and Weekly Freeman* (March 26, 1885), 3.
15. Quoted in *Kingston Journal and Weekly Freeman* (April 16, 1885), 6.
16. *Forest and Stream* (April 9, 1885), 207.
17. *The American Angler* (April 25, 1885), 261.
18. Van Dyke, *Little Rivers*, 59–60.
19. *Kingston Weekly Freeman and Journal* (July 14, 1887), 5.
20. Fitz-James Fitch, "A Trouting Outing," *Shooting And Fishing* (August 22, 1889), 326.
21. Ibid.

Chapter 11

1. Quoted in *Forest and Stream* (March 24, 1894), 250.
2. Fred Mather, New York State Fisheries Commission Annual Report, 1886, 72–73.
3. *Forest and Stream* (December 6, 1883), 367.
4. Quoted in *Forest and Stream* (May 29, 1884), 350.
5. Seth Green, New York State Fisheries Commission Annual Report, 1887, 38–39.
6. *Shooting and Fishing* (November 28, 1889), 1.
7. *Shooting and Fishing* (December 12, 1889), 127.
8. Van Cleef, "Why Fish Laws Are Not Respected," *Forest and Stream* (April 2, 1885), 188.
9. Misc. Book No. 2, Sullivan County Clerk's Office, 113.
10. *Kingston Journal and Weekly Freeman* (April 9, 1885), 5.
11. *Forest and Stream* (April 9, 1885), 207.

12. Ibid.

13. *Kingston Weekly Leader* (March 27, 1891), 5.

14. Jervis McEntee Diary, Archives of American Art, microfilm rolls, D180, D9, D30, 4707.

15. *The American Angler* (September 8, 1888), 145.

Chapter 12

1. *Catskill Recorder* (June 10, 1892), 3.

2. *New York Times* (July 15, 1894), 12.

3. *Republican Watchman* (August 31, 1894), 4.

4. Quoted in New York State Fisheries, Game and Forest Commission Annual Report, 1895.

5. *Walton Reporter* (July 6, 1895), 1.

6. *New York Times* (May 17, 1897), 5.

7. Benjamin Kent, "An Angler's Notes on the Beaverkill," in Louis Rhead, ed., *The Speckled Brook Trout*, 110.

8. *Pine Hill Sentinel* (June 15, 1895), 2.

9. *Forest and Stream* (September 15, 1906), 420.

10. Rhead, ed., *The Basses Fresh-Water and Marine*, 66.

11. Harris, "The Trouts of America," *Salmon and Trout*, 298.

12. *Ellenville Journal* (July 20, 1877), 1.

13. C. M. McDougall, "Some Peculiarities of Trout," *Forest and Stream* (May 21, 1898), 413.

14. Fitz-James Fitch, "Fishing—A Healthful Pastime," *American Agriculturist* (June 1886), 259.

15. *Republican Watchman* (June 15, 1859), 2.

16. Norris, *American Fish Culture*, 29.

17. *Roscoe-Rockland Review* (April 30, 1903), 3.

18. *The Ensign* (January 26, 1905), 7.

19. *Sullivan County Review* (June 22, 1905), 2.

20. *Hancock Herald* (June 15, 1893), 1.

21. Cheney, "Trout and Acids," *Forest and Stream* (September 1, 1900), 166.

22. *Sullivan County Review* (May 11, 1905), 1.

23. *Forest and Stream* (September 1, 1906), 341.

24. *Forest and Stream* (June 15, 1893), 1.

Chapter 13

1. Goodspeed, *Angling in America*, 221.

2. Keene, *Fly-Fishing and Fly-Making for Trout, Bass, Salmon, Etc.*, 119.

3. *The American Angler* (November 10, 1888), 289.

4. *Forest and Stream* (June 8, 1907), 900.

5. Theodore Gordon, letter to Steven Wager, November 22, 1914.

6. *Forest and Stream* (April 27, 1912), 529–530.

7. *Forest and Stream* (November 27, 1890), 372.

8. *New York Times* (May 17, 1891), 20.
9. *Forest and Stream* (April 16, 1898), 309.
10. Ibid.
11. Harris, "Methods of Fishing for Trout," in Harris and Sage, *Salmon and Trout,* 349.
12. Gill, *Practical Dry-Fly Fishing,* 169–170.
13. *Field & Stream* (June 1912), 133.
14. *New York Times* (July 6, 1913), 9.
15. La Branche, *The Dry Fly and Fast Water,* 8.
16. *Forest and Stream* (June 27, 1914), 858.
17. Ives, *Seventeen Famous Outdoorsmen,* 24.
18. Burke, *American Dry Flies and How to Tie Them,* 1.

Chapter 14

1. *New York Times* (June 24, 1900), 26.
2. Quoted in McDonald, *The Complete Fly Fisherman,* 198.
3. Jenkins, "Theodore Gordon: Random Recollections," in Gingrich, ed., *American Trout Fishing,* 25.
4. Quoted in McDonald, *The Complete Fly Fisherman,* 549.
5. Quoted in McDonald, *The Complete Fly Fisherman,* 546–547.
6. Holden, *Streamcraft,* 112.
7. McDonald, *The Complete Fly Fisherman,* 535.
8. Rhead, "The Evolution of the Trout Fly," *Forest and Stream* (November 1922), 504.
9. Quoted in Smedley, *Fly Patterns and Their Origins,* 68–69.
10. Quoted in McDonald, *The Complete Fly Fisherman,* 516.
11. Quoted in *Field & Stream* (August 1911).
12. McDonald, *The Complete Fly Fisherman,* xxi.
13. Cross, *Tying American Trout Lures,* 32.
14. Cross, *Fur, Feathers and Steel,* 2–3.
15. Ibid., 13.
16. Connett, *Any Luck?,* 28.
17. Ibid., 25.
18. McClane, *The Practical Fly Fisherman,* 228–229.
19. McClane, "Feather Merchant," *Field & Stream* (July 1955).
20. McClane, "A Fly For All Seasons," in Migel and Wright, eds., *The Masters on the Nymph,* 16.

Chapter 15

1. *Kingston Weekly Leader* (April 29, 1899).
2. *Ellenville Journal* (November 17, 1905), 1.
3. Evers, *The Catskills: From Wilderness to Woodstock,* 593.

4. Winfield T. Sherwood, "Camp Don't Hurry," *Forest and Stream* (March 2, 1907), 331.
5. Quoted in McDonald, *The Notes and Letters of Theodore Gordon,* 497.
6. Kelley, *John Burroughs:Naturalist,* 216.
7. Ingraham, *American Trout Streams,* 132.
8. *Catskill Mountain News* (April 28, 1905), 3.
9. *Forest and Stream* (December 8, 1900), 453.
10. Ibid.
11. *Roscoe-Rockland Review* (April 2, 1908), 3.
12. *Walton Reporter* (May 19, 1900), 3.
13. *Roscoe-Rockland Review* (May 2, 1901), 4.
14. *Forest and Stream* (May 25, 1907), 821.
15. *Forest and Stream* (June 15, 1907), 1.
16. *Forest and Stream* (June 29, 1907), 1019.
17. Kent, "An Angler's Notes on the Beaverkill," In Rhead, ed., *The Speckled Brook Trout,* 110.
18. *Forest and Stream* (November 15, 1902), 390–391.
19. *Forest and Stream* (September 15, 1906), 420.
20. Gordon letter to Steenrod, in McDonald, *The Complete Fly Fisherman,* 478.
21. *Kingston Weekly Leader,*(June 1, 1901), 6.
22. *Forest and Stream* (July 10, 1909), 60.
23. *Livingston Manor Times* (July 23, 1924), 1.
24. *Forest and Stream* (August 1923), 722.
25. *Forest and Stream* (September 1924), 536.
26. *Sullivan County Review* (May 18, 1916), 3.
27. Ibid.

Chapter 16

1. Theodore Gordon, "Good Fishing Near Large Cities," *Forest and Stream* (December 1916), 1237–1238.
2. *Roxbury Times* (October 20, 1917), 3.
3. *Liberty Register* (May 30, 1919), 4.
4. Ibid.
5. *Liberty Register* (May 21, 1920), 1.
6. *Liberty Register* (April 6, 1923), 4.
7. *Liberty Register* (April 13, 1923), 4.
8. Hewitt, *A Trout and Salmon Fisherman for Seventy-Five Years,* xxi.
9. Hewitt, "Better Trout Fishing," *Field & Stream* (February 1933), 49.
10. Hewitt, *A Trout And Salmon Fisherman,* 131.
11. Ibid., 145–146.
12. Wulff, "Ed Hewitt," *Rod & Reel* (November/December 1983).
13. William Chandler, *Anglers' Club Bulletin* (April 1923).

14. Quoted in McDonald, *The Complete Fly Fisherman*, 430.
15. *Ellenville Journal* (May 18, 1916), 3.
16. Wetzel, *American Fishing Books*, 202.
17. Lynn Scholz, "Louis Rhead's First Career," *The American Fly Fisher* (Winter 1985, vol. 12, no. 1), 18–24.
18. Rhead, *American Trout-Stream Insects*, 4.
19. Schaldach, *Currents and Eddies*, 50.
20. Quoted in Holden, *Angling Recollections and Practice*, 91.
21. Quoted in *The American Angler* (1917), 99.

Chapter 17

1. *Cold Brook Gazette* (May 1921), 10.
2. *Liberty Register* (April 22, 1926), 1. This same story reappeared in area newspapers again in 1946 and at that time was written as if the event had just occurred again, leading one to believe it was just a tall story or "fish tale."
3. *Sullivan County Review* (September 9, 1926), 3
4. *Walton Reporter* (April 13, 1929), 1.
5. *Sullivan County Review* (April 6, 1922), p. 1.
6. *Forest and Stream* (May 1926), 304.
7. Van Put, *The Beaverkill: The History of a River and Its People*, 199.
8. Ford, *Trout Tales*, 27.
9. Quoted in a letter from Sparse Grey Hackle (Alfred W. Miller) to the *New York Herald Tribune*, reprinted in *Liberty Register* (July 7, 1938), 7.
10. Van Put, *The Beaverkill*, 201.
11. State of New York Conservation Commission Sixteenth Annual Report, 1926, 43.
12. Heacox, *The Education of an Outdoorsman*, 54.
13. A Biological Survey of the Delaware-Susquehanna Watershed, State of New York Conservation Department, 16.
14. Quoted in John D. Gould, "Fishing-for-Fun," *The New York State Conservationist* (February-March 1960), 21.

Chapter 18

1. Corey Ford, "The Best-Loved Trout Stream of Them All," *True* (April 1952), 86.
2. Van Put, *The Beaverkill: The History of a River and Its People*, 244.
3. Quoted in McClane, *Fishing with McClane*, 114.
4. Darbee, *Catskill Flytier*, 33.
5. Percy Jennings, "The Rat Face McDougall," *Anglers' Club Bulletin* (February 1939).
6. Robert H. Boyle, "He Deftly Ties the World's Fanciest Flies," *Sports Illustrated* (June 29, 1964).
7. Cecil Heacox, "The Catskill Flytyers," *Outdoor Life* (May 1972), 158.

8. Art Flick, West Kill, N. Y., letter dated May 23, 1984. Actually, Art mentions tying the Red Quill as early as 1933, a date mentioned in *Streamside Guide.*

9. J. Michael Migel, "Fishermen—Another Endangered Species?" *The Stream Conservation Handbook,* 20.

10. *Catskill Mountain News* (June 30, 1933), 1.

11. *Biological Survey of the Delaware-Susquehanna Watershed,* 27.

12. Ibid., 29.

13. Ibid.

14. Quoted in *Catskill Mountain News* (August 2, 1935), 1.

15. McClane, *McClane's Angling World,* 155.

16. McClane, *Fishing with McClane,* xiii.

17. Heacox, *The Education of an Outdoorsman,* 174.

18. *Sullivan County Democrat* (February 7, 1923), 1.

19. New York State Conservation Department Annual Report, 1933, 184.

20. Douglas M. Thompson and Gregory N. Stull, "The Development and Historic Use of Habitat Structures in Channel Restoration in the United States: The Grand Experiment in Fisheries Management." http://www.erudit.org/revue/gpq/2002

21. Conservation Department Annual Report to the Legislature, 1934, 202.

22. New York State Conservation Department Annual Report, 1935, 260.

23. Conservation Department Annual Report to the Legislature, 1938, 201.

24. Haring, *Our Catskill Mountains,* 30.

25. *Walton Reporter* (April 12, 1935), 4.

26. Jennings, *A Book of Trout Flies,* 114.

27. Bates Jr., *Streamer Fly Tying and Fishing,* 268.

28. Bergman, *Trout,* 143.

29. A Biological Survey of the Lower Hudson Watershed, State of New York Conservation Department, Supplemental to Twenty-sixth Annual Report, 1935, 55.

30. Ibid., 33.

31. Ibid., 33–34.

32. *Walton Reporter* (June 21, 1930), 1.

33. *Walton Reporter* (April 11, 1931), 1.

34. *Biological Survey of the Delaware-Susquehanna Watershed,* 24.

35. *Liberty Register* (January 11, 1940), 4.

Chapter 19

1. *Catskill Mountain News* (January 26, 1940), 1.

2. *Liberty Register* (May 16, 1940), 1.

3. Ibid.

4. *Herald Tribune* (April 22, 1938), 25.

5. *Roxbury Times* (April 7, 1945), 3.

6. Greene, "Stocking for Production," *New York State Conservationist* (April/May 1950), 6–7.

7. *Livingston Manor Times* (August 12, 1948), 1.
8. *Liberty Register* (January 27, 1949), 1.
9. *Liberty Register* (January 27, 1949), 1.
10. *Conservationist* (April/May 1950).
11. Conservation Department Annual Report to the Legislature, 1955, 159.
12. New York State Conservation Department, Southern Fisheries District, Esopus Creek (171 H.R.), 7.
13. *Downsville News* (July 22, 1943), 2.
14. *Downsville News* (August 17, 1944), 1.
15. Joe Martin and Kermit Jaediker, "This Valley is Doomed!" *New York Daily News* (October 7, 1952), C12.
16. *Liberty Register* (May 22, 1952), 1.
17. Connell, "The West Branch of the Neversink River," 33–34. An unpublished essay for aficionados of freestone trout streams.
18. *Livingston Manor Times* (April 11, 1957), 5.

Bibliography

PUBLIC RECORDS

Delaware, Greene, Sullivan, and Ulster County Clerk's Offices: deed and mortgage books
Miscellaneous books (Sullivan County); maps placed on record, often bound in books, but earliest found in deed books.
New York State Census Records, Delaware and Sullivan Counties.
Delaware, Greene, Sullivan, and Ulster County surrogates records, wills, and probate records.
Field Books: Hardenbergh Patent Great Lot 6—1809; Delaware County Clerk's Office, Delhi, N.Y.

PUBLIC LIBRARIES

Adriance Memorial Library, Poughkeepsie, N.Y.
Albany Institute of History & Art, Albany, N.Y.
Archives of American Art, Smithsonian Institution, Washington, D.C.
Cannon Free Library, Delhi, N.Y.
Ellenville Public Library, Ellenville, N.Y.
Fairview Library, Margaretville, N.Y.
Kingston Area Library, Kingston N.Y.
Liberty Public Library, Liberty, N.Y.
Livingston Manor Free Public Library, Livingston Manor, N.Y.
Louise Adelia Read Memorial Library, Hancock, N.Y.
Mann Library, Cornell University, Ithaca, N.Y.
McDonald De Witt Library, Ulster County Community College, Stone Ridge, N.Y.

Mudd Library, Yale University, New Haven, Conn.
Munson-Williams-Proctor Institute, Utica, N.Y.
Newburgh Free Library, Newburgh, N.Y.
New-York Historical Society, New York, N.Y.
New York Public Library, New York, N.Y.
New York State Historical Association, Cooperstown, N.Y.
New York State Library, Albany, N.Y.
Orange County Community College, Middletown, N.Y.
Phoenicia Library Association, The Jerry Bartlett Memorial Angling Collection, Phoenicia, N.Y.
Roscoe Library, Roscoe, N.Y.
Sojourner Truth Library, SUNY New Paltz, N.Y.
Stamford Village Library, Stamford, N.Y.
William B. Ogden Free Library, Walton, N.Y.

NEWSPAPERS

The years indicate the period researched.
Andes Recorder (1867–1892), Delaware County Historical Society, Delhi, N.Y.
Bloomville Mirror (1853–1874), Stamford Village Library, Stamford, N.Y.
Catskill Examiner (1857–1885), New York State Library, Albany, N.Y.
Catskill Mountain News (1902–1955), Offices of the *Catskill Mountain News*, Margaretville, N.Y.
Catskill Recorder (1869–1905), New York State Library, Albany, N.Y.
Delaware Gazette (1819–1903), Cannon Free Library, Delhi, N.Y.
Delaware Republican (January 2, 1886–March 29, 1890), New York State Library, Albany, N.Y.
Downsville Herald (November 27, 1947–February 27, 1953), New York State Library, Albany, N.Y.
Downsville News (March 31, 1938–April 25, 1946), New York State Library, Albany, N.Y.
Ellenville Journal (1849–1916), Ellenville Public Library, Ellenville, N.Y.
Hancock Herald (1874–1897), Louise Adelia Read Memorial Library, Hancock, N.Y.
Kingston Argus (1873–1905), Kingston Area Library, Kingston, N.Y.
Kingston Craftsman (1820–1822), Kingston Area Library, Kingston, N.Y.
Kingston Daily Freeman (January 1, 1875–January 12, 1875; October 18, 1875–December 31, 1875; January 3, 1876–April 17, 1876; October 18, 1876–December 30, 1876), Kingston Area Library, Kingston, N.Y.
Kingston Democratic Journal (1849–1864), Kingston Area Library, Kingston, N.Y.
Kingston Press (1863–1874), Kingston Area Library, Kingston, N.Y.
Kingston Weekly Freeman and Journal (1868–1899), Kingston Area Library, Kingston, N.Y.
Kingston Weekly Leader (1887–1904), Kingston Area Library, Kingston, N.Y.
Liberty Register (1878–1967), Liberty Public Library, Liberty, N.Y.
Livingston Manor Times (1922–1960), Dr. Paul D'Amico, Livingston Manor, N.Y.
Narrowsburg Democrat (1914), Offices of the *Sullivan County Democrat*, Callicoon, N.Y.
New York American (January 1, 1827–May 14, 1832), New York State Library, Albany, N.Y.

New York Mirror (January 7, 1826–December 31, 1842), New York State Library, Albany, N.Y.

New York Sun (September 3, 1833–August 31, 1835), New York State Library, Albany, N.Y.

New York Times (1851–1950), Orange County Community College, Middletown, N.Y.

The Peoples Press (1857–1863), Kingston Area Library, Kingston, N.Y.

Pine Hill Sentinel (1885–1908), Ulster County Community College, Stone Ridge, N.Y.

Political Reformer (1839–1840), Kingston Area Library, Kingston, N.Y.

Recorder, The (Catskill) (August 4, 1911–December 29, 1916), New York State Library, Albany, N.Y.

Republican Watchman (May 19, 1829–August 30, 1918), New York State Library, Albany, N.Y.

Rondout Courier (1848–1869), Kingston Area Library, Kingston, N.Y.

Rondout Daily Freeman (1871), Kingston Area Library, Kingston, N.Y.

Rondout Weekly Freeman (1871–1872), Kingston Area Library, Kingston, N.Y.

Roscoe-Rockland Review & Sullivan County Review (1895–1941), Roscoe Central School, Roscoe, N.Y.

Roxbury Times (September 1895–June 1951), New York State Library, Albany, N.Y.

Schoharie Patriot (January 1, 1846–December 29, 1859; July 5, 1860–December 27, 1860; January 3, 1861–December 26, 1861), New York State Library, Albany, N.Y.

Stamford Mirror (1874–1886), Stamford Village Library, Stamford, N.Y.

Sullivan County Democrat (1907–1956), Offices of the *Sullivan County Democrat*, Callicoon, N.Y.

Sullivan County Record (1950–1956), Offices of the *Sullivan County Democrat*, Callicoon, N.Y.

Ulster Palladium (1830–1833), Kingston Area Library, Kingston, N.Y.

Ulster Republican (1833–1861), Kingston Area Library, Kingston, N.Y.

Ulster Sentinel (1826–1830), Kingston Area Library, Kingston, N.Y.

Walton Blade (1856–1857), William B. Ogden Free Library, Walton, N.Y.

Walton Chronicle (1877–1888), William B. Ogden Free Library, Walton, N.Y.

Walton Journal (1857–1859), William B. Ogden Free Library, Walton, N.Y.

Walton Reporter (1885–1941), William B. Ogden Free Library, Walton, N.Y.

Walton Weekly Chronicle (1869–1878), William B. Ogden Free Library, Walton, N.Y.

Windham Journal (1857–1883), New York State Library, Albany, N.Y.

BOOKS

Adams, Adeline. *John Quincy Adams Ward: An Appreciation.* New York: National Sculpture Society, 1912.

American Paradise: The World of the Hudson River School. New York: Metropolitan Museum of Art, 1987.

Baigell, Matthew. *Thomas Cole.* New York: Watson-Guptill Publications, 1981.

Barnes, Homer F. *Charles Fenno Hoffman.* New York: Columbia University Press, 1930.

Barrus, Clara, ed. *The Heart of Burroughs' Journals.* Boston & New York: Houghton Mifflin Co., 1928.

———. *John Burroughs: Boy and Man.* Garden City, N.Y.: Doubleday, Page & Co., 1920.

_____. *The Life and Letters of John Burroughs.* 1925. New York: Russell & Russell, 1968.

_____. *Our Friend John Burroughs.* Boston & New York: Houghton Miffin Co., 1914.

Bates, Joseph D., Jr. *Streamer Fly Tying and Fishing.* Harrisburg, Pa.: The Stackpole Co., 1966.

Baur, John I. H., ed. *The Autobiography of Worthington Whittredge, 1820–1910.* New York: Arno Press, 1969.

Bergman, Ray. *Trout.* 1938. New York: Alfred A. Knopf, 1964.

Biological Survey of the Delaware-Susquehanna Watershed. New York State Conservation Department Report. New York: J. B. Lyon Co., 1935.

Born, Wolfgang. *American Landscape Painting.* New Haven, Conn.: Yale University Press, 1948.

Bradley, William A. *Fly-Fishing Reminiscences of My Early Years at the Beaverkill Trout Club.* New York: private printing, 1927.

Breck, Edward. *The Way of the Woods.* 1908. New York: G. P. Putnam's Sons, The Knickerbocker Press, 1910.

Brinley, Francis. *Life of William T. Porter.* New York: D. Appleton and Co., 1860.

Brown, Henry Kirke Papers. Archives of American Art, Smithsonian Institution, Washington, D.C., microfilm rolls 2770 and 2771.

Brown, John J. *The American Angler's Guide.* 1845. New York: D. Appleton & Co., 1849, 1857, 1876.

Burke, Edgar, M.D. *American Dry Flies and How to Tie Them.* New York: Derrydale Press, 1930.

Burnaby, Rev. Andrew. *Travels through the Middle Settlements in North America in the Years 1759 and 1760.* 1775. New York: Augustus M. Kelley, Publisher, 1775.

Burroughs, John. *In the Catskills.* New York: Houghton Mifflin Co., 1910.

_____. *Locusts and Wild Honey.* 1879. Boston and New York: Houghton Mifflin Co., 1907.

_____. *My Boyhood.* Garden City, N.Y.: Doubleday, Page & Co., 1922.

_____. *Pepacton.* 1881. Boston and New York: Houghton Mifflin Co., 1904.

_____. *Wake-Robin.* Boston and New York: Houghton Mifflin Co., 1871.

Callow, James T. *Kindred Spirits.* Chapel Hill, N.C.: University of North Carolina Press, 1967.

Camp, Samuel G. *Fishing with Floating Flies.* 1913. New York: The Macmillan Co., 1923.

_____. *Taking Trout with the Dry Fly.* New York: The Macmillan Co., 1930.

Cibulka, Cheryl A. *Quiet Places: The American Landscapes of Worthington Whittredge.* Washington, D.C.: Adams Davidson Galleries Inc., 1982.

Cikovsky, Nicolai, Jr. *Sanford Robinson Gifford 1823–1880.* Austin, Tex.: University of Texas Art Museum, 1970.

Clearwater, A. T. *History of Ulster County, New York* . Kingston, N.Y.: W. J. Van Deusen, 1907.

Clemont, Clare E., and Laurence Hutten. *Artists of the 19th Century.* St. Louis: North Point Inc., 1969.

Connell, Karl. *Wintoon.* Argonaut Book Search, 1993.

Connett, Eugene V. *Any Luck?* 1933. Garden City, N.Y.: Garden City Publishing Co., Inc., 1937.

Cypress, J., Jr. Edited by Frank Forester. *Sporting Scenes and Sundry Sketches.* New York: Gould, Banks & Co., 1842.

Darbee, Harry, with Mac Francis. *Catskill Flytier.* Philadelphia and New York: J. B. Lippincott Co., 1977.

Dayton, Abram C. *Last Days of Knickerbocker Life in New York.* New York: George W. Harlan Publisher, 1882.

Delaware River Drainage Basin. New York State Department of Health and New York State Conservation Department, 1960.

DeLisser, R. Lionel. *Picturesque Catskills.* Northampton, Mass.: Picturesque Publishing Co., 1894.

————. *Picturesque Ulster.* Kingston, N.Y.: The Styles & Bruyn Publishing Co., 1896.

Dictionary of American Biography. Edited by Dumas Malone. New York: Charles Scribner's Sons, vol. X, 1936. Edited by John A. Garraty, 1965.

Dimock, A. W. *Wall Street and the Wilds.* 1915. Camden, S.C.: The Premier Press, 1993.

Downer, Alan S., ed. *The Autobiography of Joseph Jefferson.* Cambridge, Mass.: Harvard University Press, 1964.

Driscoll, John. *All That Is Glorious Around Us.* University Park, Pa: Museum of Art, Pennsylvania State University, 1981.

Dunlap, William. *A History of the Rise and Progress of the Arts of Design in the United States.* 1834. New York: Dover Publications, 2 vols., 1969.

Durand, John. *The Life and Times of A. B. Durand.* 1894. New York: Kennedy Graphics, Inc., DaCapo Press, 1970.

Eminent Literary Men. *One Hundred Years' Progress of the United States.* Hartford, Conn.: L. Stebbins, 1870.

Evers, Alf. *The Catskills: From Wilderness to Woodstock.* Garden City, N.Y.: Doubleday, 1972.

————. *In Catskill Country.* Woodstock, N.Y.: Overlook Press, 1995.

Flexner, James Thomas. *History of American Painting, vol. 3: That Wilder Image.* 1962. New York: Dover Publications, Inc., 1970.

————. *Nineteenth Century American Painting.* New York: Putnam, 1970.

Flick, Arthur B. *Streamside Guide.* 1947. New York: Crown Publishers Inc., 1969.

Foote, John Taintor. *Anglers All.* New York: Appleton-Century-Crofts, Inc., 1947.

Ford, Corey. *Trout Tales.* Bozeman, Mont.: Wilderness Adventures Press, 1995.

Forester, Frank. *Complete Manual for Young Sportsmen.* New York: Stringer & Townsend, 1856.

Francis, Austin M. *Catskill Rivers.* New York: Nick Lyons Books, 1983.

Galusha, Diane. *Liquid Assets.* Fleischmanns, N.Y.: Purple Mountain Press, 1999.

Gerdts, William H. *The Art of Henry Inman.* Washington, D.C.: The National Portrait Gallery, Smithsonian Institution, 1987.

Gerow, Joshua R. *Alder Lake.* Liberty, N.Y.: Fuelane Press, 1953.

Gill, Emlyn M. *Practical Dry-Fly Fishing.* New York: Charles Scribner's Sons, 1912.

Gingrich, Arnold. *The Fishing in Print.* New York: Winchester Press, 1974.

————. *The Joys of Trout.* New York: Crown Publishers Inc., 1973.

————. *The Well-Tempered Angler.* New York: Alfred A. Knopf, 1965.

Goodspeed, Charles E. *Angling in America.* Boston: Houghton Mifflin Co., 1939.

Goodyear, Frank H., Jr. *Thomas Doughty 1793–1856.* Philadelphia, Pa.: Academy of the Fine Arts, 1973.

————. "The Life and Art of Thomas Doughty." Master's thesis, University of Delaware, 1969.

Gordon, Theodore, and a Company of Anglers. Edited by Arnold Gingrich. *American Trout Fishing.* New York: Alfred A. Knopf, 1966.

Gould, Jay. *History of Delaware County.* 1856. Roxbury, N.Y.: Keeny & Gould, 1977.

Green, Seth. *Home Fishing and Home Waters.* New York: Orange Judd Co., 1907.

Hackle, Sparse Grey [Alfred W. Miller]. *Fishless Days, Angling Nights.* New York: Crown Publishers, Inc., 1971.

Hallock, Charles. *An Angler's Reminiscences.* Cincinnati, Ohio: Sportsmen's Review Pub. Co., 1913.

Haring, H. A. *Our Catskill Mountains.* New York: G. P. Putnam's Sons, 1931.

Harris, Neil. *The Artist in American Society.* New York: George Braziller, 1966.

Heacox, Cecil E. *The Compleat Brown Trout.* 1974. Clinton, N.J.: Amwell Press, 1983.

————. *The Education of an Outdoorsman.* New York: Winchester Press, 1976.

Heft, Lynn Harris. *Charles Lanman.* A dissertation submitted to the graduate school of Drew University, Madison, New Jersey. Ann Arbor, Mich.: Published by UMI Dissertation Services, 1996.

Herbert, William H. *Frank Forester's Fish and Fishing of the United States and British Provinces.* 1849. New York: N. A. Townsend Publisher & Co., 1864.

————. *Frank Forester's Sporting Scenes and Characters.* 1857. Philadelphia: T. B. Peterson & Brothers, 1881.

————. Edited by Will Wildwood. *Frank Forester's Fugitive Sporting Sketches.* Westfield, Wisc. (s.n.): 1879.

Hewitt, Edward R. *Better Trout Streams.* New York: Charles Scribner's Sons, 1931.

————. *Days from Seventy-Five to Ninety.* New York: Duell, Sloan and Pearce, 1957.

————. *Hewitt's Handbook of Fly Fishing.* New York: Marchbanks Press, 1933.

————. *Hewitt's Handbook of Stream Improvement.* New York: Marchbanks Press, 1934.

————. *Hewitt's Nymph Fly Fishing.* New York: Marchbanks Press, 1934.

————. *Telling on the Trout.* New York: Charles Scribner's Sons, 1926.

————. *A Trout and Salmon Fisherman for Seventy-Five Years*, 1948. New York: Abercrombie & Fitch, 1966.

Hills, John Waller. *A History of Fly Fishing for Trout.* 1921. Rockville Centre, N.Y.: Freshet Press, 1971.

History of Delaware County, N.Y., 1797–1880. New York: W. W. Munsell & Co., 1932.

History of Greene County, New York. J. B. Beers Co., 1884.

Holberton, Wakeman. *The Art of Angling.* New York: Dick & Fitzgerald, 1887.

The Home Book of the Picturesque. New York: George P. Putnam, 1852.

Holden, George Parker. *Streamcraft.* Cincinnati, Ohio: Stewart & Kidd Co., 1919.

Hornby, Eliza B. *Under Old Rooftrees.* Jersey City, N.J.: Press of Redfield Brothers, 1908.

Howat, John K. *The Hudson River and its Painters.* New York: Penguin Books, 1972.

Hunt, William Southworth. *Frank Forester: A Tragedy in Exile.* Newark, N.J.: The Cartaret Book Club, 1933.

Huntington, D. *A General View of the Fine Arts, Critical and Historical.* New York: G. P. Putnam, 1851.

Ingraham, Henry A. *American Trout Streams.* New York: Derrydale Press, 1926.

Irving, Washington. *The Sketch Book of Geoffrey Crayon, Gent.* 1820. New York: The Heritage Press, 1939.

Isham, Samuel. *The History of American Painting.* New York: The Macmillan Co., 1936.

Ives, Marguerite. *Seventeen Famous Outdoorsmen.* Chicago: The Canterbury Press, 1929.

Janson, Anthony F. *Worthington Whittredge.* Cambridge, England: Cambridge University Press, 1989.

Jennings, Preston J. *A Book of Trout Flies.* 1935. New York: Crown Publishers Inc., 1970.

Johnson, Clifton. *John Burroughs Talks.* Boston and New York: Houghton Mifflin Co., 1922.

Jordan, David Starr and Barton Warren Evermann. *American Food and Game Fishes.* New York: Doubleday, Page & Co., 1902.

Judd, David W. *Life and Writings of Frank Forester.* New York: Orange Judd Co., 1882.

Keene, J. Harrington. *Fly-Fishing and Fly-Making for Trout, Bass, Salmon, Etc.* 1887. New York: Forest and Stream Publishing Co., 1891.

Kelley, Elizabeth Burroughs. *John Burroughs: Naturalist.* West Park, N.Y.: Riverby Books, 1959.

Kennedy, William Sloane. *The Real John Burroughs.* New York: Funk & Wagnalls Co., 1924.

Knight, John Alden. *The Theory and Technique of Fresh Water Angling.* New York: Harcourt, Brace and Company, 1940.

Kudish, Michael. *The Catskill Forest: A History.* Fleischmanns, N.Y.: Purple Mountain Press, 2000.

———. "Vegetational History of the Catskill High Peaks." PhD diss., Syracuse University, 1972.

La Branche, George M. L. *The Dry Fly and Fast Water.* New York: Charles Scribner's Sons, 1914.

Lanman, Charles. *Adventures in the Wilds of the United States and British American Provinces.* Philadelphia: John W. Moore, 1856.

———. *Adventures of an Angler in Canada, Nova Scotia and the United States.* London: Richard Bentley, 1848.

———. *Essays for Summer Hours.* Boston: James Munroe Co., 1843.

———. *Haphazard Personalities.* Boston: Lea & Shepard, 1886.

———. *HAW-HO-NOO or Records of a Tourist.* Philadelphia: Lippincott, 1850.

———. *Letters from a Landscape Painter.* Boston: James Munroe Co., 1845.

———. *Private Life of Daniel Webster.* New York: Harper & Brothers, 1852.

———. *Recollections of Curious Characters and Pleasant Places.* Edinburgh: David Douglas, 1881.

Lassiter, Barbara Babcock. *American Wilderness.* New York: Doubleday & Co., Inc., 1978.

Lawall, David B. *Asher B. Durand.* New York: Garland Publishing Inc., 1978.

Leiser, Eric. *The Dettes.* Fishkill, N.Y.: Willowkill Press, 1992.

Lester, C. Edwards. *The Artists of America.* 1846. New York: Da Capo Press, 1970.

Longstreth, T. Morris. *The Catskills.* 1918. New York: The Century Co., 1921.

Marbury, Mary Orvis. *Favorite Flies and Their Histories.* 1892. Secaucus, N.J.: The Wellfleet Press, 1988.

Mather, Fred. *Men I Have Fished With.* New York: Forest and Stream Publishing Co., 1897.

———. *Modern Fish Culture.* New York: Forest and Stream Publishing Co., 1900.

———. *My Angling Friends.* New York: Forest and Stream Publishing Co., 1901.

Mayer, Alfred M., ed. *Sport with Gun and Rod.* New York: The Century Co., 1883.

McClane, A. J. *The Compleat McClane.* New York: Truman Talley Books/E. P. Dutton, 1988.

———. *Fishing with McClane.* Edited by George Reiger. Englewood Cliffs, N.J.: Prentice-Hall, Inc., 1975.

———. *McClane's Angling World.* New York: Truman Talley Books/E. P. Dutton, 1986.

————. *The Practical Fly Fisherman*. Englewood Cliffs, N.J.: Prentice-Hall, Inc., 1953.

McCoubrey, John W. *American Art 1700–1960*. Englewood Cliffs, N.J.: Prentice-Hall, Inc., 1965.

McDonald, John, ed. *The Complete Fly Fisherman*. New York: Charles Scribner's Sons, 1947.

————. *Quill Gordon*. New York: Alfred A. Knopf, 1972.

McEntee & Company. New York: Beacon Hill Fine Art, 1997.

McSpadden, J. Walker. *Famous Sculptors of America*. New York: Dodd, Mead and Co., 1924.

Minks, Louise. *The Hudson River School*. New York: Crescent Books, 1989.

Mitchell, Samuel L. *Report, in Part, of Samuel L. Mitchell on the Fishes of New-York*. New York: D. Carlisle, 1814.

Monroe, John D. *Chapters in the History of Delaware County, N. Y.* Delaware County Historical Association, 1949.

Munson-Williams-Proctor Institute. *Worthington Whittredge 1820–1910*. Exhibition Catalog. Utica, N.Y.: Munson-Williams-Proctor Institute, 1969.

Murray, David, ed. *Centennial History of Delaware County, N.Y., 1797–1897*. Delhi, N.Y.: William Clark, 1898.

Myers, Frank Daniel, III. *The Wood Chemical Industry in the Delaware Valley*. Middletown, N.Y.: Prior King Press, 1986.

Myers, Kenneth. *The Catskills: Painters, Writers, and Tourists in the Mountains 1820–1895*. Hanover and London: The Hudson River Museum of Westchester, University Press of New England, 1987.

————. *Selling the Sublime*. Yale University Press, 1990.

Noble, Louis Legrand. *The Life and Works of Thomas Cole*. 1853. Hensonville, N.Y.: Black Dome Press, 1997.

Norris, Thaddeus. *The American Angler's Book*. Philadelphia: E. H. Butler & Co., 1864.

————. *American Fish-Culture*. Philadelphia: Porter & Gates, 1868.

O'Neil, Paul. *In Praise of Trout—and Also Me*. Panacea, Fla.: Kevin Begos Pub., 1996.

Orchard, Harry Frederick (curator). *Charles Lanman—Landscapes & Nature Studies*. Morris Museum of Arts & Sciences, 1983.

Ordeman, John T. *William J. Schaldach: Artist Author Sportsman*. St. Petersburg, Fla.: private printing, 1988.

Orvis, Charles F., and A. Nelson Cheney. *Fishing with the Fly*. 1883. Rutland, Vt.: Charles E. Tuttle & Co., Inc., 1968.

Phillips, Sandra S., and Linda Weintraub. *Charmed Places*. New York: Harry N. Abrams, Inc., 1988.

Pond, Fred E. *Life & Adventures of Ned Buntline*. New York: The Cadmus Book Shop, 1919.

Quinlan, James Eldridge. *History of Sullivan County*. Liberty, N.Y.: G. M. Beebe & W. T. Morgans, 1873.

Renehan, Edward J., Jr. *John Burroughs: An American Naturalist*. Post Mills, Vt.: Chelsea Green Publishing Co., 1992.

Rhead, Louis, ed. *American Trout Stream Insects*. New York: Frederick A. Stokes Co., 1916.

————. *The Book of Fish and Fishing*. New York: Charles Scribner's Sons, 1908.

————. *Fisherman's Lures and Game-Fish Food*. New York: Charles Scribner's Sons, 1920.

————. *The Speckled Brook Trout*. New York: R. H. Russell, 1902.

Rockwell, Rev. Charles. *The Catskill Mountains and the Region Around.* 1867. New York: Taintor Bros. & Co., 1973.

Roosevelt, Robert Barnwell. *The Game Fish of the Northern States of America and British Provinces.* New York: G. W. Carleton, 1862.

Schaldach, William J. *Coverts and Casts.* 1943. Rockville Centre, N.Y.: Freshet Press, 1970.

———. *Currents and Eddies.* New York: A. S. Barnes & Co., 1944.

———. *Fish by Schaldach.* Philadelphia: J. B. Lippincott, 1937.

———. *The Wind on Your Cheek.* Rockville Centre, N.Y.: Freshet Press, 1972.

Schweizer, Paul D., ed. *Masterworks of American Art from the Munson-Williams-Proctor Institute.* New York: Harry N. Abrams, Inc., Publishers, 1989.

Scott, Genio C. *Fishing in American Waters.* New York: Harper & Brothers, 1869.

Sears, Clara Endicott. *Highlights Among the Hudson River Artists.* Boston: Houghton Mifflin Co., 1947.

Sharp, Lewis I. *John Quincy Adams Ward.* Newark, N.J.: University of Delaware Press, 1985.

Smedley, Harold. *Fly Patterns and Their Origins.* Muskegon, Mich.: Westshore Pub., 1943.

———. *Who's Who and What's What in Fly and Bait Casting in the United States.* Muskegon, Mich.: Westshore Pub., 1941.

Smith, C. Lavett. *The Inland Fishes of New York State.* Albany, N.Y.: The New York State Department of Environmental Conservation, 1985.

Smith, Mabel Parker. *Greene County, New York.* Greene County Board of Supervisors, 1963.

Street, Alfred B. *The Poems of Alfred B. Street.* Two vols. New York: Hurd & Houghton, 1867.

Sullivan, Mark W. *The Hudson River School.* Metuchen, N.J.: Scarecrow Press, Inc., 1991.

Swart, James H., and Jay A. Bloomfield. "Characteristics of New York State Lakes Gazetteer." New York State Department of Environmental Conservation, 1985.

Sweet, Frederick A. *The Hudson River School.* New York: The Art Institute of Chicago, 1945.

Sylvester, Nathaniel Bartlett. *History of Ulster County.* Philadelphia: Everts & Peck, 1880.

Takach, Mary H. *Thomas Doughty, American Painter.* Master's thesis, SUNY Binghamton, 1973.

Tuckerman, Henry. *American Artist Life.* New York: G. P. Putnam & Son, 1867.

———. *Artist Life.* New York: D. Appleton & Co., 1847.

Tuscarora Club's Forty-Year History (Millbrook, N. Y.). Portland, Me.: Southworth-Anthoensen Press, 1941.

Van Dyke, Henry. *Little Rivers.* New York: Charles Scribner's Sons, 1895.

Van Loan, Walton. *Van Loan's Catskill Mountain Guide.* New York: The Aldine Publishing Co., 1886.

Van Put, Ed. *The Beaverkill: The History of a River and Its People.* New York: Lyons & Burford, Publishers, 1996.

Van Siclen, George W., ed. *An American Edition of the Treatyse of Fysshyinge wyth an Angle, by Dame Juliana Berner.* Private printing, 1875.

Van Vechten, Vedder J., ed. *History of Greene County. Catskill, N.Y. Vol. I: 1651–1800.* 1927.

Van Winkle, William M. *Henry William Herbert [Frank Forester]: A Bibliography of His Writings 1832–1858.* Portland, Me.: The Southworth-Anthoensen Press, 1936.

Van Zandt, Roland. *The Catskill Mountain House.* New Brunswick, N.J.: Rutgers University Press, 1966.

_____. *Chronicles of the Hudson*. New Brunswick, N.J.: Rutgers University Press, 1971.

Wakefield, Manville. *To the Mountains by Rail*. Grahamsville, N.Y.: Wakefair Press, 1970.

Weir, John F. *A Memorial Catalogue of the Paintings of Sanford Robinson Gifford, N. A.* 1881. New York: Metropolitan Museum of Art, 1974.

Weiss, Ila. *Poetic Landscape*. Newark, N.J.: University of Delaware Press, 1987.

_____. *Sanford Robinson Gifford*. New York: Garland Publishing, Inc., 1977.

Wetzel, Charles M. *American Fishing Books*. 1950. Stone Harbor, N.J.: Meadow Run Press, 1990.

Whipple, Gurth. *Fifty Years of Conservation in New York State, 1885–1935*. Albany, N.Y.: J. B. Lyon Co., 1935.

White, Luke, Jr. *Henry William Herbert and the American Publishing Scene 1831–1858*. Newark, N.J.: Carteret Book Club, 1943.

Who Was Who in America, vol. I. Chicago: A. N. Marquis Co., 1962.

Willis, N. P. *Hurry-Graphs: or, Sketches of Scenery, Celebrities and Society, Taken from Life*. New Orleans: Burnett & Bostwick, 1854.

_____. *Out-Doors at Idlewild*. New York: Charles Scribner, 1855.

Yates, Norris W. *William T. Porter and the Spirit of the Times*. Baton Rouge, La.: Louisiana State University Press, 1957.

Year Book of the Holland Society of New York. New York: Knickerbocker Press, 1886–1887, 1904.

MAGAZINES AND ARTICLES

Allerton, Walter S. "Notes of the Catskill Range." *Forest and Stream*, December 14, 1876.

American Angler, The. Edited by William C. Harris. New York. A weekly journal devoted to fishing—brook, river, lake—and sea-fish culture. 1881–1895.

American Angler, The. Edited by Enos Post. Monthly. New York. 1916–1921.

American Fly-Tyer. Fitchburg, Mass. April, May, June 1941.

American Literary Magazine. Albany, N.Y.: J. Munsell, Printer. Vol. 1–5. July 1847–August 1849.

American Monthly Magazine. New York: George Dearborn. March 1833–October 1838.

American (Whig) Review. New York: Wiley & Putnam Publishers, 1845–1852.

American Sportsman, The. New York: October 1872–September 1874.

American Turf Register and Sporting Magazine. Baltimore, Md. The first of its kind in the United States; featured material on shooting, hunting, fishing, and other outdoor sports. 1829–1844.

Appleton's Journal. New York: D. Appleton & Co., April 1869–December 1881.

Ballou's Pictorial. Boston: January 6, 1855–December 24, 1859.

Bent, Ben. "Trouting Near New York—The Neversink and Streams of the Catskills." *The American Angler*, June 23, 1888.

Benton, Joel. "John Burroughs." *Scribner's Monthly*, January 1877.

Bolton, Theodore. "Henry Inman: An Account of His Life and Work." *Art Quarterly*, Autumn 1940.

Brooks, Karl L. "Catskill Study Report No. 14: The Catskills and Their Flora—An Overview." New York State Department of Environmental Conservation, 1976.

Bulletin of the American Art-Union, "Henry Inman," August 1850, 69–74.

Burroughs, John. "A Bed of Boughs." *Scribner's Magazine,* November 1877.

———. "Birch Browsings." *Atlantic Monthly,* July 1869.

———. "Heart of the Southern Catskills." *The Century,* August 1888.

———. John Burroughs Journals and Papers, Vassar College, Poughkeepsie, N.Y. Special Collections.

———. "Speckled Trout." *Atlantic Monthly,* October 1870.

———. "Springs." *Scribner's Magazine,* April 1876.

"Catalogue of the Library and Correspondence of the late Mr. Alfred B. Street." New York: The Merwin Clayton Sales Co., May 28, 1936.

"Catalogue of Works by the Late Henry Inman with a Biographical Sketch." New York: Van Norden & King, 1846.

Champney, Lizzie W. "The Summer Haunts of American Artists." *Century Illustrated Magazine,* October 1885.

Cheney, A. N. "A Synopsis of the History of Fish Culture." *Fisheries, Game and Forest Commission Report,* 1897.

———. "Trout and Acids." *Forest and Stream,* September 1, 1890.

Connell, Karl. "Julius Caesar." *Anglers' Club Bulletin,* October 1960.

Connell, Kim. "The West Branch of the Neversink." (Essay) A description of the stream and the nearby land.

Conservationist, The. New York State Conservation Department 1946–1960.

Country Life. Garden City, N.Y.: Doubleday, Page & Co., 1919–1922.

Craven, Wayne. "Henry Kirke Brown: His Search for an American Art in the 1840's." *The American Art Journal,* November 1972.

Crayon, The. New York: W. J. Stillman & J. Durand, 1855–1861.

Cross, Reuben R. *Tying American Trout Lures.* New York: Dodd, Mead and Company, Inc., 1936.

———. *Fur, Feathers And Steel.* New York: Dodd, Mead and Company, Inc., 1940.

———. *The Complete Fly Tier.* 1950. Rockville Center, N. Y.: Freshet Press, 1971.

Dearinger, David B. "Asher B. Durand and Henry Kirke Brown: An Artistic Friendship." *The American Art Journal,* vol. XX, no. 3, 1988.

Dimock, A. W. "Saving the Fish of Happy Valley." *Outing,* April 1917.

Doughty, Howard N. "Biographical Sketch of Thomas Doughty." Unpublished manuscript, New-York Historical Society, 1941.

Dwight, Henry E. "Account of the Kaatskill Mountains." *The American Journal of Science And Arts,* vol. II, 1820.

Eggert, Richard. "The Theodore Gordon Heritage, III: The Legacy." *Fly Fisherman,* December 1969.

Evers, Alf. "Catskill Cloves and Catskill Painters." *Catskill Center News,* Summer 1981.

Field & Stream. Published monthly. New York. 1898–1980.

Fitch, Ezra H. "Fishomobiling." *Field & Stream,* April 1909.

Fitch, Fitz-James. "Basket Straps, Shoes Etc." *The American Angler,* April 22, 1882.

———. "Fishing—A Healthful Pastime." *American Agriculturist,* June 1886.

———. "A Trouting Outing." *Shooting and Fishing,* August 22, 1889.

Flick Arthur B. "Fly Fishing Anyone?" *Fly Fisherman,* June 1970.

———. "Zone the Trout Fisherman." *Conservationist,* April-May 1949.

Ford, Corey. "The Best-Loved Trout Stream of Them All." *True,* 1952.

Forest and Stream. Edited from 1873 to 1880 by Charles Hallock. A journal of outdoor life, travel, nature study, shooting, fishing, and yachting. New York. 1873–1914 weekly, 1915–1930 monthly.

Forester, Frank. "Among the Mountains; or Taking Times along a Trout-Stream." *Graham's Magazine,* 1854.

Freese, John W. "Catskill Hatchery at De Bruce." *Conservationist,* February-March 1949.

"Future of the Catskills, The." New York: The Temporary State Commission to Study the Catskills. Final Report, 1975.

Gann, Michael C. "1977 Fisheries Survey White Lake P-117 Del. Lake Trout Management Program." New York State Department of Environmental Conservation, Bureau of Fisheries, Region 3.

Gerdts, William H. "Henry Inman: Genre Painter." *American Art Journal,* May 1977.

Gill, Emlyn M. "Dry-Fly Fishing with A. W. Dimock." *Field & Stream,* February 1913.

———. "Practical Dry Fly-Fishing for Beginners." Series of articles, *Field & Stream,* September–November 1911, April 1912.

———. "Why Not Introduce the Dry-Fly?" *Field & Stream,* July 1911.

Gould, John D. "Fishing-for-Fun." *The New York State Conservationist,* February-March 1960.

Graham's Magazine. Philadelphia: G. R. Graham, 1844–1856.

Greene, C. W. "Stocking for Production." *New York State Conservationist,* April-May 1950.

Hackle, Sparse Grey [Alfred W. Miller]. "A Friend of Theodore Gordon's: An Interview with Roy Steenrod." *Anglers' Club Bulletin,* June 1955.

———. "The Scandal of the Desecrated Shrine." *Sports Illustrated,* February 27, 1956.

———. "Theodore Gordon and Herman Christian." *Anglers' Club Bulletin,* June 1950.

Hallock, Charles. "Pioneer American Sportsmen." *Outing,* February 1901.

Harper's New Monthly Magazine. 1850–1874. New York: Harper & Brothers.

Heacox, Cecil E. "The Catskill Flytyers." *Outdoor Life,* May 1972.

———. "The Charmed Circle Completed." *Outdoor Life,* April 1969.

———. "The Charmed Circle of the Catskills." *Outdoor Life,* March 1969.

Heald, Bruce D. "Thomas Doughty, Landscape Artist," *The Weir Times,* July 30, 2001. http://*www.weirs.com/wtimes.*

Herbert, William H. "Trout and Trout-Fishing." *Graham's Magazine,* May 1851.

Hewitt, Edward R. "Better Trout Fishing." *Field & Stream,* February 1933.

———. "The Condition of Trout in Streams." *Field & Stream,* June 1932.

———. "Fish and Fishing." *Field & Stream,* April 1939.

———. "Midge and Nymph Fly-Fishing." *Field & Stream,* March 1933.

———. "More about Nymph Fly-Fishing." *Field & Stream,* June 1933.

———. "Stocking in 1929." *Forest and Stream,* June 1930.

———. "Trout—How, When, Where?" *Field & Stream,* June 1936.

———. "Wintering Trout in Streams." *Field & Stream,* January 1934.

Hogan, Austin S. "Fly Fishermen's Bicentennial 1761–1961." *Conservationist,* April-May 1961.

Holberton, Wakeman. "The Pleasures of Fly Fishing." *Outing Magazine,* June 1889.

_____. "That Big Trout." *Outing Magazine,* June 1893.

_____. "Where to Go A-Fishing." *Harper's Weekly Magazine,* April 18, 1891.

Holland, F. W. "Fish Farming in Western New York." *Harper's New Monthly Magazine,* December 1868.

Inglis, William. "Submerging Eight Villages in a Drinking Fountain." *Harper's Weekly Magazine,* January 11, 1908.

Ingersol, Ernest. "At the Gateway of the Catskills." *Harper's New Monthly Magazine,* May 1877.

Inman, Henry. "The Fisher Boy." *The Atlantic Souvenir,* 1830.

Irving, Washington. "The Catskill Mountains." *The Home Book of the Picturesque.* New York: G. P. Putnam's, 1851.

Jennings, Preston J. "The Dry Fly—Its Origin and Development." *Field & Stream,* June 1938.

_____. "There Is a Royal Coachman." *Esquire Magazine,* July 1956.

Johnson, Kirk. "Hunter Mountain Paintings Spurred Recovery of Land." *New York Times,* June 7, 2001, B1.

Knickerbocker, The. New York: Peabody, 1833–1840.

La Branche, George M. L. "The Dry Fly in America." Series of articles, *Field & Stream,* June, July, August, September, October, November 1912.

_____. "The Evolution of a Dry Fly Fisherman." *Recreation,* July 1904.

Lanman, Charles. "Walloniana." *The American Review,* April 1845.

Lewis, Barry. "The Art of Flytying." *Catskill-Delaware* (Callicoon, N.Y.), Summer 1986.

Lewis, E. Ana. "Art and Artists of America." *Graham's Magazine,* June 1854 and January 1855.

Lillie, Lucy C. "The Catskills." *Harper's New Monthly Magazine,* September 1883.

Literary World, The. New York: Osgood & Co., Vols. 1–13, February 1847–December 1853.

Lower Hudson River Basin Survey Series Report No. 8. New York State Department of Health, 1960.

Mabie, Hamilton. *Writers of Knickerbocker New York.* Microform, New York State Library, 1912.

Mather, Frank Jewett, Jr. "The Hudson River School." *American Magazine of Art,* June 1934.

McClane, A. J. "A Basic Fly Box." *Field & Stream,* August 1958.

_____. "Best Flies for Big Trout." *Field & Stream,* June 1964.

_____. "Brown Trout." *Field & Stream,* December 1971.

_____. "The Dry Fly on Fast Water." *Field & Stream,* January 1974.

_____. "The Rainbow." *Field & Stream,* November 1971.

McDonald, John, "Fly Fishing and Trout Flies." *Fortune Magazine,* May 1946.

McEntee Diary, Jervis McEntee Diary, Archives of American Art, Smithsonian Institution, Washington, D.C. Microfilm rolls D180, D9, D30, 4707.

New York Illustrated. Lawrence Labree, ed. New York, 1847.

New York Mirror. George P. Morris, ed. New York, January 1, 1826–December 31, 1842.

New York State Conservation Department. Annual reports, 1911–1950.

New York State Fisheries Commission. Annual reports, 1869–1895.

New York State Fisheries, Game and Forest Commission. Annual reports, 1895–1910.

Outing Magazine. Deposit, N.Y.: "The Outdoor Magazine of human interest." October 1886–March 1909.

Picton, Thomas. "Old Time Disciples of Rod and Gun." *The Rod and Gun,* September 25, 1875.

Pierce, James. "A Memoir on the Catskill Mountains with Notices of their Topography, Scenery, Mineralogy, Zoology, Economical Resources &c." *The American Journal of Science And Arts,* vol. VI, 1823.

Porter's Spirit of the Times. New York. September 6, 1856–December 31, 1859 (scattered issues).

Rhead, Louis. "Artificial Baits for Trout." *Forest and Stream,* July 1922.

_____. "Best Flies for Brook Trout." *Outing,* March 1906.

_____. "The Evolution of the Trout Fly." *Forest and Stream,* November 1922.

_____. "Fishing from Bottom to Surface." *Forest and Stream,* May 1922.

_____. "Twelve New Tiny Nature Flies." *Forest and Stream,* April 1923.

Richards, T. Addison. "The Catskills." *Harper's New Monthly Magazine,* July 1854.

Rod and Gun and American Sportsman, The. 1875–1877.

Ruff, Robin. "How to Fish the Neversink." *The American Angler,* October 1892.

Schaldach, William J. "Net Results." *Field & Stream,* February 1946.

Scholz, Lynn. "Louis Rhead's First Career." *The American Fly Fisher,* vol. 12, no. 1, 1985.

Seagears, Clayt. "For New York Waters." *Conservationist,* April-May 1951.

_____. "Homespun Hackles." *Conservationist,* June-July 1947.

Sears, George W. (Nessmuk). "The Exodus of the Trout." *The American Angler,* November 19, 1881.

Senectutus. "Early American Fly Fishing Literature." *The Anglers' Club Bulletin,* October 1954.

_____. "Fifty-four Years on the Beaverkill." *The Anglers' Club Bulletin,* February 1943.

Shanks, Wm. F. G. "Fish-Culture in America." *Harper's New Monthly Magazine,* November 1868.

Sharp, Lewis I. "John Quincy Adams Ward: Historical and Contemporary Influence." *The American Art Journal,* November 1972.

Sheldon, G. W. "An American Sculptor." *Harper's New Monthly Magazine,* June 1878.

Sherwood, Winfield T. "The Ashokan Reservoir." *Forest and Stream,* August 17, 1907.

_____. "Camp Don't Hurry." A twelve-part series. *Forest and Stream,* December 15, 1906–March 2, 1907.

Shooting and Fishing. Boston. A weekly journal of the rifle, gun and rod. November 1, 1888–October 8, 1891.

Smith, Walton M. "A Fly-Tier on the Old Neversink." *The Conservationist,* February–March 1964.

The Spirit of the Times. Edited by William T. Porter. A weekly chronicle of the turf, agriculture, field sports, literature, and the stage. New York. 1831–1861.

Street, Alfred B. "A Day's Fishing in the Callikoon." *Graham's Magazine,* October 1845.

_____. "Life in the Woods." *New York Illustrated Magazine,* 1847.

_____. "A Pic-nic at White Lake." *Graham's Magazine,* July 1847.

Sturgis, Russell. "The Work of J. Q. A. Ward." *Scribner's Magazine,* October 1902.

Sweet, Frederick A. "Asher B. Durand, Pioneer American Landscape Painter." *Art Quarterly* VIII, 1945.

Teale, Edwin. "Reuben R. Cross: Dry Flies from a Kitchen Workshop." *Outdoor Life,* December 1934.

"Temporary State Commission to Study the Catskills." Preliminary Report. Stamford, N.Y.: February 1975.

Thompson, Douglas M. and Gregory N. Stull. "The Development and Historic Use of Habitat Structures in Channel Restoration in the United States: The Grand Experiment in Fisheries Management." http://www.erudit.org/revue/gpg.

Thompson, James H. "The Father of American Fish Culture." *The American Angler*, July 1917.

Thorpe, T. B. "New-York Artists Fifty Years Ago." *Appleton's Journal*, May 25, 1872.

Townley, C. O'D. "Living American Artists." *Scribner's Monthly*, May 1871 and August 1871.

Trumble, Alfred. Article about Peekamoose Fishing Club (untitled). *The Collector*, September 15, 1896.

Turf, Field and Farm. New York. 1872; July 4, 1873–December 31, 1875; July 7, 1882–December 29, 1882; 1886; January 7, 1887–June 24, 1887.

United States Democratic Review. New York: Henry G. Langley, vol. 1–29, 1837–1851.

Van Cleef, James S. "Trout Waters and Trout Weights." *Forest and Stream*, May 21, 1898.

_____. "Why Fish Laws Are Not Respected." *Forest and Stream*, May 21, 1898.

Van Dyke, Henry. "Old-Fashioned Fishing." *Century Magazine*, August 1895.

Wiley, Morris C. William. "Rudolph King of the Esopus." *Outing Magazine*, February 1923.

Wilson, Edward L. Article on A. W. Dimock (untitled). *Wilson's Photographic Magazine*, New York, 1891.

The Woman Flyfisher's Club. Fortieth anniversary booklet, 1972.

Wulff, Lee. "Ed Hewitt." *Rod & Reel*, November/December 1983.

Index

(Italic page numbers indicate illustrations)

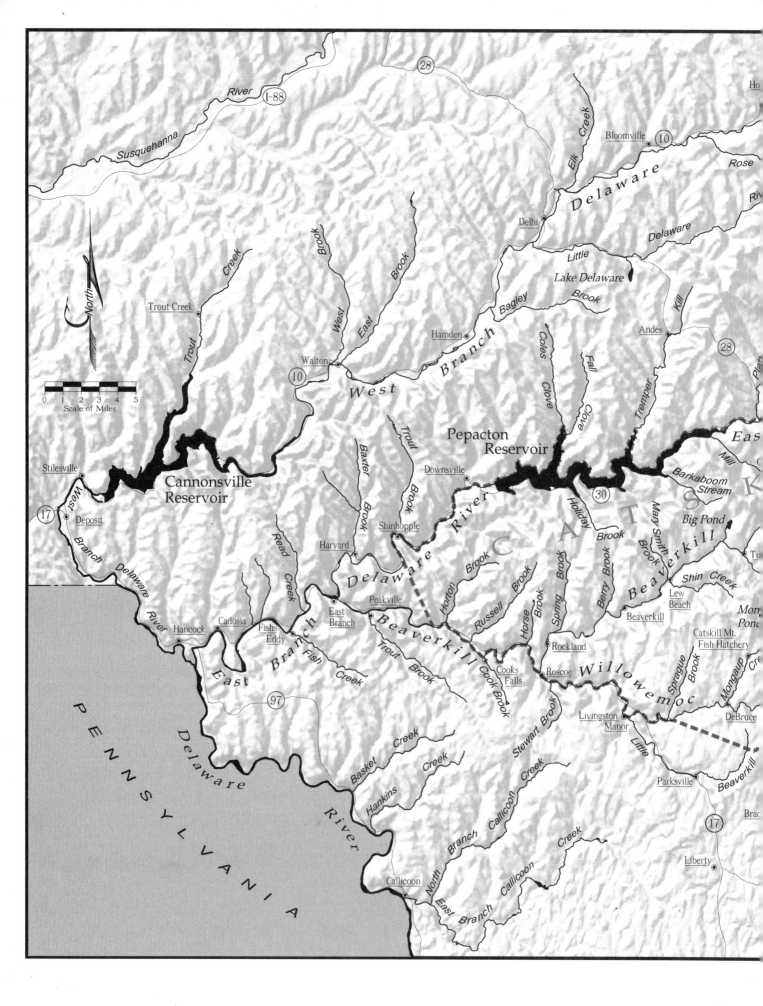